MICROCOMPUTERS

APPLICATIONS AND SOFTWARE

Felix Rodriguez
91.

SECOND EDITION

MICROCOMPUTERS
APPLICATIONS AND SOFTWARE

Dennis P. Curtin

PRENTICE HALL, Englewood Cliffs, New Jersey 07632

Curtin, Dennis, (date)
    Microcomputers: applications and software / Dennis P. Curtin. --
2nd ed.
    p.   cm.
    Includes index.
    ISBN 0-13-579830-2
    1. Microcomputers--Data processing.   2. Computer programs.
I. Title.
QA76.6.C89   1989
005.265--dc19   88-37634
                                                 CIP

This book is dedicated to Charles F. Murphy,
a good friend with whom I shared many good times,
and to his daughter, Katie, and his wife, Cindy.
Through Katie and Cindy, Chuck's unbridled enthusiasm
for life will always be with his friends.

Editorial/production supervision: Nancy Benjamin
Interior design: Maureen Eide
Cover design: Suzanne Curtin
Manufacturing buffer: Margaret Rizzi

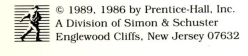

ISBN 0-13-579830-2

Prentice-Hall International (UK) Limited, *London*
Prentice-Hall of Australia Pty. Limited, *Sydney*
Prentice-Hall Canada Inc., *Toronto*
Prentice-Hall Hispanoamericana, S.A., *Mexico*
Prentice-Hall of India Private Limited, *New Delhi*
Prentice-Hall of Japan, Inc., *Tokyo*
Simon & Schuster Asia Pte. Ltd., *Singapore*
Editora Prentice-Hall do Brasil, Ltda., *Rio de Janeiro*

Contents

INTRODUCTION   xi

PART ONE
MICROCOMPUTER SYSTEMS   *1*

Topic 1-1   Information Processing in the Modern Office   5
Topic 1-2   The History of Computers   17
Topic 1-3   The Digital Revolution   41
Topic 1-4   The Microcomputer   53
Topic 1-5   Input Devices   73
Topic 1-6   Output Devices   90
Topic 1-7   External Storage Devices   107
Topic 1-8   Distribution Devices   123
Topic 1-9   Microcomputer Issues   131

PART TWO
OPERATING SYSTEMS   *139*

Topic 2-1   Typical Operating Systems   143
Topic 2-2   Loading the Operating System
                 and Executing Commands   153
Topic 2-3   Specifying Drives and Directories   163
Topic 2-4   Assigning and Listing Filenames   171
Topic 2-5   Specifying More Than One File   176
Topic 2-6   Formatting Data Disks   179
Topic 2-7   Formatting System Disks   182
Topic 2-8   Copying Files   185
Topic 2-9   Duplicating Disks   187
Topic 2-10   Comparing Disks   189
Topic 2-11   Renaming Files   191
Topic 2-12   Erasing Files   192
Topic 2-13   Checking Disks   194

Topic 2-14   Making and Removing Directories   197
Topic 2-15   Displaying and Printing ASCII
              Text Files   200
Topic 2-16   The PATH Command   202
Topic 2-17   Creating Batch Files   204
Topic 2-18   Operating System Issues   207

PART THREE
APPLICATIONS PROGRAMS   *209*

Topic 3-1   Introduction to Applications Programs   211
Topic 3-2   Loading and Quitting Applications
             Programs   218
Topic 3-3   Executing Commands   223
Topic 3-4   Saving and Retrieving Files   231
Topic 3-5   Printing Files   239
Topic 3-6   Changing Default Settings   246
Topic 3-7   Installing Applications Programs   249
Topic 3-8   Applications Programs and Data Files   252
Topic 3-9   Applications Program Issues   259

PART FOUR
WORD PROCESSING AND DESKTOP PUBLISHING APPLICATIONS   *267*

Topic 4-1   Word Processing Procedures:
              An Overview   273
Topic 4-2   Typical Word Processing Programs   279
Topic 4-3   Entering Documents   285
Topic 4-4   Editing Documents   295
Topic 4-5   Working with Blocks of Text   303
Topic 4-6   Searching and Replacing   311
Topic 4-7   Editing Aids   315
Topic 4-8   Default Formats   320
Topic 4-9   Page Breaks and Page Numbers   325
Topic 4-10   Text Alignment and Hyphenation   330
Topic 4-11   Text Emphasis, Superscripts,
              and Subscripts   336
Topic 4-12   Fonts   339
Topic 4-13   Page Layout   344
Topic 4-14   Tab Stops and Indents   352
Topic 4-15   Headers and Footers   358
Topic 4-16   Format Style Sheets   361
              Case Study   Creating a Résumé   363

Topic 4-17   Merge Printing 370
Topic 4-18   Document Assembly 377
Topic 4-19   Drawing Lines 380
Topic 4-20   Creating Special Characters 382
Topic 4-21   Printing in Columns 384
Topic 4-22   Combining Graphics with Text 386
Topic 4-23   Page Makeup 388
Topic 4-24   Glossaries 392
Topic 4-25   Math 394
Topic 4-26   Automatically Generated Lists 397
Topic 4-27   Footnotes and Endnotes 399
Topic 4-28   Sorting 401
Topic 4-29   Outlines 404
Topic 4-30   Filling Out Forms 407
Topic 4-31   Word Processing Macros 409

PART FIVE
SPREADSHEET APPLICATIONS *411*

Topic 5-1   Spreadsheet Procedures:
              An Overview 415
Topic 5-2   Getting Acquainted with Your Program 421
Topic 5-3   Typical Spreadsheet Programs 432
Topic 5-4   Labels and Numbers 436
Topic 5-5   Ranges 440
Topic 5-6   Editing Models 443
Topic 5-7   Formulas 447
Topic 5-8   Functions 455
Topic 5-9   Printing Models 463
Topic 5-10   Changing a Model's Appearance 470
Topic 5-11   Copying and Moving Data 476
Topic 5-12   Relative and Absolute Cell References 480
Case Study   Creating a Five-Year Plan 482
Topic 5-13   Windows and Fixed Titles 494
Topic 5-14   Recalculation Methods 497
Topic 5-15   Lookup Tables 500
Topic 5-16   Data Tables 504
Topic 5-17   Date and Time Functions 507
Topic 5-18   Protection and Security 509
Topic 5-19   Linking, Combining, and Extracting Files 511
Topic 5-20   Graphs 514
Topic 5-21   Data Management 516
Topic 5-22   Spreadsheet Macros 521
Topic 5-23   User-Defined Menus 526
Topic 5-24   Troubleshooting Models 528

PART SIX
DATABASE MANAGEMENT APPLICATIONS *531*

Topic 6-1   Record Management
and Database Management 534

Topic 6-2   Database Management Procedures:
An Overview 539

Topic 6-3   Typical Record and Database Management
Programs 545

Topic 6-4   Getting Acquainted with Your Program 349

Topic 6-5   Defining a Database File 553

Topic 6-6   Entering Records 561

Topic 6-7   Displaying Records 568

Case Study 1   Creating a Database of Names
and Addresses 570

Topic 6-8   Query Languages 573

Topic 6-9   Using Criteria to Display Records 576

Topic 6-10   Adding, Updating, and Deleting Records 583

Case Study 2   Using Queries and Updating
Records 585

Topic 6-11   Sorting Records 588

Topic 6-12   Indexing Records 591

Case Study 3   Sorting and Indexing Files 594

Topic 6-13   Printing Reports 597

Case Study 4   Printing Reports 601

Topic 6-14   Restructuring the Database 605

Topic 6-15   Making New Databases from Existing Files 606

Case Study 5   Joining Files 609

Topic 6-16   Writing Programs 611

Case Study 6   Writing Programs 613

Topic 6-17   Data Security 616

Topic 6-18   Hypermedia 619

PART SEVEN
GRAPHICS APPLICATIONS *623*

Topic 7-1   Business Graphics 625

Topic 7-2   Types of Business Graphs 629

Topic 7-3   Analyzing Data Graphically 637

Topic 7-4   Graph Options 642

Case Study   Creating a Graph
with Lotus 643

Topic 7-5   Interactive Graphics 646

Topic 7-6   Computer-Aided Design 649

Topic 7-7   Displaying and Printing Graphics   652
Topic 7-8   Graphics Standards   659
Topic 7-9   Audiovisual Presentations   661

PART EIGHT
COMMUNICATIONS APPLICATIONS   665

Topic 8-1   Local Area Networks   667
Topic 8-2   Wide Area Networks   676
Topic 8-3   Telecommunications Equipment   682
Topic 8-4   Communications Programs   685
Topic 8-5   Communications Settings   689
Topic 8-6   Transferring Files   697
             Case Study   Calling a Bulletin Board   700
Topic 8-7   Telecommunications Principles   705

PART NINE
OTHER APPLICATIONS   711

Topic 9-1   Project Management Programs   713
Topic 9-2   Idea and Outline Processors   717
Topic 9-3   Desktop and Personal Information
             Managers   719
Topic 9-4   Accounting Programs   721
Topic 9-5   Utility Programs   728
Topic 9-6   Expert Systems   731

GLOSSARY   733

INDEX   753

Introduction

A revolution in information processing is going on in offices, factories, and schools at this very moment. Not too many years ago, most information was processed on machines that were primarily mechanical. Words were processed on typewriters, numbers on adding machines, lists on index cards, and graphics on drafting tables. Only large companies owned computers, and they used them only for the most important corporate-level tasks, like order processing and payroll. Operating these large and complicated computers was too costly to use them to solve problems and increase productivity at the individual employee or departmental levels. All this is changing with the growing popularity of microcomputers, also called personal or desktop computers, and a large variety of easy-to-use applications programs. Computers are now accessible to almost everyone in large corporations, small businesses, professional offices, schools, and wherever else people think, create, organize, or plan.

The microcomputer's popularity comes not just from its low cost but also from its flexibility. You can use a microcomputer to prepare a financial analysis; then use it to write, edit, and illustrate a report on the results of that analysis; and finally use it to send the final document to an office halfway around the world over the telephone lines. Because of this power and flexibility, the microcomputer is becoming as familiar to everyone in business as the telephone, typewriter, and calculator.

What does this revolution mean for you, one of the people who will be using this new breed of computer? For one thing, it means you will be able to do certain tasks faster and better. It also means you can do work now that you could not have done before the arrival of the microcomputer.

- You can use word processing programs to create memos, letters, term papers, and reports, then revise them so that the results are perfect without having to retype them. You can even make a document look as though it were prepared at a professional printers using the desktop publishing features built into the latest word processing programs or available in separate packages. You can also merge names and addresses stored in the computer into form letters and send out customized copies by the hundreds or thousands—and each will be personalized. You can even print the envelopes or mailing labels for them, all automatically.

- You can use spreadsheet programs to create dynamic financial models, so that a change in one variable causes changes in the rest of the model.

You can instantly see the effects of a change. For example, you could explore the effects of various discounts on your profits.

- You can use record management or database programs for tasks as simple as keeping a phone list or as complicated as controlling inventory.

- You can use graphics programs to create graphs, not by drafting them on a board in the traditional way, but by creating them almost instantly on a microcomputer. Graphs come alive; they no longer have to show only the final results but can enhance the analysis of numbers to show trends and relationships you never saw before.

- You can use communications programs to connect your computer to other computers so that you can have instant access to the information stored in them.

This text is designed to help you understand the principles and applications of microcomputers. It can get you started on the right foot. Full understanding, however, requires some hands-on experience with a computer. After all, a computer is nothing but a sophisticated machine—it is easier to understand what the computer does while it's doing it. Trying to understand computers without practice is like trying to learn how to drive or ski by reading books. Books can give you some principles and ideas, but it's only when you first get behind the wheel, or stand at the top of the hill, that you realize there is more to it than what you read.

If you are anxious about this course, don't worry. Anxiety is a common feeling among people when they are introduced to computers. This anxiety will shortly pass and you will then be wondering why you felt it in the first place. When beginning, avoid worrying about the many unfamiliar details you have to learn. Just keep in mind that all these details boil down to a few basic steps:

1. How to insert a program disk into a disk drive. (This is rather like learning to put a cassette into your tape recorder.)
2. How to turn on the computer. In a few moments, a display appears on your screen.
3. How to move the cursor (a small, bright "pointer" on the screen) so that you can enter and edit information.
4. How to make choices from a list of commands. Called a menu, this list displays choices you select to operate the program. For example, you can select commands that save or print your work.

After you grasp these basic procedures, you can increase your understanding through further study and practice.

A NOTE TO THE INSTRUCTOR

This text and the accompanying *Microcomputer Resource Manual* are designed for the introductory course on microcomputers. They cover the principles behind, and the applications of, microcomputers. They also discuss the major types of microcomputer applications programs: word processing, spreadsheets, databases, graphics, and communications.

The Text

This text assumes the student has no previous computer experience, and can be used successfully in a course with or without a lab section. It emphasizes the principles behind computer hardware, operating systems, and applications programs. Rather than focusing on specific products, this generic approach gives students a grasp of the basic concepts behind microcomputers so that when they are faced with new or different products they will be able to adjust more easily. Texts organized around specific products inevitably limit their discussion to the features contained in those programs.

The text is organized into nine parts, each of which is subdivided into topics. Each of the 131 topics is independent of other topics so that you can select the topics to cover and present them in the order that best meets your needs. However, Parts One through Three should probably be covered first. They introduce students to the microcomputer's hardware, operating systems, and applications software. Parts Four through Nine then discuss applications programs in detail.

Many features make this text a better teaching and learning tool.

- The text is organized into topics rather than chapters. This has been done to make the text more flexible. You can tailor the text to the length of your course by selecting just those topics you choose to present. You can also present them in any order. Students also prefer a topical organization because topics are much smaller units than traditional chapters and are therefore more accessible and less intimidating.

- Each topic in this text has a parallel topic in the accompanying Resource Manual. Each topic in this Resource Manual contains several exercises designed to expand students' understanding of the principles presented in this text.

- Over 600 illustrations and accompanying captions make it easier for students to grasp the principles behind microcomputer applications.

- The coverage of operating systems focuses on the latest developments in this area, including DOS 4.0 and OS/2 and its accompanying Presentation Manager.

- The presentation of word processing includes a detailed discussion of desktop publishing. These two fields have been integrated because the trend in this area is to incorporate almost all desktop publishing features into standard word processing programs.

- The discussion of the history of computers focuses on the brief, but exciting, history of the microcomputer and introduces many of the key players who made the microcomputer successful.

- Case studies in the parts on word processing, spreadsheet, database, graphics, and telecommunications applications illustrate how problems are solved with specific programs like WordPerfect, Lotus 1-2-3, dBASE, and ProComm.

- Over 800 questions test students' understanding of the material presented in each topic.

- Tips on using computers and programs are integrated throughout the chapters on applications programs. These are based on the author's many years of practical experience with microcomputers.

- A glossary at the end of the book briefly defines hundreds of terms used in the text.

The Resource Manual

The *Microcomputer Resource Manual* accompanying this text is designed for the lab portion of the course and it includes several exercises for each topic in this text. Since each topic in this text is numbered and there is a parallel topic in the Resource Manual, students can read about the principles in this text and then find related exercises in the Resource Manual. Many of the exercises are computer-based and introduce students to introductory, intermediate, and advanced procedures for DOS (versions 1.0 through the latest 4.0 and later versions), WordPerfect, The Twin, Lotus 1-2-3, dBASE, and ProComm.

Like the text, the Resource Manual is designed so that you can custom-tailor your lab by assigning only those topics you want, in the order you want. A Roadmap in the introduction to the manual indicates which exercises use files created in previous exercises. Only in these situations is a certain order of assignment dictated.

Educational Versions of Leading Applications Programs

Prentice-Hall has made arrangements to provide you with educational versions of the programs covered in the accompanying *Microcomputer Resource Manual* (with the exception of Lotus 1-2-3). For information on their availability and how they differ from the commercial full-featured versions, contact your Prentice-Hall representative.

Other Supplements and Services

In addition to this text and its accompanying Resource Manual, other supplemental materials and services are available to support your efforts in the classroom:

Instructor's Resource Manual. The manual contains lecture outlines, helpful teaching tips, and answers to test questions.

Test Item File. Over 1000 multiple-choice, short-answer, and case questions are available on a floppy disk or as a printout.

Software Videos. These tutorial videos guide students through popular applications packages like DOS, WordPerfect, Word, Lotus 1-2-3, dBASE III Plus, and Ventura. They are free on adoption for qualifying quantities.

Educational Assistance Policy. Prentice-Hall's educational reimbursement policy is designed to assist qualifying adopters. Contact your local Prentice-Hall representative for details.

ACKNOWLEDGMENTS

This text would never have happened had I not met Les Porter at the Harvard Business School. Les had followed some of my early writing on the business applications of microcomputers and encouraged me to write a basic text on the subject. I agreed with one proviso—that he coauthor it with me. Despite being already overcommitted he agreed, and his participation in the first edition of this text provided not only support but also great assistance on many technical subjects. Janice Gogan, one of his graduate students at the time and now at Boston University, also made significant contributions. She class-tested the manuscript as it was being developed and provided insightful suggestions for improvements. Unfortunately, time

commitments resulting from a new position prevented Les from partici-
pating in this second edition. Despite not being directly involved with the
revision, his early support will always be appreciated.

Special thanks are due to those who helped turn the manuscript into a
finished book. Peggy Curtin did all the picture research and handled all contacts with the computer companies, which gave so much assistance. Nancy
Benjamin handled all aspects of production, and turned a large pile of
manuscript and illustrations into the finished text. Linda Dowell of St.
John's River Community College in Florida and Ken Kuhn at Centennial
School in British Columbia reviewed the manuscript and provided many
useful insights and suggestions for improvements. Thanks also to Suzanne
Curtin of Everex Computers who designed the covers for this text and the
Resource Manual.

And last, but by no means least, thanks to the many computer companies that responded to the author's needs with information, programs, and
illustrations. These companies are listed at the end of the book in the section "Company Trademarks." The author would especially like to thank
Jessie Kempter and Scott Brooks at IBM for their absolutely unparalleled
service; Coby Cressey, Katheryn Hinsh, and Sarah Charf at Microsoft and
Carine Bertram at the Waggoner Group for complete support from
Microsoft; and Donald LaVange and Durk Merrell for the support from
WordPerfect Corporation.

NOTE

The author and publisher of this series want to ensure that it meets your
needs, and we would appreciate your comments. If you have any suggestions for improvements or new titles to be added to the series, please write
to:

Dennis P. Curtin
c/o Editor of Introductory Computing
College Division
Prentice Hall
Englewood Cliffs, NJ 07632

Dennis P. Curtin
Marblehead, Massachusetts

Part One

MICROCOMPUTER SYSTEMS

Topic 1-1 Information Processing in the Modern Office
Topic 1-2 The History of Computers
Topic 1-3 The Digital Revolution
Topic 1-4 The Microcomputer
Topic 1-5 Input Devices
Topic 1-6 Output Devices
Topic 1-7 External Storage Devices
Topic 1-8 Distribution Devices
Topic 1-9 Microcomputer Issues

Microcomputers are used to process information in the modern business office. To use them for this purpose, you should understand the principles and concepts behind the microcomputer and the other components that make up a microcomputer system. Understanding this not only makes your work easier but also prepares you to understand and cope with future changes in technology that will affect the way you work. In this part, we introduce you to the principles and concepts behind the microcomputer system.

SYSTEM

Although most users would say they work on a microcomputer, they actually work on a microcomputer system. A **system** is a set of related parts that operate together. You encounter systems every day. For example, your circulatory system moves blood through your body. This system contains your heart, lungs, blood vessels, and so on. With these parts working together, this system distributes energy throughout your body. Your stereo is also a system. It has parts like the turntable, amplifier, and speakers, all of which work together so that you can hear music. A microcomputer system, like these other systems, comprises several interacting parts. These parts are classified as either hardware or software.

HARDWARE

FIGURE 1
The Computer System's Hardware
A typical computer system has the hardware components shown in this figure.

Hardware (Figure 1) is the physical equipment in the system, the parts you can touch, drop, and break. A **microcomputer** (also called a desktop or personal computer) is the hardware component at the center of the system, and it performs all the processing of information. Other hardware components (called **peripherals**) connect to the microcomputer so that you can both feed

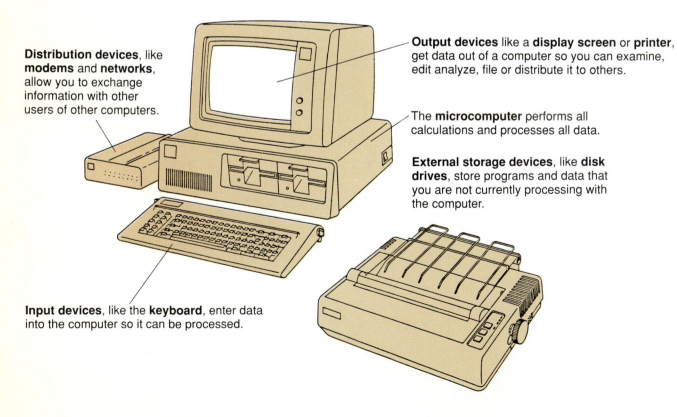

Distribution devices, like **modems** and **networks**, allow you to exchange information with other users of other computers.

Output devices like a **display screen** or **printer**, get data out of a computer so you can examine, edit analyze, file or distribute it to others.

The **microcomputer** performs all calculations and processes all data.

External storage devices, like **disk drives**, store programs and data that you are not currently processing with the computer.

Input devices, like the **keyboard**, enter data into the computer so it can be processed.

information into the computer and get the results back out to view, file, or distribute them. Typical peripherals are the keyboard, display screen, and printer.

SOFTWARE

Microcomputers are general-purpose machines with many abilities. You determine their specific applications by the software you use. This is what distinguishes microcomputers from single-purpose machines like typewriters, calculators, or dedicated word processors, machines that do only word processing. **Software** is the set of instructions, called a **program**, that tells the computer what to do and when to do it. These programs are written by professionals and then stored on disks and sold just like records or books.

The computer is like an actor, and the software is like a script. When the actor changes scripts, he or she can perform a different role. By changing the software, you can make your computer perform different functions (Figure 2). For example, if you want to use your computer for word processing, you load a word processing program into your computer's memory from the disk it is stored on. If you want to use your computer for financial analysis, you load a spreadsheet or accounting program. You do not have to learn programming to make the computer a valuable tool. Instead, you learn how to effectively use these software programs.

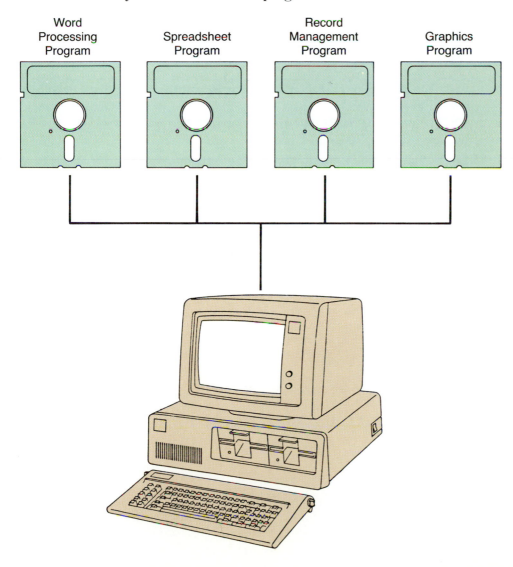

Word Processing Program   Spreadsheet Program   Record Management Program   Graphics Program

FIGURE 2
The Computer System's Software
Microcomputers allow you to load a variety of software, called programs, into memory so that you can change their applications. You can use the same piece of equipment to process words, numbers, and graphics.

Hardware and Software in the Computer Industry and Other Fields

Although the terms *hardware* and *software* are most often used in the computer field, the concepts behind them are not unique to this field. You can make similar distinctions in other industries.

Industry	Hardware	Software
Computers	Computer	WordPerfect
Movies	Camera	Gone with the Wind
Recording	Turntable	Born in the USA
Publishing	Printing press	This text
Art	Brush	Mona Lisa

SUMMARY AND KEY TERMS

- A computer **system** contains several elements including hardware and software.
- **Hardware** is the physical equipment in the system.
- **Software**, also called programs, converts the hardware to specific applications.

REVIEW QUESTIONS

1. What is a system? Try to list and describe two other systems that are not discussed in this section.
2. What is hardware? List some typical computer hardware.
3. What is software? What does it do?
4. Do you have to know how to program to use a microcomputer?

Information Processing in the Modern Office

OBJECTIVES

After completing this topic, you will be able to

- Distinguish between data processing, word processing, graphics processing, and information processing
- Describe the information processing cycle
- Explain how information processing is used in the modern office

Information is the lifeblood of the modern business. It is used to make decisions, convey actions, evaluate results, and exchange ideas. But to be useful, information must be easy to create, store, revise, and distribute. All these activities are part of information processing. Information processing has changed dramatically during your lifetime. Your parents, if they worked in an office, used equipment that was primarily mechanical though some of it was powered by electricity. Preparing written documents on a typewriter was time consuming and required much skill to get the best results. Calculations were made with adding machines or calculators and took a great deal of time. If errors were discovered, or if circumstances changed, the entire process had to be redone from scratch. Names and addresses and other important data were stored on cards or other forms of paper that were manipulated manually and stored in filing cabinets. Graphics were prepared on drafting tables.

Although these manual processes are still widely used, the computer is changing the way people work. *Technology and the American Economic Transition*, a recent study prepared by the U.S. Congressional Office of Technology Assessment, states that businesses spend 40 percent of their total investment dollars on computers and other information machines. This is double the amount spent as recently as ten years ago. The microcomputer, a computer small enough to fit on a desktop, is playing an increasingly important role. If a computer was in your parent's office, it was kept in its own air-conditioned room and was maintained and operated by a team of highly skilled technicians and programmers. Your parents didn't have to know anything about the computer because they saw only its output—paychecks, sales reports, and the like. In your home or office, a computer may be sitting on your desk. You won't be able to avoid it as your parents did. This is a two-edged sword: The computer can make you more productive than your parents, but you must learn how to use it and, more important, what to use it for. This, to make you **computer literate**, is the goal of this book. Computer literacy is not knowing technical details; it really means understanding the principles and the applications of computers. The computer is nothing more than a tool. As you may have found when working with tools around the house, knowing what a tool is and how to use it often is not enough. For example, we all know what a hammer is and how to use it, but to use it to build a house requires an understanding of how houses are built. The same is true of computers. Although you may know how to use one to analyze a financial statement, you have to know how to interpret the results.

WHAT IS INFORMATION PROCESSING?

Information processing refers to the use of computers to prepare, file, distribute, and store words, numbers, and images that communicate facts or ideas. The field of information processing is vast and includes the processing of an enormous variety of information using many processing techniques. You encounter computerized information processing systems almost every day.

- When you call to make an airline reservation, an agent enters your request into a computer. The computer then displays all the flights available, the time they depart and arrive, and their fares. If you make a reservation, your request is entered into the computer, and a seat is reserved for you.

- When you pick up your paycheck, it likely was printed by a computer. A computer also probably charged the amount of the check to the company's accounting records and calculated withholding taxes and other deductions.

- When you get into your car to drive to the store, you are driving a vehicle designed by computers. If your car is a recent model, there might be computers in the car that monitor and control some aspects of its performance. For example, more than 60 million cars with computers built into them were sold between 1982 and 1988. Typically, they control the car's ignition, brakes, dashboard displays, and stereos.

- When you open your mail, you are likely to find letters automatically generated by computers. Magazines and other businesses often use "computer mail" to try to sell you something.

- When you open your daily newspaper, you are reading a document written and set into type on computers.

- When you make a withdrawal from a bank's automatic teller machine, a computer dispenses the money and charges the withdrawal against your account.

Information processing touches all aspects of our lives. When we are born and when we die, information about us is entered into computers. In between, we read newspapers, magazines, and books created with the help of computers. The schools we attend maintain all of our records on computers. Employers pay us and promote us based on computer-processed information. In our retirement years, the government sends us social security checks processed on computers. If you were to list all of your activities in two columns—those that are influenced by information processing and those that are not—the activities not influenced by information processing would be the shorter column. This influence has happened within a very short period. In 1946, there was only one operational computer in North America. Since then, the growth has been explosive. In 1980, there was 1 computer for every 160 people. By 1985, there was 1 for every 10.

As Figure 1-1 shows, all information processed on computers falls into three broad classes: data, words, and graphics. The terms *data*, *words*, and *graphics* can be somewhat misleading because they overlap. Let's look more closely at what these terms mean.

Data Processing

Data is any information used to discuss or decide something. For example, if you were running a small store, you could carefully record the name and number of all items as they arrive from your suppliers and then record each item as it is sold. You could use these records to determine when to reorder more items and how many you should order.

When computers were first developed, their primary function was to process data like this. Large computers in company data processing departments are still largely used for this purpose. They process payrolls, keep track of inventory and sales, and solve scientific and engineering problems. All these tasks require the computer to calculate numbers, sort entries into a specified order, and find a specific record when needed. Programmers write programs for each of these tasks. Often these programs display a form on the screen that is filled in by an operator to feed information into the computer. If the form does not have a space to enter a comment, you cannot enter one. Since the purpose of the computer was to process this highly structured data, the general term **data processing** was used to describe the process. In the microcomputer field, database programs (see Part Six) are the equivalent of these highly structured data processing programs. Spreadsheet programs (see Part Five) are related to them but are more flexible and let you work with data that is not so highly structured.

Word Processing

As the information processing field matured, specialty areas emerged. **Word processing** programs were developed that made it possible to work with words so that correspondence could be written, edited, and formatted to control its final appearance. These programs allow much more flexibility than data processing programs. Instead of just entering predefined data, you can enter and manipulate data interactively. For example, you can enter

INFORMATION PROCESSING		
Words	**Data**	**Graphics**
Memos	Accounting	Illustrations
Letters	Science	Designs
Reports	Engineering	Charts and graphs
Articles	Statistics	Organization
Books	Reservations	charts
Plays		
Poems		

FIGURE 1-1
Information Processing
Information processed on computers falls into three main classes: data, words, and graphics.

a paragraph and then copy, move, delete, or change its appearance on the screen. Although you usually use word processing programs to manipulate words, a document prepared on a word processing program can also include the date or other numbers, graphic symbols like bullets (■ and ▶), lines, and even graphic images.

Graphics Processing

Later in the evolution of information processing, it became possible to create and manipulate images with the computer. **Graphics processing** programs have been developed that read images into the computer or let you draw them on the screen. These images can then be manipulated, stored, printed, and distributed just like data and words. A graphic image prepared with one of these programs can include graphic symbols, numbers, and words. For example, you can create an outline map of North America, label each location where your company has a branch office, and show the sales achieved by each office.

Information Processing

As you have seen, data, words, and graphics processed on a computer can include words, numbers, and graphics. For this reason, data processing, word processing, and graphics processing obviously do not refer to the content as much as to how the data is handled by the computer and the intent of the operator. People who do data processing focus on having the computer compile and organize data so that it can be analyzed and used for decision-making purposes. People who do word processing focus on preparing documents that can be read by others. People who do graphics processing are mostly interested in obtaining images.

Since these terms refer to distinct types of processing, the field needed a new term when new applications were introduced and when computers became powerful enough to blur the distinctions among these specialized tasks. The term **information processing** covers not only word, data, and graphics processing but also all other forms of creating, recording, storing, retrieving, distributing, and analyzing information with computers.

Until recently, each area was a specialty, requiring training and expensive equipment. The development of the inexpensive microcomputer and easy-to-use programs now make it possible for a single user to create, process, print, store, and distribute all this information (Figure 1-2). The old distinctions between the persons who prepared, distributed, and filed documents are now blurred. Today, the same person can perform all these roles.

THE INFORMATION PROCESSING CYCLE

Information processing is becoming increasingly automated, or made partially or fully automatic, through the use of machines. The microcomputer is often central to the new automated systems that make this possible. Whether done manually or on a computer, information processing is considered to have a cycle, a series of steps that follow one another in a specific order. The **information processing cycle** is generally considered to have the following five steps (Figure 1-3):

Step 1. Input

During the input stage, you enter information into the computer. You can either type it in from the keyboard or use any of the many other available input devices (see Topic 1-5).

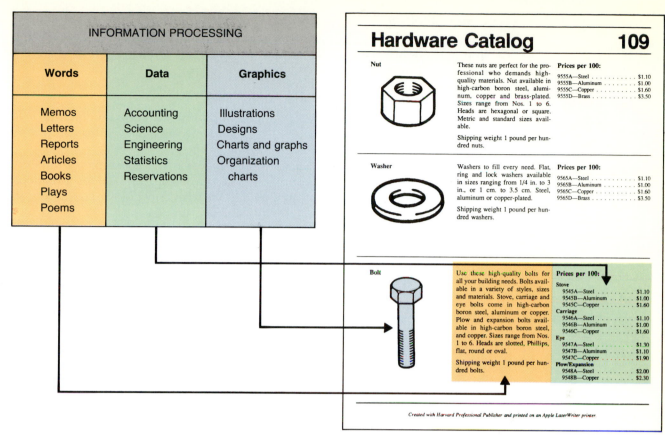

FIGURE 1-2
Combining Data, Words, and Graphics
Information processing includes words, data, and graphics. When combined, you can create documents or other files that describe, illustrate, and calculate. Courtesy of Software Publishing Corporation

Step 2. Processing

Once information is in the computer, you can process it (see Topic 1-4). For example, with a word processing program, you can edit and format text. With a spreadsheet program, you can calculate numbers and perform financial analysis.

Step 3. Output

While you are entering and processing data, it is constantly being displayed on the screen. This is one form of output. After the information is processed, you can print it out, which is another form of output (see Topic 1-6).

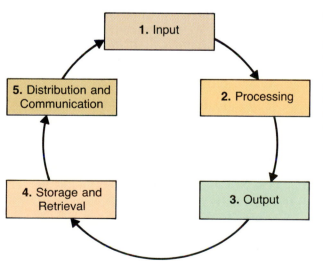

FIGURE 1-3
The Information Processing Cycle
The information processing cycle has five steps: input, processing, output, storage and retrieval, and distribution and communication.

FIGURE 1-4
Cartoon
Cartoon by Earl
Engleman. From
ComputerWorld, January
23, 1984. Reprinted with
permission.

Step 4. Storage and Retrieval

You can file copies so that you can easily locate and retrieve them if needed. You can file printed copies manually or store the information in the computer onto magnetic or optical media (see Topic 1-7).

Step 5. Distribution and Communication

You can distribute copies of the information to the intended recipients. You can send either printed copies or the data electronically to other computers over cables or telephone lines (see Topic 1-8).

All these steps undergo profound changes as they become automated. To play a central role in this revolution requires training. Today's real employment opportunities are available to those who know how to use computers (Figure 1-4).

MICROCOMPUTERS IN BUSINESS

Computers have been used in businesses since the early 1950s. These first computers were large, expensive, and complicated. As a result, separate facilities were set aside, and a professional staff was hired to program and operate them (Figure 1-5). These facilities and this staff are called the **data processing (DP) department** or **management information systems (MIS) department**. These departments manage and operate the firm's centralized computer facilities.

The Story of This Book

Let's follow the steps in this textbook's development to see how the microcomputer was used in its creation.

1. The manuscript was written and edited using Microsoft Word and an IBM AT computer. Spelling was checked with the program's spelling checker. The draft was then printed out on a laser printer and sent to the publisher's production department.

2. The production department edited the manuscript, correcting grammar and making stylistic changes and other improvements so that it would be easier for you to use.

3. Meanwhile, an interactive graphics program was used to create rough sketches of many line drawings included in the book. Another program was used to capture images of typical computer displays so that they could be illustrated in this text.

4. The files were corrected and codes were entered to indicate different design characteristics of the book.

5. The files were then sent on disks to a typesetter, a firm that sets the type used in newspapers, magazines, and books. Typesetting equipment interpreted the codes embedded in the manuscript, and the manuscript was set into the type you are now reading.

6. The publisher assembled the camera-ready copy for the book by integrating type from the typesetter, line drawings, and photographs. All this was then sent to the printer for printing.

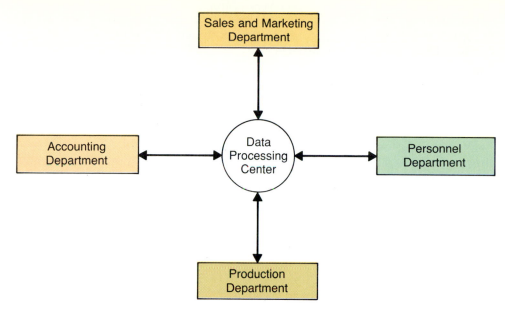

FIGURE 1-5
Data Processing Departments
Data processing departments are operated by a specialized staff. These service departments perform data processing for other departments throughout the firm.

Surprisingly, when microcomputers were introduced, large corporations were not the first to adopt them. Small businesses and professionals were the first to embrace them as a solution to several long-standing problems. Unlike large corporations where a specialized professional staff handles different aspects of the business, small firms generally have key people handle a variety of responsibilities. In professions like law and medicine, all the administrative jobs might be performed by a single person. The bookkeeper or accountant may also be the financial planner or even the receptionist. The owner might also be the sales manager, the personnel department, and the head of engineering or product development. These firms and professions do not have the funds needed to hire specialists in each of these areas. They need to increase the productivity of the people they do have.

Unburdened by committees and purchasing departments, these firms are free to experiment. When the price of a computer and accompanying software fell below $5000, they rushed to see if this was the answer to their problems. If the firm had five people and each of them could increase their productivity by 20 percent, it was the same as hiring another person, and it was less expensive. These early experiments were successful, and the microcomputer spread thorough small businesses and then into large corporations. Many of the early users in large firms had to buy their computers themselves or hide the cost under other budget items. Only in the past few years have large firms recognized the value of microcomputers and established company policies to buy and use them.

The applications of microcomputers in large and small firms are generally the same. Let's look at a few of them.

- Sales and marketing departments use microcomputers to analyze sales and maintain mailing lists of their customers.
- Production and manufacturing departments use them to analyze costs, design products or components, and control manufacturing equipment.
- Finance and accounting departments use them for financial analysis and, in smaller firms, to computerize the accounting process.

- Administration and management use them for many purposes. They analyze performance, prepare correspondence, maintain lists of phone numbers, and prepare reports.
- Design departments use them to create designs for graphics like those used in advertisements and for products.
- People in all departments use them to design, illustrate, and publish forms, brochures, catalogs, and reports.

Each of these groups performs many tasks or applications. As you will see, the computer is a general-purpose machine. You use it for specific tasks by loading an **applications program** into its memory. The applications program used depends on the task. Table 1-1 lists some typical tasks and the applications programs used to implement them.

TABLE 1-1
Tasks and Applications Programs

Task	Applications Program
Planning and budgeting	Spreadsheets
Memos, letters, and reports	Word processing
Bookkeeping and accounting	Accounting
List management	Database
Chart and graphs	Graphics
Publications	Desktop publishing
Electronic mail	Telecommunications

COMPUTERS AT WORK

Microcomputers are not just limited to office use but are also widely used in other settings.

Microcomputers in the Office
Microcomputers can be found almost anywhere in a modern office. They are used to prepare memos, letters, and reports; analyze financial data; maintain mailing lists; prepare graphics; and communicate with others in the same building or in branch offices. Courtesy of Hewlett Packard, Inc.

Primary and Secondary Schools
Microcomputers are being widely used in elementary and secondary classrooms. Courtesy of IBM Corporation.

Colleges
Students in college are increasingly putting computers to work in their classes and not just studying them. Those who use computers in their course work have a distinct advantage over those who do not use them. Courtesy of Apple Computer, Inc.

Homes
The microcomputer was introduced into the home as a game machine, but its role is changing. It is rapidly becoming a major information processing tool. When connected to optical disk players, encyclopedic information is instantly available. Courtesy of Apple Computer, Inc.

Special Education
Computers are especially valuable for the people who are physically disabled. The visual and voice capabilities make it possible for these users to learn some subjects much faster than traditional instruction techniques. Courtesy of Apple Computer, Inc.

Factories
Factory floors are becoming increasingly populated by micros. They are used for several purposes including inventory control and planning and process control. They are increasingly used to run robots—mechanical machines used to create, finish, assemble, and test products and their components. Courtesy of Apple Computer Inc.

SUMMARY AND KEY TERMS

- **Computer literacy** is understanding the principles and applications of computers. The primary application is to process **information**. Information is classified as being **data, words,** or **graphics**, but there is a great deal of overlap.

- When processing data there is a cycle, which includes **input**, **processing**, **output**, **storage and retrieval**, and **distribution and communication**.

- **Data processing departments** in companies manage and operate the firm's centralized computer facilities.

- Microcomputers are distributed throughout companies and are used by persons in departments like sales and marketing, production and manufacturing, and finance and accounting. Each of these groups performs tasks or applications using **applications programs**.

REVIEW QUESTIONS

1. What does it mean to be computer literate?
2. List as many places that computers are being used that you can think of. What information are they used to process?
3. Describe the primary application of data processing.
4. Describe the primary application of word processing.
5. Describe the primary purpose of graphics processing.
6. Describe information processing.
7. What is the definition of automation?
8. List the five steps in the information processing cycle, and briefly describe what is done at each stage.
9. What is the function of the data processing department?
10. Lists examples of how microcomputers are being used in businesses.
11. Match the tasks in column A with the applications programs used to complete them in column B.

A	B
Planning and budgeting	Database
Memos, letters, and reports	Graphics
Bookkeeping and accounting	Word processing
List management	Desktop publishing
Charts and graphs	Spreadsheets
Publications	Accounting
Electronic mail	Telecommunications

The History of Computers

OBJECTIVES

After completing this topic, you will be able to

- Describe the chronology of events that led to the development of the electronic digital computer
- Describe the key events in the development of microcomputer hardware and software

Our economies are changing from ones based on manufacturing to ones based on information. The huge increase in the amount of information generated, distributed, and stored has been possible only because of technological advances that allowed the information process to be automated. Automation has been growing dramatically as companies try to improve productivity and reduce costs so that they can remain competitive. The revolution going on in today's offices, as they convert from manual to computerized systems, has its roots in the seventeenth century.

If you stop and think about it, the fact that you can place a computer on your desk is amazing. And the story about how it got there is fascinating. If you follow television, magazine, or newspaper coverage of today's computing industry, you know it is driven by persons and technological breakthroughs. Thousands of people develop and contribute ideas that are crystalized and exploited by a few entrepreneurs. Some of these ventures result in great success, others in failure, but the tide of innovation continues. Each advance provides a stepping stone that others can build on. This isn't new; keen minds have always sought, and then exploited, the most efficient ways of making calculations and keeping pace with the explosion of information. In this topic, we look at just a few of the key people and developments that have led to the microcomputer industry.

MECHANICAL COMPUTERS

Computers, or more accurately, calculators, have been around for a long time. Some of the earliest like Stonehenge, which is thought to have been used to calculate the movement of the sun, had no moving parts.

The abacus (Figure 1-6) was probably the first calculator with moving parts, and in many areas of the world, it is still widely used. Over the years, mechanical calculators grew more and more complex. In this section, you

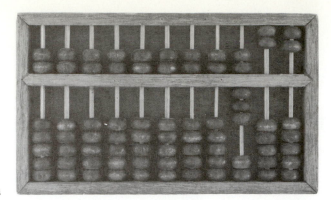

FIGURE 1-6
The Abacus
The abacus was the first calculator with moving parts. Courtesy of The Peabody Museum of Salem

meet some of the key persons during this first period of development. By no means are they the only ones who contributed to the development of calculating machines. Hundreds of other people contributed ideas and techniques on which these persons' ideas were based. Although their mechanical machines look primitive by today's standards, many of the principles they discovered are still in use in today's computers. These brief profiles don't begin to reveal the intellectual contributions of these people, many of whom also made significant contributions to science, mathematics, and philosophy.

Blaise Pascal (1623-1662): The First Commercial Failure

Blaise Pascal (Figure 1-7), a noted mathematician, scientist, and theologian, was born in Claremont, France, in 1623. He was one of the inventors of the barometer (and used it to prove that air has weight), the syringe, and the hydraulic press. In 1639, his father, Etienne Pascal, took a position with the tax service and used Blaise, who was only sixteen, to perform many of the laborious calculations required in this new position. Blaise conceived an idea for a calculator that would eliminate the drudgery of this kind of work, and for the next decade, he perfected the idea. The result was the Pascaline, a polished brass box containing a sophisticated calculating mechanism made up of gears (Figure 1-8).

FIGURE 1-7
Blaise Pascal
Blaise Pascal was one of the first to develop a calculating machine, the Pascaline. Courtesy of R.J. Proctor, 4-5-6 World

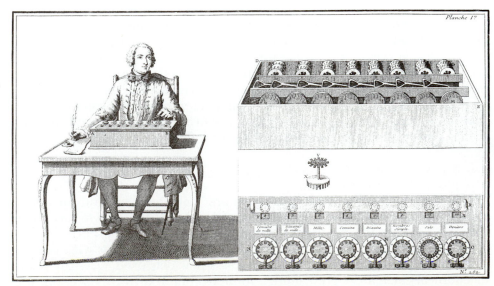

MICROCOMPUTER SYSTEMS

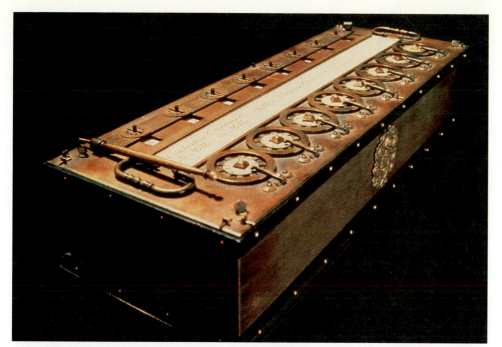

FIGURE 1-8
The Pascaline Calculator
The Pascaline had the digits from 0 to 9 arranged on wheels. When one wheel was turned in a complete revolution, it incremented the adjoining wheel one digit, much like the odometer in an automobile. Numbers could be added and subtracted as they were entered. Buyers didn't exactly rush to his door though, many feeling the simple machine was too complicated (sound familiar?). Courtesy of IBM Corporation

A Modern Version of the Pascaline

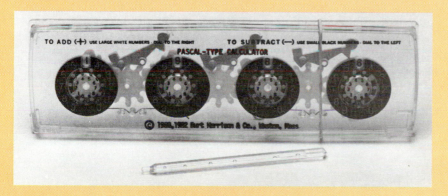

A simplified version of the Pascaline is still being manufactured and sold. Although largely a curiosity item, this inexpensive lucite unit from the Boston Computer Museum clearly shows the principles of the original.

Photo courtesy of Burt Harrison & Company, Weston, Ma.

Gottfried Wilhelm Leibniz (1646-1716): The First Commercial Success

Leibniz (Figure 1-9), one of the great minds of the seventeenth century, was born in Germany twenty-three years after Pascal. He gained fame throughout Europe for his achievements as a philosopher, jurist, historian, diplomat, and mathematician. He developed the concept of infinitesimal calculus (developed independently and at the same time by Newton).

FIGURE 1-9
Gottfried Wilhelm Leibniz
Leibniz developed the first commercially successful mechanical calculator.
Courtesy of IBM Corporation

Leibniz designed a calculator that could not only add and subtract, as did Pascal's, but also could multiply, divide, and calculate square roots (Figure 1-10). It was the first calculator that met with commercial success. A somewhat modified version, called the Arithmometer, was manufactured starting in 1862 and remained in production until the 1930s.

FIGURE 1-10
The Leibniz Calculator
The Leibniz calculator could not only add and subtract but could also multiply, divide, and calculate square roots.
Courtesy of IBM Corporation

Charles Babbage (1791-1871): The First Punched Cards

Charles Babbage (Figure 1-11), one of the founders of the Astronomical and Statistical Societies, was born in England in 1791. While a student at Cambridge University, he had an idea for a calculator that would calculate and print logarithmic tables, which were extensively used at that time in navigation.

Babbage secured several grants from the Royal Society and British government to refine and produce the machine, which he called a difference engine. After a series of problems, the machine was left uncompleted, and Babbage turned his attention to another, more powerful concept, the analytical engine (Figure 1-12).

His idea was to use punched cards, similar to those used in the

FIGURE 1-11
Charles Babbage
Babbage's mechanical calculators were the first to use punched cards to input data to be processed. However, they were never completed, so they were not commercially successful. Courtesy of IBM Corporation

Jacquard-loom to control weaving patterns (see *Punched Cards and the Jacquard-Loom*) to input both instructions and the data to be calculated.

Commercially, Babbage's inventions were failures. He spent £17,000, an enormous sum at that time, and neither of his machines was completed in his lifetime. A government official said that the only use of the analytical engine was to calculate the large amount of money Babbage spent on it. Adjusted for inflation, that sum of money would probably buy him the most powerful computer on the market today.

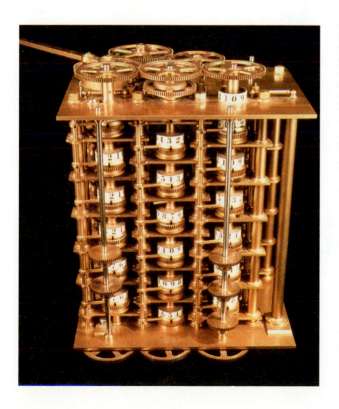

FIGURE 1-12
Babbage's Analytical Engine
Babbage's analytical engine was controlled by punched cards, still widely used until recently. The machine had two parts. The first was the "store" designed so that numbers could be stored in 1000 "registers," each capable of storing 50 digits (the first memory). The second was the "mill" (one of the first processors). When the machine was instructed to do so by the punched cards, it could retrieve the numbers, operate on them in the mill, and then store them back in the registers. Courtesy of Historical Picture Service, Chicago, Ill.

Punched Cards and the Jacquard-Loom

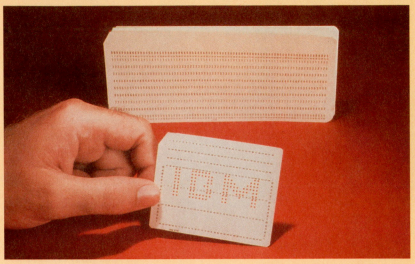

Courtesy of IBM Corporation

If you were a student a few years ago, you would have found yourself standing in a long line with a deck of punched cards in your hand waiting to turn them in so that the data processing department could run them through their computer for you. Computers were expensive, complicated, and not at all interactive. They processed data in "batches," and the program and data were often fed to them on punched cards.

Courtesy of IBM Corporation

Punched cards were first used in 1805 to control the weaving process in the Jacquard-loom, invented by Joseph Marie Jacquard. The cards were punched so that moving rods on the loom could be guided to select only certain threads. In this way, they controlled the complicated weaving patterns in the fabric.

Ada Augusta Lovelace (1815-1852): The First Programmer

While in her late twenties, Ada Lovelace (Figure 1-13), the daughter of the poet Lord Byron, became involved with the work on Babbage's analytical engine. Among her many contributions, she suggested using the machine's ability to jump from one set of punched cards to another if certain conditions were met. This meant separate sets of cards would not have to be prepared each time the same calculating process was reused. When a process was to be repeated, the machine would "jump" to the necessary set of cards and use them. This is the principle behind contemporary programmer's use of loops and subroutines. Working with Babbage, Lovelace also designed a program to compute Bernoulli numbers on the machine. Because of these contributions to the development of computers, Lovelace is considered the first programmer. In the 1970s, a new programming language, Ada, was named after her.

George Boole (1815-1864): The Founder of Information Theory

George Boole (Figure 1-14) is another of our innovators whose contributions were purely intellectual. Boole was born in England in 1815 and was a contemporary of Charles Babbage. He created no machine, but his ideas about how symbols could be used to manipulate information form the basis on which all modern computers calculate. He built on an idea introduced by Leibniz almost 200 years earlier—that "truth" could be determined by reducing statements to mathematical expressions. Called symbolic logic, Boole extensively developed this idea. He reduced statements to symbols and manipulated them by means of algebraic formulas to determine certain truths. This process has become known as Boolean algebra and is widely used in computing and philosophy.

Herman Hollerith (1860-1929): The First Empire Builder

Although the United States census survey was completed in 1880, it took more than seven years and thousands of clerks who manually tabulated the responses to publish the results. By the time the results were published, they were out of date. John Billings, in charge of vital statistics at the Bureau of the Census, mentioned to Herman Hollerith (Figure 1-15) that there should be a way to use punched cards, which had been used in the Jacquard loom to mechanize the weaving process. Taking the suggestion to heart, Hollerith began to develop the idea. By 1884, shortly after resigning from the bureau, he had made enough progress to apply for a patent on his machine.

Hollerith's tabulating machine (Figure 1-16) used cards in which clerks punched holes. The patterns of the holes described each person's response to the survey questionnaire. The cards were then inserted into a pin reader that tabulated the results. Pins going through the holes in the cards made an electrical contact that advanced the counters for each hole. The use of this electromechanical equipment allowed the bureau, in its 1890 U.S. census, to release the total population figure (62,622,250) only one month after the questionnaire returns had arrived in Washington. A complete tabulation, breaking down the responses in great detail, took only two and a half years, three times faster than the previous census.

Hollerith established the Tabulating Machine Company to commercially exploit his technology. His company manufactured the machines and cards and provided consulting services to governments around the world. In

FIGURE 1-13
Ada Augusta Lovelace
Many consider Ada Lovelace the first programmer because of her contributions to the theory behind Babbage's calculators. Courtesy of Charles Babbage Institute, Crown Copyright, National Physical Laboratories

FIGURE 1-14
George Boole
George Boole contributed the concepts of symbol logic and Boolean algebra, which are the basis for the modern computer. Picture Collection, The Branch Libraries, The New York Public Library

1911, his firm merged with three other firms to form the Computing-Tabulating-Recording Company. In 1924, the company was renamed International Business Machines Corporation, one of today's giants in the computer industry.

ELECTRONIC DIGITAL COMPUTERS

During World War II, development began in earnest on electronic computers. The discoveries and breakthroughs that resulted led directly to today's microcomputers.

The story of this period opens in 1937 with Howard Aiken of Harvard University working in conjunction with IBM. Aiken created a large electromechanical calculator. This machine, known originally as the IBM Automatic Sequence-Controlled Calculator and later as the Harvard Mark I (Figure 1-17), was a calculator, not a computer.

The first electronic digital computer was designed by John Atanasoff and Clifford Berry at Iowa State University in 1938. Their machine, called the ABC or Atanasoff-Berry Computer (Figure 1-18), was never completed, and the project was abandoned in 1942. Atanasoff had suggested that Iowa State patent the development, but nothing was done. If the idea had been patented, it would have been worth millions of dollars in royalties to the school over the life of the patent. Although not patented, Atanasoff's work was the basis for a case tried in the courts. A challenge was made to the validity of patents on the ENIAC, a later computer (see below), and the courts determined the patents were invalid on the grounds that Atanasoff was the inventor.

The first operational electronic digital computer was actually created by Konrad Zuse in Germany in 1941. But since World War II was raging at the time, this breakthrough was unknown by anyone outside Germany, and the machine was destroyed later in the war.

Beginning in 1943, major advances were made in the development of electronic digital computers at the University of Pennsylvania. There, John Mauchly and J. Presper Eckert began developing ENIAC (Electronic Numer-

FIGURE 1-15
Herman Hollerith
Hollerith developed a sophisticated tabulating machine for the U.S. Bureau of the Census. The company he founded was eventually merged with other firms. Later, this combined firm changed its name to International Business Machines Corporation, better known as IBM. Courtesy of IBM Corporation

FIGURE 1-16
Hollerith's Tabulating Machine
Hollerith's tabulating machine was the first machine to successfully process data automatically. Cards were punched with holes to record data. These cards were then fed through the machine, and the results were tabulated. The dials on the unit to the left are the equivalent of today's display screen. They always indicated the current count for each hole in the punched cards that had been tabulated. Courtesy of IBM Corporation

ical Integrator and Computer). This computer (Figure 1-19) is considered by many the first operational electronic computer primarily because Zuse's was unknown until years later, and Atanasoff's was never completed. ENIAC was initially designed to solve ballistic problems, but when it became operational in February 1946, it had opened the way to much wider applications. To program it, hundreds of wires were connected to various circuits by hand, a laborious and time-consuming process. ENIAC, however, could perform 5000 arithmetic calculations per second; it was a thousand times faster than the Harvard Mark I.

While ENIAC was being developed, John von Neumann, a professor at Princeton, joined the group at the University of Pennsylvania on a part-time basis to begin work on a second machine, EDVAC. This machine used only one tenth the equipment required by ENIAC and had one hundred times the memory. When a proposal for the machine was written, von Neumann was listed as the editor. The proposal laid out the concepts behind the modern electronic digital computer. The key concept dealt with the **stored program**. Up until this time, the data to be processed, and the instructions on how to process it, called the program, were separately fed to computers. For example, ENIAC was programmed with wires, and hundreds of hours were needed to reprogram the computer each time a new type of problem was to be solved. In the proposal, von Neumann suggested that both the data and the program be stored in memory at the same time. In this way, programs

FIGURE 1-19
ENIAC

ENIAC did not exactly fit on a desk top; it weighed 30 tons, stood 2 stories high, and covered 15,000 square feet of floor space, about the size of a suburban plot of land. It included 18,000 vacuum tubes, 70,000 resistors, 10,000 capacitors, 6000 switches, and more than a 1/2 million hand-soldered connections. When it was turned on, it used 200,000 watts of power, enough to power 600 or more modern personal computers. It's said that when it was turned on, all the lights in West Philadelphia would dim. ENIAC remains on display at the Moore School at the University of Pennsylvania although some of its parts are also displayed at the Smithsonian Institution and the Boston Computer Museum. Courtesy of IBM Corporation

could be changed with the same speed and ease as data. More than forty years later, the microcomputers you use are still based on this principle.

In 1946, Mauchly and Eckert left the university and formed the Electronic Control Company, later renamed the Eckert-Mauchly Computer Corporation. Their intent was to use their experience to design and market computers for use in business. When the company got into financial trouble due to delays in the machine's development, it was bought by Remington Rand in 1950. In 1951, Remington Rand's Univak Division delivered the firm's first computer, a UNIVAC I (Universal Automatic Computer), to the U.S. Census Bureau, and fourteen more were sold before it was replaced with a newer model. This first commercial computer became well known to the public when it was used by CBS to analyze polling responses, and it predicted that Eisenhower would win the 1952 American presidential election. UNIVAC (Figure 1-20) was the first computer to use magnetic tape to store data until it was needed. The first UNIVAC was retired in 1963 and is now on display at the Smithsonian.

Advances in computer technology have continued since the early 1950s. These advances, reflected in computers that were developed during this period, are generally classified into "generations." Each generation incorporated some major advance that made computers faster, more powerful, and more efficient. The definitions of the first three generations are generally agreed on. But the fourth and frequently discussed fifth generations are less well defined.

The First Generation: 1951-1959

The 1950s were the Eisenhower years, the period of drive-in movies, the Korean war, hula-hoops, tail-fins on big cars, saddle shoes, Elvis Presley, Buddy Holly, and the first generation of computers. One of the key charac-

FIGURE 1-20
UNIVAC
The UNIVAC I was 8 feet high, 15 feet long, covered more than 200 square feet of floor space and weighed 5 tons. UNIVAC was the first electronic digital computer sold to the business world. The first model was delivered to the U.S. Bureau of the Census and was a major improvement on Hollerith's tabulating machine, which it had used fifty years earlier. Sperry Corporation Collection, Hagley Museum and Library

teristics of this computer generation was the use of **vacuum tubes** as their active elements. These elements were large, many the size of a household light bulb. They also consumed a great deal of power and gave off large amounts of heat.

Another characteristic of this generation was the storage device that stored data and programs in the computer's main memory. At this time, memory was very expensive. Several kinds of storage were developed, including magnetic tapes and drums. The goal during this period was to make memory both faster and less expensive. The breakthrough came with MIT's development of magnetic core storage (Figure 1-21). On these early computers, punched cards, like those used on the Jacquard-loom, Babbage's differential engine, and Hollerith's tabulating machine, were used to feed data and instructions (programs) into the computer. There were no higher-level languages; rather, all programs were written in machine language, which required very detailed instructions. Typical computers of this era were the EDVAC, Whirlwind, and the IBM 700 series.

The Development of the Computer

The first electronic digital computer built in the United States, ENIAC, was unveiled at the University of Pennsylvania in 1946. It weighed 30 tons, filled the space of a two-car garage, and contained 18,000 vacuum tubes, which failed on average at the rate of one every seven minutes. It cost half a million dollars at 1946 prices.

Today, the same amount of computing power is contained in a pea-sized silicon chip. Almost any home computer costing as little as $100 can outperform ENIAC. Put another way, if the automobile and airplane businesses had developed like the computer business, a Rolls Royce would cost $2.75 and run for 3 million miles on one gallon of gas. And a Boeing 767 would cost just $500 and circle the globe in twenty minutes on five gallons of gas.

Source: Tom Forester, ed. *The Information Technology Revolution* (Cambridge, Mass.: The MIT Press, 1985).

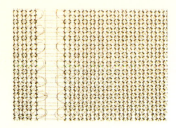

FIGURE 1-21
Magnetic Core Storage
Magnetic core storage was originally developed independently by An Wang, who later founded Wang Laboratories, one of the leading computer companies, and F. W. Viehe, who began working on improved storage techniques in the 1940s. The technique was developed further at MIT, RCA, and IBM in the early 1950s. This form of computer memory was extensively used in the 1950s and 1960s because it was much faster and more reliable than the devices previously used for computer memory. Courtesy of IBM Corporation

The Second Generation: 1959-1964

The early 1960s were the Kennedy years, the period of John Glenn orbiting the earth, the Beatles on the Ed Sullivan show, and the second generation of computers. This generation was based on the **transistor**. Although invented at Bell Labs in 1948, it was not until 1959 that the technology and production methods existed to use them in computers. These second generation computers contained approximately 10,000 individual transistors. The transistors were mounted by hand on boards and connected to each other and to other elements with wires. Transistors had several advantages over vacuum tubes. They were less expensive, faster, smaller, required less power, and gave off less heat. The first commercial computer to use them was the Philco Transac S-2000. But it was the IBM 1401 that had the greatest effect at this time. This machine sold so well it doubled the number of computers in operation and propelled IBM into its leadership position. Even today, there are still programs in operation that were developed for this early workhorse.

The Third Generation: 1964-1970

The late 1960s and early 1970s were the Nixon years, the period of the Vietnam War, hippies, the landing on the moon, the rise of Silicon Valley, and the third generation of computers. The key technological development in this generation of computers was the **integrated circuit (IC)**. The introduction of the integrated circuit and of large scale integration (LSI) made it possible to put thousands of circuits onto a single silicon chip. The complexity of the circuits that could be economically made increased dramati-

---

What Is an Electronic Digital Computer?

The development from mechanical calculators to today's computers has involved stages, with electricity becoming increasingly important at each stage. In the first stage, only mechanical parts were used, and calculators were usually operated by hand. A few calculators, like Babbage's, were larger and powered by steam. With Hollerith's tabulating machine, however, electricity began to be used to power the machines and to assist in the calculation process. From this stage on, electronics became the power behind the computer. Let's look at what the three words mean in the phrase **electronic digital computer**.

Electronic means the computer uses electronic devices, such as transistors, to process information. Earlier computers used mechanical devices like gears or electromechanical devices like relays to perform calculations.

Digital means the computer processes and stores digital signals that are based on binary arithmetic. Binary arithmetic uses only two digits, 0 and 1, to represent any familiar decimal number. The ability to use just two digits to represent any number allows numbers, letters, and other characters that can be represented by numbers to be stored in electronic devices that have only two possible states, on and off. When on, the device represents the digit 1; when off, it represents the digit 0.

Computer means a device that can store and process data based on a set of instructions or a program.

---

cally, as did the power of the computers they were used in. The number of active electronic elements in a computer rose from 10,000 to more than 0.5 million. The low cost, high reliability, small size, low power consumption, and speed of operation of these tiny chips greatly advanced the development of the computer and contributed to the development of the microcomputer. Also during this generation, magnetic disks came into use to store programs and data until they were needed by the computer; previously, they had been stored on magnetic tape.

The introduction of the IBM 360 series of computers (Figure 1-22) launched the third generation. During this period, the first minicomputer was introduced when Digital Equipment Corporation developed the PDP-1 (Programmed Data Processor). When introduced in November 1960, the PDP-1 cost about $120,000, far less expensive than the larger mainframe computers being sold at that time.

The Fourth and Fifth Generations: 1970-?

There is much disagreement about generations after the first three. Technical advances have been diverse, but none have been as profound as the steps from the vacuum tube to the transistor to the integrated circuit. Without some watershed step in technology, there is a great deal of room for disagreement. Some contend that we are already in the fifth, sixth, or later generation. Others contend that this period of refinement of existing technologies is actually the fourth generation. If one significant advance identifies this period, it is the development of the **microprocessor**, the special type of integrated circuit that is at the heart of every microcomputer. We discuss this device in detail in Topic 1-4.

At the moment, there is no fifth generation of computers; there is just a rush to develop it. The outcome is yet to be determined, but the process of getting there should be entertaining for observers and critical to the success of the winners and losers. The key to the fifth generation will be vastly expanded memory, increased operating speed, and more complex software. The goal is to make the computer easier to use and capable of solving ever more complex problems. Behind this development, rests the concept of **artificial intelligence (AI)**, the ability of a computer to simulate human reasoning. It is the hope of the fifth generation developers that this concept can be implemented on these computers.

FIGURE 1-22
The IBM 360
The IBM 360 computer launched the third generation of computers. Courtesy of IBM Corporation

MICROCOMPUTER HARDWARE— THE KEY DEVELOPMENTS

In 1972, Intel introduced a new microprocessor chip invented by one of its engineers, Marcian E. (Ted) Hoff. This microprocessor, and related ones called the 8000 series, gave birth to the entire microcomputer industry. The microprocessor's sophistication, small size, and low cost made the development of microcomputers possible. These microprocessors could do everything a large computer could do. To make them work, all that was required was to connect a keyboard and memory to them so that data and programs could be entered and stored. The microprocessor would then perform all the calculations needed to process the data; it was a computer on a chip. Additional devices, like printers or display screens, were needed to get this information out of the chip so that it could be seen. It wasn't long before these chips, and their faster and more powerful descendents, were incorporated into microcomputers by the early microcomputer developers.

1975: The MITS Altair

The cover of *Popular Electronics'* January 1975 issue (Figure 1-23) featured a new wonder, the MITS Altair 8800 computer kit. It sold for $395 in kit form or $695 assembled. The cover story began when Les Soloman, an editor at *Popular Electronics*, visited a friend in Albuquerque, New Mexico, who introduced him to Ed Roberts. At the time, Roberts' company, Micro Instrumentation and Telemetry Systems (MITS), was selling kits that could be assembled into calculators. Shortly thereafter, Roberts heard about the Intel 8008 microprocessor chip and was able to obtain an even newer version, the 8080. Working with a few friends, he developed a computer kit that any experienced hobbyist could assemble. Roberts then contacted Soloman, and Soloman agreed to do a cover story on the machine. While experimenting with the computer, Soloman thought it needed a catchy name. He asked his daughter, who was watching "Star Trek," what she would call it. "Why don't you call it Altair? That's where Enterprise is going in this episode."

This first microcomputer had no keyboard, printer, display screen, or external storage device. It was programmed using switches on the front of the case, and lights flashed for output. MITS was never adequately financed and eventually was sold to one of the companies that supplied its components.

1977: The Apple II

Because of its complexity, the MITS Altair did not achieve wide sales. The first microcomputer to do so was the Apple. The first Apple, the Apple I, was developed in a garage by Steve Jobs and Stephen Wozniak. At the time, Wozniak worked for Hewlett-Packard, and Jobs worked for Atari. They had worked together on earlier projects, including the game Breakout that ran on the Atari. Both were also members of the Homebrew Computer Club along with hundreds of other computer enthusiasts in the San Francisco Bay area. Wozniak developed a computer that he demonstrated to the club members. Jobs thought it had a market and encouraged Wozniak to join him in a company to develop and market it. They sold Jobs's Volkswagen van and Wozniak's calculator to raise $1350 to finance the development of the computer. When its design was completed in the garage of Jobs's parent's home, Jobs sold fifty Apple Is to one of the first retail computer stores

FIGURE 1-23
The MITS Altair
The MITS Altair 8800 was featured on the cover of the January 1975 issue of *Popular Electronics*. It was the first microcomputer to be widely sold in the United States. Reprinted from *Popular Electronics*, January 1975. Copyright © 1975 Ziff-Davis Publishing Company.

in the country. They used the purchase order to secure credit at an electronic supply store to buy the parts they needed to assemble the final units. The Apple I sold for $666.66, and they sold fewer than 200 partly because Wozniak insisted they also give the plans away free so that anyone could build their own.

In 1977, the Apple II was introduced. It was an improved, more elegantly packaged version of the Apple I. Unlike the Apple I, which was aimed at experienced hobbyists, the Apple II included a keyboard, a power supply, and the ability to generate color graphics. In 1978, Apple Computer introduced the first floppy disk drive for microcomputers. Until then, users had to store programs and data on slower tape cassettes. The Apple II was enthusiastically received by **hackers**, a group of people who loved electronic equipment and had been hoping for a computer they could explore long into the night. It also paved the way for the incorporation of the microcomputer into the business world. Jobs and Wozniak built Apple Computer into a major corporation; in fact, it was the fastest growing company in American history. Its sales rocketed from less than $1 million in 1977 to more than $300 million four years later. By 1983, a million Apple IIs had been sold, and another million were sold over the next twelve months. This success wasn't without a price. Both of the founders left the firm in 1985 for different reasons. Wozniak was disenchanted with working in a large corporation, which Apple had become. And Jobs was forced out by the professional managers he had hired because they felt his philosophies were no longer consistent with theirs.

1981: The IBM PC

The success of the Apple II was watched carefully by all the major computer companies, which until this time had concentrated on large, expensive computers. IBM, the world's largest computer company, was impressed with what it saw. It broke traditions and set up a special group in Boca Raton, Florida, to develop its own microcomputer, the IBM PC. This computer, introduced in 1981, set records for sales and quickly became the standard around which most other manufacturers designed their computers. Phillip Esteridge (Figure 1-24), who ran this entrepreneurial division that had such an impact on the industry, died in an airplane crash in Dallas in 1985.

1984: The Apple Macintosh

In 1983, Apple Computer introduced an easier-to-use computer called the Lisa. This computer was based partly on technology developed at Xerox's Palo Alto Research Center (PARC) in California that made it easier to use a computer by pointing to icons and pop-up menus on the screen and clicking with a mouse. The idea for the pop-up menus was developed by Dan Ingalls at PARC in the early 1970s. The idea for the mouse was developed at about the same time by Doug Engelbart at Stanford Research Center. The icons and menus that were displayed on the screen made it unnecessary for users to remember commands. The Lisa was priced at just under $10,000 and found only a limited audience. However, the Lisa led to the development of the Apple Macintosh, which was introduced in 1984. This computer was a breakthrough in the computer field. Not only was it easy to use, it also was powerful and inexpensive. When Apple introduced the Apple LaserWriter printer in 1985, it and the Macintosh led to the development of the desktop publishing field (see Part Four).

FIGURE 1-24
Phillip Esteridge
Phillip Esteridge led the IBM development team that developed the highly successful IBM PC in 1981. Courtesy of IBM Corporation

THE APPLE STORY

Apple has been a phenomenal success story. From its origins in a garage, it became the fastest growing corporation in history and led to the widespread use of microcomputers in the home and business.

All photos courtesy of Apple Computer, Inc.

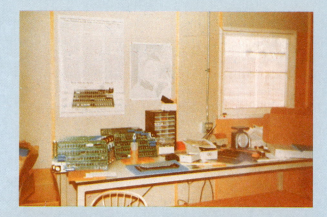

Jobs's Garage
The Apple computer was developed in Steve Jobs's garage.

Jobs and Wozniak
Steve Wozniak (left) and Steve Jobs hold one of the original Apple I boards, the heart of the computer.

The Original Apple I
The first Apple, the Apple I, had to be assembled with other components to be useful. Here a board has been installed in a briefcase.

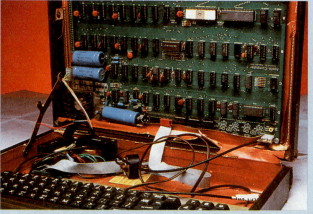

The First Apple Logo
The Apple logo is well known but wasn't developed until after the first computer was introduced. Here is the first logo developed for the computer.

The Byte Shop
This is the computer store where Steve Jobs sold the first fifty Apple I computers, giving Wozniak and him the funds they needed to continue.

The Apple II
The Apple II changed all of our lives by making an easy-to-use microcomputer widely available. Its phenomenal success led to the introduction of many other microcomputers by many manufacturers.

The Apple Macintosh
The Apple Macintosh was the first easy-to-use computer available at a reasonable price. It set the direction in user friendliness that is now being incorporated into all competing computers.

THE IBM STORY

IBM, long a leader in the computer business, introduced the IBM PC in 1981 and set the standard for almost all non-Apple business computers to come.

All photos courtesy of IBM Corporation

An Early IBM Building
The sign on this early IBM building lists some of the companies from which the world's largest computer manufacturer was formed.

Thomas J. Watson
Thomas J. Watson joined the CTR Co. in 1914 at a time when it had just over 1300 employees. His drive and foresight over the next forty-two years made IBM into the world's largest computer company. His employment at IBM spanned the entire period of the development of the modern electronic digital computer.

The IBM PC
The IBM PC was introduced in August 1981 and was soon adopted by business offices as the standard microcomputer. The standards it established are now followed by almost all other computer manufacturers.

The IBM AT
The IBM AT, which used the 80286 microprocessor, was introduced in August 1984. This computer operated much faster than previous models because the new microprocessor was so much more powerful.

The PS/2
In 1987, IBM introduced their PS/2 line of computers. Only some of the first models used the latest 80386 chip, the fastest and most powerful microprocessor available from Intel. Over the next few years, all computers in the line were converted to use this chip.

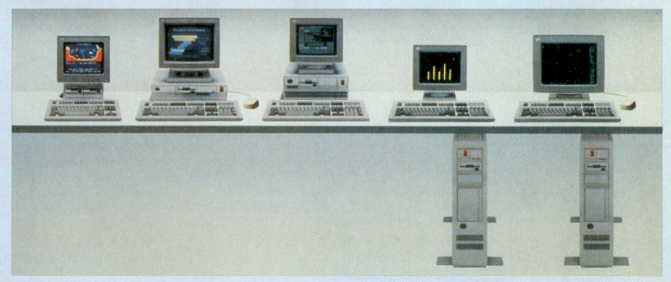

MICROCOMPUTER SOFTWARE—THE KEY DEVELOPMENTS

When microcomputers first became available, most people could not use them. They had to be programmed for each task, and programming is a skill mastered by relatively few. But the advances in microcomputer hardware were matched by equally significant advances in the programs needed to operate the hardware so that it could be used by people without a technical background. To make this possible, three kinds of software were needed: an operating system to control the computer, a programming language so that programmers could write programs, and applications programs so that people who couldn't program could still use the computer. These needs were soon filled with the introduction of new programming languages, operating systems, and applications programs.

1975: Microsoft BASIC

Bill Gates (Figure 1-25), a freshman at Harvard, and Paul Allen, a programmer at Honeywell, began experimenting with the MITS Altair as soon as it was introduced. Unfortunately, there were no applications programs available for the computer, and there was no easy way to write them. Together, they wrote a version of BASIC for the Altair. This easy-to-learn programming language had been originally developed by John Kemeny and Thomas Kurtz at Dartmouth for use on larger computers. But with its introduction for the Altair, users could begin writing their own applications programs. The success of this program led, in 1974, to the founding of Microsoft, which has become a major microcomputer software company.

1976: CP/M

Gary Kildall (Figure 1-26), who was working for Intel at the time, saw the need for an easy-to-use operating system that would control the keyboard, display monitor, and disk drives on the new microcomputers. He developed CP/M (Control Program for Microcomputers) for his own use and offered it to Intel. They rejected it because they didn't see a market for such a program. In 1976, Kildall and his wife founded Digital Research to market CP/M, which quickly became the standard operating system for the first generation of microcomputers.

1979: VisiCalc

Dan Bricklin (Figure 1-27), a graduate business student, was tired of all the erasing and recalculating required for financial analysis. He knew that there had to be a better way and that the new microcomputers might be just the tool he needed. He conceived of an electronic spreadsheet, essentially a computerized version of the timeless accountant's green, ruled ledger pad. He approached Bob Frankston (Figure 1-27) with the idea, and Frankston agreed it could be done on the microcomputers then available. The two developed the program, which was then marketed by Dan Flystra, another student from the Boston area. When introduced for the Apple II in 1979, VisiCalc (for *Visible Calculator*) caused a sensation. Until then, business people did not use microcomputers because they were still too complicated to program and use. But VisiCalc made microcomputers into a valuable tool for anyone doing financial calculations. Users could enter labels, numbers, and formulas. To make a change, they just entered a new number in place of

FIGURE 1-25
Bill Gates
Bill Gates and Paul Allen wrote the first BASIC programming language for microcomputers. The success of this program launched Microsoft Corporation, developers and publishers of many leading microcomputer programs. Courtesy of Microsoft Corporation

FIGURE 1-26
Gary Kildall
Gary Kildall wrote the first microcomputer operating system, CP/M, and formed Digital Research to develop and market it. Courtesy of Digital Research, Inc.

FIGURE 1-27
Dan Bricklin and Bob Frankston
Dan Bricklin (far left) and Bob Frankston jointly developed VisiCalc, the first commercially successful business applications program for microcomputers. Courtesy of Lotus Development Corporation

an old one. They did not have to continually erase and recalculate all the other numbers affected by this change; VisiCalc did that for them automatically. The introduction of VisiCalc is usually credited with making the Apple II the fastest selling computer of its time and with making the microcomputer acceptable in business offices. In 1985, Software Arts, the company Bricklin and Frankston had founded, was bought by Lotus Development Corporation, and the last copy of VisiCalc was shipped. In the six years of its life, it had sold more than 750,000 copies.

1979: WordStar

When the MITS Altair was introduced, one of the first applications programs developed for it was a word processing program called Electric Pencil, written by Michael Schrayer in 1975 and 1976. In 1978, Seymour Rubenstein (Figure 1-28) formed MicroPro to develop and market his own new word processing program. By August, he and John Barnaby had finished the original program, called WordMaster, and by 1979, they had revised it and renamed it WordStar. This program was to become the first standard in word processing.

FIGURE 1-28
Seymour Rubinstein
Seymour Rubinstein developed WordStar, the first widely successful microcomputer word processing program. Courtesy of Micropro International

1980: dBASE II

Wayne Ratliff (Figure 1-29) was working at the Jet Propulsion Laboratory on a data management and information retrieval system in 1977. This program was written for a large mainframe computer, but over the next few years, he transferred the system to his personal computer and improved it. In 1979, he ran ads for the program (then called Vulcan) in *Byte* magazine. In 1980, he was approached by George Tate and George Lashlee, who bought the rights to the program and renamed it dBase II. They then formed the company Ashton-Tate to market the program, which has since become the leading database management program for microcomputers. The name dBASE II was suggested by a consultant who felt the II conveyed the idea that the program was improved from an earlier version. Actually, there never was a dBase I version.

FIGURE 1-29
Wayne Ratliff
Ratliff developed dBASE II, the first successful database management program for microcomputers. Courtesy of Migent

1981: PC-DOS

IBM introduced their PC in 1981 and accompanied it with a new operating system, PC-DOS. A delegation from IBM had approached Bill Gates at Microsoft, thinking he was the owner of CP/M, then the leading operating system. Gates directed the group to Kildall at Digital Research, who actually owned the program. Kildall and IBM discussed revising the program for the IBM PC, and the next day, Kildall left on vacation. When he returned, he discovered that IBM had struck a deal with Microsoft. Bill Gates and his team at Microsoft bought a program called QDOS (Quick and Dirty DOS) from Seattle Computer Products. Using this program as their starting point, they developed an operating system called MS-DOS (for Microsoft Disk Operating System). The IBM PC version of this program was named PC-DOS. This is now the most widely used microcomputer operating system.

1983: Lotus 1-2-3

Mitch Kapor (Figure 1-30), a friend of Bricklin's and Frankston's, wrote a few programs that could be used with VisiCalc to do statistical analysis and plot graphs. He sold these programs for $1 million and used the money to start Lotus Development Corporation. Not satisfied with the amount of work involved in graphing spreadsheet data using a separate program, Kapor conceived of combining, or integrating, the two functions into a program so that graphs could be displayed by just pressing a single key. He joined with Jonathan Sachs (Figure 1-30), a programmer who had already developed three spreadsheet programs for his clients. With Kapor's guidance and experience with graphics programs and Sachs's programming talents, they developed Lotus 1-2-3. Although Kapor is widely given sole credit for the development of 1-2-3, it was actually Sachs who wrote the entire program. Just as VisiCalc had contributed greatly to the success of the Apple II, 1-2-3 made the IBM PC useful to people in business and helped it gain its leading edge in the market. Though 1-2-3 was similar to VisiCalc, it was faster, more powerful, easier to learn, and had integrated graphics and limited database capabilities.

FIGURE 1-30
Mitch Kapor and Jonathan Sachs
Mitch Kapor (top) and Jonathan Sachs developed 1-2-3, the most successful applications program developed for microcomputers. This spreadsheet is the major product of the company they co-founded, Lotus Development Corporation. Courtesy of Lotus Development Corporation

1984: VisiOn

VisiOn was a major product that failed almost before it was born. Developed by Dan Flystra's VisiCorp (the company that marketed VisiCalc), the program was designed so that you could run more than one applications program at a time. Using VisiOn, you could do word processing in one window on the screen and use a spreadsheet to calculate numbers in another window. The idea was sound and led directly to programs like Windows and IBM's Presentation Manager. However, after years of promises (contributing to the term **vaporware** to describe software that is promised but never delivered), the program was finally introduced when VisiCorp was in serious financial trouble and there was a slowdown in the industry. Much of VisiCorp's time and money was spent in a legal battle with the developers of VisiCalc, and the new program failed in the marketplace. The rights to the program were eventually sold to a large computer company, but the program never gained acceptance in the market.

1985: PageMaker

Until 1985, most microcomputer users could process information but could not present it in an attractive format. In 1984, Paul Brainard founded Aldus Corporation, where he and a team of people familiar with publishing developed a new program called PageMaker. This program, and the almost simultaneous introduction of the Apple LaserWriter laser printer, changed the way information could be presented. With these tools, users could integrate text and graphics and print documents that looked as if they had been prepared by a professional printing company. This program launched the new field of **desktop publishing**.

MICROCOMPUTER SYSTEMS

Altair, WordMaster, Tiny Troll, and Vulcan

The first developers of microcomputer hardware and software were not your typical corporate managers. They were highly creative persons, who worked on their own time with limited resources but with vivid imaginations. One of the best indicators of the way they thought was the names they originally gave their hardware and software.

The first microcomputer, the MITS Altair, was named after a planet on the "Star Trek" TV show. The first version of WordStar was called WordMaster, the first version of a program that led to Lotus 1-2-3 was called Tiny Troll, and the first version of dBase II was called Vulcan. It's not hard to imagine all these names being used in a Saturday-morning TV cartoon show.

When the developers of these products raised the funds to create their companies, most of the names were changed. And a good thing they were—its hard to imagine your banker using his or her Altair to analyze your business on Tiny Troll, keep your records on Vulcan, and write a rejection of your loan application on WordMaster.

SUMMARY AND KEY TERMS

- Today's microcomputers have evolved from mechanical calculators introduced in the seventeenth century.
- The first **electronic digital computer** was designed at Iowa State, but it never became operational. The first operational electronic digital computer was the ENIAC, which was developed at the University of Pennsylvania.
- John von Neumann developed the **stored program** concept that allowed programs to be stored in the computer's memory.
- The first computers used **vacuum tubes**, but **solid-state transistors** were then introduced. Today's computers use chips, called **integrated circuits**, on which are mounted thousands of transistors.
- A special chip called a **microprocessor** is capable of processing information.
- The first microcomputer to find a wide audience was the Apple II, and its success in the business market was largely due to the introduction of VisiCalc, the first spreadsheet program.

REVIEW QUESTIONS

1. What was the impetus behind the development of the Pascaline?
2. What was the first machine to use punched cards? What was the first computing machine to do so?
3. What was Ada Lovelace's contribution to the computer's development?
4. For what job was Hollerith's tabulating machine first used? What well-known company did his firm later become a part of?
5. What was the name of the first operational electronic digital computer? What was the first operational American computer?

6. What concept did John von Neumann contribute to the development of computers?

7. Define the three words in the phrase *electronic digital computer*.

8. Name the key technical innovations that fueled the first three computer generations.

9. What are the goals of the developers of fifth-generation computers?

10. What was the first microcomputer? The first commercially successful microcomputer?

11. What applications program led to the wide acceptance of the microcomputer in business?

TOPIC 1-3

The Digital Revolution

OBJECTIVES

After completing this topic, you will be able to

- Explain what the term *digital* means
- Describe the code and electronic device used in digital processing
- Explain how digital data is organized into bits, bytes, and words
- Describe how bytes are used to convey characters and commands

A single concept behind the computer, and almost all other equipment, is revolutionizing the field of information processing. It is the concept of **digital processing**. You may have heard this term used in connection with the music industry, where music is stored on compact discs in digital form. Digital processing simply refers to a way information, be it music or documents, is stored so that it can be processed and used. Before looking at the parts of the computer in detail, let's look at this basic concept.

Digital is derived from the word *digit*, which means a single number. When you write a check or count your change, you use the digits 0 through 9 either alone or, to convey larger numbers, in combination. The digits 1 and 9 can convey $1 or $9, or they can be combined to convey $19, $91, $19.19, and so on. This numbering system, which uses the ten digits from 0 to 9, is called the **decimal system**. You use this system when you dial the phone, look up pages in the index of a book, or address a letter to a specific street address.

The decimal system is complicated. To master the system in grade school, you had to memorize tables. For example, to add 2 + 2, you do not calculate, you recall the answer 4 from memory. To multiply 3 × 2, you recall the answer 6 from memory. If you never learned the tables or if you forget them, you may find it hard, or even impossible, to calculate with the decimal system.

Computers and other digital equipment use a simpler numbering system, the **binary system**. The binary system uses only two numbers, 0 and 1, to convey all numbers. As Table 1-2 shows, any number can be conveyed with these two digits.

Binary numbers are conveyed in an unfamiliar form, so they look much more complicated than they really are. Since binary numbers comprise only

41

TABLE 1-2
Decimal and Binary Equivalents

TABLE 1-2
Decimal and Binary Equivalents

Decimal Number	Binary Equivalent	Decimal Number	Binary Equivalent
0	0	6	110
1	1	7	111
2	10	8	1000
3	11	9	1001
4	100	10	1010
5	101	11	1011

0s and 1s, their major advantage is that they can be processed in several ways with a variety of devices:

- If you have a device that can be turned on and off, you can have on represent 1 and off represent 0.
- If you have a device that can emit high or low voltages, you can have the high voltage represent 1 and the low voltage represent 0.
- If you can align magnetic particles on a surface so that they point in opposite directions, you can have one direction represent 1 and the other direction represent 0.
- If you can have dots on a display screen be either illuminated or dark, you can have 1 illuminate a dot and 0 leave a dot dark.
- If you can have a printer that prints dots on a sheet of paper, you can have 1 tell it to print a dot and 0 leave a dot white.

All these techniques are used in microcomputers to store, process, and display information. To take it one step further, you can convey information with these numbers if you have an agreed-on code. We now see how various devices and codes can be used to convey information.

PAUL REVERE'S RIDE—THE FIRST DIGITAL REVOLUTION?

You may have heard or read Longfellow's poem *Paul Revere's Ride*. Here are a few stanzas of the poem:

> *Listen, my children, and you shall hear*
> *Of the midnight ride of Paul Revere,*
> *On the eighteenth of April, in Seventy-five;*
> *Hardly a man is now alive*
> *Who remembers that famous day and year.*
>
> *He said to his friend, "If the British march*
> *By land or sea from the town tonight,*
> *Hang a lantern aloft in the belfry arch*
> *Of the North Church as a signal light,—*
> *One, if by land, and two, if by sea;*
> *And I on the opposite shore will be,*
> *Ready to ride and spread the alarm*
> *Through every Middlesex village and farm,*
> *For the country folk to be up and to arm."*

This was a digital message. When America was a colony of England, Paul Revere was assigned the job of notifying the Minutemen who lived in the countryside if the British left Boston to attack them. He and his friend Robert Newman, the sexton of Old North Church, decided that Revere would wait on the other side of the harbor so that he had a head start should the British troops begin to move. Newman would remain in Boston to watch for any troop movements. Since Revere would be miles away, they needed a way for Newman to let him know the route the British were taking if they left Boston to attack. They decided that Newman would light one lantern in the belfry of Old North Church if the British were leaving Boston by land, and two lanterns if they were going by sea. This simple digital signal sent Paul Revere on his famous ride (Figure 1-31) that resulted in "the shot heard round the world" at the bridge in Concord.

THE TELEGRAPH—THE FIRST DIGITAL CODE

Lanterns have their limits when it comes to sending information. It is hard to spell out messages. For example, if the British had been able to take an unexpected route, Paul Revere's prearranged code would not have been able to convey the message. This problem was solved by Samuel Morse, who, co-incidentally, lived on the same shore where Paul Revere stood when he saw the lantern's light in the Old North Church. Morse invented the telegraph in the early 1800s.

With the telegraph (Figure 1-32), a sender taps on a key to send pulses

FIGURE 1-31
The First Digital Revolution
Paul Revere's ride began when he saw a lantern lit in the tower of Old North Church. Courtesy of The Bettman Archive, Inc.

A

Letters		Q	— —·—	7	— —···
		R	·—·	8	— — —··
A	·—	S	···	9	— — — —·
B	—···	T	—	0	— — — — —
C	—·—·	U	··—		
D	—··	V	···—	Punctuation	
E	·	W	·— —		
F	··—·	X	—··—	·	··· ···
G	— —·	Y	—·— —	;	—·—·—
H	····	Z	— —··	:	·—·—·
I	··	Numbers		?	··— —··
J	·— — —			!	— —··— —
K	—·—	1	·— — — —		
L	·—··	2	··— — —	Formats	
M	— —	3	···— —		
N	—·	4	····—	Underline ··— —·—	
O	— — —	5	·····	Return —··—	
P	·— —·	6	—····		

B

FIGURE 1-32
The First Digital Code
(a) The telegraph was used to send short dots and longer dashes down a wire to the recipient. (b) These dots and dashes communicated information because they followed a code. Courtesy of The Bettman Archive, Inc.

of electricity down a wire to a distant listener. At the listener's end, a device called a sounder clicks when each pulse arrives. Like the lanterns in the tower, this is a digital process. Random clicks, however, do not convey information, so Morse had to develop a code. He based the code on the pauses between the clicks, using a short pause and a long pause. (When printed, these were represented as dots and dashes.) An experimental telegraph line was constructed between Baltimore and Washington, and on May 24, 1844, a series of short and long pauses between clicks sent the historic message "What hath God wrought" down this first telegraph line.

THE TRANSISTOR—THE COMPUTER'S DIGITAL DEVICE

Like these early message systems, computers need a device that can send, process, and store information and a code that gives the information meaning. Instead of lanterns or a key to send electrical pulses in a wire, early computers used vacuum tubes, and modern computers use transistors (see the photo essay *The History of Computing Devices*). Like lanterns, transistors have only two possible states: on and off.

BITS AND BYTES—THE DIGITAL CODE

Instead of using a code of short and long pauses, as Morse did, a microcomputer uses the transistor's on and off states. The code is based on bits and groups of bits called bytes.

Bits

The smallest unit is the **bit**, a contraction of the more descriptive phrase **binary digit**. A bit is a single element in the computer, or on a disk, that is either on (indicating 1) or off (indicating 0). In the computer, on is represented by a high voltage, and off is represented by a low voltage. On a magnetic disk, the same information is stored by changing the polarity of magnetized particles on the disk's surface.

To visualize a bit, imagine a light bulb that has two states, on and off (Figure 1-33). When on, it represents the number 1; when off, it represents the number 0. You could send a message to a nearby recipient by turning the bulb on and off, but to send even a short message would take a long time.

Bytes

Since bits are small units and can convey only two possible states, they can be organized into larger units to convey more information. This larger unit is a **byte**, and it is the basic unit of information in a computer system. It usually contains 8 bits. Since each bit has two states and there are 8 bits in a byte, the total amount of information that can be conveyed is 2^8 (2 raised to the 8th power), or 256 possible combinations. These combinations can represent characters, numbers, or symbols. For example, an A, a, +, -, &, or 5 can each be communicated in 1 byte. To better understand this concept, imagine using eight light bulbs instead of one to signal the letter A. Inside the computer, the letter A is represented by the binary number 01000001. Using eight light bulbs, the letter A would be conveyed as shown in Figure 1-34.

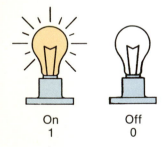

On
1

Off
0

FIGURE 1-33
The Bit
A bit is like a light bulb—it is either on to indicate 1, or off to indicate 0.

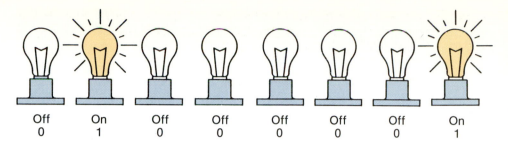

Off	On	Off	Off	Off	Off	Off	On
0	1	0	0	0	0	0	1

Words

Although bytes speed the transmission of messages, they can be conveyed even faster by sending more than one byte at a time. These larger units are called **words**. A word can contain 1, 2, or 4 bytes. Generally, however, word length is given in bits, so the equivalent word length is 8, 16, or 32 bits. If you wanted to signal the two characters A+, the A would be represented by the binary number 01000001, and the + would be represented by the binary number 0011011 (Figure 1-35).

Shorthand

Most references to a computer's digital memory, processing, storage, and communication use the byte as a unit of measurement. The number of bytes is usually given in **shorthand**. For example, you can say a computer's internal memory is 128,000 bytes or 128KB. The KB (for kilobyte) indicates a magnitude of 1000. As memory increases, the KB is replaced by an MB (for megabyte), which indicates a magnitude of 1,000,000. For example, you can say the computer's memory is 1,000,000 bytes, 1000 kilobytes, or 1 megabyte. As computer capacity expands, we will begin to encounter the next levels of magnitude: the gigabyte (1 billion bytes) and the terabyte (1 trillion bytes).

When referring to bytes in this way, the numbers are rounded so that you do not have to remember odd numbers. Bytes are calculated by raising the number 2 to various powers. For example, the number 2 raised to the 10th power is 1024. This is usually rounded off to 1000 (or 1KB). Table 1-3 shows the number 2 raised to powers between 0 and 30, the actual bytes that result, and how these bytes are expressed in shorthand as kilobytes, megabytes, or gigabytes.

Powers are not hard to understand. They are simply a number (called a base) and an exponent. The exponent tells you how many times to multiply the base times itself or the product of the previous multiplication. For example, 2^3 tells you to multiply three times. The first time, you multiply 2×2 to get 4. The second time, you multiply 2×4 to get 8, and the third time, you multiply 2×8 to get 16. If you do not remember powers from your math

FIGURE 1-34
The Byte
To understand a byte, imagine using eight light bulbs instead of one. Each letter in the alphabet could easily be assigned a pattern of lights. For example, the pattern could represent the letter A. By flashing agreed-on combinations one after another, you could quickly spell out a message a letter at a time. In digital code, each bulb can be on (for 1) or off (for 0), and the pattern can represent a code. Here, the number spelled out is 01000001, the ASCII code for the letter A.

FIGURE 1-35
Words
A word containing 16 bits is shown communicating the two characters A+ at the same time.

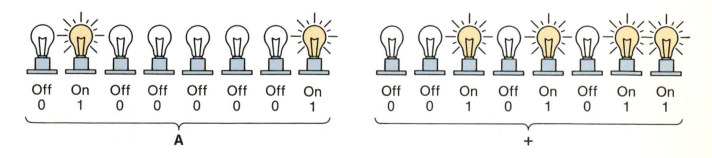

Off	On	Off	Off	Off	Off	Off	On	Off	Off	On	Off	On	Off	On	On
0	1	0	0	0	0	0	1	0	0	1	0	1	0	1	1

A   +

TABLE 1-3
Bytes, Kilobytes, Megabytes, and Gigabytes

Power	Actual	Shorthand	Power	Actual	Shorthand
2^0	1	1 byte	2^{16}	65,536	66KB
2^1	2	2 bytes	2^{17}	131,072	128KB
2^2	4	4 bytes	2^{18}	262,144	256KB
2^3	8	8 bytes	2^{19}	524,288	524KB
2^4	16	16 bytes	2^{20}	1,048,576	1MB (megabyte)
2^5	32	32 bytes	2^{21}	2,097,152	2MB
2^6	64	64 bytes	2^{22}	4,194,304	4MB
2^7	128	128 bytes	2^{23}	8,388,608	8MB
2^8	256	256 bytes	2^{24}	16,777,216	17MB
2^9	512	512 bytes	2^{25}	33,554,432	34MB
2^{10}	1,024	1KB (kilobyte)	2^{26}	67,108,864	67MB
2^{11}	2,048	2KB	2^{27}	134,217,728	134MB
2^{12}	4,096	4KB	2^{28}	268,435,456	268MB
2^{13}	8,192	8KB	2^{29}	536,870,912	537MB
2^{14}	16,384	16KB	2^{30}	1,073,741,824	1GB (gigabyte)
2^{15}	32,768	33KB			

classes, you may remember the childhood puzzle that used them. Kids would ask, "What if you put one penny in a bank on the first day and then doubled the amount every day? For example, on day two, you put two pennies in the bank; on day three, you put in four pennies; and so on. How many pennies would you have at the end of the month?" The answer was always surprising. If you look at Table 1-3, you can see that it would be 1,073,741,824 pennies after thirty days.

Characters

By themselves, bytes are meaningless. To have meaning, they must be assigned definitions that form a code. With 8 bits that can be either on (meaning 1) or off (meaning 0), there are 256 possible combinations. If all the bits are off, the byte reads 00000000. If all the bits are on, the byte reads 11111111. These two numbers, and any in between like 10000000 or 11000000, can stand for anything the computer's designer wants them to. They can represent characters, numbers, symbols, or commands to the computer.

Usually, you see these numbers converted to characters like letters, numbers, and symbols displayed on the screen. To standardize the meaning of these number combinations, the computer industry uses several codes, including

- The American Standard Code for Information Interchange, or **ASCII** (pronounced "as-key"), the code used most often on microcomputers
- The Extended Binary Coded Decimal Interchange Code, or **EBCDIC** (pronounced "eb-see-dick"), the code used most often on mainframe computers
- The American National Standards Institute, or **ANSI**

The ASCII characters are assigned two types of numbers. One number assigned to each character is an eight-digit binary number that is used inside the computer. Table 1-4 lists some typical characters and their eight-digit

TABLE 1-4
ASCII Characters

Letters		Numbers and Symbols	
A 01000001	a 01100001	0 00110000	! 00100001
B 01000010	b 01100010	1 00110001	% 00100101
C 01000011	c 01100011	2 00110010	& 00100110
D 01000100	d 01100100		
E 01000101	e 01100101		
.			
.		9 00111001	+ 00101011
.			
Z 01011010	z 01111010		

ASCII numbers. The other number is a three-digit decimal number. Figure 1-36 shows the ASCII characters in the IBM PC's character set and the three-digit decimal number assigned to each character. On many programs, you can display any of the ASCII characters on the screen by holding down the **Alt** key while you type the corresponding three-digit decimal number on the computer's numeric keypad.

	0	1	2	3	4	5	6	7	8	9
00		☺	☻	♥	♦	♣	♠	•	◘	○
01	◙	♂	♀	♪	♫	☼	►	◄	↕	‼
02	¶	§	▬	↨	↑	↓	→	←	∟	↔
03	▲	▼		!	"	#	$	%	&	'
04	(	)	*	+	,	-	.	/	0	1
05	2	3	4	5	6	7	8	9	:	;
06	<	=	>	?	@	A	B	C	D	E
07	F	G	H	I	J	K	L	M	N	O
08	P	Q	R	S	T	U	V	W	X	Y
09	Z	[	\	]	^	_	‘	a	b	c
10	d	e	f	g	h	i	j	k	l	m
11	n	o	p	q	r	s	t	u	v	w
12	x	y	z	{	¦	}	~	⌂	Ç	ü
13	é	â	ä	à	å	ç	ê	ë	è	ï
14	î	ì	Ä	Å	É	æ	Æ	ô	ö	ò
15	û	ù	ÿ	Ö	Ü	¢	£	¥	₧	ƒ
16	á	í	ó	ú	ñ	Ñ	ª	º	¿	⌐
17	¬	½	¼	¡	«	»	░	▒	▓	│
18	┤	╡	╢	╖	╕	╣	║	╗	╝	╜
19	╛	┐	└	┴	┬	├	─	┼	╞	╟
20	╚	╔	╩	╦	╠	═	╬	╧	╨	╤
21	╥	╙	╘	╒	╓	╫	╪	┘	┌	█
22	▄	▌	▐	▀	α	β	Γ	π	Σ	σ
23	µ	τ	Φ	Θ	Ω	δ	∞	φ	ε	∩
24	≡	±	≥	≤	⌠	⌡	÷	≈	°	•
25	·	√	η	²	■					

FIGURE 1-36
The IBM PC ASCII Character Set
The IBM PC character set contains ASCII characters that include letters, numbers, symbols, and graphic characters.

The characters you see on your screen are determined by which code your computer uses. The first 128 characters are almost the same. For example, if you press the letter A, the keyboard sends the computer the byte 01000001 (Figure 1-37). But if you enter a special character, for example, by holding down the **Alt** key while you type the number 169 on the numeric keypad, you may get different results, depending on which code your computer uses. On an ASCII computer, you get an upper left corner line draw character (⌐). On an ANSI computer, you get a copyright symbol, the letter c with a circle around it.

FIGURE 1-37
ASCII Characters
When you press a key on the keyboard (a), it sends a byte containing a number to the CPU (b), which sends the byte to the screen where it is displayed as a character matching the key you pressed (c).

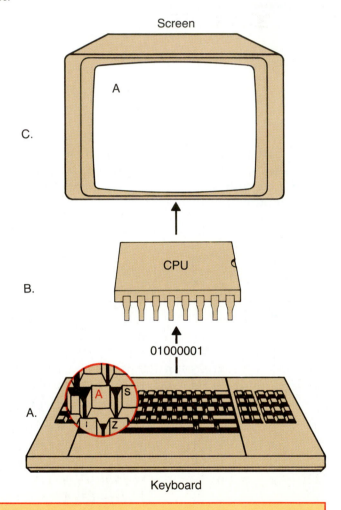

The Digital Revolution in the Home

The digital revolution isn't confined to the computer field. Computer chips are quietly at work all around you.

- Many irons use chips to measure the time when they are not moved and turn the iron off when the limit is exceeded.

- Kitchen ranges use chips to control time and temperature.

- Dishwashers use chips to diagnose problems and report them when they occur.

- Hair curling irons use chips to determine if the iron is being used, and if not, turns it off automatically.

- Microwave ovens use chips to control the time and temperature and to store programs to cook specific dishes.

THE HISTORY OF COMPUTING DEVICES

The key to the development of the microcomputer (and all other modern computers) was the development of solid-state electronics. The technology developed during this period allowed more and more electronic devices to be packed into smaller and smaller spaces. The technology also made it possible for them to operate faster, give off less heat, and be more reliable.

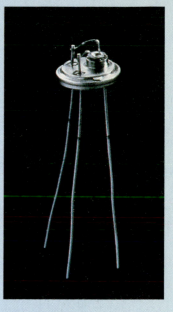

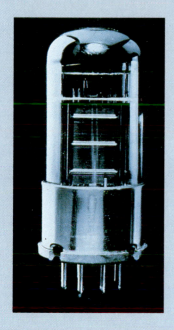

Vacuum Tubes
Until the late 1950s, all electronic equipment used vacuum tubes. Today's microcomputers would not be possible if vacuum tubes were still the only devices available.
Courtesy of IBM Corporation

The Transistor
The first step in improving on the vacuum tube occurred when John Bardeen, Walter Brattain, and William Shockley invented the transistor at Bell Labs in 1947. Unlike vacuum tubes, which used filaments and plates enclosed in a glass envelope, the transistor was a solid device that could perform the same functions in a much smaller space. The transistor also required less power and gave off less heat than vacuum tubes.

Inside the computer, transistors are not used as individual devices. Recent advances have made it possible to pack thousands, even millions, of transistors on a single silicon chip. These chips store and process large amounts of information.
Courtesy of IBM Corporation

Transistors Mounted on Boards
Before large scale integration was developed, individual transistors were hand-mounted onto circuit boards. Connecting wires were then soldered into place to connect the transistors and other components.
Courtesy of IBM Corporation

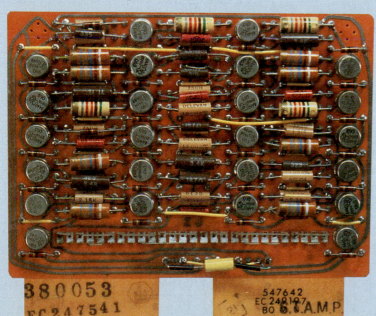

The Integrated Circuit

The next major step was when Jack Kilby, an employee at Texas Instruments, made the first working integrated circuit in 1958. A year later, Robert Noyce and Jean Hoerni at Fairchild Semiconductor developed a photographic process to create these circuits on a silicon waffer. These devices, called chips, contained thousands of transistors in the same space a single transistor occupied previously. In 1968, Noyce left Fairchild to join Gordon Moore in founding Intel Corporation, a major semiconductor manufacturer that later developed the first microprocessor, the heart of a microcomputer.

Over the next few years, advances were made in increasing the number of components that could be squeezed onto a single chip. This process, called large scale integration (LSI), led the way to very large scale integration (VLSI), which made possible the powerful chips used in today's microcomputers. What started in 1947 as a single solid-state transistor less than 1/2 inch square became, in successive steps, 1000 and then 1 million transistors in the same space in less than forty years. Courtesy of IBM Corporation

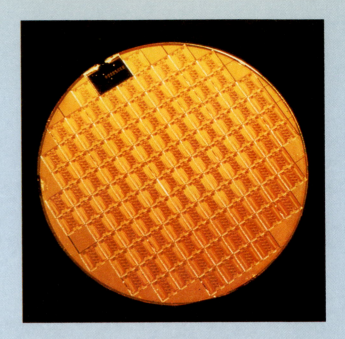

THE POWERS OF TEN

When you discuss computers and memory, some very large numbers are discussed very casually. The terms byte, kilobyte, megabyte, and gigabyte represent orders of magnitude called powers of two. Powers of ten approximate powers of two. A power of ten is calculated by raising the base 10 to a power, called an exponent. Simply stated, the exponent determines the number of zeros in the number.

- A byte is 1, approximately the number 10 raised to the power of 0.
- A kilobyte is 1000 (one thousand), approximately 10 raised to the power of 3.
- A megabyte is 1,000,000 (one million), approximately 10 raised to the power of 6.
- A gigabyte is 1,000,000,000 (one billion), approximately 10 raised to the power of 9.

The degrees of magnitude these numbers represent are extremely hard to visualize. Philip Morrison, Phylis Morrison, and the Office of Charles and Ray Eames have published a book, *The Powers of Ten*, that illustrates these and other magnitudes. In a series of illustrations, the authors move the point of view away from a scene by increments of powers of 10. In the series below, taken from this book, we have used part of this series to show the differences in magnitude involved in computers. For example, the first view shows the scene from 1 meter away, the second from 1000 meters, and so on. To visualize the magnitudes involved in a computer's memory, just imagine you are stepping back from the scene in bytes, instead of meters.

Source: The Powers of Ten. Philip and Phylis Morrison and The Office of Charles and Ray Eames. Scientific American Books, Inc. New York, 1982

1 Byte
1 Byte (10^0). An image from a vantage point of 1 meter (or an imaginary 1 byte) shows a man lying on a blanket napping after a picnic.

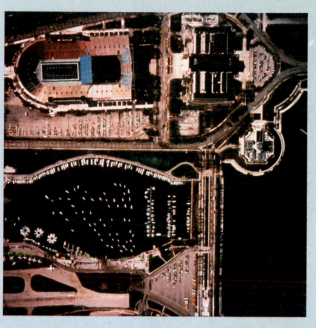

1 Kilobyte
1 Kilobyte (10^3). When the scale is increased from 1 meter to 1000 meters (or an imaginary kilobyte), the man becomes completely invisible in the large area of the countryside now shown.

1 Megabyte
1 Megabyte (10^6). Another increase in scale to 1,000,000 meters (1 megabyte) is startling. You are now looking at a large part of the Midwest, including all of Chicago and Lake Michigan.

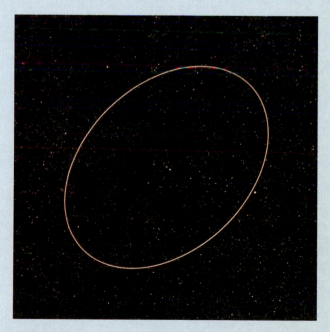

1 Gigabyte
1 Gigabyte (10^9). At the next increment, up to 1,000,000,000 meters (1 gigabyte), the earth itself becomes a small dot, and even the orbit of the moon can be seen.

SUMMARY AND KEY TERMS

■ Computers use a technique called **digital processing**. Computers contain thousands of transistors, each of which can be on or off. When on, it means 1; when off, it means 0. By grouping these signals (**bits**) into larger groups (**bytes**) and assigning a code to them (**ASCII**), letters, numbers, and symbols can be stored, processed, and communicated.

■ Bytes can be indicated using the shorthand terms **kilobyte** (thousands), **megabyte** (millions), **gigabyte** (billions), or **terabyte** (trillions). They are calculated by raising the number 2 (for the two possible states) to a **power**. For example, 2^{18} is 262,144 bytes or 262 kilobytes.

REVIEW QUESTIONS

1. What is binary arithmetic, and how is it used in computers?

2. What is the name of the digital device used inside a computer to store and process information? When thousands of these are put together, what is the device called?

3. What is the difference between a bit, a byte, and a word?

4. Memory and other devices are frequently described in terms of bytes, kilobytes, and megabytes. On the chart below, convert the bytes in column A to their equivalent kilobytes in Column B and to their equivalent megabytes in Column C.

A	B	C
Bytes	Kilobytes	Megabytes
1,000	_____ KB	
10,000	_____ KB	
100,000	_____ KB	
1,000,000	_____ KB	_____ MB

5. What is a power? Calculate the following powers:
   1^2
   2^2
   4^2
   2^3
   2^4

6. What is the name of the code used to assign characters to numbers or bytes in the computer?

7. When you press a key on the keyboard, what does it send to the computer?

8. What distinguishes the integrated circuit from the transistor?

9. Briefly describe how a chip is made.

TOPIC 1-4

The Microcomputer

OBJECTIVES

After completing this topic, you will be able to

- Explain the purpose of the central processing unit and how it works
- Describe how information is stored in a computer's memory
- Explain how peripheral equipment, like printers, are attached to the computer's ports
- Explain what a computer's architecture is
- Describe how accessory boards can be plugged into the computer to improve its performance
- List things to do and to avoid doing with your computer

The microcomputer is the central element of the computer system. Microcomputers come in many designs but can be classified according to their size and portability. Desktop computers (Figure 1-38) are relatively large, at least too large to carry easily. Portable computers (Figure 1-39) are smaller than desktop computers so that they can be carried, but you wouldn't want to carry one with you on a subway or a long trip or through a large airport terminal. Laptop computers (Figure 1-40) are the smallest models and can be carried like a small attache case or packed in a suitcase. They are not only small but are also designed so that they can run for up to eight hours on battery packs. All microcomputers, regardless of their design, have five essential components, which are shown in Figure 1-41.

THE CENTRAL PROCESSING UNIT

The heart of a computer is the **central processing unit (CPU)**. The CPU is a **microprocessor**—the device that made microcomputers possible in the first place. The microprocessor performs three key functions:

1. In conjunction with the operating system (discussed in Part Two), it coordinates all the computer's activities. It controls retrieving files from the disk, interprets data and commands you enter from the keyboard, and sends data to the printer.

FIGURE 1-38
Desktop Computers
Desktop computers, the most common microcomputer design, is a relatively large unit. Courtesy of IBM Corporation

53

FIGURE 1-39
Portable Computers
Portable computers are smaller than desktop computers so that they can be easily moved from one location to another. Courtesy of Compaq

2. It performs arithmetic calculations such as addition and subtraction using the system of binary mathematics. For example, if you enter a list of numbers in a document, many programs allow you to automatically calculate a total.

3. It performs logical operations using equal to, greater than, and less than comparisons. For example, it can be programmed to determine if your grades are higher or lower than those of other students in the same course and to print a list that ranks everyone in descending order by grade.

The microprocessor is an **integrated circuit (IC)**, a circuit that contains wires, transistors, and other electronic devices on a silicon chip. When integrated circuits were first used, each was custom designed for specific applications. A watch company would have a chip designed for a specific model of a digital watch, a calculator company for a specific calculator, and so on. Integrated circuits designed in this way had only one function, the one they were specifically designed for.

FIGURE 1-40
Laptop Computers
Laptop computers are the smallest microcomputers. They are small enough to fit on your lap on an airplane or to be packed in a larger suitcase when traveling. Courtesy of Toshiba

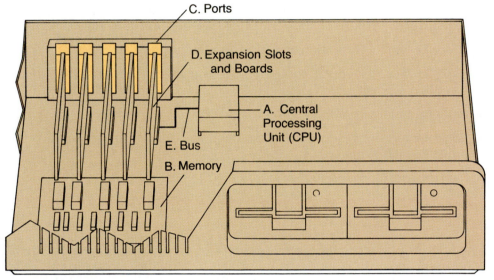

FIGURE 1-41
The Computer's Components
The computer's components include the following:

A. The central processing unit (CPU) is a microprocessor. It controls all the computer's functions, makes all calculations, and processes all data that you enter.

B. The computer's internal memory stores the programs you are using and the data you are processing. The memory is made up of small silicon chips, each containing thousands of transistors, components that store information.

C. Sockets, or ports, mounted on the outside of the computer, are used to connect peripherals like keyboards and printers. Cables connect the peripherals to the ports so that you can get data into and out of the computer.

D. Expansion slots inside many computers allow you to plug in boards or cards that contain electronic components that upgrade or expand the computer's capabilities. These boards perform many functions. Some are used to provide additional memory or ports to which peripherals can be connected. Others are the actual peripheral devices themselves. Boards containing modems or even hard disk drives can also be inserted into these slots.

E. The buses are a series of connections that are used to send messages between components.

In 1969, M.E. Hoff, an engineer at Intel Corporation, was assigned the job of designing an integrated circuit for a Japanese calculator. Instead of custom designing it to this single function, Hoff designed it so that it was programmable. By changing its program, you could change its function. It was no longer a single-function chip; it had become one with multiple functions. So the first microprocessor, the 4004, was born. It contained more than 2000 transistors and all of their interconnections on a chip less than ⅛-inch square—about the size of a ladybug.

Although powerful, microprocessors are extremely small. They are similar to the silicon chips that store data but have advanced capabilities allowing them to process the information that flows through them. Figure 1-42 shows one of the latest and most powerful microprocessors.

Microprocessor design and tooling for production is time consuming and expensive. Because this restricts the number of microprocessors, only a few of them have been used in personal computers. For example, the Intel microprocessors in all IBM microcomputers include the 8088 (1981); the 80286 (1984), called the 286; the 80386 (1986), called the 386; and the 80486 (1989) called the 486. The differences among these microprocessors are significant, but there are far greater differences among any of these chips and those produced by Motorola (which are used in Apple computers) and other manufacturers. These differences determine not only the performance of the chip but also whether programs will run on a computer using the chips.

- Programs written to run on the 8088 chip, will run on all Intel chips, including the latest version.
- Programs written for the latest chips will not run on earlier chips if they take advantage of the later chips' specific improvements.
- Programs written for any Intel chip will not run on any Motorola chip without additional hardware and software; hence IBM programs do not normally run on an Apple computer or vice versa.

Let's look at some of the features that make microprocessor chips different from one another.

The Number of Bits Processed

One of the differences among microprocessors is the number of bits of information they can process at one time. A bit, as you have seen, is the basic unit of computer information. At the moment, microprocessors are available in 8-bit, 16-bit, and 32-bit versions. Generally, the more bits a microprocessor can process at one time, the faster and more powerful it is.

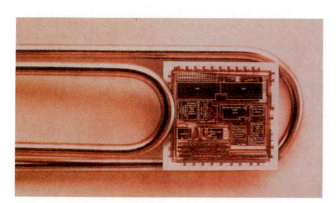

FIGURE 1-42
The Microprocessor
The microprocessor is an extremely powerful device that is used as the central processing unit (CPU) in the latest generation of microcomputers. In fact, it is as powerful as mainframe computers like those used in corporate data processing centers only a few years ago. Although the microprocessor is powerful, it is extremely small. Courtesy of AT&T Bell Labs

Faster, more powerful microprocessors make it possible to run faster, more powerful programs.

For example, as microprocessors have improved, new applications like desktop publishing have become possible. Table 1-5 shows some typical microprocessors used in microcomputers. The IBM microcomputers have always used Intel chips. The earliest IBM PCs used the 8088 or 8086. The IBM AT computers, introduced next, used the 80286. Today, the most widely used chip in new IBM PS/2 computers is the 80386 chip. Figure 1-43 shows how many of each machine were sold in 1987 and how many of each are expected to be sold in 1990.

Generally, the more bits a microprocessor can handle at one time, the faster and more powerful it is. It seems ludicrous at first to think that speed is a problem since even the slowest computer can calculate at a blinding speed. As you use the computer for more applications, however, you will soon be surprised at how impatient you become. Recalculating a large spreadsheet model, moving the cursor from the beginning to the end of a long document, and sorting a large database of names and addresses will quickly reveal a computer's lethargy.

The Instruction Set

The operations a microprocessor performs are called its **instruction set**, and the way these instructions are implemented by the program differ on

TABLE 1-5
Types of Microprocessors

Type	Manufacturer	Bits	Computers
Z80	Zilog	8	Kaypro
6502	MOS Technology	8	Apple II
8008	Intel	8	MITS Altair
8080	Intel	8	TRS-80 Model 1
8088	Intel	16	IBM PC, Compaq
68000	Motorola	32	Apple Macintosh
80826	Intel	32	IBM AT
80836	Intel	32	IBM PS/2 Model 80, Compaq 386

FIGURE 1-43
Intel Chips
In 1987, most IBM computers sold were based on either the 8088/8086 or the 80286 chips. By 1990, most will be based on the 80286 and 80386 chips. Courtesy of *InfoWorld*, February 8, 1988, page 21.

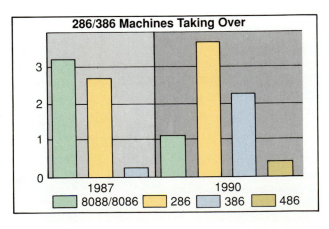

almost every microprocessor. Instruction sets can be very complicated, and the more complicated they are, the slower the microprocessor works. Microprocessors that rely heavily on instruction sets to perform almost all functions are **complete instruction set chips (CISC)**. To make computers operate faster, a new type of microprocessor, **reduced instruction set chips (RISC)**, has been introduced. RISC microprocessors operate faster than CISC microprocessors in many circumstances. They also substantially reduce the number of elements required on the chip and, hence, the cost and time involved in developing new chip designs. For example, Intel's CISC chip called the 80386 contains 275,000 transistors, whereas a RISC chip introduced by Sun Microsystems called the SPARC contains only 50,000. The lower number of elements and the reduced instruction set allow the SPARC chip to operate twice as fast as the 80386 chip. To attain these increased speeds, RISC chips perform smaller and simpler steps more often but at higher speeds. Many of the functions normally handled by a CISC chip, however, must be performed by the software, so sometimes the gains in speed are not as great as expected. Figure 1-44 shows how RISC chips are expected to take an increasingly larger share of the 32-bit microprocessor market.

Co-processors

Because the computer's microprocessor performs many functions, it often slows down at key points in the computer's operation. To relieve part of its burden, some computers include additional microprocessors, called **co-processors**, that are dedicated to specific, time-consuming tasks. These co-processors operate under the control of the CPU. For example, on the IBM PC, a special math chip can be installed to perform addition, subtraction, multiplication, division, and trigonometric operations very quickly. The more powerful models in the new IBM PS/2 line can support up to eight microprocessor chips.

MEMORY

When you load a program into the computer or enter data from the keyboard, it has to be stored where the microprocessor can quickly find it. The place where it is stored is the computer's **internal memory**. Internal mem-

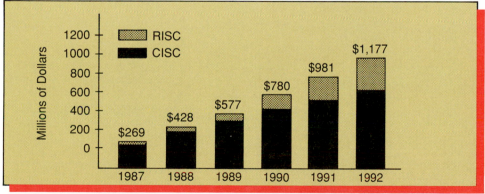

Source: Dataquest, March 1988

FIGURE 1-44
RISC vs. CISC Chips
The RISC chip is expected to take an increasingly large share of the 32-bit microprocessor market over the next few years. Courtesy of Dataquest, Inc., San Jose, Calif.

ory is divided into two parts: read-only memory (ROM) and random-access memory (RAM). The French clearly differentiate between the two types by calling RAM "live memory" (memoire vive) and ROM "dead memory" (memoire morte). Figure 1-45 shows how the Scrabble® brand crossword game is an analogy for a computer's memory.

Read-Only Memory (ROM)

Read-only memory (ROM) is static, unchanging—sometimes called **nonvolatile**—memory. Your computer can read data stored in ROM, but you cannot enter data into ROM or change the data already there. The data in ROM is permanently recorded on memory chips by the computer's manufacturer. Neither turning the computer off nor electrical power failure affect it; the data will still be there when you resume. ROM is generally used to store programs and instructions that the computer frequently needs. For example, it contains the instructions the computer follows to start up when you first turn it on.

- On the Apple Macintosh, ROM stores a large amount of information about the screen display. Programmers do not have to write these instructions each time they need them. They just instruct the computer to use the instructions already available in ROM.

- On some computers, ROM, in the form of additional plug-in chips, is used to store operating systems and applications programs so that a spreadsheet or word processing program can be loaded from ROM rather than from a disk (Figure 1-46).

The programs stored on ROM chips are put there by the manufacturer during the last stage of the chip's production. There are two basic types of

FIGURE 1-45
Read-Only Memory
The Scrabble® brand crossword game is like a computer's memory. The instruction booklet is like ROM—you can read it, but you cannot change it. The board is like RAM—you can add, remove, or move information around on it.

MICROCOMPUTER SYSTEMS

FIGURE 1-46
Plug-In ROM Chips
Some applications programs and operating systems are supplied on plug-in ROM chips. When you want to add a program, you plug in a new chip. Courtesy of GRID Systems Corporation, Mt. View, Calif.

ROM chips: PROMs (programmable ROMs) and EPROMs (erasable programmable ROMs). Special equipment is used to write or burn the programs into these chips.

- PROMs cannot be erased once they have been burned into the chip.
- EPROMs can be erased and then rewritten. EPROM chips are frequently used during the early stages of a chip's development and testing so that errors can be corrected. When they are perfect, they are distributed as PROMs.

Random-Access Memory (RAM)

When you load a program into the computer or create a word processing document or spreadsheet model, the data you enter using the keyboard is stored in **random-access memory (RAM)** (also called main, primary, or user memory). When you load a program into the computer or create a document with a word processing program, the program you load and the data you enter from the keyboard are temporarily stored in RAM. Usually, if you turn off the computer, any programs or data stored in this memory are lost; thus RAM is said to be **volatile** memory.

The term *random* comes from the way the data in memory can be located or accessed by the computer. One way to understand random is to think of the differences between a tape player and a turntable. If you want to play the third song on a tape, you must first advance the tape past the first two songs. This is called sequential access because you access each song in sequence. On a turntable, you can just lower the needle onto the track where the third song begins. This is called random access because you can randomly access songs by placing the needle anywhere on the record without first advancing through songs that precede them.

The chips used to store RAM are called dynamic or static RAM chips. Today, the chips usually used in microcomputers have a storage capacity between 64 kilobits and 1 megabit. However, 4-megabit versions have been developed and will begin to appear in newer computers. Figure 1-47 shows the years in which the latest versions were introduced.

The RAM chips used to store data come in several versions.

- The most common memory chip is a metal-oxide-semiconductor (**MOS**) chip. This is called a **dynamic RAM (DRAM)** chip because it retains its

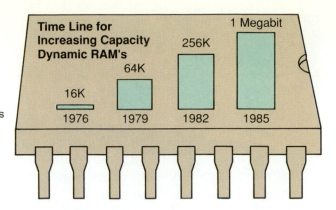

FIGURE 1-47
Dynamic RAM Chips
The capacity of ROM chips
has increased from 16KB
in 1976 to the 1MB chips
that are often found in
computers today.
Courtesy of Dataquest,
Inc., San Jose, Calif.

memory only for short periods. As a result, the computer must continually update or refresh the chip's memory between 250 and 500 times a second.

■ Another type of dynamic RAM chip, a complementary-metal-oxide-semiconductor **(CMOS)** chip is often used in portable and laptop computers that run on battery packs because CMOS chips have low power requirements. They also allow the designers to pack twice as many active elements into the same space.

■ Another form of CMOS chip is a **static RAM** chip. These chips can store data for long periods with a very low power consumption. A battery in the computer allows them to retain their memory even when the computer is turned off. This is not their only advantage; they are also much faster than dynamic RAM chips because memory does not have to be refreshed as often. For example, on an IBM PC, more than 7 percent of the CPU's power is devoted to just refreshing the computer's memory. Eliminating this requirement makes it possible for the computer to retrieve, store, and process data more quickly, thus improving the system's performance. The drawback is that static RAM chips are more expensive.

■ Another kind of RAM, called **bubble memory**, uses garnet wafers rather than metal oxide to store data. Bubble memory's big advantage is that it is nonvolatile; if the power is turned off, data stored in the memory is not lost.

Virtual Memory

Very large programs and very large files of data can strain the capacity of even a large computer's memory. To solve this problem, some operating systems (see Part Two) and many applications programs store parts of their programs or data outside RAM until needed. This type of storage is called virtual memory. On a system that uses **virtual memory**, only the parts of the program or data file currently needed are stored in the computer's memory; the rest are stored on a hard disk drive (see Topic 1-6). Although part of the programs or data files are not actually stored in the computer's memory, they are treated as if they were. When the computer needs them, it moves something in memory to the disk to make memory available. It then moves the program or data from the disk into memory. This reduces the overall cost of the system because it is cheaper to store data on a hard disk drive than it is to add additional memory chips to the computer.

Buffers

While we are talking about memory, one other important aspect should be understood. Some programs allocate a small portion of the computer's random-access memory as a buffer. Buffers have several applications.

- It's doubtful whether you can type on a typewriter faster than it can print the characters on paper. But you may be able to type faster than a computer can process your keystrokes, especially when the CPU is busily performing other tasks. To keep you from having to stop typing, keyboards have **buffers**, small areas of memory in which keystrokes are saved until the CPU is ready to accept them (Figure 1-48). If the buffer becomes full, the computer beeps, and any keys you press are not stored, so you must reenter them when the CPU empties the buffer.

- A buffer can temporarily save a record of the most recently used commands and deleted text so that the commands or deletions can be undone if you discover you made a mistake.

- A buffer (sometimes called a clipboard) is used as a storage area when you cut or copy text so that you can later retrieve it to insert elsewhere in your file.

- A print buffer (sometimes called a print spooler) can store a file so that you can work on a new file while the previous one is being printed.

Disk and Memory Caches

When a computer is operating, it is frequently moving data between the microprocessor, disk, and memory. To process data, the data must first be moved to the CPU from wherever it is stored. Since this takes time, special techniques have been developed on the latest computers to speed up this operation. The basic technique is to store data in a special area of memory called a **cache**. There are two kinds of caches: disk caches and memory caches.

Disk Caches

Moving data from the disk to the microprocessor takes a relatively long time, and this slows down the system. Getting this information from the computer's main memory is much faster than getting it from the disk. To

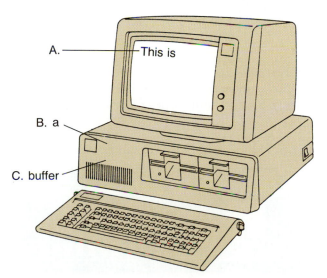

A.———This is

B. a

C. buffer

FIGURE 1-48
Keyboard Buffer
Keyboard buffers store characters when the central processing unit is busy. As you type on the keyboard, characters (in the form of numbers) are sent to the CPU. If the CPU is busy, the characters you type are stored in the buffer. As the CPU becomes available, the characters are sent to it for processing and then sent to the screen. In this illustration, the operator typed "This is a buffer." (a) The first two words have been processed by the CPU and sent to the screen. (b) The third word is being processed by the CPU. (c) The last word is being held in the buffer until the CPU is ready to accept it.

speed up a computer's operation, data that is needed often is stored in RAM. There is no improvement in speed the first time the data is needed because the computer must get it from the disk. Instead of removing it from memory when it is finished with it, it stores a copy in a special area of memory called a **disk cache**. The next time the same data is needed, the computer looks to see if it is still in the cache, and if it is, it can get to it much faster.

Memory Caches

Some computers also have a special area of memory that is reserved for a **memory cache**. The memory chips in this area are special high-speed chips from which the computer can get data much faster than from normal main memory. In these computers, the cache operates just as it does with a disk cache. When data is first used, it is copied from main memory to the high-speed cache. The next time the same data is needed, the computer first looks in the high-speed cache. If the data is still there, the computer gets it more quickly. If the data isn't still there, the computer goes to the main memory for it.

PORTS

A computer system is like a component stereo system where you use cables to connect a tape deck, turntable, and speakers to the main amplifier. The amplifier does not care what model turntable or tape deck is being connected as long as the right cables are used and they are plugged into the right sockets. The same is true of computers. The computer's external components, or peripherals, may include the printer, display screen, modem, keyboard, digitizing tablet, and mouse. You connect these peripherals to the computer with cables that connect them to **ports**, sockets mounted on the computer's cabinet. Like a stereo system, if you use the right cable and connect it to the correct socket, the peripheral will work with the computer. This is called **plug compatibility** because the computer doesn't care what peripheral is used as long as it is designed to work with one of the ports and is connected properly.

Like seaports where ships enter and leave a country, and airports where airplanes enter and leave a city, ports are where information enters and leaves the computer. Ports are generally on the back of the computers, as Figure 1-49 shows. The number and type of ports on a computer vary, but they are usually either serial or parallel.

Serial Ports

Serial ports (sometimes called RS-232-C ports or asynchronous communications ports) are where you attach modems, devices used to communicate with other computers (see Topic 1-8), and some types of printers (see Topic 1-6).

FIGURE 1-49
Ports
Ports, both serial and parallel, are sockets mounted on the back of the computer. You plug cables into these ports to connect peripherals such as printers or modems.
Courtesy of IBM Corporation

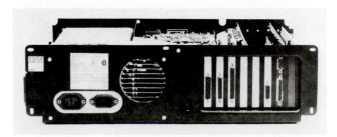

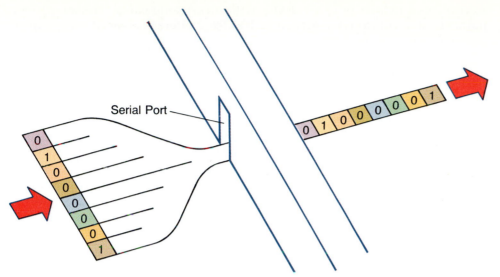

FIGURE 1-50
Serial Ports
Serial ports are like a single-lane tunnel. Information fed to it has to squeeze through the port a single bit at a time. Here, the ASCII code for the letter A is sent 1 bit at a time through the port.

When data is sent out a serial port, it is sent 1 bit at a time (Figure 1-50). Since the data is processed inside the computer 8, 16, or even 32 bits at a time, a serial port is like a narrowing on a highway at a tunnel. Data slows down, just as the highway traffic does, so that it can funnel out of the computer in single file. Serial ports provide slower communications and are therefore not ideal for printer connections. But when used with modems, serial ports are essential because the telephone lines that most modems are connected to are also serial (see Part Eight).

Parallel Ports

Parallel ports (sometimes called centronics interfaces) carry data 8 bits at a time on parallel paths (Figure 1-51). Because they can transmit data 8 bits or 1 byte at a time, they are a faster way for the computer to communicate with input and output devices. There is less narrowing than on a serial port, so traffic moves faster. Parallel ports are usually used to plug in printers.

Parallel ports have one minor disadvantage: Their signal does not travel as far as the signal from a serial port. This is important only when you want

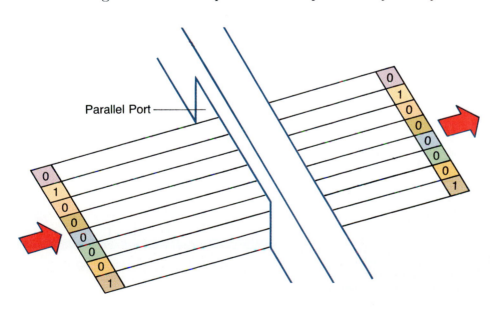

FIGURE 1-51
Parallel Ports
Parallel ports are like tunnels with almost the same number of lanes as the highway that feeds them. Information flows through faster since there is little or no constriction.

to connect a printer or other device with a very long cable. The length of a parallel cable is limited to less than 100 feet, whereas a serial cable can be up to 1000 feet long.

ARCHITECTURE

The speed of a computer isn't determined solely by the microprocessor. The language a program is written in and other factors also influence its speed. One of the main determinants of the computer's speed is its **architecture**, the way the hardware is designed. Key elements of the design include the address and data buses and the clock rate.

The computer must have connections, or circuits, along which information travels between all the components. This communication path is called a **bus**. All communications, whether internal or external, are sent along a bus. The concept behind a bus is relatively simple. There are only two ways to connect all the components: Either run wires between each component in the system or connect them all to a common set of wires—a bus.

To picture this concept, imagine a neighborhood with each house connected to every other house by a separate road or redesigned so that all houses have driveways leading to a common street (Figure 1-52). The bus design used in computers has many advantages. The bus simplifies the design, reduces the number of required circuits, and lowers the cost. A bus also allows new components to be added by simply plugging them into the bus. Many computers have expansion slots inside the cabinet for this purpose.

Microcomputers have two key buses: a data bus and an address bus.

The Data Bus

The **data bus** is used to move data between the CPU and memory and the external components like printers. This bus does not always handle the same number of bits as the microprocessor. For example, the Apple Macintosh has a 32-bit processor and a 16-bit data bus. The original IBM PC has a 16-bit microprocessor and an 8-bit data bus. Thus for the Macintosh, 16 bits are fed to and from memory at once; similarly, the IBM PC's 8-bit data bus sends 8 bits at a time. However, the Macintosh's microprocessor is designed to handle 32 bits, and the IBM PC's is designed to handle 16 bits. The ability to send and receive more data than can be processed is like the traffic buildup on a highway because the number of lanes is reduced. This slows the computer down but not by half because the computer both processes and sends information. Delays are encountered only when data is being sent. The processing speed is determined by the capacity of the

FIGURE 1-52
The Bus

a. If there are two houses, there is only one road. But as houses are added, the number of roads needed to connect them increase faster than the number of houses. By the time there are five houses, ten roads are needed. It would not take many houses before the entire neighborhood was paved in asphalt.

b. Now picture the same neighborhood with driveways leading from each house to a common street (the bus). As you can see, fewer connections are required than when all the houses are connected directly to one another. The same is true in the computer.

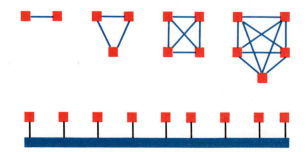

microprocessor itself. In the latest IBM PS/2 computers, the new micro channel bus architecture (MCA) avoids all delays because it can carry 32 bits to and from a 32-bit CPU microprocessor (see *Micro Channel Architecture*).

The Address Bus

The **address bus** is similar to the data bus, but it is used to communicate with specific areas in the computer's internal memory and between components in the system. When data is placed on the data bus, the address of the component, or the location in memory it is being directed to, is placed on the address bus. Thus when a component recognizes its address on the address bus, it knows that it is to read data off the data bus. When the CPU wants information from a component, it places the component's address on the address bus and then instructs the component (through another bus called the **control bus**) to write data onto the data bus.

The size of the address bus determines how much memory the CPU can address or use. Remember, any data inside a computer is in 0s or 1s. If an address bus can carry only 1 bit at a time, it can address only two memory locations: 0 and 1. If an address bus can carry 2 bits, it can address four memory locations: 0,0; 0,1; 1,0; and 1,1. This number can be calculated quickly by raising the number 2 to the power of the bits the address bus can carry. Table 1-6 shows some typical examples.

- Early 8-bit CPUs, like those in the Apple II, have a 16-bit address bus, so they could address only 65,536 individual addresses, and these computers could have only 64KB memories.
- The IBM PC introduced the 16-bit CPU that used a 20-bit address bus. This allowed it to address more than 1MB of memory.
- The Apple Macintosh uses the Motorola 68000 microprocessor, which has a 24-bit address bus, so theoretically, it can address more than 16MB of memory. Most mainframe computers do not have that much memory.
- The IBM AT introduced the 80286 chip, which also has a 24-bit address bus, so it, too, can address more than 16MB of memory.
- The IBM PS/2 computers use the 80386 chip, which has a 32-bit address bus and can theoretically address up to 4GB of memory.

The Clock Rate and Wait States

The **clock rate** determines the frequency of the computer's operations and keeps everything under control. If too many things happened at once, data

TABLE 1-6
The Address Bus and Memory

Address Bus	Formula	Addressable Memory	Example
16	2^{16}	65,536	Apple II
20	2^{20}	1,048,576	IBM PC
24	2^{24}	16,777,216	IBM AT and Macintosh
32	2^{32}	4,294,967,296	IBM PS/2

would be lost. Like the caller at a square dance or the conductor at a symphony, the clock makes everything happen only when it should. The faster the clock runs, the faster the computer can process data. Clock rates are measured in **megahertz (MHz)**—millions of cycles per second. For example, the original IBM PC 8088 chip ran at 4.77 MHz, but newer chips like the Intel 80386 are now running as fast as 40 MHz, and improvements will continue.

Some computers with a high clock speed also have **wait states**, essentially missed beats while the system waits for all components to synchronize. The fewer wait states a computer has, the faster the system runs. Wait states are built into some systems because the CPU is much faster than the memory chips. When the CPU requests information, the memory chips cannot supply it on the next cycle, so the CPU gets it on the third or later cycle. The extra cycles when data are not being sent to the CPU is called a wait state.

EXPANSION SLOTS AND BOARDS

Many users like to customize their computers to better serve their needs. To make this possible, most computers have **expansion slots** inside the cabinet into which you can plug **add-on boards** (also called add-in boards or cards) that contain electronic components (Figure 1-53). These expansion slots are connected directly to the computer's buses, so they perform just as if they were built into the computer. Computers that have these expansion slots are said to have an **open architecture** because the machine is open to new devices being plugged in. Those that do not are said to have a **closed architecture**.

Add-on boards can serve several functions. Some boards expand the computer's memory, others allow the computer to display colors or graphics, and still others connect peripherals or are the peripherals themselves. For example, you can plug in a board that controls a hard disk drive (see Topic 1-7) located elsewhere in the system, or you can plug in a board that contains the hard disk drive itself.

Since a computer has only a few slots, manufacturers have developed multifunction boards. These boards combine two or more tasks that might once have required two or more boards. Here are some of the functions typically combined on these boards.

FIGURE 1-53
Expansion Slots and Add-On Boards
Expansion slots inside the computer allow you to plug in add-on boards that expand the computer's capabilities. Courtesy of IBM Corporation

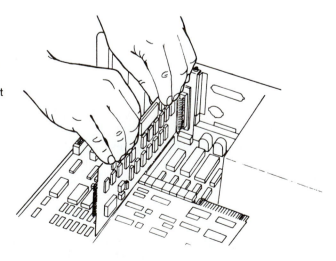

Micro Channel Architecture

When IBM introduced their PS/2 line of computers, they radically redesigned the buses so that they could carry either 16 or 32 bits at a time. This new bus design, called **micro channel architecture (MCA)**, has many benefits besides its increased speed. Chet Heath, IBM's chief designer on the project, told *InfoWorld* that the following advantages are offered:

- Smaller add-on boards are possible. (However, boards designed for older IBM bus designs cannot be used with the MCA bus.)

- Installation of add-on boards is easier and faster because you can install them with software rather than with DIP switches. Each add-on board has its own unique ID number and comes with a disk that contains a text file called an Adapter Definition File (ADF). This file contains information telling the computer what resources the board needs to operate. When you install the board, the information in this file is automatically copied to nonvolatile RAM in the computer. Then, each time you turn on the computer, the information in this file is used to automatically set up the system.

- Lower electromagnetic emissions prevent distortion of nearby radios and televisions.

- Higher reliability and lower repair costs should be seen.

- Support of up to eight microprocessor chips. Moreover, the bus is processor independent; any microprocessor, including those made for Apple computers, can run on it.

- Support of up to eight communications ports instead of the two supported on earlier models.

- Additional random-access memory.
- A faster microprocessor. For example, there are **accelerator boards** that let you upgrade IBM AT computers that use the Intel 8088 or 80286 chip to the newer 80386 chip.
- A clock and battery to automatically set the computer's clock when the machine is turned on.
- A serial port or parallel port or both to connect peripherals like printers to the computer.
- Graphics processors and memory that display data on the screen in color or with more sharpness.
- A hard disk drive.

One of the problems with installing add-on boards is that tiny switches, called **DIP switches**, must be set to tell the board what system you have installed it in. This makes installation difficult and is the leading cause of service calls finding no problem, just wrong switch settings. One reason that IBM introduced the micro channel architecture in its PS/2 line of computers is to allow these settings to be made automatically using software when the board is installed.

CARING FOR YOUR COMPUTER

Computers are rugged and will provide good service with minimal maintenance if you treat them properly. Here are a few important dos and don'ts that will ensure you get the maximum life out of your equipment.

DO turn down the screen intensity if you will not be working on the computer for a while so that an image is not burned into its phosphor surface.

DO use a surge protector, a device that you plug into an outlet and then plug the computer into. This device protects the computer from any surges that might come down the power line. Surges occur when the power company restores service after it has been lost or when a nearby line is struck by lightning. A surge temporarily increases the current in the line, much like a wave of water is created if you suddenly remove a dam from a river. This surge, or wave of current, can damage a computer.

DON'T get it wet.

DON'T use it during lightning storms. Better yet, to be completely safe, unplug it when it is lightning.

DON'T drop it.

DON'T smoke around it.

DON'T leave it where it is exposed to direct sunlight.

DON'T turn the computer off more than is necessary. Computers, like other electronic equipment, are harmed more by the surge of power that runs through them when you first turn them on than they are by being left on all the time. Many users never turn their computers off; others just turn them off at the end of the day or on weekends.

DON'T use an ultrasonic humidifier without a mineral filter nearby the computer. These units do not evaporate water and leave minerals behind. They break the water and the minerals into small particles that are then distributed throughout the room. When the particles land on a computer, the water evaporates, leaving behind a powder that can damage sensitive equipment.

THE DEVELOPMENT OF THE MICROPROCESSOR

The design for a chip begins as a large drawing of the thousands of elements, like transistors, and their connections—the integrated circuit that is to be built into the chip. Many of these drawings are so complicated that they could not be designed without the aid of computers. In a sense, computer chips are therefore used to design other computer chips. The finished drawing is then photographically reduced to the final size of the actual chip.

Silicon, extracted from quartz rocks, is purified and grown into crystals. These crystals are then sliced into thin wafers about 4 inches across. The wafers are coated with a very thin film of metallic-oxide and a top layer of light sensitive material (called the photoresist). Infrared light is projected through the photographic image of the original drawing onto the wafer. The part of the wafer exposed to the light hardens while the part shielded by the parts of the negative remain soft. These softer parts are then removed with solvents, leaving small depressions that are then filled with a deposit of metal. This process is repeated for additional layers.

Over the past thirty years, there has been steady progress in increasing the number of active elements that can be mounted on a single chip. Just glancing at these photographs clearly shows the increasing complexity of the chips over the years.

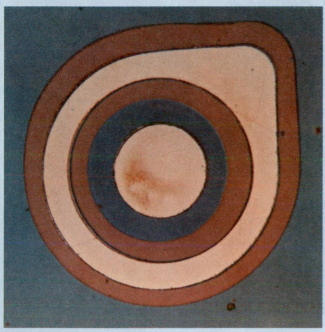

1959
The first planar transistor contained a single element. Courtesy of National Semiconductor

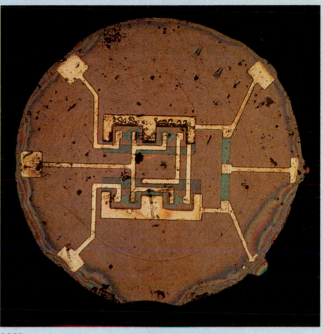

1961
The first integrated circuit on a single chip contained four transistors. Courtesy of National Semiconductor

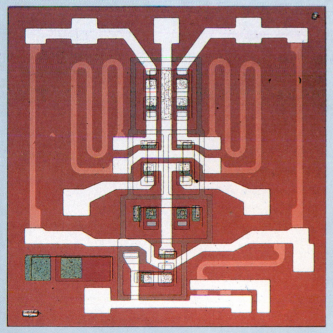

1964
The first chip designed for consumer applications contained five transistors. Courtesy of National Semiconductor

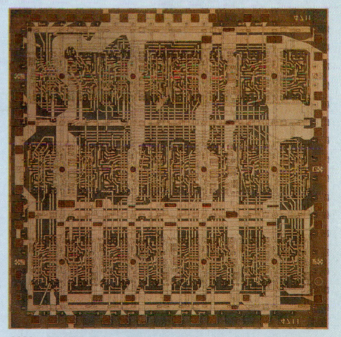

1968
A logic chip contained 180 transistors. Courtesy of National Semiconductor

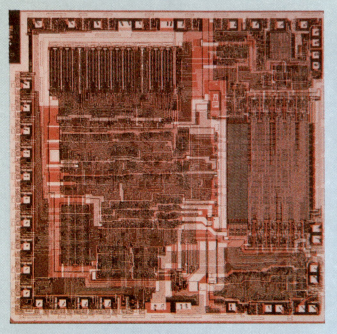

1987
The Intel 80386 chip is the latest and most powerful microprocessor. It contains 275,000 transistors. Courtesy of Intel

1978
The first 16-bit chip to contain a complete microprocessor contained 20,000 transistors. Courtesy of National Semiconductor

Silicon Wafers
An integrated circuit is created on a wafer of silicon, cut apart, and mounted into plastic mounts about ¼-by-1 inch so that they can be more easily handled and connected to other elements in the computer. The chip contains hundreds of thousands of transistors. Courtesy of The Computer Museum and Inmos Corporation

The Circuits on a Chip
The circuits on a chip are very small. This photo of a chip could easily be mistaken for an aerial view taken of a city from a nearby mountain. Actually, the large object on the left is an ordinary grain of salt. The "landscape" on the right is actually a close-up of the circuits on a chip. Courtesy of Xerox Corporation

- The microcomputer contains a special chip called a **microprocessor** that acts as the **central processing unit (CPU)**. The CPU coordinates the computer's activities and performs arithmetic and logical calculations. Programs written for one microprocessor may not run on another microprocessor.

- Microprocessors differ in the amount of information they can process at one time. The more they can process in one step, the more powerful they are.

- Microprocessors have built-in **instruction sets** that perform operations. Those with a complete instruction set are called **CISC chips**. Those with a reduced set are called **RISC chips**, and they operate faster.

- Many computers have more than one microprocessor. Those that perform specific functions are called **co-processors**.

- Microprocessors store data in and retrieve data from **internal memory**. There are two basic types of internal memory: **read-only memory (ROM)** and **random-access memory (RAM)**. ROM is unchangeable, but your programs and data are stored in RAM. Since you can change the data in RAM, it is called **volatile** memory.

- RAM chips come in several versions. The most common are **dynamic RAM chips (DRAM)**, which must be constantly refreshed. **Static RAM chips** are more expensive, but because they don't have to be refreshed as often, they don't load down the microprocessor, so it can operate faster on other tasks.

- Since RAM is limited, some computers use **virtual memory** to store programs and data on a disk until needed.

- Certain areas of memory are also reserved for **buffers** and **caches**. Buffers temporarily store data that is being sent to the printer, typed from the keyboard, or perhaps deleted. Caches store the most recent information processed by the CPU, so if it's needed again, the CPU can get to it faster.

- Data are sent out of the computer via **ports. Serial ports** send data a bit at a time, and **parallel ports** send it a byte at a time.

- The design of a computer's circuits is called its **architecture**. One of the key elements of a computer's architecture is its **bus**, the circuits along which signals are sent between components.

- Ports and other components in the computer are connected to the computer's **data bus**. It is sent to the device that is specified on the **address bus**. The number of bits that an address bus can carry at the one time determines the amount of memory that the microprocessor can address.

- All the computer's communications are controlled by the computer's clock.

- If the computer's memory chips are not as fast as the microprocessor, the computer must miss a beat when storing or retrieving information. This missed beat is called a **wait state**.

- The bus frequently has **expansion slots** into which you can plug **add-on boards** to improve the performance of your system.

1. List three types of microcomputers in descending order of their size and weight.
2. List three functions performed by the computer's central processing unit (CPU).
3. What kind of chip is used for the central processing unit?
4. What are the primary differences between 8-bit, 16-bit, and 32-bit microprocessors?

5. What is the purpose of the microprocessors instruction set? What two types of sets are used, and what are their advantages and disadvantages?

6. Describe the purpose of a co-processor.

7. Describe the differences between RAM and ROM.

8. Do all random access memories lose their data when power is turned off?

9. What does the term *virtual memory* mean?

10. Describe the function of a buffer. List and describe the functions of at least two buffers.

11. What are caches? List and describe two types of caches.

12. What is the function of a port? List the two kinds of ports on a computer, and describe the basic difference between them.

13. What does the term *architecture* mean?

14. Describe the purpose of the data bus.

15. Describe the purpose of the address bus.

16. What is micro channel architecture? Who introduced it?

17. What is a clock rate? What is a wait state?

18. What is the purpose of the expansion slots inside a computer? What can they be used for?

19. What are some typical functions performed by add-on boards?

20. What is a DIP switch? What is it used for?

21. List four things you should never do with your computer.

22. List two things you should always do with your computer.

23. Match the items in column A with their description in column B.

A	B
_____ Central processing unit (CPU)	A. Storage for documents and programs
_____ Expansion slots and boards	B. Used to attached peripherals like printers
_____ Memory	C. Processes data and controls computer operations
_____ Ports	D. Used to expand the computer's capabilities

24. What is the difference between a memory chip and a microprocessor chip?

TOPIC 1-5

Input Devices

OBJECTIVES

After completing this topic, you will be able to

- Describe the keys on the computer's keyboard

- Explain how scanners work, and list the differences between scanners that read text and those that read images

- Explain why voice input to the computer has not yet been fully developed

- Describe other input devices like graphics tablets, mice, joysticks, trackballs, and touch screens

Input devices are used to enter data into the computer where it can be processed. All computers come equipped with a keyboard, but several other input devices are also available that can enter data into your computer for processing. For example, you can scan text or images into your computer, or you can give it verbal instructions in special applications.

TEXT INPUT DEVICES

You usually enter data that you want to process by typing it on the computer's keyboard or scanning it in with a text scanner that can recognize characters. As you type or scan a document, the information is fed to the CPU and then either executed (if a command) or stored in memory (if data).

Keyboards

Keyboards vary in design and layout from computer to computer, but all have essentially the same types of keys. However, the names of the keys and their locations vary somewhat from keyboard to keyboard. For example, Figure 1-54 shows the original IBM PC keyboard, and Figure 1-55 shows the enhanced keyboard introduced with the IBM AT. The main differences between the old and new keyboards are the locations of the function keys and the directional arrow keys. When using either keyboard, keep the following points in mind:

- Many keys have an **autorepeat feature**; that is, if you hold them down, they continue entering the key's character or repeating its function until you release the key.

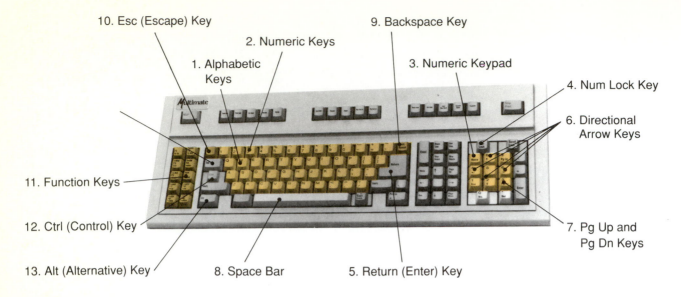

10. Esc (Escape) Key

2. Numeric Keys

9. Backspace Key

1. Alphabetic Keys

3. Numeric Keypad

4. Num Lock Key

6. Directional Arrow Keys

11. Function Keys

12. Ctrl (Control) Key

13. Alt (Alternative) Key

8. Space Bar

5. Return (Enter) Key

7. Pg Up and Pg Dn Keys

FIGURE 1-54
Typical Keyboard
The typical microcomputer keyboard has several different types of keys. Courtesy of IBM Corporation

FIGURE 1-55
Enhanced Keyboard
The enhanced keyboard has the function keys arranged above the main keyboard instead of grouped at the side. It also has a separate cursor movement keypad. Courtesy of IBM Corporation

■ To enter uppercase letters, either hold down **Shift** while typing a letter or press **Caps Lock**. An indicator on the screen usually tells you if **Caps Lock** is engaged or not. **Caps Lock** is like a **toggle** switch: If it is not engaged when you press it, it becomes engaged; if it is engaged when you press it, it becomes disengaged.

■ You enter numbers using either the number keys at the top of the keyboard or, if your computer has one, the numeric keypad at the right of the keyboard. If some of the keys on the numeric keypad also move the cursor, you must press **Num Lock** to switch back and forth between entering numbers and moving the cursor. Often, an indicator on the screen tells you if **Num Lock** is engaged or not.

■ If you are an experienced typist and are used to typing a lowercase **L** for 1 or an uppercase **O** for 0 (zero), do not do this on your computer. The computer treats numbers and letters differently, and although you usually won't have problems, you could run into difficulties by disregarding this distinction.

1. Function Keys

2. Separate Cursor and Screen Control Keys

3. Separate Cursor Movement Keypad

The most common layout of the alphabetic keys is identical to the layout on a typewriter. This layout is called a **QWERTY keyboard** because those are the first six keys on the upper row of letter keys. There are also several other arrangements, such as the **Dvorak keyboard**, named after its developer, Dr. August Dvorak. Many people claim, and research studies support, that designs like Dvorak's are more efficient. These claims make sense. An accomplished pianist can hit up to 2000 keys a minute, the equivalent of typing almost 400 words a minute. Compare this to a typist who can rarely attain speeds of more than 100 words a minute on a much smaller, easier-to-reach keyboard. The difference in speed is not caused by a difference in talent but by the inefficiency of the QWERTY keyboard's design. Still, despite its limitations, most people are familiar with the standard QWERTY keyboard, and other keyboards have not gained wide acceptance.

A person writing a software program (called a **programmer**) can assign any function he or she chooses to each of the keys on the keyboard. Thus the actual function that each key performs varies from program to program. But in general, here is what each of the keys is normally used for.

1. Alphabetic keys are arranged on the keyboard just as they are on a typewriter. When you press them, they enter lowercase letters. If you hold down the **Shift** key when you press the letter keys, or if you engage the **Caps Lock** key, you enter uppercase (capital) letters (Figure 1-56). If you engage **Caps Lock** and then hold down **Shift** while typing, you enter lowercase letters.

2. Numeric keys are located above the alphabetic keys and are labeled with both numbers and symbols. When you press these keys, you enter either the indicated numbers or, if you hold down **Shift**, the indicated symbols.

3. On many keyboards, there is a separate set of number keys arranged like those on a calculator. With this **numeric keypad**, you can enter numbers more quickly. But on some computers, the numeric keypad

FIGURE 1-56
Uppercase and Lowercase
The terms *uppercase* and *lowercase* come from the typesetting field. When type was set by hand, all the characters were stored in a type case. The typesetter selected individual characters from the case and assembled them into words, sentences, paragraphs, and pages. The capital letters were stored in the upper part of the case, and the other letters in the lower part, hence the terms. Courtesy of The Bettman Archive, Inc.

It May Be Taps for Old Keyboard

The familiar typewriter keyboard used around the world for more than a century may be replaced in the microelectronic age by a faster, simpler arrangement that lets many touch typists cruise at speeds of 100 words a minute or more.

Directory assistance operators across the country already are using the new system. State governments in Oregon and New Jersey have begun converting their typing operations, and federal agencies such as the Department of Agriculture are experimenting with the new keyboard. Many insurance firms and large manufacturers are boarding the bandwagon.

Efficiency experts have argued for decades that the standard keyboard, known as "QWERTY" after the first six letters of a top row, is slow and unproductive. Indeed, it was designed that way.

Christopher Latham Sholes, father of the typewriter, laid out the QWERTY keyboard in the 1870s. His first machines kept jamming when typists went too fast. To slow things down, he spread the most common letters—e, t, o, a, n, i—all over the board and ensured that frequent combinations (such as "ed") had to be struck by the same finger—the slowest motion.

By the 1930s, typewriters mechanically were fast enough to keep up with most typists, but the purposely inefficient QWERTY held sway because nobody pushed hard for change; nobody, that is, except August Dvorak, a University of Washington psychologist who devoted his life to an anti-qwerty crusade.

Dvorak, a pioneer of "ergonomics"—the study of the interaction between man and machine—designed a keyboard built for speed, putting all five vowels and the five most common consonants on the center, right under the fingers.

With the letters on Dvorak's home row—AOEUIDHTNS—the typist can produce about 3,000 common English words. The

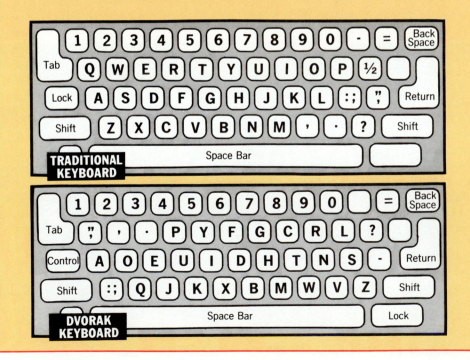

QWERTY and Dvorak Keyboards
Source: T.R. Reid, Washington Post, 1985. Reprinted with permission.

QWERTY keyboard's home row—ASDFGHJKL—makes fewer than 100 common words.

Dvorak's design also permits a much faster two-handed rhythm by splitting the strokes evenly between right and left. With QWERTY, the left hand does almost 60 percent of the typing; on Dvorak's keyboard, each hand types 50 percent of the letters.

"When you see Dvorak typists, it looks like their hands aren't even moving," said Patricia Kaplus, a supervisor in an Oregon government office that has made the switch. "You don't have to jump from row to row, so it's faster and more accurate."

Dvorak set forth his new arrangement in his 1936 study, "Typewriting Behavior." He then set out to sell it to the world.

A U.S. Navy study found that the Dvorak board would increase typing speed by 25 percent or more, and the Navy ordered 2,000 Dvorak typewriters during World War II, when there was an acute shortage of typists. But the war ended before the system got going.

Consumer advocate Ralph Nader—who has had a Dvorak typewriter for years but says he never found time to master it—charges that the typing industry deliberately held back despite Dvorak's demonstrated superiority.

"The typewriter companies and the secretary schools don't want an increase in productivity," Nader said. "They don't want an office to get the same work out of two typists that used to take three."

Donald Seaton, a Smith-Corona executive who does his typing on Dvorak, said his firm offered a Dvorak keyboard in its catalogue for years but phased out the model due to limited demand.

QWERTY is not quitting quietly. Industry officials estimate that there are 30 million standard QWERTY keyboards in use today, and about one tenth as many with Dvorak capability. Most typing schools still concentrate on QWERTY.

Professor Dvorak died in 1975—just before the breakthrough that has made his keyboard accessible to every home and office.

The invention of electronic keyboards controlled by a programmed microchip has made it possible to switch from QWERTY to Dvorak and back with the touch of a key. "Ever since they put the chip into a keyboard, there's been a groundswell (for the faster version)," said Virginia Russell, founder and head of the International Dvorak Federation in Brandon, Vt.

Many computer firms, including Apple, are building in Dvorak conversion capability as standard equipment on their keyboards today, and plenty of low-cost programs are available to reprogram keyboards on other computers. For older keyboards that convert to DVORAK, a typist can buy stick-on letters to mark the key tops or new key tops to snap over the old ones. Keyboard makers such as Keytronics and Wico are producing boards that have both the QWERTY and Dvorak letter stamped on each key top—often in contrasting colors.

Professor Richard Land of the Harvard University Instructional Laboratories said an ordinary typist normally will go from about 40 to more than 60 words per minute after switching to Dvorak.

Source: T. R. Reid. *Washington Post*, 1985. Reprinted with permission.

serves a second purpose. It contains the directional arrow keys (see 5). If the numeric keypad serves this dual function, **Num Lock** must be engaged to enter numbers. When it is not engaged, the keys on the numeric keypad move the cursor.

4. The **Return** key (also called the **Enter** key) is often pressed as the final keystroke.

   ■ When sending commands to the computer. You often have to type, or otherwise indicate, a command and then press **Return** to send the command to the CPU.

   ■ When ending paragraphs of lines of text before they reach the right margin. But unlike a typewriter, you don't have to press it to end lines within a paragraph.

5. Cursor movement keys move the **cursor**, a reverse video (a dark character against a light background or vice versa) or underline character, around the screen. You use the cursor to point to where you want to enter or edit data on the screen. Because keyboards vary and program designers can change their functions, the keys used to move the cursor also vary. Generally, the directional arrow keys (Figure 1-57) move the cursor one line or character at a time. On most programs, the **PgUp** and **PgDn** keys move the cursor a screen or page at a time.

6. The **Spacebar** enters spaces. On a typewriter, pressing **Spacebar** moves the print element over existing text, but on a computer, pressing **Spacebar** pushes the next characters, if any, to the right. On a few programs, it is also used to move a highlight to choices listed on a menu when the menu is activated. These menus list commands you can choose from by highlighting them and then pressing **Return**.

7. The **Backspace** key backs the cursor up. If the program assigns this key the ability to delete characters you back it over, it is called a **destructive backspace**. This lets you quickly back over and delete characters when you discover a mistake while entering text.

8. The **Esc** (Escape) key (or other designated key) is often used to cancel a command in progress if you change your mind before completing the command.

FIGURE 1-57
Directional Arrow Keys
The directional arrow keys move the cursor on the screen. They are sometimes referred to as north (up), south (down), left (west), and right (east).

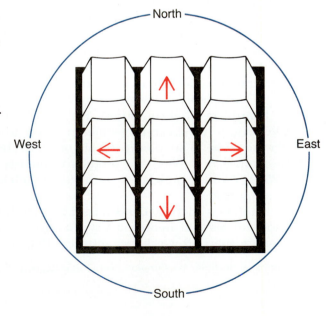

MICROCOMPUTER SYSTEMS

9. Computer manufacturers recognize the need for special keys to which software designers can assign frequently used tasks. They have therefore added special keys that can be used for this purpose. These **function keys** (often designated **F1**, **F2**, **F3**, and so on) perform functions assigned to them by the programmer. For example, on a word processing program, function keys are often assigned to select, copy, move, or delete text. On some keyboards, the function keys are grouped at the side of the keyboard. On other computers, they are the top row of keys.

10. Many keys are assigned more than one function. For instance, pressing the right directional arrow key may move the cursor one column or character at a time, but pressing the right directional arrow key while holding down the **Ctrl** (Control) key may move the cursor several columns or characters at a time. Pressing the letter **B** enters the letter alone, but pressing **B** while holding down the **Alt** (Alternate) key might enter a code that tells the printer to begin boldfacing text. Neither **Ctrl** nor **Alt** sends characters to the computer; they change what is sent when you press other keys. Using combinations of keys in this way lets the software designers assign many more functions to the keyboard than there are keys available. This is much like the standard typewriter, which uses **Shift** to type uppercase letters. Using this approach, fifty-two characters (twenty-six uppercase and twenty-six lowercase letters) can be generated with only twenty-six keys.

11. The **Tab** key moves the cursor to the next tab stop. The **Backtab** key, which is usually the same key as **Tab** but pressed along with **Shift**, does the same thing but moves the cursor in the opposite direction.

Text Scanning Devices

When you type text into a computer and then print it out on a printer, you are actually converting the text from a digital form (the form used by the computer) to a printed form. Until recently, this conversion process has been like a one-way street. It was not possible to easily convert printed copy into an electronic form that could be processed by a computer or word processing program. For example, if a document has already been typed and printed, it is time consuming to rekeyboard it back into the computer. To make the conversion from printed text to electronic text more efficient, **scanners** have been developed (Figure 1-58).

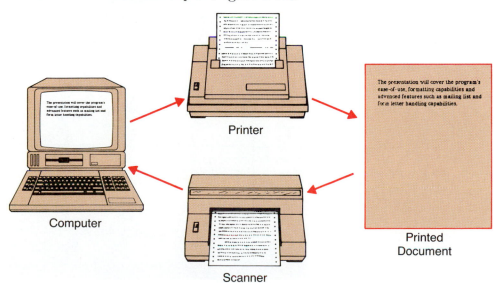

Printer

Computer

Scanner

Printed Document

FIGURE 1-58
Scanning
Scanning is like reversing the process of printing. Printing converts the document from an electronic to a printed form, and scanning converts it from a printed to an electronic form.

Bar Codes and Bar Code Scanners

One of the most widely used scanners is the **bar code scanner** (Figure 1-59) that reads universal product codes (UPCs). Made up of bars of different widths and spacing, these codes convey alphabetic and numeric information about products. Information stored in a bar code might include a serial number, price, date, and time. UPC bar codes can be scanned with either a hand-held wand or a built-in scanner like those in supermarkets. Bar code scanners read the code and convert it into an electronic form that can be processed by a computer.

Bar code scanners are extremely accurate, fast, and inexpensive—features that have made them familiar at supermarket checkout counters, where the checkout person uses them to read the bar code labels on cans, boxes, and bags. These supermarket scanners are connected to a computer that contains a complete list of product names and prices for each different bar code in the store. When the scanner reads the bar code on, say, a can of beans, the computer looks up the product number the bar code represents and returns its name and price to the register at the checkout counter.

The information collected by the computer when these devices are used can also have additional benefits. For example, they allow the store to track inventory and perform marketing analyses. With instant feedback, the managers can know what products are selling, measure the effect of prices and discounts, and compare one product's sales with another's.

Optical Character Recognition (OCR) Devices

Many business documents are not as easy for a computer to read as bar codes are. Documents may be typed or printed using any number of different typefaces. Because converting this text into digital form is more complicated, it is done with **optical character recognition (OCR)** devices.

The first OCRs could not distinguish between different typefaces, so a special OCR typeface was developed (Figure 1-60). When a document was

FIGURE 1-59
Bar Code Scanners
Bar code readers can convert the universal product codes (UPCs) on products and other items into an electronic form the computer can process.
Courtesy of NCR Corporation

typed using this special typeface, it could be easily scanned into the computer. Unfortunately, this approach requires planning ahead which documents might be scanned. The OCR typeface is also not attractive enough to use in most business letters and reports.

Recent improvements now make it possible for OCR scanners to read many different typefaces with a high degree of reliability. The devices vary widely in design, but the principle behind them is the same. In one type, the document remains fixed while a scanner moves down it a line at a time. In another type, the document is fed into the scanner and moved slowly past the scanner (Figure 1-61).

The scanner reads the pattern of dark characters against a light background and converts each character to its digital ASCII number (Figure 1-62). This ASCII number is then stored in the computer's memory or on a disk. Since the text is converted into its ASCII numbers, it can be stored, displayed, printed, and otherwise manipulated just as if it had been entered into the computer through the keyboard. Text you enter with one of these devices can be edited by word processors and processed by other programs that accept ASCII input.

Although these scanners are ideal for converting text documents into electronic form, they cannot convert graphs and other illustrations. They also cannot read corrections and notes made with a pencil or pen. These must be manually entered into the computer after the main body of the document has been scanned.

GRAPHICS INPUT DEVICES

Besides scanning textual documents to convert them from printed to electronic form, input devices let you scan graphic images into the computer or create them directly on the screen. Until recently, there was no reason for most users to understand how these devices work since computer graphics

---

THIS IS AN
OCR TYPEFACE

FIGURE 1-60
OCR Characters
OCR typefaces were originally designed because scanners could read only a few typefaces. To simplify this, standard typefaces were used when a document was prepared for scanning.

FIGURE 1-61
OCR Scanner
An OCR scanner scans documents into the computer a character at a time so that the text can be manipulated just as if it had been entered through the keyboard. Courtesy of Dest Corporation

FIGURE 1-62
Scanning Text
As an OCR scanner pauses on a line of text, it compares each character with the characters stored in its memory. If it finds a match, it looks up the ASCII number of the character in its memory and sends that number to the CPU, which displays it on the screen and stores it in memory. Here the scanner has scanned the first line of text in the document (a) and has found a match for the letter A and displayed it on the screen (b).

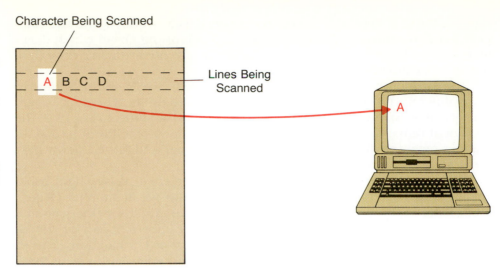

A. The Document

B. The Screen

were not widely used in documents. Charts, graphs, and illustrations were prepared separately and inserted into documents after they were printed. But now it is possible to create these images on a microcomputer and insert them directly into a document while you are working on it. With desktop publishing becoming more widespread, the use of graphics in documents will only increase.

Graphics Scanners

Graphics scanners (also called image digitizers) (Figure 1-63) are becoming more and more useful now that desktop publishing programs allow you to combine text and graphics in documents.

As you have just seen, text scanners, like bar code readers and OCR de-

FIGURE 1-63
Graphics Scanners
Graphics scanners (also called image digitizers) scan images, converting each point or pixel on the document into electronic signals that are sent to the computer. Unlike text scanners, the electronic signals do not indicate characters. Courtesy of Dest Corporation

MICROCOMPUTER SYSTEMS

vices, convert printed documents into electronic form so that the characters, letters, numbers, and symbols can be manipulated by the computer just as if they had been entered through the keyboard. Many documents, however, are not primarily textual. These documents contain images: photographs, line drawings, charts, maps, and so on. To scan graphic images like these into the computer, graphics scanners are used to convert the printed image into digital form. Instead of converting the image into characters, graphics scanners take a digital picture of it, much as a copy machine does. The difference, of course, is that the copy is stored in the computer in digital form.

Unlike text characters, graphic images are not converted into ASCII codes. Thus text scanned into the computer with a graphics scanner cannot be edited with a word processing program. To convert these images, parts of which are either dark or light, into digital form, the scanner divides the printed image into a grid of small dots, called picture elements or **pixels**. For each pixel on the document, a corresponding pixel is on the screen (Figure 1-64). This one-to-one correspondence between pixels on the document and pixels on the screen lets a duplicate of the original be read into the computer and displayed. As the image is scanned, the scanner determines if each of these pixels is light or dark. If dark, the scanner assigns it the value 0. If light, it assigns it the value 1. These values are fed into the computer and stored in memory. When the scanning is completed, the entire image is stored in the computer's memory as a series of numeric values, one for the level of brightness of each pixel in the image. When it is displayed on the screen, the digitizing process is reversed—the numeric value of each pixel in the original image is used to control the brightness of its corresponding pixel on the display screen. Once the image has been stored in the computer's memory and displayed on the screen, it can be manipulated by a program designed to work with images of this kind.

Graphics scanners are available in several versions, including 1 bit, 8 bits, 16 bits. Scanners that use 1 bit to store an image can scan only black and white images because with 1 bit you can specify only if a pixel is black or white. Many images, like photographs, have intermediate gray tones, and more information is needed to accurately scan these. The spectrum of tones

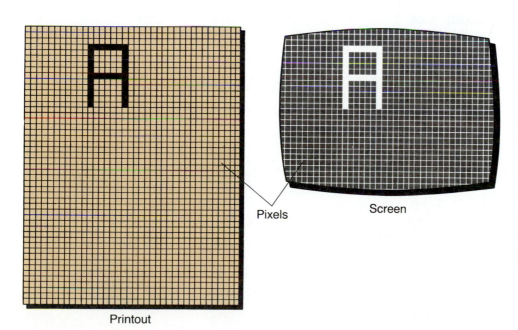

Pixels

Screen

Printout

FIGURE 1-64
Scanning Graphic Images
There is a one-to-one correspondence between pixels on a document and pixels on the screen. If the pixel on the document is light, the scanner sends the value 1 to the computer, which then illuminates the corresponding pixel on the screen. If the pixel on the document is dark, the scanner sends the value 0 to the computer, and the corresponding pixel on the screen is left dark.

FIGURE 1-65
Gray Scale
8-bit graphics scanners
can store up to 256 values
to reproduce images, like
photographs, that have
many tones. The
arrangement of tones from
light to dark is called a
gray scale.

in these images is called a **gray scale**. When arranged from darkest to lightest, they look like Figure 1-65. When these images are scanned with a 1-bit scanner, the tones are approximated with a process called **dithering**. However, 8-bit scanners can store up to 256 tones ($2^8 = 256$), so they can be used to scan images of this kind. They can also scan color images and assign any one of 256 colors to each dot being scanned.

The number of bytes required to store a graphic image depends on the number of bits assigned to each pixel. For example, an 8½-by-11-inch image printed 300 dots to the inch has almost 8-million pixels. To store a graphic image of this size, a 1-bit scanner requires almost 1MB of memory. An 8-bit scanner requires almost 8MB. Since these file sizes would create serious storage problems, scanners use a special procedure called **file compression** to store the files in much less space on the disk.

Graphics Tablets

One of the most interesting devices for creating graphics on the screen is a **graphics tablet** (also called a digitizing tablet or graphics pad). These devices are like electronic pantographs. Pantographs have been used for hundreds of years to make copies of images. As Figure 1-66 shows, they have two pens connected by a mechanism. When a drawing is traced with one of the pens, the other pen moves in the same pattern, duplicating the original drawing.

The electronic pantograph, or graphics tablet, is simply a pad with an associated penlike stylus (Figure 1-67). You move the stylus across the surface of the pad to trace existing drawings laid on top of the pad, to create new drawings, or to execute commands. The pad always knows the stylus

FIGURE 1-66
Pantographs
Pantographs were
developed to trace
drawings. As you trace the
drawing with one pen, the
arm moves, and the other
pen makes a copy of the
original drawing. Courtesy
of Historical Pictures
Services, Chicago, Ill.

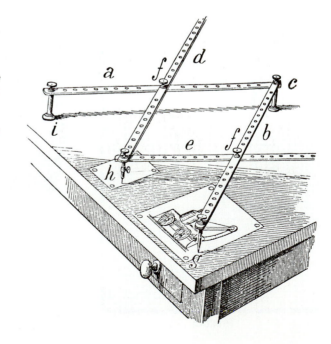

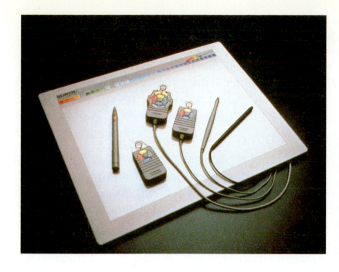

FIGURE 1-67
Graphics Tablet
A graphics tablet is like an electronic pantograph. As you draw on the pad, it sends electronic signals to the computer, and the image appears on the screen. Courtesy of Kurta

position because the pad is broken up into a grid of individual pixels. The screen is also divided into pixels, so if you press on a given pixel on the pad, the corresponding pixel on the screen is illuminated. To draw a line, you press on one pixel after another, and the corresponding pixels on the screen are illuminated to display a line. This graphic device lets you use the same kind of hand motion you use when sketching.

Light Pens

Light pens are hand-held devices that let you draw directly on the screen (Figure 1-68). There is no tablet between the pen and the screen as with a graphics tablet. You simply hold the pen against the screen, and the image is "painted" on the computer's screen by a beam of electrons that sweeps across and down the screen a line at a time. When you hold a light pen against the screen, the pen senses the electron beam as it sweeps by. Knowing where the electron beam is at any time, the computer calculates the pen's position and places a dot at that point on the screen on the next scan.

VOICE INPUT DEVICES

Despite the incredibly fast processing speed of the computer, it is slowed down by the keyboard. To process information, you must first enter it into the computer, and people can type only so fast. Ideally, people should be able

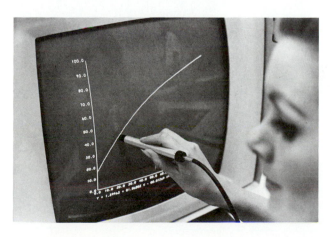

FIGURE 1-68
Light Pens
A light pen can be used to draw directly on the display screen. Courtesy of IBM Corporation

to talk to the computer as they talk to friends and co-workers. This would not only make the process faster but would also make the computer accessible to those who do not know how to type. It is not yet possible to converse with your computer, but **voice input devices** have been developed that, though limited, do convert the human voice into a signal the computer can understand. This is not a simple task. A recent article in *The Economist* uses the following two sentences to illustrate the difficulty:

This new display can recognize speech.
This nudist play can wreck a nice beach.

Read each sentence aloud. To tell the difference between them requires very good hearing. Even then you probably could not tell the difference unless the words were pronounced very carefully. Imagine how difficult it is to program a computer so that it can tell the difference!

Advances are slowly being made, and systems have been developed that can understand up to 20,000 words (Figure 1-69). To use one of these systems, you must first "train" the computer to make it familiar with the way you pronounce each word. To do so, each word in the program's vocabulary is displayed on the screen, and you speak each aloud into a microphone. The computer then stores your pronunciation along with the matching word displayed on the screen. This computerized match is called a **voice template**. The next time you speak to the computer, it quickly matches the pattern of your voice against the voice templates stored in its memory. If it finds a match, it can display the word or execute the command.

This approach limits the computer to a small vocabulary. As you add words, training the computer takes longer. More words require more computer memory, and it then takes the computer longer to search though the larger number of voice templates for a match. Despite these limitations, the approach is useful when there are a limited number of commands or when larger amounts of information can be conveyed by relatively few code words. For example, let's say you wanted to know all the details about items in your company's inventory. These details might include the price, size, quantity in stock, and color. The details for each product could then be stored in the computer and assigned names or numbers. A typewriter might be assigned the stock number 100, and a copy machine the number 200. To display the details about an item, you would only have to say, "DISPLAY." The computer might then ask, "DISPLAY WHAT?" and you would respond, "ONE," pause for a moment, and then say, "HUNDRED" to display details about the type-

FIGURE 1-69
Voice Input
Voice input devices allow you to enter data and commands with your voice by converting speech into electronic signals.
Courtesy of The Voice Connection

MICROCOMPUTER SYSTEMS

writer. You could also say, "TWO," pause, and then say, "HUNDRED" to display details about the copy machine. In this way, a great deal of information can be manipulated with a limited vocabulary.

OTHER TYPES OF INPUT DEVICES

Several other input devices have been developed to make data entry easier or for special purposes.

Mice

An increasingly common input device is the **mouse**. One type of mouse houses a rolling ball and one or more buttons that you press to execute commands (Figure 1-70). As you move the mouse around on a flat, smooth surface, the ball rolls and feeds electrical signals to the computer to move the cursor on the screen. There are also optical mice, which use a mirrorlike pad to reflect a tiny beam of light.

Trackballs

Trackballs are like an upside-down mouse. Instead of moving them around on a flat surface, they remain stationary while you spin a ball exposed on their top surface to move the cursor on the screen. The direction you spin the ball determines the direction the cursor moves.

Joysticks

Joysticks are familiar to anyone who has played electronic arcade games. When attached to a microcomputer, the joystick is used much like a mouse, but instead of using a rolling ball, the unit has a movable stick that can be used to position the cursor on the screen. Buttons mounted on the stick, or elsewhere on the unit, can be pressed to execute commands.

Touch Screens

Some computers have **touch screens** that are sensitive to your touch (Figure 1-71). You use your finger to point to a command displayed on the screen, and it is executed. Many techniques are used to make the screens sensitive to touch.

FIGURE 1-70
Mouse
A mouse is a device that you move across a smooth surface. As you do so, the cursor moves on the screen so that you can draw lines and make selections from menus by pressing the buttons on the mouse. Courtesy of Apple Computer, Inc.

FIGURE 1-71
Touch Screens
Some computers have touch-sensitive screens. You use your finger to point to a command displayed on the screen, and it is executed. Courtesy of IBM Corporation

1. Infrared screens surround the screen with pairs of light-emitting diodes (LEDs) and photo detector cells so that they cover the screen with an invisible grid of light. The LEDs emit infrared light, and the detectors receive it, much like the devices used to automatically open doors. When you touch the screen, some of the beams are broken, and the computer then calculates the position of your finger.

2. Pressure-sensitive screens use two sheets of mylar assembled so that they are separated by a small space. Each sheet of mylar contains rows of invisible wires, and the sheets are assembled so that the wires run horizontally in one sheet and vertically in the other. When you apply pressure to the screen, the wires at that spot make contact, and a circuit is closed.

3. Capacitive screens use a device that senses changes in capacitance when and where you touch the screen with a stylus.

SUMMARY AND KEY TERMS

- Data is usually entered into the computer through the **keyboard**.
- **Scanners** allow you to speed up the input process by scanning printed material so that you do not have to retype it. Some of these devices scan just text, and others scan graphics.
- Data scanned into the computer with a **text scanner** can be manipulated by applications programs like word processors a character at a time just as if it had been entered from the keyboard. Typical text scanners are **bar code scanners** and **optical character recognition (OCR)** devices.
- Data scanned in with a **graphics scanner** is more like a picture; individual characters cannot be manipulated as text can be.
- There are also other input devices like **graphics tablets, light pens, mice, trackballs, touch screens,** and **joysticks**. The most promising is **voice input,** which allows you to give commands to your computer.

REVIEW QUESTIONS

1. What does it mean when you say a key autorepeats? How do you make it do so? How do you stop it?
2. What does it mean when you say a key toggles?

3. What is a Dvorak keyboard? How does it differ from the QWERTY keyboard? Why isn't the Dvorak keyboard more popular?

4. What is the purpose of a numeric keypad?

5. What are cursor movement keys?

6. Match the keys in column A with their functions in column B.

A	B
Spacebar	Enters uppercase letters when engaged
Backspace	Cancels commands
Caps Lock	Toggles the numeric keypad between entering numbers and moving the cursor
Shift	Enter commands
Num Lock	Deletes characters
Return	Enters spaces
Esc	Enters uppercase letters when held down

7. What are function keys, and what are they used for?

8. List two types of text scanners, and describe how they differ.

9. What is the difference between text and graphics scanners?

10. What is a pixel?

11. What is a graphics tablet used for?

12. What is the first step you must complete when using most voice input systems?

13. List as many input devices as you can think of, and describe what they are best used for.

Output Devices

OBJECTIVES

After completing this topic, you will be able to

- Distinguish between the various types of computer display screens
- Explain how images are displayed on the screen, and list the differences between character and graphics screens
- Describe the types of color monitors that are available
- Explain how printers form characters and transfer them to paper
- List the differences among types of printers
- List and describe common printer accessories

When working on a computer, you want to be able to see what you are working on. You also want to print your work on paper so that you can take it with you, share it with others, or file it for later reference. The devices you use to do this are called **output devices** because they get information out of the computer.

DISPLAY SCREENS

The **display screen** (also called a video display or display monitor) attached to your microcomputer gives you instant feedback while you are working. This screen is a window into your computer's memory. As you type text on the keyboard, it is entered into memory and copied (echoed) to the screen so that you can see it. Since you spend most of your time looking at the display screen, its quality and capabilities are important. For example, some screens display only text characters, whereas others also display graphics. Some display an image in a single color, and others in multiple colors.

Inside a Display Screen

Display screens fall into two main classes: cathode ray tubes and flat-panel displays.

Cathode Ray Tubes (CRTs)

Most microcomputers are equipped with a **cathode ray tube (CRT)** because these displays create the best image. Many CRTs display twenty-four or twenty-five lines of eighty characters each, but some display up to sixty-six lines, enough to show a full 8½-by-11-inch page of text. Displays capable of showing the full page (Figure 1-72) are highly desirable but still quite expensive. With the increasing popularity of desktop publishing, however, these full-page displays will inevitably become more popular and less expensive.

Flat-Panel Displays

CRTs are bulky, so portable computers must use flat-panel displays (Figure 1-73). On these displays, the image is created using various technologies, all of which offer advantages and disadvantages, with the tradeoffs usually being made between readability, power consumption, and cost. Since these screens are most often used in portable computers, power consumption is a major concern. If a display requires too much power, the battery life be-

FIGURE 1-72
Full-Screen Displays
Full-page display screens are ideal for most word processing purposes. They are especially useful when you are formatting pages with a desktop publishing program. Courtesy of IBM Corporation

FIGURE 1-73
Flat-Panel Displays
Flat-panel displays create an image with LEDs or LCDs. They are widely used in portable computers because of their small size and light weight. Courtesy of IBM Corporation

TABLE 1-7
Flat-Panel Technologies

Type	Readability	Battery Life	Cost
Liquid crystal displays (LCDs)	Lowest	Longest	Lowest
Light-emitting diodes (LEDs)	Low	Long	Low
Gas plasma	High	Shortest	High
Electroluminescent	Highest	Short	Highest

tween recharges is very short, perhaps as short as one hour. Lower power consumption can increase a battery's life to six or more hours. Table 1-7 lists the four basic types of flat-panel displays and their advantages and disadvantages.

Liquid crystal displays (LCDs) do not create an image by generating light. Instead, they change the reflectance of areas of the screen so that light is either reflected or absorbed. Characters appear as black against a silver background. In some lighting, these displays are hard to read, and they cannot be read at all in the dark. To reduce this problem, some LCDs are now backlit or use other technologies to increase their contrast. Their major advantage is that they consume very little power, so they are ideal in portable, battery-operated computers.

Light-emitting diode (LED) displays have many very small light-emitting diodes arranged in a grid on the screen. By lighting the appropriate diodes, an image of light characters appears against a dark background.

Gas plasma displays sandwich small bubbles of gas between two glass plates. The two outer sheets of glass contain transparent electrical conductors arranged in rows, so when they are assembled at 90-degree angles to each other, they form a grid. When any two wires on the grid are charged with electricity, the gas in the bubble between which they intersect is illuminated.

Electroluminescent displays create characters by illuminating small diodes on the screen's surface. Characters appear light against a dark background.

Monochrome and Color Screens

Displays are also classified as either monochrome or color.

Monochrome Displays

Monochrome screens display a single color, usually green or amber characters against a black background. On some of these screens, you can reverse the display so that dark characters are displayed against a light background.

Color Displays

Color displays have become increasingly popular. To generate colors, three dots or thin stripes of phosphor (red, green, and blue) must be illuminated to create a single dot from which characters are created (Figure 1-74). The size, or **pitch**, of the dots (or stripes) determines how sharp a character displayed on the screen will appear. High-quality monitors have a pitch of 0.31 mm (about ⅓ of a millimeter) or less. Not long ago, even the best color monitors could not provide the **resolution**—that is, sharpness of characters—

Dots

Stripes

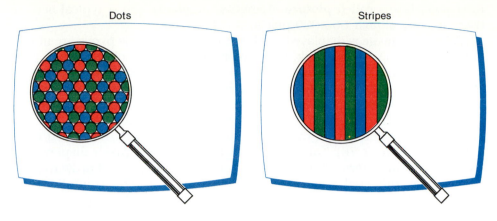

FIGURE 1-74
Color Displays
A color CRT has three sets of dots or stripes, one for each of the primary colors (red, green, and blue). By illuminating combinations of these sets of dots, any color can be displayed.

that monochrome screens could. Using a color graphics card, enhanced color graphics adapter, or the new graphics chips built into the computer itself, a much higher resolution image can be sent to the screen.

When the computer communicates with the display screen, it has to send a stream of information including the colors of the characters to be displayed (called the **dot stream**) to illuminate the screen. Computers send these signals as either a composite signal or an RGB signal.

Composite color displays are just like a television set. The signals for the three primary colors, red, green, and blue, are combined into a single composite signal when fed from the computer to the display. Though generally inexpensive, composite color displays give relatively poor quality.

RGB color displays (RGB stands for red, green, blue) are fed three separate video inputs from the computer. A separate input is used for red, green, and blue. The image is sharper and the cost higher than a composite color display.

How Images Are Displayed

Besides categorizing display monitors as either monochrome or color, they can be categorized by how the image is created on the screen. Two approaches are used: graphics based and character based. The computer system's hardware and software determine which approach is used. To understand the differences between character-based and graphics-based displays, you first must understand how images are created on the screen.

Picture Elements

All images displayed on a screen are created with dots. To do this, the screen is divided into a grid, as shown in Figure 1-75. The grid divides the screen

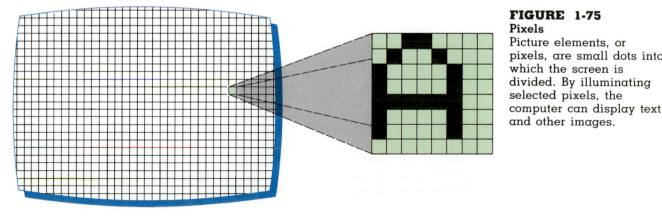

FIGURE 1-75
Pixels
Picture elements, or pixels, are small dots into which the screen is divided. By illuminating selected pixels, the computer can display text and other images.

into small boxes called **picture elements,** or **pixels**. On a typical screen, there may be almost 800,000 pixels.

When an image is displayed on the screen, some of the pixels are illuminated, and some are left dark. On a color monitor, the colors of each pixel can also be set to one of many colors. The illuminated or colored pixels on the screen are arranged into patterns that form characters and other images on the screen.

The number of pixels, and hence the resolution (sharpness) of the display, is determined by the number of rows and columns the screen is divided into (Figure 1-76). Table 1-8 shows the number of pixels displayed on typical IBM computers when equipped with the appropriate hardware. The resolution is indicated by the number of pixels displayed horizontally on the screen by the number displayed vertically. For example, a resolution of 640-by-480 pixels indicates the screen has 640 pixels horizontally and 480 vertically. The number of pixels on a screen, and the number of colors or shades of gray that can be displayed, are limited by the amount of video memory the computer has. For example, a monochrome display on a screen with 320-by-200 pixels requires only 8KB of memory. There are 64,000 pixels (320 by 200), and only 1 bit is needed for each pixel, so you require 64,000 bits or 8000 bytes. To display any of 256 colors, however, you need 1 byte for each pixel ($2^8 = 256$), so you need 64KB of memory. On a very high resolution screen with 1024-by-768 pixels, you have a total of 768,432 pixels, so you would need more than 98KB of video memory.

Although all screens display characters that are composed of pixels, these characters are generated either as characters or as graphics. Understanding the differences between these two approaches is important because they determine what you can display on the screen.

FIGURE 1-76
Resolution
High-resolution displays divide the screen into more pixels than a low-resolution screen does. The result is a sharper image because each character is formed from more dots.

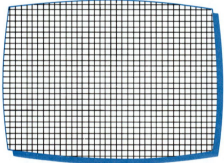

High Resolution

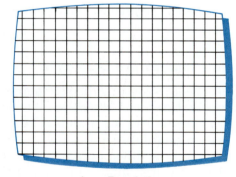

Low Resolution

TABLE 1-8
Typical IBM Computer Displays

Type of Display Adapter	Number of Pixels	Number of Colors
Monochrome	Text only	1
Color graphics card	320 by 200	4
	640 by 200	2
Enhanced graphics adapter	320 by 200	4
	640 by 200	2
	640 by 350	16
	640 by 350	1
	720 by 400	(text)
IBM PS/2 Color Display 8512	640 by 480 (graphics)	256
IBM PS/2 Color Display 8514	1024 by 768	256

Graphics Displays

If you are using a graphics display, some programs display the image on the screen using a technique called **bit mapping** (also called memory mapping or all points addressable). A bit-mapped display stores each of the screen's pixels in one or more bits of memory. Thus there is a one-to-one relation between the pixels on the screen and the pixels stored in memory. As Figure 1-77 shows, if the bit in memory is a 1, the corresponding pixel on the screen is illuminated. If the bit in memory is a 0, the pixel is not illuminated.

By approximately setting the values in memory, any kind of image can be displayed on the screen. For example, Figure 1-78 shows a bit-mapped display of three different typefaces. Because the image is created in memory and then sent to the screen, the wide variations are possible. Table 1-9 describes the advantages and disadvantages of graphic displays.

Applications programs are becoming increasingly sophisticated. In some programs, it is now possible to combine text and illustrations on the same page or to change the size and style of characters. These features are easier to use if you can see on the screen exactly what you will get when you print the document. For this reason, graphics displays, and programs that take advantage of them, are becoming increasingly common.

To use a program that utilizes bit mapping, you must have a graphics display screen. If your computer does not have graphics built in, you also

FIGURE 1-77
Graphics Display
A graphics display allocates memory for each pixel on the screen. If the memory for a pixel contains a 1, the corresponding pixel on the screen is illuminated. If the memory for a pixel contains a 0, the corresponding pixel is left dark.

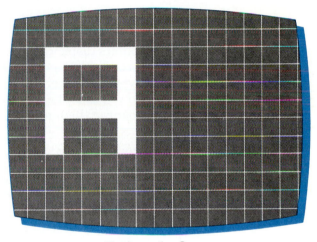

Bits in Memory

Pixels on the Screen

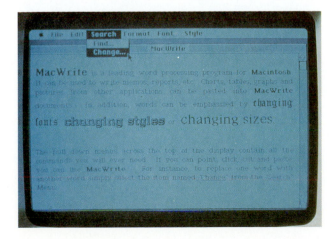

FIGURE 1-78
Graphic Display of Characters
A graphics display is more versatile than a character display. For example, a character can be displayed in more than one size or typestyle. Courtesy of Apple Computer, Inc.

TABLE 1-9
Advantages and Disadvantages of Graphic Displays

- They require a lot of memory.
- They operate slowly.
- A graphics display can display different fonts, type sizes, and enhancements like italics and proportional spacing.
- Both text and graphics can be displayed on the screen at the same time, which is especially important in desktop publishing applications (Figure 1-79).

must insert a graphics card into one of the expansion slots. There are three standard graphics add-on boards: CGA, EGA, and VGA.

Color graphics adapters (CGA) display 320-by-200 resolution in 4 colors.

Enhanced color graphics adapters (EGA), introduced in 1986, display 640-by-350 resolution in 16 colors. Extended EGA boards, introduced later, display 640-by-480 resolution in 16 colors and 320-by-200 resolution in 256 colors.

Video graphics array (VGA) was introduced with IBM's PS/2 line of computers in 1987 and is being added to older computers with add-on boards. This standard displays 640-by-480 resolution in 16 colors and 320-by-200 resolution in 256 colors.

To display various typestyles and type sizes on the screen, the computer also must have access to the necessary characters. For example, many computers display all text on the screen in the same size and style because there is only one type of character (called a font). But other computers can display type that is very large and very small. To do so, additional characters (other fonts) must be made available to the computer. These are usually added by loading them into the computer's memory or adding additional ROM chips.

Character Displays

When text is displayed on some screens such as the IBM monochrome monitor, bit mapping is not used. Instead, the computer stores the ASCII value of each character in memory. A character generator (a special ROM chip) then converts these values into the dot pattern needed to create characters on the screen.

FIGURE 1-79
Graphics Display of Text and Graphics
Both text and graphics can be displayed on a graphics display. Courtesy of Software Publishing Corporation

This type of character display requires much less memory than does a bit-mapped graphics display. A character (or text) display can also be updated by the computer much faster, so there is less screen flicker, and you can move more quickly through text displayed on the screen. The character generator stores specific characters in its memory. Figure 1-36 in Topic 1-3 shows the characters in the IBM PC character set. These characters, and no others, are stored in the computer's ROM, so they are the only characters that can be displayed on the screen. Table 1-10 describes the advantages and disadvantages of character displays.

PRINTERS

The second most widely used output device is the printer. Having a printer is essential if the data you process with your computer is to be filed or physically distributed to others. Until recently, you had to choose between an expensive printer that printed letter-quality characters like a typewriter and an inexpensive printer that created each character from a pattern of dots. These differences have narrowed, however, and today you have a wide variety of printers and prices to choose from. The quality of all types of printers has improved dramatically.

Some printers come in 80-column and 132-column widths. An 80-column printer prints on standard 8½-by-11-inch paper. A 132-column printer can print on 8½-by-11-inch or 11-by-14-inch paper. This wide-carriage printer is ideal for printing wide spreadsheet models. Although wide-carriage printers cost more, they are often a good investment because of their flexibility.

Data can be sent to a printer through either a serial port or a parallel port. The type of port you have on your computer determines whether you need a serial or parallel printer. On computers with expansion slots, you can buy an add-on board that provides either or both of these ports.

Hundreds of printers are available, and nearly all of them have unique features. There are, however, at least two ways to categorize printers: by how they form characters and by how the characters are transferred to paper.

TABLE 1-10
Advantages and Disadvantages of Character Displays

- They require little memory.
- They operate very quickly.
- They can display only the characters in the computer's character set.
- They can display only simple graphics using the graphic characters in the character set. For example, the IBM character set has ruled lines and corners so that you can create boxes. But you cannot create circles because these are not stored in the character set.
- Programmers and users cannot create their own characters and graphics; they must use those included in the character set.
- Characters must occupy a fixed position on the screen; they cannot be offset half a line or half a column. This prevents you from seeing on the screen the effects of proportional spacing, different type sizes, subscripts, and superscripts.
- A character display cannot display italic type.

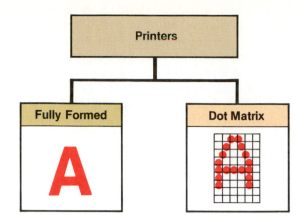

FIGURE 1-80
How Printers Form Characters
Printers can form characters in two ways: as fully formed characters or as dot-matrix characters.

How Characters Are Formed

As Figure 1-80 shows, printers use one of two approaches when they form letters. Either characters are printed as fully formed characters, similar to the characters a typewriter prints, or they are created by arranging a series of dots on the paper, much as characters are displayed on the screen.

Fully Formed Character Printers

Fully formed character printers print solid characters using a type element with raised characters like those on a typewriter. The two basic type elements these printers use are print wheels and thimbles.

Printers using **print wheels** are commonly called daisy-wheel printers. The term *daisy wheel* comes from the way individual characters are arranged on flexible "petals" radiating from the center of the type element (Figure 1-81). **Thimbles** also have raised characters, but they are arranged on an inverted thimble (Figure 1-82).

Table 1-11 describes the advantages and disadvantages of fully formed character printers.

Dot-Matrix Printers

Dot-matrix printers form characters using an array of dots. Because the spacing of the dots affects the resolution and **density**, or quality, of the characters, the closer the dots, the closer to letter quality the characters will appear (Figure 1-83). Table 1-12 describes the advantages and disadvantages of dot-matrix printers.

FIGURE 1-81
Daisy Wheels
A daisy wheel is named after its shape. Petals with raised characters radiate from the center. Courtesy of Qume Corporation, San Jose, Calif.

FIGURE 1-82
Thimbles
Thimbles work just like daisy wheels, but the characters are on petals that take the shape of a thimble. Courtesy of NEC Information Systems, Inc.

TABLE 1-11
Advantages and Disadvantages of Fully Formed Character Printers

- They transfer sharp, crisp characters onto the paper.
- They are relatively slow.
- They cannot print graphics.
- Typefaces and type sizes can be changed only by changing the type element. To do this, you have to stop the printer. This is so time consuming that most users use the same typestyle and type size for the entire document.

TABLE 1-12
Advantages and Disadvantages of Dot-Matrix Printers

■ They can print any image on the paper. The image does not have to be available on a print element, as it does on a fully formed character printer. Any image that can be created in memory or displayed on the screen can be printed on a dot-matrix printer.

■ You can use a wide range of fonts (typestyles and type sizes) within the same document (Figure 1-84). The ease with which you can do this depends on the program you are using.

■ They can print graphics (Figure 1-85). Since the **printhead**—the element that forms the printed image on the paper—scans the entire page, dots can be printed anywhere. If the dots are close enough, solid, dark areas can be printed. This ability to print dots anywhere on the page is called **all points addressable (APA).**

■ The less expensive models do not print characters as clearly as fully formed character printers or more expensive dot-matrix printers.

FIGURE 1-83
Print Quality
The quality of the character is determined by the spacing of the dots. This enlargement of a dot-matrix character shows that the closer the dots are, the more like letter quality the character is.

This is 10pt Times Roman	This is 10pt Helvetica
This is 12pt Times Roman	This is 12pt Helvetica
This is 10pt Times Roman bold	**This is 10pt Helvetica bold**
This is 12pt Times Roman bold	**This is 12pt Helvetica bold**
This is 10pt Times Roman italic	*This is 10pt Helvetica italic*
This is 12pt Times Roman italic	*This is 12pt Helvetica italic*

FIGURE 1-84
Fonts
Fonts are different typestyles and sizes. The fonts shown here were all printed on the same printer.

FIGURE 1-85
Graphics
Graphics can be printed on a dot-matrix printer. By varying the spacing between the dots, an illusion of brightness can be created. Here an enlargement of a small area of the illustration clearly shows how the image is formed from dots. Courtesy of Xerox Corp.

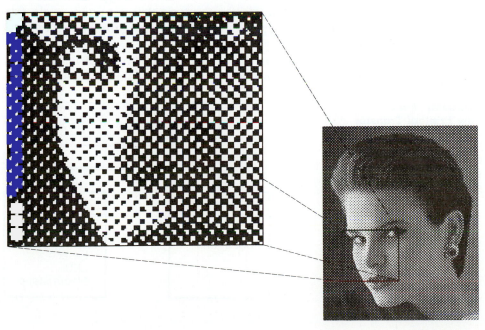

How Characters Are Transferred to Paper

Printers can also be categorized by how they transfer the characters to paper. The two methods of transfer are impact and nonimpact (Figure 1-86). Although most printers used with microcomputers print one character at a time, some like laser printers print a full page at a time using xerography technology.

Impact Printers

Impact printers create an image on the paper using a mechanical printhead that strikes an inked ribbon against the surface of the paper. There are two types of impact printers: fully formed character printers and dot-matrix impact printers.

Fully formed character printers (Figure 1-87) use a type element with raised, fully formed characters, much like the type element used on electric typewriters. A character on this type element is struck against an inked ribbon to transfer the character to the paper.

Dot-matrix impact printers use a printhead containing pins, or wires, arranged in a column to print characters. As the printhead passes across

FIGURE 1-86
How Printers Transfer Characters
Printers transfer characters to the paper by either impact or nonimpact technology.

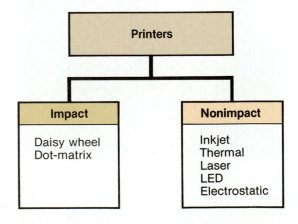

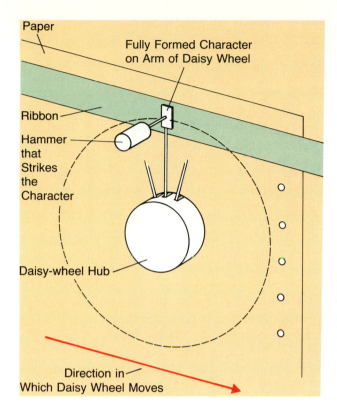

Paper

Fully Formed Character
on Arm of Daisy Wheel

Ribbon

Hammer
that
Strikes
the
Character

Daisy-wheel Hub

Direction in
Which Daisy Wheel Moves

FIGURE 1-87
Fully Formed Characters
A fully formed character
printer transfers the
character to the paper
when a hammer strikes
the character against an
inked ribbon sandwiched
between the characters
and the paper.

the paper (Figure 1-88), the computer tells it which pins in the printhead are to be fired to form a particular character. As the pins are fired, they strike an inked ribbon against the paper. The printed dots are arranged in an invisible matrix—often seven columns across and nine lines deep.

The number of wires and dots determines the character's resolution. Older, less expensive printers usually use nine pins to create characters. The latest, and more expensive, printers have eighteen or twenty-four wires in their printhead.

Nonimpact Printers

Nonimpact printers do not use an inked ribbon. Characters are transferred to the paper using sprayed ink, electrostatic charges and toner, or heat. All nonimpact printers, however, form characters with patterns, much like those in a dot-matrix impact printer. Extensive research and development

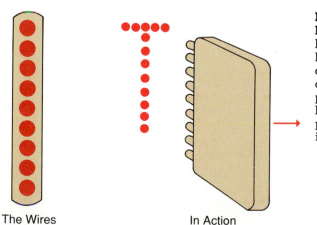

The Wires   In Action

FIGURE 1-88
Dot-Matrix Impact Printers
Dot-matrix impact printers
have a printhead that
contains pins. The pins
are fired against the
paper, and the ribbon
between the printhead and
paper creates an inked
image on the paper.

Printer Speed

The speed of a printer is generally given in **characters per second (CPS)**. Printers do not usually print at the advertised speed because these speeds are generally for straight text only. If you use boldfacing, underlining, or any other character enhancements, the printer will print at a slower speed because the print element must make more than one pass over the material.

Density is controlled on a fully formed character printer by striking the same character in the same position one or more times. On an impact printer that forms characters with dots, density is controlled by shifting the printhead between normal printing positions to create overlapping dots (Figure 1-89).

Many dot-matrix impact printers offer at least two modes. In **draft** mode, they print quickly, but since the density is light (fewer dots are used to increase the speed), the characters are light and obviously formed from a series of dots. In **near-letter-quality (NLQ)** mode, they either make more than one pass over each character, slightly offsetting the printhead on each pass, or they use more pins in the matrix to form the characters. These techniques increase the character's density and make them look more like fully formed characters. NLQ, however, slows down the printer because of the number of dots transferred for each character.

is occurring in this area, and great advances are being made. These printers are quickly replacing impact printers as the most popular type of printer. Nonimpact printers offer many advantages, including their speed and quietness. Their one drawback is they cannot print multipart forms that require impact to print the image through the carbon paper. Ink-jet, thermal, laser, LED, and electrostatic printers are all nonimpact printers.

Ink-jet printers use moving nozzles to focus a stream of ink onto the paper. The number of nozzles determines the printer's resolution. Color ink-jet printers use three separate jets, one for each of the primary colors (red, green, and blue). When used for printing in color, all ink jets can work simultaneously, thus speeding up the printing since the printer does not have to make successive passes for each color. Ink-jet printers are very quiet.

Thermal printers use a dot-matrix printhead and heat-sensitive paper to create images. Recent models, however, no longer require heat-sensitive paper but can print on any paper. The printhead of a thermal printer com-

FIGURE 1-89
Dot-Matrix Density
Density is changed on a dot-matrix printer by printing the same character more than once with the printhead slightly offset. (a) This character has been created with a single set of dots. (b) This character has been printed by shifting the printhead to print a second set of dots overlapping the first.

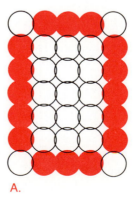
A.

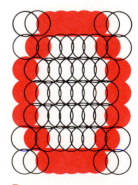
B.

FIGURE 1-90
Laser Printer
Laser printers are usually
sheet fed and print only
on 8½-by-11-inch paper.
They are quiet and give
good results. Courtesy of
Hewlett-Packard Company

prises a grid of wires. When an electric current is applied to any pair of wires, heat is generated where they intersect, leaving a dot on the paper.

Laser printers (Figure 1-90), an increasingly popular type of printer, also form characters using dots. They are very fast, usually printing eight or more pages per minute, and their cost has fallen to where they are now competitive with other types of printers. Unlike all the other printers described in this section, these are **page printers** because they print an entire page at a time before ejecting it from the printer. Other printers are **line printers** because they print a line and then advance the paper to the next line. Only after all lines have been printed, is the paper ejected from the printer.

The resolution of laser printers is greater than most other dot-matrix printers because of the much higher number of dots and their greater density. Most laser printers can print 300 dots per inch although printers with 400 or more dots per inch are available. Despite the great number of dots, laser printers are fast because the dots are not transferred to the paper with mechanical devices that strike a ribbon.

Laser printers provide extremely high quality. Figure 1-91 shows a

FIGURE 1-91
Laser Printer Output
Laser printers can print
both text and graphics
and are very close to
letter quality. The dots
making up the image are
so closely spaced that
they look like characters
typed on a typewriter.
Courtesy of Software
Publishing Corporation

FIGURE 1-92
How Laser Printers Work
Laser printers first focus a laser beam onto a
moving drum using a mirror. The moving drum is
charged with electricity. As the drum revolves, it
is scanned by the laser, and the image is
"painted" onto the drum. The intensity of the laser
beam is varied, and at selected points, it removes
the electrical charge from the drum to form
invisible characters with a neutral charge.
Charged toner is then electrostatically attracted to
these characters. This toner is transferred to the
paper and fused to it by heat and pressure as it is
pressed against the revolving drum.

sample (text and graphics) of laser printing. The technology of laser printers
is similar to that of office copiers. They print images in two steps (Figure
1-92). Current laser printers can print in only one color, but strides are being made in the development of color laser printers. Moreover, laser printers
are now available that print on both sides of a sheet of paper at the same
time. This process is called **duplex printing**.

LED printers have many of the same performance characteristics as
laser printers, but instead of using a laser to create the image, they use an
array of light-emitting diodes.

Electrostatic printers use a dot-matrix printhead to apply electrostatic
charges to the surface of the paper. When the paper is passed through
toner, the toner adheres to the charged areas, making the image visible.
This process is similar to that used in copy machines.

Printer Accessories

Printers require supplies and accessories for specific purposes.

Paper

Most printers accept both single sheets of paper and **continuous form paper** (also called fan-fold), which has perforated margins with holes. These
holes are engaged by a tractor or pin feed to pull the paper through the
printer one sheet after another and keep it aligned. After the printout is
completed, the holes can be used to hold the paper in special binders, or
they can be torn off. Continuous form paper is available as single sheets or
as multipart carbon forms. It can also be preprinted with specially designed
forms or company letterheads on each sheet.

Ribbons or Toner

Inked ribbons or other supplies like toner are needed to transfer the characters to the paper. Supplies depend on the type of printer being used. Both
cloth and film ribbons are available. Cloth ribbons are more economical, but
film ribbons produce sharper characters on the paper.

Fonts

Many newer printers can print type in various styles, or **fonts**. Some fonts
may be permanently stored in the printer's memory (ROM). Others are avail-

Off to the Printers

Once information has been entered into the computer, it is usually printed on a nearby printer. Documents like catalogs, annual reports, magazine articles, books, and important reports, however, need to be printed with a higher quality than a printer can provide. To do this, the document is sent on a disk or over the phone lines to a typesetter. These service businesses set the document into type so that the printer can make plates from which multiple copies are then printed. The result is a high-quality document at a cost lower than if the document had been sent to the printer as typed copy. The need to rekeyboard and, in some cases, reformat the document has been eliminated.

able on cartridges or stored on disks. Font cartridges are plugged into the printer when you want access to the fonts they contain. Printers using this system can print only the fonts stored in ROM or on the cartridge plugged into the printer. Fonts stored on disks, called **downloadable fonts**, are more flexible. You can choose from the fonts on the disk and load them into the printer's RAM when you need them. This way the printer has access to any fonts you want to use. We describe fonts in detail in Part Three.

Sheet Feeders

When using single sheets of paper or envelopes, **sheet feeders** (also called bins) are needed. Sheet feeders hold as many as 500 sheets of stationery and feed them to the printer one sheet at a time. When printing letterhead, two sheet feeders are needed. One holds the letterhead used for the first sheet, and the other holds the nonletterhead paper used for subsequent sheets. On many printers, sheet feeders are accessories, but on laser printers, they are built in because laser printers do not accept continuous form paper.

Tractor Feeds

Tractor feeds are used with continuous form paper to move it smoothly through the printer. When long printouts are made without a tractor drive, the paper can gradually become skewed in the printer. Tractor feeds built into the printer are called **pin feeds**.

Soundproof Enclosures

Soundproof enclosures are insulated covers that are placed over a printer. They are often used with impact printers to reduce the noise level and usually have a hinged door so that you can gain access to the printer.

Switches

Switches can be used to connect two or more printers to the same port on a computer. These let you switch quickly between a fast dot-matrix impact printer used for draft copies and a fully formed character or laser printer used for a final copy.

SUMMARY AND KEY TERMS

- **Display screens** are either based on **cathode ray tubes (CRTs)** or some form of **flat-panel** device. Typical flat-panel devices include **LCDs, LEDs, gas plasmas,** and **electroluminescent diodes**.

- Display screens can also be **monochrome** or **color**. Color displays are either composite or RGB. **Composite displays** send all colors in a combined signal. **RGB displays** send each color as a separate signal.

- **Character displays** can display only the **character set**, a fixed set of characters supplied with the computer. Because of the versatility of graphic displays, all computers will eventually have them. Their only drawback is that they operate more slowly, so it takes a powerful computer to use them effectively.

- **Graphic displays** allow you to display anything on the screen that can be represented by a fine pattern of dots. Each dot is called a **pixel**. The number of pixels determines the screen's **resolution**. The processes of storing the information for each dot on the screen is called **bit mapping**. To use a bit-mapped display, your computer must have a **graphics card** add-on board, or the same circuits must be built into the computer. Typical add-on boards include **CGA, EGA,** and **VGA**.

- Printers also fall into two categories, those that print with **fully formed characters** like a typewriter and those that create images with a fine pattern of dots (**dot-matrix printers**). The images are transferred to the paper with **impact** or with some form of **nonimpact** technology. Almost all microcomputer printers are now dot-matrix, nonimpact printers. The image is transferred to the paper using any one of several technologies, the most popular being a **laser**.

REVIEW QUESTIONS

1. Describe the two basic types of display screens.
2. What is the difference between a composite color display and an RGB display?
3. What do the terms *low resolution* and *high resolution* refer to?
4. What is the primary difference among CGA, EGA, and VGA?
5. What is the difference between a graphics display and a character display? What are their advantages and disadvantages?
6. What are the two methods used by printers to form images? What are the advantages and disadvantages of each?
7. What are the two methods used by printers to transfer characters to paper? List some examples of each.
8. On printers that form characters from dots, what determines the sharpness or resolution of the characters?
9. What are fonts?
10. What are printer sheet feeders used for?

External Storage Devices

OBJECTIVES

After completing this topic, you will be able to

- List and describe the main features of floppy disks
- Explain how floppy disks and hard disk drives work
- Describe how data are stored on magnetic media
- Describe the uses for magnetic tape
- Describe optical disks and the major differences between the three types
- List and describe ways to protect and secure your data

The memory in your computer is a limited resource, yet it must serve many uses. Not only do you load different applications programs, you also create files for your own work, and there can be a lot of them. The computer's memory is not large enough to store all the programs, documents, and other computer-generated files you work on. Moreover, most memory will lose its data when you turn the computer off.

For these reasons, **external storage** (also called auxiliary or secondary storage), another form of more permanent storage, is provided (Figure 1-93). You use this storage to store programs and data that you are not using at the moment. Once data is stored on these storage media, you can reload it into the computer's memory without having to rekeyboard it.

In Topic 1-2, we introduced you to some early methods of external stor-

FIGURE 1-93
External Storage
External storage is used to permanently store data files. It is a more permanent form of storage than the computer's memory. When you are finished working on a document on the screen, you store it on the external storage device. You can then clear it from the computer's memory. When you need the document later, you retrieve it from the external storage device and transfer it to the computer's memory.

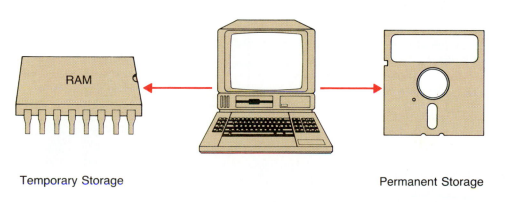

Temporary Storage   RAM   Permanent Storage

107

age. Documents were stored on different kinds of media, including embossed cylinders, paper tape, and magnetic cards. Today's computers usually use magnetic disks or magnetic tape to store documents and programs. But new storage devices have been introduced that use lasers and light to store even more data.

External storage media and the devices used to store and retrieve data on them, fall into four major classes.

1. Floppy disks and floppy disk drives are the most common external storage media and devices.

2. Hard disk drives with built-in or removable rigid platters have become increasingly popular because of their capacity and speed.

3. Magnetic tape, once a major storage medium, is now used along with tape drives primarily as a backup device.

4. Optical disks and disk drives that store and retrieve data with lasers are the latest external storage media and devices.

FLOPPY DISKS

Floppy disks are available in three sizes: 8, 5¼, and 3½ inches (Figure 1-94). Each size works only with drives specifically designed to accept it. Although floppy disks come in various sizes and styles, they all have certain features in common (Figure 1-95). If you were to remove the plastic jacket or housing of a floppy disk (Figure 1-96), you would find a round piece of plastic covered with a metallic oxide, similar to the magnetic recording material used on audio and video tapes. The round disk is sandwiched between two sheets of a soft feltlike material, which is impregnated with a lubricant that protects the disk when it is spinning in the drive.

FLOPPY DISK DRIVES

The **floppy disk drive** (Figure 1-97) is the device the floppy disk is inserted into so that you can store data to and retrieve data from it. Inside the floppy disk drives are parts you should be familiar with.

1. Two clamps designed to close on the large center hole in the disk and clamp it tightly. Either these clamps are connected mechanically to the disk drive door and clamp the disk when the door is closed or they are controlled electrically and close when the disk drive is ready to spin.

FIGURE 1-94
Floppy Disk Sizes
Floppy disks come in three different sizes. Disk drives are designed to accept one of the sizes.

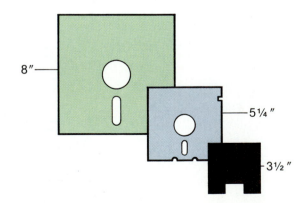

8″

5¼″

3½″

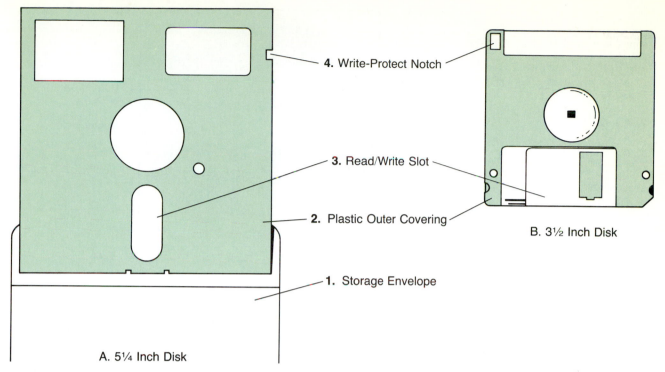

4. Write-Protect Notch

3. Read/Write Slot

2. Plastic Outer Covering

B. 3½ Inch Disk

1. Storage Envelope

A. 5¼ Inch Disk

FIGURE 1-95
Floppy Disk Characteristics
The outside appearance of 5¼-inch and 3½-inch disks varies, but both have many features in common.

1. A **storage envelope** protects 5¼- and 8-inch disks from scratches, dust, and fingerprints. Some envelopes are treated to eliminate the static buildup that attracts abrasive grit. These envelopes are not used on the better-protected 3½-inch disks.

2. A **plastic outer covering** protects the disk itself while allowing it to spin smoothly inside the jacket. 5¼- and 8-inch disks are protected by flexible plastic jackets, and 3½-inch disks are mounted in a rigid plastic housing. The jacket or housing is permanently sealed and contains lubricants and cleaning agents that prolong the life of the disk.

3. The **read/write slot** in the jacket is where the disk drive's **read/write head** contacts the surface of the disk. This read/write head stores data on (writes) and retrieves data from (reads) the surface of the disk as the disk spins inside the drive. On 3½-inch disks, the read/write slot is protected by a sliding metal cover called the shutter. When you insert the disk into the drive, this shutter is automatically pushed aside so that the read/write slot is exposed and the drive can come in contact with the floppy disk within.

4. The **write-protect notch** allows you to write on a disk when it is uncovered and prevents you from writing on the disk when it is covered. To write-protect a 5½- or 8-inch disk, you cover the write-protect notch with tape. On 3½-inch disks, you press a sliding tab to cover the write-protect hole. A switch, or photoelectric circuit, inside the disk drive determines if the write-protect notch is uncovered. If it finds it is covered, the switch disables the drive's ability to write information onto the disk. Permanently write-protected disks, which some programs are distributed on, have no notch. This is to prevent you from inadvertently erasing irreplaceable files that are stored on the disk.

2. A motor, connected to the clamps, spins them and the disk they are tightly holding. The disk spins, inside its outer jacket, at 300 rpm (almost ten times faster than a 33⅓ album spins on your record turntable).

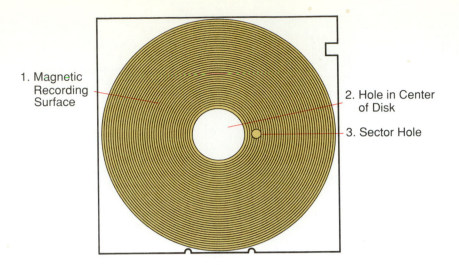

1. Magnetic Recording Surface

2. Hole in Center of Disk

3. Sector Hole

FIGURE 1-96

Inside a Floppy Disk

The inside of a floppy disk is a plastic disk coated with magnetic material similar to that used on cassette and video tapes. The blank disk has three key features:

1. The disk's **magnetic recording surface** on which the data is stored covers a band around the disk.

2. The large hole in the center of the disk is used by the drive to align and spin the disk. This hole is sometimes reinforced with a plastic hub, and on 3½-inch disks, it is covered by a metal hub.

3. The disk's **sector hole** is punched through the disk and is used by the computer to know where to store data to and retrieve data from the disk. A light and a photoelectric cell inside the disk drive, much like the ones that automatically open doors for you at the supermarket, are positioned on either side of the sector hole in a 5¼-inch disk's plastic cover or at the top of the read/write slot on a 3½-inch disk. As the disk spins inside its outer cover, the hole in the disk aligns with one of these openings once each revolution. When the holes are aligned, light shines through them, and the photoelectric cell signals the computer so that it can keep itself oriented to the disk's position, much as a ship can orient itself from a lighthouse beacon.

3. Two read/write heads that record data onto the disk and retrieve data from it are connected to a second motor so that they can move freely over the entire width of the disk's recording surface, much like the play-back arm on a record turntable can move to follow the grooves. On a single-sided drive, one head is used; on a double-sided drive, one head is mounted on either side of the disk. These heads come in contact with the spinning disk and either store (write) information on it or copy (read) information from it.

4. A switch, or photoelectric circuit, determines if the write-protect notch (if there is one) is uncovered. If it finds it's covered, the switch disables the drive's ability to write information onto the disk.

5. Electronic circuits, in conjunction with the computer and the operating system, control the mechanical parts of the drive.

6. A light and a photoelectric cell are positioned on either side of the sector hole in the outer plastic cover of the disk. As the disk spins inside its

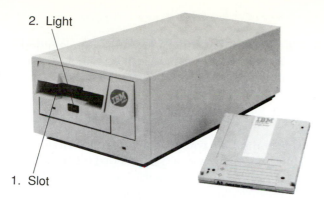

2. Light

1. Slot

FIGURE 1-97
The Floppy Disk Drive
The floppy disk drive has two parts that you should be very familiar with: the drive's slot and the drive's light.

1. The **slot** is where you insert a floppy disk into the drive. On 5¼-inch drives, the slot has a door that you must open before inserting or removing a disk. To insert a disk, you open the door, insert the disk into the slot, and then close the door. The door must be fully closed, or you can encounter problems. On 3½-inch drives, the slot does not have a door. You just press the disk into the slot firmly until it locks into place. To remove the disk from the slot, you press a lever that releases it from the drive.

2. The **light** on the front of the drive goes on when the drive is operating. When the light is on, you should not open the door or eject a disk. Doing so can damage the disk and cause you to lose data. If you make a mistake, and the drive spins when the door is open or without a disk inserted, do not close the door or insert a disk. In a few moments, a message will usually appear telling you the drive's door is open or no disk is in the drive. When the light goes out, close the door or insert a disk and follow the instructions displayed on the screen. Courtesy of IBM Corporation

envelope, the hole in the disk aligns with the hole in the jacket once each revolution. When the holes are aligned, light shines through the hole, and the photosensitive cell signals the computer so that it can keep itself oriented to the position of the disk, much as a ship can orient itself from a lighthouse beacon.

Floppy Disk Storage Capacity

The size of a disk does not determine how much data you can store on it. This is determined by the processes used in its manufacture and the ability of the disk drive to pack more data on the disk. Over the past few years, steady progress has been made in storing data on disks so that today's floppy disk can store much more information than its predecessors. For example, a few years ago, most disk drives could store data on only one side of the disk, but now almost all new disk drives store data on both sides. This simple improvement doubled the storage capacity of the disk. Disks and disk drives have also been improved so that they can store more data on each side of the disk.

The disks you buy must be appropriate for the system you want to use them on. There are several terms on the box and disk labels that you should be familiar with. Knowing the number of sides, the density, and the sectors used by your system allows you to select and use the correct disks with your system.

Sides

Disks are rated as being single or double sided. Single-sided disks can store data on only one side of the disk. Double-sided disks can store data on both sides of the disk if your system's disk drive is capable of doing so.

Density

Data are stored on a disk on **tracks**, narrow concentric bands around the disk somewhat like the grooves in a 33⅓ record (although a record's groove is one continuous spiral and not a series of concentric circles). To store more data, the tracks are placed closer together. The spacing of these tracks is measured as **tracks per inch (TPI)**. The maximum density that can be used to store data on a disk is indicated on the disk label and box.

- **Single-density disks** can store data on 24 TPI.
- **Double-density disks** can store data on 48 TPI or up to 360KB.
- **Quad-density disks** (also called high-capacity disks) can store data on 96 TPI. Whereas a regular double-sided, double-density 5¼-inch floppy disk and disk drive can store 360KB of data, a quad-density disk can store 1.2MB of data. The newer 3½-inch floppy disk systems can store 720KB per side or 1.44MB on a double-sided disk. These smaller disks can store more data than the larger 5¼-inch disks because they store data on 135 TPI.

When using 5¼-inch disks with different TPI ratings, keep the following points in mind:

- If you format a 96 TPI disk on a system that can read and write only 48 TPI disks, they are formatted as 48 TPI disks. You cannot use their additional storage capacity.
- To use 48 TPI disks on a system designed for 96 TPI disks, you must format them as 48 TPI disks before you store data on them.
- You cannot retrieve files stored on a 96 TPI disk using a disk drive that can read and write only 48 TPI.

Sectors

When data is stored on a track, the track is divided into **sectors**, smaller sections of the track that make it easier for the drive to locate the data it needs. On most microcomputers, the tracks are divided into sectors when the disk is first prepared to be used with your computer (called **formatting** the disk). These disks are called **soft sectored** and contain only one sector hole. On some computers, the sectors on the disk are specified when the disk is manufactured by punching a number of sector holes in the disk. These disks are called **hard sectored**. Soft-sectored disks can be used on many computers since they are customized for each just before using them. Hard-sectored disks can generally be used only with the computer they were designed for.

Floppy Disk Storage

When you first start working on a microcomputer, the number of disks you work with is manageable. But before long, keeping disks filed in an orderly way can present quite a problem. Several disk filing systems have been de-

veloped. They include plastic sleeves that can be inserted in three-ring binders, plastic cases (Figure 1-98), and sophisticated filing cabinets for large collections.

HARD DISK DRIVES

Hard disk drives (also called fixed disks or Winchester disk drives after their code name while being developed at IBM) were not commonly used with microcomputers until recently because of their high cost.

But over the past few years, their cost has dropped dramatically. Lower cost and superior performance have made hard disk drives the first choice of serious computer users. Moreover, their storage capacity greatly reduces the number of disk "swaps" that have to be made when working with floppy disk drives. Since many applications programs come on several floppy disks, this can save a great deal of time.

Instead of a floppy disk, hard disk drives use rigid metal platters to store data (Figure 1-99). This allows them to store data more densely. This increased density plus the number of platters greatly increases their storage capacity. Hard disk drives generally provide 10, 20, 40, or more megabytes

FIGURE 1-99
Hard Disk Drives
Hard disks use metal
platters instead of plastic
disks to store data. Photo
courtesy of Seagate

of storage capacity. As Figure 1-100 shows, a hard disk can store much more information than a floppy disk.

A hard disk drive spins at 3600 rpm, about ten times faster than a floppy disk drive, allowing data to be stored and retrieved faster. For example, an IBM XT hard disk drive transfers data twenty times faster than a floppy disk drive.

In a floppy disk drive, the read/write heads are in contact with the disk. In a hard disk drive, they fly over its surface on a cushion of air with a space smaller than a piece of dust separating the head from the rapidly spinning disk. To imagine the small tolerances involved, picture a large airplane flying at high speed 1/20 of an inch above the ground without making contact. With the high speeds and small spaces involved, even a particle can cause the read/write head to come into contact with the disk's surface, creating a **head crash**. With the disk spinning at almost 60 mph, this can cause a lot of damage to the disk and the data stored on it.

Figure 1-101 shows the distance between the disk and the head compared to some typical items that can cause damage. To prevent these objects from damaging the drive or affecting its performance, hard disks are hermetically sealed in a case. When you use a hard disk drive, the read/write head is positioned on the disk where data is stored. If you are going to move your computer, use the **park program** (found on a disk that comes with your computer) to "park" the read/write head. This program moves the read/write head to a section of the disk that has no data, thus preventing the head from damaging data on the disk should it move. Even slightly jarring your computer may damage your files.

Even hard disks eventually become full. When there is no room for additional files, you must either delete files (after copying those that you want to save onto floppy disks) or add a larger disk drive. A few hard disk drives now come with removable disks that make this unnecessary since you can insert a new disk just as you do on a floppy disk system.

FIGURE 1-100
Hard Disk Storage
Hard disks can store much more information than floppy disks because the data is stored more closely together. For example, 45 tracks on one IBM hard disk can fit between two lines on a fingerprint. This disk can store almost 26 million bits in 1 square inch. Courtesy of IBM Corporation

FIGURE 1-101
Hard Disk Tolerances
Hard disks have very small tolerances. When the read/write head is flying over the surface of the disk, the two are so close that smoke, a dust particle, a hair, or even a fingerprint could cause the head to crash.

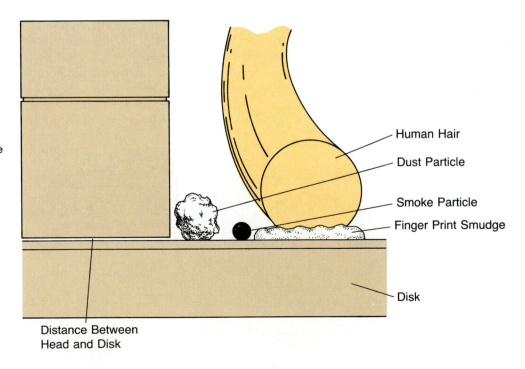

Human Hair
Dust Particle
Smoke Particle
Finger Print Smudge
Disk
Distance Between Head and Disk

HOW DATA IS STORED TO AND RETRIEVED FROM A DISK

Data is stored on a disk magnetically. If you have ever played with two magnets, you know that when held end to end, they attract each other. When one of them is reversed, they repel each other. This is caused by a difference in polarity. Opposite polarities attract, and identical polarities repel. These two magnetic states are used to record data on a disk much as on and off, or 1 and 0, are used to store data in the computer's memory.

As the disk spins, electrical signals in the read/write head change the polarity of magnetic particles on the disk's surface to record 0s and 1s, as Figure 1-102 shows. When you are retrieving a file from the disk, the effect is reversed. The polarity of the disk immediately under the read/write head induces an electrical current in the read/write head that is transmitted to the computer in the form of 0s and 1s.

The kind of external storage medium a computer uses affects the amount of data that can be stored and the time it takes to save files to and retrieve them from storage. These characteristics are expressed as storage capacity, access time, and data transfer rate.

Storage Capacity

As you have seen, **storage capacity** depends on several factors. Generally, hard disks are capable of storing larger amounts of data than floppy disks. Hard disk storage capacity is generally 10, 20, 40 or more megabytes. Typical floppy disks can store between 360KB and 1.44MB.

Access Time

When you execute a command that requires the computer to find information stored externally, it takes time to find it. The time it takes to do this is the **access time**.

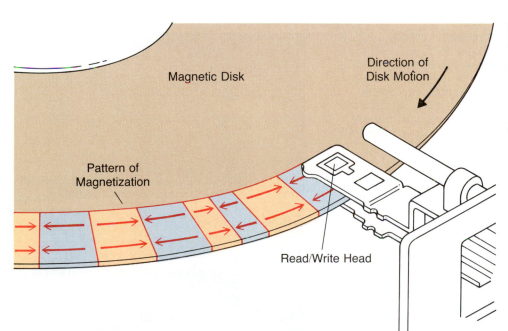

Magnetic Disk

Direction of Disk Motion

Pattern of Magnetization

Read/Write Head

FIGURE 1-102
How Data Is Stored on a Disk
Data is stored magnetically as the drive's read/write head moves over the disk. If the polarity of the magnetized area points in one direction, it is a 1; in the other, it is a 0.

Data Transfer Rate

Once the computer has located the data in the external storage device, it must transfer it to memory. The rate at which data can be transferred is the **data transfer rate**. Hard disk drives generally have the fastest data transfer rates, and tapes the slowest; floppy disk drives are somewhere in between.

MAGNETIC TAPE

Magnetic tape was once a major storage medium for microcomputers. The problem with magnetic tape, however, is its slow speed. For data to be retrieved, the tape has to first be advanced to the place where it is stored. It cannot be accessed randomly as on a disk. This is much like the difference between a song recorded on a cassette tape and a record. On the record, you can lower the needle directly onto any song, whereas on a cassette tape, you have to first advance the tape to the song you want to hear. Moreover, when the desired data is located on a computer tape, it is then transferred into the computer's memory more slowly than it is from a disk. For these reasons, magnetic tape is now used mostly as a backup medium for hard disk files (Figure 1-103).

OPTICAL DISKS

One of the most recent and far-reaching developments in the microcomputer field is the new technology of **optical disks**. Data are stored on and retrieved from these disks with a laser. These disks currently come in three forms: CD-ROM disks, write-once, read-many (WORM) disks, and erasable optical disks.

CD-ROM Disks

CD-ROM disks (Figure 1-104) are similar in concept to the compact disks (CDs) now popular in the music recording industry. These disks can store so much information that it is measured in gigabytes. A small 4¾-inch CD-ROM can store up to 550MB of data, or more than ½GB. This is equivalent

FIGURE 1-103
Magnetic Tape
Tape drives used to back up the files on a hard disk are similar to cassette players. They record data on large-format cassette tapes. Courtesy of Everex

FIGURE 1-104
Optical Disks
Optical disks and disk drives have become popular in offices that need to access large amounts of data quickly. Parts catalogs, reference files, and listings of all kinds will be stored on the optical disks. Courtesy of Phillips Subsystems & Peripherals

to more than 1500 floppy disks. Larger CD-ROMs can store up to 20GB, and that limit will be exceeded long before you read this text.

Combined with search and retrieve software, these disks are changing the way information is stored, distributed, and accessed. One of the first optical disks to be published is the *Microsoft's Bookshelf CD-ROM Reference Library*. This CD-ROM disk contains ten of the most widely used reference works, including *The World Almanac and Book of Facts*, *Bartlett's Familiar Quotations*, *The Chicago Manual of Style*, and the *U.S. ZIP Code Directory*. It also includes search and retrieve software, which makes it possible to look for information while working on another program. With just a few keystrokes, you can find information in any of these references and insert it into a document on the screen.

Another CD-ROM disk contains all forty-seven of the U.S. Postal Service ZIP + 4 Code information on a single disk (Figure 1-105). These nine-digit ZIP codes identify areas of cities but also apartment buildings, office suites,

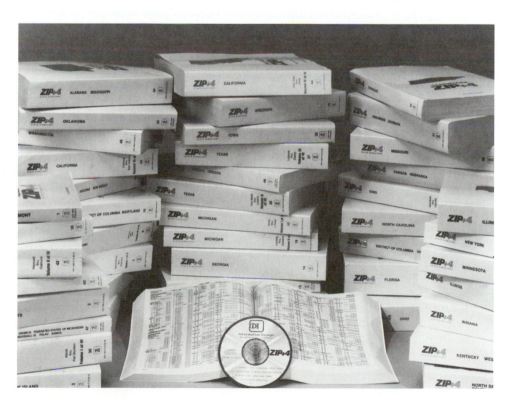

FIGURE 1-105
Reference Works on Optical Disks
The single optical disk shown here contains all the ZIP codes listed in the bound volumes. Courtesy of Information Update, Inc.

and floor numbers in commercial buildings. Software with the disk can check a new address as it is being entered and display the full address and ZIP code for approval.

The possibilities for CD-ROM are unlimited. Parts catalogs, stock market reports, reference books, library card index files, and telephone directories are just some of the items that can be distributed and used more effectively with this new technology.

WORM Disks

Unlike a magnetic medium, where the information can be recorded and then erased when not needed, many optical disks cannot be erased. For example, CD-ROM disks are prerecorded, and you cannot save your own data on them. However, another type of optical disk, **write-once, read-many (WORM) disks**, is making it possible for you to store data. To record data on a WORM disk, a laser actually burns microscopic pits into its surface. The storage area on these disks is so vast that you can afford to record the same file in different places on the disk each time you make changes. The old version is not erased, it is just ignored. Eventually the disk will be filled, but even the early versions of these disks store up to 200MB of data. With this much space, they will not be filled quickly.

Erasable Optical Disks

Major efforts have been made to make optical disks reusable. Since most technologies use a laser to burn pits into the disks surface to record data, removing the pits is a problem. Tandy Corporation was the first firm to announce a low-cost **erasable optical disk**. This optical disk system, called CD-THOR, uses two lasers and a disk coated with a dye-polymer. The first laser records data on the disk by raising pimples on the dye-polymer surface instead of burning pits. Each pimple represents a digital 1, and each space without a pimple represents a digital 0. The second laser then smoothes out the pimples when the data is no longer needed. When refined, the optical disk will seriously challenge the hard disk drive as an external storage device for large amounts of data.

PROTECTING YOUR FILES

When you enter data into the computer, it is not stored permanently until you save it onto disks. But even then the data is not protected from loss or damage or from being seen by unauthorized persons.

Security

If you work on a computer with floppy disk drives, you can secure your work by removing the floppy disks and taking them with you. On a hard disk system, this is not possible. Protecting sensitive data on hard disks from other users who have access to the computer is difficult. One way to provide security is to encrypt (or code) files using an **encryption program**. Then, only users who know an assigned password can gain access to the files.

Another way to provide security is by using hard disk drives with removable media (see *Removable Media*). The media can be removed and stored separately from the computer.

Removable Media

Drives with removable media are an ideal way to protect your files. This drive, called a Bernoulli box, uses high-capacity floppy disks to store 10MB or more. The disks can then be removed from the drive and stored elsewhere until needed again. The more interesting aspect of this device is how it operates. The unit uses floppy disks instead of rigid disks—for a reason. As the floppy disk is spun inside the drive, air currents between it and the stationary

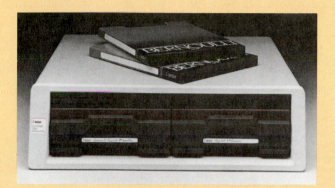

read/write head are generated. These air currents cause the disk to bulge up close to the head. If by any chance the flow of air is interrupted, for example by dust, smoke, or shock, the air flow is broken, and the disk drops back away from the head. This prevents damage if anything goes wrong. In a hard disk drive, these problems can cause the head to crash and damage the disk. In a Bernoulli box, the head doesn't move, and if one of these problems is encountered, the floppy disk just falls away from it with no damage being caused.

Photo courtesy of Iomega, Inc.

Backup Copies

It is also wise to make a **backup copy** (a duplicate) of the files on a hard disk so that they are not damaged in the event of a head crash or other problem. The least expensive, but most time-consuming, way is to back them up on floppy disks.

More expensive hard disks have a built-in backup system that copies files from the hard disk onto a tape using a tape drive. These tapes can then be removed for safekeeping. It is also possible to use a video tape cassette player to back up a hard disk if you have the appropriate hardware and software to connect them.

Caring for Your Disks

Disks, both hard and floppy, are very reliable storage media. However, the data they contain can be lost or damaged if you do not take a few precautions. Floppy disks are relatively durable under ordinary conditions and

The Laser Card—A Novel in Your Wallet

As technology improves, more and more information can be stored in less and less space. The same technology used to create video laser disks and compact audio disks can be used to store data for computers.

This figure shows a credit-card-sized Drexon Laser Card. It uses an optical process to record permanently up to 2MB of digitized data—about 800 pages of typed information. The data strip encapsulated within the card can be read using low-cost optical systems.

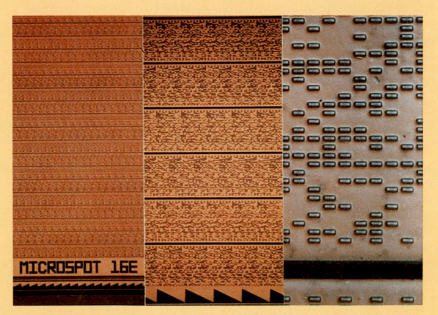

Data are stored on the strip using laser energy to record patterns of extremely small pits representing digital information. This figure shows the circular pits recorded on the card with a laser enlarged 2500 times.

Photos courtesy of Drexler Technology Corporation.

have a useful life of about forty hours' spinning time. But that life can be shortened or abruptly ended by improper handling. Proper care ensures that disks will accurately store and play back the data you need.

Care of Hard Disks

DON'T drop or jar them. They are very sensitive.

DO use the park program to move the drive's read/write head to a safe place on the disk before moving the computer.

Care of Floppy Disk Drives

DON'T use commercial cleaning kits too often. Overuse can cause problems with the drive.

DO insert the cardboard protectors that came with the computer into the disk drives, and close the doors when moving the computer.

Care of Floppy Disks

DO keep disks in their protective storage envelopes. These envelopes reduce static buildup, which can attract dust that might scratch the disk.

DO keep disks dry, away from sneezes, coffee, or anything wet. A wet disk is a ruined disk.

DO prevent disks from getting too hot or too cold. They should be stored at temperatures of 50°-150°F (10°-52°C). Extremes of temperature can destroy a disk's sensitivity, so treat them the same way you treat photographic film; that is, keep them out of direct sunlight, do not leave them in a car exposed to temperature extremes, and so forth.

DO keep disks at least 2 feet away from magnets. The magnets found in copy stands, telephones, radios or stereo speakers, vacuum cleaners, televisions, air conditioners, novelty items, electric motors, or even some cabinet latches can ruin a disk's sensitivity.

DO always make backup copies of your important disks, and save them a safe distance from your working area. Make sure the same accident cannot happen to both the disk and its backup copy. The information on the disk is usually worth much more than the disk itself, so don't take chances.

DO load disks into the drive gently. Otherwise, they may bend, center improperly, or rotate in an elliptical orbit that misses data.

DON'T touch a disk's recording surface. Handle them only by their protective covers.

DON'T use a hard-tipped pen to write on a disk label that is affixed to the disk. This can crease the disk inside the protective cover and cause you to lose data. Write on the label before putting affixing it to the disk, or use a felt-tip pen with very light pressure.

DON'T leave a disk in a nonoperating disk drive with the door closed for more than an hour. Open the drive door to lift the read/write head from the surface of the disk.

DON'T insert or remove a disk from the drive when the disk drive is running (that is, when the red light is on).

DON'T bend, fold, or crimp disks.

DON'T use paper clips to attach a floppy disk to a file folder or copy of a printout. Special folders are available that let you keep disks and printed documents together.

DON'T expose disks to static electricity. In dry climates or in heated buildings, static builds up when you walk on carpeted and some other kinds of floors. If you experience shocks when you touch metal objects, you are discharging the static that has built up. If you touch a disk when still charged with this static, you can damage the data. To prevent this, increase the humidity in the air, use static-proof carpets, or touch something like a typewriter to discharge the static before you pick up a disk.

Even with the best of care, floppy disks can last only so long. Close to the end of their useful life, they show their own form of senility by losing information or giving invalid commands. These are signs that it is time to replace the disk, which ideally, you have already made another backup copy of.

SUMMARY AND KEY TERMS

- Since memory in the computer is so limited, **external storage devices** are used to store programs and data until needed.
- There are basically four types of external storage, and each type has its own **media** and hardware. The most common forms of storage are **floppy disks** and **hard disk drives**.
- When moving a computer with a hard disk, you should always move the read/write head to a safe place on the disk with the drive's **park program**.
- The amount of data stored on these disks is partly based on their **density**, measured in **tracks per inch (TPI)**.
- How fast data are stored and retrieved is based on the **access time** and the **data transfer rate**.
- The other two types of external storage are magnetic tape and optical disks. **Magnetic tape** is used almost exclusively to back up hard disk drives. **Optical disks** are extremely promising. Their immense storage capacity makes them the ideal storage media once they are available in an erasable format. At the moment, you can buy them prerecorded (**CD-ROM**) or so that you can record your own data on them only once (**WORM**).

REVIEW QUESTIONS

1. List and briefly describe the four main types of external storage media and devices.
2. What is the purpose of the write-protect notch on a floppy disk, and how do you use it?
3. Describe the purpose of the red light on the front of a disk drive.
4. What is a Winchester disk drive? What other names are used for the same device?
5. List at least three advantages a hard disk drive has over floppy disks and disk drives.
6. When you are going to move a microcomputer, what preventive step should you take to protect the hard disk drive?
7. What two factors determine the amount of information that can be stored on a disk?
8. What are the two factors that determine how fast a drive can store data to and retrieve data from a disk?
9. What is the primary use of tape storage when used with a microcomputer?
10. What is CD-ROM, and what is it used for?
11. What is the major advantage of optical disks over other types of storage media?
12. What is a WORM disk?
13. What is the difference between a WORM disk and an erasable optical disk?
14. Why do you make backup copies of important disks?
15. List three things you should do to protect floppy disks and three things you should not do.

Distribution Devices

OBJECTIVES

After completing this topic, you will be able to

- Describe how computers are organized in business
- Describe how microcomputers can communicate with mainframe computers
- Explain the function of a modem
- Describe the different types of modems available
- Explain how you send documents to and from your computer using facsimile

Information processing is performed throughout large and small companies and in professional offices. Users sit at **workstations** (also called terminals, video display terminals (VDTs), or microcomputers). Each workstation has a display screen and a keyboard. The way these workstations are organized and the other equipment they have depend on the technology the company is using. The basic approaches are centralized, decentralized, or a combination of the two.

THE ORGANIZATION OF COMPUTERS IN BUSINESS

Computers are found throughout the modern business world. The ways these computers are organized varies widely from company to company and even within departments in the same company.

Centralized Information Processing

When information processing was first introduced into businesses in the 1950s, the systems available were expensive. This led to their being organized into a central system called a data processing (DP) department, which is operated by a specialized staff. Workstations connected to this centralized system are usually **dumb terminals**; that is, they lack the ability to process data on their own. They have only a screen and a keyboard. To work, a dumb terminal must be connected to a central computer that can process data for it. The terminal is used only to send information to the computer and receive information from it.

Decentralized Information Processing

With the development of low-cost microcomputers, information processing became more decentralized. **Standalone microcomputers**, which were not tied into a larger system, began to appear throughout the corporation. Each standalone microcomputer is a complete system that includes a computer, keyboard, display screen, and printer (Figure 1-106). At the heart of most standalone systems is a microcomputer that has the ability to process information without being connected to a central computer. A standalone system like this is used by a single person or shared by several people who use it at different times. Although the standalone units are not operated by a specialized staff, they may be supervised by a manager from the company's management information systems (MIS) department. This manager approves the purchase of hardware and software and provides training and support to the users.

Combined Centralized and Decentralized Information Processing

With recent advances in technology, it has become possible to combine the best features of centralized and decentralized information processing systems. If you were to walk through a modern office, you would see computer workstations throughout the building. Each workstation is either a microcomputer or a dumb terminal, and you cannot tell the difference just by looking at it. The significant differences are inside the cabinet. As you have learned, dumb terminals cannot function unless connected to the central computer, whereas intelligent computers can process information even though not connected to the central computer.

Workstations in these systems are frequently organized into two types of systems: local area networks and multiuser computer systems.

A **local area network (LAN)** (Figure 1-107) is a group of computers that are connected so that they can exchange messages and files and share resources like printers. Systems organized into a network are usually supervised by a **network manager**. This person can be a member of either the department the network is located in or the MIS department. The network manager is responsible for supervising the use of the system and authorizes or denies users access to specific files. An authorized user, for example, may be authorized access to correspondence files but denied access to financial analysis files.

FIGURE 1-106
Standalone Workstations
A standalone workstation has everything an operator needs to do word and information processing. The workstation is not connected to other computers. Courtesy of IBM Corporation

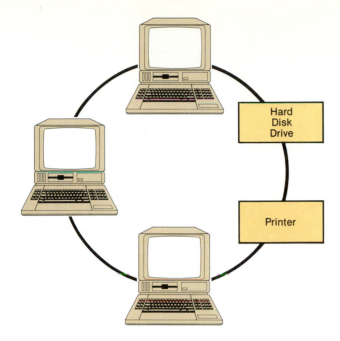

FIGURE 1-107
Networks
A computer network combines the best features of centralized and standalone systems. Users can work individually or share documents and resources like printers with other users on the network.

Sneaker Net

Networks are often either too expensive or too complicated for users. These people sometimes refer to their Sneaker Net or Walk Net. On these networks, the computers are not connected by wires but by users who walk from one workstation to another to deliver a file or a printout. Not only are these networks less expensive and less complicated, but the users get some exercise.

A **multiuser computer system** has a central computer that does the processing for the other workstations connected to it (Figure 1-108). These workstations can be either computers or dumb terminals.

COMMUNICATING WITH MAINFRAME COMPUTERS

Managers in large corporations need to speed up their access to data stored on the mainframe computer. Even if they have a microcomputer on their desks, they often must wait for a printout from the DP department and then rekey the data they are interested in. Ideally, they could connect their microcomputer to the mainframe and access the data directly.

Although this is highly desirable and will eventually be the way all managers work, several technical and organizational problems must first be solved.

Technical Problems

Most companies own a wide variety of microcomputers. Each of these works somewhat differently and may not be compatible. The cost of connecting these computers to the mainframe is a serious consideration, as is the quality of the connections now available. Mainframes can be accessed by either modems or coaxial cable. The first option requires that the mainframe and each computer be provided with a modem. Communications between them

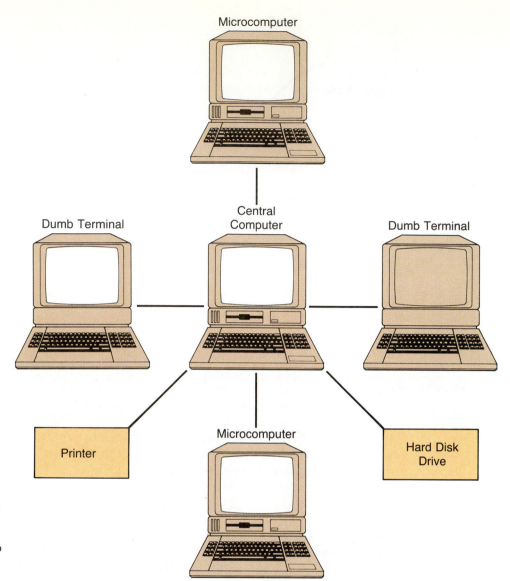

Microcomputer

Dumb Terminal   Central Computer   Dumb Terminal

Printer   Microcomputer   Hard Disk Drive

FIGURE 1-108
Multiuser Systems
A multiuser computer system is similar to a network, but all processing is done by a central computer to which workstations are connected. The workstations can be dumb terminals or intelligent computers.

occur over existing telephone lines. A better alternative, since it allows direct connections, is to connect the mainframe and computers with coaxial cable. But this cable may have to be run through walls and ceilings—not a minor inconvenience and expense.

Security Problems

Even when it is possible to connect computers to the mainframe, there are serious issues about preserving the integrity of the database and ensuring that users access only what they are authorized to see. Therefore, connections with mainframe computers generally take one of three forms.

1. The microcomputer acts like a dumb terminal so that it can see data in the mainframe's database but not manipulate it. In this case, the microcomputer is just like any other terminal in the company.

2. The microcomputer can **download** data, or copy it from the mainframe to the microcomputer, so that it can be manipulated with spreadsheet, graphics, database, and word processing programs. This eliminates the need for the manager to rekey all information to be analyzed or used.

3. The microcomputer can **upload** data, or copy it from the microcomputer to the mainframe. This means files can be created or modified on the microcomputer and then sent back to be stored in the mainframe's database. This, more than any other method, presents the most problems. In a large corporation, few things are as important or as well protected as the records stored in the mainframe. Many companies even go so far as to make backup copies of their disks and have them stored in bomb-proof shelters buried deep within mountains. The idea of someone's being able to modify data in these files is disturbing to DP managers who are responsible for the integrity of these records.

MODEMS

A **modem** is a communications device that links computers connected by telephone lines. With modems, you can send data from your computer to another similarly equipped computer located anywhere you can reach by phone (Figure 1-109). This is called **telecommunications** (see Part Eight).

The reason you need a modem to telecommunicate is simple: The computer generates digital signals, but telephone lines are designed to carry analog signals. When you transmit a message, the modem at the sending end converts the computer's digital signals into analog signals (modulation) so that they can be transmitted effectively over telephone lines. The modem at the receiving end then converts the analog signals back into digital signals (demodulation) so that they can be used by the computer. The name *modem* derives from *mo*dulate-*dem*odulate. We discuss this process in more detail in Part Eight.

FIGURE 1-109
Modems
Modems must be used at both ends of the telephone circuit. The sender can then transmit data over the telephone lines to the modem at the other end. The receiving modem can be connected either to another computer or to a printer.

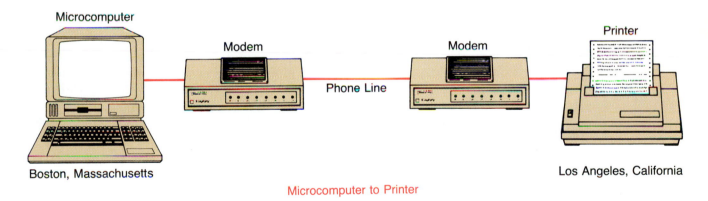

Microcomputer

Modem   Modem   Printer

Phone Line

Boston, Massachusetts   Los Angeles, California

Microcomputer to Printer

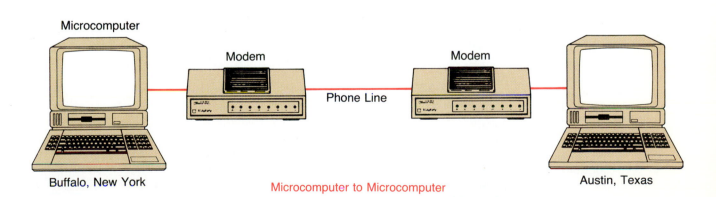

Microcomputer

Modem   Modem

Phone Line

Buffalo, New York   Austin, Texas

Microcomputer to Microcomputer

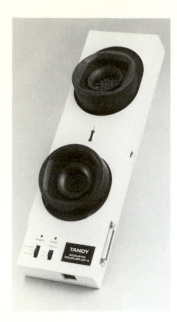

FIGURE 1-110
Acoustic Coupler Modems
Acoustic coupler modems have cups into which you press the telephone's handset. They also have switches to turn the modem on and off and to switch between data and voice communications. Courtesy of Radio Shack, a division of Tandy Corporation

FIGURE 1-111
Direct Connect Modems
Direct connect modems plug directly into the phone line so that you do not need a phone to use them. They come in two basic versions: a modem on a board plugs into an expansion slot in the computer, and a standalone modem connects to the computer's serial port. Courtesy of U.S. Robotics

The type of modem determines how it is connected to the computer and phone lines. As you have seen, data inside the computer is processed 8, 16, or 32 bits at a time. Since most telephone lines can handle only 1 bit at a time, the data must be sent from the computer to the modem serially, 1 bit at a time. To do this, you need to connect your modem to a serial port on your computer. A serial port converts the parallel signal used by the computer into a serial signal suitable for transmission over telephone wires.

Acoustic Coupler Modems

An **acoustic coupler modem** (Figure 1-110) is a low-speed modem that has a rubber cradle into which you place the telephone's handset. A speaker in the sending end of the modem "talks" into the microphone in the telephone's mouthpiece. These signals are then transmitted over the telephone lines. A microphone in the receiving end of the modem "listens" to the telephone's earpiece for data received from the remote computer. The data is then passed on to the computer.

Though generally inexpensive, acoustic couplers have several drawbacks. They often require you to manually dial the number you want to call. And when you connect with another computer, you must flip a switch to go from voice to data transmission. These modems have fairly high error rates because the modem picks up any background noise in the room, and this can garble the data transmission. Moreover, a telephone always feeds some of the transmitted signal back into the earpiece so that you can hear what you are saying. This telephone feedback confuses acoustic coupler modems. The transmit volume has to be set very low so that the modem does not interpret this feedback as a signal.

Direct-Connect Modems

A **direct-connect modem** (Figure 1-111) is connected to the computer and phone lines with cables so that no background noise can interfere with the data. Because there is less noise, data can be transmitted faster than with acoustic couplers. There are two types of direct-connect modems: A modem on a board plugs into an expansion slot in the computer, and a standalone modem connects to the computer's serial port with a cable. Both types are then connected to the telephone's wall jack with a standard phone cable.

FACSIMILE MACHINES

Until recently, you could distribute the documents that you created on your computer in only two ways, either as electronic digital signals or as printed copy. Today, you can distribute them electronically over a network, or you can use a modem to connect to a remote computer. And you can distribute printed copy through the mail, or you can use a **facsimile (fax) machine** (Table 1-13).

TABLE 1-13
Methods of Document Distribution

Sender	Recipient	Method of Distribution
Printout	Printout	Facsimile to facsimile
Digital	Digital	Computer to computer
Digital	Printout	Computer to facsimile
Printout	Digital	Facsimile to computer

FIGURE 1-112
Facsimile Machines
Facsimile machines have a document tray into which you place the document you want to send. You dial the number of another fax, and the document is drawn through the scanner and converted into digital signals. These signals are sent over the telephone lines, and the receiving fax reverses the process and converts the signals back into a printed image. Courtesy of Fujitsu Imaging Systems of America, Inc.

A facsimile machine (Figure 1-112) is like a copy machine where you insert the original document into your machine, and a copy comes out on another facsimile machine anywhere else in the world.

Since the cost of fax machines has dropped, they have become widespread. To send a document on a fax machine, you insert the document into the fax's document tray, and then dial the phone number of another fax machine. When the other fax answers the call, your fax automatically feeds the document through its scanner. This scanner converts the document into digital signals. These signals are sent over the phone line to the recipient's fax machine, which reverses the process. It converts the digital signals back into an image, which it prints out. When the transmission is completed, both machines hang up.

With an add-on board, it is even possible for you to send a document to someone's fax machine directly from your computer (Figure 1-113), or for someone with a fax machine to send a document directly to your computer. This speeds up the process since you don't have to first make a printout and then walk to a fax machine. These add-on boards are installed into one of the expansion slots in your computer and then connected to the telephone jack on the wall with a cable.

VOICE MAIL

One of the big problems in business is phone-tag. This is where you call someone, discover he or she isn't there, and then leave a message for the person to return your call. When the person does call back, you aren't there,

FIGURE 1-113
Microcomputer-based Facsimile
Microcomputer-based facsimile is now possible by inserting an expansion board into one of your computer's ports. With this board, you can send documents directly from your files to another fax.

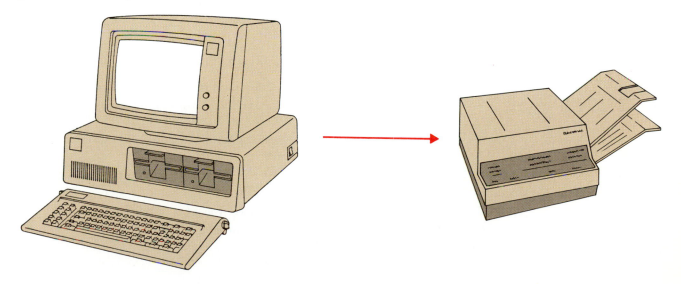

so he or she leaves a message for you. A microcomputer-based solution to this problem has been introduced. Called **voice mail**, it automates phone answering and messaging. To use these systems, you insert an add-on board and run the voice mail software. When someone calls your phone, the computer answers, and a digitized voice tells the caller to leave a message. When the caller does so, it is digitized and stored on your disk. You can then play back recorded messages by pressing a few keys on the computer's keyboard or by dialing your phone from a touch-tone phone. Sophisticated systems also have an **automated attendant** that routes callers to the right person when they press keys of a touch-tone phone. For example, the attendant answers the phone and tells the caller to press 1 to reach marketing, 2 to reach service, or 3 to place an order. The voice mail system then routes the call to the appropriate department. If no one answers, a digitized voice asks the caller to leave a message.

SUMMARY AND KEY TERMS

- The system that a user sits at when working on a computer is called a **workstation**.

- Data in a computer can be sent to other computers over a **local area network (LAN)** or multiuser system. Both systems use wires or cables to connect the computers. The workstations connected to either system can be computers or **dumb terminals.**

- Decentralized computers that are not connected to other computers are called **standalone** systems.

- Computers can be connected to mainframe computers, but this presents serious security problems.

- You can also connect with other computers over the phone lines. To do so, both computers must have a **modem** to convert the computer's digital signals into the analog signals that the telephone lines carry.

- Modems come as **acoustic couplers** or **direct connect** units. Acoustic couplers have cups into which you plug the phone's handset. A direct connect modem either attaches directly to the computer with cables or is plugged into the expansion slot as an add-on board.

- If you want to send images, rather than files, you can send them by **facsimile**. You can add a facsimile board to your computer and then send documents to other computers with similar boards or to any fax machine.

REVIEW QUESTIONS

1. What is the difference between a dumb terminal and an intelligent computer?
2. Computers are connected on local area networks or as multiuser systems. What is the basic difference between these two arrangements?
3. Describe two reasons why networks are used to connect microcomputers?
4. What is the function of a modem?
5. List two types of modems, and describe the differences between them.
6. What is the purpose of a facsimile machine?
7. What is voice mail, and briefly how does it work?
8. Give an example of how an automated attendant works.

Microcomputer Issues

OBJECTIVES

After completing this topic, you will be able to

- Describe the causes of health problems that might arise when working on a microcomputer, and explain how to avoid them

- Describe why training is important

- Describe some security issues that arise when microcomputers are used

- Explain why compatibility between computers is important but also difficult to obtain

When the microcomputer became available, it presented a real challenge to the data processing department. Up till then, computing power had been centralized. The availability of the inexpensive microcomputer now made it possible to decentralize this power. Computers could be distributed throughout the corporation. This distribution of computers raised several significant issues that have yet to be resolved to everybody's satisfaction.

ERGONOMICS AND HEALTH

The medical and physical effects of working long hours on video displays are not fully known. It is suspected that some problems can result. Complaints generally concern vision and muscle strain. But you can avoid most, if not all, of these problems.

Your eyes were made for most efficient seeing at a far distance. Working on video display equipment calls for intense concentration on a task close at hand, usually no more than a couple of feet away. When your eyes change focus from far, their natural state, to near, several different muscles are called into action. A muscle inside the eye changes the shape of the eye's lens to focus sharply and clearly on the display screen. Other muscles turn both eyes inward, pointing them together at the same character on the screen, and still other muscles move the eyes quickly from one character or word to another.

Users complain most often of headaches, blurred vision at both near and far viewing distances, itching and burning eyes, eye fatigue, flickering sensations, and double vision.

Those who do research in **ergonomics**, the study of the interaction of people and machines, have developed several suggestions that users should follow to reduce or eliminate any potential problems.

- Use an adjustable chair, which can be a vision aid by enabling you to sit at a proper angle to the display screen (Figure 1-114). Generally, the top of the display screen should be 10 degrees above, and the center of the screen 20 degrees below, your straight-ahead seeing position. The distance from your eyes to the screen should be 14 to 20 inches.

- Place your reference material as close as possible to the display screen to avoid frequent large eye and head movements. A copy stand is very useful for this.

- Place your reference material the same distance from your eyes as the display screen is to avoid having to change focus when you look from one to the other. Every time your eyes change focus, it requires muscles to work inside the eye. Frequent changes may cause you to feel tired.

Lighting and glare control can also make a difference. The following recommendations are designed to maximize comfort, accuracy, and productivity and to minimize eye fatigue and other complaints:

- Although lighting needs vary from person to person, check that overall illumination for video display equipment is between 30 and 50 footcandles, which is less than the customary office lighting level. Display screen brightness should be three or four times greater than room light. A lower level of room lighting can be achieved by using fewer bulbs or fluorescent lights and by replacing cool white fluorescent tubes with cool white deluxe tubes that provide less light but a more comfortable and pleasing atmosphere.

- Adjust the characters on the display screen to contrast well with the screen background.

- Minimize reflected glare on display screens by placing the screens so that windows and other sources of light are behind you. Do not sit facing an unshaded window or other bright light source. Make use of drapes and shades to reduce glare. Small hoods can be attached to extend above the display screen to shield it from overhead light if necessary. You can also use nonreflective surfaces or buy antiglare filters that fit over the screen.

FIGURE 1-114
Positioning Your Materials
Positioning your display screen correctly can reduce the strain of working at a microcomputer and make your work healthier and more enjoyable.

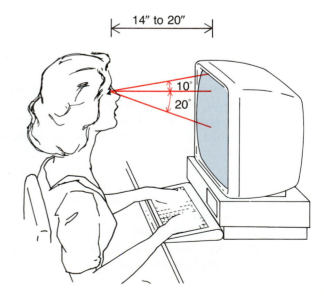

14" to 20"

10°

20°

- Use localized lighting like flexible lamps for other desk work as required. They are shielded and must be placed to avoid glare on the work surface of the display screen.
- Avoid white or light colored clothing if it causes a reflection on the screen.

Taking rest breaks can often solve many problems. Because word and information processing generally requires intense concentration on the document and screen, rest is important. The National Institute of Occupational Safety and Health (NIOSH) recommends a fifteen minute break after two hours of continuous work for users having moderate visual demands or moderate workload (less than 60 percent of your time looking at the screen) and a fifteen minute break every hour for users having high visual demands, high workloads, or repetitive work tasks.

VDT User Vision Checklist

Your workspace and vision care habits: Do they measure up?

- ☐ Correct angle and distance from screen to eyes (see Figure 1-114)
- ☐ Reference material placed near the screen
- ☐ Reference material and screen same distance from eyes
- ☐ Screen brightness properly adjusted
- ☐ Proper overall room lighting
- ☐ Windows and other sources of bright light shielded
- ☐ Proper lamps for reference material
- ☐ Sources of screen reflection eliminated
- ☐ Fifteen minute break every two hours for moderate users
- ☐ Fifteen minute break every hour for frequent users

TRAINING

The large variety of computers has caused a training nightmare. No single person can master them all. As a result, a network of knowledgeable people has emerged in many companies that is only now being recognized and addressed. These people, generally the pioneers who introduced the microcomputer in the firm, are continually sought out by people who have recently gained access to a computer. They answer their questions and help get them started. They obviously provide a valuable service, but it takes time and detracts from their performance in their own job. Many companies are now formally recognizing the skills of these people and are changing their job descriptions to acknowledge the contribution they make. Some larger companies have organized **information centers (ICs)**, whose staff are responsible for providing training and other services.

When new employees are hired or new programs introduced into a company, users must be trained. The responsibility for this training is usually assigned to the IC or MIS department. The high cost of this training makes companies reluctant to introduce new programs and has led to the standardization of programs within each company. Most companies specify that you can use no more than one or two programs in each of the main applications categories. If you use an unauthorized program, the company may not supply training, and the files you create may be unusable by other employees.

SECURITY

When computer power is centralized, security can be ensured. Only people authorized to have access to information are allowed to see it. Security is important for everyone, not just management. For example, no one should be able to see your salary or medical records stored on the computer unless there is a genuine need to and management authorizes it. When computers are sitting on desks throughout the firm, security becomes a serious problem. The DP department can use access codes to prevent unauthorized persons from seeing information in the main computer, but these can be lost or stolen. Moreover, people often use their microcomputers for sensitive

Protecting Privacy and Security in the Micro Environment

Early this year I visited a major American manufacturing firm whose engineering, sales, and administrative staffs are heavy users of personal computers. A company executive explained, "We're providing our professionals with a powerful analytic tool that they can use at any moment they need it—at the office, at home, or on the road. We want them to be experimental and to have computing power at their fingertips."

However, this firm has become increasingly concerned with threats to the confidentiality and security of company data. Within the past year company officers discovered that employees were taking terminals home, accessing the mainframe with an ID code, and storing their personal files on the mainframe system—all in violation of company rules. They also found that an employee was authorizing complimentary product orders from a microcomputer that bypassed the regular sales-order system controls. In addition, a full account of the access procedures for getting into the company telecommunications system suddenly appeared on a hacker's bulletin board.

The experiences and dilemma of this company are typical among business, government, and nonprofit organizations. We found the same concerns among 110 organizations examined in a recently completed two-year study: "Project on the Workplace Impact of Using VDTs in the Office." All of the surveyed managers reported experiences of and worries about breaches of confidentiality and security.

At several newspapers we visited, management gave reporters a private file in which they could store confidential notes and sources and told them that no one else could get into their file. In fact, the security was so weak, that other reporters and editors soon learned how to browse these private files.

At a law office where attorneys use both a dedicated word processor and a micro system, the office manager became concerned about the security of highly sensitive client data. After creating an empty file and marking it Confidential, the office manager found that during the first week of its existence, eight attempts had been made to access the file from inside the firm.

At a high-technology company, a manager made adjustments in the electronic mail system so that all messages to other executives but not to him appeared on his terminal. He said he "just wanted to keep informed about what people were saying to one another."

work, and most microcomputers have very poor security devices, if any at all.

COMPATIBILITY

As you'll see, each computer has its own characteristics. Programs that run on one computer may not run on others. When microcomputers first became available, most firms didn't have a policy on which model and brand to buy. Thus a great many computers entered the firm by a variety of routes. The result is a large investment in equipment that can't be integrated. **Computer compatibility**, the ability of one computer to run the same soft-

At one bank, personnel officers with personal computers were creating their own automated files on employees. They recorded matters of discipline, lateness, absentee counts, and other matters, especially when they thought "potential Equal Employment Opportunity (EEO) issues might arise." This violated the bank's employee-privacy rules and could also have been a serious problem in EEO or unjust discharge cases.

In at least a dozen organizations we visited, company officers told us that professional employees had downloaded proprietary information or valuable customer lists from the mainframes onto floppy disks, which they had taken off the premises and sold to competitors.

Although we found that most management information services executives and security professionals are concerned about these issues, more than 90 percent of the organizations we visited from 1982 to 1984 had not:

- done a risk assessment of new privacy and security exposures in their organizations
- conducted a sensitivity analysis to classify types of information handled in the micro environment
- issued any policy statements or guidelines to instruct end users in their responsibilities
- trained end users in safeguarding sensitive personal or proprietary data

Fortunately, this seems to be changing. In 1985 when we sampled some of the organizations visited earlier, we found that about half had created privacy and security task forces to draw up policy guidelines for micro users, issued handbooks on microcomputer confidentiality and security techniques, and set specific responsibilities for managers to assure that their employees will comply with privacy and security policies.

It is clear that inexpensive desktop computers and powerful off-the-shelf software represent a resource that can unlock the creativity of millions of professional and managerial users. But with these powerful tools comes duty of trusteeship for sensitive personal and proprietary information. Any organization that does not address this issue now and does not provide data security training for its microcomputer users is risking serious future trouble.

Source: Reprinted with permission from *Lotus Magazine.*

ware as another, is becoming increasingly important now that many firms want to connect all these individual computers into a network so that they can exchange files.

In the early days of microcomputers, several conflicting standards prevented programs from being run on various computers. The dominance of IBM and Apple has reduced the number of standards, but all programs still do not run on all computers. To run a program on a particular computer, the program must be designed for, or compatible with, that computer. Let's look at two aspects of this problem that have arisen with the introduction of the IBM PS/2 computers. Compatibility problems arise because some of the computers in these new machines use different microprocessor chips.

More than 9 million IBM PCs or compatible computers are installed in businesses. All these computers use the 8086 or 8088 microprocessor chips made by Intel. The more powerful models in the new PS/2 line use new chips, the Intel 80286 or 80236. When the Intel 286 and 386 chips were being developed, one of the goals was to make them compatible with previous chips, specifically the 8086 and 8088 chips used in IBM PCs. This compatibility lets the newer chips run all software developed for the earlier, slower chips. To do this, the 286 and 386 chips have three modes—real, virtual, and protected—that you can switch between by pressing designated keys.

Real mode is used to run applications programs written for earlier chips. The term *real* comes from the chip's acting as if it were a real 8086 or 8088 chip. Real mode has the following features:

- It is essentially a much faster 8086 or 8088 chip.
- It addresses as much as 1MB of memory.
- It does not use the advanced features of the 286 and 386 chips.
- It cannot do **multitasking**, that is, run more than one program at a time. But this shortcoming can be overcome by using EMS (see Topic 2-18).

Virtual 8086 mode is an extension of real mode that you can use to run existing applications with the following differences:

- You can run multiple existing applications simultaneously as if they were running on different computers.
- It makes it relatively easy to use EMS to address as much as 8MB of RAM per application.

Protected mode refers to the way the chip prevents programs running at the same time (multitasking) from interfering with one another by trying to use one anothers' memory space. This is important because if two programs try to store data in the same area of memory, one or both of the programs will crash. Protected mode has the following features:

- It will not run existing 8086 or 8080 applications programs but will run programs written specifically for the 80286.
- It can do multitasking.
- When used on a 286 chip, it addresses as much as 16MB of conventional memory and uses as much as 1GB of virtual memory (memory on the hard disk treated as if it were memory inside the computer's chips).
- When used on a 386 chip, it addresses as much as 4GB of conventional memory and uses as much as 64TB (64 terabytes, or 64 trillion bytes) of virtual memory.

- Health problems associated with computers derive from the poor design of workstations. With a little planning for the lighting, chairs and desks, and positioning of work materials, these problems can be reduced or eliminated. **Ergonomics** determines the correct design of a workstation.

- Companies that use microcomputers have additional responsibilities. They must train new users and protect data from unauthorized users.

- **Computer compatibility** is becoming a problem as new and more powerful computers are introduced. To reduce the problem, the microprocessors used in the new IBM PS/2 line are compatible with older software. When you run new software, you run it in **protected mode** so that you can run more than one program at the same time, and they are protected from each other. You run older software in **real mode**, but since the computer cannot ensure that one program won't erase data needed by the other, you can run only one of these programs at a time.

1. What is ergonomics? Why is it important?
2. List three things you can do to avoid vision and muscle strain problems when working at a microcomputer.
3. What is the difference between real mode and protected mode?
4. What is virtual 8086 mode?

Part Two

OPERATING SYSTEMS

Topic 2-1   Typical Operating Systems
Topic 2-2   Loading the Operating System and Executing Commands
Topic 2-3   Specifying Drives and Directories
Topic 2-4   Assigning and Listing Filenames
Topic 2-5   Specifying More Than One File
Topic 2-6   Formatting Data Disks
Topic 2-7   Formatting System Disks
Topic 2-8   Copying Files
Topic 2-9   Duplicating Disks
Topic 2-10   Comparing Disks
Topic 2-11   Renaming Files
Topic 2-12   Erasing Files
Topic 2-13   Checking Disks
Topic 2-14   Making and Removing Directories
Topic 2-15   Displaying and Printing ASCII Text Files
Topic 2-16   The PATH Command
Topic 2-17   Creating Batch Files
Topic 2-18   Operating System Issues

As you saw in Part One, the central processing unit is the heart of the computer's hardware. All activity in the computer revolves around it. But you use software to give instructions to the hardware. Although you do your computer work on applications programs, the heart of the computer's software is the **operating system**. The operating system coordinates activity between you and the computer and between parts of the computer. Through the operating system, you tell the computer to run your word processing, spreadsheet, or database applications program; save your work into a file on the disk; print a file; and so forth.

All applications programs that operate on a microcomputer require an operating system. This operating system software is sometimes hidden from you behind menus, dialog boxes, and icons. This is especially true of computers like the Apple Macintosh or IBM computers running Windows or OS/2 with Presentation Manager. When using a computer with one of these operating systems, you have to know only how to point and click with a mouse. But on other computers, like those that run MS-DOS or PC-DOS, you need to know a little more about the operating system to take full advantage of what the system offers.

Because the operating system coordinates activity between any applications program you run and the computer hardware, you must load the operating system into the computer's memory before you load an applications program (Figure 2-1). Most applications programs that you buy from publishers do not contain the operating system. To use these programs, you must first load the operating system from another disk, or copy the appropriate operating system program files to the applications program disk or to your hard disk. This is necessary because the operating system may have been written by one company and the applications program by another. Even if the same company publishes both, they are not sure which version of their operating system you may be using, so they cannot anticipate which version to put on the disk.

FIGURE 2-1
The Operating System and Applications Programs
The operating system communicates between applications programs and the hardware. The operating system must always be loaded into the computer's memory before any applications are loaded.

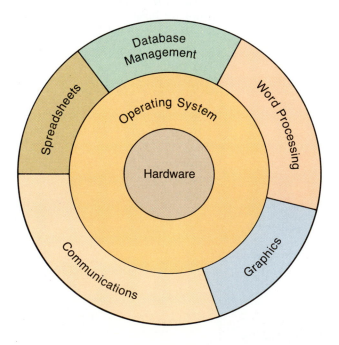

THE FUNCTIONS OF AN OPERATING SYSTEM

The primary functions of the operating system are to coordinate, or supervise, the activities of the computer and allow you to manage your files. It decides where programs and data are stored in the computer's memory and handles communication among the computer's components, the applications programs, and you—the user. The operating system controls your computer without your involvement or awareness. In this respect, it is like your body's respiratory system, which keeps you breathing and your heart beating even though you are hardly aware of it.

Picture a busy intersection at rush hour with no traffic lights and no police officer (Figure 2-2). No one approaching the intersection knows what to do or when to do it. The traffic backs up, and tempers flare. The solution is the installation of traffic lights or a police officer to tell people when to stop and go. In your computer, this function is handled by the operating system's input/output manager and command processor.

The **input/output (I/O) manager** coordinates the computer's communications with all peripheral devices. For example, it coordinates the flow of data to the display screen and to other output devices like printers and modems. It also controls the flow of data to and from the disk drives.

The **command processor** interprets what you enter from the keyboard or other input devices. In this respect, it is rather like an interpreter (Figure 2-3). If you spoke only English and tried to carry on a discussion with some-

FIGURE 2-2
The Operating System
Coordinates Traffic
Intersections without traffic control are confusing. Those with traffic control are more efficient. Everyone knows when to stop and when to go. The operating system performs traffic control functions within the computer.

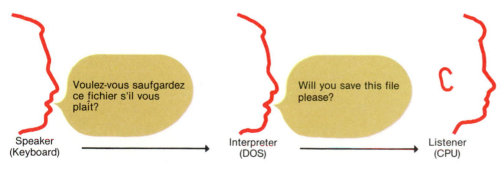

Speaker (Keyboard) → Interpreter (DOS) → Listener (CPU)

Voulez-vous saufgardez ce fichier s'il vous plaît?

Will you save this file please?

FIGURE 2-3
The Operating System
Interprets
Command processing is a form of interpreting. The commands you enter on the keyboard are interpreted by the operating system and sent to the central processing unit.

one who spoke only French, you both would need an interpreter to translate what was being said so that you could understand each other. The same is true of a computer. When you use an applications program, the program's commands are interpreted by the operating system for the hardware. For example, on one program, you might save a file you are working on by holding down the **Ctrl** key while you press the letters **K** and **D**; on another, you might press the **F10** function key and then press **Return**. The operating system interprets these commands and instructs the disk drive to spin while it copies the file to the disk from the computer's internal memory.

In addition to the things the operating system does automatically, it contains **utility programs** that you use to manage your files. You use these utility programs to perform tasks such as copying files and preparing disks for use on your computer.

SUMMARY AND KEY TERMS

- The **operating system** controls the computer's operations and must always be loaded before you load an applications program. This is true for all computers.
- The operating system's **input/output manager** coordinates communications between the components of the computer system.
- The **command processor** interprets your commands.
- The operating system's **utility programs** are used to manage your files.

REVIEW QUESTIONS

1. Why does a computer need an operating system?
2. When do you load the operating system?
3. What is the function of the input/output manager?
4. What is the function of the command processor?
5. What are the operating system's utility programs used for?

TOPIC 2-1

Typical Operating Systems

OBJECTIVES

After completing this topic, you will be able to

- List and describe some of the most common operating systems
- Understand the basic differences between versions of operating systems
- Describe the difference between a singletasking and multitasking operating system
- Describe operating system environments

Although all computers use an operating system, not all use the same one. Over the years, a variety of operating systems have been developed. Operating systems are the most complex programs used by microcomputers. They have to interact between the system's hardware and applications programs, and they are usually specific to the hardware and software they are being used with. If you have an IBM PC computer, you are probably using PC-DOS or IBM-OS/2. If you have an IBM PC compatible computer, you are probably using MS-DOS or MS-OS/2, slight variations on the IBM versions.

Applications programs written for one operating system often will not run on another. Moreover, data files created under one operating system may not be read by another. Thus it is important to have at least some understanding of the types of operating systems available. For example, many applications programs are written to run on a specific operating system like PC-DOS or MS-DOS. For the program to run on the Apple Macintosh, the program's publisher has to write a different version of the program. Even programs written for one IBM PC operating system may not run on another. If they do, the program may not take advantage of the full features offered by the operating system unless it is adapted to do so.

Operating systems are either portable or proprietary.

- **Portable operating systems** are designed so that they can be modified slightly to run on a variety of computers.
- **Proprietary operating systems** are designed to run on a single brand of computer.

143

CP/M

When the first microcomputers were developed, they had no operating systems. This made it difficult for both users and programmers. In 1973, Gary Kildall wrote an operating system called **CP/M** (Control Program for Microcomputers). One of the key features of this program was its structure. All the parts specific to hardware were grouped into one of the program's modules, called **BIOS** (Basic Input Output System). This made it easy to convert the program to run on a variety of computers; only this small section of the program had to be revised. This ease of conversion quickly made CP/M the most widely used microcomputer operating system for the first generation of 8-bit microcomputers. It was widely used until the IBM PC began to dominate the microcomputer market.

MS-DOS AND PC-DOS

When IBM developed the IBM PC, they used a new 16-bit microprocessor, so they needed a new operating system. IBM contracted the development of the new operating system to Bill Gates at Microsoft. Bill and his team developed an operating system called **MS-DOS** (Microsoft Disk Operating System). The IBM PC version of this program was named **PC-DOS**. (Throughout the remainder of this text, we refer to both versions as DOS.) The PC-DOS version usually runs on IBM PC computers, and the MS-DOS version usually runs on compatibles made by manufacturers other than IBM. These two versions of the operating system are essentially identical in the way they work and the commands you use to operate them; usually they are interchangeable.

Because DOS commands are cryptic and hard to remember, several programs, called **shells**, have been developed (Figure 2-4). You load one of these shells into the computer's memory *after you load DOS*, and it displays menus and lists of files. Using the menus, you can execute many of the most frequently used DOS commands without having to remember how to type them. With the introduction of DOS 4.0, the menus offered by these shells were built into the operating system. This version allows you to execute many of the most commonly used commands from these menus (Figure 2-5). DOS 4.0 also includes on-line help, which you can display at any time by pressing **F1**.

FIGURE 2-4
DOS Shells
Since DOS commands are so cryptic, many people use DOS shells, programs that help you navigate directories and select operating system commands from menus.

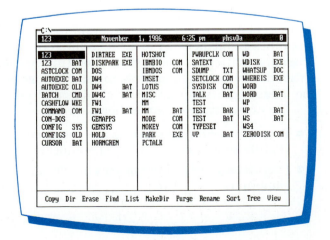

OPERATING SYSTEMS

Display Title

Action Bar

Group Contents

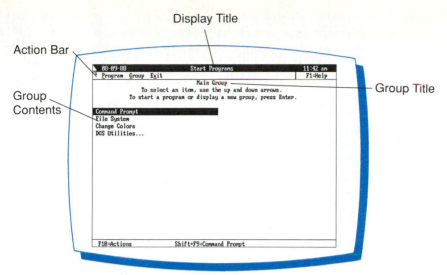

Group Title

A. The Start Program Screen

FIGURE 2-5
DOS 4.0
DOS 4.0 contains a shell, a menu-driven interface. When you load DOS (or type DOSSHELL and press **Return** from the system prompt), the Start Program screen is displayed (a). When you select File System from the menu, the File System screen is displayed (b). This screen displays drive indicators and the files in the current directory. When you press **F10**, the menu bar at the top of the screen is activated (c), and the pull-down menus list the file commands you can use. To return to the DOS prompt at any time, you just press **F3**.

Display Title

Action Bar
Drive Identifier
Path Area

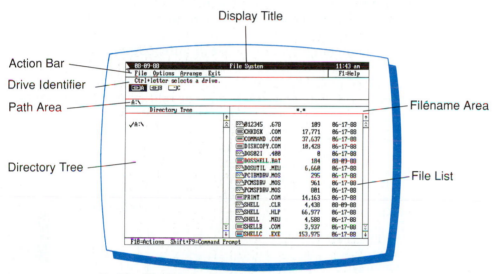

Filename Area

File List

Directory Tree

B. The File System Screen

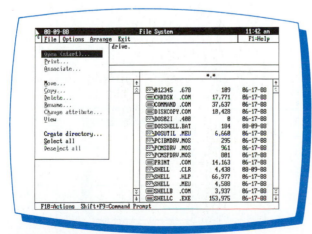

C. Pull-Down Menus

Since the IBM PC set the standard for microcomputers, MS-DOS and PC-DOS have been the most widely used operating systems. But today, they are being replaced on some computers by a new operating system named OS/2.

IBM OPERATING SYSTEM/2™

Operating System/2 (OS/2) was developed to overcome the built-in limitations of DOS (Figure 2-6). DOS operating systems are not user friendly, they run only one applications program at a time, and they can address only 640KB of memory. They also make it difficult for microcomputers to exchange information with mainframes, which are used by many corporations. In an attempt to solve these problems, IBM and Microsoft introduced OS/2 when IBM introduced their IBM Personal System/2 computers. Like DOS, there are two versions, IBM-OS/2 for IBM computers and MS-OS/2 for all other computers. Unlike DOS, Microsoft does not sell a retail version of the OS/2 operating system. Instead, they sell it to other computer companies (called original equipment manufacturers, or **OEMs**) and customize it for them. This OEM version has an option that lets you choose DOS or OS/2 when you first turn on the computer; the IBM version does not offer this option. (Throughout the remainder of this text, we refer to both versions as OS/2.)

To run OS/2, your computer must have an Intel 80286 or 80386 microprocessor. These microprocessors are found in IBM AT computers and some of the more advanced models in IBM's more recent PS/2 line of computers. OS/2 is available in two versions: the Standard Edition and the Extended Edition.

FIGURE 2-6
OS/2
Operating System/2 removes the 640KB barrier imposed by DOS. It allows the computer to address up to 16MB of memory. This allows you to run larger programs (and more of them) and to create larger files. Courtesy of IBM Corporation. *Source:* Information Systems Group, 900 King Street, Rye Brook, NY 10573 (ISG 008 04/02/87)

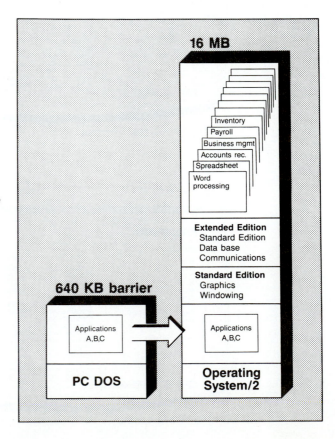

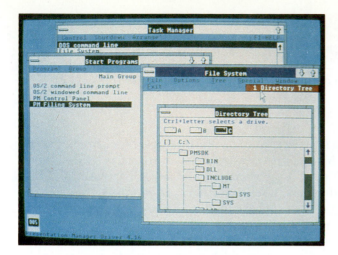

FIGURE 2-7
Presentation Manager
Presentation Manager is the new graphical interface for Operating System/2. It allows you to load more than one program into memory so that you can quickly switch between them. It also allows you to perform many operating system functions, like copying files without having to learn the cryptic commands usually required. The Start Programs window lists the programs that can be run. To run a program, you just select it from the menu. The Task Manager window displays the programs currently running in memory. You can quickly switch between them from this screen. The File System window lists files on the default disk and directory and provides menus you use to copy, delete, and rename files. Courtesy of Microsoft

The Standard Edition comes in two versions, 1.0 and 1.1. Both versions make it possible to address as many as 16MB of memory instead of the 640KB addressable by DOS. This makes running larger programs and creating larger files possible. Version 1.1 also incorporates a graphics display and features a built-in **Presentation Manager**™ based on Microsoft's Windows program (Figure 2-7). Presentation Manager allows you to divide the screen into windows in which multiple applications programs can be displayed and run at the same time.

One of the key advantages of Presentation Manager is that it gives a common look to most programs that are developed to take advantage of its features. For example, it allows you to operate the computer using pull-down menus and standardized commands to load programs; call up help; cancel commands; format disks; copy, rename, and erase files; and quit to return to the operating system. To ease the use of advanced features like fonts, Presentation Manager includes libraries of drivers, the programs needed to communicate between your computer and peripherals like the screen and printer. Previously, these drivers had to be supplied with each program, and standards varied widely from publisher to publisher. Programmers now write their programs to address Presentation Manager, and it in turn handles all communications with the peripheral devices.

The Extended Edition contains all the functions of the Standard Edition and includes a Communications Manager and Database Manager. The Communications Manager improves communications with other computers, including IBM's mainframes. The Database Manager is a relational database management system.

OS/2 supports two types of applications programs: DOS programs and OS/2 programs.

- DOS programs were initially written to run under DOS. These programs run in **real mode** in a **compatibility box**. Real mode simply means the operating system is using the microprocessor mode that runs programs designed for the original Intel 8086 or 8088 chips that are in all the original IBM PCs. You can run only one of these programs at a time, and they can take up only 500KB of memory.

- OS/2 programs were written especially for OS/2. These programs run in **protected mode**, so they are protected from each other by the operating system. Protecting a program from another simply means the operating system does not allow different programs to use the same memory locations. If they were to do so, the system might crash.

APPLE DOS AND PRODOS

When Apple introduced the Apple II, it contained a proprietary operating system called Apple DOS. This operating system was later modified so that it would work with a hard disk drive. This later version was named ProDOS.

MACINTOSH OPERATING SYSTEM

The proprietary operating system that runs on the Apple Macintosh was designed to be easy to use. Many of the features that it introduced have been incorporated into IBM PC operating systems like OS/2's Presentation Manager. Instead of using commands, it features menus and **icons**, small representative images, which you select by pointing to with a mouse and then clicking one of the mouse's buttons. For example, to retrieve a file, you use the mouse to move a pointer on the screen to point to the term *File* displayed at the top of the screen. You then click a button on the mouse, and a list of choices descends into the screen area.

UNIX

UNIX is a portable, multiuser, multitasking operating system. It was originally developed at AT&T's Bell Labs in 1973, and revised versions were introduced later. The current AT&T version is System V. There is much debate about this operating system becoming a standard for the next generation of microcomputers. Because of its popularity in certain circles, various versions have been developed that are based on, but slightly different from, the original. Examples are XENIX, VENIX, MICRONIX, Berkeley, and the recent Apple version A/UX and IBM's microcomputer version of AIX.

Unlike all the operating systems that we have discussed, this operating system has one key advantage: It is not tied to a specific microprocessor. It can easily be modified to run on any of them. This allows the program to run on microcomputers, minicomputers, and mainframes—a great advantage given the trend to tie all these computers into networks. Recently, several companies have banded together to develop new versions of this operating system. These versions will have a solution to the old, unfriendly command line where you had to type cryptic and complicated commands. They will also have a graphic interface much like the Apple Macintosh's and IBM's Presentation Manager. This interface (Figure 2-8) will make the operating system much easier for nonprogrammers to use.

FIGURE 2-8
UNIX's Open Look Interface
One of the groups developing a new, more user-friendly version of UNIX call their graphical interface Open Look. This menu-driven interface makes UNIX much easier to use because many commands are executed from pull-down menus. Courtesy of Infoworld

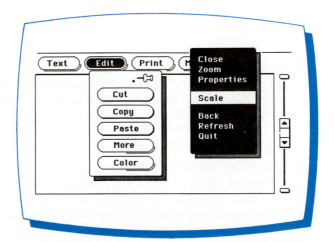

OPERATING SYSTEMS

OPERATING SYSTEM VERSIONS

As computers have evolved, so have operating systems. When major changes are made in the operating system, it is released as a new version. For example, PC-DOS was initially released as version 1.0, and over the years, versions 2.0 and 3.0 have been released. Minor changes also are introduced periodically. These are usually identified with numbers following the decimal point. For example, DOS is available in versions 3.0, 3.1, 3.2, 3.3, and 4.0. Normally, programs that run on an early version will also run on a later version. Table 2-1 lists some of the differences among versions of DOS. Table 2-2 lists the basic differences among versions of OS/2.

TABLE 2-1
MS-DOS and PC-DOS Versions

Version	Description
DOS 1.0	Original version
DOS 2.0	Added support for hard disk drives
DOS 3.0	Added support for local area networks
DOS 3.2	Added support for 3½-inch floppy disk drives
DOS 3.3	Added additional commands
DOS 4.0	Added menus to execute commands, on-line help, and allows users to address hard disks larger than 32MB

TABLE 2-2
OS/2 Versions

Version	Description
Standard Edition 1.0	Original version
Standard Edition 1.1	Added Presentation Manager
Extended Edition 1.0	Original version with database and telecommunications features
Extended Edition 1.1	Added Presentation Manager
	Added support for hard disks larger than 32MB and Token Ring and PC Network local area networks

SINGLETASKING, MULTITASKING, AND MULTIUSER OPERATING SYSTEMS

One way to classify operating systems is by the number of programs they can run at one time and the number of users that can work on computers or terminals connected to a central computer. Generally, operating systems are classified as singletasking, multitasking, or multiuser.

Singletasking Operating Systems

Many of the most common operating systems are still **singletasking**. This means only one program can be run on the computer at a time. If you are working on a spreadsheet program and want to use another program for word processing, you must remove the first program from the computer's memory and then load the other program. A singletasking operating system cannot handle both programs at the same time. Typical singletasking operating systems include MS-DOS, PC-DOS, and CP/M.

Multitasking Operating Systems

Some new operating systems allow you to run more than one program at a time and switch between or among the programs currently in memory. This is called **multitasking** (also called concurrent processing). To use more than one program, you load them, one after another, into the computer's memory. You then use the operating system's commands to move between the programs. The program you are currently working on is in the **foreground**. The other programs, which you are not currently working on, are in the **background**. Multitasking operating systems include OS/2, UNIX, and Apple's Multifinder OS.

Another way to do multitasking is to load a **memory resident program** (also called a terminate and stay resident, or TSR, program). These programs are in memory whenever you are using another program. When you want access to them, you press one or more designated keys, and the memory resident program appears on the screen. When finished, you press one or more other keys, and the original applications program reappears. But unlike a true multitasking operating system, the program in the background does not continue to function.

Multiuser Operating Systems

Some users, especially in large companies, connect several computers, called **workstations**, to a central computer so that the central computer's CPU is shared by all the workstations. When this is done, the computer must run an operating system that supports all these computers. The individual workstations can either be microcomputers or dumb terminals.

OPERATING SYSTEM ENVIRONMENTS

Operating system environments like Digital Research's GEM (Graphics Environment Manager), Quarterdeck's DESQview, and Microsoft's Windows (Figure 2-9) make using the computer easier and more efficient. They act much like OS/2's Presentation Manager.

They feature menus you can choose commands from to copy, rename, or delete files; prepare disks for use; and perform many other standard operating system tasks. Using DOS without the aid of an operating system environment, you perform these tasks by typing cryptic commands that you must either memorize or look up each time you want to use them.

Operating system environments also let you multitask by splitting the screen into **windows**, portions of the screen surrounded by a frame. You can run your favorite spreadsheet in one window and your favorite word processor in another.

With these operating environments, you can copy and move data between programs. For example, with Microsoft's Windows, you first select the part of the text that you want to copy or move. You then select the operating environment's *Cut* or *Copy* command to move or copy the selected text to the clipboard. You then switch to the other program, and use the *Paste* command to move the text from the clipboard to this program.

Three levels of compatibility determine how successfully programs will run with an operating environment like Windows.

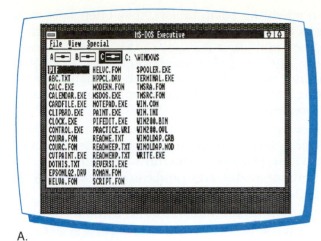

A.

B.

C.

FIGURE 2-9
Microsoft Windows
Microsoft Windows, a typical operating system environment, allows you to load more than one program into memory so that you can quickly switch between them. It also allows you to perform many operating system functions, like copying files without having to learn the cryptic commands usually required. The Windows screen (a) lists some of the programs that can be run. To run a program, you just select it from the menu. To use DOS commands, you highlight a file, and then pull down the File menu (b). When you select *Copy* from the menu, a dialog box appears where you enter the path you want to copy the file to (c).
Courtesy of Microsoft

■ DOS programs have their own unique ways of communicating with the keyboard and display monitor. For these programs to run under an operating environment, the publishers must provide utilities that allow them to do so. Even then, it is unlikely they will take advantage of all the operating environment's capabilities. For example, when these programs are run under an operating environment, they often take over the screen looking just as they do when they run on their own. Thus pull-down menus, windows, and other features of the operating environment cannot be used. When moved to the background, DOS programs often do not continue to function, so a database management program cannot be sorting a file in the background while you are working on a memo in the foreground.

- Operating-environment-aware programs use the same standard DOS commands as the operating environment to communicate with the monitor and keyboard. These programs will run successfully in the operating environment without modification and can take advantage of its many features like pull-down menus and windows.

- Operating-environment-specific programs cannot run without the integrating environment program, which becomes the operating system for these programs. These programs take full advantage of all features offered by the operating environment.

SUMMARY AND KEY TERMS

- **Portable operating systems** can be easily modified to run on other computers. **Proprietary operating systems** are designed to run on a single brand of computer.

- Typical operating systems include CP/M, MS-DOS and PC-DOS, Operating System/2, Apple DOS, and UNIX.

- OS/2 Standard Edition 1.1 includes a **Presentation Manager** that allows you to divide the screen into windows and execute commands from menus.

- Since DOS commands can be cryptic, **shells** have been developed that allow you to execute DOS commands by making menu selections.

- When improvements are made in an operating system, a new **version** is released. These new versions are usually compatible with earlier versions.

- **Singletasking operating systems** allow you to run one program at a time, whereas **multitasking operating systems** allow you to run more than one.

- When working with a singletasking operating system, you can simulate multiprocessing when using **memory resident programs**.

- **Operating system environments** are not actually operating systems but expand on them. For example, they have menus just like shells but also allow you to divide the screen into windows and to run more than one program even if the operating system is not multitasking.

REVIEW QUESTIONS

1. What is the basic difference between a portable and a proprietary operating system?
2. What is an operating system shell?
3. What is the difference between the OS/2 Standard Edition and Extended Edition?
4. What is the purpose of OS/2's Presentation Manager?
5. What is the purpose of OS/2's compatibility box?
6. What are versions of operating systems?
7. What is the difference between a singletasking and a multitasking operating system?
8. What is the purpose of an operating system environment like Windows?

Loading the Operating System and Executing Commands

OBJECTIVES

After completing this topic, you will be able to

- Explain the difference between a warm boot and a cold boot
- Describe how you load the operating system
- Describe the difference between an internal and external command
- Describe how you execute commands on command line operating systems and those with graphic interfaces
- List some basic operating system commands
- Describe the keys you press to print a record of your operating system sessions

To use an operating system's utilities, or to run an applications program, you must first load the operating system. This is called **booting** the system. Once the operating system is loaded, you can load your applications programs or use the operating system's commands to manage your files.

LOADING THE OPERATING SYSTEM

If you are already running an applications program, you do not have to boot the system to return to DOS since it is already in memory. You just use the applications program's *Quit* command, and that returns you to the operating system prompt. You can load the operating system from either a floppy disk that you insert into drive A (Figure 2-10) or from a hard disk. If loading it from a hard disk, be sure to open the door to drive A if it contains a disk so that the program does not try to load the operating system from that drive.

There are two ways to boot a computer system, depending on whether the computer is off or on.

- A **cold boot** means the computer is off and you turn it on.
- A **warm boot** means the computer is already on. You warm boot the system by inserting a disk with the necessary operating system files into drive A, closing the drive's door, and then pressing the keys specified by the computer's manufacturer. For example, on an IBM PC, you hold

FIGURE 2-10
Inserting the Operating System Disk into Drive A
Because computers always look to drive A first when you boot the system, you always insert the operating system disk into drive A when booting a floppy disk system. On a hard disk system, you leave the drive A door open so that the computer looks to the hard disk drive for the operating system files.

down **Ctrl** and **Alt** while pressing **Del**. This command clears all data from the computer's memory. Since it has almost the same effect as turning the computer off and then back on again, use it with caution.

When you boot the computer, the following happens:

1. The computer first executes a small program that is stored in ROM. This program instructs the computer to run diagnostic tests, which include checking the computer's memory to make certain it is operating correctly. If the computer finds a problem, it displays a message on the screen indicating where the problem is located.

2. Once memory is checked, the computer checks if a disk is in drive A. If it finds one, the program in ROM executes the two system programs on the disk. If it does not find a disk in drive A, it loads the two programs from the hard disk drive (drive C). (See *What Happens When You Format a Disk?* in Topic 2-7 for a more complete discussion of these two programs.)

3. Once the two system programs are executed, the computer looks for a program called COMMAND.COM and executes this program. This program contains the internal commands for the operating system. Executing the COMMAND.COM program loads a copy of the operating system into RAM. This program remains in RAM as long as the computer has power.

4. The computer next looks for a **batch file** on the disk called AUTO EXEC.BAT (see Topic 2-17). If this file is present, the computer executes whatever programs are listed there. If there is no AUTO EXEC.BAT file (and if there is no clock set by a command that is also in the batch file), the computer asks you to enter the date and time so that it can reset its internal clock. It is important to enter the date and time because the computer uses this information to date- and time-stamp your files. When you save a file, the computer automatically records the date and time. The date and time are helpful if you have several files containing the same document and you forget which is the most recent.

5. At last, the operating system is loaded. The screen display depends on the operating system that you are using.

Loading DOS

If you have loaded DOS 3.3 or an earlier version, the **system prompt** is displayed. It will be A> if you loaded from a floppy disk (Figure 2-11) or C> if you loaded from a hard disk. The system prompt tells you that you are in DOS and that the default, or active, disk drive is drive A or C. From this system prompt, you can execute DOS utility programs or start an applications program.

If you loaded DOS 4.0 or a later version, either the system prompt or the Start Program screen, called the Shell, is displayed (see Figure 2-5). If the Start Program screen is not displayed, you can display it any time the system prompt is on the screen by typing DOSSHELL and then pressing **Return**. From the Shell, you can execute DOS commands or load programs, or you can press **F3** to return to the system prompt.

Loading OS/2 with Presentation Manager

If you load OS/2 with Presentation Manager, the Presentation Manager screen is displayed (see Figure 2-7). You can also use the Presentation Manager to execute many of the most often used commands more easily. Presentation Manager has three components: Task Manager, Start Programs, and File System.

- Task Manager lists the programs currently running.
- Start Programs lists all programs on the disk. You can run any program just by selecting it from the list. You can run up to twelve OS/2 compatible programs and one DOS program. To start an OS/2 compatible program, you select its name from a list. To start a DOS program, you select *DOS Command Prompt* from the list (you must have requested DOS compatibility when you installed OS/2), and the system prompt appears on the screen so that you can execute DOS commands or run an applications program. This is called the compatibility box since it allows you to run programs that are compatible with DOS. The system prompt looks only slightly different from the DOS prompt. For example, it displays the C> prompt as C:\> and also displays a help message telling you to press **Ctrl-Esc** to return to the Program Selector or type HELP for help.
- File System lists files (or displays them with icons). You can copy or move them between directories by pointing to them with a mouse and dragging them to the appropriate directory.

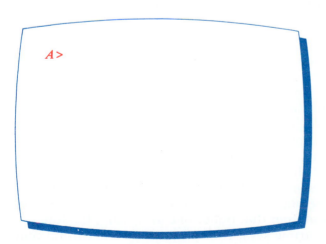

A>

FIGURE 2-11
The DOS Screen Display
When you load DOS 3.3 or earlier, the screen displays the system prompt.

EXECUTING COMMANDS

Once the operating system is loaded, you can use the operating system's commands or load an applications program (see Topic 3-3). When using operating system commands, you should understand the difference between internal and external commands. You should also know how to execute commands with the two basic types of operating system interfaces: command line interfaces, where you enter commands at the system prompt, and menu operated interfaces, where you execute commands by making choices from menus.

Internal and External Commands

Internal commands are built into the operating system, so they are available whenever the operating system prompt $A>$, $B>$, or $C>$ is displayed on the screen. Internal commands are automatically loaded into the computer's memory whenever you load DOS. They are contained in a file named COMMAND.COM.

External commands are stored in separate program files on the operating system disk until you need them. These commands are used less often than internal commands, so not loading them into memory until they are needed leaves room for other programs and data.

To use an external command, you must insert a disk with the necessary utility program on it into one of the disk drives. You then type the utility program's name and press **Return**. If the external command's utility program is on the disk in the default drive, you have to type only its name to execute the command. For example, let's say you want to use the CHKDSK command to check a disk in drive B (see Topic 2-13), and the operating system disk is in drive A. If the default drive is A, all you have to type is CHKDSK B: . But if the default drive is B, you have to type A: CHKDSK B: .

If you enter an external DOS command, and its program is not on the disk in the specified drive, the computer tells you it cannot find the command. When this occurs, check what commands are on the disk and if you specified the correct command. If you frequently use an external command, copy the appropriate program file from the DOS disk onto an applications program disk or your hard disk drive so that you do not have to swap disks when you need it.

Executing Commands from System Prompt Interfaces

When you work with DOS 3.3 or earlier, or display the command prompt when running DOS 4.0 or OS/2, one of the system prompts $A>$, $B>$, or $C>$ (or $A:\>$, $B:\>$, or $C:\>$ on OS/2) is displayed on the screen. When working with computers, you often encounter **prompts**, which are simply requests for you to supply the computer with information it needs. Some prompts, like the operating system prompt, are cryptic. Others are more helpful; for example, a prompt may ask *Do you want to save this file? (Y/N)*. To enter responses to these prompts, you type them, and then press **Return**. Additional prompts may appear on the screen during the execution of the command. You answer those prompts and sometimes press **Return**. When the command is finished executing, the system prompt reappears.

The commands you type when working with DOS are stored in a buffer. You can recall the command from that buffer to edit it using the function keys and the left and right arrow keys. DOS provides several editing commands that are executed by pressing function keys. These commands, described in Table 2-3, allow you to correct mistakes or repeat commands without having to retype the entire command.

Executing Commands from Menu Interfaces

On DOS 4.0's Shell and OS/2's Presentation Manager, many of the most frequently used commands are listed on menus. These menus have been developed to make the operating system easier to use. These systems display filenames, menus, dialog boxes, and icons so that you can execute commands without remembering cryptic commands and details on how to enter them. These interfaces can be operated either from the keyboard or with a mouse. When using a mouse, you can select filenames and drives by pointing to them and then clicking one or more of the mouse's buttons. You can then click on one of the pull-down menu commands to execute a command like copying or deleting the selected file(s). If using the keyboard, you press **F10** to pull down menus and make menu choices.

On DOS 4.0, to load the Shell, you type DOSSHELL from the system prompt, and then press **Return**. This displays the Start Program screen (see Figure 2-5).

■ You can select any of the choices, like *File System*, that are listed on the Group Contents part of the screen by highlighting them with the selection cursor and then pressing **Return**.

■ You can press **F10** to pull down the menus listed on the Action Bar at the top of the screen. You then select any command by highlighting it and pressing **Return** (or clicking on it with a mouse button). You can press **Esc** to cancel a command without executing it, or you can press **F3** to return to the system prompt (or to the Start Program screen from the File System).

TABLE 2-3 **Correcting Mistakes**	
Key	**Description**
Del	Deletes the current character from the buffer.
Esc	Cancels the editing up to that point and restores the buffer.
F1 or l	Advances and reveals one character from the buffer.
k	Moves back one character.
F3	Advances and reveals the remaining characters in the buffer. If you press this key after executing a command, the entire command reappears on the command line so that you can just press **Return** to execute it again. If you are using the same command over and over again, for example, to look at the directories on a series of disks you are inserting one after another into drive B, you do not have to keep retyping DIR B:. Just type it the first time, and then press **Return.** The next time, press **F3** to display the same command on the prompt line, and then press **Return** to execute it.
F5	Accepts the edited line and returns to the beginning for further editing.

If you are using DOS 4.0 or Presentation Manager, only the most often used commands are listed on the menus. But you can run commands that are not listed by running another copy of COMMAND.COM.

- On DOS 4.0, you select *Command Prompt* from the Start Program screen. This displays the system prompt. You can also press **Shift-F9** from any point in the Shell to do the same thing.

- On OS/2, you display the Start Program menu, and then select *OS/2 command line prompt*. If using a mouse, point to the command, and then click the mouse's button twice very quickly. If using the keyboard, press the arrow keys to highlight the command name, and then press **Return**. When the system prompt appears on the screen, enter the command(s) you want to run.

When finished with the command prompt, type EXIT and then press **Return** to remove the second copy of COMMAND.COM from memory and return to where you were before you displayed the system prompt.

Source and Target Drives

When executing commands, you should understand the source and target disks, drives, or directories. The **source** is the disk, directory, or file that you want the action performed on. The **target** is the disk, directory, or file that you want to be affected by the source. For example, when you want a listing of the files on a disk, that disk is the target disk. When you copy files from one disk to another, the disk you copy from is the source disk, and the disk you copy to is the target disk.

If you have only one floppy disk drive, specify the source drive as drive A and the target drive as drive B. The operating system will then prompt you to swap disks whenever it needs access to the source or target disk and it is not in the drive.

DOS UTILITY PROGRAMS

Normally, the operating system handles its functions without your direct involvement. But all operating systems include several built-in commands and separate utility programs that you must understand to manage your files. You use these commands and utility programs to prepare disks for use on the computer and to copy, rename, erase, and otherwise manage files you have saved on your disks. Although these commands are discussed in detail in the following topics, Table 2-4 lists many commonly used DOS and OS/2 commands. Here is how to read this table.

- **To Perform This Task** lists many tasks that you might want to perform.

- **At This Prompt** indicates the system prompt that should be on the screen when you perform the task. There are also ways to perform the same tasks with other prompts on the screen, as you will see in the topics in this part.

- **Insert This Disk Into Drive A** specifies the disk that should be in drive A when you first execute the command. Sometimes it specifies N/A, the DOS disk, a source disk, or a target disk. N/A means it does not matter what disk is in drive A. When it specifies the DOS disk, it means the command is a separate utility program (an external command) and not a utility program that is loaded with the rest of the operating system (an internal command). The source and target disks are the disks you want the task performed on.

TABLE 2-4
Summary of DOS and OS/2 Commands

To Perform This Task	At This Prompt	Insert This Disk Into Drive A	Insert This Disk Into Drive B	Type This Command and Press Return	See Topic
Display version of DOS in memory	A$, B$, or C$	N/A	N/A	VER	2-2
Display of change system date	A$, B$, or C$	N/A	N/A	DATE	2-2
Display of change system time	A$, B$, or C$	N/A	N/A	TIME	2-2
Clear the screen display	A$, B$, or C$	N/A	N/A	CLS	2-2
To change the default drive to A	B$ or C$	Any disk	N/A	A:	2-3
To change the default drive to B	A$ or C$	N/A	Any disk	B:	2-3
To change the default drive to C	A$ or B$	N/A	N/A	C:	2-3
Change to a new directory	B$ or C$	N/A	Target disk	CD\DIRECTORY	2-3
Return to root directory	B$ or C$	N/A	Target disk	CD\	2-3
Move up one level in directories	B$ or C$	N/A	Target disk	CD..	2-3
List files on disk in drive A	A$	Target disk	N/A	DIR, DIR/P, or DIR/W	2-4
	B$	Target disk	N/A	DIR A:, DIR A:/P, or DIR A:/W	2-4
List files on disk in drive B	A$	N/A	Target disk	DIR B:, DIR B:/P, or DIR B:/W	2-4
	B$	N/A	Target disk	DIR, DIR/P, or DIR/W	2-4
Display directories on disk	B$ or C$	N/A	Target disk	TREE	2-4
Display directories and files on disk	B$ or C$	N/A	Target disk	TREE/F	2-4
Send list of files on drive A to printer connected to LPT1	A$	Target disk	N/A	DIR A:>LPT1	2-4
Send list of files on drive A to file on disk in drive B	A$	Source disk	Target disk	DIR A:>B:FILENAME.EXT	2-3
Format a data disk in drive B	A$	DOS	Blank disk	FORMAT B:	2-6
Format a system disk in drive B	A$	DOS	Blank disk	FORMAT B:/S	2-7
Copy a single file from A to B	A$	Source disk	Target disk	COPY FILENAME.EXT B:	2-8
	B$	Source disk	Target disk	COPY A:FILENAME.EXT	2-8
Copy all files from A to B	A$	Source disk	Target disk	COPY *.*. B:	2-8
	B$	Source disk	Target disk	COPY A:*.*	2-8
Duplicate a disk in A to B	A$	DOS (then source)	Target disk	DISKCOPY A: B:	2-9
Compare the disks in A and B	A$	DOS (then source)	Target disk	DISKCOMP A: B:	2-10
Rename a file on a disk in drive A	A$	Target disk	N/A	RENAME A:OLDNAME.EXT NEWNAME.EXT	2-11
	B$	Target disk	N/A	RENAME A:OLDNAME.EXT A: NEWNAME.EXT	2-11
Erase a single file on disk in drive A	A$	Target disk	N/A	ERASE FILENAME.EXT	2-12
	B$	Target disk	N/A	ERASE A:FILENAME.EXT	2-12
Erase all files on disk in drive A	A$	Target disk	N/A	ERASE *.*	2-12
	B$	Target disk	N/A	ERASE A:*.*	2-12
Check the files on disk in drive B	A$	DOS	Target disk	CHKDSK B:	2-13
Make a new directory	B$ or C$	N/A	Target disk	MD\DIRECTORY	2-14
Display an ASCII text file on drive A	A$	Target disk	N/A	TYPE FILENAME.EXT	2-15
Display an ASCII text file on drive B	A$	N/A	Target disk	TYPE B:FILENAME.EXT	2-15
Print an ASCII text file on drive B	A$	DOS	Target disk	PRINT B:FILENAME.EXT	2-15
Create a batch file on disk in drive A	A$	Target disk	N/A	COPY CON FILENAME.BAT	2-17

- **Insert This Disk Into Drive B** specifies the disk that should be in drive B when you first execute the command.
- **Type This Command and Press Return** specifies the command that you type to perform the function. After typing the command, you press **Return** to execute it.
- **See Topic** lists the topic in Part Two where the command is discussed in detail.

PRINTING TEXT ON THE SCREEN

When working with DOS commands, you can make printouts of the information that appears on the screen. One command makes a "snapshot" of the screen, and the other prints all text that appears on the screen until you turn it off.

Capturing a Still Picture of the Screen

If you want to print the text on the screen, be sure the printer is on and has paper in it; then hold down **Shift** and press **PrtSc** (**Print Screen** on the IBM PC). This tells the computer to print whatever is on the screen. The computer freezes the screen, even in the middle of a procedure, and sends a copy of the image on the screen to the printer. This command sends the screen display as well as any text you have entered. As a result, many of the characters on the screen may not be printed correctly if they are not supported by your printer. While a printout is being made, the computer will not accept any additional input from the keyboard.

If you want to print graphics, you can use the GRAPHICS program that is included on the DOS disk for versions 2.0 and later. You must load this program into the computer's memory before loading your applications program. When you then hold down **Shift** and press **PrtSc**, the GRAPHICS program will send, or **dump**, the graphics that appear on the screen to the printer. But this works only with programs like Microsoft Excel, PageMaker, and Ventura Desktop Publisher that use a bit-mapped screen display (see Topic 1-6).

To advance the printed page out of your printer (since **Shift-PrtSc** does not automatically do so unless a page is filled)

1. Press the printer's on-line switch to take it off line.
2. Press the printer's form-feed switch to advance or eject the page.
3. Press the printer's on-line switch to put it back on line.

Capturing a Moving Picture of the Screen

If you want to have a running, printed record of what you are doing while working on the computer, hold down **Ctrl** and press **PrtSc** to send screen text to the printer. From then on, a copy of whatever the computer sends to

Useful DOS and OS/2 Commands

There are some useful commands that you can use when the system prompt is on the screen.

VER lists the version of the operating system currently in memory.

DATE displays the current date and a prompt that asks if you want to change it. If so, enter a new date, and then press **Return**. If not, just press **Return**. When you enter the date, you enter it with numbers for the day, year, and month and separate them with slashes or hyphens, for example, 12/05/89 or 12-05-89.

TIME displays the current time and a prompt that asks if you want to change it. If so, enter a new time, and then press **Return**. If not, just press **Return**. When you enter the time, you enter it with numbers for the hour and minutes and separate them with a colon, for example, 10:00. If you also want to display seconds and hundreds of seconds, add them to the end of the command separated by a period, for example, 10:00:05.00.

PROMPT allows you to change the prompt. For example, to display the current directory, type PROMPT PG and then press **Return**.

CLS clears the screen.

VOL displays the volume name on the disk, if any.

Ctrl-C cancels a command in progress.

the screen will also be sent to the printer. After executing this command, you can turn it off by holding down **Ctrl** and pressing **PrtSc** again.

This command works from DOS but does not work when most applications programs are displayed on the screen.

SUMMARY AND KEY TERMS

- Loading the operating system is called **booting** the system. If the computer is off, it is called a **cold boot**. If the system is already on, it is called a **warm boot**.

- DOS has **internal** and **external** commands. The internal commands are part of the COMMAND.COM file and are always available whenever the system prompt is displayed on the screen. External commands are stored in their own files. To use them, the file must be on a disk in one of the drives.

- When executing commands, the **source drive** is the drive that contains a file you want to manage. The **target drive** is the drive you want to copy it to.

- To capture a still picture of the screen on an IBM computer, you press **PrtSc**. To capture a moving picture, you press **Ctrl-PrtSc** (the same commands turn printing off).

REVIEW QUESTIONS

1. What does booting a computer mean?
2. What is the difference between a warm and a cold boot? How do you do each?
3. What is the basic difference between an internal and an external DOS command?

4. What does the *A*> prompt mean? The *B*> prompt?

5. Describe the source and target drives.

6. Why would you want to use the VER command to find out which version of DOS is in your computer's memory?

7. When typing DOS commands, do you have to be careful with the case of the letters you type?

8. What command do you use to change the system's date?

9. What command do you use to change the system's time?

10. What command do you use to change the system prompt?

11. Using Table 2-4 as a guide, match the DOS commands in column A with the function they perform in column B.

A	B
FORMAT	Displays an ASCII text file on the screen
COPY	Displays a list of files on the disk
DISKCOPY	Compares two disks
DISKCOMP	Copies two or more files
TYPE	Prints an ASCII text file
PRINT	Tells you if there are any noncontiguous sectors on a disk
CHKDSK	
DIR	Changes the name of a file
RENAME	Prepares a disk so that you can store data on it
FORMAT/S	Prepares a system disk that is self-booting
	Makes an exact duplicate of a disk

12. What command do you use to clear the screen?

13. Name and describe three function keys that can be used with DOS.

14. What command captures a still picture of the screen?

15. What command captures a moving picture of the screen?

16. What switch on the printer do you use to take the printer off line and then put it back on line?

17. What switch on the printer do you press to advance the paper to the top of the next sheet?

Specifying Drives and Directories

OBJECTIVES

After completing this topic, you will be able to

- Describe the difference between the default drive and other drives
- Describe the commands you use to change the default drive
- Explain the way hard disks are organized into directories and subdirectories and how to move between them
- Describe the command that you can use to change the system prompt
- Describe paths and explain how you specify them

Since most computers have two or more disk drives, you often must tell the computer which drive to use, or **address**. For example, you do this when you run a program or copy, save, or retrieve files. When addressing the drive, the operating system spins the disk in the drive so that it can read information from, or write information to, the disk.

THE DEFAULT AND OTHER DRIVES

When you first turn on your computer and load the operating system, drive A spins. If a disk in that drive contains the necessary operating system files, the operating system is loaded. Drive A operates because the computer's designers have placed a program in the computer's ROM telling it that it should address this drive when first turned on. Since it addresses drive A automatically, drive A is the **default drive** (Figure 2-12). The DOS system

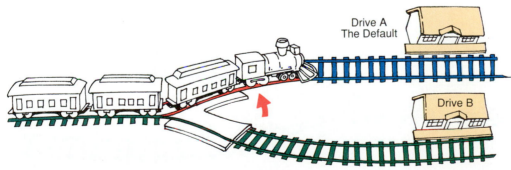

Drive A
The Default

Drive B

FIGURE 2-12
The Default Drive
The default drive is the drive the computer automatically addresses when you save and retrieve files. It's like a model railroad set where you can set a switch to send a train down one track or another.

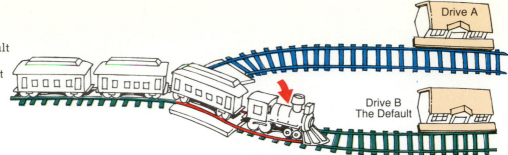

prompt indicating that drive A is the default drive is *A>*. On Presentation Manager, the drive A icon is highlighted to indicate the same thing.

Although you cannot change the default drive that the computer addresses when you first turn it on, you can, and often do, copy, rename, delete, and save files from a drive other than the default drive. There are two ways to do this: You can change the default drive, or you can specify the other drive in the command.

Changing the Default Drive

Whenever the operating system is on the screen, you can quickly change the default drive (Figure 2-13).

- To do so with the system prompt on the screen, type the letter of the drive, a colon (:), and then press **Return**. For example, to change the default drive from A to B, type B: and then press **Return**. The system prompt changes from *A>* to *B>*.

- From the DOS 4.0 Shell, you select *File System* from the Start Program screen, highlight the drive indicator, and then press **Return**. You can also hold down **Ctrl** and press the letter of the drive.

- From Presentation Manager, you use the mouse pointer to point to the drive icon that represents the drive that you want to be the default, and then click one of the mouse's buttons. If you are using Presentation Manager with the keyboard, you hold down **Ctrl** and press the letter of the drive. The default drive's icon is always highlighted on the screen.

Specifying the Other Drive

To copy a file to a drive other than the default drive, or to delete or rename a file on such a drive, you must specify the drive in the command (Figure 2-14). For example, if the default drive is set to A, and you want to copy a file

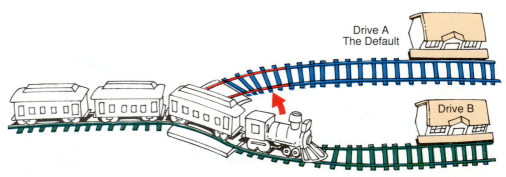

named LETTER on drive A to drive B, you would type either COPY A: LETTER B: or COPY LETTER B: . In the first command, you specified both drives, so the command reads "copy the file named LETTER in drive A to drive B." In the second command, you did not specify drive A. You do not have to because drive A is the default drive, and you never need to specify the default drive except as a precaution. This command reads "copy the file named LETTER in the default drive to drive B."

DIRECTORIES AND SUBDIRECTORIES

Most operating systems, including DOS and OS/2, are able to divide a hard disk into directories, which help you organize files on these disks. Imagine if you used a file drawer to store all of your memos, letters, and reports. Before long, the drawer would become so crowded that you could not find anything. But with a little organization and planning, the documents could be organized into folders, making it easier to locate the needed document (Figure 2-15).

A hard disk is like an empty drawer in a new filing cabinet: It provides a lot of storage space but no organization (Figure 2-16). To make it easier to find items in the drawer, you can divide it into categories with hanging folders. You can file documents directly into the hanging folders, or you can divide them into finer categories with manila folders. A **directory** is like a hanging folder, and a **subdirectory** is like a manila folder within a hanging folder. A file is a letter, report, or other document within either a directory or a subdirectory.

To work with directories, you have to know how to change the default directory or specify paths. Directories on a hard disk drive are organized in a hierarchy (Figure 2-17). The main directory, the one not below any other directories, is the **root directory**. Below it, several directories have been created. These directories can hold files or subdirectories.

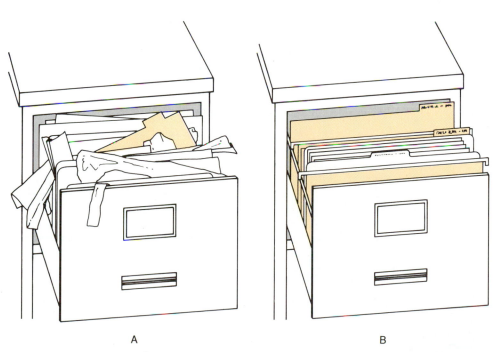

A

B

FIGURE 2-15
File Drawers
Unorganized file drawers make it difficult to find files when you need them (a). Organized file drawers make it easy to find the file you want (b).

FIGURE 2-16
Hard Disks
A new hard disk is like an empty file drawer (a). It has lots of room for files but no organization. You can divide the hard disk into directories, which is like dividing the file drawer with hanging folders (b). You can then subdivide the directories into smaller subdirectories, which is like dividing the hanging folders with manila folders (c). You can then save files in any of these subdirectories the same way you would file a document in one of the manila folders (d).

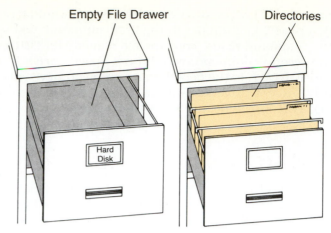

A. A new hard disk is like an empty file drawer. It has lots of room for files, but no organization.

B. You can divide the hard disk into directories, which is like dividing the file drawer with hanging folders.

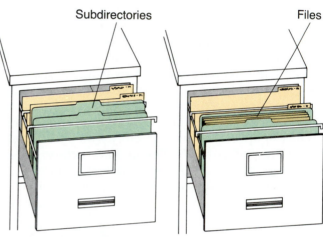

C. You can then subdivide the directories into smaller subdirectories, which is like dividing the hanging folders with manila folders.

D. You can then save files in any of these subdirectories the same way would file a document inone of the manila folders.

FIGURE 2-17
Directories
On the hard disk, directories and subdirectories are organized into a treelike hierarchy. The topmost directory is called the root directory. Directories below it are called directories. When directories are subdivided into additional directories, they are called subdirectories.

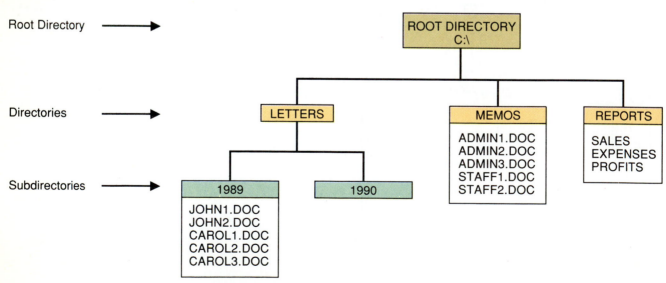

Root Directory ➡

Directories ➡

Subdirectories ➡

ROOT DIRECTORY C:

LETTERS

MEMOS
ADMIN1.DOC
ADMIN2.DOC
ADMIN3.DOC
STAFF1.DOC
STAFF2.DOC

REPORTS
SALES
EXPENSES
PROFITS

1989
JOHN1.DOC
JOHN2.DOC
CAROL1.DOC
CAROL2.DOC
CAROL3.DOC

1990

Changing Directories

To change default directories, you use the commands that move you through directories (Figure 2-18). To change directories from the system prompt, you use the CD (Change Directory) command. There are several versions of this command.

- To change the default directory, type CD\ the name of the drive and directory, and then press **Return**. For example, to make 1988 the default directory, type CD C:\ 1988 and then press **Return**.

- To return to the root directory, type CD\ and then press **Return**. For example, if you are in the 1988 directory, type CD\ and then press **Return**.

- To move up one level, type CD. . and then press **Return**. For example, if you are in the 1988 directory, type CD\ .. and then press **Return** to make LETTERS the default directory.

When changing directories, it is easy to get lost. It's claimed that in Maine, when someone from out of state asks directions, a native will respond, "If you don't know where you are, you don't belong here." The same is true of directories. To change the system prompt so that it displays the default directory, you type PROMPT PG (Figure 2-19).

When using DOS 4.0's Shell, you first display the File System screen. You then press **Tab** to move the selection cursor to the directory tree, highlight the desired directory, and then press **Return**.

Specifying Paths

When you are using a computer with a hard disk drive, you not only must specify a drive, you also must specify a default directory in many commands. This is essential because most hard disk drives are divided into directories to make them more manageable. Specifying the drive and directories is called specifying a **path** (Figure 2-20).

Paths are instructions to the program that tell it what subdirectory a file is located in. It is like telling someone that "the last letter to ACME Hardware is in the manila folder labeled ACME in the hanging folder labeled Hardware in the third file cabinet from the right." These precise instructions make it easy to locate the file.

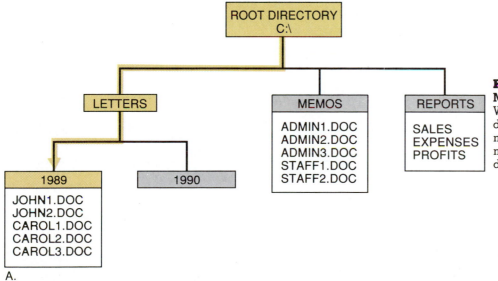

A.

FIGURE 2-18
Moving through Directories
When a hard disk contains directories, you can easily move between them to make any directory the default.

a. You change the default directory with the CD or CHDIR command. For example, to make the subdirectory 1989 the default directory, you type **CD\LETTERS\1989** and then press **Return**.

b. To move up one directory, for example, from 1989 to LETTERS, you type **CD..** and then press **Return**.

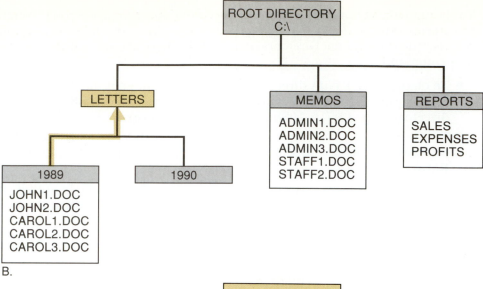

B.

c. To return to the root directory, for example, from 1989 to C:\, you type **CD** and then press **Return**.

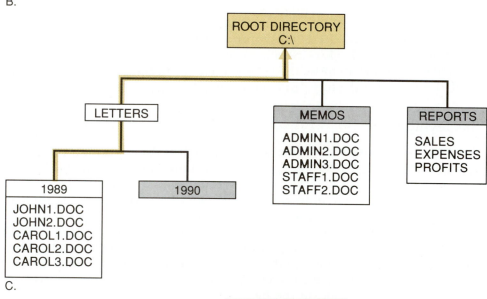

C.

d. To move between directories (c), type the complete path following the CD command. For example, to make the 1989 directory the default directory, you type **CD\LETTERS\1990** and then press **Return**.

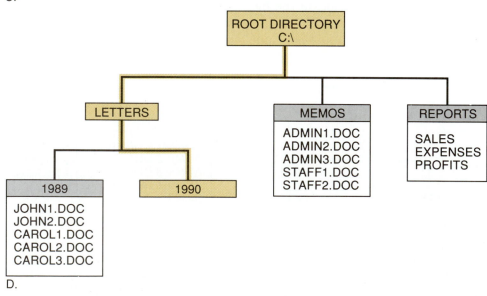

D.

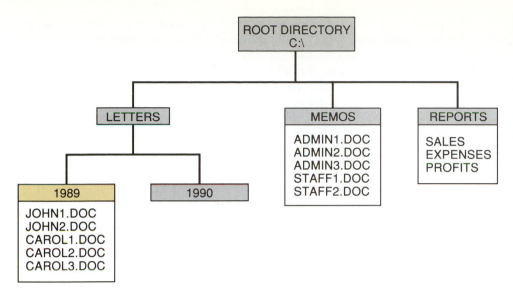

FIGURE 2-19
Changing the Prompt
If you type **PROMPT PG**
and then press **Return**, the
prompt changes to indicate
the default directory. For
example, when 1989 is the
default directory, the
prompt reads
C:\LETTERS\1989>.

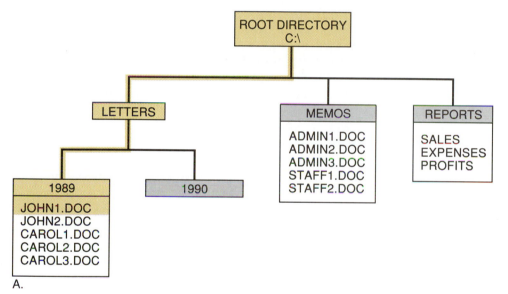

A.

FIGURE 2-20
Path
When a hard disk drive is
subdivided into a number
of directories and
subdirectories, you have to
specify paths. For
example, to specify a
specific file, you have to
specify the complete path.
(a) To specify the file
JOHN1.DOC, you specify
the path as
C:\LETTERS\1989\
JOHN1.DOC. (b) To specify
the file SALES, you specify
the path as
C:\REPORTS\SALES.

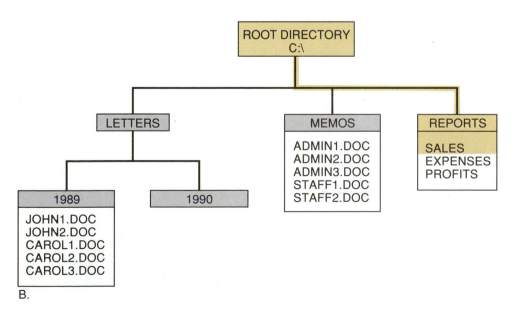

B.

To specify a path, you must indicate the drive, then the name of all subdirectories, and then the filename. All elements must be separated from one another by backslashes (\). For example, to copy a memo named JOHN.DOC from drive A to the MEMO subdirectory on drive C, you type COPY A:\ JOHN. DOC C:\ MEMO. To copy the same file to the LETTER subdirectory, you type COPY A:\ JOHN. DOC C:\ LETTER.

If you just type COPY A:\ JOHN. DOC C:\ the file is copied to the root directory on drive C. If you type COPY A:\ JOHN. DOC C: no slash following the C: command), the file is copied to the current default directory on drive C. The slash is always required to address the root directory.

SUMMARY AND KEY TERMS

- When specifying commands, you have to tell the program what drive to **address**. This spins the disk so that the data can be read into the computer or stored on the disk.

- The **default drive** is the drive the computer addresses unless you specify another drive.

- To change the default drive, you type its letter, a colon, and then press **Return**.

- To specify a drive other than the default, you must enter its address in the command. For example, to display a directory of the files on the default drive, you type DIR and then press **Return**. To display them on drive B, when that is not the default drive, you type DIR B: and then press **Return.**

- A hard disk drive can be divided into **directories** and **subdirectories**. The highest level directory is called the **root directory.**

- To change directories, you use the **CD** command. For example, to change to a directory named LETTERS, you type CD LETTERS and then press **Return**.

- To change the system prompt so that it always displays the current directory, you use the **PROMPT PG** command.

- When working on a hard disk drive, you must know how to specify **paths**. To do so, you specify the drive and any directories between the root directory and the file. For example, to copy a file on drive C from the directory LETTERS to the directory MEMOS, type COPY C:\ LETTERS\FILENAME C:\ MEMOS\.

REVIEW QUESTIONS

1. What is the default drive?
2. Using MS-DOS or PC-DOS, how do you change the default drive?
3. If you want to direct a file to a drive other than the default drive, how do you do so?
4. What is the topmost directory on a hard disk called?
5. What command do you use to change directories? What command to move up one level?
6. In the following examples, you are given the name of a file and the drive and directory it is stored on. Write out the path you would specify to direct the file to the indicated drive and directory.

Filename	Drive	Directory	Path
LETTER1.DOC	C	LETTERS	_____
LETTER2.DOC	D	1987	_____
LETTER3.DOC	C	Root Directory	_____

Assigning and Listing Filenames

OBJECTIVES

After completing this topic, you will be able to

- List the characters that you can use when assigning filenames
- Describe the commands that you use to display and print a list of files or directories on a disk

When working on a computer, you save your work in files on a disk. The operating system uses filenames to keep track of individual files. Here, we introduce you to filenames and how to list the names of files on your disks.

ASSIGNING FILENAMES

The files for the programs you use have already been assigned names. When you use these programs to create and save your own work, you must assign names to your files. The number and type of characters that you can use in a file's name are determined by the operating system you are using. Some operating systems are designed so that you can use long descriptive filenames. Others require you to use short cryptic names. For example, with DOS or OS/2, you can create filenames that have only eight characters and an optional period and three-character extension (Figure 2-21). The characters that are allowed are called **legal characters**, and they are listed in Table 2-5. Using any other character results in a name the computer will not accept.

You can type filenames in uppercase letters, lowercase letters, or a combination of uppercase and lowercase. If you do not use uppercase letters, the computer automatically converts your characters into uppercase.

Extensions are made up of a period (.) followed by up to three of the same characters that can be used for filenames. Often you do not enter the extension; the applications program you use enters it for you. As you use different programs, you will discover that each employs its own extension to identify files that it creates. The extension is also reserved for special uses. For instance, .EXE and .COM are used for program files, and .BAT is used for batch files (see Topic 2-17).

Each filename you use must be unique if the file is not stored on a separate disk or in a separate directory on a hard disk drive. If you assign the

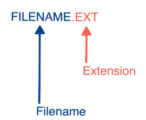

FIGURE 2-21
Filenames
Filenames have two parts, the filename and an extension.

TABLE 2-5

Characters That Can Be Used in Filenames

Characters	Examples
Letters	A through Z (uppercase or lowercase)
Numbers	0 through 9
Characters	! @ # $ % ^ & ( ) - _ { } ~ ´ `

same name and extension as a file that is already on the disk, the new file will overwrite the previous file and erase it. However, you can use the same filename with different extensions, for example, LETTER.DOC and LETTER .BAK. You can also use the same extension with different filenames.

LISTING FILES

Since a disk can hold many files, it is often necessary to find out what files are on a particular disk or in a particular directory. The names of the files on a disk are held in a directory. You can display the directory any time the operating system is on the screen.

To display files from the system prompt, you use the DIR command. Besides listing the filenames, the DIR command also displays

- The size of each file in bytes
- The date and time the file was last saved (useful only if you set the date and time each time you turn on the computer)
- The number of files on the disk
- How much free space is left on the disk

In its simplest form, the DIR command lists the directory of the disk in the default drive (Figure 2-22). For example, with the operating system A> prompt on the screen

- To list the files on the disk in drive A, type DIR or DIR A: and then press **Return**.
- To list the files on the disk in drive B, type DIR B: and then press **Return**.

FIGURE 2-22

Directory Listings
The DIR command lists all files on the disk or in the specified directory.

```
Volume in drive A has no label
Directory of A:\

COMMAND    COM    33612    5-15-87    3:20a
ANSI       SYS     1651    5-15-87    3:20a
ASSIGN     COM     1523    5-15-87    3:20a
ATTRIB     EXE     8234    5-15-87    3:20a
BACKUP     COM    17216    5-15-87    3:20a
CHKDSK     COM     9819    5-15-87    3:20a
COMP       COM     3241    5-15-87    3:20a
DISKCOMP   COM     5776    5-15-87    3:20a
DISKCOPY   COM     6224    5-15-87    3:20a
DRIVER     SYS     1350    5-15-87    3:20a
EDLIN      COM     7495    5-15-87    3:20a
FDISK      COM     6731    5-15-87    3:20a
MORE       COM      282    5-15-87    3:20a
PRINT      COM     8963    5-15-87    3:20a
RECOVER    COM     4284    5-15-87    3:20a
REPLACE    EXE     6354    5-15-87    3:20a
RESTORE    COM    16912    5-15-87    3:20a
SELECT     COM     4425    5-15-87    3:20a
SHARE      EXE     8544    5-15-87    3:20a
SORT       EXE     1898    5-15-87    3:20a
SUBST      EXE     9898    5-15-87    3:20a
SYS        COM     3751    5-15-87    3:20a
TREE       COM     7056    5-15-87    3:20a
VDISK      SYS     2831    5-15-87    3:20a
XCOPY      EXE     8308    5-15-87    3:20a
DIRLIST            1696    5-18-88    5:37a

    38 File(s)    99328 bytes free
```

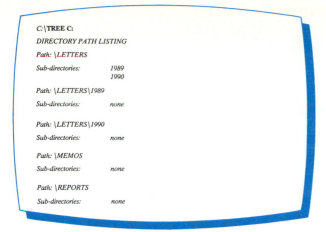

```
C:\TREE C:

DIRECTORY PATH LISTING

Path: \LETTERS

Sub-directories:         1989
                        1990

Path: \LETTERS\1989

Sub-directories:         none


Path: \LETTERS\1990

Sub-directories:         none


Path: \MEMOS

Sub-directories:         none


Path: \REPORTS

Sub-directories:         none
```

FIGURE 2-23
The TREE Command
The TREE command lists just the directories on the disk.

- To list the files in the subdirectory LETTERS, make that the default directory, type DIR and then press **Return**. You can also be in another directory and type DIR C: \LETTERS and then press **Return**.

If a list of files is too long to be displayed on the screen, some of the filenames will quickly scroll up and off the screen. Two commands prevent this: DIR/W and DIR/P. The /W and /P following the command are called **switches** and modify the basic command.

- The /W switch tells the DIR command to display the files horizontally instead of vertically. DIR/W drops the file size, date, and time information to make room for a horizontal listing of filenames. Because only the filenames are displayed and they are arranged horizontally on the screen, many filenames can be displayed on the screen at one time.

- The /P switch tells the DIR command to display files until the screen is full. To display additional files, simply press any key. Since most screens can display only twenty-three filenames, DIR/P is useful when more than twenty-three files are on a disk. If you use the regular DIR command, the topmost filenames scroll off the screen too quickly to read them.

When you want a list of your hard disk's organization, you use the TREE command (Figure 2-23). When you want a list of the directories, and the files they contain, you use the TREE/F command (Figure 2-24). This com-

FIGURE 2-24
The TREE/F Command
The TREE/F command lists directories and files on the disk.

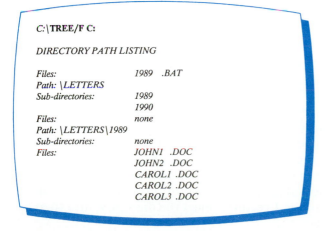

```
C:\TREE/F C:

DIRECTORY PATH LISTING

Files:                  1989   .BAT
Path: \LETTERS
Sub-directories:        1989
                        1990
Files:                  none
Path: \LETTERS\1989
Sub-directories:        none
Files:                  JOHN1  .DOC
                        JOHN2  .DOC
                        CAROL1 .DOC
                        CAROL2 .DOC
                        CAROL3 .DOC
```

```
Path: \LETTERS\1990
Sub-directories:        none
Files:                  none
Path: \MEMOS
Sub-directories:        none
Files:                  ADMIN1 .DOC
                        ADMIN2 .DOC
                        ADMIN3 .DOC
                        STAFF1 .DOC
                        STAFF2 .DOC

Path: \REPORTS
Sub-directories:        none
Files:                  SALES
                        EXPENSES
                        PROFITS
```

TABLE 2-6
Sorting Directory Listings

To Sort By	Type
Filename	DIR : SORT or DIR B: : SORT
Extension	DIR : SORT/+10 or DIR B: : SORT/+10
File size	DIR : SORT/+14 or DIR B: : SORT/+14
Date	DIR : SORT/+24 or DIR B: : SORT/+24

mand, unlike the DIR command, lists files in all directories, not just the one you specify.

You can also list files so that they are sorted. To do so, you use the SORT command. SORT is an external command, so it must be on the disk when you use this command. Table 2-6 describes the versions of the command that you can use to sort directory listings.

If you are using DOS 4.0 or Presentation Manager, files in the current directory are automatically listed whenever the Filing System Directory Tree is displayed on the screen. To display a list of files on another drive, or in another directory, make that drive or directory the default. To sort the list of files on DOS 4.0, you pull down the Options menu, and then select *Display Options*.

PRINTING OR STORING LISTS OF FILES

When you use the DIR command, you can use the DOS and OS/2 redirection feature to print the directory or store it in a disk file for future reference.

Storing a Directory Listing in a Disk File

When storing the list in a file, there are two redirection characters that you can use when entering the command from the system prompt. The > character stores the list in a file and erases the file's previous contents, if any. The >> characters append the list to the end of the specified file. For example, to store the directory listing in a file named DIRLIST, type DIR> DIRLIST and then press **Return**. To append the directory listing of another disk or directory to the end of the same file, type DIR>>DIRLIST and then press **Return**. You can retrieve the file with any applications program that can read ASCII text files. You can also display it on the screen with the TYPE command or print it with the PRINT command (see Topic 2-16).

Printing a Directory Listing

You can also redirect the listing to the printer so that you have a file copy. To do so from the command line, turn on the printer, type DIR>LPT1 and then press **Return**.

If you are using Presentation Manager, you can print a listing of the files in either the current directory or any other directory listed on the screen. To print the current directory, press **Spacebar** so that no files are selected. (Or hold down **Shift**, point to the previously selected item, and then click the mouse button.) Select *File* to pull down the menu, select *Print* to display a dialog box that lists the selected or current directory, and then select *OK*. To print a list of the files in another directory, select the directory, and then use the same menu commands.

- **Filenames** on DOS computers can have eight characters and a three-character **extension** (separated from the filename by a period).

- You can use only **legal** (that is, allowable) characters in a filename. Characters that you cannot use are **illegal**.

- The command you use to list the files on a disk is **DIR**, which is an internal command.

- To display a long list of filenames, you can follow the DIR command with **switches**. For example, **DIR/W** displays filenames across the screen, and **DIR/P** displays a screenful of names and then stops until you press a key to continue.

- To display a list of directories on a hard disk drive, you use the **TREE** command. To display a list of directories and the files they contain, you use the **TREE/F** command.

- To sort a list of files displayed with the DIR command, you use the **SORT** command. For example, to display the files on drive B sorted by filename, you type DIR B: :SORT and then press **Return**.

- To send a list of filenames to a file on the disk, you use the > **redirection character**. For example, to store a list of filenames in a file named FILENAME, you type DIR>FILENAME and then press **Return**.

- To send a list of files to the printer, you use the same redirection character (>). For example, to print the filenames on a printer attached to the LPT1 port, you type DIR>LPT1 and then press **Return**.

1. Why do you have to give a file a name?

2. What are the two parts of a filename called? How many characters are allowed for each part? What are the parts separated with?

3. Indicate whether the filenames listed below are legal or illegal on a PC-DOS or MS-DOS system.

FILENAME.DOC	_____ Legal	_____ Illegal
FILE/DOC	_____ Legal	_____ Illegal
LETTER.DOCUMENT	_____ Legal	_____ Illegal
DOCUMENTS.DOC	_____ Legal	_____ Illegal
MEMO JOHN.DOC	_____ Legal	_____ Illegal
MEMO^5.DOC	_____ Legal	_____ Illegal
99999.999	_____ Legal	_____ Illegal
2	_____ Legal	_____ Illegal
2_2	_____ Legal	_____ Illegal

4. Is the DIR command an internal or external command?

5. What information does the DIR command give you in addition to a list of filenames?

6. If drive A is the default drive, what command do you use to display a list of files on the disk in that drive? In drive B?

7. If drive B is the default drive, what command do you use to display a list of files on the disk in that drive? In drive A?

8. What is a switch?

9. What switch do you use to display filenames horizontally across the screen?

10. What switch do you use to display filenames a page at a time?

11. What command do you use when you want to display the directories on a hard disk? When you want to display both the directories and the files?

12. What command do you use when you want to sort files in the directory?

13. What is the name of the character that you use to direct the list of files to the printer of a file? What is the character?

TOPIC 2-5

Specifying More Than One File

OBJECTIVES

After completing this topic, you will be able to

- Explain how to specify files with wildcards and what they do
- Describe how to select files with Presentation Manager

In many operating system commands, you specify the name of a file. Frequently, however, you want to work with groups of files. For example, when making a backup disk, you might want to copy all the files from one disk to another. Instead of copying one file at a time, you can copy several files at once.

When entering commands from the system prompt, you specify groups of files using wildcards. A **wildcard** is simply a character that stands for one or more other characters, much like a wildcard in a card game. DOS and OS/2 wildcards are the question mark (?) and the asterisk (*).

The question mark can be used to substitute for any single character (Figure 2-25).

- BOO?.EXE will stand for any filename that has four characters and that begins with BOO, followed by a single character and the extension .EXE, for example, BOOT.EXE or BOOK.EXE.
- BO??.EXE will stand for any filename that has four or fewer characters and that begins with BO, followed by any two characters and the extension .EXE, for example, BOOT.EXE or BORE.EXE.
- B??.??? will stand for any filename that has three or fewer characters and that begins with B, followed by any extension of three or fewer characters, for example, BAD.PRT or BO.DOC.
- ????.??? will stand for any filename that has four or fewer characters, followed by any extension of three or fewer characters (including no extension), for example, LOV.EX, TEXT, TEXT.1, EYE.DOC, WORD.CH6, NAME.LST, or READ.ME.

The asterisk is more powerful; it represents any character in a given position and all following characters (Figure 2-26).

- *.* will stand for any filename with any extension.

176

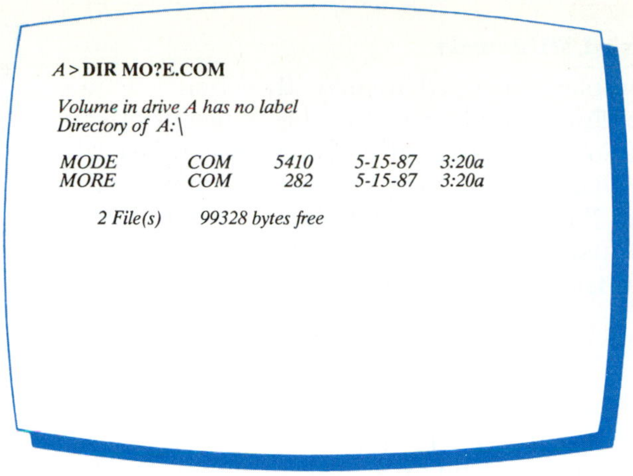

FIGURE 2-25

```
A > DIR MO?E.COM

Volume in drive A has no label
Directory of A:\

MODE      COM     5410    5-15-87   3:20a
MORE      COM      282    5-15-87   3:20a

    2 File(s)    99328 bytes free
```

FIGURE 2-25
The Question Mark Wildcard
The question mark wildcard stands for a specific character in the position of the question mark. For example, typing the command DIR MO?E.COM and then pressing **Return** displays the two files shown here.

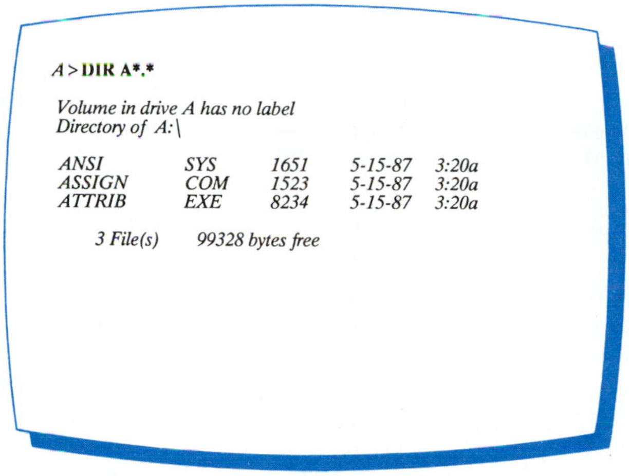

```
A > DIR A*.*

Volume in drive A has no label
Directory of A:\

ANSI      SYS     1651    5-15-87   3:20a
ASSIGN    COM     1523    5-15-87   3:20a
ATTRIB    EXE     8234    5-15-87   3:20a

    3 File(s)    99328 bytes free
```

FIGURE 2-26
The Asterisk Wildcard
The asterisk wildcard stands for any group of characters from the position of the asterisk to the end of the filename or the end of the extension. For example, typing the command A*.* and then pressing **Return** lists all files that begin with the letter A.

- B*.* will stand for any filename that begins with B, followed by any extension, for example, BOOT.SYS or BOTTLE.DOC.
- B*.EXE will stand for any filename that begins with B, followed by the extension .EXE, for example, BRAIN.EXE or BYLAWS.EXE.
- *.EXE will stand for any filename with the extension .EXE, for example, GRAPHICS.EXE or INCOME.EXE.

When using DOS 4.0's Shell, you display the File System screen, and then press **Tab** to move the selection cursor to the *File List*. You select and unselect individual files by highlighting them and then pressing **Spacebar**. You can also select and unselect all files by pulling down the File menu and then selecting *Select all* or *Deselect all*.

When using Presentation Manager, you select one or more files as follows:

- If using a mouse, you hold down **Shift**, and click the files you want to select.
- If using the keyboard, you press the arrow keys or type the first character in the filename. If more than one file begins with the same letter, press that letter repeatedly until the appropriate file is selected. To unselect a filename, press **Spacebar**. To select a group of adjacent files, select the first, hold down **Shift**, and then press the arrow keys to high-

> ### Previewing the Effects of Wildcards
> Wildcards can cause problems if used incorrectly when you are copying or deleting files. For example, you can delete files that you did not intend to delete. For this reason, it is always wise to use the DIR command with the wildcards you plan on using to preview the files that will be affected. For example, if you plan to delete all files with the extension .BAK using the command DEL *.BAK, first type DIR *.BAK to display a list of the files that would be deleted.

light additional files. To select nonadjacent files, hold down **Ctrl**, and press the arrow keys to move a dotted box over the filename. Release **Ctrl**, and press **Spacebar** to select the file. Repeat this command to select additional files.

SUMMARY AND KEY TERMS

- To specify more than one filename in a command on DOS computers, you use **wildcards**.
- The **question mark** wildcard stands for any character in the position you enter it in.
- The **asterisk** wildcard stands for any character in the position you enter it in and all the characters that follow in either the filename or the extension.

REVIEW QUESTIONS

1. What are wildcards used for?
2. What two wildcards are used with MS-DOS and PC-DOS? Describe what each does.
3. What are the advantages of using wildcards? What are the potential disadvantages?
4. If you are using commands that erase or copy files, how can you preview the results the commands will have?

Formatting Data Disks

OBJECTIVES

After completing this topic, you will be able to

- Describe how to format a disk you save files on
- Understand the importance of labeling your disks
- Explain why you label your disks

When you buy new blank disks to store your data files, they usually have to be prepared to run on your computer. (The only exception is when disks are made to run with a particular computer such as the Apple Macintosh.) Most disks are designed to be used on numerous computers. Since many computers and their operating system use different methods to save files, the blank disks must be customized for each type of system. This process is called **formatting**. (To see what happens when you format a disk, see *What Happens When You Format a Disk?* in Topic 2-7.)

The FORMAT command completely erases any data on a disk. You therefore must be careful with this command. You should never format a previously used disk or a program disk unless you are sure you will not need any of the files on it. You also should never format a hard disk drive unless you are willing to lose every file on the disk.

To format a disk, insert the DOS disk into drive A, or change to the directory that contains the FORMAT utility program. Type FORMAT and then press **Return**. For example, to format a disk in drive B on a floppy disk system, insert the DOS disk into drive A. Type A: and then press **Return** to make drive A the default drive. Type FORMAT B: and then press **Return**. A prompt asks you to insert the disk to be formatted. Insert the disk to be formatted into drive B, and then press the designated key to continue. A message tells you the disk is being formatted. In a few moments, a message tells you the formatting is completed and asks if you want to format another disk (Figure 2-27). If so, insert another disk, and then press Y to continue. If not, press N.

When formatting disks from the system prompt, you can use the FORMAT command or add switches to control the type of format.

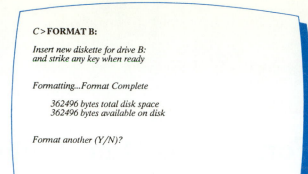

FIGURE 2-27
DOS 3.3 Format Complete Message
When a disk has been formatted, the formatting complete message appears on the screen. The message indicates the total disk space, the number of bad sectors (if any), and the space available on the disk.

- You can add a volume name that identifies the disk. The volume name is displayed when you use the DIR command. You can also display the volume name with the LABEL command (an internal command) from the system prompt. To format a disk and add a volume name, type FORMAT B: /V instead of FORMAT. When you add the /V option, a prompt appears asking you to enter the volume name. Type a name up to eleven characters long, and then press **Return**.

- To format a disk in a high-capacity drive (one that can store 1.2MB on a disk), type FORMAT/4. This command formats a disk so that you can use it to store files on a regular 360KB drive. You can also use it in the high-capacity drive, but you can only store 360KB of data, not 1.2MB.

Labeling Your Disks

An unwritten rule among computer users is that an unlabeled disk contains no valuable files. People often do not take the time to check an unlabeled disk to see what files, if any, it contains. Thus the first step when you use a disk is to label it. Always write the disk title, your name, the date, and the operating system version that you are using on the labels.

> Program Disk -- Duplicate
> Name: John Smith
> Date: 1/10/88   Format: DOS 3.3

Be sure also to fill out labels before you affix them to the disks. If you write on a label that is already on a disk, you can damage the disk if you press down too hard. If you must write on a label that is already on a disk, use a felt-tip pen, and write very gently. Do not apply pressure.

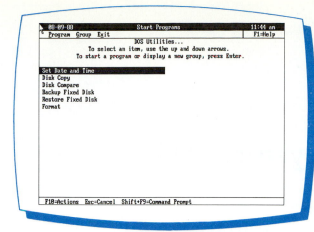

FIGURE 2-28
The DOS 4.0 DOS Utilities Screen
The DOS Utilities screen lists the commands that affect the disk as a whole.

When using DOS 4.0's Shell, you select *DOS Utilities* from the Start Programs Main Group, and then select *Format* from the DOS Utilities Main Group (Figure 2-28). This displays a pop-up box in which you enter the letter of the drive that contains the disk you want to format. For example, to format the disk in drive B, you type B: and then press **Return**.

■ To use a new disk on your computer, you must first format it with the **FORMAT** command. This is an external command.

■ You can use switches following the FORMAT command. For example, to add a volume name to a disk being formatted in drive B, type FORMAT B: /V and then press **Return**. To format a disk on a high-capacity drive so that it can be read by a regular 360KB drive, type FORMAT B: /4 and then press **Return**.

■ After formatting a disk, you should always label it.

SUMMARY AND KEY TERMS

1. Why do you format a disk?
2. What command do you use to format a disk?
3. Why must you be careful when using the command?
4. What would you do if you found an unlabeled disk in the computer lab? Would you use it for your own files or try to find out whose it is?
5. Why should you write out a label before you stick it onto a disk?

REVIEW QUESTIONS

TOPIC 2-7

Formatting System Disks

OBJECTIVES

After completing this topic, you will be able to

- Describe how to format a disk you save program files on so that it is self-booting

- Explain what happens when you format a disk

Most applications program disks can be set up so that when you turn on the computer with a program disk in drive A, the computer automatically starts the program you want. But as you have seen, most disks are not shipped with the operating system files that make this possible. If you turn on the computer with one of these disks in drive A, an error message will tell you that it is a nonsystem disk and ask you to replace it and then press a specified key to continue.

When you want to load a program without first having to load the operating system from another disk, you format the program disk as a system disk. The command you use to do this is a version of the FORMAT command. Disks formatted in this way are called **self-booting** disks because both the operating system and the program can be loaded from the same disk.

To format a system disk, you add the /S switch to the FORMAT command. For example, to format a disk in drive B as a system disk, insert the operating system disk into drive A (or change to the directory that contains the FORMAT utility program), type FORMAT B: /S and then press **Return**. A prompt asks you to insert the disk to be formatted into drive B. Insert the disk to be formatted into drive B, and then press the designated key to continue.

The FORMAT/S command tells the operating system to copy the system files to the disk in drive B. Like the FORMAT command, the FORMAT/S command completely erases any data on a disk. You should never use this command to format an original program disk or any disk that contains files you do not want to lose. You also should never format a hard disk drive unless you are willing to lose every file on the disk.

Although the FORMAT/S command completely erases any data on a disk, there are times when you want to transfer the system files to an applications program disk that already contains files. You can do so without reformatting the disk and erasing files by using the SYS command. This command transfers the operating system files IBMBIO.COM, IBMDOS .COM, and COMMAND.COM to a disk that was previously formatted to receive them (with either the FORMAT/S or the FORMAT/B command, which

What Happens When You Format a Disk?

The FORMAT command tries to write combinations of 0s and 1s to the surface of the disk and then read that data back. This enables the computer to detect any area of the disk surface that is not usable. Here is what happens when you format a disk.

1. When you execute the FORMAT command, the disk drive clamps the disk to be formatted and begins to spin it.

2. The disk drive's photoelectric cell finds the sector hole in the disk. It uses the sector hole as a reference point.

3. Once the drive is oriented, it begins to magnetically mark tracks and sectors on the disk's surface. It divides the disk into tracks and sectors, an invisible magnetic pattern that looks something like a dart board (Figure 2-29). This breaks the disk's surface into smaller sections so that it is easier to locate and store data. Without these smaller sections, the drive would have the same problem a letter carrier would have trying to deliver a letter addressed to Chicago, Illinois. Tracks run in concentric rings around the disk, and sectors radiate from the center in pie-shaped wedges. The number of tracks affects the amount of data that can be stored on the disk. For example, DOS 2.0 and later versions create 40 sectors on a 5¼-inch disk. Each track is divided into 9 sectors for a total of 360 sectors (40 × 9 = 360). Each sector is designed to hold 512 bytes of data. It also checks the disk surface for unusable spots. If it finds any bad sectors, it marks them so that data is not stored on them.

4. Finally, the computer assigns specific functions to the first few sectors on the first track. The first sector on a system disk (sector 0) is reserved for the boot record, which is used by the operating system and other programs to load themselves. This is not needed on a disk that will just be used to store data from applications programs you use, but the FORMAT command always leaves room for it anyway. The file allocation table (FAT) is used by the operating system to keep a record of which tracks and sectors have been assigned to which files and the order in which they should be read, which sectors are bad, and which are free. Because the FAT is so important, two copies are kept, one in sectors 1 and 2 and the second in sectors 3 and 4. Without this table, the operating system would not be able to locate any files on the disk when it was asked to retrieve them. Finally, the next seven sectors are used for a directory for filenames and related information.

5. Once the disk is formatted, the message reads *362496 bytes total disk space*. But a disk holds 368,640 bytes, so what happened to the missing 6144 bytes? As the table shows, the missing bytes hold the housekeeping items just described.

Sectors	Use
0	Boot area
1-4	FAT
5-11	Directory
12-719	User's data

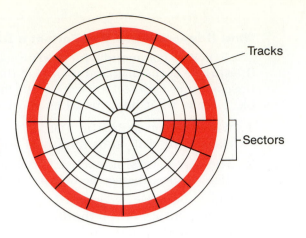

FIGURE 2-29
Formatted Disk
One way to visualize a formatted disk is as a dart board. Tracks run in circles around the disk. The number of tracks per inch determines the density of the disk and the amount of data that can be stored on it. A high-density disk has more tracks per inch than a low-density disk and can therefore store more data. Since tracks can store a great deal of data, the computer divides them into sectors, which makes it easier to find a location on the disk. These sectors are like pie-shaped wedges that radiate from the center of the disk. Each track is divided into the same number of sectors. When playing darts, you try to place the dart into the appropriate track and sector. Your computer does the same thing; it looks for a free sector in the first track to store data and later looks to that same sector to retrieve the data.

reserves room for the files but does not copy them). This command does not erase any of the files on the disk other than the operating system files if they were previously copied there. This command is also useful when you want to update the version of the operating system on an existing disk. To use this command from the system prompt, insert the DOS disk into drive A, and then close the drive's door. Type A: and then press **Return** if necessary to make drive A the default drive. Type SYS B: and then press **Return**. In a moment, a message tells you that the system files were transferred, and the system prompt reappears. If you get the message *No room*, the program disk was not formatted as a system disk. Format a blank disk as a system disk, and then copy the program's files to the new disk.

When using DOS 4.0's Shell, you select *DOS Utilities* from the Start Programs Main Group, and then select *Format* from the DOS Utilities Main Group. This displays a pop-up box in which you enter the letter of the drive that contains the disk you want to format and add any parameters (like /S). For example, to format the disk in drive B as a system disk, you type B: /S and then press **Return**.

SUMMARY AND KEY TERMS

- A disk that you can use to load both the operating system and an applications program is called a **self-booting disk** or a **system disk**. It contains the necessary operating system files.

- The command you use to format a disk as a system disk is **FORMAT/S**. This is an external command.

- To transfer the operating system files to a disk without formatting it, you use the **SYS** command. To use this command, the target disk must have been formatted so that there is room for the operating system files.

- When you format a disk, it is divided into concentric **tracks** and pie-shaped **sectors.**

REVIEW QUESTIONS

1. What is the difference between a system disk and a data disk?
2. Why would you want to copy the operating system files to an applications disk?
3. What files are copied to a system disk?
4. Why is DOS not already on a program disk when you buy it?
5. What command do you use to transfer system files to a disk without formatting the disk and erasing the files already on it? Can you do this with any disks?
6. When you format a disk, what does DOS do to the disk?

OPERATING SYSTEMS

Copying Files

OBJECTIVES

After completing this topic, you will be able to

- Describe how to copy one or more files
- Explain why you write-protect disks that you are copying from

When you want a copy of one or more files, you use the COPY command (an internal command). This command copies one or more specified files from a disk in one drive or directory to a disk in another drive or directory. The COPY command is often used to make backup copies of important files.

When you use the COPY command, you must specify three things.

1. What is to be copied—the files
2. Which disk they are to be copied from—the source disk
3. Which disk they are to be copied to—the target disk

When specifying the source and target, you must specify the path and filename (Figure 2-30). For example, with the operating system A> prompt on the screen, the disk that files are being copied from in drive A, and the disk that files are being copied to in drive B

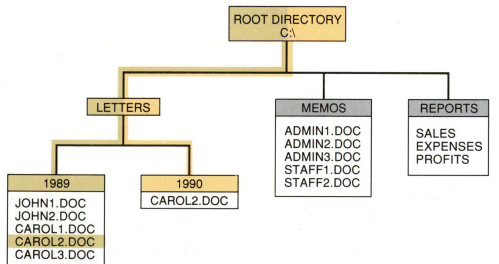

FIGURE 2-30
Copying Files Between Directories
When you want to copy a file from one directory to another, you must indicate the drive, the name of the subdirectory, and the filename. All three must be separated from one another by backslashes (\). For example, to copy the file named JOHN1.DOC from the 1989 subdirectory to the 1990 subdirectory, you type COPY C:\LETTERS\CAROL2.DOC C:\LETTERS\1990 and then press **Return**.

- To copy a file named FILENAME.EXT, type COPY A:FILENAME.EXT B: and then press **Return**.
- To copy a file named LETTER.DOC to a directory named LETTERS on drive C, type COPY LETTER.DOC C:\LETTERS and then press **Return**.

When used from the system prompt, you can also use wildcards to copy more than one file.

- To copy all files, type COPY A:*.* B: and then press **Return**.
- To copy all files named with the extension .EXT, type COPY A:*.EXT B: and then press **Return**.

If you are using DOS 4.0's Shell, you first display the File System screen and select the file(s) to be copied. You then pull down the File menu and select *Copy* to display a pop-up box. You enter the path and filename where you want the file copied, and then press **Return**.

SUMMARY AND KEY TERMS

- The command you use to copy files is **COPY**, an internal command.
- You can use wildcards to copy groups of files. For example, COPY A:*.* B: copies all files on the disk in drive A to the disk in drive B.
- When copying files, you should **write-protect** the source disk.

REVIEW QUESTIONS

1. What command do you use to copy files?
2. Is the command an internal or external command?
3. When the default drive is set to A, and you want to copy a file named FILENAME.EXT from drive A to drive B, what command do you enter?
4. When the default drive is set to A, and you want to copy a file named FILENAME.EXT from drive B to drive A, what command do you enter?
5. What is the purpose of the write-protect notch on a floppy disk? What can you do when it is covered with tape, and what can you not do? What can you do when it is not covered?
6. Why would you not use a piece of clear tape to cover the write-protect notch?
7. If you want to make a copy of a file on the same disk as the original file, can you use the same name for both files?

Duplicating Disks

OBJECTIVES

After completing this topic, you will be able to

- Describe how to make a duplicate of a disk
- Explain the differences between a disk that has been copied and one that has been duplicated

As you have seen, you can use the COPY command with wildcards to copy all the files from one disk to another to make a backup copy. The DISKCOPY command (an external command) also lets you make a backup copy of a disk. So why are there two commands to do the same thing?

- The DISKCOPY command does not require you to format the disk you are copying the files to. The DISKCOPY command automatically formats the disk before it begins to copy the files. This means you cannot use this command to copy files to a disk that already contains files unless you want to erase the existing files.
- The COPY command does not make an exact duplicate of a disk. It copies the files but not their exact location on the disk. When you want to make an exact duplicate of a disk, use the DISKCOPY command. If a disk is full and files are stored in noncontiguous sectors (see Topic 2-10), it takes the drive longer to save and retrieve them. The COPY *.* command will copy them so that they are all on contiguous sectors, but the DISKCOPY command will not. If you are making backup copies, it is better to use the COPY *.* command.

To duplicate a disk from the system prompt, insert the operating system disk into drive A, type DISKCOPY A: B: and then press **Return**. A prompt asks you to insert the source and target disks (Figure 2-31). Insert the source disk (the one you are copying from) into drive A. (Write-protect it so that you do not inadvertently erase it.) Insert the target disk (the one you are copying to) into drive B, and then press the specified key to continue. When the first disk is duplicated, a prompt asks if you want to duplicate more. Press the specified keys to quit or continue.

When using DOS 4.0's Shell, you select *DOS Utilities* from the Start Programs Main Group, and then select *Disk Copy* to display a pop-up box. You enter the source and target drives, and then press **Return**.

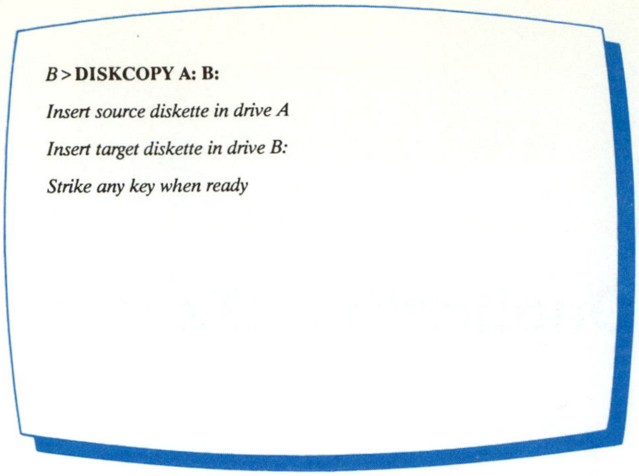

> *B* > **DISKCOPY A: B:**
>
> *Insert source diskette in drive A*
>
> *Insert target diskette in drive B:*
>
> *Strike any key when ready*

FIGURE 2-31
DOS 3.3 DISKCOPY Prompt
The DISKCOPY prompt
asks you to insert the
source disk (the disk you
are copying from) and the
target disk (the disk you
are copying to).

SUMMARY AND KEY TERMS

- The command you use to duplicate a disk is **DISKCOPY**, an external command.
- DISKCOPY makes an exact bit-by-bit duplicate disk.

REVIEW QUESTIONS

1. What command do you use to duplicate disks?
2. Is the command an internal or external command?
3. When would you not want to use the command?
4. What are the differences between this command and the COPY *.* command?
5. Why is it preferable to use the COPY command when making a backup copy of files?

Comparing Disks

OBJECTIVE

After completing this topic, you will be able to

■ Describe the command you use to compare two disks to see if they are identical

After you duplicate a disk with the DISKCOPY command, you can use the DISKCOMP command (an external command) to check that the disks are identical. This command does not compare disks copied with the COPY command because it compares disk bit by bit, not file by file.

To compare disks from the system prompt, insert the DOS disk into drive A. Type `DISKCOMP A: B:` and then press **Return**. A message asks you to insert the two disks to be compared (Figure 2-32). Do so, and then press the specified key to continue. When the disks are compared, a message indicates how they compared and asks if you want to compare additional disks. Press the specified keys to continue or quit.

When using DOS 4.0's Shell, you select *DOS Utilities* from the Start Programs Main Group, and then select *Disk Compare* to display a pop-up box. You enter the source and target drives, and then press **Return**.

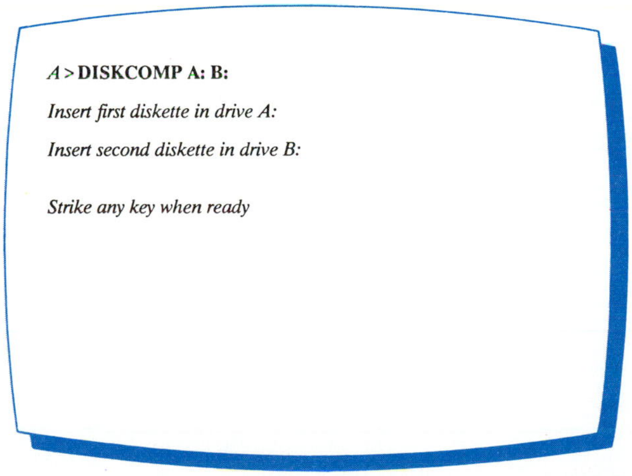

FIGURE 2-32
The DISKCOMP Prompt
The DISKCOMP prompt asks you to insert the disks to be compared.

A > DISKCOMP A: B:

Insert first diskette in drive A:

Insert second diskette in drive B:

Strike any key when ready

SUMMARY AND KEY TERMS

■ The command you use to compare duplicated disks is **DISKCOMP**, an external command.

■ If disks do not compare exactly, make another copy with the DISKCOPY command.

REVIEW QUESTIONS

1. What command do you use to compare disks?

2. Is the command an internal or external command?

3. Can you use the command to compare disks you copied with the COPY command?

4. What should you do if the command finds that your disks do not exactly match?

Renaming Files

OBJECTIVE

After completing this topic, you will be able to

- Describe how to rename files on a disk

There are times when you want to change the name of a file after it has been saved. To do this, you use the RENAME command (an internal command). You can also use REN, a shorter version of the command, to do the same thing.

When using this command from the system prompt, you must specify the old name and the new name. For example, when the *A>* prompt is on the screen and a disk in drive B has a file named OLDNAME.EXT that you want to change to NEWNAME.EXT, you type RENAME B:OLDNAME.EXT NEWNAME.EXT and then press **Return**.

You can also change the name of a file while copying it. For example, when the *A>* prompt is on the screen and a disk in drive A has a file named OLDNAME.EXT that you want to change to NEWNAME.EXT and copy to drive B, you type COPY A:OLDNAME.EXT B:NEWNAME.EXT and then press **Return**.

If you are using DOS 4.0's Shell, you first display the File System screen and select the file to be renamed. You then pull down the File menu and select *Rename* to display a pop-up box. You enter the new filename, and then press **Return**.

SUMMARY AND KEY TERMS

- The command you use to rename a file is **RENAME** (or **REN**), which is an internal command.
- You can also rename a file while copying it.

REVIEW QUESTIONS

1. What command do you use to rename files on a disk?
2. Is the command an internal or external command?
3. Can you rename a file while copying it? If so, how?

Erasing Files

OBJECTIVE

After completing this topic, you will be able to

- Describe how to erase unneeded files from a disk

Monitoring the amount of free space on a disk is important because many applications programs misbehave when you ask them to save files on a full disk, or they may create temporary files that take up a lot of space. Most people tend to keep files long after they are useful. It is good practice to occasionally use the DIR command to list the files on a disk and then the ERASE command (an internal command) to delete any files no longer needed. You can also use the DEL command to erase files from the disk. It works just like the ERASE command.

For example, with the *A>* prompt on the screen and a disk in drive B that you want to erase a file named FILENAME.EXT from, you type ERASE B:FILENAME.EXT and then press **Return**.

You can use wildcards with the ERASE command, but it is dangerous to do so. Miscalculating even slightly the effects that wildcards have can cause the wrong files to be deleted. One way to use them safely is to preview what files will be affected by specifying the planned wildcards with the DIR command (see Topic 2-5). If only the files you want to delete are listed, the same wildcards are safe to use with the ERASE command.

If you are using DOS 4.0's Shell, you first display the File System screen and select the file to be deleted. You then pull down the File menu and select *Delete* to display a pop-up box that lists the selected file. To delete the file, you press **Return**.

The ERASE command does not actually erase a file from the disk. It merely changes the first letter of its name in the file directory to CHR$(299). All programs that access the directory know that if a filename begins with this character, the file has been deleted, and new files can be saved in the space previously reserved for the deleted file. If you save another file on this disk, it might be saved on top of, and thus erase, the file you "erased" with the ERASE command. If you ever erase a file by mistake, do not save any files on the disk because utility programs are available that you can use to put its name back in the directory so that you can retrieve it from the disk.

- The commands you use to erase files are **ERASE** or **DEL**, both of which are internal commands.
- When using wildcards with these commands, you should preview the results with the DIR command.
- When you erase files, they are not actually erased from the disk. Just their name is changed in the directory. You can recover files that you inadvertently deleted using special utility programs if you do not save other files onto the disk first.

1. What two commands do you use to erase files?
2. Are these commands internal or external commands?
3. Why must you be careful when using wildcards to erase files?
4. When using wildcards to erase groups of files, how can you preview the names of the files to be deleted?
5. Can you retrieve a file that you inadvertently erased? What should you do to salvage it?

Checking Disks

OBJECTIVE

After completing this topic, you will be able to

■ Describe the command you use to check a disk

When you save a file on a new disk, it is stored neatly on adjacent sectors around adjacent tracks on the disk. But after the disk begins to fill up and you delete some files, the disk drive has to work harder to store a file. It tends to store different parts of the file wherever it can find free sectors. After a while, a file may end up scattered all over the disk on **noncontiguous sectors** (Figure 2-33). Files stored this way (called **fragmented files**) take longer to save and retrieve and put increased wear and tear on the drive because the drive's read/write head must keep moving over the disk's surface to reach parts of the file. Parts of these files can also become lost if the drive cannot find all the sections.

You can check your disks with the CHKDSK command (an external command) to see if any files are scattered. To check a disk, type CHKDSK and then press **Return**. The screen indicates the following information about the disk (Figure 2-34):

FIGURE 2-33
Contiguous and Noncontiguous Sectors
A disk with noncontiguous sectors (a) has a file stored in sectors that are not adjacent to each other. A disk with contiguous sectors (b) stores the file in adjacent sectors.

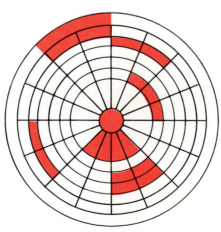

A. Noncontiguous

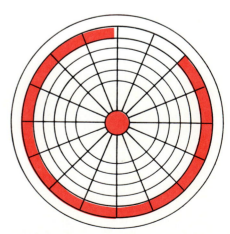

B. Contiguous

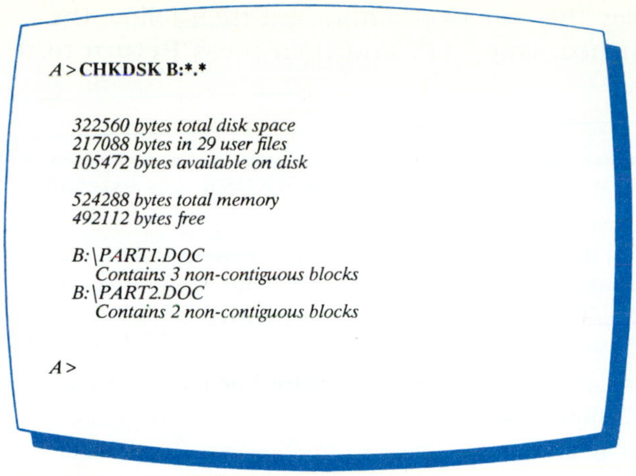

```
A > CHKDSK B:*.*

     322560 bytes total disk space
     217088 bytes in 29 user files
     105472 bytes available on disk

     524288 bytes total memory
     492112 bytes free

     B:\PART1.DOC
         Contains 3 non-contiguous blocks
     B:\PART2.DOC
         Contains 2 non-contiguous blocks


A >
```

FIGURE 2-34
The CHKDSK Screen Display
If the CHKDSK *.* command finds that files have been fragmented, the screen tells you there are noncontiguous sectors. If your disk has these, you should copy the files to a new disk.

- The total disk space on the disk
- The number of bytes in your files and the number of files
- The number of hidden files (if any)
- The space that remains available on the disk for additional files
- The total amount of memory your computer has
- The amount of memory that is free (that is, not currently used by the programs you have loaded into memory)

You can also use variations of the command.

- To check a single file, you type CHKDSK FILENAME (where FILENAME is the name of the file).
- To check the status of all files on a disk, you type CHKDSK *.* (or CHKDSK B:*.*), and then press **Return**. In a moment, the screen tells you if all files are contiguous or shows you the files that are noncontiguous, or scattered. Contiguous means the files are stored in adjacent sectors, as they should be. To save the files so that they are contiguous, copy all the files to a new formatted disk with the COPY *.* command. The DISKCOPY command will copy the noncontiguous files exactly as they are, so nothing is gained.

If sectors of a file become scattered, the operating system may not be able to find sections called **clusters**. The CHKDSK command occasionally displays a message telling you the disk has lost clusters and asks if you want them fixed. To do so, you should be familiar with two other variations of the CHKDSK command.

- To have a series of messages displayed as the disk is checked, type CHKDSK B:/V (or CHKDSK B:*.*/V), and then press **Return**.
- To correct any errors discovered by the CHKDSK command, type CHKDSK B:/F (or CHKDSK B:*.*/F), and then press **Return**. This command stores the lost clusters in a file named FILEnnnn.CHK (where nnnn is a sequential number) in the root directory. You can then retrieve this file to see if it contains any useful data that you want to recover. You can retrieve the file with any applications program that reads ASCII text files (see Topic 3-7). You can also send all errors to a file by typing CHKDSK C:>FILENAME.

If you are using DOS 4.0, the CHKDSK command is not listed on the menus. To use this command, select *Command Prompt* from the Start Pro-

CHECKING DISKS

grams Main Group to display the system prompt, and then follow the instructions above. When finished, type EXIT and then press **Return** to return to the Shell.

SUMMARY AND KEY TERMS

- The command you use to check your disks is **CHKDSK**, an external command.
- When files are deleted and then new files are saved onto a disk, the file may be stored in **noncontiguous sectors**. To find files like this, use the **CHKDSK** *.* command. To rearrange such files, copy the files to a new disk with the COPY *.* command.
- To have a series of messages displayed when checking the files on a disk, use the **CHKDSK** *.*/**V** command.
- When a file is stored, it is stored in a group of adjacent sectors, called **clusters**.
- To fix errors on a disk when a message tells you it contains lost clusters, use the **CHKDSK** *.*/**F** command.

REVIEW QUESTIONS

1. What command do you use to check disks?
2. Is the command an internal or external command?
3. What happens to files, when the disk begins to get full, that makes the drive work harder and take longer to retrieve and save the files?
4. If you get a message telling you your files have noncontiguous sectors, what does it mean?
5. If a disk has noncontiguous sectors, how can you fix the files so that they are all in adjacent sectors on the disk?
6. What is the difference between the CHKDSK and CHKDSK *.* commands?

Making and Removing Directories

OBJECTIVE

After completing this topic, you will be able to

- Describe the commands you use to make and remove directories

When you want to organize your work on a hard disk drive, you create directories. When they are no longer needed, you remove them (after first deleting all the files they contain).

To make a directory from the system prompt, you type MKDIR (or MD), followed by name of the directory you are creating (Figure 2-35). If you are creating a directory more than one level down, you must specify the complete path starting at the root directory.

To remove a directory from the system prompt, you must first delete all the files that it contains. To do so, make the directory to be removed the default directory. Then type DEL *.*. A prompt asks *Are you sure (Y/N)?* Press Y to delete all the files. Next, you have to move to the directory above the one to be removed. To do so, type CD.. and then press **Return**. Now,

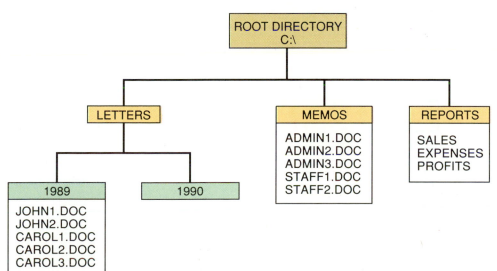

FIGURE 2-35
Making Directories
You make new directories with the MKDIR command. For example, to make the three directories off the root directory, you type MD\LETTERS and then press **Return**
MD\MEMOS and then press **Return**
MD\REPORTS and then press **Return**
To make the two subdirectories off the LETTERS directory, you type
MD\LETTERS\1989 and then press **Return**
MD\LETTERS\1990 and then press **Return**

197

FIGURE 2-36

Removing Directories
When you are done with a directory's files, you can delete them and then delete the directory. For example, if you want to delete the 1990 directory (a), you first delete the files that it contains (b). You can then delete the directory with the RD or RMDIR command. (c) For example, to remove the 1990 directory, you type RD LETTERS\1990 and then press **Return**.

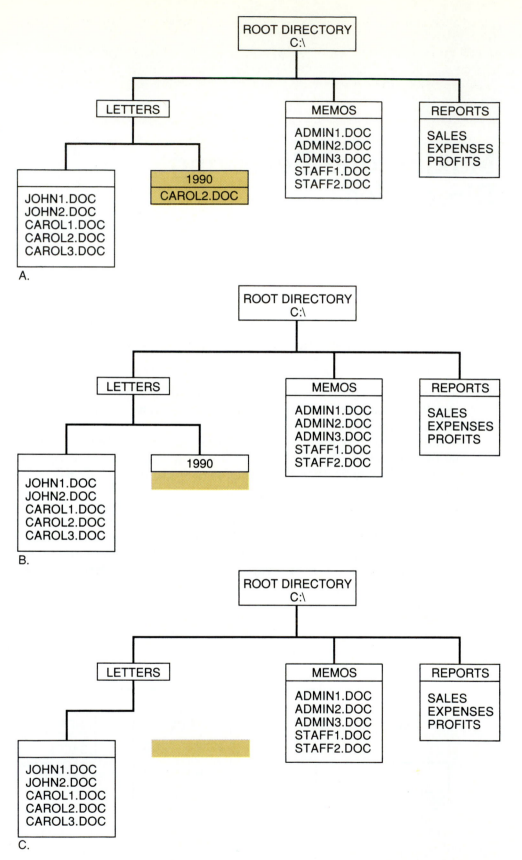

OPERATING SYSTEMS

type RMDIR (or RD), followed by the name of the directory you are removing (Figure 2-36).

If you are using DOS 4.0's Shell, you first display the File System screen. You then pull down the File menu and select *Create Directory* to display a pop-up box. You enter the name of the new directory as described above, and then press **Return**.

- The command you use to make new directories on a disk is **MKDIR** (or **MD**), which is an internal command.
- The command you use to remove a directory is RMDIR (or RD), which is an internal command. To remove a directory, it must contain no files.

1. What command do you use to make directories?
2. What command do you use to remove directories?
3. Are these commands internal or external commands?
4. What must you do before you can remove a directory from a hard disk?

Displaying and Printing ASCII Text Files

OBJECTIVES

After completing this topic, you will be able to

- Describe how to display an ASCII text file on the screen
- Describe how to print an ASCII text file

When you save files, you can save them in two, and sometimes three, formats: binary, ASCII, and print file, as you will see in Part Three. Those saved in an ASCII format or printed to files on the disk can be displayed on the screen or printed from the operating system using the TYPE and PRINT commands.

DISPLAYING ASCII TEXT FILES

To display an ASCII text file from the system prompt, you use the TYPE command (an internal command). To use this command, type TYPE followed by the file's name. When you display a file with the TYPE command, you can freeze it on the screen while it is scrolling by pressing **Ctrl-S**. To resume scrolling, press **Spacebar** or any other key.

If you are using DOS 4.0's Shell, you first display the File System screen and select the file to be displayed. You then pull down the File menu and select *View* to display the contents of the file. When finished, press **Esc** to return to the File System screen.

PRINTING ASCII TEXT FILES

To print an ASCII text file from the system prompt, you use the PRINT command. To do so, type PRINT followed by the file's name. (You can use wildcards to print a group of files.) When you use the PRINT command the first time in a session, a prompt asks you for the name of the print device and suggests LPT1 (the normal printer port). If your printer is attached to that port, you just press **Return** to print the file. If your printer is attached to a different port, for example, LPT2, COM1, or COM2, you type the name of the port, and then press **Return**. You are asked for the port only when you first use the command. If you want to change the port later in the session, you must either reboot the system or redirect the output with the >LPT2 or

>COM1 commands. For example, to send the output to LPT2, type PRINT FILENAME.EXT>LPT2.

When printing files from the system prompt, there are additional commands you can use.

- To display files in the print queue if there is more than one, type PRINT and then press **Return**.
- To stop printing a file, type PRINT/T and then press **Return**.
- To remove a file from the print queue, type PRINT FILENAME/C (where FILENAME is the name of the file to be removed from the queue).
- To add a file to the print queue, type PRINT FILENAME/P (where FILENAME is the name of the file to be added to the queue).

If you are using DOS 4.0's Shell, you first display the File System screen and select the ASCII text file to be printed. You then pull down the File menu and select *Print* to print the contents of the file.

SUMMARY AND KEY TERMS

- The command you use to display an ASCII text file on the screen is **TYPE**. To freeze a file scrolling on the screen, press **Ctrl-S**. To resume scrolling, press any other key.
- The command you use to print an ASCII text file is **PRINT**, an external command. To stop a file being printed with this command, use the **PRINT/T** command.

REVIEW QUESTIONS

1. What command do you use to display ASCII files on the screen?
2. Is the command an internal or external command?
3. What command do you use to print ASCII text files?
4. Is the command an internal or external command?
5. What command do you use to stop files that have been started printing from the system prompt?

Topic 2-16

The PATH Command

OBJECTIVE

After completing this topic, you will be able to

■ Explain how you can load programs on a hard disk without changing directories

You normally have to make a directory containing a program the default directory before you can execute the program. The PATH command lets you load a program regardless of where you are in the disk's directories. Ordinarily, you put the PATH command in the AUTOEXEC.BAT file so that you do not have to type it each time you load the program (see Topic 2-17).

To enter the PATH command (Figure 2-37), type PATH followed by the directories the operating system should look in for the program files you want to execute. For example, to be able to load programs in the root directory and directories named DOS and WORD, type PATH C:\ C:\DOS;C:\WORD. You must separate each of the directories with a semicolon.

FIGURE 2-37
The PATH Command
If you want to be able to run programs from any directory, you enter a PATH command after loading the operating system. (Or enter it in the AUTOEXEC batch file so that it loads automatically when you boot the system.) For example, to run programs from any of the directories shown here, you type PATH C:\;C:\DOS;C:\WORD;C:\123 and then press **Return**.

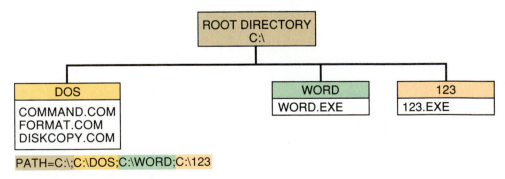

202

- The **PATH** command allows you to run programs from one directory while you are in another. If you do not use this command, you can run programs only from the current directory.
- The directories you want to be able to run programs from must be listed following the PATH command. Each directory is separated from the next with a semicolon.
- You do not have to type the PATH command each time you turn on your computer if you list it in the AUTOEXEC.BAT file.

1. What is the purpose of the PATH command?
2. When you enter the PATH command, what character do you use to separate different directories?
3. If you do not want to enter the PATH command each time you turn on the computer, what can you do?

Creating Batch Files

OBJECTIVES

After completing this topic, you will be able to

■ Explain the purpose of batch files

■ Describe how to create a batch file

■ Describe how to execute a bath file

■ Explain the command you use to display the contents of a batch file

Suppose you have a disk with a word processing program and the operating system files on it. Each time you use this disk to start the system, the computer asks you to enter the date and time. When the system prompt appears, you must type the name of the program to load it. To speed things up, you can set up the program disk so that the program loads automatically. With batch files, you can tell the computer to do a series of tasks by entering a single command or by just turning on the computer with the disk containing the batch file in drive A.

For example, let's assume you have a program called CLOCK that automatically answers the computer's prompts for the date and time when you turn it on. You also have two programs on the same disk that you want to load into the computer's memory. One of the programs, DESKTOP, is a memory resident program with a built-in phone dialer and appointment calendar. The second program, GOODWORD, is the word processing program that you use. They are each in their own directories. You also want to be able to load these programs from any directory and to run DOS external commands without changing to the DOS directory where they are stored. To do so, you need to add a PATH command.

To manually answer the date and time prompts, load both programs, and enter the PATH command from the keyboard, you would type the following each time you turned on the computer:

Type   11/10/89 and then press **Return**.

Type   11:20 and then press **Return**.

Type   PATH C:\DESKTOP;C:\GOODWORD;C:\DOS and then press **Return**.

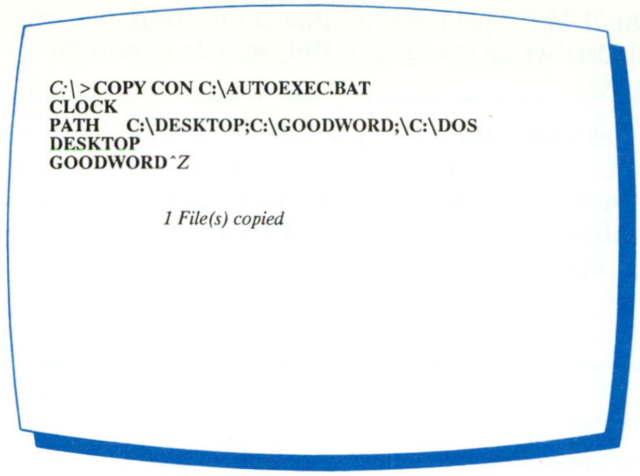

```
C:\>COPY CON C:\AUTOEXEC.BAT
CLOCK
PATH    C:\DESKTOP;C:\GOODWORD;\C:\DOS
DESKTOP
GOODWORD^Z

        1 File(s) copied
```

FIGURE 2-38
Batch Files
Batch files are a way to store keystrokes. When you type the batch file's name, the keystrokes are automatically executed. To create a batch file, you can use a word processing program or the COPY CON command, which copies typed text to the console.

Type   DESKTOP and then press **Return**.

Type   GOODWORD and then press **Return**.

You can replace these sixty-five keystrokes with a single batch file (AUTOEXEC.BAT) that automatically executes these commands when you turn on the computer (Figure 2-38). For example, to create an AUTOEXEC.BAT file, follow these five steps. The same procedures work when creating batch files that do not execute automatically when you turn on the computer.

1. Load the operating system so that the *C>* prompt is displayed on the screen. (If you are creating the batch file on a floppy disk, the prompt should read *A>*, and you should insert the program disk you want to create a batch file on in drive A.)

2. Type COPY CON A: AUTOEXEC. BAT and then press **Return**. The COPY CON command tells the computer to copy anything you type on the keyboard to the specified file. The filename specification, A:AUTOEXEC.BAT, indicates the drive the commands you type are copied on to and the name of the file they are to be copied in to. You use the name AUTOEXEC.BAT because this is the file the computer looks for automatically whenever you turn it on.

3. Now type in the commands you want executed just as you would normally enter them from the keyboard.

    Type   CLOCK and then press **Return**.

    Type   PATH C: \DESKTOP; C: \GOODWORD; C: \DOS and then press **Return**.

    Type   DESKTOP and then press **Return**.

    Type   GOODWORD (but do not press **Return**).

4. To tell the computer you are finished entering commands, hold down **Ctrl** while you press the letter Z. On an IBM PC, you can just press the **F6** function key.

5. To save the commands in the AUTOEXEC.BAT file, press **Return**. The drive spins, and in a moment, the *A>* prompt reappears. You can now execute the batch file by typing its name AUTOEXEC and then pressing **Return** or by turning on the computer with the disk on which it is

stored in drive A. On the IBM PC and compatible computers, you can also hold down **Alt** and **Ctrl** while you press **Del**, which is similar to turning off the computer.

You can create other batch files using the same procedure. Just use any legal filename other than AUTOEXEC, and add the extension .BAT. To run the batch file, type the file's name (not including the extension), and then press **Return**. To see the contents of an AUTOEXEC.BAT file, or any other batch file, use the TYPE command.

SUMMARY AND KEY TERMS

- A **batch file** stores a series of commands that you can then execute by typing the batch file's name.
- To start creating a batch file from the operating system prompt, you use the **COPY CON** command, an internal command. To end it, you press **Ctrl-Z,** and then press **Return**.
- A batch file named **AUTOEXEC.BAT** is automatically executed whenever you turn on the computer.

REVIEW QUESTIONS

1. What are batch files, and what are they used for?
2. What does an AUTOEXEC.BAT file do?
3. What is the command you type to begin entering a batch file from the system prompt?
4. What key(s) do you press to end a batch file and save it to the disk?

Operating System Issues

OBJECTIVE

After completing this topic, you will be able to

- Describe how operating systems address memory and the techniques used to increase the memory they can address

In the early days of microcomputers, several conflicting standards prevented programs from being run on a variety of computers. The dominance of IBM and Apple have reduced the variety of standards, but all programs still do not run on all computers. To run a program on a particular computer, the program must be designed for, or compatible with, that computer. **Compatibility** is a major issue in the microcomputer field. One compatibility issue concerns operating systems.

For example, newer computers and newer operating systems can run more than one program at the same time and address up to 16MB of memory. This is a major improvement, but millions of older computers use the original 8088 and 8086 chips and run the original DOS operating system. One of the limitations of this operating system is its inability to address more than 640KB of memory. Since the operating system takes up part of this memory, and applications programs take up a lot more of it, the memory available for data files and other programs is limited. To correct this deficiency, several schemes have been developed that allow you to add additional memory to your computer and use it to store data or run programs. These schemes let DOS use part of the 640KB that it can address (called conventional, lower, or base memory) to address additional memory above 640KB (called expanded or upper memory).

On DOS computers, memory can be divided into conventional, extended, and expanded (Figure 2-39).

Conventional memory is any memory up to 640KB. The operating system can address this memory directly.

Extended memory is memory from 1MB to 16MB on computers that use the 80286 and 80386 chips. On a computer running DOS, this memory cannot be used to run programs, but it can be used to store data files. On computers using the 286 and 386 chips running OS/2, you can use this memory just like conventional memory. On computers running DOS or using the 8088 and 8086 chips, you cannot address this memory directly

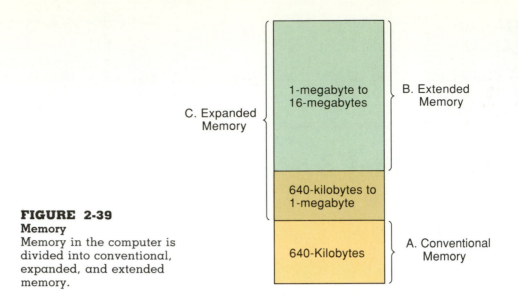

FIGURE 2-39
Memory
Memory in the computer is divided into conventional, expanded, and extended memory.

C. Expanded Memory

B. Extended Memory

1-megabyte to 16-megabytes

640-kilobytes to 1-megabyte

640-Kilobytes

A. Conventional Memory

because the chips can address only up to 1MB of memory, and DOS can address only 640KB.

Expanded memory is memory that is physically in the computer but that cannot normally be addressed by the operating system. To use it, you must use some form of **paging** (also called bank-memory switching). The computer uses a 64KB block of memory normally reserved for keeping track of the system's hardware. It swaps data from above 640KB into this "window" when needed and assigns a block of memory so that data stored above 640KB can be swapped in and out of conventional memory. The ability to do this requires an **expanded memory scheme (EMS)**. Moreover, your computer must have the necessary hardware (an expanded memory add-on board) and a special program (an expanded memory manager), and your applications software must be designed to address this memory. Many leading applications programs have been adapted so that they can address it.

Until recently, there were several competing expanded memory schemes. In 1987, some computer companies got together and introduced a combined and improved scheme, EMS 4.0. This scheme not only allows you to address up to 32MB of memory but also allows you to do multitasking.

SUMMARY AND KEY TERMS

- DOS is limited to addressing 640KB of memory.
- Memory is divided into **conventional, extended,** and **expanded** memory.
- On DOS computers, the first 640KB of memory is conventional memory.
- Extended memory is any memory from 1MB to 16MB.
- Expanded memory is memory that is inside the computer but that DOS cannot address directly. To address it, you need to use an **expanded memory scheme (EMS)**. The scheme must be supported by your hardware and software.

REVIEW QUESTIONS

1. What is conventional memory?
2. What is extended memory, and what purpose does it serve?
3. What is expanded memory, and what purpose does it serve?
4. What is an expanded memory scheme? Why do you need to use it?

Part Three

APPLICATIONS PROGRAMS

Topic 3-1   Introduction to Applications Programs
Topic 3-2   Loading and Quitting Applications Programs
Topic 3-3   Executing Commands
Topic 3-4   Saving and Retrieving Files
Topic 3-5   Printing Files
Topic 3-6   Changing Default Settings
Topic 3-7   Installing Applications Programs
Topic 3-8   Applications Programs and Data Files
Topic 3-9   Applications Program Issues

In this part, and those that follow, we introduce you to the major applications programs that run on microcomputers. What are applications programs? They are programs designed to convert the general-purpose computer into a working tool for a specific application. Typical applications might be writing a letter, term paper, or report, or preparing a budget or sales analysis. The programs you use for these specific applications are applications programs. For example, a word processing program is applied to the writing of letters and reports. A spreadsheet program is applied to the preparation of budgets and sales forecasts. In many jobs, you are expected to become familiar with several applications programs so that you can process all the company's information.

All applications programs are designed to make you more productive, and they will, once you have gained sufficient experience with them. Learning these programs requires experience more than anything else. The best way to learn these programs is with a combination of reading and hands-on use. Begin by reading enough about them to become familiar with their principles, then get some hands-on experience, and then read some more. Continue this cycle of reading and hands-on use until you have mastered the program. You will soon find you have learned enough about a program to make it into a useful tool for the work you want to do. This is an exciting point to reach. In a very short time, you will see how a word processing program will outperform the best, and most expensive, conventional typewriter or how a spreadsheet program is far superior to the best calculator. This is also a critical point because it's easy to stop learning when you have already achieved so much. You experience relief at having gotten the hard part behind you and satisfaction at making the program do your bidding. We want to encourage you to continue, however, because at this point, you will have laid the foundation for further learning. Around the corner lie solutions to problems you would not otherwise discover.

This part and those that follow are designed to give you the principles behind applications programs. Much of what we discuss is not covered in the manuals that accompany these programs. For example, every word processing manual we have seen assumes you know what a hanging indent, widow, and running header are and when to use them. In this book, you learn what these, and hundreds of other such things, are and *why* you would want to use them.

Each part of this book is designed to put specific programs into a broader perspective so that you can understand how the actual programs you work on fit into the range of available programs. Of course, not everything we discuss applies to every applications program; no one program offers all that can be offered.

REVIEW QUESTIONS

1. What are applications programs?
2. What is the best way to learn an applications program?

Introduction to Applications Programs

OBJECTIVE

After completing this topic, you will be able to

- Describe the most common types of applications programs, and explain what they are used for

Before looking at how applications programs work, let's first look at some of the most popular types of applications programs. We discuss all these programs (and many others) in greater detail in Parts Four through Nine of this text.

WORD PROCESSING AND DESKTOP PUBLISHING PROGRAMS

Word processing programs are used to enter and edit text. They are typically used to prepare memos, letters, reports, manuscripts, contracts, and other types of documents. In addition to entering and editing, these programs allow you to format documents to control how they look when printed. For example, you can set margins and tab stops or boldface headings. A few years ago, the editing and formatting tasks were done with separate programs. You would first enter and edit the document on a text editing program. When you were finished editing, you would load a separate text formatting program to format the document. Eventually these two tasks were combined into the modern word processing program (Figure 3-1).

Since the introduction of the laser printer, new formatting procedures are available. For example, you can print in different type sizes and typestyles, and you can combine graphics with text. Although word processing programs are powerful, a new class of programs has been introduced to implement all the new formatting possibilities. These new programs are called **desktop publishing programs** (also called *page makeup*, *page composition*, or *page processing* programs). These programs, which offer a wide selection of typestyles, make it easy to organize type into columns, add ruled lines, and combine text with graphics on the same page. Desktop publishing programs are among the newest software available, and they are still being refined. Generally, first you enter and edit a document on a word processing program, and then you transfer it to a desktop pub-

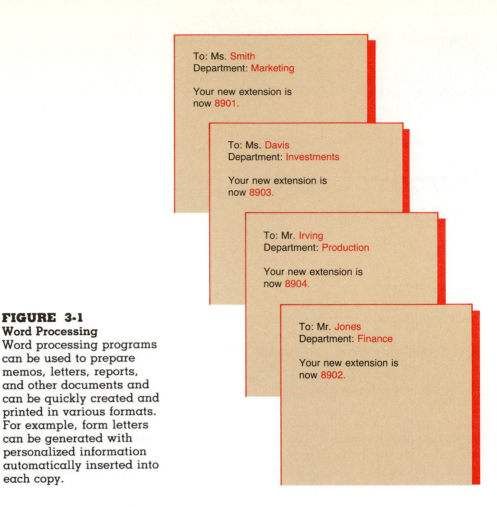

To: Ms. Smith
Department: Marketing

Your new extension is
now 8901.

To: Ms. Davis
Department: Investments

Your new extension is
now 8903.

To: Mr. Irving
Department: Production

Your new extension is
now 8904.

To: Mr. Jones
Department: Finance

Your new extension is
now 8902.

FIGURE 3-1
Word Processing
Word processing programs can be used to prepare memos, letters, reports, and other documents and can be quickly created and printed in various formats. For example, form letters can be generated with personalized information automatically inserted into each copy.

lishing program, where you lay out and design the final document. Word processing programs are better at editing than at formatting, and desktop publishing programs are better at formatting than at editing. In essence, it is like the old days when editing was done on one program and formatting on another. Increasingly, however, the features offered by desktop publishing programs are being incorporated into word processing programs, just as formatting was previously combined with editing (Figure 3-2).

SPREADSHEET PROGRAMS

Until recently, bookkeeping, accounting, and other forms of financial analysis were done by entering numbers on the pages of an accountant's ledger pad (Figure 3-3). Gathering data and calculating totals on these spreadsheets took a long time. And doing what-if analyses to see how changes would affect the outcome was laborious.

Spreadsheet programs (Figure 3-4) have taken the drudgery out of working with numbers. On a spreadsheet, you quickly create a model of a situation by entering labels, numbers, and formulas. You use the program's built-in functions to perform complicated calculations like your monthly payments on a loan. You then use the completed model to explore what-if questions. For example, when you change the interest rate for the loan, the spreadsheet instantly recalculates your new monthly payment. The models created with spreadsheet programs are often incorporated into business reports and other documents by transferring the labels and numbers to a word processing program.

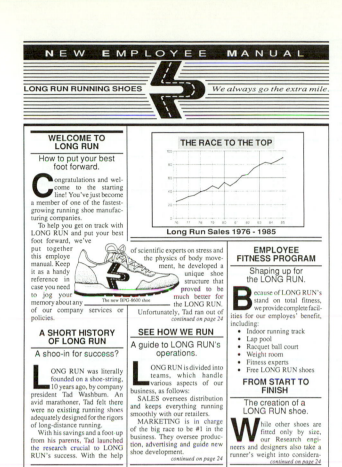

continued on page 24

FIGURE 3-2
Desktop Publishing Programs
Desktop publishing makes it possible to prepare documents that rival those prepared by professional printing services. Desktop publishing allows you to combine text and graphics, print in multiple columns, and change formats so that type is printed in different sizes and styles where desired. You can then print the finished document on a high-quality laser printer. You can distribute the document or send it to a printer to print multiple copies. Desktop publishing opens up a whole new world of opportunities since you can now inexpensively generate typeset-quality copy for newsletters, catalogs, advertising brochures, reports, articles, and books. Courtesy of Software Publishing Corporation

DATABASE PROGRAMS

You use **database management programs** (sometimes called *record or file management programs*) for tasks as simple as keeping a phone list or as complicated as controlling inventory. A **database** is any logically connected collection of data. The concept behind database management programs is

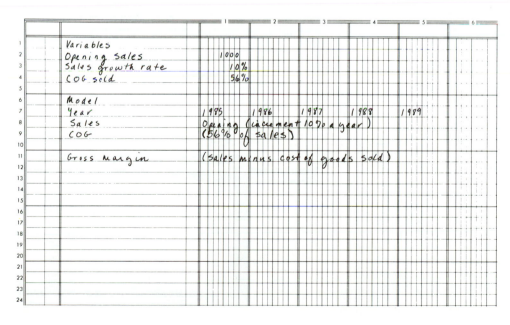

FIGURE 3-3
Ledger Pads
An accountant's ledger pad has ruled lines into which labels and numbers are written to keep financial records or do financial analysis.

FIGURE 3-4
Spreadsheet
A spreadsheet program is an electronic ledger pad. You can move the cursor around the screen and enter labels, numbers, or formulas in each of the boxes (called cells). The formulas can refer to numbers in other cells so that if you change the numbers, the formula instantly calculates a new result. Electronic spreadsheets are large, having thousands of rows and columns. Since you usually cannot see the entire spreadsheet on the screen at once, you can move around the spreadsheet.
Spreadsheet programs can be used to perform financial analysis. For example, you can use one of these programs to prepare a department's annual budget.

	A	B	C	D	E	F
1	PART 1. VARIABLES					
2	Opening Sales	$1,000				
3	Sales growth rate	10%				
4	Cost of goods sold	56%				
5						
6	PART 2. MODEL					
7	Year	1989	1990	1991	1992	1993
8	Sales	1,000	1,100	1,210	1,331	1,464
9	Cost of goods sold	560	616	678	745	820
10	Gross margin	440	484	532	586	644
11						
12						
13						
14						
15						
16						
17						
18						
19						
20						

simple: They allow you to store information in an organized way so that you can retrieve or update it when you need to (Figure 3-5).

These programs do the same things you can do with a set of index cards, but they let you do it faster and more easily. You can store large amounts of information like mailing lists, inventory records, or billing and collection information in lists stored as files. You can then sort, edit, add to, or delete from the information in these files. Database management programs are often used to maintain mailing lists, which are then used to automatically print names and addresses on letters, envelopes, and mailing labels. They are also frequently integrated into other applications programs, like word processing and spreadsheet programs.

FIGURE 3-5
Database Management Programs
Database management programs allow you to enter information by filling out a form on the computer screen (a) and the information is then stored in tables in memory and on the disk (b). You then use the program's commands to sort the information, display selected records, or print reports. Database programs can be used to store and manipulate information. Courtesy of Microsoft Corporation

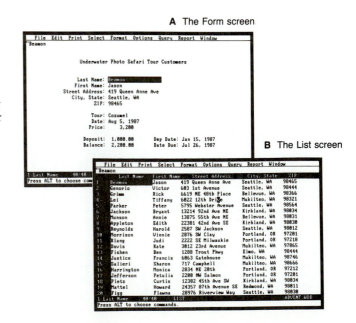

A The Form screen

B The List screen

GRAPHICS PROGRAMS

The saying "a picture is worth a thousand words" appropriately applies to computer graphics. In a glance, graphics can convey information that would be difficult to put into words. You can easily use your microcomputer to generate graphics. Two kinds of **graphics programs** are business graphics programs and interactive graphics programs.

Business graphics programs, which are often integrated into spreadsheet programs, create charts and graphs that represent numeric data (Figure 3-6). **Interactive graphics programs** generate original, free-form art and designs (Figure 3-7). These programs are called interactive because you create, edit, and manipulate the images directly on the screen. Business and interactive graphics programs are being used more and more to create images that are then incorporated into word processed or desktop published documents.

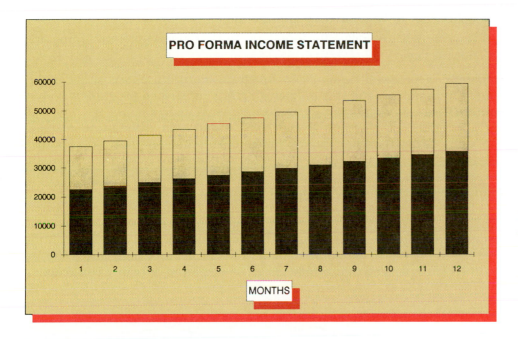

FIGURE 3-6
Business Graphs
A business graph can convey a great deal of information in a single picture. Here a stacked bar graph represents expenses and profits for a 12-month period.

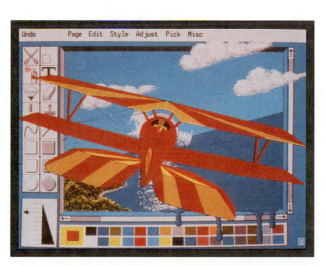

FIGURE 3-7
Line Drawings
Interactive graphics programs allow you to draw and manipulate an illustration on the screen. Graphics programs can be used to prepare art or create and polish graphs for presentations. Courtesy of Z-Soft Corporation

COMMUNICATIONS PROGRAMS

To communicate with other computers, your computer and the computers you want to communicate with must be connected to a telephone line (Figure 3-8). A **communications program** is then used so that the computers can call one another and exchange data. These programs store phone numbers you use to call another computer. Once connected, you can also specify the names of files to be sent or received.

INTEGRATED PROGRAMS

Most programs do one task and thus are called **standalone programs**. But several programs are available that combine two or more of the five basic types of applications programs—word processing, database management, spreadsheets, graphics, and communications (Figure 3-9). These **integrated programs** try to meet the following standards:

- Use common commands or command structures in all functions
- Allow data to be shared by all functions
- Have sufficiently powerful functions so that standalone programs are not needed

Generally, a program designed to integrate many functions must make some compromises, and it is unlikely that any integrated program will ever contain the best program for all five functions. Moreover, many users found early versions of these programs complicated and difficult to learn—especially if they used one function most of the time and only occasionally used the others. Newer integrated programs now stress ease of use. Though these programs are not as powerful as some of the early integrated programs, they meet most of the needs that many users have.

The most successful integrated programs combine only two or three functions. For example, many word processing programs have built-in database management programs so that you can maintain and use mailing lists to send out form letters. And many spreadsheet programs have built-in graphics programs so that numbers can be displayed or printed as graphs.

FIGURE 3-8
Telecommunications Programs
Communications programs allow you to send a message to another user's microcomputer in the same building, on the same campus, or anywhere in the world that can be reached with a telephone call. The recipient checks his or her "electronic mailbox" to find the message. These electronic message services are both public and private. Typical public services include EasyLink (Western Union), MCI Mail, and AT&T Mail. Private electronic mail services are also set up and used by individual companies. More and more firms are setting up these networks because it is less expensive to send a message electronically than to send it by courier, regardless of the distance.

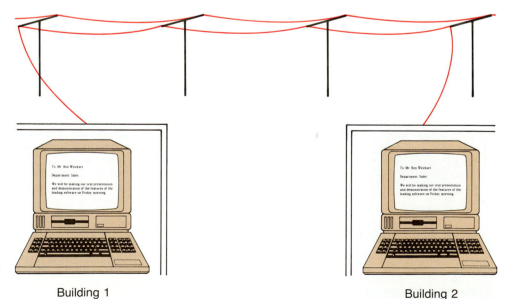

Building 1   Building 2

APPLICATIONS PROGRAMS

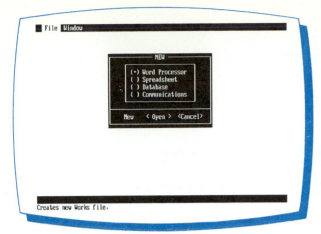

FIGURE 3-9
Integrated Programs
An integrated program, like Microsoft Works, combines several applications. The Main menu lists the available applications; for example, you can display a spreadsheet, a word processor, a graph program, a database, and a communications program.

- **Word processing programs** are used to enter, edit, and format text.
- **Desktop publishing programs** offer additional formatting possibilities. Many desktop publishing features are being added to the latest versions of word processing programs.
- **Spreadsheet programs** are like electronic versions of the accountant's ledger pad. They are used to enter labels, numbers, and formulas to analyze financial and other numeric data.
- **Database management programs** are used to organize lists or other collections of data so that you can find data quickly and easily.
- **Graphics programs** are used to graph business data or to create art and designs.
- **Communications programs** are used to send and receive data over telephone lines.
- **Integrated programs** combine one of more of the basic functions of word processing, spreadsheets, database management, graphics, and communications.

1. What are word processing programs used for?
2. What is a desktop publishing program?
3. What is a spreadsheet program used for?
4. What similarities are there between an accountant's ledger pad and a spreadsheet program?
5. What is a database management program used for in word processing?
6. What two kinds of graphics programs are widely used in business?
7. What is a communications program used for?
8. What is an integrated program? What are the five most commonly integrated applications?

TOPIC 3-2

Loading and Quitting Applications Programs

OBJECTIVES

After completing this topic, you will be able to

- Explain how to load an applications program from the system prompt or Presentation Manager

- Explain why it is important to quit a program properly

Before you can use an applications program, you must turn on the computer and load the operating system (called **booting** the system); you then load the program. The way you load a program depends on whether you are loading it from the system prompt or from Presentation Manager.

LOADING A PROGRAM FROM THE SYSTEM PROMPT

The way you load a program from a floppy disk depends on how your program disk has been set up. There are three basic variations of a program disk.

- If your program disk does not contain the operating system files needed to load it, you must first load the operating system from the operating system program disk by booting the system. On the IBM PC, this disk is labeled PC-DOS, MS-DOS, IBM OS/2, or MS OS/2. When the system prompt appears, you remove the operating system disk, insert the applications program disk, and type the name you use to load the program.

- If the needed operating system files have already been copied to your applications program disk, the disk is **self-booting**. It is called self-booting because you can load both the operating system and the applications program from the same disk. When you format a blank disk as a system disk and then copy the applications program's files to it, you have created a self-booting program disk.

- If your disk is self-booting and contains an AUTOEXEC.BAT file (see Topic 2-17), the operating system and the program are loaded automatically when you boot the program.

218

Loading a Program from a Floppy Disk Drive

When loading a program from a floppy disk drive, follow these steps.

1. **Insert a self-booting disk into drive A.** Drive A is usually the one on the left if your drives are side by side or the one on top if they are above each other. On a floppy disk system, you always load programs from drive A, the start-up drive (Figure 3-10).

   ■ If the program disk is self-booting, insert it into drive A, and then close the drive's door.

   ■ If the program disk is not self-booting, insert the operating system disk (which is always self-booting) into drive A, and then close the drive's door.

2. **Boot the system.**

   ■ If the computer is off, turn it on. If your computer does not have a built-in clock, you are prompted to enter the date and time. Enter the date in the format month/day/year (for example, type 1/1/89) or month-day-year (for example, type 1-1-89), and then press Return. Enter the time in the format hour:minute (for example, type 10:15), and then press **Return**. You can enter time in twenty-four-hour format if you desire; for example, you can type either 14:00 or 2:00 for 2 P.M.

   ■ If the computer is already on and the *A>* prompt is displayed, go to step 3. If a prompt other than *A>* is displayed, type A: and press **Return** to make drive A the default drive, and then go to step 3.

   ■ If the computer is on but another program is displayed, quit the program to return to the operating system prompt.

3. **Load the program.**

   ■ If the disk has an AUTOEXEC.BAT file, the program loads automatically when you boot the system. The program appears on the screen without your having to specify a command.

   ■ If the program disk does not have an AUTOEXEC.BAT file, the *A>* prompt appears on the screen when you boot the system or quit another program. If you loaded the operating system from a different disk, remove it, and insert the applications program disk into drive A. To load the program, type a command (usually a contraction of the program's name), and then press **Return**. For example, to load WordPerfect, type WP and then press **Return**; to load Lotus 1-2-3, type LOTUS and then press **Return**; and to load Microsoft Works, type WORKS and then press **Return**.

   If the program is on two disks, remove the first one and insert the second when prompted to do so; then press the key specified to continue.

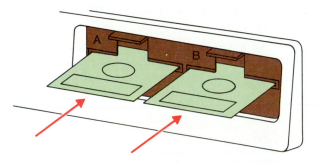

Operating System and
Program Disks in Drive A

Data Disk in Drive B

FIGURE 3-10
Loading a Program from a Floppy Disk
When loading an applications program from a floppy disk, you always insert the program disk into drive A. If you are also saving your work on a floppy disk, you insert a data disk into drive B.

Loading the Program from a Hard Disk Drive

Most hard disk systems are set up so that the operating system appears automatically whenever you turn on the computer without a disk in drive A. Thus you just load whatever program you want to use. To load a program from a hard disk follow these steps.

1. **Boot the system.**

   - If the computer is off, open the door of drive A so that the computer does not try to load a program from the disk in that drive. Turn the computer on, and then enter the date and time if prompted to do so.

   - If the computer is already on and the C> prompt is displayed, go to step 2.

   - If the computer is on but another program is displayed on the screen, quit the program to return to the operating system prompt.

2. **Change directories.** To load a program from a hard disk drive, you make the drive and directory that contains the program files the current directory (unless you previously entered a PATH command that refers to the directory in which the program file is stored—see Topic 2-16). If the current drive is not drive C, type C: (or any other drive that contains the program's files), and then press **Return** to display the C> prompt. You then specify the directory to load the program from. This is either the root directory or the subdirectory in which the program's files are stored.

   - Some programs automatically create a batch file in the root directory when the program is first installed on the hard disk drive. If there is a batch file that loads the program from the root directory, make it the default directory. Type CD\ (for change directory), and then press **Return**.

   - If you want to load the program from the directory that contains the program files, type CD\ and the name of the directory, and then press **Return**. For example, to change to a directory named WORD, type CD\WORD and then press **Return**.

3. Load the program. Type the program's abbreviation, and then press **Return**. For example, to load a program that uses the name WORD, type WORD and then press **Return**.

LOADING A PROGRAM FROM PRESENTATION MANAGER

If you use Presentation Manager, you display the Start Programs Window and then load programs in one of two ways.

- If you are using a mouse, by pointing to the programs on the screen and then clicking one of the buttons
- If you are using the keyboard, by pressing the arrow keys to move the highlight over the desired program's name and then pressing **Return**

Since Presentation Manager is the user interface for OS/2, you can load up to twelve OS/2 programs and one DOS program.

QUITTING THE PROGRAM

At the end of a session, you quit the program you are working on to load another program or turn the computer off. It is always advisable to quit a program using the commands or menu choices designed for this purpose.

Although you can quit a program by simply turning off the computer, this is a bad habit to get into because some day you will do it without thinking and may lose files as a result.

Moreover, many programs create temporary files on the disk while you are working. The program then deletes these files when you quit the program. If you do not use the Quit command, these files remain on the disk, and your own files may be corrupted. For example, many applications programs print a file to the disk before sending it to the printer. It then automatically erases the file from the disk when it is no longer needed. The only time you see these files is if you display a directory of the disk on which they are stored before they are deleted or if the computer shuts down for some reason before it erases them. If you simply turn off the computer, these files will remain on the disk. Other programs create temporary files on the disk while you edit. If you turn off the computer, the regular document files may not reflect any of the changes stored in the temporary files created by the program.

When you use the Quit command to leave a program, it returns you to the computer's operating system. Some programs check documents on the screen to see if any changes have been made that you have not yet saved. If documents like this are found, the program asks if you want to save them before quitting. After you indicate whether you want to save or abandon the documents, the operating system screen is displayed. If you are using DOS, the A> or C> prompt (depending on the drive you have returned to) appears. If you loaded the program from Presentation Manager, the Presentation Manager screen reappears. You can now load another program, format disks or copy files, or turn off the computer to quit for the day.

If you are quitting for the day (or for any period longer than about an hour), you should do four things.

- Make a backup copy of any files you created so that you have at least the original and one copy.

- Use the display monitor's controls to dim the screen so that an image will not be "burned" into its phosphor surface.

- Open the floppy disk drive doors to lift the disk drives' read/write head off the disks. This prevents the read/write heads from leaving an indentation in the disks' surface.

- Remove your disks from the disk drives. This prevents their loss, increases security, and ensures that no one mistakenly erases them.

Turning Off Your Computer

There are two schools of thought on turning off computers (or other electronic equipment). Some people prefer to turn them off whenever they are not using them, and others never turn them off. The reason for not turning a computer off is that the surge of electricity that goes through it when you turn it on can cause more damage than leaving the computer on for long periods. To be conservative, turn the computer off only when you will not be using it for extended periods. Do not turn it on and off several times during the day; it is probably less harmful if you turn it off only at the end of the day.

SUMMARY AND KEY TERMS

- You load an applications program after you load the operating system. You can load both from the same disk if the disk is a self-booting system disk.
- A self-booting disk with an AUTOEXEC.BAT file automatically loads both the operating system and the applications program.
- Incorrectly quitting a program can cause problems if the program creates temporary files on the disk.
- When you quit a session, you should make backup copies of your files, dim the screen's image, open the doors of floppy disk drives, and remove your disks.

REVIEW QUESTIONS

1. How do you load a program that does not have the operating system files on it?
2. List the three steps you would follow to load a program from a floppy disk drive.
3. List the three steps you would follow to load a program from a hard disk drive.
4. What two ways are there to quit a program when you are done? Which one should you use?
5. If you are quitting for the day, what steps should you take?
6. What is the difference between clearing the screen and quitting the program?

Executing Commands

OBJECTIVES

After completing this topic, you will be able to

- Describe on-line help features
- Explain how to use function keys and type commands
- Describe menus and how you use them
- Explain how to respond to prompts and dialog boxes
- Explain how you cancel a command in progress
- Explain what error messages are

One of the main differences among programs is the number of commands they have and the way you execute them. To use a program, it is not necessary for you to know all the commands because many of them are for advanced features that you learn if you need them. There are two ways to execute commands when operating an applications program: typing the commands or selecting them from a menu. These two approaches are not mutually exclusive, and most programs now combine them so that users have the benefits of both.

Most programs come with a **quick reference card** that lists many of the program's commands and briefly describes how you execute them (Figure 3-11). These cards are useful when you cannot remember a specific command. Until you are very familiar with a program, you should always keep a quick reference card handy when you are working on the computer.

USING ON-LINE HELP

One function key on the keyboard is usually designated by the program as the **help key**. If you need help at any time, pressing this key displays text that describes the program's commands and how to use them (Figure 3-12).

If the help screens are **context sensitive**, the help displayed may be directly related to what you are trying to do at the moment. For example, if you have begun the sequence of commands to save a file and cannot remember how to complete the sequence, pressing the help key displays help on saving files.

223

Feature	Keystrokes
Advance Line	Shift-F1
Advance Up/Down	Shift-F1
Alignment Character	Shift-F8
Append Block (Block on)	Ctrl-F4
Auto Hyphenation	Shift-F8, 5
Auto Rewrite	Ctrl-F3
Backspace	←
Binding Width	Shift-F7, 3
Block	Alt-F4
Block, Cut/Copy (Block on)	Ctrl-F4
Block Protect (Block on)	Alt-F8
Bold	F6
Cancel	F1
Cancel Hyphenation	F1
Case Conversion (Block on)	Shift-F3
Center	Shift-F6
Center Page Top to Bottom	Alt-F8
Change Directory	F5, =
Change Print Options	Shift-F7
Colors	Ctrl-F3
Column, Cut/Copy (Block on)	Ctrl-F4
Columns, Text	Alt-F7
Column Display	Alt-F7
Concordance	Alt-F5, 6, 5
Conditional End of Page	Shift-F8
Copy	F5, ←
Create Directory	F5, =
Ctrl/Alt Key Mapping	Ctrl-F3
Date	Shift-F5
Delete	Del
Delete (List Files)	F5, ←
Delete Directory (List Files)	F5, ←
Delete to End of Line (EOL)	Ctrl-End
Delete to End of Page (EOP)	Ctrl-PgDn
Delete to Left Word Boundary	Home, ←
Delete to Right Word Boundary	Home, Del
Delete Word	Ctrl-←
Display All Print Jobs	Shift-F7, 4
Display Printers and Fonts	Shift-F7, 4
Document Comments	Ctrl-F5
Document Conversion	Ctrl-F5
Document Summary	Ctrl-F5
DOS Text File	Ctrl-F5
Endnote	Ctrl-F7
Enter (or Return)	←
Escape	Esc
Exit	F7
Flush Right	Alt-F6
Font	Ctrl-F8
Footnote	Ctrl-F7
Full Text (Print)	Shift-F7

Feature	Keystrokes
Generate	Alt-F5, 6
"Go" (Resume Printing)	Shift-F7, 4
Go to DOS	Ctrl-F1
Hard Page	Ctrl-←
Hard Return	←
Hard Space	Home, Space Bar
Headers or Footers	Alt-F8
Help	F3
Home	Home
Hyphen	-
Hyphenation On/Off	Shift-F8, 5
H-Zone	Shift-F8, 5
Indent	F4
Indent	Shift-F4
Index	Alt-F5
Insert Printer Command	Ctrl-F8
Justification On/Off	Ctrl-F8
Line Draw	Ctrl-F3
Line Format	Shift-F8
Line Numbering	Shift-F8
Lines per Inch	Ctrl-F8
Lists Files	F5, ←
List (Block on)	Alt-F5
Locked Documents	Ctrl-F5
Look	F5, ←
Macro	Alt-F10
Macro Def	Ctrl-F10
Margin Release	Shift-←
Margins	Shift-F8
Mark Text	Alt-F5
Math	Alt-F7
Merge	Ctrl-F9
Merge Codes	Alt-F9
Merge E	Shift-F9
Merge R	F9
Minus Sign	Home, =
Move	Ctrl-F4
Name Search	F5, ←
New Number (Footnote)	Ctrl-F7
New Page Number	Alt-F8
Number of Copies	Shift-F7, 3
Outline	Alt-F5
Overstrike	Shift-F1
Page Format	Alt-F8
Page Length	Alt-F8
Page Number Column Positions	Alt-F8
Page Number Position	Alt-F8
Page (Print)	Shift-F7
Paragraph Number	Alt-F5
Pitch	Ctrl-F8
Preview a Document	Shift-F7
Print	Shift-F7

Feature	Keystrokes
Print (List Files)	F5, ←
Print a Document	Shift-F7, 4
Print Block (Block on)	Shift-F7
Print Format	Ctrl-F8
Printer Control	Shift-F7
Printer Number	Shift-F7, 3
Proportional Spacing	Ctrl-F8, 1
Rectangle, Cut/Copy (Block on)	Ctrl-F4
Redline	Alt-F5
Remove	Alt-F5, 6
Rename	F5, ←
Replace	Alt-F2
Replace, Extended	Home, Alt-F2
Retrieve	Shift-F10
Retrieve (List Files)	F5, ←
Retrieve Column (Move)	Ctrl-F4
Retrieve Rectangle (Move)	Ctrl-F4
Retrieve Text (Move)	Ctrl-F4
Reveal Codes	Alt-F3
Rewrite	Ctrl-F3, Ctrl-F3
Rush Print Job	Shift-F7, 4
Save	F10
Screen	Ctrl-F3
Search	F2
Search, Extended	Home, F2
Search	Shift-F2
Search, Extended	Home, Shift-F2
Select Print Options	Shift-F7, 4
Select Printers	Shift-F7, 4
Sheet Feeder Bin Number	Ctrl-F8
Shell	Ctrl-F1
Short Form Marking	Alt-F5
Soft Hyphen	Ctrl--
Sort	Ctrl-F9
Sorting Sequences	Ctrl-F9
Spacing	Shift-F8
Spell	Ctrl-F2
Split Screen	Ctrl-F3, 1
Stop Printing	Shift-F7, 4
Strikeout (Block on)	Alt-F5
Super/Subscript	Shift-F1
Suppress Page Format	Alt-F8
Switch	Shift-F3
Tab	→
Tab Align	Ctrl-F6
Tab Ruler	Ctrl-F3, 1
Table of Authorities (Block on)	Alt-F5
Table of Contents (Block on)	Alt-F5
Tab Set	Shift-F8
Text In (List Files)	F5, ←
Text In/Out	Ctrl-F5
Text Lines	Alt-F8, 4

Features	Keystrokes
Thesaurus	Alt-F1
Time	Shift-F5, 2
Top Margin	Alt-F8
Type-thru	Ins
Typeover	Ins
Undelete	Shift-F7
Underline	F1
Underline Style	F8
Widow/Orphan	Ctrl-F8
Window	Alt-F8
Word Count	Ctrl-F3
Word Search	Ctrl-F2
	F5, ←

Cursor Control

Go To	Ctrl-Home
Word Left	Ctrl-←
Word Right	Ctrl-→
Screen Left	Home, ←
Screen Right	Home, →
Screen Down	+ or Home, ↓
Screen Up	- or Home, ↑
Page Down	PgDn
Page Up	PgUp
Beginning of Text	Home, Home, ↑
End of Text	Home, Home, ↓
Beginning of Line (text)	Home, Home, ←
Beginning of Line (codes)	Home, Home, Home, ←
	Home, ←
End of Line	Home, Home, →

FIGURE 3-11

Quick Reference Card

A quick reference card lists many of the program's commands in a summarized form. Courtesy of WordPerfect Corporation

Most help screens also have a table of contents, an index, or a menu, that lists all the topics help is available for. By selecting a topic from this list, you can look up information on any topic at any time.

When you have finished with help, you press the key specified, or select *Quit* or *Resume* from the Help menu to return to where you were in your procedure before you asked for help.

USING FUNCTION KEYS AND TYPING COMMANDS

One way to execute commands is to press function keys, or other designated keys, and then type the commands. Typing commands is fast, especially for touch-typists. For example, if the program's command to save a file is to hold down the **Ctrl** key while you press the letters **K** and **S**, you can execute the command without looking at the keyboard or screen.

Computer keyboards have several function keys whose sole purpose is

FIGURE 3-12

Help Screens

A help screen displays instructions on the screen when you press the key designated as the Help key. You can then press other keys to find topics of interest. When finished, you press another key to remove the help screen and return to your document. This illustration shows one of the WordPerfect help screens.

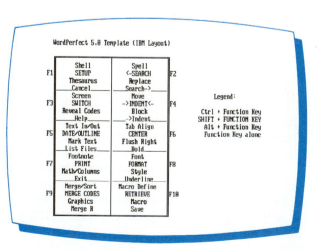

to perform tasks assigned to them by the program's author. For example, on a database program, the function key **F10** may be assigned the task of adding a record, whereas on a word processing program, **F10** may be assigned the task of saving a document.

Many keys are assigned more than one task; for example, pressing the right arrow key may move the cursor one column or character at a time, but pressing the right arrow key while holding down **Ctrl** may move the cursor several columns or characters at a time. The **Ctrl** key does not send characters to the computer; rather, it changes what is sent when other keys are pressed. Using combinations of keys in this way allows software designers to assign many more tasks to the keyboard than there are keys.

When you use these control keys—usually the **Ctrl, Alt,** and **Shift** keys—the sequence you press them in is important. For example, to use the **Ctrl** and right arrow keys together, you press the **Ctrl** key and hold it down while you quickly press the right arrow key. On many commands, if you hold down both keys, the computer keeps repeating the command, causing unexpected results.

Programs that assign specific task to keys often supply a plastic or cardboard **keyboard template** (Figure 3-13) that fits over some of the keys (usually the function keys). These templates briefly describe the tasks assigned to each key so that you need not memorize them.

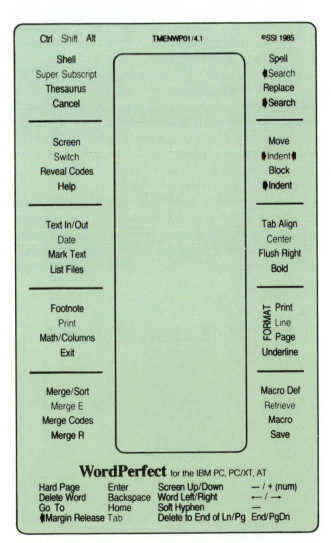

FIGURE 3-13
Keyboard Template
A keyboard template usually fits over the keyboard's function keys and provides a quick guide to the program's commands. For example, the WordPerfect keyboard template fits over the function keys and lists the keys and combinations of keys you press to execute commands. Courtesy of WordPerfect Corporation

USING MENUS

Another way to execute commands is to use **menus** (Figure 3-14). Choosing commands from a menu is easy because you need not memorize commands. Menus are like those you get in a restaurant—they list available choices. To execute commands on a **menu-driven program**, you usually have four options.

- Use designated keys to highlight a selection with a **menu pointer**, and you then press **Return** to execute the highlighted command.
- Type the number preceding the command or the first character in the command's name. On some programs, you must press **Return** after doing this.
- Point to the menu choice with a mouse pointer, and then click one of the buttons on the mouse to execute the command.
- On some systems, you can also select from the menu by pointing to a choice on a touch-sensitive screen or graphics tablet.

Many menu-driven programs use more than one level of menus. These **multilevel menus** allow numerous commands to be listed on a relatively narrow screen. Choosing many of the commands listed on the menu just displays another menu on the screen. Getting to the actual command you want to execute occasionally means you must select a series of commands from the displayed **submenus** (Figure 3-15). As you make selections from multilevel menus, you are actually working your way through a **menu tree**, which, like a family tree, is simply an arrangement of menu commands.

As you work your way through the commands shown on the menu tree, you may find you are on the wrong branch or decide not to continue for some other reason. Usually, **Esc** is designated as the key that returns you to your starting point. Some programs designate **Esc**, or another key, as the key you can retrace, a command at a time, your steps with to back out of the menu. Sometimes you retrace your steps only part way so that you can continue the command down a different branch of the tree.

Often, the menu disappears when you complete a command, and you are returned to where you were before you began executing the command. In some cases, you must select *Quit* or *Exit* on the menu or press a designated key to remove the menu. These **sticky menus** stay on the screen, anticipating you will want to use more than one of the listed choices. For example, you might want to boldface, italicize, or underline the same phrase

FIGURE 3-14

Menus

On programs with pull-down menus, when you select a choice from a menu bar at the top of the screen, a list of related commands descends from the choice. This pull-down menu lists specific commands that you can choose by highlighting them and then pressing **Return**.

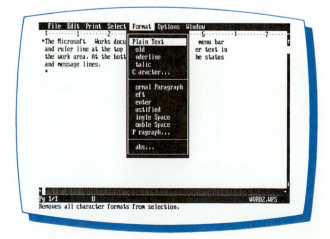

APPLICATIONS PROGRAMS

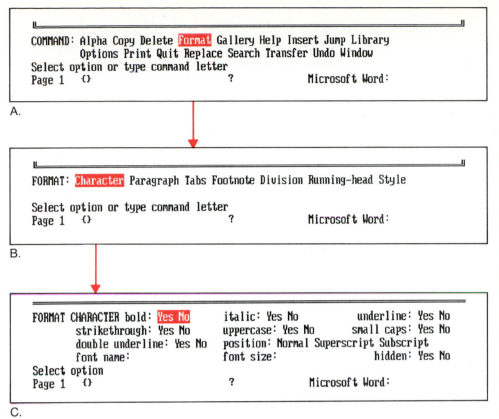

```
┌─────────────────────────────────────────────────────────────────┐
│  ╓─────────────────────────────────────────────────────────────╖ │
│  ║                                                               ║ │
│  COMMAND: Alpha Copy Delete [Format] Gallery Help Insert Jump Library │
│          Options Print Quit Replace Search Transfer Undo Window   │
│  Select option or type command letter                             │
│  Page 1   {}                      ?            Microsoft Word:     │
│                                                                   │
└─────────────────────────────────────────────────────────────────┘
A.
```

```
┌─────────────────────────────────────────────────────────────────┐
│  ╓─────────────────────────────────────────────────────────────╖ │
│  ║                                                               ║ │
│  FORMAT: [Character] Paragraph Tabs Footnote Division Running-head Style │
│                                                                   │
│  Select option or type command letter                             │
│  Page 1   {}                      ?            Microsoft Word:     │
│                                                                   │
└─────────────────────────────────────────────────────────────────┘
B.
```

```
┌─────────────────────────────────────────────────────────────────┐
│  ═════════════════════════════════════════════════════════════   │
│  FORMAT CHARACTER bold: [Yes No]    italic: Yes No      underline: Yes No │
│         strikethrough: Yes No   uppercase: Yes No    small caps: Yes No │
│         double underline: Yes No position: Normal Superscript Subscript │
│         font name:              font size:            hidden: Yes No │
│  Select option                                                    │
│  Page 1   {}                      ?            Microsoft Word:     │
└─────────────────────────────────────────────────────────────────┘
C.
```

FIGURE 3-15
Multilevel Menus
Multilevel menus frequently display a submenu when you make a menu choice. For example, when you press **Esc** on Microsoft's Word, the menu at the bottom of the screen is activated. When you move the highlight over the menu choice *Format* (a) and press **Return** a new menu appears (b) that lists format commands. When you highlight *Character* and press **Return** a third menu appears (c) that lists all the formats that you can apply to characters.

in a document. If the menu were to automatically disappear when you make a selection, you would have to repeat the entire sequence of commands to select again from the same menu. Since the menu remains on the screen, you can make several choices and remove the menu only when you are finished.

Some programs, when you first load them, display a list of the major program functions. This **Main menu** (Figure 3-16) lists all the program's main functions. From the Main menu, you initiate most functions, such as opening new files, retrieving existing files, or printing documents. It is also the menu you return to after these functions have been completed. For example, when you work with a word processing program, you can create new documents, retrieve old ones for editing, print documents, change the program's settings, check spelling, and perform several other functions.

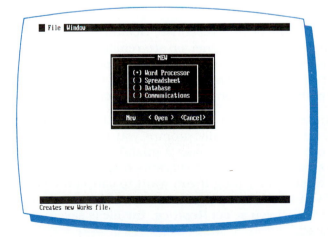

FIGURE 3-16
A Main Menu
When you load some programs, they display a Main menu that lists the program's functions. To select one of them, you type the number or letter that corresponds to your choice, and then press **Return** or click on the choice with a mouse. This illustration shows the Microsoft Works Main menu.

RESPONDING TO PROMPTS AND DIALOG BOXES

When executing commands, programs often ask you to enter information they need to complete the command, for example, a page number to print, the name of a file to save or retrieve, or a word to be searched for. The text that appears on the screen asking you to supply this information generally appears as either a prompt or a dialog box.

Prompts

Many commands display **prompts**, lines of text at the top or bottom of the screen that ask you to enter the information the computer needs. You answer prompts in one of three ways.

- You type information from the keyboard, and then press **Return**. You can type information in lowercase letters, uppercase letters, or both; for example, filename, FILENAME, and FileName are all the same.
- You make a choice from a menu.
- You press **Return** to accept the default response. Default responses either are entered by the program's designer or are remembered by the program as your previous responses to the same prompts. If the program displays default responses, you can type over them to enter a new response, or you can make another choice from the menu.

Critical commands, like those that erase a file you are working on or that save files on top of earlier versions, generally prompt you to confirm the command so that you do not inadvertently make a mistake. For example, when saving a file for the second time, many programs display a message telling you the file already exists and asking if you want to cancel the command or replace the file. If you select *Cancel*, you return to where you were before you began the command. If you select *Replace*, the file is saved, and the previous version is erased.

Dialog Boxes

Some programs display **dialog boxes** (also called fill-in forms or settings sheets) that list command choices (Figure 3-17). You can enter responses into spaces in the dialog box or press designated keys to indicate, for example, margin widths, page length, or which pages to print. After filling in the form, you press a designated key to continue. The way you move the cursor between the choices on the screen varies. Using a keyboard, the keys most commonly used for this are **Tab** and **Backtab**. When you have made all the necessary changes, you press **Return** to continue. If using a mouse, you point to a blank and click. You then type the response and press **Return**, or point to *OK* and click.

CANCELING A COMMAND IN PROGRESS

When you begin a command, you can either complete the sequence of commands or menu selections or cancel them by pressing **Esc** or other designated keys. Canceling the command sequence returns you to where you were before you began the command.

ERROR MESSAGES

If you make any errors when executing commands, the computer often beeps and displays an **error message**. On some programs, you must then press **Esc** or **Return** before you can enter any further commands or data.

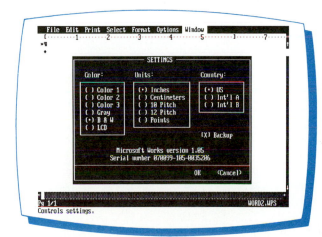

FIGURE 3-17
Dialog Boxes
Dialog boxes or fill-in forms provide spaces you can enter responses into or lists of choices you can choose from. The Microsoft Works form shown here is used to control the screen display.

- Most applications programs have **on-line help** that you display by pressing a designated key. If the help is **context sensitive**, it displays help on the procedure you are attempting.

- On most programs, you execute commands by typing them or selecting choices from menus. The most frequently used commands are usually assigned to function keys.

- Many menus have more than one level. When you select a menu command, another menu is displayed. One key, usually **Esc**, is designated as the key that cancels a command or backs you up one level.

- If a menu does not automatically disappear when you make a selection, it is a **sticky menu**.

- **Main menus** are those displayed on some multifunction programs when you load them. The Main menu lists all the program's main functions.

- When executing commands, you often must provide the computer with information. You enter this information when a **prompt** or **dialog box** is displayed on the screen.
- If you make a mistake when operating a program, an **error message** is usually displayed.

REVIEW QUESTIONS

1. What is a quick reference card?
2. What are help screens? What does it mean when they are context sensitive?
3. What is a keyboard template?
4. What is a menu?
5. How do you select choices from a pull-down menu?
6. What is a multilevel menu?
7. What is a sticky menu?
8. What is a Main menu? What are some of the typical commands that would be listed on a Main menu?
9. What are the advantages and disadvantages of commands and menus?
10. What is a prompt? What three ways are there to answer prompts?
11. What is a dialog box?
12. If you make a mistake when using menus or commands, what key is usually assigned to cancel the command?
13. What are error messages?

Saving and Retrieving Files

OBJECTIVES

After completing this topic, you will be able to

- Describe how to name and save data files
- Describe how to retrieve files
- Explain how to specify drives and directories
- Describe how to keep track of your files

One of the primary functions of all applications programs is saving and retrieving files. Most programs let you specify the drive a file is to be saved on, and if you are using a hard disk drive, you can also specify the directory. Later, when retrieving the files, you must specify the same drive and directory.

NAMING AND SAVING FILES

You should frequently save the file you are working on. If you turn off the computer, experience a power failure, encounter hardware problems, or make a mistake, you may lose files that are in the computer's memory. Your files are not safe from these disasters until you save them onto a disk—a more permanent form of storage. When you save a data file, the program copies it from the computer's memory onto a disk (Figure 3-18). When working on a computer, you should always save your file

- Before experimenting with unfamiliar commands
- Before making major revisions
- Before printing (in case something goes wrong during the process)
- Before quitting the program

There are usually two ways to save a file.

- One command saves the file but also leaves it in memory and on the screen so that you can continue working on it.
- The other command saves your work in a file on the disk, removes it from memory, and clears the screen or returns you to the Main menu so that you can create a new file, select another function, or quit the program.

231

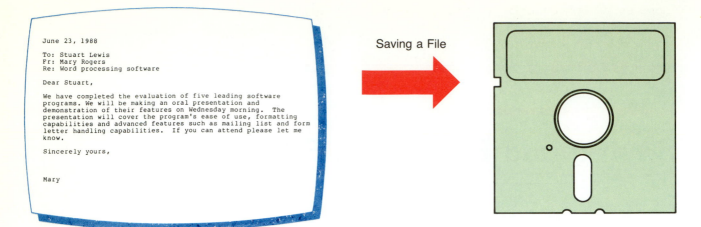

June 23, 1988

To: Stuart Lewis
Fr: Mary Rogers
Re: Word processing software

Dear Stuart,

We have completed the evaluation of five leading software
programs. We will be making an oral presentation and
demonstration of their features on Wednesday morning. The
presentation will cover the program's ease of use, formatting
capabilities and advanced features such as mailing list and form
letter handling capabilities. If you can attend please let me
know.

Sincerely yours,

Mary

Saving a File

FIGURE 3-18
Saving a File
When you save a file, the
computer copies the
version currently on the
screen and stored in the
computer's memory to a
file on the disk. You can
retrieve it later by copying
it from the disk back into
the computer's memory.

Each file saved onto a disk must have a unique name. You can assign the same name only under the following circumstances:

■ When you save the files onto different disks

■ When you save the files in different directories on a hard disk drive (see Topic 2-3)

The operating system generally determines the name you can give a file. (We discussed the rules for DOS and OS/2 filenames in detail in Topic 2-4.)

■ If you specify an illegal filename, the program normally does not accept it and prompts you to enter a correct filename.

■ If you enter a filename with more than eight characters, some programs accept it but then use only the first eight characters. If, for example, you save a file named FILENAME1 and later create and save another file named FILENAME2, the program overwrites and erases the first file, and then only one file, named FILENAME, is on the disk. The operating system assumes they are the same file because the first eight characters are identical.

■ The extension can be from one to three characters long and must be separated from the filename by a period. Often, the extension is added automatically by the program to identify the program that generated it. Some programs, on different occasions, assign more than one extension, as shown in the following examples:

When you save a file the first time, and if you have not specified an extension, the program may automatically add one, for example, .DOC.

When you save a file the second and subsequent times, the previous version may be saved as a back copy. The program may add an extension like .BAK to the file to indicate it is a back copy.

When you save a file so that another program can work with it, the extension .TXT may be added to indicate it is an ASCII text file. When you print to the disk, the program may add the extension .PRT.

When you are working with hundreds of files, the limitations that the operating system imposes make the naming of files difficult. Each file must have a unique name, and yet you must be able to recognize it later when it is listed on a directory. A few programs allow you to get around the operating system's limitations on naming files.

- Some programs use an indexing system. When you name a file, you can give it a name longer than the operating system allows. The program then stores this name in an index and assigns a number to it. It is the number, rather than the name, that the program uses to store and find the file on the disk.

- Other programs use a file folder system. You begin by opening a file folder within which you can create and store several documents. The entire folder is stored on the disk as a single file. Thus its name must follow the operating system's conventions. The files within the folder, however, are managed by the applications program, so they can have longer and more descriptive names.

Protecting Yourself Against Serious Mistakes

If you ever make a serious mistake, for example, inadvertently delete a major section of a file—or think you may have—you might want to save the file under a new name so that you don't overwrite the most recently saved version. This way you can compare the two versions on the screen one at a time, or make printouts, before deciding which version to continue with.

RETRIEVING FILES

After you have created and saved a file on a disk, you can retrieve it later for further work. To retrieve the file, you must

- Insert the disk it was saved on into the disk drive if you are working on a floppy disk system.

- Specify the drive and directory it is stored in if it is not stored on the default drive and directory.

When you execute the program's *Retrieve* command, many programs display a list of the filenames on the disk to guide you (Figure 3-19). You can retrieve a file in one of three ways.

- By entering the filename and then pressing **Return**

FIGURE 3-19
Retrieving Aides
When you want to retrieve a file, most programs allow you to display a list of the files on the disk or in the current directory. You retrieve a specific file either by moving a highlight over it and pressing **Return** or by selecting the *Retrieve* choice from a menu. These illustrations show the (a) Word and (b) WordPerfect screens.

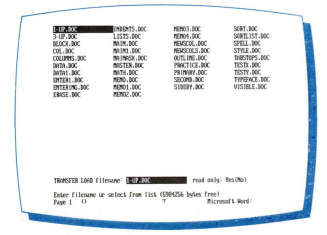

A. Word

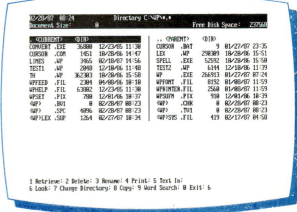

B. WordPerfect

- By pointing to the filename on the list with a highlight and then pressing **Return** or clicking with the mouse
- By pointing to the filename on the list with a highlight and then selecting the *Retrieve* command from a menu

When the file is retrieved, the disk drive operates, and the computer copies the file from the disk into the computer's memory and displays it on the screen (Figure 3-20). The copy of the file on the disk remains unchanged until you change the file in memory and then save it back onto the disk, at which time it overwrites the old file.

On programs that automatically save back copies, you can retrieve the previously saved version of the file if you make a major mistake with the most recently saved version.

When you retrieve a file from the disk, you must know its name. Most programs include one or more aids to guide you when you cannot remember a file's name.

Search

Some programs have a command that searches files for keywords. If a match is found, the program lists the names of the files containing the information you searched for. Depending on the program, the *Search* command looks for a keyword in one of three places.

- The filenames on the disk.
- The summary screen that you filled out when you opened the file. For example, if you entered the description Letter to John Doe, 1/10/88, you can search for Letter, John, Doe, or 1/10/88.
- Within the file itself. For example, if there is a file on the disk with the name Mary in it, you can search for that name.

Preview or Look

A few programs let you preview or look at files on the disk. You specify the filename, and it is displayed on the screen. If it is not the file you want, you press a key, and the file is cleared from the screen. This command does not actually load the entire file, so you cannot edit it. But it does provide a way for you to quickly scan the contents of several files until you find the one you want.

FIGURE 3-20
Retrieving a File
Retrieving a file from the disk copies it from the disk into the computer's memory. The copy of the file on the disk remains unchanged.

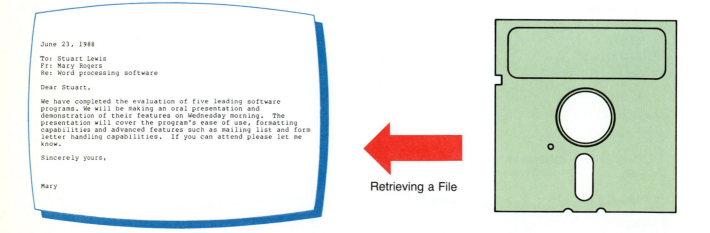

Retrieving a File

Comments

Some programs allow you to enter comments about a file when you first create or save it. They also have a command that displays both the names of the files on the disk and the comments you entered to help you identify them.

SPECIFYING DRIVES AND DIRECTORIES

When you run applications programs, you will find that they usually come from the publisher with the default drive for data files set to drive B. But all programs allow you to change the default drive so that when you use a *Save* or *Retrieve* command, the computer automatically addresses the drive you specify as the default drive. When you load an applications program, you almost always leave the program disk in drive A because the program's designers have told the program to look for the files it needs on the disk in that drive. They have specified that drive A is the default drive for program files. When you save files to or retrieve files from the data disk, most applications programs will automatically address drive B. This is because the program's designers have specified that drive B is the default drive for data files.

As you saw in Topic 2-3, your program saves files to and retrieves files from the default drive and directory unless you specify otherwise. You can specify another drive and directory in one of two ways (Figure 3-21).

- You can specify a path in the *Save* or *Retrieve* command.
- You can change the applications program's default drive and directory.

Specifying a Path

When the prompt asks you to enter a filename, you can precede the name with a path. For example, to save a file named JOHN.DOC to a subdirectory named LETTERS on drive C, you might begin by issuing the program's *Save* command. When a prompt appears that reads something like *Name of file to save:* you type C:\LETTERS\JOHN.DOC and then press **Return**. The file is then saved to the subdirectory LETTERS on drive C. If you just type JOHN.DOC and then press **Return**, the file is saved to the default drive.

Changing the Default Drive and Directory

Usually two commands change the default drive and directory.

- One command changes it for the current session. When you leave the program and reload it, the old default drive is again made the default drive.

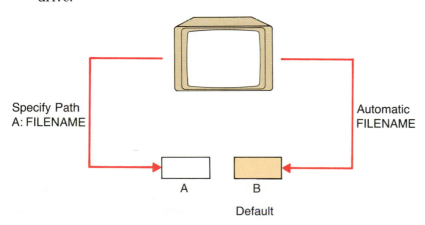

FIGURE 3-21
Default and Other Drives
When the default drive is set to drive B and you save or retrieve a file, the program automatically sends it to or tries to retrieve it from that drive when you specify just the file's name. To save it to or retrieve it from a disk in another drive, you have to specify the drive when you enter the filename, for example, B:FILENAME. If you are using a hard disk drive, you also have to specify a default directory. To save the file to or retrieve the file from a different directory, you have to specify the drive and path, for example, C:\LETTERS\FILENAME.

Specify Path
A:FILENAME

Automatic
FILENAME

A

B

Default

- Another command changes the default permanently (until you use the same command to change it again). The drive and directory you specify are saved in a special **configuration file** (see Topic 3-6). Whenever you load the program, it checks this configuration file for the drive and directory you have set to be the default.

KEEPING TRACK OF FILES

As the number of files you work on increases, so does the problem of being able to find them later when you need them. You should develop a system for naming files. But since many operating systems limit filenames to eight characters, this can be a real problem. Two months from now, will you remember if the filename OPRAT contains business files or biology files?

The limitations on filenames makes it impossible to identify each document with a fully descriptive name. Most companies and experienced users, therefore, have a rigid system of assigning filenames or numbers to each file. These names or numbers are often entered into a log along with more descriptive information about the files. Figure 3-22 shows a typical log. If a name is used, it should logically relate to the file's contents. Above all, the system that files are designated by should be consistent and understood by everyone responsible for assigning names or retrieving files.

A typical file naming system might use the eight filename characters as follows:

- A file number can be assigned. For example, the numbers 00000000 through 99999999 allow 100 million documents to be stored without duplicating a number.

- Abbreviations for the sender and recipient can be used.

FIGURE 3-22
Document Log
A document log helps you easily locate files.

Date	Filename	DiskOperator	Description
1/1/88	MEMO 1001	100 DPC	Memo from x to y
1/2/88	LTR10008	110 DS	Letter from x to y

- Dates, possibly combined with other information, can be used. For example, a letter by JH completed January 1, 1988, can be coded as JH1188, JH010188, or JH1-1-88.
- Version numbers can be added to filenames. For example, if you revise a file named JOHN1, you can rename it JOHN2 when you save it again.

Besides the filename or file number, a good log will contain some or all of the following information about each file:

- The name of the originator
- The name of the person who did the processing
- The type of file, for example, letter, report, or budget
- A brief description of the file
- The name of the intended recipient
- The name or number of the disk it is stored on
- The retention date, that is, the date on or after which the document can be permanently removed from electronic storage in the absence of other instructions

Other techniques you can use to simplify managing your files include

- The operating system automatically adds the date and time to a file when you save it. These can be seen using the DIR command (or other command) described in Topic 2-4. These can be used to tell one version of a file from another when they have been saved on different disks using the same filename. Periodically print out directories of the files on your disks.
- Most disks come with a package of labels. Use one of these labels to assign a number and perhaps a descriptive title to each disk, for example, Disk 1: Letters, Disk 2: Spreadsheet Files, Disk 3: Reports.
- If using a hard disk, store related files in their own directories.
- Always erase unneeded files from your disks (see Topic 2-12). If you print a file and are certain you will never need it again, delete it immediately. If you leave it, the next time you see the filename, you may not remember if it is important.

- There are usually two commands to save a file. One saves it and leaves it on the screen. The other saves it and removes it from memory.
- Many programs automatically assign extensions to the files you save. The extension is based on the command you use to save the file.
- Many programs save your most recent version on top of the one you previously saved. This is dangerous since many mistakes are found only after saving a file. Some programs automatically create a backup file; the previous version is renamed, and then the most recent version is saved under the original filename.
- Some programs let you enter descriptive comments about files so that you don't have to rely on the limited number of characters allowed in the filename to identify them.
- When you save a file, it is saved to the default drive and directory unless you specify a path in front of the filename.

SUMMARY AND KEY TERMS

REVIEW QUESTIONS

1. What happens to a file you are working on if you turn off the computer without first saving the file onto a disk?

2. List four stages at which it is prudent to save your files.

3. Why would you save a file before printing it?

4. What two ways are usually provided to save files?

5. Why would you want to abandon a file instead of saving it?

6. You are working on a document named MEMO.DOC and want to save it on a disk or in a directory other than the default. For each of the following, specify the path and filename you would specify:

To save the file on		I would specify this path
	Drive	**Directory**
B:	None	_____
A:	None	_____
C:	Root	_____
C:	LETTERS	_____
C:	LETTERS\1987	_____

7. Assume you are writing three term papers for each of your classes on a computer. List the filename you would assign to each paper so that you could later identify the course and the papers from them.

Printing Files

OBJECTIVES

After completing this topic, you will be able to

- Describe how you load continuous form paper
- Describe the printer's controls
- Explain why you would print to a disk
- Explain how to manage a print queue
- Describe printing options
- Explain how to set up a printer

When you want to send a file to the printer, you first load the printer with paper, align the paper, and turn the printer on. The way you load paper varies, depending on the type of printer and paper you are using. If you are using single sheets, you usually stack them in a paper tray or bin. If you are using continuous form paper, you feed it into the printer as shown in Figure 3-23.

The settings you can make on the printer vary. Many have some or all of the following switches:

- On/Off turns the power to the printer on and off. Knowing when to use this switch is important.

  If you turn the printer off while it is operating, all data in its buffer will be lost. When you turn the printer back on, your document may resume printing, but a large block will have been missed.

  If you have canceled a print job and want to start over, turning the computer off and back on is a good way to ensure that text from the previous job does not remain in the buffer.

  If after you turn the printer off, you turn it back on, it resets the top of the form so that the printer considers the line that the print element is resting on the top line of the sheet of paper. It uses this line as the starting point when calculating top margins and page length. This is useful since you can adjust your paper in the printer, and just turn it off and then back on to set the top of the form.

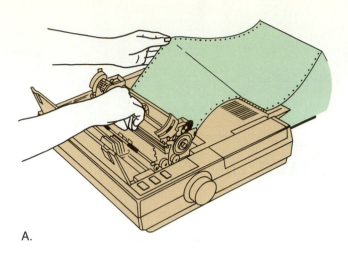

A.

FIGURE 3-23
Loading Continuous Form Paper
To load continuous form paper into a printer, you feed it through a slot, around the platen, and back out of the printer (a). In the process, you engage the holes in the perforated, tear-off margins with the tractor or pin feed mechanism (b). Courtesy of Epson

B.

- Off-Line/On-Line connects the printer to and disconnects it from the computer. The printer must be on line to print documents, but it must be off line to use some of the other switches on the printer like Form Feed and Line Feed.

- Form Feed advances a sheet of paper out of the printer. If the printer has an automatic sheet feeder or tractor feed, it inserts a new sheet. For this switch to work, the printer must be off line.

- Line Feed advances paper in the printer by one line. This is useful when making fine adjustments to the paper's position in the printer. For this switch to work, the printer must be off line.

- Letter Quality/Draft Quality switches the printer between its high-quality but slower letter-quality mode and its lower-quality but faster draft-quality mode.

- Font changes the default font (see Topic 4-12) so that the entire document is printed in that font unless you specified otherwise by entering font change codes within the document.

Because the computer is generally tied up while the printer is printing, you lose time when you print out files, especially if the files are long. Many programs solve this problem by printing the document to a temporary file on

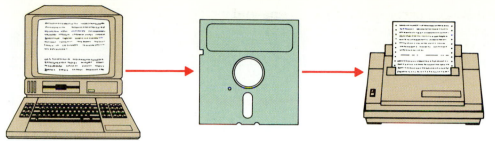

FIGURE 3-24
Printing a File
When you print a
document, it is first printed
to a temporary file on the
disk. The program then
allows you to continue
editing while it sends the
file on the disk to the
printer.

the disk. The program then sends that file to the printer (Figure 3-24) and returns control of the computer back to you so that you can work on other files. When the file has been printed, the program automatically deletes the temporary file from the disk. In effect, the computer does two things at the same time: It prints the file in the background while you work on another file in the foreground. However, when you execute a command (for example, to move the cursor from the beginning to the end of the file you are working on), the computer may take more time than usual because it must wait for the CPU to be temporarily freed from printing.

PRINTING TO THE DISK

Many programs allow you to send your print output to a disk instead of to the printer. A **print file** is created just like a printout on the printer. The only difference is that the output is sent to a file on a disk instead of to the printer. When printed on the disk, they are similar to ASCII files, but all format commands you have used are interpreted. That is, headers, footers, page numbers, top and bottom margins, and other formats that would appear on a printout all appear in the print file. You might create a print file for three reasons.

- You can retrieve the file and preview how it looks when printed because all commands that show their effects only when printed (for example, page numbers, running heads, and running feet) appear in the print file.

- If your operating system supports it, you can print these files from DOS and **queue** them—that is, specify the sequence the files are printed in—so that they print one after another unattended.

- If you are using some programs, like spreadsheet or graphics programs, you can print their data to a file and then retrieve them into a document on the screen so that you do not have to reenter the data.

Documents printed to a disk often are assigned the same filename as the original file but are differentiated from it by an extension that is automatically added to the filename. For example, if the original document is called LETTER, its file is named LETTER.DOC, and the print file is named LETTER.PRT or LETTER.PRN.

MANAGING A PRINT QUEUE

When you print a document, it is sent to the printer. If while the first document is still being printed, you specify that additional documents be printed, they are stored in a **print queue**, a line of jobs waiting to be printed (Figure 3-25). The jobs appear in the queue in the order you specify. But you can manage the print queue, including the current job being printed, with the following options:

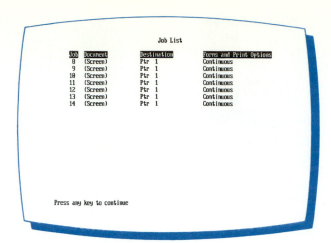

Job List

Job	Document	Destination	Forms and Print Options
8	(Screen)	Ptr 1	Continuous
9	(Screen)	Ptr 1	Continuous
10	(Screen)	Ptr 1	Continuous
11	(Screen)	Ptr 1	Continuous
12	(Screen)	Ptr 1	Continuous
13	(Screen)	Ptr 1	Continuous
14	(Screen)	Ptr 1	Continuous

Press any key to continue

FIGURE 3-25
Print Queue
A print queue contains the current job being printed and all other print jobs you have requested.

- *Change position* moves a print job higher or lower in the queue waiting to be printed. If you expedite a print job, the program may ask if you want to interrupt the document that is printing. If you indicate that you do, the printer finishes the current page, prints the expedited document, and then resumes printing the original document.

- *Pause* temporarily stops the printer so that you can continue printing exactly where you left off. You can use this command to pause the printer while you change paper or load more paper. On some programs, you can send a printer control code from within a document to pause the printer so that you can change the type element on a fully formed character printer to, for example, italicize a key section.

- *Resume* restarts a printer after you have made it pause. The printer resumes printing the document from where it stopped.

- *Stop* stops the printer so that you can start over from the beginning or return to another task. Unlike *Pause*, you cannot resume printing; you must repeat the *Print* commands to begin again. This is helpful when you notice something is wrong, for example, when the paper is improperly inserted or the margins incorrectly set.

- *Cancel* deletes a specified job from the print queue so that it is not printed.

PRINTING OPTIONS

Most applications programs provide several options you can use when printing documents.

- *Printer selection* allows you to specify the printer you want the job printed on. This is useful when you have a special printer for draft copies and another for final copies or when you have a local printer and a remote one.

- *Continuous form or single sheets* can usually be specified. If you select the setting for single sheets, the printer pauses after completing each page so that you can insert a new sheet and then resume printing.

- *Pages to be printed* can usually be specified. This is helpful when you are making corrections to individual pages. Certain pages can be reprinted without reprinting the entire document. The pages you specify are called a range. For example, you can print from the beginning of the document to a specific page, all pages between two specified pages, or from a specified page to the end of the document. Some programs allow you to specify individual pages and ranges together. For example, the command to print pages 1-6,9,11,15-20 would print pages 1 through 6, pages 9 and 11, and then pages 15 through 20.

- *To printer or disk* can be specified. If you select the printer, a copy is printed on the printer. If you select the disk, a copy is printed to the disk, just as if it had been sent to the printer. All format commands are interpreted; for example, all margins are set as you request, and page numbers, headers, and footers, if any, are printed.

- *Number of copies* can be specified so that you can avoid having to photocopy your documents after printing.

- *Draft* is used to print documents more quickly. The *Draft* command causes the printer to ignore commands, like boldfacing, that slow it down. This command must be supported by the printer and can sometimes be set on the printer rather than the program.

- *Bin selection* specifies the bin that the paper for the job is stored in. Some programs allow you to print on paper stored in two or more bins. For example, when you are printing business correspondence, the first page is printed on letterhead paper, which is stored in one bin, and the second and subsequent pages are printed on plain paper, which is stored in another bin.

- *Document summary sheet* prints out the summary sheet you filled out to describe the document when you first created it (see Topic 4-2).

- *Portrait or landscape* refers to the orientation of the printout on the page (Figure 3-26). **Portrait mode** is like a normal document; that is, text is printed across the width of the page. **Landscape mode**, which is useful when you are printing wide tables and illustrations, rotates the image 90 degrees so that it is printed along the length of the page. To use landscape mode, it must be supported by your printer, and all printers do not support this mode because they do not have the necessary landscape fonts.

FIGURE 3-26
Portrait and Landscape Mode
Portrait and landscape modes change the orientation of the printout on the page. (a) In portrait mode, the document is printed across the width of the page. (b) In landscape mode, the document is turned 90 degrees and printed across the length of the page. Courtesy of Xerox Corporation

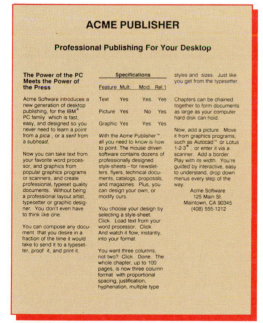

A. Portrait Mode

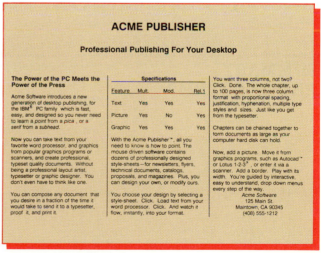

B. Landscape Mode

PRINTER SETUP

Before you can print documents, you must tell your program what printer you are using and what port it is connected to. This is sometimes done when you install the program the first time you use it (see Topic 3-7). If you change printers, you must run the install program again to tell the program you have done so unless you specified more than one printer when you installed the program.

Installing Printers

The install program copies the necessary driver from the install or utility disk (see Topic 3-6). This driver lets your program "talk" to your printer. If you do not use the correct driver, you may get strange results when you print a document. When installing the program, you also must tell the program what port the printer is connected to. The choices are usually LPT1 and LPT2 for parallel printers and COM1 and COM2 for serial printers.

Specifying Printers

Many programs allow you to install more than one printer when you run the install program. Then, when you print a document, you can select the printer you want it printed on.

Testing Printers

For best results, you have to use a printer capable of supporting the options offered by your program. For example, not all printers can print italic text or superscripts and subscripts even though your word processor offers these features. The best way to find out if your printer supports certain features is to make a trial printout using all the program's commands you are interested in. For example, you can boldface words, change fonts, use proportional spacing, and indent paragraphs. When you print the document, you see how they appear. Many programs provide special printer test files that you can use for this purpose.

SUMMARY AND KEY TERMS

- The printer has several controls. For example, **Off-Line/On-Line** connects and disconnects the printer from the computer, **Form Feed** advances the paper out of the printer, and **Font** changes the default printer font.

- When printing to a disk, all print functions are interpreted—for example, margins and headers and footers are added. The file on the disk is called a **print file**. This feature allows you to preview the finished results before sending copy to the printer. It also allows you to print the files later using DOS.

- Some programs allow you to work on one file while another is being printed. This is a great time saver since you can continue working while printing.

- If a program allows you to print a file before the first is finished, the print jobs waiting to be printed are added to the **print queue**. These programs usually have commands that change the order of the jobs in the queue, cancel jobs, or pause and then restart them.

- Most applications program provide several print options, including a choice of printers if you have more than one, the type of paper, and the number of copies.

■ Before using an applications program to print a file, you must tell the program what kind of printer you are using and what port it is connected to. This is called installing the printer.

REVIEW QUESTIONS

1. What does it mean to say a printer is on line or off line?
2. What happens when you turn a printer off and then back on while a job is printing?
3. Why would you want to print to the disk instead of to the printer?
4. What is a print queue?
5. List some typical printer options, and describe them.
6. Why do you set up a printer before you use it? What do you do when you set one up?

PRINTING FILES

245

Changing Default Settings

OBJECTIVES

After completing this topic, you will be able to

- Explain what default settings are
- Describe how you override default settings
- Explain how you change system default settings

All applications programs have commands to modify certain settings. But when you use these programs, you do not always have to use all these commands. For example, almost every word processing program automatically prints documents so that they are single spaced with 1-inch margins on an 8½-by-11-inch sheet of paper without your telling it to do so. The program's designers have made certain assumptions about what they feel average users want. These assumptions are the program's **default settings**. Figure 4-46 in Topic 4-8 shows some typical default settings for a word processing program. You can use these default settings as is, override them throughout a specific document, or change them for all documents. Similar commands are used to override default settings on all applications programs.

OVERRIDING DEFAULT SETTINGS

When you load an applications program, default settings have already been made for you. For example, when you load a word processing program and open a new document, margins may be 1 inch on all sides and text aligned with the left margin and single spaced. If you want different margins or want to center or double space some or all of the text, you must override the default settings at the appropriate place in the document. Depending on the program, you can format a document before, during, or after you have entered it. Before entering text, you might change the margins or page length. While entering text, you might boldface and underline keywords and titles. After entering text, you might change the position of page numbers on the page.

You can easily experiment with formats until you find the ones you like. Formatting and data entry are separate operations, so if you want, for example, to change margins after you have entered text, you just use the margin commands. Unlike a typewritten document, you do not have to reenter the text each time you change the format.

How you override the default format settings varies from program to program. Generally, you do so by making menu selections, filling out dialog boxes, or inserting codes.

Whether or not you see them, many formats are created by entering codes at selected points in the document (Figure 3-27). For example, common settings like page breaks or character emphasis like boldfacing are controlled by codes. When you print the document, these codes arrive at the printer and give it instructions. A code might tell the printer to advance to the top of the next page after printing fifty-four lines, begin and then stop boldfacing, print a page number at the bottom of the page, or indent a paragraph five spaces from the left margin. These codes are usually hidden unless you use the command that displays them.

Generally, two types of codes are used in files, open and paired codes.

Open codes begin a format that affects large sections of the file, for example, a change in margins. These codes affect the file from where they are entered to the end of the file or until another code of the same type changes the format again.

Paired codes have one code that begins a format and another that ends it. For example, one code starts boldfacing, and another code ends it. If you enter only the code that starts a format, or insert data between the code that starts the format and the code that ends it, some text will likely be formatted in a way you do not want. Entering paired codes on most programs is simple because you first select the text you want to format by highlighting it. When you execute the format command, codes are entered automatically at the beginning and end of the highlighted section.

CHANGING SYSTEM DEFAULT SETTINGS

When you first load a program, the default settings automatically take effect. For example, if your default left margin is in column 10 and your default right margin is in column 65, these settings will be in effect when you open a new document. These **system defaults** are saved in a configuration file that the program reads when you first load it. You can change the system default settings on many programs. If you find you are changing margins, turning off page numbers, or changing other formats for most of your files, you will find it much faster to change the program's system default settings.

To change system default settings, you usually select a command from the menu or run a special install or setup program (see Topic

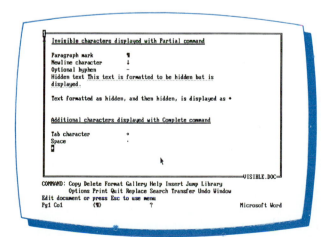

FIGURE 3-27

Codes in a Document
When you change formats in a file, you are actually entering codes that control the printer. On many programs, these codes are hidden from view, but many programs allow you to display them when editing. This illustration shows codes displayed on Microsoft Word's screen.

3-7)—sometimes the same one you used to originally install the program. When the system default menu is displayed on the screen, you can change several settings so that they are the ones that are then used automatically unless you override them. The system default settings you can change vary from program to program but usually include

- Margins and page size
- Default drives and directories for files
- The color and number of lines on the screen

When you change these settings, they are saved in the configuration file that the program reads when you first load it.

SUMMARY AND KEY TERMS

- All programs come with many of the settings already made for you. These are called the **default settings**.
- You can override the default settings to change formats within a file. To do so, you enter **codes** into the document.
- Instead of overriding default settings, you can change the **system default settings** on many programs. Any changes you make are automatically used when you create new files.

REVIEW QUESTIONS

1. What are default settings?
2. How do you override default settings?
3. When you enter codes, what two kinds do you usually enter?
4. How do you permanently change default settings? Why would you want to do so?

TOPIC 3-7

Installing Applications Programs

OBJECTIVES

After completing this topic, you will be able to

- Explain why you have to back up and install programs
- Describe what a driver is, and explain why it is important
- Explain what emulation does and why it is important

Before you actually use a new applications program, a few preparatory steps are usually required. You may find that these steps already have been done for you by the time you get a program. It's unlikely that you will have to do them until you are working on your own, with your own programs.

MAKING BACKUP COPIES

It is always wise to make a backup copy of any important program disk in case something goes wrong and you damage files on the original copy. Because some applications program disks are **copy protected**, meaning you can't freely make copies of them, you may not always be able to do this. In those cases, the software publisher usually supplies a backup copy when you buy the program. Other programs allow you to copy a program a predetermined number of times—at least enough times to make one backup copy or to copy the program's files onto a hard disk drive.

INSTALLING APPLICATIONS PROGRAMS

Software companies obviously want their programs to run on the largest number of computer setups. Since computer components can be mixed and matched, programmers are never sure what devices will be connected to the computer their program is being used on. To overcome this problem, software companies frequently include an **installation program** that installs their applications program so that it will work with your display monitor, printer, disk drives, and other equipment.

Installing a program is generally a one-time task unless you change equipment, for example, when you add a new printer. The program may then have to be reinstalled. The specific installation procedures vary from program to program, but the principles are the same. When you first use a program, you run the installation program that comes with it. When you run this program, it displays prompts or lists of choices on the screen. You answer the prompts or select choices from the lists to tell the program what type of display monitor, printer, and other peripherals you are using. You can also specify default drives for program and data files and, sometimes, change the way files are formatted on the screen.

Drivers

Based on the information you supply, the program then knows what **drivers** to use. Drivers are small programs that translate the programmer's generic instructions into instructions for a specific piece of hardware. Programs using drivers do not have to be revised by the software companies when new devices become available because the program addresses only the drivers, not the device itself. As new components become available, software companies just add new drivers.

Applications programs generally have a library of drivers, one for each specific hardware item (Figure 3-28). For example, there may be a driver for a specific model of a dot-matrix impact printer and another for a specific model of laser printer. If you tell the installation program what printer you are using, it knows to use that driver.

For a program to run on your system, it must contain drivers that communicate between the program (which can run on a wide variety of systems) and your specific equipment. If you have a piece of hardware that the program does not include a driver for, you may be unable to use it with the program (Figure 3-29). Using a printer or display screen without the correct driver can give totally unexpected results. Type that you expected to appear small may be large, headers and footers may not print, or margins may be incorrect. When buying applications programs, always be sure it contains the drivers you need to have it work with your equipment.

FIGURE 3-28
Drivers
Drivers translate your program's commands into commands that peripheral devices can understand. For example, if you boldface a word on the screen, the driver translates that command into one the printer needs to boldface the word.

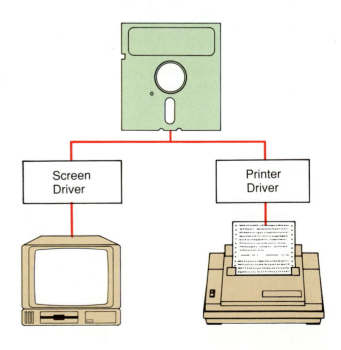

Screen Driver

Printer Driver

FIGURE 3-29
Reprinted from
INFOSYSTEMS, May 1985,
(C) Hitchcock Publishing
Company

"Your hardware doesn't like your software and they both despise your printer!"

Emulation

As you have seen, many different types of printers and display screens are available. Unfortunately, there are no agreed-on standards for the way these components work. Thus each manufacturer has its own way of doing things, and you may not be able to display or print a file on your screen or printer if the program does not supply the necessary drivers. To help solve this problem, many components are designed to be able to act like, or **emulate**, other components of the same type from different manufacturers. When installing a program, if drivers are not supplied for your equipment, you can specify a different device if your equipment has the ability to emulate it. For example, many laser printers can emulate the Hewlett-Packard LaserJet, and many display screens can emulate IBM's enhanced graphics adapter (EGA). If your program does not list the drivers for your printer or screen, but your printer or screen can emulate these two leading sellers, you can select their drivers, and the program will run correctly.

SUMMARY AND KEY TERMS

- You should always make backup copies of important program disks.
- Before using many applications programs, you have to **install** them. This procedure tells the program what system you are running it on and specifies what **drivers** it is to use to communicate with the system.
- If you have a piece of equipment for which a driver is not provided, it may be able to **emulate** one for which there is a driver. If you specify that driver, the program and equipment work together correctly.

REVIEW QUESTIONS

1. Why do you make backup copies of program disks?
2. Why do you install a program the first time you use it? When do you have to reinstall the program?
3. What is the purpose of a driver? What happens when you use a program that does not have a driver for your printer?
4. What does it mean when you say a printer emulates another printer?

TOPIC 3-8

Applications Programs and Data Files

OBJECTIVES

After completing this topic, you will be able to

- Explain the difference between memory-based and disk-based programs and data files

- Describe the various types of data files and how they differ from one another

- Describe how you can use operating system commands to manage your files from within an applications program

The computer's memory is a valuable, but limited, resource. Hence, the way applications programs and data files are stored in memory is a key feature of how a program operates.

APPLICATIONS PROGRAMS AND MEMORY

Applications programs operate in memory in two basic ways, memory based or disk based. Some programs let you choose either method.

Memory-Based Programs

Memory-based programs are entirely loaded into RAM when you load the program from its disk (Figure 3-30). The remaining memory is available for data that you enter. Memory-based programs have more advantages than disadvantages.

- Since the entire program is in memory, it can perform its functions quickly because everything the program needs is accessible.

- Since the entire program is in memory, the program disk can be removed from the disk drive, making it available for another disk.

- The main disadvantage is that these programs can take up a lot of the computer's available memory, leaving little for your own files.

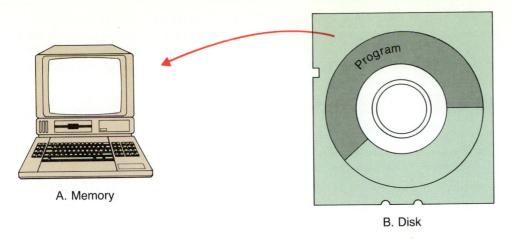

A. Memory

B. Disk

FIGURE 3-30
Memory-Based Programs
A memory-based program loads the entire program from the disk (b) into the computer's memory (a).

Disk-Based Programs

Disk-based programs are so large that loading them entirely into memory would leave little memory available for the files you are working on. Thus disk-based programs load only part of the program into memory; the rest of the program, using *virtual memory*, remains on the disk until needed (Figure 3-31). This lets a large program run in a small amount of memory. Pro-

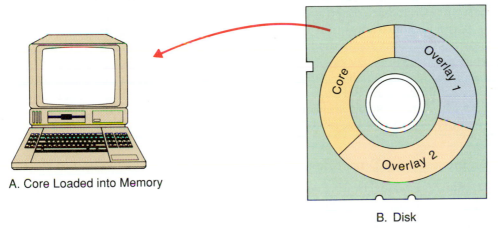

A. Core Loaded into Memory

B. Disk

FIGURE 3-31
Disk-Based Programs
A disk-based program initially loads only the program's core (a). The program's overlay files remain on the disk until you execute a command stored in these files. The core then reads the appropriate overlay file into memory (you will hear the drive operate), and that overlay file completes the command (b).

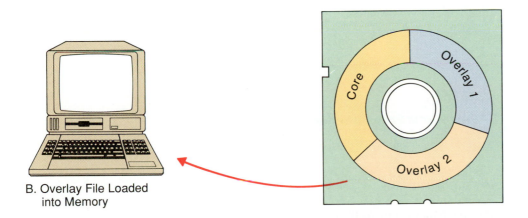

B. Overlay File Loaded into Memory

grams of this kind have two parts. The **core**, or kernel, is that part of the program always in memory. It executes the most often used commands and calls other parts of the program, the **overlay files**, into memory when they are needed. When you execute a command, the disk drive often operates because the command often is not in memory; thus the core goes to the disk to load the necessary overlay file. You can sometimes identify these files in your disk directory because they frequently have the extension .OVR. There are advantages and disadvantages to disk-based programs.

- Disk-based programs usually do not take up as much memory as do memory-based programs, so you can work on larger files.
- Since a disk-based program must go to the disk occasionally for those parts of the program or data files it needs, these programs are slower than memory-based programs. Retrieving overlay files from a disk slows down the execution of commands.
- Since the program leaves part of its own files on the disk, the disk must be left in the drive so that the program can find these files when it needs them.

DATA FILES AND MEMORY

When you use an applications program to create a document, spreadsheet model, or database, you store your work on a disk in a **data file** so that you can retrieve it later. Each type of applications program creates its own type of data file. For example, files you create with a word processing program are called document files, those you create with a spreadsheet program are worksheet files, those you create with a database management program are record or database files, and those you create with a graphics program are picture files (Table 3-1).

The data files you are working on are handled in two ways: They can be memory based or disk based.

Memory-Based Data Files

Memory-based programs keep the entire file you are working on in memory. These programs have advantages and disadvantages.

- The size of files created on memory-based programs is limited by the available memory.
- You move through large memory-based files more quickly.

TABLE 3-1
Applications Programs and Their Files

Type of Applications Program	Name of Files
Word processing	Document files
Desktop publishing	Document files
Spreadsheet	Worksheet files
Database management files	Database or record
Graphics	Picture files

Disk-Based Data Files

Other programs keep only part of long files in memory and store other parts on a disk (Figure 3-32). For example, when you are using word processing program that stores part of the file on a disk, the disk drive will operate when you are working on a long file and move the cursor to a distant part of the file. The program has to retrieve from the disk the part of the file you are moving to because it is not in memory at that moment. When a program stores data on the disk as if it were storing it in memory, it is called virtual memory. Disk-based programs have advantages and disadvantages.

- The size of files created on disk-based programs is limited only by the amount of storage space on the disk.
- You move through large disk-based data files more slowly since the program may have to retrieve sections of the file from the disk.

FILE TYPES

Applications programs are often capable of saving files in various formats. Many programs automatically add an extension to the filename to differentiate one type of file from another.

Binary Files

The files you create with a program are usually saved in a binary format. Along with ASCII characters, most programs use additional bytes that are coded to represent commands. These coded characters are used for many formatting commands specific to the program. For example, when you underline words, add page numbers, change margins or line spacing, or add headers and footers, you are actually entering codes into the document. These codes are specific to the program you are using; there is no standard. Thus these codes cannot be interpreted by other programs. Files containing these codes are called **binary files**. To use binary files with another program, the program-specific codes must be either removed or converted into codes the program will understand. This is generally done by saving them with a command designed for this purpose or by using a separate program to convert them.

Binary files are usually saved with an extension specific to the program you are working on. Some programs automatically add an extension, for example, .DOC (for document), to every file you save. Other programs do not automatically add an extension, but you can add one. Different extensions let you distinguish among files created with different programs.

FIGURE 3-32
Disk-Based Data Files
Some programs store parts of your file on the disk while you are working on it so that you can work with files that are too large to fit into the computer's memory.

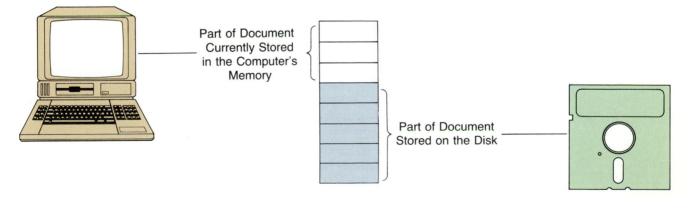

Part of Document Currently Stored in the Computer's Memory

Part of Document Stored on the Disk

ASCII Files

ASCII files are saved in a standard format. When saved in this format, they can be used by other programs or transmitted by a modem over telephone lines. When you use a word processing system and indent, boldface, set spacing, and the like, the program is inserting formatting or printer control codes throughout your text. These control codes are specific to your program and can rarely be interpreted by other programs. Nor can they be telecommunicated using a modem without first making special provisions. Many programs, therefore, allow you to save files as ASCII text files. When saved in this way, all control codes specific to the program are removed from the file. These files are identified with various extensions, two of the most common being .TXT (for text) and .ASC (for ASCII).

Print Files

Print files are like ASCII files, but all format commands you have entered into the file are interpreted. A print file is created just like a printout on the printer. The only difference is that the output is sent to a file on a disk instead of to the printer. For example, headers, footers, page numbers, top and bottom margins, and other formats that would appear on a printout also appear in the print file on the disk. Print files are created so that you can preview the results of format commands before actually printing the file on paper. They also can be printed directly from the operating system and, in some cases, can be used (as ASCII files can be) by other programs. For example, using print files, you can exchange formatted text between programs. You can create a file using a spreadsheet or graphics program and then print it to the disk. You can then load a word processing program and these print files into a document. Print files are usually identified with an extension like .PRT or .PRN (for print).

EXCHANGING FILES BETWEEN PROGRAMS

What if twenty manufacturers made twenty different kinds of record turntables and twenty recording companies produced twenty different kinds of records? If you changed turntables, you might have to buy an entirely new record collection. It is unlikely that the music business would be successful if it operated like this. But as shortsighted as it sounds, this is the way it is in the computer field. Apple computers cannot run IBM PC programs or files. Files created with WordPerfect cannot be edited with WordStar. This incompatibility causes problems for companies that use more than one program. The incompatibility arises from two causes: file storage techniques and file formats.

File Storage Techniques

As you saw in Part Two, the operating system controls the way files are saved on a disk. When you format a disk, you customize it for use with your equipment and operating system. When you then save data onto the disk, the operating system saves it using its own specific storage techniques. If you then take the disk to another computer running a different operating system, you cannot retrieve the files from the disk. For example, a disk used with an Apple Macintosh cannot be read by an IBM PS/2 even though both computers use 3½-inch disks.

To transfer the files, you usually have to send the disk to an outside service that has the hardware and software that can convert the files for you.

When you upgrade from one type of floppy disk to another, the problem is not as serious. For example, the millions of users of IBM PCs have stored their work on 5¼-inch floppy disks. But the new IBM PS/2 computers use 3½-inch floppy disks. To use old files on the new machines, users must either add a 5¼-inch floppy disk drive to their new system or have someone who has done so copy their files for them.

File Formats

As you have seen, the ASCII code stores characters in a computer in a standard way. This standardization lets you exchange files between programs. The problem is that data files you create do not contain only ASCII characters. When you use many formatting commands, for example, those to underline or boldface text, change margins, and enter subscripts or superscripts, the program enters codes that tell the printer what to do. These codes are not standardized. To transfer files to another program, you have two choices: Save the file in a format that can be read by another program, or convert the file into another format using a file conversion program.

Saving a File in a Format That Can Be Read by Another Program

What if you want to insert a spreadsheet model or database file into a report? Or what if you want to insert a table in a document into a spreadsheet model or a database file? Do you have to retype everything? The answer is no if your program allows you to save files in an ASCII text format. When you save a file as an ASCII text file, you remove any special codes so that the file contains only ASCII characters. When you retrieve the file with another program, you have to reformat it.

Converting a File into Another Format

What if you want to transfer a model created on one spreadsheet program to a database or vice versa? Since each program uses its own unique ways to code data, files can't be used directly; they first must be converted. As you have seen, saving files as ASCII or print files converts all formulas and numeric values to text characters. If one of these files were retrieved by another spreadsheet program, all the characters would be treated as labels. To allow you to transfer files, special utility programs have been developed. Instead of removing codes, you can use a utility program to convert the codes entered with one program into those used by another.

USING OPERATING SYSTEM FUNCTIONS FROM WITHIN APPLICATIONS PROGRAMS

As you saw in Part Two, you can use the operating system's utilities to format disks, copy files, and accomplish other file management tasks. There are times when you want to perform these tasks while working on a program. But to quit the program, return to DOS, perform the tasks, and then reload the program is time consuming. Therefore, most applications programs let you execute DOS commands without quitting. There are two approaches.

- The program has commands that perform the most common operating system commands. For example, you use the applications program's commands to copy or rename a file instead of the operating system's commands.

■ The program allows you to access the operating system to perform these tasks without actually leaving the application program. When you use this command, the system prompt appears on the screen. You can then use any of the standard operating system's commands. When finished, you type a command, usually EXIT and then press **Return**. This returns you to where you were before you accessed the operating system.

SUMMARY AND KEY TERMS

■ Some programs are **memory based**: the entire program is loaded into memory. Other programs are **disk based**: only the **core** of the program is loaded into memory. Other parts of disk-based programs, called **overlay files,** are stored on the disk until needed. This is called **virtual memory** because the program is using the disk as if it were internal memory.

■ The files that you create when working on an applications program are called **data files**.

■ The maximum size of data files on programs that use **memory-based data files** is limited by the available computer memory; on programs that use **disk-based data files**, their size is limited only by the amount of available disk storage space. Those that use virtual memory allow you to create extremely long files. But using the disk in this way slows the program down since it takes time for the section to be reloaded into memory.

■ Most programs codes into files that make them incompatible with other programs. These are called **binary files**. Saving files as **ASCII files** removes these codes so that the text can be used by other programs or transmitted by electronic mail.

■ The compatibility of data files is determined by the computer's storage techniques and the program's file formats.

■ Saving files in an ASCII format allows you to exchange data between spreadsheets, word processors, and record files.

■ File conversion converts the codes entered into a file into codes that can be read by another program. This conversion is done with a utility program.

REVIEW QUESTIONS

1. What is the difference between a disk-based program and a memory-based program? List one advantage and one disadvantage of each.
2. What is the difference between disk-based data files and memory-based data files? List one advantage and one disadvantage of each.
3. What is a data file? List four types of data files.
4. What is a binary file?
5. What is an ASCII file?
6. What is the difference between files that are stored in ASCII and binary formats?
7. What is a print file? How do print files differ from ASCII files?
8. What prevents you from using the information stored on an IBM disk on an Apple computer?
9. What prevents you from editing a file created on one word processing program with another program?
10. What format do you save files in when you want to exchange them between programs?
11. What operation can you perform to convert a file created on one program so that it can be used by another program?
12. Why would you want to access the operating system without leaving an applications program?

Applications Program Issues

OBJECTIVES

After completing this topic, you will be able to

- Explain some of the major issues that arise for users of applications software

- Explain what clones are, and describe how they differ from the programs they emulate

- Describe viruses and how to avoid them

When you use microcomputers and applications software programs, you should understand the following issues.

COPY PROTECTION

Software publishers have done an outstanding job at producing and providing useful, powerful, easy-to-use software. Users generally appreciate this and pay well for the privilege of using it. However, one issue that deeply divides users and publishers is copy protection. Most software publishers feel the investment they have made and the risks they have taken justify their charging a high price for their products. Most people who understand the principles of business agree with them. But publishers, rightly or wrongly, do not trust users. They feel users would copy unprotected disks and freely distribute them to friends and co-workers. To discourage this theft, many software publishers copy protect their program disks so that users cannot copy them. This seems reasonable.

But copy protection presents serious difficulties for users. The first problem occurs when an important disk containing a program is lost or damaged, especially if the firm that produced it is no longer in business. Generally, publishers provide a backup copy along with the original disk, but this disk could also be lost or damaged, leaving the user unable to use valuable files. The second problem occurs when computers are connected into networks. Some publishers code their program disks with "keys" that must be checked by the computer when the program is first loaded. This means a copy of the disk must be provided for every computer in the network. These same keys affect people who use computers with hard disk drives. Hard disk drives (see Topic 1-7) have one major convenience: You can store many programs on a hard disk so that you do not have to keep swapping floppy disks. The program disk that contains a key, however, must be inserted into the disk drive when the program is loaded even when the program is already stored on the hard disk drive.

PIRACY

Several firms have produced special programs designed to copy disks that have been copy protected. The rationale for these programs is that users need backup copies in case something goes wrong with the primary disk. But some users, and almost all software companies, feel a different rationale predominates—that these programs are used to copy programs so that they can be distributed to others. Called **piracy**, this practice costs software companies lost revenues, and they are increasingly taking legal action to prevent the distribution, sale, and use of these disks, especially in large corporations. Corporations are even being held accountable for the actions of employees who use these programs to copy disks.

LICENSING

When you walk into a computer store and pay $100 or more for a program, you may think you have bought the program, but usually you would be wrong. You have actually bought the **license**, or right, to use the program and its documentation. The physical materials still belong to the publisher. Read these licenses carefully; they spell out your rights in detail (Figure 3-33).

SITE LICENSING

As corporations and other large organizations have become more dominant in the software market, they have become increasingly forceful in setting the terms they are willing to accept when they buy applications programs. More and more firms are demanding site licenses. A **site license** allows a company either to run programs on networks without having a copy for each workstation or to make a limited number of copies for use within a single department or location. Site licenses reduce the companies total software costs, lessen the likelihood of violating the publisher's legal rights, and make it easier on all network users since they do not need individual copies of the program.

DOCUMENTATION

Computer and software manuals, called **documentation**, are the computer industry's Achilles heel. Much of what you are expected to read and understand has been written by programmers for programmers. The reason we point this out is simple—you are not nearly as dumb as some of this material will make you feel.

We all need patience and help to overcome the shortcomings of documentation. Most users do not rely entirely on the documentation that comes with their hardware and software. They take courses, use on-screen tutorials, read books, talk to other users, and join users groups. Not only does this make them more knowledgeable, but it also gives them a better sense of the excitement of being in a new field. When the field has matured to where the computer is as easy to use as a telephone, people will no longer feel the

The TWIN™ Educational Version Program License Agreement

READ THE FOLLOWING TERMS AND CONDITIONS CAREFULLY BEFORE OPENING THE DISKETTE ENVELOPE. OPENING THE DISKETTE ENVELOPE CONSTITUTES YOUR ACCEPTANCE OF THESE TERMS AND CONDITIONS. IF YOU DO NOT AGREE TO THESE TERMS AND CONDITIONS, YOU MUST PROMPTLY RETURN THE ENTIRE PACKAGE WITH THE DISKETTE ENVELOPE UNOPENED AND YOUR PAYMENT WILL BE REFUNDED.

Mosaic Software, Inc. and Prentice-Hall, Inc. provide this program and license its use for educational purposes only. You assume responsibility for the selection of the product to achieve your intended results, and for the installation, use and results obtained from the program.

LICENSE

As licensed owner, you may:

a. use the program on a single machine.

b. copy the program into any machine-readable or printed form for back-up or modification purposes in support of your use of the program on a single machine.

c. transfer the program and the license to another party if the other party agrees to accept the terms and conditions of this Agreement. If you transfer the program to another party, you must transfer all copies of the program, in either written, printed, or machine-readable form, at the same time to the same party or destroy any additional copies of the program in your possession; this includes all modifications and portions of the program therein or elsewhere contained.

You must reproduce and include the copyright notice on any and all copies you create.

YOU MAY NOT USE, COPY, MODIFY, OR TRANSFER THE PROGRAM, OR ANY COPY, MODIFICATION IN WHOLE OR IN PART, EXCEPT AS EXPRESSLY PROVIDED FOR IN THIS LICENSE.

IF YOU TRANSFER POSSESSION OF ANY COPY OF THE PROGRAM TO ANOTHER PARTY, YOUR LICENSE IS TERMINATED.

This program is copyrighted and protected by the copyright laws of the United States. Any copying of this program unless authorized by Mosaic Software, Inc. and Prentice-Hall, Inc. is illegal and prohibited by law.

TERM

Your license is effective until terminated. You may terminate your license at any time by destroying the program, including all copies and modifications in any form. Your license will also terminate upon conditions and terms set forth elsewhere in this Agreement or if you fail to comply with any term or condition of this Agreement. You agree upon such a termination of your license to destroy the program and all copies in any form that you hold in your possession.

LIMITED WARRANTY

The Package, including the program, is provided "as is" without warranty of any kind, either expressed or implied, including, but not limited to the implied warranties of merchantability and fitness for a particular purpose. The entire risk as to the quality and performance of the program is with you. Should the program prove defective, you (and not Mosaic Software, Inc. or Prentice-Hall, Inc.) assume the entire cost of all necessary servicing, repair or correction. Some states do not allow the exclusion of implied warranties so the above exclusion may not apply to you. This warranty gives you specific legal rights and you may also have other rights which vary from state to state.

Mosaic Software, Inc. and Prentice-Hall, Inc. do not warrant that the functions contained in the program will meet your requirements or that the operation of the program will be uninterrupted or error free.

FIGURE 3-33
License Agreement
Courtesy of Prentice-Hall, Inc.

frustrations they now feel, but they will also no longer feel the accomplishment of having mastered something new and different.

SUPPORT

Many leading software publishers offer **support** for their programs. This support usually consists of a technical representative you can call if you have a problem. Some of these support services charge a fee.

TRAINING

When new employees are hired or new programs introduced into a company, users must be trained. The responsibility for this training is usually assigned to the management information systems (MIS) department or the information center (IC). The high cost of this training makes companies reluctant to introduce new programs and has led to the standardization of programs within each company. Most companies specify that you can use no more than one or two programs in each of the main applications categories. If you use an unauthorized program, the company may not supply training, and the files you create may be unusable by other employees.

PROGRAM UPDATES

Companies that publish programs generally update them every one or two years. **Updates** (also called upgrades) generally include corrected old features as well as new features that improve the program.

When new versions are prepared that contain only corrections, users are not informed of their availability unless they have registered with the company. Most programs come with a card that you fill out and return to the company to become a registered user. The better publishing companies notify registered owners when new versions are available.

New versions generally build on the previous version so that you have to learn only the new features. Generally, new versions of a program can work on any files created with earlier versions. This may be a one-way street, however, because files created with the new version may not be usable with earlier versions of the program.

Updates are not free, but publishers usually offer attractive discounts to get previous users to buy the update. This process of releasing new versions is occasionally misused. Publishers know it is easier to sell updates to their existing customers than it is to attract new customers. The fact that files created on the new version usually cannot be used by earlier versions forces users who exchange files to buy the new update. If only a few users buy the update and others do not, the files created by those using the new version cannot be shared by those who chose not to upgrade. This is called a **forced upgrade**, and users should both resist and object to this practice. When faced with a new version, you should be an informed consumer. Find out what features the new program has. If it does not have any that you need, you probably should not buy the new version.

CLONES

Over the past few years, a few spreadsheet, database, and word processing programs have become standards in their areas of application. These standards are a two-edged sword. On the one hand, they simplify training because there is a large pool of people familiar with these programs, and new users have to be trained on only one program. On the other hand, users have become increasingly frustrated by high prices, copy protection, the lack of site licenses, and the forced upgrade polices imposed on them by the companies that publish these standard programs. The trade journals and end-user publications are full of complaints about the rigidness of these policies. This frustration has been heard by entrepreneurs who have rushed to fill the needs of these users. The result has been the development of **clones**, or compatible programs that are almost indistinguishable from the standards. The ingredients for a successful clone are simple.

- They must use the same command structure as the leading program in the field so that users do not have to familiarize themselves with new and different commands.

- They must be able to retrieve files created on the leading program and save files that the leading program can retrieve.

- They must have features not available on the leading program, and they must improve on its power, flexibility, and usefulness.

- They must have a lower price, must not be copy protected, and must be available through a site license; moreover, upgrades must be inexpensive and offer real improvements on the previous version.

- They must overcome the users' mental block that clones are somehow

Bugs: Who Made the Mistake?

Occasionally when you are working with an applications program, something doesn't work the way you expect. Most users immediately conclude that they did something wrong. But this isn't always so. Sometimes the problem was caused by an error in the program itself. These programming errors are called **bugs**.

The source of the term *bug* is often credited to Grace Hopper. She used it to describe a problem caused when a moth flew into the contacts of the Mark II computer. Actually, the term was used before by Thomas Edison. Here is an extract from a letter he wrote that clearly uses the term in its modern computer context.

I have the right principle and am on the right track, but time, hard work, and some good luck are necessary too. It has been just so in all of my inventions. The first step is an intuition, and comes with a burst, then difficulties arise—this thing gives out and then - 'Bugs' - as such little faults and difficulties are called—show themselves and months of intense watching, study, and labor are requisite before commercial success—or failure—is certainly reached.

Letter from Thomas Edison to Theodore Puskas (November 13, 1878)

inferior, just as it has been overcome in the hardware field. A few years ago, clones of leading computers held a small market share. Today, they control more than 50 percent of the market, and that share is growing daily. The same recognition by users, that quality and value are more important than brand names, is now rapidly occurring in the software field.

VIRUSES

One of the fastest growing problems in the microcomputer field is the introduction of **viruses** by antisocial users. A virus is a small program, either stored on a disk by itself or appended to an existing file called a **Trojan horse**. When the file is loaded or the Trojan-horse program is run, the virus loads itself into the computer's memory. Once there, it can secretly attach itself to other files or programs or store itself on any other disks run on the computer, including the hard disk. What happens next, depends on the intent of the vandal that created the virus.

- The virus may cause problems immediately.
- It may count specific occurrences, for example, how many times it is copied, and then cause damage.
- It may look at the computer's clock and cause damage on a specific date.
- It may reproduce itself and then cause damage. Like a biological virus, a computer virus can infect other files and then be spread from them (Figure 3-34).

The number of instances in which viruses cause damage is increasing (see *The Viruses Are Coming*). Once introduced, viruses are hard to detect and remove. Thankfully, several programs have been developed to locate and remove viruses. For individual users, the best defense is to use only commercial programs and not to exchange files with other users. Especially avoid downloading files from public bulletin boards (see Topic 8-6).

FIGURE 3-34
How a Rogue Program Spreads
Reprinted by permission of The New York Times Company.

1. A programmer creates a program that can secretly bind to another program or a computer operating system and copy itself.

2. The program is placed on a floppy diskette or hidden in a program sent to an electronic information service, or electronic bulletin board, where information is exchanged by computer over telephone lines.

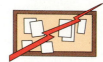

3. When an unknowing user inserts the floppy diskette in a computer or retrieves data containing the rogue program from another computer via telephone, a new computer is infected.

4. Once inside the new computer, the program copies itself onto a new floppy diskette or the computer's hard disk.

5. Later, the program is activated according to instructions originally embedded within it by the programmer. It might be set off on a certain date or after making a certain number of copies of itself. The instructions can be as benign as displaying a message or as destructive as the erasure of all the data stored in the computer.

The Viruses Are Coming

- A virus introduced into the computers at several universities counted the number of times it copied itself to other disks. When it had reproduced itself four times, it erased all files on the current disks in the computer.

- ARC, a major shareware program used to compress files so that they take up less space on the disk and can be telecommunicated faster, was altered and then uploaded to bulletin board systems. When it was then downloaded to a user's computer and run, it erased the part of the hard disk that is needed to boot the computer.

- A Christmas message sent over IBM's worldwide network looked up the mailing list of each person it was sent to and then sent itself to all those people. The cascade effect as it was sent to more and more people slowed down the system and eventually brought it to a halt.

- A virus attached to Aldus's Freehand program displayed a peace message on users' screens on March 2, 1988, the anniversary of Apple's introduction of the Macintosh II. This was the first virus to be distributed in a commercial software program. The program infected several hundred thousand computers.

- A stack for Apple's Hypercard was uploaded to CompuServe. It contained the same peace message distributed on Freehand and displayed the message on the screen of any other user who downloaded the file.

- Some program disks are **copy protected** so that you cannot make copies of them.

- Making unauthorized copies of programs is called **piracy**.

- When you buy an applications program, you have actually bought only a **license** to use it. To use it on more than one computer, for example, to run it on a network, you buy a separate **site license**.

- Since **documentation** often leaves much to be desired, many publishers also offer **support** for their products. To use this support, you must register with the company and sometimes pay a fee.

- When new features are added to an existing program, it is released by the publisher as an **update**. Some updates should be bought and others not. You should make an informed decision. When the publisher puts the old version out of production and arranges it so that older versions cannot read the new update's files, it is called a **forced upgrade**. It is forced because if one person in your office needs a copy of the program, they can buy only a version whose files cannot be read by other users, forcing them to also upgrade.

- **Clones** are inexpensive versions of leading programs. Many clones are actually superior to the program they are based on.

- **Viruses** are programs or altered programs that copy themselves onto other disks. When triggered, they display messages or cause damage.

1. What does it mean when a disk is copy protected? Why is copy protection sometimes necessary?

2. Do you think it is legal or ethical to copy disks when a publisher has asked you not to? Why or why not?

3. When you buy a program, do you usually buy all rights to it?

4. What is the purpose of a site license?

5. What is a bug?

6. What are program updates? Should you always buy them?

7. What are clones? List some of the ingredients for a successful clone.

8. What is a virus? What is one way to avoid them?

Part Four

WORD PROCESSING AND DESKTOP PUBLISHING APPLICATIONS

Topic 4-1   Word Processing Procedures: An Overview

Topic 4-2   Typical Word Processing Programs

Topic 4-3   Entering Documents

Topic 4-4   Editing Documents

Topic 4-5   Working with Blocks of Text

Topic 4-6   Searching and Replacing

Topic 4-7   Editing Aids

Topic 4-8   Default Formats

Topic 4-9   Page Breaks and Page Numbers

Topic 4-10   Text Alignment and Hyphenation

Topic 4-11   Text Emphasis, Superscripts, and Subscripts

Topic 4-12   Fonts

Topic 4-13   Page Layout

Topic 4-14   Tab Stops and Indents

Topic 4-15   Headers and Footers

Topic 4-16   Format Style Sheets

Case Study   Creating a Resume

Topic 4-17   Merge Printing

Topic 4-18   Document Assembly

Topic 4-19   Drawing Lines

Topic 4-20   Creating Special Characters

Topic 4-21   Printing in Columns

Topic 4-22   Combining Graphics with Text

Topic 4-23   Page Makeup

Topic 4-24   Glossaries

Topic 4-25   Math

Topic 4-26   Automatically Generated Lists

Topic 4-27   Footnotes and Endnotes

Topic 4-28   Sorting

Topic 4-29   Outlines

Topic 4-30   Filling Out Forms

Topic 4-31   Word Processing Macros

Word processing is probably the most common application of microcomputers. The ease with which you can draft and revise memos, letters, reports, and other documents with a word processing program increases both the speed and quality of your writing. You can enter, edit, change, reorganize, format, and print text without having to retype all of it each time you make a change. This ease of use encourages you to revise and reorganize your material more frequently so that you can express your ideas more clearly.

Until recently, word processing could be done only on **dedicated word processors**. They are called dedicated because word processing is all that you can do on these machines. But over the past few years, word processing programs have been developed for microcomputers that improve on the features of these more expensive dedicated word processors.

Many word processing programs are on the market. All of them allow you to accomplish the basic word processing functions, like entering, editing, formatting, and printing text. They differ from one another in two major respects: the features they offer and the procedures you follow to obtain specific results.

The number of features offered by word processing programs increases almost daily. A few years ago, a program that allowed you to enter, edit, format, and print a document was considered sufficient. These functions alone were such an improvement to the typewriter that many people switched to microcomputer-based word processing systems. Newer programs, however, have added built-in spelling checkers and thesauruses and the ability to draw lines, make calculations, print in multiple columns, and so on. Gradually, features once considered exotic have become standard. Today, programs that lack these features are considered inferior or incomplete. The improvements are continuing. Features considered exotic today, like those found in desktop publishing programs, will be considered standard tomorrow.

Keeping abreast of this rapidly developing technology is an adventure. But you cannot keep up unless you have a solid understanding of the many features that are now offered and those that are soon to be offered. In this part, we help you gain this understanding. We introduce you to the features now available on all programs and to some features not yet widely available. When you have finished the course that this text is based on, you will be prepared to work with virtually all word processing programs now and in the future.

HOW THIS PART IS ORGANIZED

To introduce you to word processing procedures, we have organized Part Four into thirty-one topics. These topics are familiar because they are not limited to microcomputer-based word processing. They discuss the same results you might want to obtain if typing on a typewriter. For example, topics include controlling page breaks and page numbers, entering headers and footers, emphasizing characters, aligning text with margins, and using tabs and indents.

Organizing the discussion of word processing around these familiar topics makes it easier for you to find the information you need. The results discussed under these topics are seldom discussed in the manuals that accompany word processing programs. The writers of these manuals assume you know what indents, enumerations, outlines, and margins are and that you know how, when, and where to use them. In this part, we not only discuss these results, we also illustrate them. These illustrations help you picture the results, and some provide examples you can use to practice the procedures you follow to obtain them on your own word processing system.

Each topic explains the procedures you follow to obtain the desired result. Because these procedures vary from program to program, each topic describes several of the approaches used. This overview prepares you to use any word processing program.

WORD PROCESSING TERMINOLOGY

As you study word processing procedures, you will find that the terminology is not standardized. The variety of terms applied to the same items or procedures causes confusion and makes the subject sound more complicated than it really is. Table 4-1 shows some of the generic terms we use in this part and the terms five leading programs use for the same items. In this part, we introduce you to the principles behind these and other terms so that you will be able to understand them regardless of the names they are given by the publishers of these and other programs.

The applications of word processing software are almost endless, ranging from the same tasks that can be done on a typewriter (for example, writing memos, letters, and reports) to entire new kinds of tasks that aren't possible without the power of the computer. Let's look at some.

TABLE 4-1
Word Processing Terms

Generic Term	DisplayWrite 4	Microsoft Word	WordStar	MultiMate	WordPerfect
Hard carriage return	Required carrier return	Paragraph mark return	Hard carriage return		Hard return
Soft carriage return			Soft carriage return		Soft return
Hard hyphen	Required hyphen	Hard hyphen	Hard hyphen		Hyphen
Soft hyphen	Syllable hyphen	Normal or optional hyphens	Soft hyphen	Soft hyphen	Soft hyphen
Hard space	Required space	Required space	Hard space	Hard space	Hard space
Soft space		Soft space	Soft space		Soft space
Hard page break	Required page end	Hard page break	Hard page break	Required page break	Hard page break
Soft page break	Auto page end	Soft page break	Soft page break		Soft page break
Insert mode	Insert	Insert	Insert on	Insert	Insert
Typeover mode	Typeover	Overtype	Insert off	Strikeover	Typeover
Word-wrap	Auto carrier return	Wordwrap (one word)	Word-wrap	Word-wrap	Word-wrap
Paragraph reforming	Line adjust		Aligning	Adjusted	Rewrite
Typewriter mode	N/A	Print direct	N/A	Typewriter mode	Type-thru
Primary file	Shell document	Main document	Master document	Merge document	Primary document
Secondary file	Variables document	Data document	Data file	Merge datafile	Secondary file

- Memos, letters, and reports can be quickly entered, edited, revised, saved, and printed in various formats.

- Form documents can be prepared and used over and over again, with just a name or phrase changed here and there. Contracts, sales letters, and collection notices are typical form documents. You can use a word processor to create and save the form document's **boilerplate**—the part of the document that never changes.

    You can then retrieve the boilerplate whenever you need it and insert the data that personalizes the document for a specific use. Some word processors can be used in conjunction with databases that store mailing lists and other data. By coding form documents to indicate what, and where, information from the database should be inserted, tens, hundreds, or thousands of personalized form letters can be printed. The same database can then be used to print the corresponding envelopes or mailing labels.

- Electronic mail documents can be prepared for telecommunication over telephone lines with a modem. Many services have been introduced to instantly transmit letters and other documents to other computer users. Some of the better known of these services are The Source, EasyLink (Western Union), MCI Mail, and CompuServe. You can enter your message when connected to these services, but this is time consuming and expensive. Moreover, the editing capabilities on these systems are limited. It is usually faster, easier, and cheaper to prepare these documents using your own word processor and then send them (called uploading) to the service's computer to be distributed, thus minimizing the time and expense of being connected to the service. On some systems, you can **broadcast** copies of your letter to several recipients at the same time.

- Copy for printing can be prepared on a computer. Recent advances in computerized typesetting make it possible to lay out and illustrate text on your word processing system so that codes embedded in the text with the word processor can be used to control a powerful typesetter. The text can also be sent to a relatively inexpensive, but very high quality, laser printer that prints your material using a much wider variety of typestyles and type sizes than those found on a regular printer. This printed copy can then be distributed as is or used as camera-ready copy to make plates to print copies. This emerging technology opens up a new world of opportunities since you can now inexpensively generate typeset-quality copy for catalogs, advertising circulars, reports, articles, and books.

A NOTE ON DESKTOP PUBLISHING

In the early days of computers, people who used them for word processing had to use two programs. One program, a text editor, was used to enter and edit text. When the document was completed, a second program, a text formatter, was used to format the document for printing. Today, we find ourselves in a similar position though at a much higher level. One of the fastest growing areas within word processing is desktop publishing, which makes it possible to produce documents that look like the documents printed by professional printers. A complete desktop publishing system lets you print text using a variety of fonts (typestyles and typefaces); it also lets you combine line art and digitized photographs on the same page. A complete system lets you print in columns and add special textures, patterns,

The History of Word Processing

You may be surprised to learn how short the history of word processing really is. From the first primitive "automatic typewriters" developed in the early part of this century to today's sophisticated microcomputer-based programs is only a very short period—most of the major advances have been made in your lifetime. Here are some of the key points in the history of word processing:

1918 Hooven introduced an automatic typewriter that could record keystrokes on an embossed cylinder for later playback.

1932 The Automatic Typewriter Company introduced the "Auto-Typist," which used paper tape similar to that used on player pianos to record and play back keystrokes made on a typewriter. This typewriter was being manufactured and sold as recently as the late 1970s.

1964 IBM introduced the IBM MT/ST (Magnetic Tape/Selectric Typewriter), which married a magnetic tape storage unit to a selectric typewriter so that text could be stored and then played back again.

1969 IBM introduced the IBM MC/ST (Magnetic Card/Selectric Typewriter), which replaced the magnetic tape storage unit with a magnetic card unit. Each magnetic card could hold a single page of typed text.

1972 Lexitron introduced the first video display unit so that type could be displayed and edited on a screen before printing.

1973 Vydec introduced the first word processor that used magnetic disks and a disk drive to store documents.

1978 MicroPro International introduced WordStar to run on a wide variety of microcomputers.

The major names in word processing have all entered the field within the past thirty years. The dates on which some of them introduced their first word processing products are all surprisingly recent:

1964	IBM
1971	Olivetti
1972	Wang
1973	Videc
1974	Xerox
1975	Digital Equipment Corporation

and lines. Desktop publishing programs that improve the printed quality of documents are being widely used to create forms, newsletters, manuals, charts, brochures, letterheads, logos, catalogs, and reports.

Today, word processing and desktop publishing programs have only some overlap. Word processing programs are better for entering and editing documents, and desktop publishing programs are better for formatting them. Thus text is normally created with a word processing program and then transferred to a desktop publishing program where you format and lay it out for printing. The overlap between word processing and desktop publishing will rapidly increase over the next few years. You will see more and more desktop publishing features incorporated into word processing programs. Increasingly, you will be able to create, edit, format, and lay out sophisticated documents on the same program. Because these two fields are so closely allied, we treat them together in this part. Topics that apply to desktop publishing include 4-12, 4-16, and 4-19 through 4-23.

REVIEW QUESTIONS

1. What is a dedicated word processor?

2. List and describe four common applications of word processing. Can you think of one that is not mentioned in the text?

3. Briefly describe desktop publishing, and list some of its applications.

Word Processing Procedures: An Overview

OBJECTIVE

After completing this topic, you will be able to

- List and describe the basic steps you follow when preparing a document

In Topic 1-1, we introduced you to the five steps in the information processing cycle: input, processing, output, storage and retrieval, and distribution and communications. Let's now look at how a word processing program is used in this cycle, from loading the program to clearing the screen or quitting. Later in this part, we explain these procedures in detail. We also introduce you to the many variations that programs offer for each of these procedures.

STEP 1: LOAD THE PROGRAM

The first step in word processing is loading the program. To do so, you first load the computer's operating system and then the word processing program into the computer's memory from the disks they are stored on. If you are using a computer with floppy disk drives, you also insert a formatted data disk into drive B.

STEP 2: OPEN A NEW DOCUMENT (OR EDIT AN EXISTING ONE)

When you load the program, it usually displays a copyright notice and then does one of two things: It displays either the document screen (Figure 4-1) or a Main menu (Figure 4-2). If a Main menu appears, it lists choices you can select from, usually by typing a number preceding the desired choice. When you select the choice that opens a new document, the document screen appears. However you get there, once the document screen appears, you are ready to enter text.

Naming Documents

Depending on the word processor you are using, you may have to name the document file before creating (typing and editing) it. Other programs are designed so that you don't assign a name until you save the document.

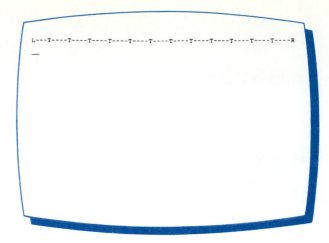

```
L---T----T----T----T----T----T----T----T----T----T----R
—
```

FIGURE 4-1
The Document Screen
The document screen
always displays a cursor.

```
1. Create a new document
2. Edit an existing document
3. Save the document
4. Print document
5. Check spelling
6. Quit the program

       Enter choice:__
```

FIGURE 4-2
The Main Menu
On some programs, you
have to make a choice
from the Main menu to
display the document
screen.

Retrieving Existing Documents

If you created the memo earlier and saved it onto a disk, you must first retrieve it from that disk. You retrieve existing documents for editing using the *Edit Existing Document, Retrieve,* or *Load* command and then specifying the filename assigned when it was created and saved. When you retrieve a file from the disk, it is "copied" into memory; the document file on the disk remains unchanged.

STEP 3: ENTER THE DOCUMENT

The document screen always displays a cursor, a one-character wide underline or box. The cursor indicates where the next character you type will appear. When you type a character, it appears on the screen, and the cursor moves one space to the right. The text you enter is not only displayed on the screen (Figure 4-3), it is also stored in the computer's memory.

Entering text on a word processor is similar to entering it on a typewriter. The main difference is that you do not have to press **Return** at the end of each line (as you have to press the carriage return on a typewriter); the program automatically does that for you. You have to press **Return** only at the end of paragraphs and when you want a line to end before the right margin is reached.

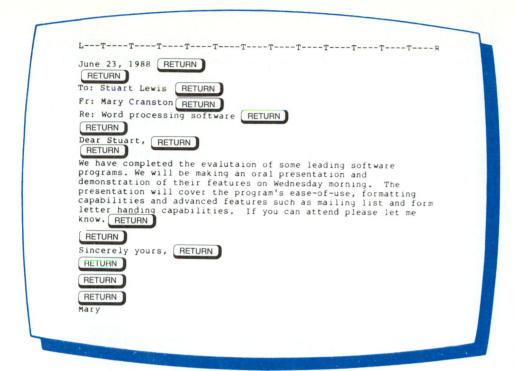

FIGURE 4-3
Entering the Document
You enter a document by typing, pressing **Return** only at the end of paragraphs.

STEP 4: EDIT AND REVISE THE DOCUMENT

After you enter the document, you proofread it and correct any mistakes. Generally, it is easier to proofread a printout of a document than to proofread the document on the screen (Figure 4-4).

To edit a document on the screen after you have proofread it, you use the cursor movement keys to move the cursor through the text of the document. You can then delete or insert characters, words, or phrases, or you can select blocks—large sections of text—to copy, move, or delete in one step. You can also use advanced editing features like search and replace and spell checking to speed up the editing.

```
        June 23, 1988

        To: Stuart Lewis
        Fr: Mary Rogers
        Re: Word processing software

        Dear Stuart,

        We have completed the evalutaion of some leading software
        programs. We will be making an oral presentation and
        demonstration of their features on Wednesday morning.  The
        presentation will cover the program's ease of use, formatting
        capabilities and advanced features such as mailing list and
        form letter handing capabilities.  If you can attend please
        let me know.

        Sincerely yours,


        Mary
```

FIGURE 4-4
Editing the Document
You edit a document by moving the cursor and inserting or deleting text.

STEP 5: FORMAT THE DOCUMENT

You format a document to control its layout and appearance (Figure 4-5). You can format a document at any time—before you enter the document, while you enter it, or after you enter it. You can change margins, emphasize keywords by boldfacing them, or indent paragraphs. You do not need to know much about formatting when you begin word processing since nearly every program is already set to print a document single spaced on an 8½-by-11-inch sheet of paper. These default settings anticipate the most frequent applications of word processing programs—the preparation of memos, letters, and reports.

STEP 6: SAVE THE DOCUMENT

When you have completed the document, you save it before printing. To save the document, you use the program's *Save* command, and the document on the screen and in memory is copied to a file on the disk. If the document is long, you normally would have saved it several times while entering it so that it would not be lost if the power failed or something else went wrong. Most programs have two save commands.

- One command saves the file and leaves it on the screen so that you can continue working on it.
- The other command saves the file and returns you to the Main menu (if any) or clears the document from the screen so that you can create a new document or retrieve an existing one.

STEP 7: PRINT THE DOCUMENT

You make a printout using the program's *Print* command. This command sends the document to the printer, where it is printed using the formats you specified in Step 5 (Figure 4-6).

FIGURE 4-5
Formatting the Document
You can format a document to change its layout or appearance.

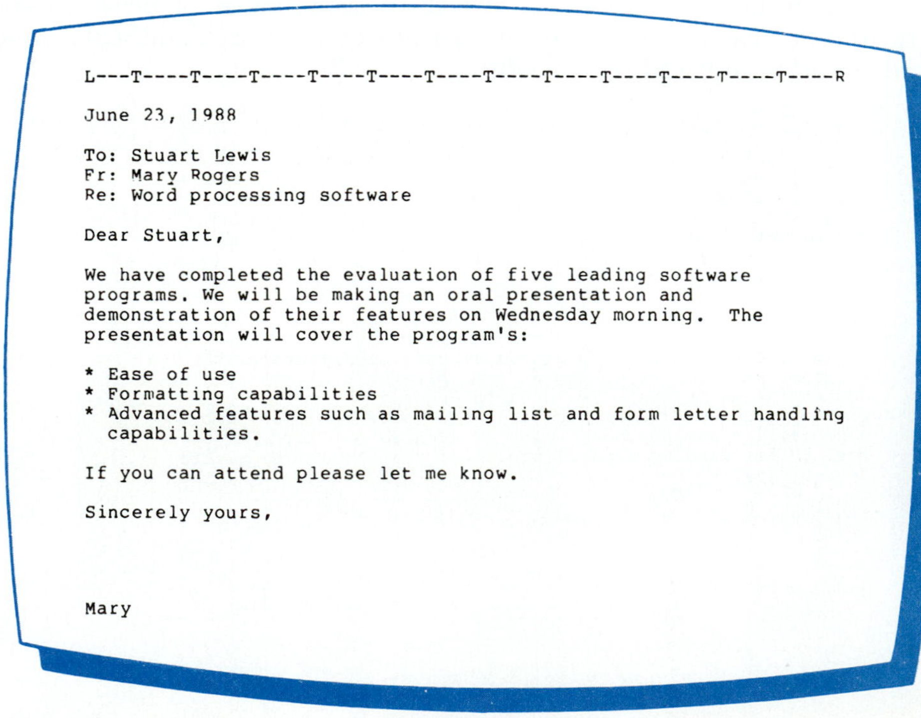

```
L---T----T----T----T----T----T----T----T----T----T----T----R

June 23, 1988

To: Stuart Lewis
Fr: Mary Rogers
Re: Word processing software

Dear Stuart,

We have completed the evaluation of five leading software
programs. We will be making an oral presentation and
demonstration of their features on Wednesday morning.   The
presentation will cover the program's:

* Ease of use
* Formatting capabilities
* Advanced features such as mailing list and form letter handling
  capabilities.

If you can attend please let me know.

Sincerely yours,


Mary
```

WORD PROCESSING AND DESKTOP PUBLISHING APPLICATIONS

```
June 23, 1988

To: Stuart Lewis
Fr: Mary Rogers
Re: Word processing software

Dear Stuart,

We have completed the evaluation of five leading software
programs. We will be making an oral presentation and
demonstration of their features on Wednesday morning.  The
presentation will cover the program's:

* Ease of use
* Formatting capabilities
* Advanced features such as mailing list and form letter handling
  capabilities.

If you can attend please let me know.

Sincerely yours,


Mary
```

FIGURE 4-6
Printing the Document
Most programs are set so
that documents are
automatically printed on
8½-by-11-inch paper with
1-inch margins.

STEP 8: CONTINUE OR QUIT

When you have finished a document, you have three choices: open a new document, retrieve an existing document, or quit the program.

Open a New Document or Edit an Old One

If you want to open a new document or edit an old one, you first clear the existing document from the screen and the computer's memory. You then open a new document or retrieve an existing one just as you did in Step 2.

Quit the Program

If you are done for the day or want to run another program, you select the *Quit* command. This command removes the program and any document you are working on from the computer's memory and from the screen. In a moment, the operating system prompt or Presentation Manager reappears. Since this command removes from memory the document and program you are working on, you must save the document before quitting, or it is lost.

- Word processing follows the information processing cycle. You input, process, output, store and retrieve, and distribute documents.
- When creating a new document, on some programs, you name it when you open it; on other programs, you name it the first time you save it.
- When you want to edit an existing document, you retrieve it from the file on the disk.
- You enter a document much as you do on a typewriter, but you do not have to press **Return** at the end of lines, just at the end of paragraphs.
- To edit a document, you move the cursor through the text and insert or delete characters, words, or larger sections.

SUMMARY AND KEY TERMS

- You format a document to control its layout and appearance.
- When finished with a document, you save it. You can then retrieve another document, clear the screen to create a new document, or quit the program and return to the operating system.

REVIEW QUESTIONS

1. List the eight steps in the word processing cycle, and briefly describe each of them.
2. What does it mean to open a new document file?
3. What does it mean to format a document?

Typical Word Processing Programs

OBJECTIVES

After completing this topic, you will be able to

- Describe how you open a document
- Identify the key elements on a word processing document screen
- Explain what windows and split screens are used for
- Describe some typical word processing programs

When you work with a word processing program, you can create new documents, retrieve old ones for editing, print documents, change the program's settings, check spelling, and perform several other functions. Before you can create a new document, you must first open a new document file.

- On some programs, this happens automatically when you load the program.
- On many programs, you do this by selecting *Create New Document*, or a similar choice, from the Main menu. Some programs prompt you to assign a name to the file when you first open it; others prompt you to assign a name the first time you save the file.
- If you are already working on a document and want to open a new one, you first save or abandon the current file. This either clears the document screen so that you can enter a new document or returns you to the Main menu so that you can open another new document file.

Some programs display a summary screen or comment screen when you open a new document file. You use this screen to describe the file (Figure 4-7).

When you open a new document, the document screen is blank, like a piece of blank writing paper. Many programs, however, display ruler lines or other helpful features to guide you. The document screen is a window into your computer's memory. It shows only part of a document, which can be many pages longer or wider than your screen. Document screen displays vary widely from program to program, but most have all or some of the elements shown in Figure 4-8.

FIGURE 4-7
Document Summary Screen
A typical document summary screen has spaces (called fields) where you enter the filename and information that describes it. This illustration shows the WordPerfect document summary screen.

```
Document Summary

        System Filename          (Not named yet)
        Date of Creation         July 22, 1988
    1 - Descriptive Filename
    2 - Subject/Account
    3 - Author
    4 - Typist
    5 - Comments
    ┌──────────────────────────────────────────┐
    │                                            │
    │                                            │
    └──────────────────────────────────────────┘

    Selection: 0
```

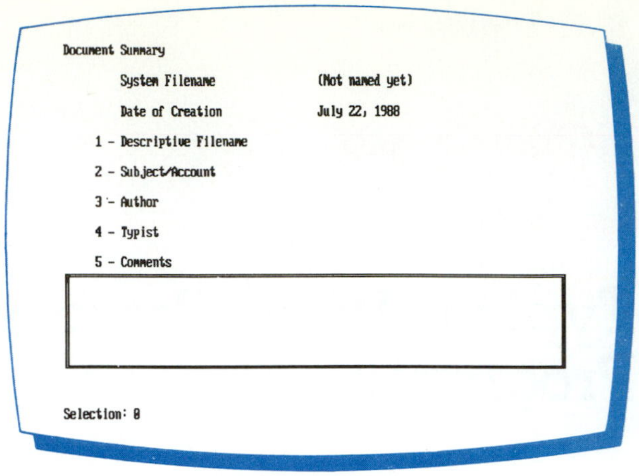

WINDOWS AND SPLIT SCREENS

Many programs allow you to split the screen or divide it into **windows** (Figure 4-9). You use this feature to display either different parts of the same document or different documents. Windows make it easy to compare, copy, or move text within the same document or between two or more different documents.

TYPICAL WORDPROCESSING PROGRAMS

WordPerfect is a memory-based, menu-driven program. When you load the program, the document screen is immediately displayed (Figure 4-10). Menus are displayed when you press function keys.

Microsoft Word is a disk-based, menu-driven program. Its menu and messages are displayed at the bottom of the screen (Figure 4-11).

WordStar is a disk-based, command-driven program. There are several versions designed to run on a variety of computers. The program requires you to enter codes to perform most of the basic commands. It displays a Main menu when you load the program (Figure 4-12). When you press D to open a new document, the document screen appears (Figure 4-13).

MultiMate Advantage II is a disk-based, command-driven program for the IBM PC and compatibles. It was the first microcomputer-based word processing program to emulate the Wang dedicated word processor. Since the program operates similarly to this widely installed system, it quickly gained popularity among people who had experience on the Wang. The MultiMate Main menu (Figure 4-14) lists nine choices. When you open a document, first a document summary screen appears (Figure 4-15) and then the document screen (Figure 4-16).

Besides the standalone word processing programs described here, word processors are included in almost all integrated programs. Figure 4-17 shows Microsoft Works' document screen, which displays a menu bar at the top of the screen.

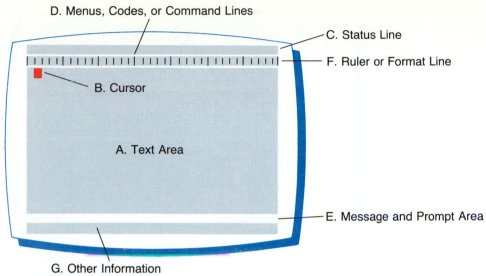

D. Menus, Codes, or Command Lines

C. Status Line

F. Ruler or Format Line

B. Cursor

A. Text Area

E. Message and Prompt Area

G. Other Information

FIGURE 4-8
Typical Document Screen
A typical document screen contains a cursor and other information to guide you when entering documents.

A. The **text area** is where you enter text. Most display screens can display text up to eighty characters wide and twenty-four lines long. Some screens, however, can display up to sixty-six lines, the same number usually printed on an 8½-by-11 inch sheet of paper. Portable, or laptop, computers often have a smaller screen displaying only twelve or sixteen lines of text. The actual number of lines of text displayed varies according to the number of lines occupied by a particular word processing program's menus, ruler lines, and so on.

B. The **cursor** is a bright, one-character-wide reverse video highlight (the character highlighted by the cursor appears dark against a bright background) or underline character. It moves as you enter text to indicate where the next character you type will appear. After you have entered text, you can move the cursor with the cursor movement keys to point to places in the document where you want to insert, delete, format, copy, or move text.

C. The **status line** at the top or bottom of the screen indicates the position of the cursor by column, row, and page. This information is helpful since it shows you where text will appear on the page when you print it out. Additional information, such as the default drive and the name of the file currently on the screen, is also often displayed on this line.

D. **Menus**, **codes**, or **command lines** that describe or execute commands may be listed at the top or bottom of the screen. You use these commands to save or retrieve files, copy or move text, and so on.

E. **Message** and **prompt** areas, located at either the top or bottom of the screen, guide you when you execute commands. Messages inform you about what the program is doing or has just finished doing. They require no action on your part. For example, when you save a document, a message may appear that reads *Saving file B:MEMO*. Error messages also appear when you do something wrong. For example, if you press the wrong key, a message may read *Invalid key*.
Prompts are similar to messages, but they ask you to supply information or tell you what to do next to continue a procedure. For example, when you set a margin, the program needs to know which column you want to set it in and may display a prompt such as *Enter column number for left margin*.

F. The **ruler** or **format line**, or a similar guide, is displayed on many screens so that you know where margins and tab stops are set. Frequently, you can turn these ruler or format lines on and off.

G. Other information is also displayed on many screens. For example, indicators may indicate if **Caps Lock**, **Num Lock**, or **Scroll Lock** are engaged or if you are currently in insert or typeover mode.

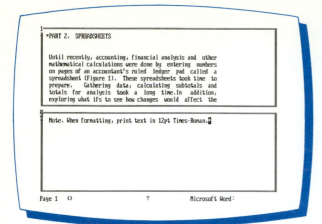

A. Horizontal Window

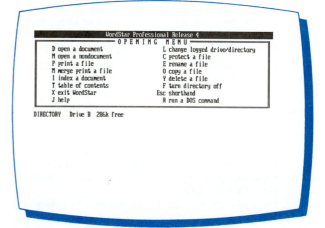

B. Vertical Window

FIGURE 4-9
Windows
Windows and split screens can be used to display different parts of the same document or different documents. This makes it easy to compare documents or copy and move text from one document to another. These illustrations show a horizontal window (a) and a vertical window (b) on Microsoft Word.

FIGURE 4-10
The WordPerfect Document Screen
The WordPerfect document screen shows only a cursor and a status line at the bottom of the screen.

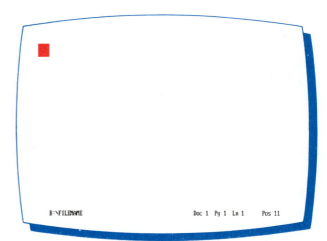

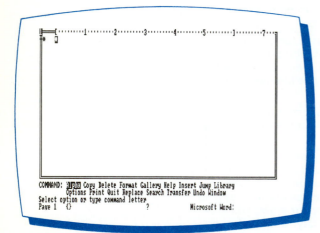

FIGURE 4-11
The Microsoft Word Document Screen
To execute commands, you press **Esc** to activate the menu. You then

- Press the arrow keys to move the menu-pointer (the bright highlight) to the command you want to use, and then press **Return**.

- Type the first letter in any command.

- Point to any of the menu commands with a mouse and click.

FIGURE 4-12
The WordStar Main Menu
The WordStar Main menu appears when you load the program. It displays a list of commands you select from by pressing the indicated letter. For example, you press **D** for *open a document* to open a new or existing document.

FIGURE 4-13
The WordStar Document Screen
The commands listed at the top of the screen briefly
describe the commands available to you. The line
at the very top of the screen (called the status line)
tells you the name of the document you are editing,
the position of the cursor by page, line, and
column, and displays other important information.
On version 3.3 (and later versions), the tasks
assigned to function keys are displayed on the
bottom of the screen.

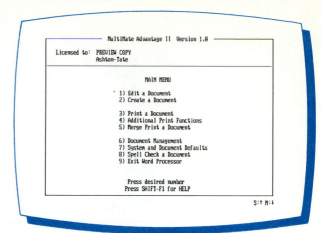

FIGURE 4-14
The MultiMate Main Menu
To make a selection from MultiMate's Main menu,
you just enter its number, and then press **Return**.
For example, you press **1** for *Edit a Document* to
retrieve an exiting document from the disk. You
press **2** for *Create a Document* to open a new
document.

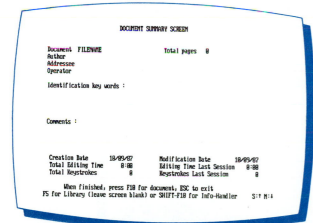

FIGURE 4-15
The MultiMate Document Summary Screen
You can enter descriptive information on this page,
including the name of the author and the name of
the person it is being sent to. The document
summary also displays information that you don't
have to enter, such as the length in pages, and
date the document was created, the
date it was last modified (edited), and a summary
of the keystrokes used to create and edit it.

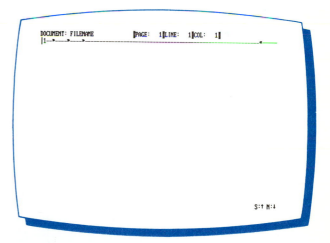

FIGURE 4-16
The MultiMate Document Screen
The MultiMate document screen contains a line at
the top of the screen indicating the name of the
document and the current position of the cursor by
page, line, and column. Below this line is the ruler
line showing left and right margins and tab stops.

FIGURE 4-17
The Microsoft Works Document Screen
The Microsoft Works word processor displays a menu bar at the top of the screen. When you press **Alt**, or click on one of the menu names, a menu listing commands is pulled down. Just below the menu bar is a ruler line that you use to set margins and tab stops.

REVIEW QUESTIONS

1. This screen illustration has some typical elements. Match the letters with the labels.

   a. Status line
   b. Cursor
   c. Ruler line
   d. Menu

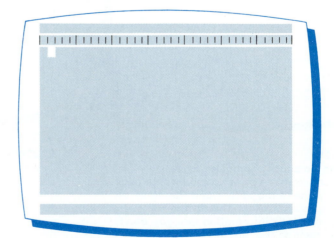

2. What is the purpose of split screens or windows?

3. List four popular word processing programs.

Entering Documents

OBJECTIVES

After completing this topic, you will be able to

- Describe how to enter text
- Explain the difference between hard and soft carriage returns, hyphens, and spaces
- Describe how the screen scrolls on document-oriented and page-oriented programs
- Describe the purpose of typewriter mode

Entering text with a word processing program is no more difficult than typing it on a typewriter; in many ways, it is easier. With both, you use the keyboard to enter letters, numbers, and symbols.

KEYBOARDING

On a word processing program, the cursor, a bright one-character-wide underline or rectangle, indicates where the next character you type will appear. When you open a new document, the cursor rests in the upper left-hand corner of the screen. As you type characters, they appear where the cursor is, and the cursor moves one space to the right.

Word Wrap

When you are typing paragraphs, you do not have to press **Return** at the end of each line. The program automatically does this for you. Unlike a typewriter, when the end of a line is reached, the word processing program calculates whether the word being entered fits on the line. If it will not fit, the program automatically begins a new line of text by moving the entire word to the next line. Called **word wrap** (Figure 4-18), this function is common to all word processing programs.

Some programs give you the option of switching word wrap off so that words do not automatically wrap to the beginning of the next line. On these programs, you almost always leave word wrap on. The only time you turn it off is when you are creating special line-oriented files, for example, pro-

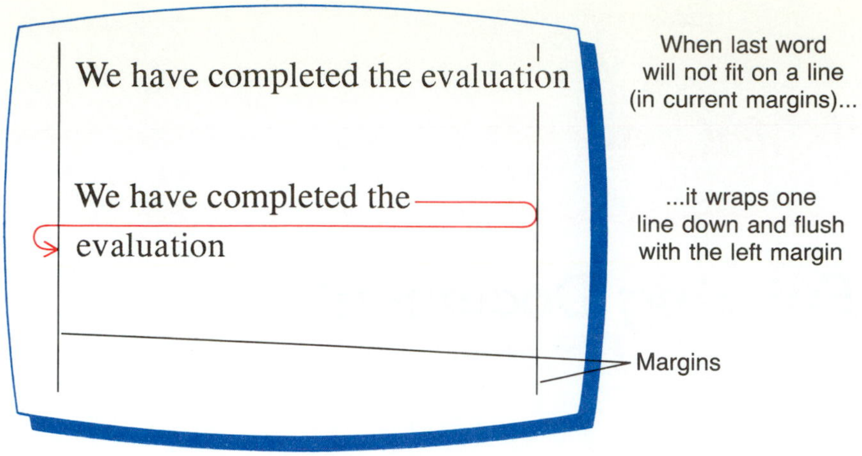

FIGURE 4-18
Word Wrap
Unlike a typewriter, when you reach the end of a line, the program calculates whether the word you enter fits on the line. If it will not fit, the program moves, or wraps, the entire word to the beginning of the next line.

When last word will not fit on a line (in current margins)...

...it wraps one line down and flush with the left margin

Margins

We have completed the evaluation

We have completed the evaluation

grams or some types of record files used to merge print multiple copies (see Topic 4-17).

Carriage Returns

Carriage returns are codes in the document that move the cursor and printer down one line and back to the left margin. Word processing programs have two kinds of carriage returns: soft and hard.

Soft Carriage Returns

The computer automatically enters **soft carriage returns** at the end of a line as you enter text whenever it wraps a word to the next line. Soft carriage returns automatically adjust their position if you revise the text so that they no longer fall at the end of a line. For example, when you insert or delete text or when you change the margins, existing soft carriage returns are deleted, and new ones are inserted at the end of each line.

Hard Carriage Returns

You press **Return** to enter a **hard carriage return** (also called a required return) when you want to end a line before you reach the right margin, for example

- To enter inside address, salutations, or headings.
- To insert a blank line, as you do following an inside address, the date, and the closing of a letter. Each time you press **Return**, you insert another blank line.
- To start a new paragraph, you press **Return** twice—once to end the current paragraph and then again to insert a blank line before starting the first line of the next paragraph. Each time you press **Return**, the cursor moves down another line.

If you then add or delete text, lines that end with hard carriage returns are not automatically rearranged, as are those that end with soft carriage returns.

You can enter hard carriage returns as you type a document (Figure 4-19), or you can enter them into existing text (Figure 4-20). All programs treat carriage returns just like any other character, so you can delete them just like other characters with the **Backspace** or **Del** key. Some programs display hard carriage returns on the screen with graphic symbols. Others

WORD PROCESSING AND DESKTOP PUBLISHING APPLICATIONS

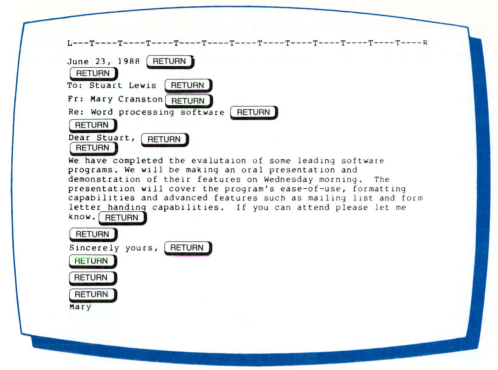

L---T----T----T----T----T----T----T----T----T----T---R

June 23, 1988 [RETURN]
[RETURN]
To: Stuart Lewis [RETURN]
Fr: Mary Cranston [RETURN]
Re: Word processing software [RETURN]
[RETURN]
Dear Stuart, [RETURN]
[RETURN]
We have completed the evalutaion of some leading software
programs. We will be making an oral presentation and
demonstration of their features on Wednesday morning. The
presentation will cover the program's ease-of-use, formatting
capabilities and advanced features such as mailing list and form
letter handing capabilities. If you can attend please let me
know. [RETURN]
[RETURN]
Sincerely yours, [RETURN]
[RETURN]
[RETURN]
[RETURN]
Mary

FIGURE 4-19
Carriage Returns as You Enter Text
When entering hard carriage returns as you enter text, you press **Return** to end a line before it reaches the right margin or at the end of a paragraph to start a new one. The cursor moves down a line and back to the left margin. You press **Return** again to insert a blank line before starting the first line of the next paragraph. Each time you press **Return**, the cursor moves down another line.

use a special command to see where they have been entered (see *Displaying Hidden Characters and Codes* in Topic 4-4). It helps to know where hard carriage returns are because to remove them you must delete them as you would any other character.

Most programs use hard carriage returns to define paragraphs. These programs define a paragraph as any text from the top of the document to the next hard carriage return or any text between two hard carriage returns. Knowing how your program defines paragraphs is important because some of the commands you will learn about select, copy, and move paragraphs.

Entering Spaces

When entering text, you press **Spacebar** to insert spaces, just as you do on a typewriter. But when you press it in existing text, how it behaves depends on whether the program is in insert or typeover mode (see Topic 4-4). In in-

FIGURE 4-20
Hard Carriage Returns in Existing Text
You enter hard carriage returns in existing text whenever you want to break an existing paragraph or line into two paragraphs or lines. To do so, you move the cursor to where you want to break the text and then press **Return**. This inserts a hard carriage return and moves the cursor, the character it was highlighting, and all text to its right, down one line and back to the left margin. If you press **Return** a second time, a blank line is inserted.

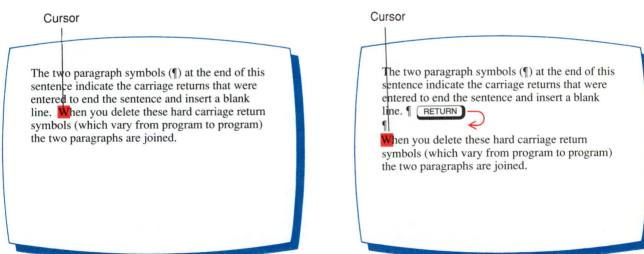

Cursor

The two paragraph symbols (¶) at the end of this sentence indicate the carriage returns that were entered to end the sentence and insert a blank line. When you delete these hard carriage return symbols (which vary from program to program) the two paragraphs are joined.

Cursor

The two paragraph symbols (¶) at the end of this sentence indicate the carriage returns that were entered to end the sentence and insert a blank line. ¶ [RETURN]
¶
When you delete these hard carriage return symbols (which vary from program to program) the two paragraphs are joined.

sert mode, pressing **Spacebar** inserts a space, and text to the right of the cursor moves over to make room for it. In typeover mode, pressing **Spacebar** deletes the character in that position and moves the cursor to the right; text to the right of the cursor does not move over. Like carriage returns, there are both soft and hard spaces.

Soft Spaces

When you press **Spacebar** in a document, it enters a **soft space**. If the word following the space does not fit on the line, the word wraps at the space to the next line. Soft spaces are also automatically entered on programs to justify lines of text (see Topic 4-10).

Hard Spaces

Certain phrases (for example, a title like Henry VIII, a time like 8 P.M., or an address like 32 Elm Street), though they contain spaces, should not be printed on different lines. To keep the two or more parts of the phrase together, you enter **hard spaces** (also called required spaces). This way, if the phrase does not fit on one line, it all wraps to the next line.

If you are using justified text, hard spaces also prevent the program from inserting unwanted soft spaces in formulas and computer commands.

Hyphens

You normally enter hyphens with the **Hyphen** key on the top row of the keyboard. Like carriage returns and spaces, hyphens can be either soft or hard.

Soft Hyphens

Soft hyphens (also called *syllable* or *optional* hyphens) are not like other characters in a word. If the word containing a soft hyphen does not fit at the end of the line, the part of the word or phrase following the soft hyphen may wrap to the next line. The first part of the word or phrase and the hyphen then remain on the first line. There are two kinds of soft hyphens, visible and invisible.

Visible soft hyphens, those you enter with the **Hyphen** key, appear on the screen and print out wherever they fall in the document.

Invisible soft hyphens, those you enter with a special command or that are automatically entered during paragraph reforming (see Topic 4-4) or hyphenation (see Topic 4-10), appear on the screen and print out only if they fall at the end of a line.

Hard Hyphens

Hard hyphens (also called *required* hyphens), which you usually enter with a special command, print out wherever they appear in the paragraph and will not wrap at the right margin. If a word or phrase hyphenated with a hard hyphen does not fit on a line, the entire word or phrase wraps to the next line. For example, to keep the entire phrase *son-in-law* on the same line, you enter hard hyphens between the words.

Dashes

If you want to enter dashes—perhaps to indicate an interruption in thought—use two hyphens. The first hyphen should be a hard hyphen, and the second should be a soft hyphen. If the two words on either side of a dash do not both fit on the same line, the phrase wraps after the soft hyphen, leaving the dash at the end of the first line.

Repeat Command

Many programs have a **repeat command**, which repeats keystrokes a specified number of times. This command is useful when entering hyphen characters for ruled lines or when repeating a command. To use the repeat command, you press a specified key that puts the computer into repeat mode. You then enter the character or command you want repeated. How you indicate the number of times the character or command is to be repeated varies from program to program.

CORRECTING MISTAKES

There are several ways to correct mistakes, but you usually use the **Backspace** key to do so. If you make any mistakes—and notice them immediately—press **Backspace** to move the cursor to the left and delete the incorrectly typed characters (Figure 4-21). You can then correctly type the characters. If pressing **Backspace** deletes the character to its left, it is called a destructive backspace. But if pressing **Backspace** simply moves the cursor to the left through the text, it is just like the left arrow key. Some programs let you choose how you want the **Backspace** key to work. In Topics 4-4 and 4-5, we discuss the commands that delete text.

SCROLLING

As you enter text, the screen gradually fills up. When the last line on the screen is filled, the text begins to **scroll**, or move, up a line at a time so that the line you are entering is always displayed on the screen. To make room for the new text, text at the top of the document scrolls off the top of the screen (Figure 4-22). But it is not gone for good; you can scroll back to it whenever you want. You can scroll the screen vertically and horizontally to see the text.

■ You use vertical scrolling when the document is longer than the screen (Figure 4-23). The effects vertical scrolling has depend on whether the program is document oriented or page oriented; each reacts differently to vertical scrolling.

FIGURE 4-21
Destructive Backspace
A destructive backspace deletes the character to the left of the cursor when you press **Backspace**. (a) Here, the cursor is positioned to the right of the *t* in *at*. (b) When you press **Backspace**, the cursor moves one space to the left and deletes the *t*.

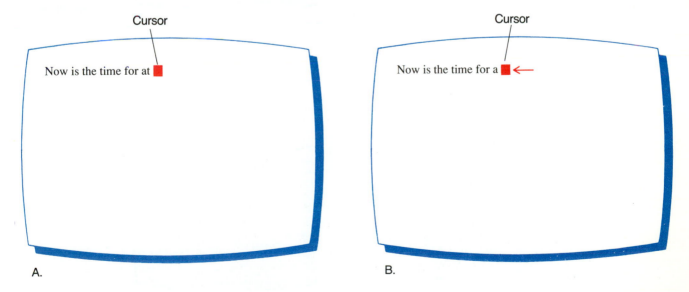

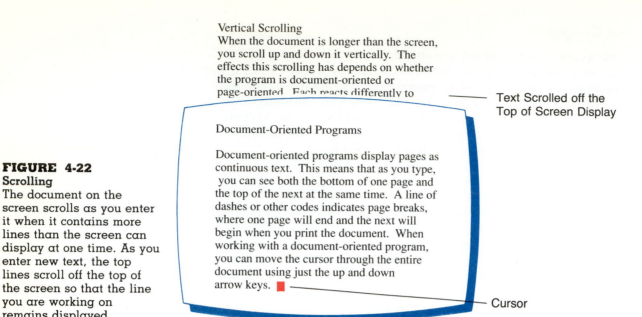

Vertical Scrolling
When the document is longer than the screen, you scroll up and down it vertically. The effects this scrolling has depends on whether the program is document-oriented or page-oriented. Each reacts differently to

Document-Oriented Programs

Document-oriented programs display pages as continuous text. This means that as you type, you can see both the bottom of one page and the top of the next at the same time. A line of dashes or other codes indicates page breaks, where one page will end and the next will begin when you print the document. When working with a document-oriented program, you can move the cursor through the entire document using just the up and down arrow keys. ■

Text Scrolled off the
Top of Screen Display

Cursor

FIGURE 4-22
Scrolling
The document on the screen scrolls as you enter it when it contains more lines than the screen can display at one time. As you enter new text, the top lines scroll off the top of the screen so that the line you are working on remains displayed.

■ You use horizontal scrolling when the document is wider than the screen (Figure 4-24).

Document-Oriented Programs

Document-oriented programs display pages as continuous text; that is, as you type, you can see the bottom of one page and the top of the next at the

FIGURE 4-23
Scrolling the Screen Vertically
You can scroll the screen vertically using the four directional arrow keys or other cursor movement commands.

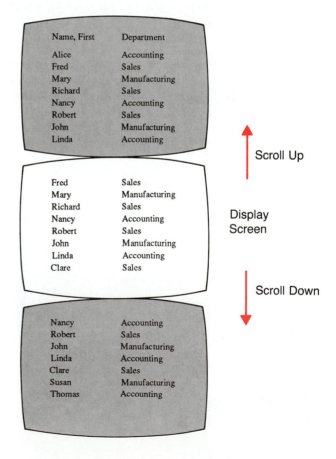

Name, First	Department
Alice	Accounting
Fred	Sales
Mary	Manufacturing
Richard	Sales
Nancy	Accounting
Robert	Sales
John	Manufacturing
Linda	Accounting

Scroll Up

Fred	Sales
Mary	Manufacturing
Richard	Sales
Nancy	Accounting
Robert	Sales
John	Manufacturing
Linda	Accounting
Clare	Sales

Display Screen

Scroll Down

Nancy	Accounting
Robert	Sales
John	Manufacturing
Linda	Accounting
Clare	Sales
Susan	Manufacturing
Thomas	Accounting

Display Screen

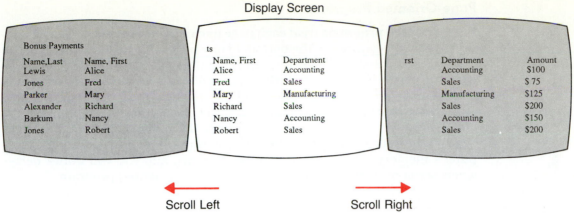

Bonus Payments			
Name,Last	Name, First		
Lewis	Alice		
Jones	Fred		
Parker	Mary		
Alexander	Richard		
Barkum	Nancy		
Jones	Robert		

ts		
Name, First	Department	
Alice	Accounting	
Fred	Sales	
Mary	Manufacturing	
Richard	Sales	
Nancy	Accounting	
Robert	Sales	

rst	Department	Amount
	Accounting	$100
	Sales	$ 75
	Manufacturing	$125
	Sales	$200
	Accounting	$150
	Sales	$200

← Scroll Left   Scroll Right →

FIGURE 4-24
Scrolling the Screen Horizontally
You can scroll the screen horizontally when your document is wider than the screen.

same time (Figure 4-25). A line of dashes or other codes indicate **page breaks**, where one page will end and the next will begin when you print the document. When working on a document-oriented program, you can move the cursor through the entire document using only the up and down arrow keys.

FIGURE 4-25
Document-Oriented Programs
Document-oriented programs display the document as a continuous text. You can scroll up and down through the text as if it were one long scroll, and you can see the top of one page and the bottom of another on the screen at the same time.

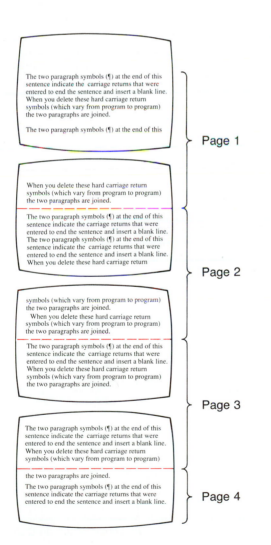

Page-Oriented Programs

Page-oriented programs treat each page like individual sheets of paper (Figure 4-26). You cannot see the bottom of one page and the top of the next on the screen at the same time. You can scroll through only the displayed page with the arrow keys. To scroll through another page, you must execute a next page or previous page command. Some page-oriented programs hold only the current page in memory; all other pages they store on the disk. When you move from one page to another, the program saves the current page on the disk and retrieves the page you want from the disk into the computer's memory. This slows the program down, and you will notice delays when scrolling through a document on a page-oriented program.

TYPEWRITER MODE

Normally, you enter text, save it in a file on a disk, and print it from that file. But some programs have a **typewriter mode** (also called *type-through* or *print direct mode*) that you can use when writing brief memos, addressing envelopes, or filling out preprinted forms.

As you type characters in this mode, the printer simultaneously prints them (Figure 4-27). On some programs, word wrap does not work in this mode, so you have to press **Return** to end each line, just as you do on a typewriter. On other programs, you can type lines and paragraphs, and text is printed only when you press **Return**. Until you press **Return**, you can edit the line or paragraph just as you edit any other text on the screen. This feature partly depends on your printer. For example, a laser printer cannot print text a character, line, or paragraph at a time; it can print only complete pages. If you want to print out less than a page, you must press the on-line button to take the printer off line, and then press the form-feed button to advance the page out of the printer.

FIGURE 4-26
Page-Oriented Programs
Page-oriented programs display text in pages. You can scroll through the page displayed on the screen, but to scroll through the next or previous page, you must first display that page on the screen.

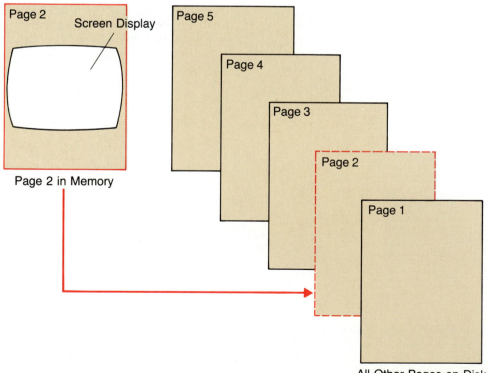

Page 2

Screen Display

Page 2 in Memory

Page 5

Page 4

Page 3

Page 2

Page 1

All Other Pages on Disk

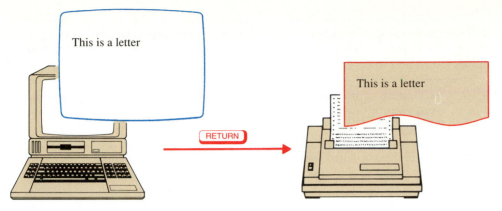

OTHER ENTERING PROCEDURES

Several commands simplify entering text. For example, instead of typing the date and time, many programs have a command that automatically enters them for you. The date and time it enters is read from the computer's clock. If you do not correctly enter the date and time when first turning on the computer, the date and time are incorrectly shown. There are two versions of this command: One enters the date or time as text, and the other enters a function.

- Dates and times entered as text are calculated from the computer's clock and then entered into the document. They are displayed and printed just as if you had typed them yourself.

- Date and time functions entered into a document calculate the date and time from the computer's clock and either display them in the document or display just a code. Whenever you retrieve the document from the disk or print the document, the function reads the system's clock and displays or prints the current date or time. Programs that have this function usually allow you to customize how the date and time are displayed. For example, you can display dates as *January 10, 1988, 1/1/88,* or *Jan 88,* and you can display time as *2 PM, 2:00 PM,* or *14:00* hours.

- When you type text and a word does not fit on the end of the line, it **wraps** to the next line.

- **Carriage returns** are codes that move the cursor and printer down one line and back to the left margin. There are three types of carriage returns: **hard**, **soft**, and **conditional**.

- **Spaces** are normally entered to separate words. There are two kinds of spaces: soft and hard. Words connected by **soft spaces** will break at the end of a line. Those connected by **hard spaces** are glued together and will not break at the end of the line.

- Programs have at least two kinds of **hyphens**: soft and hard. **Soft hyphens**, like soft spaces, will break at the end of a line. **Hard hyphens**, like hard spaces, will not.

- Some programs have a **repeat command** that repeats characters a specified number of times. This is extremely useful when you are entering ruled lines used to highlight tables, headings, and so on.

SUMMARY AND KEY TERMS

- When entering text, you can correct mistakes by pressing **Del** or **Backspace**. **Del** deletes the character highlighted by the cursor. If **Backspace** deletes the character to its left, it is called a **destructive backspace**.

- As you fill the screen, text **scrolls** off the top to make room for new lines at the bottom of the screen. You can then use **vertical scrolling** to move up and down through text longer than the screen. You can also use **horizontal scrolling** to move sideways though text wider than the screen.

- **Document-oriented programs** display text in one continuous strip. **Page-oriented programs** display one or more pages in memory and store the other pages on the disk until you scroll to them.

- **Typewriter mode** sends characters you type directly to the printer so that you can address envelopes and write short memos that you don't need to save or heavily edit.

- Some programs allow you to automatically enter dates and times. Some programs automatically calculate the current date and time whenever you retrieve or print the document. You might use this feature for documents that go through a series of revisions so that you can tell one version from another.

REVIEW QUESTIONS

1. Describe word wrap. When does it happen?
2. What are carriage returns? What is the difference between hard and soft carriage returns?
3. How do you break a paragraph into two paragraphs?
4. If you press **Spacebar** to move the cursor, what happens if the program is in insert mode? In typeover mode?
5. What is the difference between hard and soft spaces? When would you want to use a hard space?
6. What is the difference between hard and soft hyphens? When would you want to use a hard hyphen? What is the difference between a visible and an invisible soft hyphen?
7. How do you enter a dash?
8. What is a *Repeat* command?
9. What is the most common way to correct mistakes when entering text?
10. What happens to the document on display when you scroll the screen?
11. What is the difference between a document-oriented and a page-oriented program?
12. What is typewriter mode, and when would you use it?
13. What are two ways you can enter dates and times on some programs?

Editing Documents

OBJECTIVES

After completing this topic, you will be able to

- Describe how to get around a document and make changes
- Describe the differences between inserting and typing over existing text
- Describe hidden codes, and explain why you display them
- Explain how to delete text and undo the deletion if you make a mistake
- Describe paragraph reforming and document repaginating

After you type a document, you proofread, edit, and revise it. Editing refers to correcting mistakes and making minor changes. Revising implies more significant changes in organization or approach. To edit or revise a document on the screen, you use the cursor movement keys or commands to move the cursor through the document to delete or insert characters, words, or phrases. You can also mark **blocks**, large sections of text that you can copy, move, or delete in one step (see Topic 4-5).

MOVING THE CURSOR AND SCROLLING THE SCREEN

Word processing programs provide you with several ways to move the cursor through a document. You can move the cursor a character or line at a time with the directional arrow keys (Figure 4-28). You can also move the cursor in larger jumps with commands; the longer your document, the more important these commands become. If your computer has **PgUp** and **PgDn** keys, you use them to scroll through the text a screen or page at a time. Other keys, like **Home** and **End**, move the cursor to the top or bottom of the screen or document or to the beginning or end of a line. Some other commands use **Ctrl**, or another key, as an amplifier. For example, when you press the down arrow key, the cursor usually moves down one line at a time. But when you press the down arrow key while holding down **Ctrl**, the cursor may jump much farther, perhaps to the end of a sentence or paragraph or to the bottom of the screen depending on the program you are using. Table 4-2

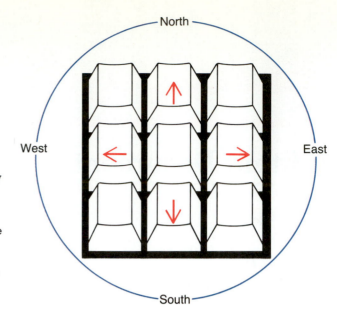

FIGURE 4-28
Directional Arrow Keys
The four directional arrow keys (sometimes called cursor movement keys) move the cursor a character or line at a time in the direction of the arrow. The directional arrow keys are north (up), south (down), east (right), and west (left).

lists some of the typical cursor movement commands that make moving the cursor fast and easy.

When moving the cursor with the designated arrow keys, you will notice

- When you move the cursor along a line of text, it moves through the text and does not affect it.
- When you move the cursor past the rightmost character on a line, it usually jumps down to the beginning of the next line.
- When you move the cursor past the leftmost character on a line, it usually jumps up to the end of the above line.
- If the document is longer than the number of lines displayed on the screen, it can be scrolled into view by moving the cursor to the top or bottom of the screen and pressing the up or down arrow keys. Instead of moving off the screen, the cursor stays on the top or bottom row, and the text scrolls into view.

TABLE 4-2
Cursor Movement Commands

Cursor Movement Commands	Enter Commands for Your Program
To the next character	_____
To the next word	_____
To the next line	_____
To the end of a line	_____
To the beginning of a line	_____
To the end of a sentence	_____
To the beginning of a sentence	_____
To the end of a paragraph	_____
To the beginning of a paragraph	_____
To the end of a document	_____
To the beginning of a document	_____
To the top and bottom of the screen	_____
To a specified line	_____
To a specified page	_____

- You cannot move the cursor off the screen, and you usually cannot move it past the last line of text in the document.

You can move the cursor directly to a specific point in a document without having to scroll to it. The way programs do this varies. Some programs let you assign names to lines of text or insert markers that you can instantly move the cursor to. Other programs automatically number every page and line of text so that you can move directly to any page or line you specify.

Some programs and computers are designed so that you can point a mouse or simply touch the screen to move the cursor through a document.

INSERTING OR REPLACING TEXT

To edit text, you move the cursor through the document and delete and insert characters as needed. Most word processing programs allow you to toggle, or switch, between inserting characters and typing over and replacing characters already there. A command that toggles is like a light switch—it has only two states, on or off. This command switches between insert and typeover mode.

Insert Mode

When you set the command to insert mode, the existing text moves over and down to make room for the new text. On most programs, you can actually watch text rearrange itself on the screen. On others, like those that emulate Wang dedicated word processors, you use a different approach called drop-down. You first move the cursor to where you want to insert characters. You then press **Ins**, or execute an insert command. The screen clears so that only the line below the cursor appears on the bottom line of the screen. You then enter the text you want to insert. When you finish, you press **Ins** again, and the original text reappears on the screen with the new text inserted.

Typeover Mode

When you set the command to **typeover mode** (also called *replace*, *overtype*, *strikeover*, or *insert-off*), the new text types over and erases existing text while text to the right and below does not move. This is useful when entering or editing tables or lists arranged in columns. In typeover mode, you can enter new text without causing characters in columns to the right to shift out of alignment. If you press **Spacebar** in typeover mode, you erase the character highlighted by the cursor.

DISPLAYING HIDDEN CHARACTERS AND CODES

As you create a document, usually just the letters and numbers you type are displayed on the screen. However, you often enter invisible **control codes** (also called *printer control* or *format* codes) into the document. On all programs, control codes are entered whenever you press **Return**, **Tab**, or **Spacebar**. You also enter these codes when you use formatting commands, for example, to center, indent, or underline text. Control codes usually do not appear on the screen and never in the printout. They control how your text is displayed on the screen and printed on a page.

Many programs allow you to display these codes (Figure 4-29), which makes editing much easier. By displaying the codes, you can see where carriage returns and other formatting codes are located, which makes it simple

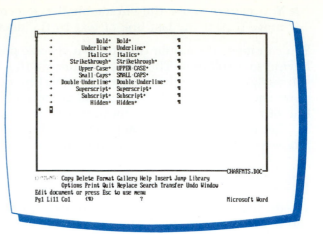

FIGURE 4-29
Hidden Codes
Displaying hidden codes is useful when editing because it lets you see the codes that you may want to delete or change. Here, you see some of the hidden codes displayed on Microsoft Word.

to delete or change them. Hard and soft hyphens are also displayed differently so that you can tell them apart. The codes displayed vary from program to program, but they include

- Spaces
- Tabs
- Hard carriage returns
- Printer control codes for italics, boldfacing, superscripts and subscripts, and so on
- Hard and soft hyphens

DELETING TEXT

As you have seen, you can delete words a character at a time with **Backspace** or **Del**. On most programs, pressing **Backspace** deletes the character to the left of the cursor, whereas pressing **Del** erases the character highlighted by the cursor. If you hold down either key, the computer's autorepeat feature causes it to delete one character after another until you release the key. That is, holding down **Backspace** deletes one character after another to the left of the cursor, and holding down **Del** deletes one character after another to the right of the cursor.

Table 4-3 lists many of the commands that delete specific sections of text. You can also use special commands to delete blocks of text (see Topic 4-5). When text is deleted, all text to its right and below moves over and up to fill the space vacated.

UNDOING MISTAKES

Deleting text removes it from the screen and the computer's memory. With many programs, this means you lose the text unless you save it before you delete it. Some programs have an **undo** command (also called an undelete command) that stores deletions in a buffer—a small portion of the computer's memory allocated to saving material that you delete (Figure 4-30). You can recover a deletion if you notice the mistake soon enough.

Buffers store only the most recent deletions (and sometimes other commands), and they do not permanently store material. Thus you must undo mistakes immediately. Depending on the amount of material you have deleted and the size of the undo buffer, you may be able to recover only part of the deleted material.

TABLE 4-3
Delete Commands

Delete Commands	Enter Commands for Your Program
By character	_____
By word	_____
By line	_____
By sentence	_____
By paragraph	_____
To end of line	_____
To beginning of line	_____
To end of sentence	_____
To beginning of sentence	_____
To end of paragraph	_____
To beginning of paragraph	_____
To end of document	_____
To beginning of document	_____

JOINING LINES OF TEXT SEPARATED BY CARRIAGE RETURNS

When editing, you often want to delete blank lines, join two lines, or join paragraphs that were separated by hard carriage returns. Though not necessarily displayed on the screen, hard carriage returns are much like other characters you enter in a document; therefore, you delete them as you would other characters. Some programs let you display hard carriage returns, making it easy for you to find them if you want to delete them (see *Displaying Hidden Characters and Codes*).

To join two lines or two paragraphs (Figure 4-31), move the cursor one space to the right of the punctuation mark at the end of the first line or paragraph. Use your program's delete keys or commands to delete carriage returns until the line or paragraph below jumps up to join the line above. If necessary, you then use **Spacebar** to insert spaces between the last word of

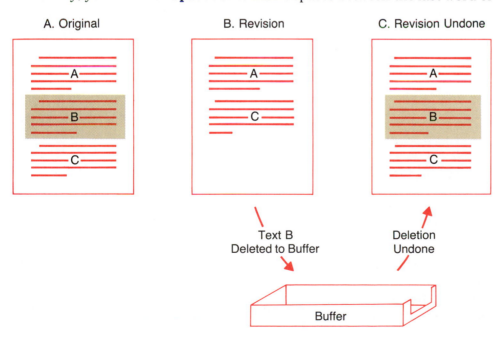

A. Original   B. Revision   C. Revision Undone

Text B
Deleted to Buffer

Deletion
Undone

Buffer

FIGURE 4-30
Undoing Mistakes
Undoing mistakes copies the deleted text from the buffer back into the document. (a) Here, a block of text is selected. (b) When you delete it, it is removed from the screen and stored in the computer's buffer. (c) Undoing the deletion moves the block from the buffer back into the document.

The two paragraph symbols (¶) at the end of this sentence indicate the carriage returns that were entered to end the sentence and insert a blank line.¶
¶
When you delete these hard carriage return symbols (which vary from program to program) the two paragraphs are joined.

A. Paragraphs Separated by Hard Carriage Returns

The two paragraph symbols (¶) at the end of this sentence indicate the carriage returns that were entered to end the sentence and insert a blank line. When you delete these hard carriage return symbols (which vary from program to program) the two paragraphs are joined.

B. Paragraphs Joined by Deleting Hard Carriage Returns

FIGURE 4-31
Joining Lines of Text
Joining lines of text is done by deleting the hard carriage returns that keep them separated. (a) Here, two paragraphs have been separated by two hard carriage returns. (b) Deleting these carriage returns joins the two paragraphs.

the first paragraph and the first word of what was the second paragraph. On some programs, you may also have to reform the paragraph to realign it with the margins.

PARAGRAPH REFORMING AND REPAGINATION

When editing a document, you often add or delete text, which changes the length of paragraphs or pages. When you do this, the text below the changes must be reformed so that it aligns with the left and right margins, and it must be repaginated so that text appears on the appropriate pages.

Reforming Paragraphs

When you make changes to a paragraph that affect its length or margins, most programs automatically realign it with the margins (Figure 4-32). This is called **automatic paragraph reforming** (also called *line adjust* or *paragraph aligning*). But on some programs, you must manually reform paragraphs, or at least you are given the option to do so.

On some programs, when you reform a paragraph, the cursor stops if a word will not fit at the end of the line. You are then given the opportunity to hyphenate the word to avoid an extremely ragged-right margin (see Topic 4-10).

FIGURE 4-32
Reforming Paragraphs
Reforming paragraphs aligns the revised text with the left and right margins. This figure shows the original unedited paragraph, the edited paragraph, and the reformed paragraph.

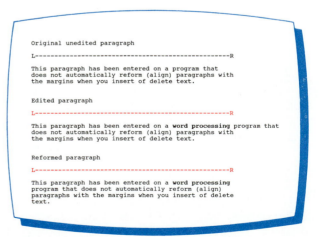

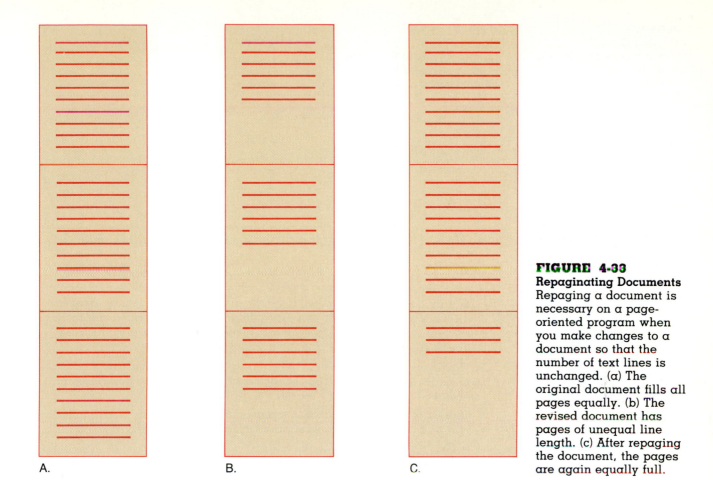

A.   B.   C.

FIGURE 4-33
Repaginating Documents
Repaging a document is
necessary on a page-
oriented program when
you make changes to a
document so that the
number of text lines is
unchanged. (a) The
original document fills all
pages equally. (b) The
revised document has
pages of unequal line
length. (c) After repaging
the document, the pages
are again equally full.

Repaginating the Document

If you make any changes that affect a document's length on a page-oriented program, you must repaginate your document to display all text on the appropriate pages (Figure 4-33).

OTHER EDITING PROCEDURES

Some word processing programs have other commands that are useful in special situations.

Changing Case

Some programs let you change the case of characters after you have entered them. For example, if you type a heading as **Financial Results—1987**, you can use the change case command to change it to **FINANCIAL RESULTS—1987** without having to retype it. Several variations of the change case command are possible (Figure 4-34).

Transposing Characters

Some word processing programs let you transpose characters (Figure 4-35). To do so, you select the two adjacent characters, and then execute the transpose command.

FIGURE 4-34
Changing Case
Changing case commands change the case of lowercase and uppercase letters.

	Before	After
From lowercase to uppercase	case	CASE
From uppercase to lowercase	CASE	case
First letter made uppercase	case	Case

FIGURE 4-35
Transposing Characters
Transposing characters reverses the order of the selected characters.

Before transposing last two letters	Teh
After transposing last two letters	The

SUMMARY AND KEY TERMS

- To edit a document, you use the program's commands that move the cursor.

- Some programs allow you to move the cursor directly to a specific point in a document without having to scroll to it. The way programs are set up to do this varies. Some allow you to assign names to lines of text or to insert markers you can instantly move the cursor to. Other programs automatically number every line or page of text so that you can move directly to any line or page.

- When you use **insert mode**, characters to the right of new text move to make room for it. When you use **typeover mode**, the text doesn't move, and the new text replaces the old.

- **Hidden codes** are entered when you press **Return** or **Tab** or when you format text. Many programs allow you to display these codes so that you can more easily edit them.

- You can delete text with the program's commands that delete predefined sections like words, sentences, and paragraphs.

- If you delete text by mistake, you can use the program's *Undo* command to restore it.

- If you want to join lines or paragraphs separated by hard carriage returns, you just delete the carriage returns.

- When text is inserted into or deleted from existing text, some programs automatically **reform** the text to realign it with the margins. Other programs require that you do this manually.

- If you insert or delete enough text to affect the number of lines on a page, page-oriented programs require you to **repaginate** the document so that each page has the same number of lines.

- Some programs have commands that change the case of selected text or transpose characters.

REVIEW QUESTIONS

1. What does scrolling the screen mean? When does it scroll?
2. What is the cursor used for, and how do you move it?
3. What is the basic difference between insert mode and typeover mode? What does to insert text mean? To replace (or type over) text?
4. What are hidden characters? Why would you want to be able to display them?
5. Describe three ways of deleting text.
6. What is the *Undo* command? Describe how it works.
7. If two lines or paragraphs were separated by a carriage return, how would you join them?
8. What is paragraph reforming? When is a paragraph reformed?
9. What does repagination mean? When do you repaginate a document?

WORD PROCESSING AND DESKTOP PUBLISHING APPLICATIONS

Working with Blocks of Text

OBJECTIVES

After completing this topic, you will be able to

- Describe what a block of text is and how you select, copy, move, and delete blocks

- Explain what column mode is and how to use it

If you are revising typewritten copy, at some point you will likely take a pair of scissors and some glue and reorganize your work by cutting and pasting. With a word processing program, you do this electronically. Blocks of text are the sections you cut from one place in a document and then paste to another place.

DEFINITION OF BLOCKS

A block of text can be a character, word, phrase, sentence, paragraph, group of paragraphs, or an entire document.

Line Blocks

When working with blocks of text, you usually copy, move, or delete lines of text (Figure 4-36). The block can begin or end anywhere on the lines. Many

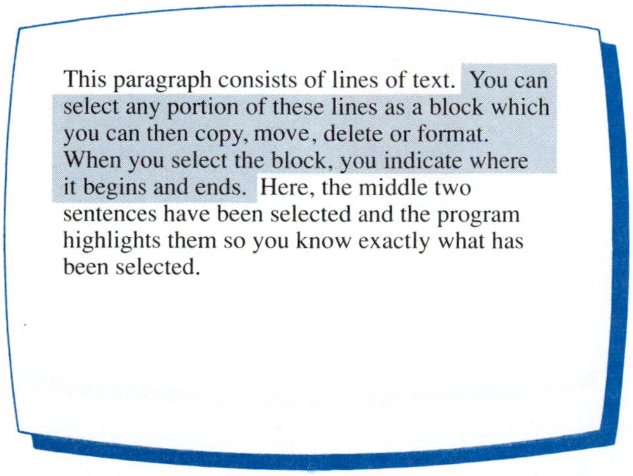

FIGURE 4-36
Line Block
Line blocks can be characters, words, phrases, sentences, or paragraphs.

This paragraph consists of lines of text. You can select any portion of these lines as a block which you can then copy, move, delete or format. When you select the block, you indicate where it begins and ends. Here, the middle two sentences have been selected and the program highlights them so you know exactly what has been selected.

programs also have predefined blocks that you can select with a single command. Predefined blocks include those listed in Table 4-4.

Column Blocks

Many word processors also allow you to work with columns of text (Figure 4-37). This feature, called **column mode**, is useful when revising or formatting tables or other text aligned in columns. For example, what if you want to reorganize a table by copying, moving, or deleting one of the columns? If the program works only with lines, you must painstakingly copy, move, or delete the entries in the selected column one line at a time. But with column mode, you can select a column and then copy, move, or delete it all at once. Columns are usually defined as text separated by tabs and, on some programs, by spaces.

Rectangular Blocks

Rectangular blocks are like column blocks, but they have no conditions; that is, they can begin in any column on any line (Figure 4-38). These blocks are usually parts of line drawings. When you delete or move a rectangular block, the existing lines do not reform with the margins; rather, each line

TABLE 4-4
Cursor Movement Commands

Predefined Blocks	Enter Commands for Your Program
A word	_____
A line	_____
A sentence	_____
A paragraph	_____
To the end of a line	_____
To the beginning of a line	_____
To the end of a sentence	_____
To the beginning of a sentence	_____
To the end of a paragraph	_____
To the beginning of a paragraph	_____
To the end of a document	_____
To the beginning of a document	_____

FIGURE 4-37
Column Mode
If a program has a column mode, you can copy, move, or delete entire columns in one step. This figure shows the second column highlighted so that one of these operations can be performed on it.

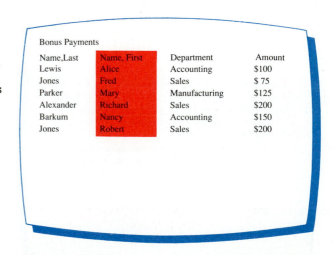

Bonus Payments			
Name,Last	Name, First	Department	Amount
Lewis	Alice	Accounting	$100
Jones	Fred	Sales	$ 75
Parker	Mary	Manufacturing	$125
Alexander	Richard	Sales	$200
Barkum	Nancy	Accounting	$150
Jones	Robert	Sales	$200

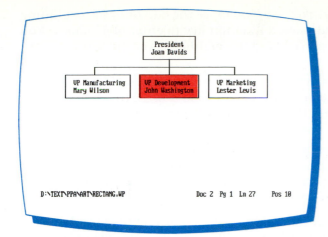

FIGURE 4-38
Rectangular Block
Rectangular blocks are any portion of the document defined by specifying an upper left-hand and lower right-hand corner.

closes up individually, Thus deleting a rectangle from a paragraph turns it into nonsense. Each line reads correctly up to where the block was deleted and then continues with the text that was on the same line on the other side of the deleted block.

PERFORMING OPERATIONS ON BLOCKS

You can perform several operations on blocks of text, including

- Copying or moving the block within the document on the screen
- Copying or moving the block to another file on the disk
- Deleting the block
- Formatting the block, for example, boldfacing, italicizing, or underlining it (see Topic 4-11)

Selecting a Block

Depending on your program, you use one of two approaches to work with a block of text: Either you first select the block (highlight it), and then indicate the function, or you first indicate the function, and then select the block.

To select a block of text, you indicate the beginning and end of the block (Figure 4-39). You do this in one of three ways.

FIGURE 4-39
Selecting a Block
Selecting a block marks the beginning and end of the block so that the commands used to copy, move, or delete it apply only to that section of the document. The selected block is usually highlighted. You can select a line block (a) or a column block (b).

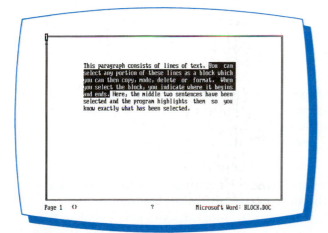

A. Selecting a Line Block

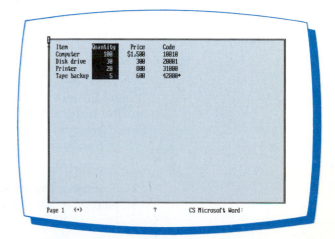

B. Selecting a Column Block

- You highlight the block. To do so, you move the cursor to the beginning or end of the block, and press a function key to enter block mode. You then use the arrow keys to expand the highlight over the text you want included in the block.

- You enter control codes at the beginning and end of the block. They are called control codes because you usually hold down Ctrl while you type other characters to enter the codes. These codes do not print out; they are used only to mark the block.

- You select specific types of blocks by pressing an amount key that tells the program you want to select the word, sentence, or paragraph the cursor is positioned in. You then press a designated key to copy, move, delete, or format the selected block.

A selected block usually appears highlighted so that it stands out from the text you have not selected. It may be in a different color, dimmer or brighter than the rest of the document, or highlighted in **reverse video** (dark characters against a bright background).

When you select a block of text, any hidden codes in the block are also selected. Since you normally do not see these codes, you can encounter problems. For example, if the first word in a block is boldfaced, and you do not include the boldface code at the beginning of the word in the selected block, the word will not be boldfaced in the location you copy or move it to. In fact, all text from the code you left behind to the new position of the block may be boldfaced.

Copying a Block

Copying a block leaves the original block unchanged and duplicates the block in a new position in the document (Figure 4-40). If you copy the block into existing text, the text moves over or down to make room for it.

On many programs, you copy selected blocks by moving the cursor to where you want to insert the copied block and then issuing a *Copy* command. Some programs do this in two steps (Figure 4-41).

1. You copy the block to a buffer (sometimes called a clipboard, scrapbook, or scrap).

2. You move the cursor to where you want to insert the copied text, and then you **paste**, or copy, the block from this buffer. Since the buffer stores only the most recent block, you usually must insert it into the new position before executing any other commands that store text in the buffer.

Moving a Block

When you move a selected block, it is first copied to the cursor's position, and then the old block is deleted, and the text closes up to fill the space the block was moved from (Figure 4-42).

Again, some programs use two steps.

1. You **cut**, or move, the block to the buffer.

2. You move the cursor to where you want to insert the text, and then you paste the block from the buffer back into the document.

A. Copying a Line Block

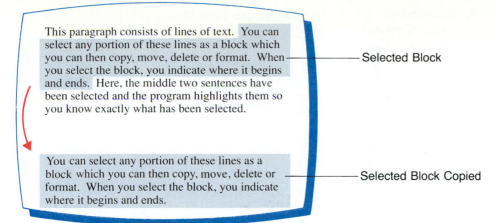

This paragraph consists of lines of text. You can select any portion of these lines as a block which you can then copy, move, delete or format. When you select the block, you indicate where it begins and ends. Here, the middle two sentences have been selected and the program highlights them so you know exactly what has been selected.

— Selected Block

You can select any portion of these lines as a block which you can then copy, move, delete or format. When you select the block, you indicate where it begins and ends.

— Selected Block Copied

B. Copying a Column Block

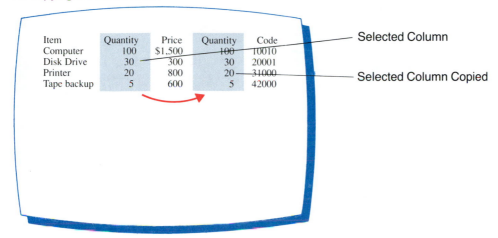

Item	Quantity	Price	Quantity	Code
Computer	100	$1,500	100	10010
Disk Drive	30	300	30	20001
Printer	20	800	20	31000
Tape backup	5	600	5	42000

— Selected Column

— Selected Column Copied

FIGURE 4-40
Copying a Block
Copying a block leaves the original block unchanged and makes a duplicate of the block at the position of the cursor. You can copy a line block (a) or a column block (b). When you copy a selected column into other columns, the columns to the right move over to make room for it.

Deleting a Block

Deleting a block deletes the selected block from the screen and the computer's memory (Figure 4-43). Some programs temporarily store the deleted block in a buffer so that you can undo the deletion if you change your mind (see Topic 4-4).

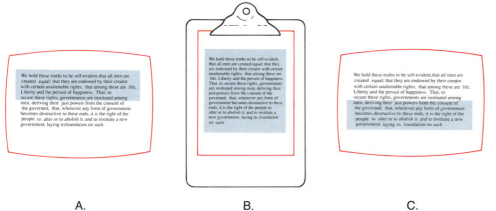

A.　　　　　B.　　　　　C.

FIGURE 4-41
A Clipboard
On programs that use a clipboard, (a) you copy (and move text) by first selecting a block. (b) Then you copy or delete the block to the clipboard. (c) Next you move the cursor to where you want to copy or move the block from the clipboard back into the document.

A. Selected Line Block

This paragraph consists of lines of text.
You can select any portion of these lines
as a block which you can then copy, mode,
delete or format. When you select the
block, you indicate where it begins and ends.
Here, the middle two sentences have been
selected and the program highlights them so
you know exactly what has been selected.

B. Selected Line Block Moved

This paragraph consists of lines of text. Here, the
middle two sentences have been selected and the
program highlights them so you know exactly
what has been selected.

You can select any portion of these lines as a block
which you can then copy, mode, delete or format.
When you select the block, you indicate where
it begins and ends.

Selected Block
Shown Already Deleted

Selected Block Moved

A. Selected Column Block

Item	Quantity	Price	Code
Computer	100	$1,500	10010
Disk Drive	30	300	20001
Printer	20	800	31000
Tape backup	5	600	42000

B. Selected Column Block Moved

Item	Code	Quantity	Price
Computer	10010	100	1,500
Disk krive	20001	30	300
Printer	31000	20	800
Tape backup	42000	5	600

FIGURE 4-42
Moving a Block
Moving a block deletes the block from its original position in the document and copies it to the position of the cursor. You can move a line block (a) or a column block (b). When you move a selected column, the columns originally arranged in one order are arranged in a different order.

Copying or Moving a Block to a Disk File

You can copy or move selected blocks from the file you are working on to their own files on the disk (Figure 4-44), or you can append them to the end of existing files. This is sometimes called **writing blocks**.

When you write a selected block to its own file on the disk, you have the choice of copying or moving it.

- If you copy the block, it remains unchanged on the screen.
- If you move the block, it is deleted from the document on the screen.

Either a new file with the name you specify is created on the disk or the block is appended to the end of the file you specified. You can retrieve the new file and edit it just like any other document file. It can also be copied or read into another position in the document you read it from or into any other document.

Moving blocks is often used to break large documents into smaller, more manageable files. Working on smaller documents has several advantages.

- You can get around them more easily.
- You can save and retrieve them faster.

WORD PROCESSING AND DESKTOP PUBLISHING APPLICATIONS

A. Selected Line Block

This paragraph consists of lines of text. You can select any portion of these lines as a block which you can then copy, move, delete or format. When you select the block, you indicate where it begins and ends. Here, the middle two sentences have been selected and the program highlights them so you know exactly what has been selected.

B. Selected Block Deleted

This paragraph consists of lines of text. Here, the middle two sentences have been selected and the program highlights them so you know exactly what has been selected.

A. Selected Column Block

Item	Quantity	Price	Code
Computer	100	$1,500	10010
Disk drive	30	300	20001
Printer	20	800	31000
Tape backup	5	600	42000

B. Selected Column Block Deleted

Item	Price	Code
Computer	$1,500	10010
Disk drive	300	20001
Printer	800	31000
Tape backup	600	42000

- You are less likely to run out of memory.
- You are less likely to lose your entire document if you make a catastrophic mistake.

When copying or moving extremely large blocks of text within a document, you might want to use an intermediate step of copying the block to its own file and then reading it back into the appropriate place in the file (see Topic 4-18). This requires less memory for the transfer and reduces the chance of encountering problems if there is not enough memory.

FIGURE 4-43
Deleting a Block
Deleting a block removes it from the document on the screen and the computer's memory. The text below the deleted block moves up to fill the space (a). When you delete a column, the columns to the right move over to fill the vacated space (b).

When you write a selected block to its own file on the disk, you have the choice of copying or moving it.

If you copy the block, it remains unchanged on the screen. If you move the block, it is deleted from the document on the screen.

In either case, a new file with the name you specify is created on the disk or the block is appended to the end of the file that you specified. You can retrieve the new file and edit it just like any other document file. It can also be "read" into another position in the document from which you read it, or into any other document.

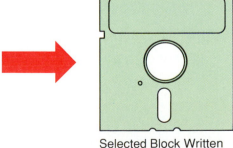

Selected Block Written
(Copied) to a File on a Disk

FIGURE 4-44
Copy a Block to Its Own File
Writing a selected block copies or moves it from the document on the screen to a file on the disk.

SUMMARY AND KEY TERMS

- When large sections of text are to be copied, moved, or deleted, you select the **block**, and then perform the operation. Blocks can be lines, columns, or rectangles.

- **Column mode** allows you to work with columns as well as lines of text. This feature is extremely valuable when you are editing, formatting, and reorganizing such text.

- You **select a block** by highlighting it, entering codes at the beginning and end, or by pressing a specific key.

- **Copying a block** inserts a duplicate copy of the selected block at the cursor's position.

- **Moving a block** inserts a duplicate copy of the block at the cursor's position and then deletes it from the original location.

- **Deleting a block** removes the selected block from the document and the computer's memory. Some programs temporarily store it in a buffer so that you can undo the deletion.

- Blocks of text can be copied or written to their own file on a disk.

REVIEW QUESTIONS

1. What is a block of text? What kinds of blocks can you work with?
2. What is column mode? When would you use it?
3. What operations can you perform on blocks?
4. How do you select blocks?
5. What is the difference between moving and copying a block of text?
6. What are the advantages of being able to copy or move a block to a file on the disk?

Searching and Replacing

OBJECTIVES

After completing this topic, you will be able to

- Explain how to search for words or phrases and how to search for and then replace them

- Describe typical search and search and replace options

When you want to find text in a document, you **search** for it. If you want to replace it with new text, you **search and replace** it. You can search or search and replace any string of characters. Letters, words, numbers, symbols, sentences, codes, and so on that appear in sequence are strings. Table 4-5 lists some examples of strings.

SEARCH

When you use the *Search* command, you are prompted to enter the string you want to find. If the specified string is found, the program moves the cursor to the beginning or end of the string or highlights it in some other way. The program may then display a prompt asking if you want to quit the operation or find the next occurrence. Or the search might end automatically, and you then use another command to continue the search. You might search for strings for several reasons.

- You can use the command to find a section of a document. Just enter a

TABLE 4-5
Examples of Strings

Character	Example
Letters	a
Words	president
Numbers	$100.00
Symbols	→
Numbers and letters	100 Elm Street
Sentences	Thank you for your consideration.
Codes	*[PgBrk], CR*

keyword that appears in the section's title or contents, and the *Search* command finds it.

- You can use the command to check words that you frequently misspell, especially those you misspell in more than one way. For example, using wildcards (see *Wildcards*), you can find all occurrences of the word *similar* even if they have been misspelled *similar*, *simelar*, and *similer*.

SEARCH AND REPLACE

When you use the *Search and Replace* command (sometimes called just *Replace*), you specify the string you want to find and the string you want to replace it with. If the string is found, the program highlights it and usually displays a prompt or menu offering you options; for example, you can

- Replace it
- Leave it unchanged
- Find the next occurrence
- Quit the search and replace operation

Normally, you use the *Search and Replace* command to replace misspelled words with their correct spelling. But it also has other useful applications, including saving typing time. If a word or phrase appears repeatedly in a document, you can substitute an unusual character (or characters) that are unlikely to appear elsewhere in the document instead of repeatedly entering the word or phrase. Later, you can search and replace these characters with the actual word or phrase. For example, if you often refer to a book title in a long report, you can enter an abbreviation wherever the title is to appear. Then you can search and replace the abbreviation with the actual title.

SEARCH AND REPLACE OPTIONS

Both search and search and replace are powerful editing tools. Wildcards and other options make them even more so.

Wildcards

When you enter a string to be searched for, you can use wildcards to substitute for any character or characters. The symbols for these wildcards vary from program to program, but the principles are the same.

- The wildcard ? may stand for any character that appears in this position. Searching for *h?t*, would find *hot*, *hat*, *hit*, and so on.
- The wildcard * may stand for any characters in or after this position, for example, *Mac** finds *MacWilliams*, *MacCarney*, *Macintosh*, and so on. And *t*t* finds *tot*, *treat*, and *toast*.

Other Options

When using search or search and replace, you may use several options to control the process. Not every program offers all these options. And programs that do offer them frequently call them other names.

- *Automatic* or *Global* finds all occurrences of a string and automatically replaces them with the new string. You are not prompted to confirm the replacement. Be careful with commands that affect the entire document in this way. Sometimes the command will not differentiate between whole words or parts of words, for example, *row* and *arrow*. This command also ignores context. For example, if the document contains the sentences *He can read very well* and *She read the book just before class*, and you search and replace *read* with *write*, the second sentence would read *She write the book just before class*.

- *Manual* or *Pause for approval* or *Confirm* finds the specified string and then pauses. A prompt offers you the choice of replacing the string or leaving it unchanged.

- *Ignore case* finds all occurrences of a string, whether some or all of the characters are uppercase or lowercase. This is useful because words falling at the beginning of a sentence are capitalized, whereas the same word falling elsewhere in a sentence may not be. A few programs ignore the case when searching but replace strings using the same case. That is, if the found string is capitalized, the replacement is capitalized; if the found string is lowercase, the replacement is lowercase.

- *Find whole words only* avoids the problem of replacing parts of words when you intended to replace only whole words. For example, searching and replacing *row* with *column* converts *arrow* into *arcolumn* and *rowboat* into *columnboat*. When you specify this option, you should be aware that searching for a singular will not find plurals or possessives. For example, searching for *desk* will not find *desks*.

TIPS: Searching and Replacing

- You can use spaces as part of the search and replace operation. For example, searching and replacing *row* with *column* converts *arrow* into *arcolumn* and *rowboat* into *columnboat*. But searching for *(space)row(space)* finds only whole words spelled *row* with a space before and a space after them. This approach will not find words followed by a punctuation mark. To do so, you must repeat the procedure, this time specifying *(space)row*.

- You can delete strings by replacing them with nothing. When prompted for the word to find, you type in the word to be deleted. When prompted for the word to replace it with, leave it blank. When the search and replace is completed, all the specified strings are deleted.

- To replace strings that may or may not begin with the same case, search for and replace all characters but the first. For example, if *Toggel* is to be replaced with *toggle*, searching for *oggel* and replacing with *oggle* leaves the case of the first letter unchanged since it is not included in the replacement operation.

- Some programs allow you to search and replace special characters, for example, spaces, tab stops, and carriage returns. To search for these kinds of characters, you usually answer the prompt *Search for?* by entering a special symbol, pressing a function key, or holding down **Ctrl** while pressing other keys on the keyboard. This option is useful when editing a document's format.

- Some programs search in both directions from the cursor's position. Others search from the cursor's position to the end of the file. When using one of these other programs, you should move the cursor to the beginning of the file before you execute the search or replace command if you want the entire file searched or replaced.

SUMMARY AND KEY TERMS

- Any group of adjacent characters (including spaces) is called a **string**.
- **Search** is used to find strings; **search and replace** is used to find one string and replace it with another.
- Search and search and replace features include wildcards, global or selective replacement, ignore case, and find whole words only.

REVIEW QUESTIONS

1. What is a string? Give some examples.
2. What is the search command, and what is it used for?
3. What is the search and replace command, and what is it used for?
4. What is a wildcard used for?
5. List and describe three options available when you want to search or search and replace.

Editing Aids

OBJECTIVE

After completing this topic, you will be able to

- Describe editing aids like spelling checkers, thesauruses, style and grammar checkers, and document compare features

Spelling checkers, thesauruses, and style and grammar checkers are invaluable aids when you are editing important documents.

SPELLING CHECKERS

Spelling checkers check all words in a file against a main dictionary and any supplemental dictionaries that you specify. Any words not found in the dictionaries are either flagged with special characters or highlighted. You can then decide whether to change them, leave them as is, or in some cases, add them to the dictionary. Good spelling checkers do not simply flag questionable words; they also list spelling suggestions that you can accept or reject.

When Misspelled Words Are Found

When spelling checkers find misspellings varies, but generally, it is either when you type them or when you run the spelling checker program.

A spelling checker that finds misspellings as you type monitors each word and immediately flags any word it does not find in its dictionary.

Most spelling checkers find misspellings only when you load the spelling checker program and execute a command. Some of these programs stop at each word that it does not find in its dictionary and offer you options, including leaving it unchanged or replacing it with a suggested word. Others check the entire document without your intervention. When checking is completed, all words the program could not find in its dictionary are displayed in reverse video or low intensity or are underlined or listed on the screen one at a time. You can then correct the word, add it to the dictionary, or leave it unchanged.

How Misspelled Words Are Found

Spelling checkers compare your text against either a root word dictionary or a literal dictionary.

- A **root word dictionary** contains only word roots; it does not include prefixes and suffixes.

- A **literal dictionary** contains exact spellings of complete words. They are much longer than root word dictionaries because they contain various entries for each root word.

How would these two types of dictionaries deal with the word *preplan*? If you spelled it incorrectly as *preplane*, the root word dictionary would assume it was spelled correctly because the word's root, *plane*, is spelled correctly. The literal dictionary, however, would flag it since the word *preplane* would not be found in the dictionary.

What Misspelled Words Are Not Found

Spelling checkers are nice, but you cannot entirely rely on them. They check only for spelling, not usage. For example, spelling checkers would find no problems in the sentence *Eye wood like two except you invitation, butt can not. Unfortunately, their are another things i half too due.* It may be an exceptionally fine example of bad grammar, but each word is spelled correctly. Because of this limitation, you must proofread documents carefully for content and context. This cannot be stressed enough.

Spelling Checker Options

When a word is flagged because the spelling checker program cannot find it in its dictionary, the program offers you options that might include one or more of the following:

- *Replace* replaces the flagged word in the text with one of the words suggested by the program.

- *Skip* or *Ignore* skips the flagged word and continues, leaving the word unchanged. This choice tells the program to assume the word is spelled correctly. Sometimes it causes the program to ignore later occurrences of the word in the document.

- *Add to dictionary* is selected when the word is spelled correctly and you want to add it to the dictionary. When you add a word to the dictionary, it is usually added to a supplemental dictionary. Most programs let you specify the supplemental dictionary it is to be added to. This way you can create a series of special-purpose dictionaries. Many users create a supplemental dictionary for names and addresses and another for technical terms used in their fields. At least one program allows you to add a word to a document dictionary. Words added to this dictionary are no longer flagged when you spell check the document again. This dictionary is attached only to the document from which words were added to it.

- *Edit* is used when a typo is found that you can correct without waiting for the program to suggest replacement words. It also is useful when the word is misspelled so badly that the program cannot suggest alternative spellings.

- *Look up* is used to find specific words, for example, when you are typing and are unsure of a word's spelling. The look-up function allows you to enter the word, and the dictionary suggests possible correct spellings.

- *Phonetic* finds words in the dictionary using an **algorithm** (a set of rules) that looks for words sounding like the word you enter. For example, you could type *catigory*, *catagory*, *katagory*, or *kaatagory* to find the correct spelling of the word *category*.

Dictionary Maintenance

Since the dictionary is the heart of the spelling checker, its maintenance is important. You need to be able to add words to it, delete words from it, and correct words in it.

The dictionaries provided with many spelling checkers contain more than 100,000 words, but they are not necessarily the words you use in your business. Ideally, you can create and maintain several separate supplemental dictionaries. Although you can add words to a supplemental dictionary while checking a document, others allow you to create the dictionary directly by listing words in a special file.

Adding a misspelled word to the dictionary by mistake is easy. If you do not discover the mistake and delete it from the dictionary, any further misspellings will not be found. The program will just check your current misspelling against the misspelled word you added to the dictionary and assume the word in the document is spelled correctly.

Some programs store their supplemental dictionaries as normal document files. You can edit and create these dictionaries just like any other files. Other programs store their dictionaries in a special format so that you must convert them from one format to another when retrieving them for editing or saving a new or revised dictionary.

THESAURUSES

When using a **thesaurus**, you can highlight a word and request the thesaurus to display a list of synonyms. For example, when the word *wicked* is highlighted, the thesaurus may display the synonyms *sinful*, *erring*, *nefarious*, *wayward*, *dissolute*, *vile*, and *vicious*. You can then select one of the suggested words to replace the word highlighted in the document, look up another word, or quit the thesaurus and return to the document.

STYLE AND GRAMMAR CHECKERS

Style and grammar checkers look beyond spelling to the structure of your text. For example, RightWriter can analyze documents created on any word processing program. After analyzing the document, it summarizes the analysis (Figure 4-45) and inserts comments into the document that you can use to improve your writing. Typical comments that the program inserts include

- *Wordy* indicates the phrase is wordy or redundant and suggests you phrase it more strongly.
- *Weak* indicates the phrase is weak and suggests you rephrase it more strongly.
- *Negative* indicates the phrase contains a double negative or is negatively worded.
- *Colloquial* indicates the word is colloquial or slang.
- *Overused* indicates the phase is trite or overused.
- *Passive voice* indicates the phrase is in the passive voice.

```
<<** SUMMARY **>>

OVERALL CRITIQUE FOR: test
READABILITY INDEX: 11.39
· Readers need an 11th grade level of education to understand.

        Total Number of Words in Document:   75
        Total Number of Words within Sentences:   75
        Total Number of Sentences:   4
        Total Number of Syllables:  125

STRENGTH INDEX:  0.00
The writing can be made more direct by using:
                        — the active voice
                        — shorter sentences

DESCRIPTIVE INDEX:   0.61
The use of adjectives and adverbs is within the normal range.

JARGON INDEX:     0.42
The writing contains a good deal of jargon.

SENTENCE STRUCTURE RECOMMENDATIONS:
            14.  Consider using more predicate verbs.

            <<WORDS TO REVIEW >>
Review the following list for negative words (N), colloquial
    words (C), jargon (J), misspellings (?), misused words (?),
 or words which your reader may not understand (?).
EXPEDITIOUSLY(J) 1    INDICATIVE(?)  1   MULTIPLICITY(J)  1
            REPS(?) 1       TERRIBLE(N)   1
        <<END OF WORDS TO REVIEW LIST >>
```

FIGURE 4-45
Grammar and Style Checkers
RightWriter checks your documents grammar and style and displays a summary of the analysis. Courtesy of RightSoft

■ *Offensive* indicates the word is sexist or might give offense to many people.

DOCUMENT COMPARE

Documents sometimes go through many revisions before the final version is printed and distributed. All changes are not necessarily good ones, but it gets hard to keep track of them from version to version. A **document compare feature** is therefore useful. This feature compares two versions of a document and highlights the differences between them. For example, CompareRite will highlight, in whatever format you specify, all additions and deletions made to an edited version of a document.

OTHER EDITING AIDS

Besides these editing aids, other features found on some programs are also useful in specific situations.

Redlining and Strikeout

When a document is written by one person and edited by another, or edited by one person and typed by another, some phrases or paragraphs have to be flagged for further consideration. Some paragraphs may be proposed for insertion and some for deletion. A few programs allow you to use **redlining** to indicate text proposed for insertion and **strikeout** to indicate text proposed for deletion. Redlining puts markers in the margin on lines that have been redlined or prints a screen over it when you print the document. These highlights indicate that the material is proposed for insertion. Strikeout puts a strikeout character (- or /) through text proposed for deletion.

After final changes are decided on or approved, a special command deletes all text that has been struck out and removes all redlining from text that has been redlined.

Word Count

Some programs have a command that counts the words in a document or in a selected block. This command is useful when preparing documents with strict length limitations. Typical applications are when typing assigned reports and other school-related projects or when processing articles for magazines and newspapers.

- **Spelling checkers** find and correct misspellings. Some run from within the program; others are separate packages. Some suggest replacements; others only flag mistakes.
- Many programs allow you to add your own words to the dictionary or to create your own **supplemental dictionaries** for special purposes.
- A **thesaurus** suggests synonyms for a highlighted word.
- **Grammar and style checkers** check your text for style and usage. Some run from within the program; others are separate packages.
- If you have two versions of the same document and want to see how they differ, you can use the program's **document compare** feature.
- **Redlining** and **strikeout** are related features on many programs. Redlining highlights added text, and strikeout highlights deleted text. After reviewing the change, you can then automatically remove redlining and delete the struckout text.

1. What is the purpose of a spelling checker?
2. What is the difference between a root word and a literal dictionary? How would each deal with the misspelled word *preplane* for *preplan*?
3. What is the purpose of a thesaurus?
4. What is the purpose of a style and grammar checker?
5. What is a document compare feature, and when would you want to use it?
6. What is redlining? Strikeout? How are they related on some programs?

TOPIC 4-8

Default Formats

OBJECTIVES

After completing this topic, you will be able to

- Explain what default settings are and how you change them
- Describe how some programs allow you to preview on the screen how the finished document will appear when printed

---

As you saw in Part Three, all applications programs have default settings and commands you can use to override them. Figure 4-46 shows some typical word processing default settings. You can use these default settings as is, override them throughout a specific document, or change them for all documents.

LEVELS OF FORMATTING

Formatting documents for printing is done on three levels.

1. Page formats affect the entire page. Examples are margins, headers, and footers.
2. Line or paragraph formats affect individual lines or paragraphs. Examples are paragraph indents, breaking and joining lines of text, and page breaks.
3. Character formats affect individual characters. Examples are boldfacing, underlining, subscripts, and superscripts.

OVERRIDING DEFAULT FORMAT SETTINGS

When you load a word processing program and open a new document, any text you enter is automatically formatted using the default settings. For example, margins may be 1 inch on all sides and text aligned with the left margin and single spaced. If you want different margins or want to center or double space some or all of the text, you must override the default settings at the appropriate place in the document. Depending on the program, you can format a document before, while, or after entering it. Before entering text, you might change the margins or page length. While entering text, you might boldface and underline keywords and titles. After entering text, you might change the position of page numbers on the page.

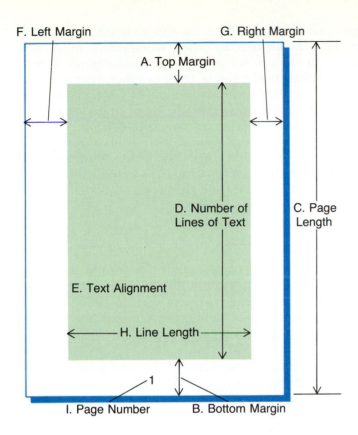

F. Left Margin   G. Right Margin

A. Top Margin

D. Number of
Lines of Text

C. Page
Length

E. Text Alignment

H. Line Length

1

I. Page Number   B. Bottom Margin

FIGURE 4-46
Default Document Formats
Default settings vary from program to program but include the following:

A. The top margin is the distance, measured in lines, from the top of the page to the first printed line.

B. The bottom margin is the distance, measured in lines, from the last printed line to the bottom of the page.

C. Page length is the distance, measured in lines, from the top to the bottom of the page.

D. The number of lines of text that can be printed on a page is calculated by subtracting the number of lines in the top and bottom margin settings from the number of lines in the page length.

E. The text is aligned with the left margin. The right margin can be ragged or justified so that it is evenly aligned with the right margin.

F. The left margin is the distance in from the left edge of the page that the first character in each line of text prints.

G. The right margin is the distance from where the last character on a line can print to the right edge of the page.

H. The line length is the distance between the left and right margin settings.

I. Page numbers may or may not be printed on each page of a document. If they are printed, the position of the page numbers may vary.

You can easily experiment with formats until you find the ones you like. Formatting and text entry are separate operations, so if you want, for example, to change margins after you have entered text, you just use the margin commands. Unlike a typewritten document, you do not have to reenter the text each time you change the format.

How you override the default format settings varies from program to program and from command to command. Generally, there are two methods: inserting codes and inserting format lines.

Inserting Codes

Whether or not you see them, many formats are created by entering codes at selected points in the document (Figure 4-47). For example, common set-

document and these codes arrive at the printer they give it instructions.
[MARGIN CODE]
     For example, a code might tell the printer to advance to the top of the next page after printing 54 lines, print a page number at the bottom of the page, indent a paragraph 5 spaces from the left margin and so on. Usually, these codes are hidden unless you use the display hidden codes command (see Topic 7).
[MARGIN CODE]
Many codes must be entered in pairs, one code to begin a format and another

FIGURE 4-47
Format Codes
Format codes are entered into a document to change formats. These codes are usually hidden, but on most programs, you can display them for editing. Here, a code has been entered to change the margins after the first paragraph. A second code has then been entered to restore the margins to their original settings. The text above the first code is formatted by the program's default settings. The first code affects all text between it and the second code. The second code affects all text from it to the end of the document.

tings like hard carriage returns, spaces, tabs, alignment between margins, and emphasized characters are controlled by codes. When you print the document, these codes arrive at the printer and give it instructions. A code might tell the printer to advance to the top of the next page after printing fifty-four lines, print a page number at the bottom of the page, or indent a paragraph five spaces from the left margin. Usually, these codes are hidden unless you use the *Display Hidden Codes* command (see Topic 4-4).

Many codes must be entered in pairs, one code to begin a format and another to end it; for example, one code starts boldfacing, and one code ends it. If you enter only the code that starts a format, or insert text between the code that starts the format and the code that ends it, some text will likely be formatted in a way you did not intend.

Inserting Format Lines

Some programs group several related commands on a **format line** (also called an *alternate format line* or a *division line*). You can insert these format lines throughout the document wherever you want to change one or more of the settings it controls (Figure 4-48). Typical format line settings are for left and right margins, tab stops, text alignment, headers and footers, and page numbers.

Format lines affect all text below them down to the next format line or the end of the document, whichever occurs first. The default format line is always at the top of the document. If you do not change it and do not enter a new format line elsewhere in the document, the entire document uses the default format settings. If you enter a new format line halfway through the document, the top half uses the default settings, and the bottom half uses the ones you entered halfway down.

Some programs have a standard default format line that you can insert below a format line where you changed settings. This default format line reestablishes the default formats for all text below it. For example, you might enter a new format line to change margins and tab stops above a table. You can then insert the default format line below the table to reestablish the default formats for the rest of the document.

CHANGING SYSTEM DEFAULT FORMAT SETTINGS

When you first load a program, the system default settings are in effect. These system defaults are saved in a configuration file that the program

FIGURE 4-48

Format Lines

Format lines group related commands. Here, a format line has been inserted below the first paragraph to change both margins and line spacing from the default settings that control text at the top of the document. A second format line has been inserted below the second paragraph to restore the margins and line spacing to their original settings. When you enter a new format line, the settings you change affect the document to the next format line or the end of the document.

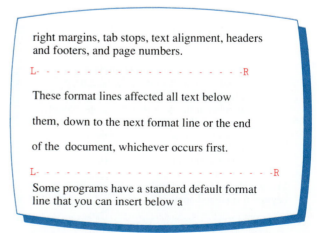

right margins, tab stops, text alignment, headers and footers, and page numbers.

L- -R

These format lines affected all text below

them, down to the next format line or the end

of the document, whichever occurs first.

L- -R

Some programs have a standard default format line that you can insert below a reads when you first load it. You can change the system default settings on many programs (see Topic 3-5).

DOCUMENT PREVIEW

If you use several formatting commands, you may have a hard time visualizing what the document will look like when it is printed. Many formatting commands do not show their effects on the screen. For example, few programs display headers, footers, footnotes, top and bottom margins, and font changes on the screen. To help, some programs have a *Document Preview* command that displays a page on the screen the same way it will look when printed.

One of the more recent goals of those who develop word processing programs has been to allow you to see on the screen exactly what your document will look like when you print it out. This is called **WYSIWYG** (pronounced "whizzy-wig") or "what you see is what you get." WYSIWYG is important in desktop publishing applications, but it is also important in standard word processing applications. Some of the latest word processing programs provide WYSIWYG, whereas others have *Document Preview* commands that let you see how the document will look when it is printed (Figure 4-49). Though you cannot edit the document when it is displayed with this command, you can see where improvements might be made before you print it out.

What is displayed on your screen depends on both your program and your computer system. For example, you cannot see headers and footers unless the program is designed to display them, and you cannot see italic type or subscripts and superscripts unless you have a graphics display. Despite these limitations, you usually get a good idea of how the document will look when printed from what you see on the screen. Table 4-6 lists some of the most common formats and indicates where they are usually seen—on the screen, on the printout, or both.

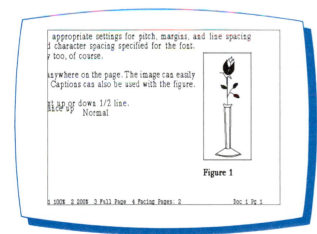

FIGURE 4-49
Document Preview
Desktop publishing features are being introduced into word processing programs. Here, you see a WordPerfect 5.0 screen display of a page that has graphics integrated into the document.

TABLE 4-6
On-Screen and Off-Screen Formatting

Command	Character Display	Graphics Display	Printout
Boldface	■	■	■
Underline	■	■	■
Italics		■	■
Font changes		■	■
Text alignment	■	■	■
Tab stops	■	■	■
Paragraph indents	■	■	■
Margins—left and right	■	■	■
Line length	■	■	■
Page offset			■
Headers and footers			■
Page numbers			■
Font changes		■	■
Margins—top and bottom			■
Page breaks	■	■	■
Page length			■
Line spacing	■	■	■
Lines per inch		■	■
Superscripts and subscripts		■	■

SUMMARY AND KEY TERMS

- **Default formats** are formats that were entered by the program's designers. You can change or override them when required.
- You can format a document on three levels using **page formats**, **line** or **paragraph formats**, or **character formats**.
- You override default format settings by entering codes or **format lines**.
- If you want to change the default settings for your program, you change the **system format settings**.
- What you see is what you get—or is it? Many word processing systems will print exactly what you see on the screen, including line spacing and margins. Others will not; some things are displayed on the screen, but many appear only when the document is printed. Many programs offer a **document preview** feature that allows you to see on the screen exactly how your document will look when printed. Other programs always display the document on the screen in the way it will print. These programs are called **WYSIWYG** (what you see is what you get).

REVIEW QUESTIONS

1. What are default formats? List some of the typical default settings used for printing documents.
2. What are the three levels you can format text on?
3. How do you override default formats?
4. How do you permanently change default formats? Why would you want to do so?
5. What is a document preview command?
6. What is the definition of WYSIWYG?

WORD PROCESSING AND DESKTOP PUBLISHING APPLICATIONS

Page Breaks and Page Numbers

OBJECTIVE

After completing this topic, you will be able to

- Describe how to control page breaks and page numbers

When you print a document, you can control where page breaks fall and page numbers are printed.

PAGE BREAKS

A **page break** is where the printer stops printing lines on the current sheet of paper, advances the paper to the top of the next page, and resumes printing on that page. The way the printer advances to the next page depends on your printer and the kind of paper you are using.

- If you are hand-feeding the printer single sheets of paper, the printer ejects the current sheet and pauses at a page break. You then insert a new sheet and press a designated key to resume printing.
- If you are printing on single sheets of paper on a printer with an automatic sheet feeder, the printer does not pause at a page break; rather, it ejects the current sheet, automatically feeds another sheet, and resumes printing.
- If you are printing on continuous form paper, the printer stops printing at a page break, advances the paper to the top of the next page, and then resumes printing.

Controlling where page breaks occur is important when printing multipage documents because there are certain places where you want to avoid page breaks.

- Letters should not end with the closing of the letter at the top of the second page.
- Reports, term papers, and other important documents should often have major sections begin at the top of a new page.
- Tables and the like should be kept together so that they do not break with one part on one page and the rest on the next page (Figure 4-50).

A.

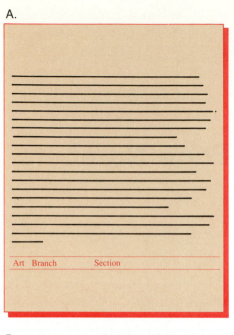

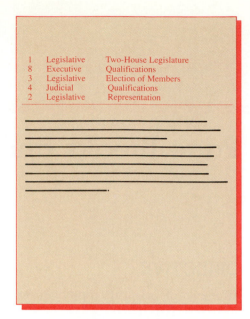

B.

FIGURE 4-50
Incorrect Page Breaks
There are places where you do not want pages to break, for example, in the middle of a table (a). You can prevent bad page breaks by entering a hard or conditional page break above the table so that the entire table prints on the next page (b).

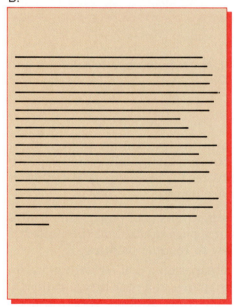

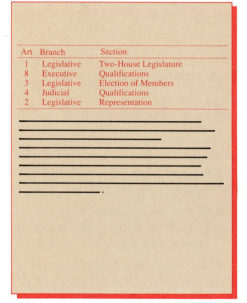

■ The first or last line of a paragraph should never be printed by itself at the bottom or top of a page. You should always have at least two lines of a paragraph together on a page. If the first line of a paragraph prints by itself at the bottom of page, it is a **widow**. If the last line of a paragraph prints by itself at the top of a page, it is an **orphan**.

Page breaks are especially easy to control when your program has a **dynamic page display**, which shows on the screen where page breaks will occur. To control them, word processing programs have three kinds of page breaks: soft, hard, and conditional.

Soft Page Breaks

When you enter or edit a document, some programs automatically insert page breaks and automatically adjust them when necessary. Other programs do so only when you paginate or repaginate the document. Either

WORD PROCESSING AND DESKTOP PUBLISHING APPLICATIONS

way, the page breaks inserted automatically are **soft page breaks**. If you edit the document so that the length of one or more pages changes, the soft page breaks are relocated automatically or when you repaginate the document.

Hard Page Breaks

Normally, page breaks occur automatically when a page is full, but you can also force them to fall at selected points in a document. To force a page break, you insert a **hard page break** (also called a required page end) where you want text to start printing at the top of the next page. If you are using a page-oriented program, repaging the document rearranges soft page breaks, if necessary, but not hard page breaks. To change a hard page break, you must delete the code you entered to create it.

Conditional Page Breaks

Forced page breaks created with hard page break codes give you a lot of control, but they sometimes create problems. For example, if you find a table broken by a page break, you may insert a hard page break just above the table so that it starts printing on a new page. Later, you add or delete a section of text above the table, and then print the document. The table now prints on a new page even though there is room for it on the previous page. You can prevent unwanted page breaks like these with a **conditional page break**. This command inserts a special version of the soft page break code that tells the printer, "If this section fits in the remaining space on this page, print it here; otherwise, advance the paper, and begin printing it at the top of the next page." If the section is too long for a single page, it breaks as necessary and continues printing on the second and subsequent pages.

This command is extremely useful when you want to

- Keep the lines of a table on the same page as the table headings
- Keep an illustration on the same page
- Keep a heading and at least the first two lines of the following text on the same page

Widows and Orphans

Most programs have a command that prevents widows and orphans from occurring in your printed documents (Figure 4-51). This command prevents the first line of a paragraph from printing by itself at the bottom of a page and the last line of a paragraph from printing by itself at the top of the next page. If the program calculates that only the first line will print at the bottom of the page, it moves the entire paragraph to the next page. If it calculates that only the last line will print at the top of the next page, it moves another line to accompany it. Thus no three-line paragraphs will be split; the entire paragraph will move to the next page if it will not print on the current page. On some programs, you can specify the minimum number of lines to appear at the top and bottom of a page.

PAGE NUMBERS

Page numbers can be printed on every page of a multipage document, turned off when printing a single-page letter, or turned off for the first page and on for the second page when printing a two-page letter. This on-off control is sufficient for many documents, but most programs give you much

A. Widow at Top of Page

chosen

The history of the present King of Great

B. Orphan at Bottom of Page

FIGURE 4-51
Widows and Orphans
Widows and orphans can be prevented. (a) A widow occurs when the last line of a paragraph prints at the top of a new page. (b) An orphan occurs when the first line of a new paragraph prints at the bottom of a page.

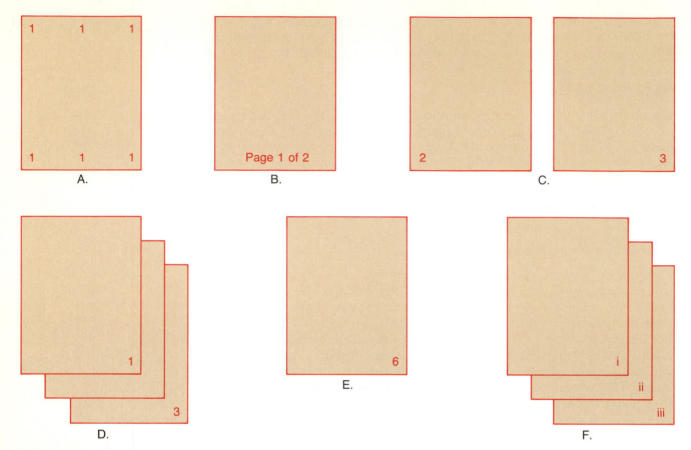

FIGURE 4-52
Page Number Options
You can control where and how page numbers are printed: centered or aligned with the left or right margin (a), combined with text (b), printed on alternate sides of the pages (c), skipped (d), started at any desired number (e), printed in Arabic or Roman numerals (f).

greater control over page numbers. Figure 4-52 shows some of the options you have when printing page numbers.

The way you enter page numbers varies. On some programs, there are special page numbering commands. On others, you enter page numbers in headers and footers (see Topic 4-15).

On document-oriented programs, pages are renumbered automatically when text is inserted or deleted and text on the following pages moves up or down a page. On page-oriented programs, you have to repaginate the document each time changes of this kind are made. Some programs allow you to specify that the document be automatically repaginated when you print or save it.

TIPS: Page Breaks and Page Numbers

When creating a document, you may occasionally refer to a page number (or any other kind of number) elsewhere in the document. But what happens if you revise the document so that the reference no longer refers to the correct page or if you change any number later referred to? **Symbolic referencing** (also called *automatic referencing*), one of the latest developments in word processing programs, solves this problem. Using this feature, whenever you change a number, all references to it automatically change.

WORD PROCESSING AND DESKTOP PUBLISHING APPLICATIONS

- **Page breaks** determine where the printer stops printing on a page and advances to the top of the next page.
- When laying out important documents, you should be able to see on the screen where page breaks will occur. This is called a **dynamic page break display**.
- There are three kinds of page breaks: **soft**, **hard** and **conditional**.
- A **widow** is the last line of a paragraph printed by itself at the top of a page. An **orphan** is the first line of a paragraph printed by itself at the bottom of a page.
- Most programs allow you to print **page numbers** on multipage documents. They can be printed at the top or bottom of the page and aligned flush left, centered, or flush right. You can also print them on odd or even pages only or alternate them for a document that is to be copied on both sides of the paper so that they appear only on the outside corner of each page.
- Some programs provide **symbolic referencing** so that you can enter a code that refers to a number elsewhere in the document. The code always reflects the same number as the number it refers to. If you change the number, the code displays the new number.

1. What is a page break? Why would you want to control them?
2. What is the difference between a soft and a hard page break?
3. What is a conditional page break command?
4. What are the differences between a hard page break and a conditional page break?
5. What are widows and orphans, and why do you want to prevent their occurring?
6. What two ways do programs use to print page numbers?
7. What is symbolic referencing?

Text Alignment and Hyphenation

OBJECTIVES

After completing this topic, you will be able to

- Explain how to align text with the left and right margins and center it between them
- Describe justified text
- Explain hyphenation and how to use it

Among the most useful features of word processing programs are those you use to align text with the margins. These commands give you a great deal of control over the way your printed document looks. Unlike a typewriter, a word processing program allows you to experiment with alignments. If you do not like the results you get with one alignment, you can change it without having to reenter the text. How you align text varies from program to program.

- On some programs, you select the text to be aligned and execute an alignment command.
- On other programs, you enter codes or format lines wherever you want to change the alignment.

HORIZONTAL ALIGNMENT

The commands that align text affect entire paragraphs, that is, any section of text that ends with a hard carriage return. To align more than one paragraph, you must either select all the paragraphs and then align them or enter an alignment code above and below the paragraphs to be aligned. A few programs require you to enter an alignment code for each paragraph individually.

You have four choices when aligning text with the left and right margins (Figure 4-53): You can align it flush with the left margin, flush with the right margin, flush with both margins, or center it between the margins.

Flush Left and Flush Right

Text is normally aligned with the left margin when you create documents. This text is **flush left**. But there are times when you might want to align it with the right margin, when entering dates and page numbers, for example.

Left-aligned text has its left edge flush with the left margin and its right margin ragged. Right-aligned text has its right edge flush with the right margin and its left edge ragged. Justified text is aligned with both the left and right margins. The alignment is achieved by inserting spaces between words and characters on the lines. Centered text is equally spaced between the left and right margins.

A.

Left-aligned text has its left edge flush with the left margin and its right margin ragged. Right-aligned text has its right edge flush with the right margin and its left edge ragged. Justified text is aligned with both the left and right margins. The alignment is achieved by inserting spaces between words and characters on the lines. Centered text is equally spaced between the left and right margins.

B.

Left-aligned text has its left edge flush with the left margin and its right margin ragged. Right-aligned text has its right edge flush with the right margin and its left edge ragged. Justified text is aligned with both the left and right margins. The alignment is achieved by inserting spaces between words and characters on the lines. Centered text is equally spaced between the left and right margins.

C.

Left-aligned text has its left edge flush with the left margin and its right margin ragged. Right-aligned text has its right edge flush with the right margin and its left edge ragged. Justified text is aligned with both the left and right margins. The alignment is achieved by inserting spaces between words and characters on the lines. Centered text is equally spaced between the left and right margins.

D.

FIGURE 4-53
Aligning Text with the Left and Right Margins
You can align text with or between the left and right margins. (a) Left-aligned text has its left edge flush with the left margin and its right margin ragged. This is the default setting for many programs. (b) Right-aligned text has its right edge flush with the right margin and its left margin ragged. (c) Justified text is aligned evenly with both the left and right margins, except lines ending with a hard carriage return. You find this alignment most frequently in books, magazines, and other published materials. (d) Centered text is equally spaced between the left and right margins.

This text is **flush right**. When text is aligned with one margin, the other margin is not aligned. Unaligned margins are **ragged right** or **ragged left**.

Centered

Centered text is normally centered between the left margin and the right margin. But many programs let you change the point that text is centered on (Figure 4-54). On some, you do this by centering text in a tab stop column (see Topic 4-14). On others, you point to the desired column with the cursor, and then execute the centering command.

Justified

Justified text is aligned flush with both the left and right margins. To justify text so that it aligns with both margins, the program inserts spaces of

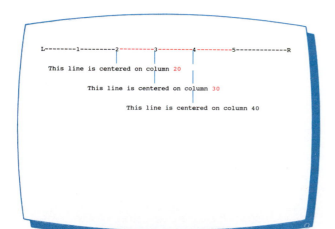

FIGURE 4-54
Text Centered on a Column
Text can also be centered on a specified column or tab stop. Here three lines are centered on different columns.

varying width between words to expand the lines. On the screen, lines are justified by inserting full-character spaces between words; when printed, most programs do the same. The result is that large white spaces are occasionally inserted between words to justify lines.

A few programs can insert spaces as small as 1/120 inch between words and letters to expand the line. This **microspace justification** (also called *microjustification* or *horizontal motion index*) when supported by the program and printer gives a finished appearance to printed text. If your program and printer do not support microspace justification, you may decide, after comparing justified to unjustified printouts, that unjustified text not only looks better but also is easier to read.

VERTICAL ALIGNMENT

A few word processing programs have a command that centers text vertically on the page between the top and bottom margins (Figure 4-55). This command is useful when you are formatting title pages for documents. Generally, the effects of vertical alignment are seen only on the printout of the document; they are not usually displayed on the screen.

RETURNING TEXT TO ORIGINAL MARGINS

After you change the alignment of text, you may decide you prefer it the way it was originally. You can easily return the text to its default alignment. The way you do this varies from program to program.

- You use a command similar to the one you used to change the alignment. For example, if you used a center command, you now use an align left command.

FIGURE 4-55
Text Centered Vertically
Text can be centered vertically on the page. This is useful when you are printing title pages for documents.

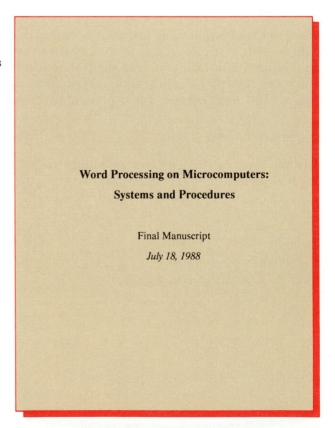

Word Processing on Microcomputers:

Systems and Procedures

Final Manuscript

July 18, 1988

- You delete codes or spaces that you entered when you originally changed the alignment.
- You delete or revise a format line.
- You change printer specifications at the time you print the document.

HYPHENATION

Programs that automatically reform paragraphs often have a separate *Hyphenation* command (Figure 4-56). Hyphenating text is similar to paragraph reforming, but the hyphens you enter with this command are soft hyphens (see Topic 4-3).

To hyphenate a document, you move the cursor to the top of the document, and execute the *Hyphenation* command. The program then scrolls through the text, or you do so manually. When a word falls within the hyphenation zone (see *Hyphenation Zones*), the program pauses and suggests where you might place a hyphen. You then have three options: You can accept the suggestion, use the directional arrow keys to move the cursor to where you want the hyphen, or tell the program not to hyphenate.

- If you hyphenate the word, the hyphen is the last character on the line; the rest of the word wraps to the beginning of the next line.
- If you do not hyphenate, the entire word wraps to the next line.

In either case, scrolling then resumes until another candidate for hyphenation is found or the end of the document is reached.

You should always hyphenate just before printing. The slightest change in the wording or punctuation of paragraph may change the position of words so that hyphenated words no longer fall at the end of lines. When this happens, you have to hyphenate the document again.

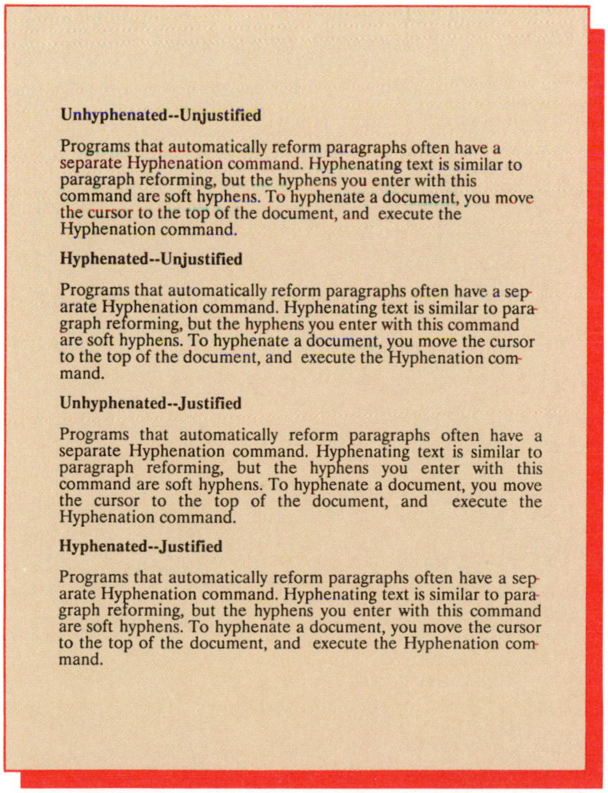

FIGURE 4-56
Hyphenated Text
Hyphenated text has a more even right margin. This also reduces the white space between words in justified text.

Unhyphenated--Unjustified

Programs that automatically reform paragraphs often have a separate Hyphenation command. Hyphenating text is similar to paragraph reforming, but the hyphens you enter with this command are soft hyphens. To hyphenate a document, you move the cursor to the top of the document, and execute the Hyphenation command.

Hyphenated--Unjustified

Programs that automatically reform paragraphs often have a separate Hyphenation command. Hyphenating text is similar to paragraph reforming, but the hyphens you enter with this command are soft hyphens. To hyphenate a document, you move the cursor to the top of the document, and execute the Hyphenation command.

Unhyphenated--Justified

Programs that automatically reform paragraphs often have a separate Hyphenation command. Hyphenating text is similar to paragraph reforming, but the hyphens you enter with this command are soft hyphens. To hyphenate a document, you move the cursor to the top of the document, and execute the Hyphenation command.

Hyphenated--Justified

Programs that automatically reform paragraphs often have a separate Hyphenation command. Hyphenating text is similar to paragraph reforming, but the hyphens you enter with this command are soft hyphens. To hyphenate a document, you move the cursor to the top of the document, and execute the Hyphenation command.

Hyphenation Zones

Some programs allow you to control hyphenation by changing the hyphenation zone at the right margin (Figure 4-57). The **hyphenation zone** is a specified number of columns on either side of the right margin setting. If a word begins before or at the left edge of the hyphenation zone and extends past its right edge, you are asked if you want to hyphenate it.

How a Program Knows Where to Hyphenate

When you hyphenate a document, the program suggests where you might place the hyphen in a word, and a prompt asks if you want to accept the suggestion. Programs determine where a word should be hyphenated in one of two ways: dictionaries and algorithms.

Hyphenation dictionaries are built into some programs. When a candidate for hyphenation is found, the program looks the word up and suggests you hyphenate it the way the dictionary lists it.

Hyphenation algorithms are built-in rules of hyphenation. Some programs use these rules, instead of a dictionary, to determine where words should be hyphenated. Typical hyphenation rules include

- When possible, hyphenate between syllables.
- Do not hyphenate so that a single letter is left at the end of the line.
- Do not hyphenate so that fewer than three characters are at the beginning of the next line.
- Hyphenate hyphenated compound words, like *computer-based*, only at the hyphen.
- Hyphenate nonhyphenated compound words, like *microcomputer*, only between the words (between *micro* and *computer*).
- Do not hyphenate names or other proper nouns.

FIGURE 4-57
Hyphenation Zone
You can revise the hyphenation zone. Here, the left edge of the zone has been set eight columns to the left of the left margin. The right edge of the zone has been set in the same column as the left margin. When a word begins at or before the left edge of the zone and extends past the right edge, you are asked if you want to hyphenate it. The narrower the zone, the more words there are hyphenated but the less ragged the right margin.

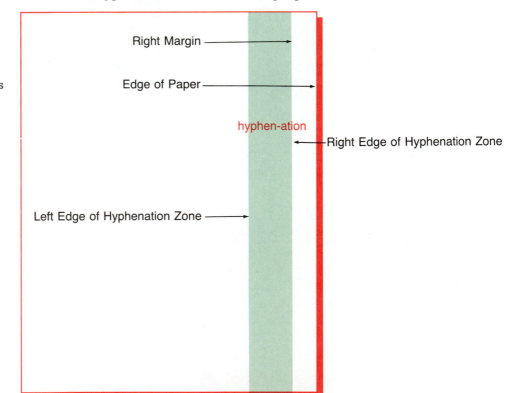

Right Margin

Edge of Paper

hyphen-ation

Right Edge of Hyphenation Zone

Left Edge of Hyphenation Zone

WORD PROCESSING AND DESKTOP PUBLISHING APPLICATIONS

TIPS: Text Alignment and Hyphenation

- Text is justified only if the line or paragraph ends with a hard carriage return. Therefore, always press **Return** after entering the last line or paragraph in a document, or it will not be justified.
- **Proportional spacing**, the allotment of space for characters based on their width, adds to the attractiveness of justified text (see Topic 4-12).
- Hyphenation can also improve the appearance of justified text.
- Justification is not always used. Because word processing is becoming so prevalent in the office, higher volumes of output are being achieved. Many letters you receive are actually form letters generated on a computer with little or no operator involvement. Justified text is a dead giveaway that the document was prepared on a computer. Although most offices want higher volume, they are unwilling to sacrifice personalization. Therefore, many word processing operators, supervisors, and even management personnel choose to keep unjustified text their standard.

SUMMARY AND KEY TERMS

- Text can be aligned with the left or right margins, centered, or justified. When text is aligned flush with the left or right margins, the other margin is **ragged**. **Justified text** is flush with both the left and right margins.
- Some programs will insert spaces between letters as well as words to better align a line with both margins. This is called **microspace justification**, and it greatly enhances the appearance of justified documents, but it must be supported by the printer.
- **Vertical centering** centers a section of text between the top and bottom margins.
- **Hyphenation** automatically inserts soft hyphens to give a more even look to the right margin.
- Where words are hyphenated is determined by the **hyphenation zone**. If a word at the end of a line begins before or at the left edge of the zone and extends past its right edge, you are prompted to hyphenate it. A hyphen position is suggested by the program based on a **hyphenation dictionary** or **algorithm**.

REVIEW QUESTIONS

1. List four ways you can align text, and give some examples of when you might want to use the alignments.
2. Describe the difference between justification and microspace justification.
3. Why do you hyphenate a document? When do you do so?
4. What is a hyphenation zone?

Text Emphasis, Superscripts, and Subscripts

OBJECTIVES

After completing this topic, you will be able to

- Describe how to emphasize words with boldface and underlines
- Describe how to enter superscripts and subscripts

Word processing programs offer several formats you can use to emphasize text. For example, you can boldface or underline headings, keywords, disclaimers, and book titles (Figure 4-58). You can use these formats for individual characters, words, lines, paragraphs, or entire documents. You can also combine them; for example, you can both boldface and underline a heading.

How you assign these formats varies. On some programs, you select the text, and then choose the format from a menu. On others, you enter codes at the beginning and end of the text to be emphasized. If you are using the latest dot-matrix printers (including laser printers), you achieve the same result by changing fonts (see Topic 4-12). To use these formats in combinations, for example, to both boldface and underline a phrase, you enter the command for each format individually.

FIGURE 4-58
Text Emphasis
Text can be emphasized by changing its format. (a) Boldfaced text is darker than regular text and can emphasize section and table headings or keywords in a document. (b) Text can be struck out to indicate that it will be dropped in the next version or to cancel clauses in contracts and other agreements. (c) You can use boldfacing and underscoring in combination. Underscored, or underlined, text can be used for titles of books and articles. Continuous underscoring (d) underlines both characters and spaces, whereas noncontinuous underscoring (e) underlines only characters. (f) Underlines can be either single or double; these forms are used when preparing financial statements.

```
(a)  Boldface
(b)  Strikethrough
(c)  Boldface and underscore
(d)  Continuous underscoring
(e)  Non-continous underscoring

(f)  Single and double underscoring

     $1,000
     -  300   --- Single underscore
     $  700   --- Double underscore
```

BOLDFACE

Boldfaced text is darker than normal text and can be used to emphasize section and table headings or keywords in a document. Impact printers print boldfaced characters by striking the character two or three times. Laser printers must have access to a separate boldfaced font since they cannot restrike the same characters to create a darker image (see Topic 4-12). Some programs have two boldface commands: One command strikes the character three times for boldface, and another strikes the character twice for doublestrike.

UNDERLINE

Underlining (also called *underscoring*) can be used to indicate titles of books or articles or to divide sections in financial reports. There are a two basic underscore styles, continuous and noncontinuous, and some programs offer you a choice. Continuous style underscores words and the spaces between the words. To obtain continuous underscoring on some programs, you must enter hard spaces between words (see Topic 4-3). Noncontinuous style underscores words but not the spaces between them.

Some programs also offer both single and double underline options. These are useful when you are creating financial statements and other documents with subtotals and totals. Although some programs offer these options, they also must be supported by the printer type element or font.

STRIKEOUT

Strikeout (also called *overstrike* or *strike-through*) can be used to indicate where deletions have been made when one person edits a document and another reviews the changes. It can indicate what text is to be dropped in the next version of a document or to cancel clauses in contracts or other agreements. Some strikeout commands also make a line of hyphens into a continuous line that you can use to separate elements in a table. Most programs use the hyphen symbol to strike out text, but a few allow you to choose the character. On some programs, struck-out text can be automatically deleted (see Topic 4-7).

OTHER EFFECTS

Besides boldfacing, underlining, and striking out characters, some programs offer additional formats. For example, if you have a color printer, you can change colors to emphasize words and phrases. And shadow print prints each letter with a shadowy effect.

SUPERSCRIPTS AND SUBSCRIPTS

Most word processors, especially those used by technical, scientific, and engineering writers and typists, allow you to enter **superscripts** above and **subscripts** below the normal line of text. Superscripts and subscripts can be used to print copyright marks, trademark symbols, formulas, and footnote numbers (Figure 4-59).

- Some programs print a superscript above and a subscript below the line of text. If the program does not allow you to control the distance they print above and below the lines, you may have to double space the text

FIGURE 4-59
Superscripts and Subscripts
Superscripts print above the line, and subscripts below the line. They have several applications. For example, you can use them to create fractions, formulas, trademark symbols, copyright symbols, registration marks, temperature degrees, and footnote symbols.

A superscript is printed above the center of the line.

A subscript is printed below the center of the line.

	Before	After
Fractions	1/2	$^1/_2$
Formulas	H2O	H_2O
Trademark symbols	Trademarkstm	Trademarks^{tm}
Copyright symbols	Copyrights(c)	Copyrights$^{(c)}$
Registration marks	RegisteredR	Registered^R
Temperature degrees	70o	70°

to provide enough room for the superscripts and subscripts. To use superscripts and subscripts with these programs, your printer must be able to print them in the desired position. That is, it must be able to advance the paper forward and backward to print characters above and below the line it is currently printing.

■ Other programs print the superscripts and subscripts on the same line as the text but in smaller type. The superscript on these programs is printed in small type above the center of the line, and the subscript is printed in small type below the center of the line.

SUMMARY AND KEY TERMS

■ Types of emphasis include **boldface**, **doublestrike**, **underline**, **shadow print**, and **strikeout**. They can even be used in combinations. Character attributes can be assigned to a character, word, paragraph, block, or entire document.

■ **Superscripts** print above the center of the line, and **subscripts** print below it. They are used to add footnote references as well as in math and science formulas.

REVIEW QUESTIONS

1. List two ways to emphasize text.
2. What is the difference between continuous and noncontinuous underlining?
3. Describe superscripts and subscripts, and give examples of when you might want to use them.

WORD PROCESSING AND DESKTOP PUBLISHING APPLICATIONS

Fonts

OBJECTIVES

After completing this topic, you will be able to

- Describe a font and its features and how to change fonts
- Understand the difference between fixed pitch and proportional spacing
- List the types of fonts that are available

One of the hallmarks of professionally prepared documents is the selective use of different styles and sizes of type. This text, for example, uses one typestyle and type size for main headings, another for less important headings, another for the text itself, and still another for captions. The visual quality of the final text is much higher than that of the draft it was prepared from.

The ways you could emphasize text on a word processing program were once limited to boldface, underline, italic, and pitch. Today, a much wider selection is available because of fonts.

A **font** is a complete set of the characters you need to print a document in one typestyle and type size. Special characters are also included in many fonts, for example, foreign language characters, Greek characters, mathematical symbols, and graphics characters. Pick up a typeball from a typewriter, and you are holding a font (Figure 4-60). The importance of fonts has increased as word processing technology has improved and, especially, as printers have become able to print a wide variety of typestyles and type sizes. Fonts are available in many designs or typefaces, each typeface has several typestyles, and each typestyle comes in various sizes (Figure 4-61). Fonts can also have a fixed pitch or be proportionally spaced. Let's look at these characteristics of fonts.

FIGURE 4-60
A Typeball Font
The characters on a typeball are all the same size and all have the same style, so they are a font. Courtesy of International Business Machines Corporation

TYPEFACES

Typeface refers to the type's particular design. Typical typefaces include Elite, Pica, Gothic, Helvetica, Times Roman, and Baskerville.

TYPESTYLES

Most typefaces come in several variations called **typestyles**, for example, light, medium, bold, extra bold, italic, expanded, and condensed. These var-

TYPEFACE	TYPESTYLE	TYPE SIZE
Times Roman	Normal	8 point
Helvetica	**Bold**	10 point
Courier	*Italic*	12 point
		14 point

FIGURE 4-61
Fonts
Fonts come in many typefaces. Each typeface has several variations called typestyles, and each typestyle comes in several sizes.

iations are important, especially when you are printing on a laser printer. Since a laser printer cannot backspace over a character to make it darker, it must have access to a normal version of the selected typestyle to print regular text and a bold or italic version to print boldfaced or italicized text. If the printer has access only to Times Roman Normal and Times Roman Bold, you cannot print text in Times Roman Italic.

TYPE SIZES

Type size, the size of the printed character, is specified either by pitch or in points.

Pitch

Pitch refers to the number of characters printed per inch. If you are typing on a typewriter, you can generally switch from 10 pitch to 12 pitch. This means the typewriter can print either 10 or 12 characters per inch. You can do the same on a word processing program (Figure 4-62). Changing the pitch changes letter spacing and affects the number of characters printed per inch and per line.

Points

The size of type is specified in **points**. Each point equals 0.0138 (about 1/72) inch. Because the size of the type determines both its horizontal and vertical size, it determines how many characters can be printed on a line and the number of lines that can be printed on a page. Changing the size of type in a

FIGURE 4-62
Pitch
You can change pitch in a document if this command is supported by the printer. For example, you can change from elite (a) to pica (b).

A. Elite
```
The number of characters printed horizontally per inch — called
"pitch" — can be controlled on many printers or programs. On
letter-quality printers that use fully-formed characters, pitch
can only be changed by changing the type-element on the printer.
On dot-matrix printers, pitch can be changed by sending control
codes to the printer. Some programs allow you to embed control
codes in the document so you can use more than one pitch in the
same document.

This paragraph has been printed using Elite.
```

B. Pica
```
The number of characters printed horizontally per inch -- called
"pitch" -- can be controlled on many printers or programs. On
letter-quality printers that use fully-formed characters, pitch
can only be changed by changing the type-element on the printer.
On dot-matrix printers, pitch can be changed by sending control
codes to the printer. Some programs allow you to embed control
codes in the document so you can use more than one pitch in the
same document.

This paragraph has been printed using Pica.
```

FIGURE 4-63
Type Size

document can dramatically affect the number of characters that fit on a line and the number of lines that fit on a page (Figure 4-63). On programs where you specify margins in characters and lines, you may have to change the margins when you change the type size. On programs where you specify margins in inches, you do not have to change the margins when you change the type size. The program calculates the number of characters that will fit on a line while retaining the left and right margins.

Type size affects both the number of characters per line and the number of lines per page. (a) For example, if you print a document in a small type size, the number of characters per line and number of lines per page is quite large. The same text printed in a larger size allows fewer characters per line and fewer lines per page (b).

FIXED PITCH AND PROPORTIONAL SPACING

The size of a character determines how many characters can be printed per inch or per line. All programs and printers support fixed pitch, and many also support proportional spacing (Figure 4-64). A letter typed with a **fixed pitch** uses the same space for each letter, whether a wide W or a narrow I. **Proportional spacing** varies the space between the characters depending on the width of the letter. Proportionally spaced, a W is given more space than an I.

On some programs, you can also kern text. **Kerning** controls the spacing between letters to give a very finished appearance to the text. Though related to proportional spacing, kerning goes one step further, as Figure 4-65 shows.

FIGURE 4-64
Fixed Pitch and Proportional Spacing
Fonts with fixed pitch differ from those with proportional spacing. (a) Fixed pitch allocates the same space to each character whether it is a wide W or a narrow I. (b) Proportional spacing allocates more space for wide characters than for narrow ones.

A. Fixed Pitch

B. Proportional Spacing

FIGURE 4-65
Kerning
Kerning is a further extension of proportional spacing. Proportional spacing considers the width of a character when it assigns letter spaces. Kerning also considers the characters a letter is next to. Some characters are set so that they actually overlap, as an uppercase T overlaps an adjacent lowercase a.

CHANGING FONTS

We are today in a transition period between old-style fully formed character printers and the latest laser printers that form images from dots. Because of this, the way you change fonts varies from program to program.

You change fonts for characters, words, or phrases by entering codes into the document. These codes do not appear in your printouts, but they instruct the printer what to do. You often must enter these codes in pairs, one at the beginning of the text you want printed with a different font and one at the end. You enter these codes by typing them or by selecting a font from a menu.

When you print the document, the codes tell the printer what font to use. For the printer to change fonts, it must be able to access them. Fully formed character printers can change fonts only if the program allows you to enter **stop codes**, which instruct the printer to pause so that you can change type elements.

Dot-matrix printers can change fonts only if the font is available to the printer when needed. The number of fonts that can be made available is limited, so the number of fonts that can be used in a document is also limited. Except in special applications, this is not a serious problem. Good design dictates that font changes be sparingly used. Too many fonts on the same page gives a cluttered, amateurish appearance to a document.

Fonts are made available to the printer in five ways: internally, in a cartridge, downloaded into the printer's memory, stored on a font server, or electronically generated by an algorithm.

- **Internal fonts** are stored in the printer's memory and are always available. All the latest dot-matrix printers have a few fonts stored in ROM inside the printer.

- **Font cartridges** (Figure 4-66) are cartridges that you plug into the printer. To change a font cartridge, you have to turn off the printer, plug in the new cartridge, and then turn on the printer.

- **Downloadable fonts** (also called soft fonts) come on disks just like other software. To use them, you download, or transfer, the desired fonts into the printer's memory so that the printer has access to them when it needs them. One technique to increase the available number of fonts is to have the printer load only those fonts needed at the time. When it needs another font, it removes the current font from its memory and downloads another from the disk. Although this slows down the printer, it increases the number of fonts available for a document.

- **Font servers** are like hard disk drives on which many fonts are stored. But since the fonts enter the printer through a separate channel, the printer is not slowed down as it prints a document and changes fonts.

FIGURE 4-66
Font Cartridges
Font cartridges contain several fonts and are plugged into the printer to make these fonts available when they are specified in a document that you want to print. Photo courtesy of Hewlett-Packard Company

- On most printers, the fonts are actually stored in memory when their characters are being used. The fonts take up a great deal of memory, and this limits the number of fonts available at any one time. The latest technology does not save fonts, it saves **algorithms**, the rules fonts are generated by. These rules then generate the needed characters in the desired font. Because algorithms take up much less space in the computer's memory, many fonts can be made available on line.

EDITING FONT CHANGES

If you change your mind after specifying font changes in a document, you might want to remove them entirely or change to a new font. How you do this depends on the program. On some programs, you select the text again, and then select an attribute such as *Normal*. On others, you display and then delete the codes that the program entered when you specified the fonts.

TIPS: Fonts

Although your program may offer a variety of fonts, not all screens can display them. Graphics displays can display fonts exactly as they will appear when printed if the program provides screen fonts that match the printer fonts they supply. Character displays either do not show the font changes at all or show them in a modified form, for example, displaying italicized text as underlined text.

SUMMARY AND KEY TERMS

- A **font** is a complete set of characters.
- **Typeface** refers to a particular design like Times Roman or Courier.
- **Typestyles** refer to variations in a typeface such as normal, italic, or bold.
- **Type sizes** are given in pitch or points. **Pitch** refers to the number of characters that print per inch. **Points** refer to both the horizontal and vertical size of the type.
- Type is either fixed pitch or proportionally spaced. **Fixed pitch** type allocates the same space to every character regardless of its size. **Proportionally spaced** type allocates less space to narrower characters.
- **Kerning** moves pairs of letters closer together if there is room.
- You change fonts by entering font change codes into the document or by entering **stop codes** that pause the printer so that you can change the font.
- Fonts are stored in the printer in font cartridges. **Soft fonts** are stored on disks or **font servers** from which they are **downloaded** to the printer when needed. Some programs create fonts using algorithms.
- The fonts that are displayed on the screen depend on the **screen fonts** available to the computer.

REVIEW QUESTIONS

1. What is a font?
2. What three terms are used to describe a font?
3. What is pitch? Points?
4. Describe the difference between fixed pitch and proportional spacing.
5. What does the term *kern* mean?
6. List and describe four places where fonts are stored.

TOPIC 4-13

Page Layout

OBJECTIVES

After completing this topic, you will be able to

- Explain page offset, gutter margins, and margin release
- Describe how to calculate and change left and right margins
- Describe how to calculate and control vertical spacing, lines per inch, lines per page, page length, and line spacing

As you have seen, most word processing programs have default settings that print a document single spaced on 8½-by-11-inch paper with 1-inch margins. You can change these settings to vary line spacing and margins or to print on different-sized paper.

HORIZONTAL LAYOUT

Margin settings determine where the first and last characters on a line are printed. You can change margins for an entire document or for individual paragraphs (Figure 4-67). The left and right margin settings determine the length of lines printed (Figure 4-68). The way you specify left and right margins varies.

- On older programs, you set the left and right margins in characters or columns. The line length is the difference between the two. For example, if the left margin is in column 10 and the right margin is in column 65, the maximum line length is fifty-five characters.
- On the latest programs, you set the left and right margins in inches. If you set both margins at 1 inch, the length of the lines is the width of the paper minus the margins. On an 8½-by-11-inch sheet, the length of lines with 1-inch margins is 6½ inches. Margins set in inches make it much easier to change pitch and fonts and to use proportional spacing because the margins are retained despite how many characters are printed per inch. The program does all the calculations needed to retain the margins on the printed page.

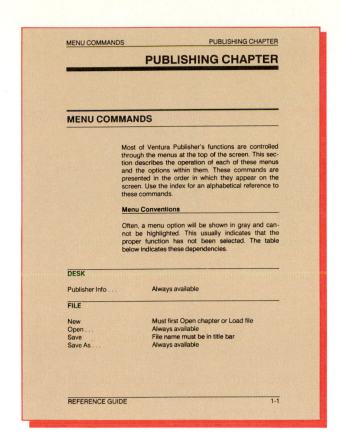

PUBLISHING CHAPTER

MENU COMMANDS

Most of Ventura Publisher's functions are controlled through the menus at the top of the screen. This section describes the operation of each of these menus and the options within them. These commands are presented in the order in which they appear on the screen. Use the index for an alphabetical reference to these commands.

Menu Conventions

Often, a menu option will be shown in gray and cannot be highlighted. This usually indicates that the proper function has not been selected. The table below indicates these dependencies.

DESK

Publisher Info . . .	Always available

FILE

New	Must first Open chapter or Load file
Open . . .	Always available
Save	File name must be in title bar
Save As . . .	Always available

REFERENCE GUIDE   1-1

FIGURE 4-67
Left and Right Margins
You can change margins selectively to improve a document's appearance and impact. For example, this figure shows headings flush with the left margin and text margins changed so that the text stands out from the rest of the document.

Page Offset

Some word processing programs treat margins on the screen and margins on the printout separately. On these programs, text aligned with column 1, the far left margin on the screen, is printed in column 1, the left edge of the paper, unless you specify how many columns it should be offset (Figure 4-69). The **page offset** command shifts the entire block of text left or right on the paper. It has the same effect as shifting the paper in the printer or changing both the left and right margins by the same amount.

A. Left Margin   C. Line Length   B. Right Margin

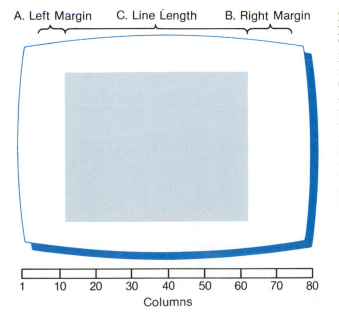

1   10   20   30   40   50   60   70   80

Columns

FIGURE 4-68
Margins and Line Length
There is a relationship between left and right margins and line length. (a) The left margin determines how far in from the left edge of the page the text is printed. (b) The right margin determines how far in the right margin the text stops printing. (c) The line length is the total page width minus left and right margins.

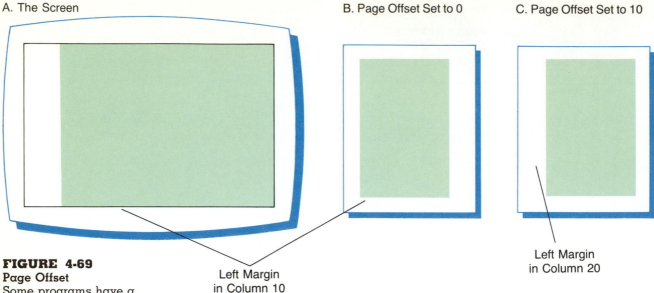

A. The Screen

B. Page Offset Set to 0

C. Page Offset Set to 10

Left Margin
in Column 20

Left Margin
in Column 10

FIGURE 4-69
Page Offset
Some programs have a page offset command that lets you shift the text block right or left on the page without changing the margins. (a) For example, text displayed on the screen has its left margin set in column 10. (b) When the document is printed without changing the page offset, the left margin is ten characters in from the left edge of the page. (c) But if the page offset is changed to 10, the left margin is printed twenty characters in from the left edge of the page.

FIGURE 4-70
Gutter Margin
The gutter margin command adds to the width of the margin on odd and even pages. Here, the first three pages of a document are printed (a) with and (b) without a gutter margin. On those printed without, the text blocks are centered between the left and right edges of the pages. On those using a gutter margin, however, the left margin is increased by the number of columns specified in the gutter margin command. On the second and subsequent pages, the margin is increased on the binding side—the right margin on even pages and the left margin on odd pages.

Gutter Margins

The **gutter margin** command (also called binding margin command) is a specialized version of the page offset command. You use this command when you want to reproduce bound copies of a document that is printed or copied on both sides of the pages. This command increases the width of the margin by a specified amount on the side of the pages to be bound or three-hole punched (Figure 4-70).

Entering Text to the Left of the Left Margin

When you set the left margin setting in any column other than the first, the cursor does not automatically move to columns to the left of the margin.

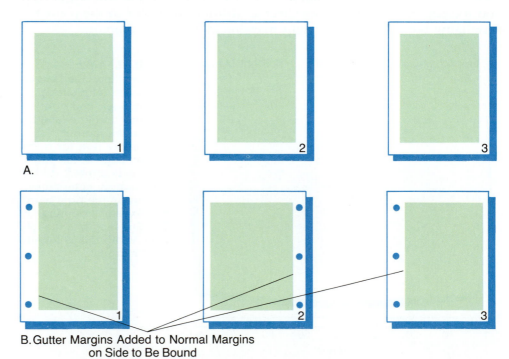

A.

B. Gutter Margins Added to Normal Margins
on Side to Be Bound

WORD PROCESSING AND DESKTOP PUBLISHING APPLICATIONS

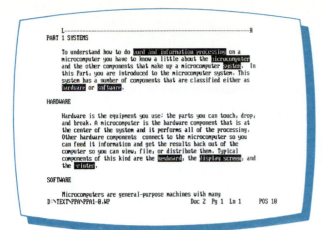

```
L--------------------------------------------------R
PART 1 SYSTEMS

   To understand how to do word and information processing on a
   microcomputer you have to know a little about the microcomputer
   and the other components that make up a microcomputer system. In
   this Part, you are introduced to the microcomputer system. This
   system has a number of components that are classified either as
   hardware or software.

HARDWARE

   Hardware is the equipment you use; the parts you can touch, drop,
   and break. A microcomputer is the hardware component that is at
   the center of the system and it performs all of the processing.
   Other hardware components connect to the microcomputer so you
   can feed it information and get the results back out of the
   computer so you can view, file, or distribute them. Typical
   components of this kind are the keyboard, the display screen, and
   the printer.

SOFTWARE

   Microcomputers are general-purpose machines with many
D:\TEXT\PPA\PPA1-0.WP            Doc 2  Pg 1  Ln 1       POS 18
```

FIGURE 4-71
Margin Release
You can use the margin release command to enter headings or other text in the left margin area. It can also be used for hanging indents, enumerations, and other effects.

When words wrap or when you press **Return**, the cursor always returns to the left margin setting. To enter text to the left of the left margin (Figure 4-71), you use the **margin release** command.

Calculating Left and Right Margins

On many programs, you specify margin settings in characters; for example, you set the left margin in column 10 and the right margin in column 75. To calculate the number of characters to specify for a given setting, you can use a type scale or a regular ruler.

You can measure a page with a type scale, which is marked in characters per inch for several pitches (Figure 4-72), and then directly read the number of characters that fit in a given space.

You can use a regular ruler to measure the distance in inches, and then use simple arithmetic to convert inches to characters. For example, here is how you would calculate a left margin setting.

1. Measure the distance from the left edge of the paper to where you want the first characters of the text to print. Let's say it is 1½ inches.

2. Determine the pitch, that is, how many characters per inch you will be printing. This can be controlled from your program or printer, but it is usually set to 10 or 12 unless you specify otherwise.

3. Multiply the desired margin spacing in inches by the pitch.
   1.5 inches × 10 characters per inch = 15 characters
   or
   1.5 inches × 12 characters per inch = 18 characters

4. Set the left margin to the calculated number of characters. When you print the document, the first character in each line will now print in column 15 or 18 on the paper.

VERTICAL LAYOUT

Top and bottom margins determine the number of lines left blank at the top and bottom of a page and the line that the first line of text prints on. These margins, the page length setting, and the lines printed per inch all affect the number of text lines printed on the page (Figure 4-73). Since these settings are interrelated, programs control them in one of two ways.

FIGURE 4-72
Type Scale
A type scale can be used to make horizontal measurements on a page. It indicates the number of characters printed per inch. Courtesy of Charrette Inc.

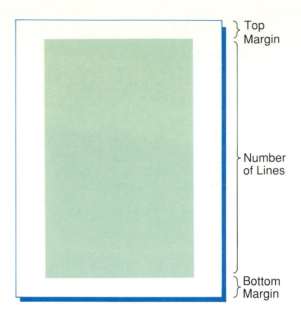

FIGURE 4-73
Vertical Spacing
Vertical spacing of a document is controlled by the page length, the top and bottom margins, and the lines printed per inch.

- On some programs, you set the top and bottom margins in lines, and the number of text lines is set indirectly. For example, if you specify six lines for both the top and bottom margins and a page length of sixty-six lines, fifty-four text lines can be printed on the page (66 − 12 = 54).

- On other programs, you set the top and bottom margins and the page length in inches. The program then calculates the space available for text lines. For example, if you specify 1-inch top and bottom margins, the program calculates that 9 inches can be used for text. Programs that allow you to set top and bottom margins and page lengths in inches make it easier to change type sizes. If you enlarge or reduce the type, the program automatically recalculates how many lines fit on a page.

Lines per Inch

A printer normally prints six lines per inch. You can change this setting for individual paragraphs or for an entire document (Figure 4-74).

Lines per Page

The number of lines on a page is calculated by multiplying the length of the page in inches by the number of lines printed per inch. For example, if the page is 11 inches long and the printer prints six lines per inch, the number of printable lines on a page is sixty-six. If the printer prints eight lines per inch, the number of printable lines on a page is eighty-eight. The number of text lines that are actually printed on a page is determined by three variables (Figure 4-75).

- The length of the paper
- How many lines the printer prints per inch
- How many lines are reserved for the top and bottom margins

For example, if you print six lines per inch on a page that is 11 inches long, you can print a maximum of sixty-six lines. If you reserve six lines for the top and bottom margins, you can print fifty-four lines on the page. If you use only three lines for the top and bottom margins, you can print sixty lines on the page.

(a) Six lines per inch

You can change the number of lines printed per inch: (a) shows a paragraph that has been printed 6 lines per inch, the normal setting, and (b) shows a paragraph printed 8 lines per inch to print the lines closer together.

(b) Eight lines per inch

You can change the number of lines printed per inch: (a) shows a paragraph that has been printed 6 lines per inch, the normal setting, and (b) shows a paragraph printed 8 lines per inch to print the lines closer together.

FIGURE 4-74
Lines per Inch
You can change the number of lines printed per inch. A paragraph can be printed six lines to the inch (a), the normal setting, or eight lines to the inch (b) to print lines closer together.

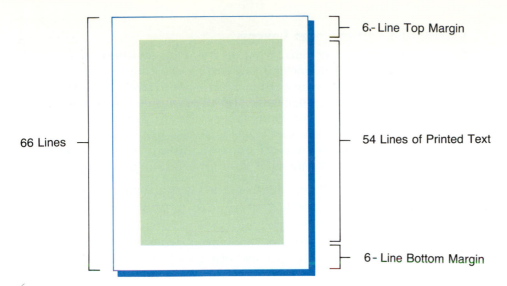

6.- Line Top Margin

66 Lines

54 Lines of Printed Text

6- Line Bottom Margin

FIGURE 4-75
Calculating Vertical Layout
The number of text lines printed on a page is calculated using the top and bottom margins, the page length, and the number of lines printed per inch. In this illustration, you would calculate the number of text lines that can be printed as follows:

Lines printed per inch (6) $\times$ page length (11 inches) = 66

Lines reserved for top (6) and bottom (6) margins = 12

Total lines printed per page = 54

Line Spacing

You can change line spacing for an entire document or for individual paragraphs (Figure 4-76). Some programs display the specified line spacing on the screen; other programs always display single spacing on the screen to make it faster to scroll through the document. When you print the document, the line spacing is whatever you have specified.

Leading

On some newer programs that include desktop publishing features, you control the space between lines by specifying **leading**, the distance between the bottom of one line and the top of the next.

Page Length

The page length setting determines where the printer stops printing and advances to the top of the next form. When using continuous form paper, envelopes, or labels, you measure the page length from the top of one sheet to the top of the next sheet. If this measurement is 11 inches, you set the page length to 11 inches, or the equivalent number of lines, and then the top, bottom, and number of lines per page settings are adjusted for the new page length.

Calculating Vertical Page Layouts

Settings that control vertical layout on the page are often given in lines, but you generally measure in inches. To calculate vertical spacing settings, you can use either a line scale to read the number of lines directly or a regular ruler and then simple arithmetic to convert inches to lines. For example, if you want to have the first line of a letter print below a letterhead, here is how you do it. (Although you are calculating the top margin setting, the same method is used to calculate the bottom margin or page length.)

1. Measure the vertical distance from the top of the paper to where you want the top of the first line of text to print. Let's say the distance is 1½ inches.

2. Find out how many lines per inch your program and printer prints. Unless you have specified otherwise, this is usually set to 6.

3. Multiply the vertical distance by the number of lines per inch.
   1.5 inches × 6 lines per inch = 9 lines

   or

   1.5 inches × 8 lines per inch = 12 lines

4. Set the top margin settings to the calculated number of lines. If the program asks you to specify the first line that text is printed on, add 1 to either setting; for example, enter line 10 or line 13. When the page is printed, the printer advances that number of lines before printing the first line of text.

If you are setting the bottom margin, it leaves the indicated number of lines between the last line of text and the bottom of the page.

If you are changing page length, it prints the indicated number of lines per page, including blank lines for top and bottom margins, before advancing to the top of the next sheet.

TIPS: Page Layout

- Although you can adjust the top and bottom margins when you align the paper in the printer, it does not have the same effect as when you use commands to control them. Setting them with the program causes a corresponding change in the number of lines of text that are printed on the page so that the bottom margin falls where it should. Shifting the paper in the printer just moves both the top and bottom margins up or down the same number of lines, perhaps even causing the last line to print at the top of the next page.

- If you set the top margin so that the first line of text prints below a letterhead, you should return it to its default setting on the second and subsequent pages.

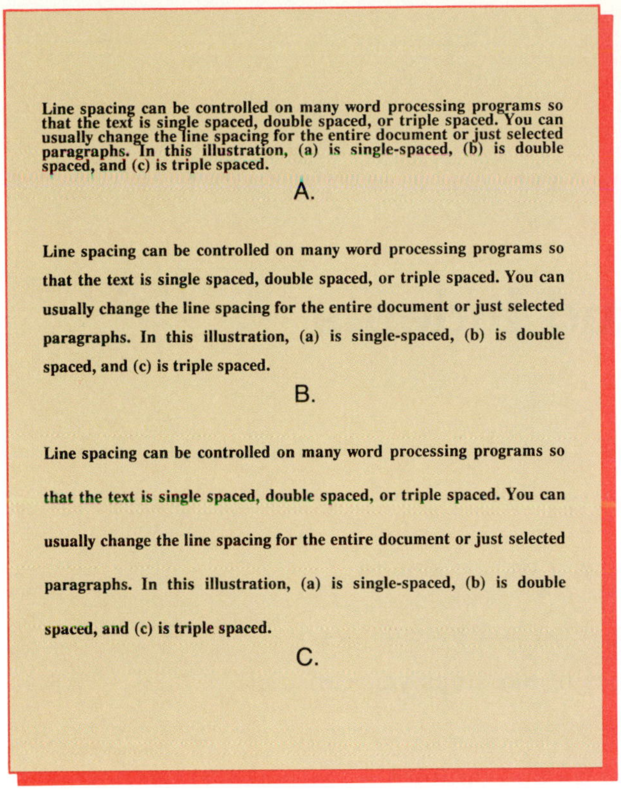

Line spacing can be controlled on many word processing programs so that the text is single spaced, double spaced, or triple spaced. You can usually change the line spacing for the entire document or just selected paragraphs. In this illustration, (a) is single-spaced, (b) is double spaced, and (c) is triple spaced.

A.

Line spacing can be controlled on many word processing programs so that the text is single spaced, double spaced, or triple spaced. You can usually change the line spacing for the entire document or just selected paragraphs. In this illustration, (a) is single-spaced, (b) is double spaced, and (c) is triple spaced.

B.

Line spacing can be controlled on many word processing programs so that the text is single spaced, double spaced, or triple spaced. You can usually change the line spacing for the entire document or just selected paragraphs. In this illustration, (a) is single-spaced, (b) is double spaced, and (c) is triple spaced.

C.

FIGURE 4-76
Line Spacing
Line spacing can be changed throughout a document. Here, (a) one paragraph is single spaced, (b) another is double spaced, and (c) a third is triple spaced.

SUMMARY AND KEY TERMS

- **Left and right margins** can be set for the entire document or set paragraph by paragraph.
- **Page offset** shifts the entire block of text left or right on the page.
- **Gutter margins** alternate on odd and even pages so that you can print the pages back to back and then bind or three-hole punch them.
- **Margin release** is used to enter text to the left of the left margin.
- **Top and bottom margins** are the lines left blank at the top and bottom of the page.
- **Lines per inch** determines the spacing between lines.
- **Lines per page** is the length of the page (in inches) times the number of lines printed per inch.
- **Page length** determines where the printer advances to the top of the next page.
- **Line spacing** specifies if lines are printed single, double, or triple spaced.
- **Leading** is the distance between the bottom of one line and the top of the next.

REVIEW QUESTIONS

1. What two ways are used by programs to set left and right margins?
2. What is the page offset?
3. What is a gutter margin command, and when would you want to use it?
4. What command do you use to enter text to the left of the left margin?
5. What does changing the lines per inch do?
6. What does changing the line spacing do?
7. What does the term *leading* mean?

Tab Stops and Indents

OBJECTIVES

After completing this topic, you will be able to

- Describe how to use tab stops and indents
- Explain the different types of tab stops you can use
- Describe how you set tab stops
- Describe how to enter tables and outlines.

Tab stops on a word processor are much like those on a typewriter. You can position them at intervals across the width of the screen and beyond. When you press **Tab** in insert mode, the cursor jumps to the next tab stop. When you press **Backtab**, the cursor moves to the left to the previous tab stop. On most programs, you can set both text tabs and decimal tabs. You can then use these tab settings to align columns or indent paragraphs.

TEXT TABS

You use tabs to indent paragraphs or lists or to create tables with aligned columns (Figure 4-77). You can align text with tab stops as you enter the text or after you have entered it.

- To align text with a tab stop as you enter the text, press **Tab** until the cursor is in the desired tab column, and then type the text. If you type enough text to reach past the right margin, the second and subsequent lines wrap back to and align with the left margin, not with the tab stop.

- To align text with a tab stop after you have entered the text, position the cursor on or under the first character in the text to be aligned. When you then press **Tab**, or **Ins** and then **Tab,** the cursor and all text to its right moves to the next tab stop. On many programs, you must be in insert mode to do this. If you are in typeover mode, pressing **Tab** may just move the cursor through the text.

Many programs allow you to change the way text aligns with tabs stops, as Figure 4-78 shows.

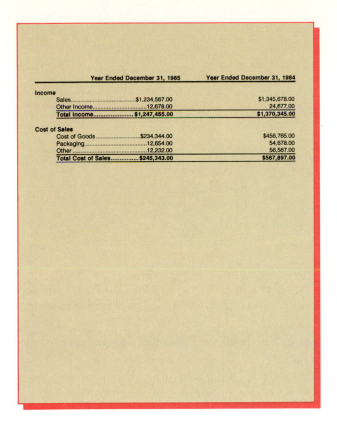

	Year Ended December 31, 1985	Year Ended December 31, 1984
Income		
Sales......................................$1,234,567.00		$1,345,678.00
Other Income..........................12,678.00		24,677.00
Total Income....................$1,247,455.00		$1,370,345.00
Cost of Sales		
Cost of Goods.........................$234,344.00		$456,765.00
Packaging................................12,654.00		54,678.00
Other.......................................12,232.00		56,567.00
Total Cost of Sales..............$245,343.00		$567,897.00

FIGURE 4-77
Tables
Tables are created using tab stops at or around which text is aligned into columns.

DECIMAL TABS

Columns of numbers, including those containing decimal points, can be aligned with programs that include a **decimal tab** feature (Figure 4-79). All programs allow you to align decimal points, but some allow you to change the alignment character. This is useful when you want to align dollar signs ($) or when you are writing to a foreign country that uses commas where we use decimal points, and vice versa. (For example, where we write $1,000.50, people in some countries write $1.000,50.) To align numbers with decimal tabs

1. Position decimal tab stops in the desired columns.
2. Press **Tab**, or another designated key, to move the cursor to the decimal tab position. On many programs, an indicator on the screen shows when the cursor is in a decimal tab column.

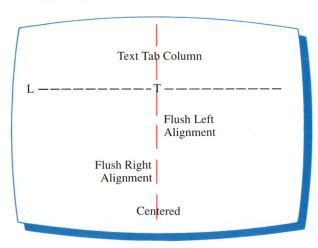

FIGURE 4-78
Tab Alignment
Text can be aligned with tab stops in several ways. It is normally aligned flush left in the tab column. On programs where you can change tab alignment, you can also align it flush right or center it on the tab column.

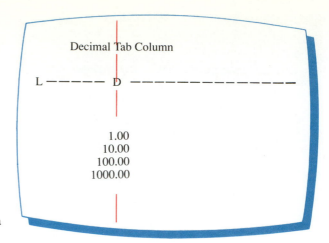

FIGURE 4-79
Decimal Tabs
Decimals can be aligned with decimal tab stops so that they are all aligned in the same column.

Decimal Tab Column

L — — — — — D — — — — — — — — — — — —

1.00
10.00
100.00
1000.00

3. Enter the part of the number preceding the decimal point. As you do so, the numbers you enter move to the left while the cursor remains in the decimal tab column.

4. Enter a decimal point (using the period key or other alignment character that you have specified).

5. Type the numbers that follow the decimal point. As you do so, the decimal remains fixed in place, and all numbers are entered to the right of it.

If your program does not allow you to right align text with tab stops, you can achieve the same result by using decimal tab stops. Just follow the preceding steps, but do not enter a decimal point.

INDENTS

As Figure 4-80 shows, you can indent paragraphs in many ways. The number of characters you indent is up to you, but five characters is the standard text indent. Normally, when you enter text, you execute the indent command, and it stays in effect until you press **Return**. At that point, text aligns with the original margins. The way you indent text that has already been entered varies. On some programs, you select blocks of text, and then use an indent command. On others, you change margin settings, or insert a format line.

On most programs, indents are made to tab stops. To change indents, you may have to change tab stops. On other programs, the amount of the indent is specified independently of the tab stop settings.

One of the major applications of indents is for number lists, called **enumerations** (Figure 4-81). To get the correct indenting, you may have to change tab stops. When creating outlines and some other documents, you occasionally need more than one level of enumeration to show topics and subtopics. These are done the same way as enumerations with one level except you calculate each subsequent level of indent from the indent of the level above instead of from the left margin.

SETTING TAB STOPS

Programs normally have default tab stops set every five columns. You can change these settings by adding or deleting tab stops. There are two ways to do this.

Indents can take a number of forms. You can indent the first line of a paragraph (a) or the entire paragraph (b) from the left margin. You can indent the paragraph from both margins (c) or create a hanging indent so the first line is flush with the left margin and the rest of the paragraph is indented (d).

A.

Indents can take a number of forms. You can indent the first line of a paragraph (a) or the entire paragraph (b) from the left margin. You can indent the paragraph from both margins (c) or create a hanging indent so the first line is flush with the left margin and the rest of the paragraph is indented (d).

B.

Indents can take a number of forms. You can indent the first line of a paragraph (a) or the entire paragraph (b) from the left margin. You can indent the paragraph from both margins (c) or create a hanging indent so the first line is flush with the left margin and the rest of the paragraph is indented (d).

C.

Indents can take a number of forms.

(a) You can indent the first line of a paragraph a specified number of characters from the left margin.
(b) You can indent the entire paragraph a specified number of characters from the left margin.
(c) You can indent the paragraph a specfied number of characters from both margins.
(d) You can create a hanging indent so the first line is flush with the left margin and the rest of the paragraph is indented.

D.

FIGURE 4-80
Indents
Indents can take several forms. (a) You can indent the first line of a paragraph, or paragraphs, a specified number of characters. (b) You can indent one or more paragraphs to offset them from other text in the document. This indent is the same as changing the left margin. (c) You can create double indents to indent one or more paragraphs from both the left and right margins to specified tab stops. This sets off these paragraphs from the rest of the text. A double indent is the same as temporarily changing the left and right margins. (d) You can create a hanging indent (also called a reverse indent or an outdent) so that the first line remains flush with the left margin and the rest of the paragraph is indented.

When you use hanging indents to create enumerations, the largest number you use determines the amount of the indent that you specify for all entries. Set the indent to the number of digits in the largest number and add three spaces, one for the period and two for blank spaces before the endented paragraph. Also, insert spaces in front of numbers where needed to align decimal points. For example

1. If you plan on using only the numbers 1 through 9, you indent 4 characters.
2. If you plan on using the numbers 1 through 99, but not more than 99, you indent 5 characters.
3. If you plan on using the numbers 1 through 999, you indent 6 characters.

A.

 1. If you plan on using only the numbers 1 through 9, you indent 4 characters.
10. If you plan on using the numbers 1 through 99, but not more than 99, you indent 5 characters.
99. If you plan on using the numbers 1 through 999, you indent 6 characters.

B.

  1. If you plan on using only the numbers 1 through 9, you indent 4 characters.
 10. If you plan on using the numbers 1 through 99, but not more than 99, you indent 5 characters.
999. If you plan on using the numbers 1 through 999, you indent 6 characters.

C.

FIGURE 4-81
Hanging Indents and Enumerated Lists
Hanging indents are especially useful when you are preparing numbered outlines or lists where some or all of the entries run more than one line long. The numbers in the list stand off by themselves, but the text following them is indented and aligned. When you create enumerations with single-digit numbers (or letters), the decimal points automatically align (a). If you use numbers with more than two digits, your largest number determines the indent for all entries. For example, if your list includes the numbers 1 through 99 (b), you indent five characters to leave room for two digits, a period, and two spaces. If your list includes the numbers 1 through 999 (c), you indent six characters to leave room for three digits, a period, and two spaces.

- You can change the tab stops for part or all of an individual document.
- You can change the system defaults so that new default tab settings appear when you open a new document.

To change tab stops, you usually display a ruler or format line, move the cursor to it, and then use the appropriate commands to revise the current tab settings. Most programs have several tab stop settings that you can enter. For example, you may enter an L for a left-aligned tab, an R for a right-aligned tab, a C for a centered tab, and a period or D for a decimal tab stop.

When you have changed the position of tab stops, you may want to return them to their original default settings. How you do this varies from program to program.

- Some programs have a command that automatically does this.
- In other programs, you individually move, delete, or insert tabs.

Most programs allow you to change tab settings throughout a document by entering a new format line or tab code where you want the settings to change. The new tab stops affect all text that follows until either the end of the document or the next format line or tab code.

ENTERING TABLES AND OUTLINES

Many word processing programs let you easily set up tables, outlines, and other heavily indented text. When you create tables and outlines, you can tab text into columns, align decimal places, and add ruled lines to separate sections. A few programs also are able to sum rows and columns of numbers so that these calculations can be made right in the document (see Topic 4-25).

Tables

Tables that consist of more than one column can be set up easily using a word processing program. Here are some of the word processing commands used to enter and edit tables.

- Tab stops align headings and entries in columns.
- Decimal alignment aligns entries with decimal points.
- Column mode moves, copies, or formats columns of text rather than lines.
- Replacement (typeover) mode prevents text in columns to the right of where you are making a change from being forced over when entries are made or edited.
- Paragraph indents align multiline entries. Some programs allow you to use paragraph indents for each column; others allow only one column to be indented.
- Hanging indents indent enumerated lists so that the numbers are left hanging.
- Ruled lines separate headings from listings and indicate the end of a table. Some programs also allow you to enter vertical ruled lines to separate columns.

Outlines

You can quickly and easily create outlines using a word processing program (Figure 4-82).

- Tab stops indent subsections.
- Decimal alignment numbers sections and aligns the decimal points.
- Hanging indents align multiline entries.

A. Standard Outline Numbering

   I. THIS IS A LEVEL 1 ENTRY
      A. This is a level 2 Entry
         1. This is a level 3 entry
  II. THIS IS ANOTHER LEVEL 1 ENTRY

B. Legal Outline Numbering

  1. THIS IS A LEVEL 1 ENTRY
    1.1 This is a level 2 Entry
      1.1.1. This is a level 3 entry
  2. THIS IS ANOTHER LEVEL 1 ENTRY

FIGURE 4-82
An Outline
Outlines use indents to
indicate levels.

SUMMARY AND KEY TERMS

- **Tab stops** are used to indent text and align tables and lists. You can align text flush left, flush right, or center it on a tab stop.
- **Decimal tabs** are used to quickly align columns of numbers containing decimal points.
- Paragraphs can be **indented** so that the first line is indented from the rest of the paragraph or the first line is kept aligned with the left margin and the rest of the paragraph is indented.
- You set tab stops by entering or revising a ruler line or inserting a code.

REVIEW QUESTIONS

1. When would you use regular tab stops?
2. In what ways can you align text with a tab stop?
3. When would you use decimal tab stops?
4. List and describe three ways to indent text.
5. What is a hanging indent? What is it used for?

TOPIC 4-15

Headers and Footers

OBJECTIVE

After completing this topic, you will be able to

■ Describe how to add headers and footers to a document and control their position

You can add headers and footers to your document. **Headers** are text printed at the top of the page in the space reserved for the top margin. **Footers** are text printed at the bottom of the page in the space reserved for the bottom margin. The advantage of using the *Header* and *Footer* commands is that you enter the text only once, and it is then printed on any pages you specify. Headers and footers (Figure 4-83) can be printed on a single page or on every page of a document. When printed on more than one page of a document, they are called **running heads** or **running feet**.

When you enter headers and footers, the program normally aligns them flush left on a specific line of the page. As Figure 4-84 shows, you can change this alignment or use other variations.

FIGURE 4-83
Headers and Footers
Headers are lines of text that are printed in the top margin of each page of a document. Footers are the same but are printed in the bottom margin of the page.

Header

Word Processing

February 2, 1990   2

Footer

FIGURE 4-84

Header and Footer Options
You have several options available when entering headers and footers: aligned with the left or right edge of the page or centered (a), printed on any blank margin line (b), changed throughout the document (c), multiline (d), printed with page numbers (e), or discontinued on selected pages (f).

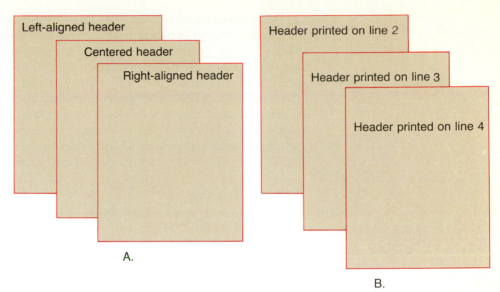

A.

B.

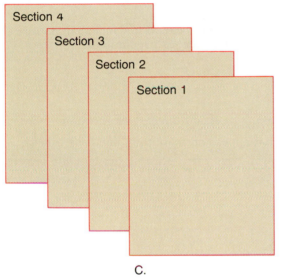

C.

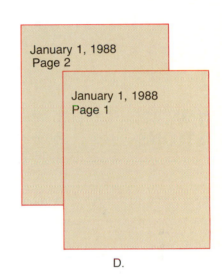

D.

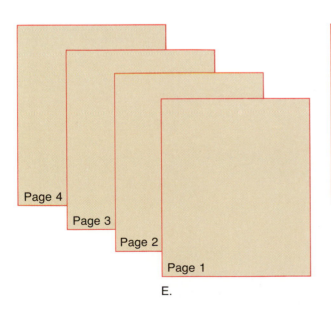

E.

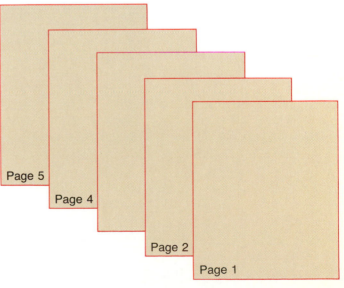

F.

Many programs can automatically number, date, and time-stamp pages of a document as it is printed. These features are special forms of headers or footers. Unlike headers and footers that simply repeat text, these features are calculated by the program. Although you can manually enter page numbers, dates, and times into a header or footer, some programs also let you enter special symbols or codes into them. These codes calculate and print the current page number or read the current date and time from the computer's clock. The advantage of using the clock is that the dates and times change automatically each time the document is printed; thus it is easier to keep track of the various versions of the same document.

SUMMARY AND KEY TERMS

- **Headers** and **footers** are printed at the top and bottom of the page. When printed on more than one page, they are called **running heads** and **running feet**.
- Some programs allow you to control the horizontal and vertical placement of headers and footers, change them as needed throughout a document, and print them on more than one line.
- Some programs allow you to enter codes in headers and footers that automatically calculate and print the date, time, or page number.

REVIEW QUESTIONS

1. What are headers and footers? Why are they used?
2. What are headers and footers that appear on more than one page called?
3. List and describe some options you have when printing headers and footers.

Format Style Sheets

OBJECTIVE

After completing this topic, you will be able to

- Describe how formats can be created, saved, and reused with style sheets

Some programs allow you to define and save the definition of frequently used formats on **style sheets** (Figure 4-85). For example, you can specify that main headings are to be uppercase and boldfaced, subheadings initial capital only and underlined, and the body of the text printed in 10-point Times Roman type. You specify these definitions on the style sheet.

- On some programs, you assign each format an abbreviation, for example, MH for main headings, SH for subheadings, and TX for body text. You then use these abbreviations, not the normal formatting commands, to mark the text. For example, you select a main head, and type

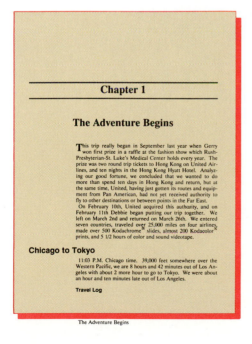
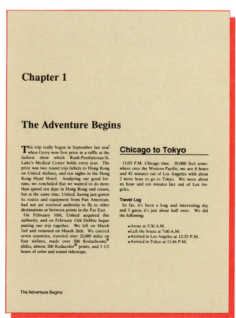

FIGURE 4-85
Style Sheet
Style sheets are used to define characteristics of typical elements in a document. Each definition is coded with an abbreviation. When you format the document, you use these abbreviations, not the actual formatting command. If you change the definition, the format of the document changes.

MH to format it. The main head will then print as uppercase and boldfaced.

- On other programs, you define the style and add it to a menu that lists all the styles you have defined. When assigning the style to text, you select the style from the menu.

So far, you have not saved much time, but now the real power of a style sheet becomes evident. Assume you have formatted a hundred headings and decide that you want to change the format. Without a style sheet, you have to reformat each individually. But with a style sheet, you change only the definition, and all formatted text is automatically changed. For example, you could change the definition of main headings from uppercase and boldfaced to uppercase and underlined, and all main heads are automatically reformatted.

You can also save the style sheet that contains these definitions so that you can use it with any document you create. When you create new documents, you use the existing style sheets to format them for printing, which saves you time and standardizes your formats.

You can create a standard style sheet for each class of documents (memos, letters, reports, and so on) and then use that style sheet each time one of these is created. This ensures that all versions are uniform. You can also create different style sheets for the same class of documents. For example, you can print double-spaced draft copies to make editing easier, and then you can print single-spaced final copies. This lets you print the same document in a variety of formats with little additional effort.

SUMMARY AND KEY TERMS

- If you use a variety of standard styles when creating documents—for example, when creating memos, letters, and reports—some programs allow you to create and then save these styles for use again. The files these formats are saved in are called **style sheets**.
- Typical style elements entered on a style sheet include margin settings, page-numbering options, and headers and footers.
- Some programs provide a library of standard style sheets that can be used as is or modified.

REVIEW QUESTIONS

1. What is a style sheet?
2. What is the main advantage of using one?

CASE STUDY
Creating a Résumé

Creating documents is an equal mix of writing, editing, organizing, and formatting. You have to understand how to express yourself; no word processing program can help you do that. But a word processing program does make it easy to edit and revise your writing so that your ideas are more clearly expressed. In the topics in this part, we introduce you to the individual procedures you use to create documents. In this case study, we look at how you put these procedures together to prepare a résumé. From this, you should get a good idea of how to effectively use a word processing program.

Step 1: Planning the Résumé   The power of a word processing program is directly related to your ability to create documents that not only express what you want to say but also are attractive and easy to read. Here you want to create a résumé, so the first step is to gather the information you will need—a list of the jobs you've held, your educational background, and the names of some references (Figure A). You can also make notes on achievements or other experiences that you want to mention.

Name and address
Phone number
Objectives
Entry level position in industrial or graphic design.
Education
Industrial Design, 1987.
Skills; CADD, Engineering Drawing, photography.
Work experience
Curtin & London; Summer 1984.
Prepared and produced a catalog on business and computer books.
Learned microcomputer-based word processing (WordStar) and
spreadsheets (SuperCalc).
Crooked Stick Golf Club; Summer 1985.
Groundskeeper
Special landscaping tournaments.
Purdue Memorial Union — Sweet Shop; 1/84 through 5/87.
Trained new employees.
Received and distributed inventory.
Supervised receipts.
Prepared and served all food items.
Marriott Hotel; Summer 1986.
Supervised receipts and closed out accounts at end of shift.
Handled customer calls
Coordinated waiters and waitresses.
Campus Graphic; 12/86 through 5/87.
Developed business plan for a start-up. Current projects include
restaurant menus and textbook illustrations.
Professional Societies
Purdue I.D.S.A. Student Chapter.
I.D.S.A. Student Chapter fund raising committee.
Honors and activities
Merit Award; Art and Design Exhibition (color photography).
Purdue Distinguished Student
Dean's List.
Participant in Purdue University student phonathon.
References

FIGURE A
Planning the Résumé
When planning a résumé, or any other document, you make a list of the items that you want to be sure to cover.

Step 2: Loading the Program After you have planned your résumé, you load the word processing program if it is not already on the screen. If you are planning to save your work, you also insert a formatted data disk into drive B, and then close that drive's door.

Step 3: Entering the Résumé Once you have gathered your information, you enter text into the document (Figure B). You are not now concerned with how the document looks. You just want to put down the facts and express yourself as clearly as possible.

FIGURE B
Entering the Résumé
When entering the résumé you concentrate on getting down the correct facts.

SUZANNE CURTIN
107 Fowler Street
West Lafayette, IN 47906
[317] 743-9812

OBJECTIVE
A position leading to a career in industrial or graphic design.

EDUCATION
Purdue University; B.A., Industrial Design, 1987.
Technical Skills; CADD, Engineering Drawing, photography.

WORK EXPERIENCE
Curtin & London; Marblehead, MA; Summer 1984.
Developed, wrote copy for, and implemented a direct mail catalog on small business and computer books. Learned word processing (WordStar) and spreadsheets (SuperCalc).
Crooked Stick Golf Club; Carmel, Indiana; Summer 1985.
Groundskeeper for 18-hole course.
Purdue Memorial Union - Sweet Shop; January 1984 - May 1987.
Trained all recently hired new employees on operational procedures. Received inventory and supervised receipts. Prepared and served all food items.
Marriott Hotel; Boston, MA, Summer 1986.
Supervised all receipts and closed out accounts at the end of shift. Handled all customer calls and coordinated waiters and waitresses.
Campus Graphic; West Lafayette, Indiana; December 1986 - May 1987.
Developed the beginning business plan for a freelance design service managed by myself and two other designers. Current design projects include restaurant menus and textbook illustrations.

PROFESSIONAL SOCIETIES
Member of Purdue I.D.S.A Student Chapter.
Member I.D.S.A Student Chapter fund raising committee.

HONORS AND ACTIVITIES
Merit Award; Purdue University Art & Design Exhibition (color photography).
Purdue Distinguished Student, Dean's List.
Participant in Purdue University student phonathon.

REFERENCES AVAILABLE UPON REQUEST.

Step 4: Editing and Revising the Résumé   After you have entered the text, you focus on expressing your ideas more clearly. You should also correct any spelling and grammatical mistakes (Figure C).

SUZANNE CURTIN
107 Fowler Street
West Lafayette, IN 47906
[317] 743-9812

OBJECTIVE
An entry level position leading to a career in *the field of* industrial or graphic design.

EDUCATION
Purdue University; *West Lafayette, Indiana*; B.A., Industrial Design, 1987.
Technical Skills; CADD, Engineering Drawing, *B&W and Color* photography.

WORK EXPERIENCE
Curtin & London, *Publishers*; Marblehead, MA; Summer 1984.
Developed, *designed*, wrote copy for, and ~~implemented~~ *produced* a direct mail catalog on ~~small~~ business and computer books. Learned *microcomputer-based* word processing (WordStar) and spreadsheets (SuperCalc).
Crooked Stick Golf Club; Carmel, Indiana; Summer 1985.
Groundskeeper for 18-hole course. *Special landscaping and overtime for tournaments*
Purdue Memorial Union - Sweet Shop; January 1984 - May 1987.
Trained all ~~recently hired~~ new employees on operational *and safety* procedures.
Received *and distributed* inventory and supervised receipts. Prepared and served all food items.
Marriott Hotel; Boston, MA, Summer 1986.
Supervised all receipts and closed out accounts at the end of shift. Handled all customer calls and coordinated waiters and waitresses.
Campus Graphic; West Lafayette, Indiana; December 1986 - May 1987.
Developed the ~~beginning~~ business plan for a *start-up* freelance design service managed by myself and two other designers. Current design projects include restaurant menus and textbook illustrations.

PROFESSIONAL SOCIETIES
Active member of Purdue I.D.S.A Student Chapter.
Member I.D.S.A Student Chapter fund raising committee.

HONORS AND ACTIVITIES
Merit Award; Purdue University Art & Design Exhibition (color photography).
Purdue Distinguished Student, Dean's List.
Participant in Purdue University student phonathon.

REFERENCES AVAILABLE UPON REQUEST.

FIGURE C
Editing and Revising the Résumé
When editing the résumé, you insert and delete words and phrases to make it read better.

Step 5: Organizing the Résumé Next, be sure everything is in the right order. If you feel the organization can be improved, you can move blocks of text to do so (Figure D).

SUZANNE CURTIN
107 Fowler Street
West Lafayette, IN 47906
[317]743-9812

OBJECTIVE
An entry level position leading to a career in the field of industrial or graphic design.

EDUCATION
Purdue University; West Lafayette, Indiana; B.A., Industrial Design, 1987.
Technical Skills; CADD, Engineering Drawing, B&W and Color photography.

WORK EXPERIENCE
Campus Graphic; West Lafayette, Indiana; December 1986 - May 1987.
Developed the business plan for a start-up freelance design service managed by myself and two other designers. Current design projects include restaurant menus and textbook illustrations.
Marriott Hotel; Boston, MA, Summer 1986.
Supervised all receipts and closed out accounts at the end of shift. Handled all customer calls and coordinated waiters and waitresses.
Purdue Memorial Union - Sweet Shop; January 1984 - May 1987.
Trained all new employees on operational and safety procedures. Received and distributed inventory and supervised receipts. Prepared and served all food items.
Crooked Stick Golf Club; Carmel, Indiana; Summer 1985.
Groundskeeper for 18-hole course. Special landscaping and overtime for tournaments.
Curtin & London, Publishers; Marblehead, MA; Summer 1984.
Developed, designed, wrote copy for, and produced a direct mail catalog on business and computer books. Learned microcomputer-based word processing (WordStar) and spreadsheets (SuperCalc).

HONORS AND ACTIVITIES
Merit Award; Purdue University Art & Design Exhibition (color photography).
Purdue Distinguished Student, Dean's List.
Participant in Purdue University student phonathon.

PROFESSIONAL SOCIETIES
Active member of Purdue I.D.S.A Student Chapter.
Member I.D.S.A Student Chapter fund raising committee.

REFERENCES AVAILABLE UPON REQUEST.

Step 6: Formatting the Résumé   Once everything is said the way you want to say it, you can concentrate on formatting the document (Figure E).

FIGURE E
Formatting the Résumé
Finally, you format the résumé so that it has maximum impact. You center headings, add ruled lines, and indent the job listing so that it reads more clearly.

Step 7: Printing the Résumé Now, you print out the result (Figure F). Be sure to carefully proofread this printout. You may find mistakes that you did not notice on the screen. If so, correct them, and then make a new printout.

FIGURE F
Printing the Résumé
The last step is to print out the résumé for mailing.

SUZANNE CURTIN
107 Fowler Street
West Lafayette, IN 47906
[317]743-9812

OBJECTIVE

An entry level position leading to a career in the field of industrial or graphic design.

EDUCATION

Purdue University; West Lafayette, Indiana; B.A., Industrial Design, 1989.
Technical Skills; CADD, Engineering Drawing, B&W and Color photography.

WORK EXPERIENCE

Campus Graphic; West Lafayette, Indiana; December 1988 - May 1989.
   Developed the business plan for a start-up freelance design service managed by myself and two other designers. Current design projects include restaurant menus and textbook illustrations.
Marriott Hotel; Boston, MA, Summer 1988.
   Supervised all receipts and closed out accounts at the end of shift. Handled all customer calls and coordinated waiters and waitresses.
Purdue Memorial Union - Sweet Shop; January 1986 - May 1989.
   Trained all new employees on operational and safety procedures. Received and distributed inventory and supervised receipts. Prepared and served all food items.
Crooked Stick Golf Club; Carmel, Indiana; Summer 1987.
   Groundskeeper for 18-hole course. Special landscaping and overtime for tournaments.
Curtin & London, Publishers; Marblehead, MA; Summer 1986.
   Developed, designed, wrote copy for, and produced a direct mail catalog on business and computer books. Learned microcomputer-based word processing (WordStar) and spreadsheets (SuperCalc).

HONORS AND ACTIVITIES

Merit Award; Purdue University Art & Design Exhibition (color photography).
Purdue Distinguished Student, Dean's List.
Participant in Purdue University student phonathon.

PROFESSIONAL SOCIETIES

Active member of Purdue I.D.S.A Student Chapter.
Member I.D.S.A Student Chapter fund raising committee.

REFERENCES

AVAILABLE UPON REQUEST.

Writing on a Word Processing Program

Writing on a word processor is different from typing on a typewriter; it can even make you a better writer. Sure, you have to type either way. The only difference is that when you enter text on your computer, you don't have to hit the **Return** key at the end of each line—the program automatically wraps any text that won't fit on the current line to the next line. There is a different attitude, though, that makes a world of difference. Typing on a conventional typewriter is like carving something in stone; changes and revisions are time consuming and difficult. This forces you to carefully think out everything before you write; ideas that don't have a direct bearing on the sentence you are writing at the moment have to be put on hold—to be integrated later or perhaps forgotten. You have to think about what you are doing on at least five levels.

1. What to write (the content)
2. Where to write it (the layout)
3. How to say it (the style)
4. How to structure it (the grammar)
5. What order to put it in (the organization)

Word processors make changes, revisions, and reorganizations so easy that you don't have to think on all these levels at the same time. You can make separate passes through the document for each aspect of your writing. The ease of making revisions tends to encourage you to rewrite and make changes in organization. Since good writing is generally the result of extensive revision and rewriting—of polishing ideas and expressing them more clearly—the ease of doing so on the computer can help you become a better writer.

When you prepare a written document with a word processing program, you go through several steps. These steps don't always happen in a specific order. Many writers approach a project on many levels simultaneously. For example, after preparing a rough outline, some writers may complete one or two sections to develop their style and then work on the rest of the document. Other writers work through all parts of the document in stages. As you gain experience, you will find the approach that best suits your personality.

Here are some of the "steps" in creating a document.

1. Create a rough outline. It doesn't have to be formal or numbered. Your purpose is to list the major topics in roughly the order you want to present them in.
2. Break down major sections of the outline into subsections. Think about each section, and decide what subtopics have a bearing on it.
3. Enter ideas, notes, and text as they come to mind. You don't have to worry too much now about typos, misspellings, or perfect expressions. Here you're trying to establish the content, approach, and organization of your document.
4. Save the file periodically so that your work isn't lost if you make a serious mistake or if you experience an equipment malfunction or power failure. When enough work has been invested so that you would tear out your hair if you lost the file, make a backup copy on another disk.
5. Gather more data (research), and enter it where appropriate. Think carefully about each of the topics, and enter any new facts or ideas that come to you so that they aren't forgotten (much as you would use index cards to gather facts for a term paper).
6. Write for content, expanding on ideas to express them more completely.
7. Reorganize the material. After you determine the basic ideas and have written a rough draft, you can move text around to organize the material better.
8. Rewrite for style. Express your ideas more clearly, build bridges between concepts, combine ideas that appear in more than one place, and break up ideas that have developed into a series of subtopics.
9. Edit and revise for spelling and grammar. Surprisingly, word processors have their limits when you're writing and revising documents. Many people find it difficult, if not impossible, to rewrite for style on the screen. They need to make printouts and jot changes here and there. Others can't find misspellings on the screen; they need to make a printout to find and correct them. Once you have determined these changes, you can easily integrate them into the document on the screen.
10. Format the document. When to format and style a document using tabs, changing margins, boldfacing key points, and the like is a personal decision. Some people format as they create a document. Others do it after final editing and just before printing since any changes may require them to reformat and restyle some or all of the sections.
11. Print the final copy, and proofread the printout. If you find any mistakes, correct them, and then make another printout.

Merge Printing

OBJECTIVES

After completing this topic, you will be able to

- Explain the purpose of merge printing
- Describe how to code a primary document
- Describe a secondary file
- Explain how to merge the primary document and secondary file

Instead of individually entering and editing tens, hundreds, or thousands of letters or other documents, merge printing lets you enter one document and then enter personalized data into each copy as it is being printed. This can greatly increase your speed in preparing documents like form letters for billing or scheduling appointments, which are essentially the same except for minor changes from copy to copy. For example, you can maintain a mailing list for existing or prospective customers and regularly send them personalized letters using merge printing.

The data that personalizes each form letter, like the name and address, can be entered from the keyboard or kept in a separate file from which it is automatically inserted into the form letter during printing. When stored in a separate file, the information can be easily kept up to date and used to automatically print letters, envelopes, and mailing labels.

The first step in merge printing form letters is to create the needed files. When using this feature, you enter the information that is to be printed into every document in the **primary document** (also called the *template, shell document, main document, master document,* or *merge document*). Data to be inserted into this primary document to personalize each copy when it is printed are called **variables**. You can enter these variables directly from the keyboard or store them in a second file, a **secondary file** (also called a *data file, database,* or *variables file*). When you then **merge print** the primary document, it is printed over and over again, with the variables specific to each copy entered manually from the keyboard or inserted automatically from the secondary file (Figure 4-86).

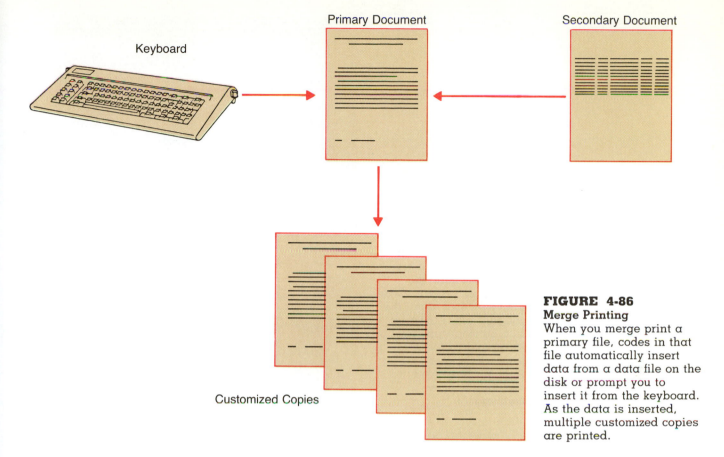

Keyboard

Primary Document

Secondary Document

Customized Copies

FIGURE 4-86
Merge Printing
When you merge print a
primary file, codes in that
file automatically insert
data from a data file on the
disk or prompt you to
insert it from the keyboard.
As the data is inserted,
multiple customized copies
are printed.

THE PRIMARY DOCUMENT

The primary document contains the unchanging parts of the document
(sometimes called the boilerplate). You also insert codes (sometimes called
merge codes or merge instructions) into this document to indicate where
the variables are to be merged during printing (Figure 4-87). Typical codes
you can insert include

- Secondary filename specifies the name of the file in which the data to be
  merged is stored.

- **Variable names** (also called *field names*) are inserted throughout the
  document wherever data is to be inserted from the secondary file or the
  keyboard. If data are being inserted from a secondary file, these variable
  names refer to fields (also called variables) in that file (see *The Secondary File*). For example, one variable name code might specify that the
  person's name is to be inserted from the secondary file, and another
  code might specify that the person's street address is to be inserted.
  The variable name codes are entered into the primary document where
  this data is to be inserted. When the document is merge printed, the
  codes are replaced with data from the secondary file.

- A **stop merge** code pauses the printer so that you can enter data from
  the keyboard. Most programs allow you to create prompts that appear
  on the screen when the document is being merge printed to remind you
  of the information to enter. The stop merge code refers to a variable
  name in the document. For example, you can enter a code that displays
  the prompt *Enter amount due:* and enter the variable name AMOUNT
  into the body of a letter. When you merge print the document, as the

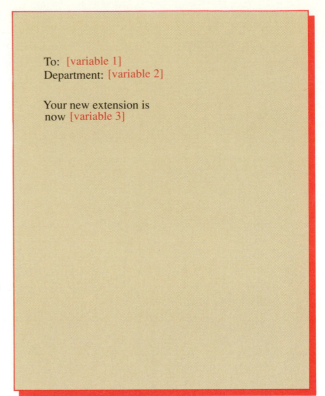

To: [variable 1]
Department: [variable 2]

Your new extension is
now [variable 3]

FIGURE 4-87
The Primary Document
The codes in a primary
document control the
merge print process. Codes
can be entered to tell the
program where to insert
data automatically from a
separate data file or to
pause the printer so that
data can be entered
manually from the
keyboard.

program encounters the stop merge code in each copy, it displays the
prompt. You type the amount due, and then press a designated key to
continue. The program inserts the amount you typed into the body of
the letter in place of the AMOUNT variable name and continues
printing.

- **IF statements** can be used in special circumstances to change the text
that is printed. For example, what if you want to send a bill to a customer, and your company's policy is to pay freight charges on all orders
over $100? You can enter an IF statement into the primary document
that prints one phrase if the order is less than $100 and another phrase
if it is $100 or more. For example, for orders under $100, it might print
Since your order is less than $100, freight charges have been added.
For orders of $100 or more, it might print *Since your order is for $100
or more, we pay all freight charges.* The different versions of the text
specified in the IF statement can be entered into the primary document
or stored in separate files on the disk. The IF statement that determines
what phrase or file to print must refer to another field in the secondary
file. In this example, the IF statement might read

IF AMOUNT DUE>100 THEN FILE-1 OTHERWISE FILE-2

In English, this would read "If the amount in the AMOUNT DUE field in the
secondary file is less than $100, then print the text stored in File-1. If the
amount in that field is $100 or more, print the text stored in File-2."

Set variable is a code entered into the primary file to enter the same
data into each copy for a specified variable. This is useful for information
that changes from day to day but that you do not want to store in the data
file and do not want to enter manually from the keyboard because it appears
in every copy. For example, what if you routinely send a letter to your customers informing them of the price of an item, and the price changes

monthly? The primary file would include a variable name code indicating where the price should be printed in the document. You then enter a set variable code at the top of the document that might read as follows:

SET PRICE = $100

When you print the document, the price of $100 is printed in place of the price variable name code in all copies. If the price changes, you open the primary document, and then change the set variable.

SET PRICE = $125

The next time you merge print the document, the new price is printed in all copies.

THE SECONDARY FILE

The secondary file stores the variables that you want inserted into each copy of the primary document when you merge print it. The variables you enter into a secondary file must be organized so that the program can easily find it when you merge print. To understand how a program finds the needed information to insert into the copies, you must first understand how data are stored in fields and records in a secondary file (Figure 4-88).

Fields

A **field** is a specific piece of information, for example, a person's name. Fields can be names (Smith), numbers (100.10), names and numbers (100 Main Street), or formulas (100*3).

All programs have rules that you must follow when you enter information into the fields in a secondary file.

- If the entry contains commas or colons, you might have to enclose it in double quotation marks. For example, you would enter a name as **"Smith, John"**.

- If the entry contains quotation marks, you might have to enter them in pairs and then enclose the entire entry in another set of quotation marks, for example, **"Charles""Fats""Waller"**.

- The entry might have a length limitation.

When you first create a record file, you should plan so that the data are effectively organized.

	Field	Record
Variable 1	Variable 2	Variable 3
Ms Smith	Marketing	8901
Mr. Jones	Finance	8902
Ms Davis	Investments	8903
Mr. Irving	Production	8904

FIGURE 4-88
The Secondary File
Fields and records in a secondary file are used to organize the data in a record file. A field is a specific piece of information, for example, a name (Mr. Jones), a department (Finance), or a phone extension (8902). A record is a collection of fields that describe a specific item or person, for example, Mr. Jones, Finance, 8902.

- If you want to be able to sort a mailing list by ZIP codes, they must be entered into a separate field.
- If you want to use the last name in the salutation, it must be in a separate field. If you have only one field for the entire name, your letter might read Dear Mr. John Smith instead of Dear Mr. Smith.
- The number of lines used in addresses varies. One address might require only three lines, and another might require five. Set up your fields for the most number of lines. If a particular address is shorter, you can leave those fields blank.

Records

Related fields are stored together as **records**, for example, a person's name, address, and phone number make up a record. Each record must have the same fields, and data must be entered in the same order into each record. The fields in each record are separated from each other by a **delimiter**, usually a comma or colon. If a field is to be left empty in a record, the delimiter that ends the field must be entered anyway so that the program knows the field is empty. For example, if you have three fields for name, company, and street, and the program requires you to separate the fields with a comma, a record containing all entries might be

John Smith,Word Corporation,100 Elm Street

whereas a record without a company entry might appear as

Mary Hernandez,,200 Main Street

Relating the Primary Document and Secondary File

When you code the primary document, you enter variable names that specify what information is to be inserted into the copies when they are merge printed. These variable names refer to the fields in the secondary file. For example, your secondary file may have fields in each record for the person's name, street address, city, state, ZIP code, and salutation. Depending on the program, you assign names to these fields in the primary document or the secondary file. For example, you may name them as follows:

NAME,STREET,CITY,STATE,ZIP,SALUTATION

When you insert variable name codes into the primary document, the codes refer to these field names. When you merge print the primary document and secondary file, data from the fields in each record are inserted into each copy in place of the variable name that refers to them.

You may refer to all the fields in the secondary file or just to some of them. For example, a primary document used to print letters might refer to all the fields mentioned above, but a primary document used to print envelopes would not refer to the salutation field.

MERGE PRINTING

Merge printing is the process of printing multiple copies of the primary document, each with a different set of variables (Figure 4-89). If you manually enter the variables, prompts can be displayed on the screen telling you what to enter, for example, *Enter amount due:*. When you enter the requested information and press **Return**, the merge continues.

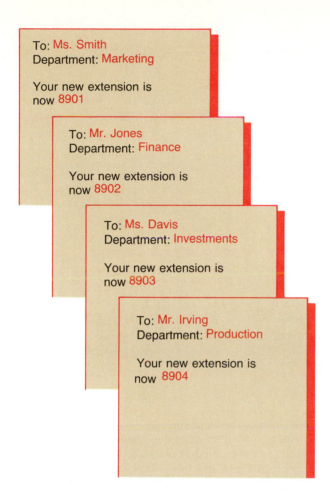

To: Ms. Smith
Department: Marketing

Your new extension is
now 8901

To: Mr. Jones
Department: Finance

Your new extension is
now 8902

To: Ms. Davis
Department: Investments

Your new extension is
now 8903

To: Mr. Irving
Department: Production

Your new extension is
now 8904

FIGURE 4-89
Merge Printing the Primary and Secondary Documents
Merge printing the primary document creates multiple copies of the form letter. If a code in the primary document specifies that data is to be inserted automatically, the program goes to the specified file and field for the information to be inserted.

If you enter the variables from a secondary file, the merge printing is automatic. As the first letter is being printed, the program stops at each code in the primary document, goes to the first record in the secondary file and inserts data from the specified field, and then continues printing. After all the requested fields from the first record have been inserted, the first copy advances from the printer, and the second copy is printed. But this time, the program inserts data from the second record in the secondary file. This continues until all the records in the secondary file have been used.

MERGE PRINTING ENVELOPES AND LABELS

If you maintain a list of names and addresses, you can use it not only to address letters but also to print envelopes and mailing labels. Envelopes can be fed to the printer from a bin or by using continuous form envelopes. Mailing labels normally come in several forms, called 1-up labels, 2-up labels, 3-up labels, and so on (Figure 4-90). If you print on 1-up labels, you simply code the primary document as you did the form letter. You then must specify new page length, top and bottom margin settings, and begin printing.

Because you must specify horizontal spacing, 2-up and 3-up labels present a special problem. The program also must be able to work with the record file so that it can print a line of just names and then a line of just addresses. Instead of proceeding through each field in a record, as it would with a letter, it must access the same field in several records before it moves down to the next line. Some programs are able to do this, but many are not.

WordPerfect Procedures Manual MASTER	WordPerfect Procedures Manual BACKUP	DisplayWrite 4 Procedures Manual MASTER
DisplayWrite 4 Procedures Manual BACKUP	Microsoft WORD Procedures Manual MASTER	Microsoft WORD Procedures Manual BACKUP
MultiMate Advantage II Procedures Manual MASTER	MultiMate Advantage II Procedures Manual BACKUP	WordStar 4 Procedures Manual MASTER

A. 1-Up Labels

B. 3-Up Labels

FIGURE 4-90
Merge Printing Labels
Labels are available in several forms. Typical examples are (a) 1-up labels and (b) 3-up labels.

TIPS: Printing Form Letters

Some programs allow you to sort record files so that documents are printed in a specified order (see Topic 4-28). This is often useful; for example, you can print mailing labels that are sorted by ZIP code so that you can take advantage of bulk rates for presorted mail.

SUMMARY AND KEY TERMS

- **Merge printing** is used to print many copies of a form document with data entered manually or from a record file in specific places to customize each copy. It can also be used to prepare mailing labels and envelopes.

- The **primary document** contains the text that is to appear in all printed copies and **merge codes**, called **variable names**, that indicate where customized information is to be inserted.

- The **secondary file** contains the information, **called variables**, that is to be inserted in place of the merge codes in the primary document when it is merge printed. The data in this file is organized into **fields** and **records**.

- In addition to merge codes that assign variable names, you can enter merge codes that stop the merge at selected points so that you can enter information from the keyboard or calculate IF statements.

- You can use a secondary file to automatically merge print envelopes and labels.

REVIEW QUESTIONS

1. What are the two files you need for automatic merge printing?
2. Describe a primary document and what its function is.
3. List and describe the two basic codes you can enter in a primary document.
4. Describe a secondary file and what its function is.
5. Describe fields, records, and record files.

TOPIC 4-18

Document Assembly

OBJECTIVE

After completing this topic, you will be able to

- Explain how to assemble documents on the screen or when printing them

You can maintain parts of a document in separate files on a disk and assemble them into documents as needed. This procedure is useful in a variety of situations.

- An author can store book manuscripts and reports in several files to make them easier to manage and edit. When printing documents stored in this way, one file after another can be printed in a specified sequence while the program sequentially numbers each page.
- An attorney can keep a library of contract clauses on a disk and then assemble them as he or she chooses to print custom contracts, inserting additional data as needed.

There are two ways to assemble large documents: on the screen or while printing.

ASSEMBLING DOCUMENTS ON THE SCREEN

Most programs allow you to insert text from another file stored on the disk into the document you are working on (sometimes called reading, merging, or including a file). This is helpful when you are extensively revising long documents. There are also times when parts of a file are stored separately and then combined just before printing. To insert a file on the disk into a document on the screen, you follow two steps.

1. Position the cursor where you want the file on the disk to be inserted.
2. Execute the program's command that inserts files, and specify the name of the file on the disk.

Most programs read in the entire file. If the file contains more text than you want, you can delete unwanted sections once they have been read into the file you are working on. Other programs display the file you want to read text from so that you can select a specific block.

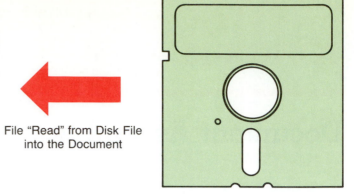

separately and then combined just before printing. To insert a file on the disk into a document on the screen you follow these two steps:

1. Position the cursor at the place where you want the file on the disk to be inserted.
2. Execute the program's command that inserts files and specify the name of the file on the disk.

Most programs read in the entire file. If the file contains more text than you want, you can delete unwanted sections once they have been

File "Read" from Disk File into the Document

FIGURE 4-91
Reading a File
Reading a file from the disk copies it into the document on the screen.

When you read a document into a file, it is copied from a file on the disk and inserted into the document on the screen at the cursor's position (Figure 4-91). All text below the cursor moves down to make room for the inserted text.

Some programs use a different concept, called a **master document**. You open a file, and then insert codes that refer to the names of other files. You then expand, or generate, this master document, and the files referred to by the codes are assembled on the screen.

ASSEMBLING DOCUMENTS WHILE PRINTING

To assemble a document while printing, you create a primary document, and then enter codes into it that indicate the names of files on the disk to be

FIGURE 4-92
Assembling Documents While Printing
Document assembly is done by coding a primary document (a). The codes specify what files are to be inserted at that point in the document. When the program encounters a code (b), it stops printing the primary document and begins printing the specified file from the disk. When it has finished printing that file, it resumes printing the primary document.

A. Primary Document

B. Code

We hold these truths to be self-evident, that all men are created equal; that they are endowed by their creator with certain unalienable rights;

that, whenever any form of government becomes destructive to these ends, it is the right of the people to alter or to abolish it,

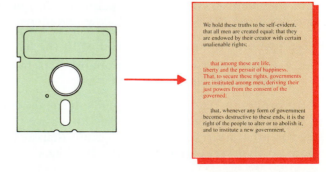

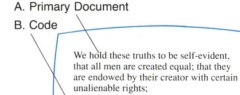

inserted. You then merge print the primary document. When the program encounters a code, it prints the specified file from the disk (Figure 4-92).

The files you insert into a primary document can also have codes that refer to other files. This is called **nesting**. Many programs allow you to nest files up to seven or more levels. For example, you can code a primary document to insert a clause on renting an apartment. The code might refer to a file named RENT. The RENT file might have a code that inserts a clause on the monthly rental charge stored in a file named COST. When you merge print the primary file, the following happens:

1. The primary document is printed until the program encounters the code that refers to the file named RENT.
2. The RENT file is printed until the program encounters the code that refers to the COST file.
3. The COST file is printed until it is finished.
4. The program resumes printing the RENT file until it is finished.
5. The program resumes printing the primary document.

REVIEW QUESTIONS

1. Describe two ways to assemble documents stored in separate files on the disk.
2. What does the term *nesting* mean?
3. What is a master document?

Drawing Lines

OBJECTIVE

After completing this topic, you will be able to

- Describe how to draw lines to create tables and boxes

Many word processing programs now include the ability to draw lines. Using the line draw feature, you can draw lines in tables to separate elements from one another and around text to create boxes. Programs allow you one or more ways to draw lines or boxes in a document.

- On some programs, you first select the character you want to work with. You then use the directional arrow keys to move the cursor around the screen. As you move the cursor, you paint a line with the selected character. There are also commands that let you erase any lines you have mistakenly entered.

- On other programs, you can select one or more paragraphs, and then use a menu command that draws a line on one or more sides or encloses the paragraphs in a box. This approach is preferred because the size of the lines or boxes automatically changes if you change margins or add or delete text.

FIGURE 4-93
Lines and Boxes
Line draw character (a) can be used to make a document more attractive. For example, you can draw lines and boxes (b) or create illustrations like an organization chart (c).

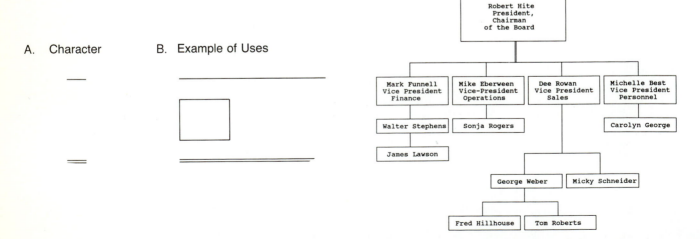

A. Character

B. Example of Uses

Organization Chart

The IBM PC character set has several graphics characters that you can create lines and boxes with. This line drawing can highlight headings, create organization charts (Figure 4-93), and make attractive tables (Figure 4-94). To print out line drawings, your printer must have a font that contains the line drawing graphics characters. Since some fonts contain the line draw characters and some do not, you may have to specify a different font to print them if your program allows you to do so.

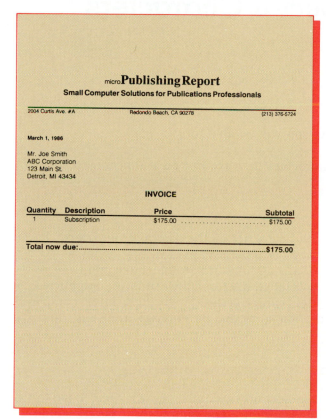

FIGURE 4-94
Tables
Lines can also be used to separate elements in a table. Courtesy of Xerox Corporation

- Some programs allow you to select line draw characters and then draw lines on the screen by pressing the cursor movement keys.
- Some programs have commands that automatically add lines of boxes to selected paragraphs. If you add or delete text, the size of the lines or boxes automatically adjusts.

1. What are the two ways programs let you draw lines and boxes?
2. List as many uses for a program's line draw capability as you can think of.
3. If the line drawings you create do not print out on your printer, what is the reason?

TOPIC 4-20

Creating Special Characters

OBJECTIVE

After completing this topic, you will be able to

■ Explain how to enter characters that are not on the keyboard

Special characters are any characters not on the computer keyboard. These include graphics symbols, Greek letters, foreign currency symbols, foreign language accents, and almost any other character used to communicate information. To print these special characters, they must be supported by your printer. Special characters can be created with the printer, composed on the computer, selected from a menu, or entered from the numeric keypad.

OVERPRINTING SPECIAL CHARACTERS

What if you are preparing a report on international sales and have to express some amounts in pounds sterling? The symbol for this is £, a character not found on many keyboards or supported by many printers. To simulate the character, you can print an uppercase L with a superimposed hyphen. The end result, Ł, is achieved by **overtyping** (also called *overprinting* or *overstriking*), printing the two characters over each other. This technique is accomplished by telling the printer to back up one space after it prints the first character so that it can print the second character in the same position.

COMPOSING SPECIAL CHARACTERS

Composing characters is a version of overtyping, but instead of entering a code to back the printer up each time you want to enter the symbol, you create it once, and the printer automatically backs up. Composing characters is useful when entering **digraphs** (a pair of letters representing a single sound) and **diacriticals** (a mark or symbol used to indicate a sound). To compose a character, you execute the *Compose* command, type the two characters you want to print over each other, and assign them to a combination of keys. For example, to create the pound sterling symbol, you begin the *Compose* command, type the uppercase **L** and the - (hyphen), and then specify that the symbol be assigned to the **Alt-$** keys. Then, whenever you want to enter the pound sterling symbol, you simply hold down **Alt** and press **$**.

SELECTING SPECIAL CHARACTERS

On some programs, you can display a menu of the special characters available in the computer's character set. The IBM character set (see Figure 1-36 in Topic 1-3) includes several characters not found on the keyboard. Programs that allow you to select these characters can display them on the screen for you to choose from. You then assign the desired characters to a combination of keys. For example, you might assign a right arrow symbol (→), to the keys **Alt-R**. Whenever you hold down **Alt** and press **R**, the right arrow symbol is entered into the document at the cursor's position.

TYPING ASCII CODES

Almost all programs allow you to enter special characters by holding down **Alt** while you type their ASCII decimal codes on the numeric keypad. When you do so, and then release **Alt**, the character is displayed on the screen. You can enter any of the codes shown in Figure 1-36 in Topic 1-3. To find the code, first locate the character you want to enter in that figure, and then read across to the left column numbers for the first two digits and to the top row for the third. For example, the up arrow is 024, music notes are 013 and 014, and the 1/2 character is 171.

- **Overprinting characters** allows you to create special symbols or accents by printing one over another: for example, printing a dash (-) over an uppercase L prints an acceptable British pound sterling symbol. Overprinting a single quotation mark (' or ') on a character adds an accent mark to a letter.
- **Composing** a character allows you to specify two characters that are printed together.
- **Selecting** characters from a menu and assigning them to a combination of keys allows you to quickly enter the character by pressing those keys.
- Most programs allow you to enter special characters by holding down **Alt** and **typing** the character's three-digit decimal number on the numeric keypad.

SUMMARY AND KEY TERMS

---

1. List and briefly describe three ways to create special characters that are not on the keyboard.
2. How do you enter special characters using their three-digit decimal code?

REVIEW QUESTIONS

TOPIC 4-21

Printing in Columns

OBJECTIVES

After completing this topic, you will be able to

- Explain how to print in multiple columns
- Describe the differences between newspaper-style and parallel-style columns

Normally, text is printed in one column on a sheet of paper, but some programs let you specify that it be printed in two or more columns. Some programs display the columns on the screen; others just show the results when you print the document. The two basic types of text columns are newspaper columns and parallel columns.

NEWSPAPER-STYLE COLUMNS

Newspaper-style columns (Figure 4-95) (also called snaking columns) are like those you see in newspapers, newsletters, and books. Text flows from column to column. As you enter text, it gradually fills the first column. When that column is full, text flows into the next column. When the last column on the page is full, text starts to fill the first column on the next page. If you add text to or delete text from any of the columns, the remaining text adjusts to keep the columns full.

PARALLEL-STYLE COLUMNS

Parallel-style columns (Figure 4-96) (also called side-by-side columns) align related text side by side. This style is used when showing the same text in two languages; annotating a script with marginal notes; or creating tables of text for schedules, product descriptions, and the like. Text does not flow from one column to another, as in newspaper columns. You enter and edit text in each column independently.

AST Research Inc.	(714) 863 1333	Creative Strategies Resrch Inter	(408) 249 7550
Abaton Technology	(818) 905 9399	Cybertext Corp.	(707) 822 7079
Addison-Wesley Publishing Co.	(617) 944 3700	Data Transforms	(303) 832 1501
Adobe Systems Inc.	(415) 852 0271	Data Change, Inc.	(404) 441 1332
Adserve Media Systems, Inc.	(212) 213 5700	Data Frontiers, Inc.	(716) 467 3125
Advanced Technologies Int'l	(408) 748 1688	Data Recording Systems, Inc.	(516) 293 2400
AFIPS	(703) 620 8926	Data Sytems of Connecticut Inc.	(203) 877 5451
Airus	(503) 684 3000	Datacopy	(415) 965 7900
Allied Linotype	(516) 434 2000	Datalogics Inc.	(312) 266 4444
Allotype Typographics	(313) 577 3035	Datamate Co.	(800) 262 7276
Alpha Software Corp.	(617) 229 2924	Dataquest Inc.	(408) 971 9000
AlphaGraphics	(602) 882 4100	Datek Information Services, Inc.	(617) 893 9130
Altertext	(617) 426 0009	DayFlo Inc.	(714) 476 3044
American Business Press	(212) 661 5360	DecisionWare, Inc.	(813) 383 6059
Amgraf, Inc.	(816) 474 4797	Decision Resources	(203) 222 1974
Amrron Data Services	(714) 859 8333	Desktop Graphics	(302) 736 9098
Apple Computer, Inc.	(408) 996 1010	Dest Corporation	(408) 946 7100
Applied Publishing Technologies	(202) 872 1190	Dicomed Corp.	(612) 885 3000
Archtype	(617) 482 2739	Diconix Inc.	(513) 259 3100
Arrix Logic Systems Inc.	(416) 292 6425	Digital Equipment Corp.	(603) 884 5111
Ashton-Tate	(213) 329 8000	Digital Technology International	(801) 226 2984
AST Research Inc.	(714) 863 1333	Dunn Instruments	(415) 957 1600
Autographix	(617) 890 8558	Dunn Technology Inc.	(619) 758 9460
Autologic	(805) 498 9611	Eastman Kodak	(800) 445 6325
Automatic Fulfillment Services	(201) 366 8722	Eikonix Corporation	(617) 275 5070
Autospec Inc.	(408) 649 0890	Electronic Information Technology	(201) 227 1447
Award Software Inc.	(408) 395 2773	The Electronic Publisher	(816) 637 7233
Beach Media Inc.	(619) 226 6726	Emerging Technology Consultants	(303) 447 9495
Bell & Howell Company	(312) 262 1600	Epsilon	(617) 273 0250
BPAA	(212) 661 0222	Epson America, Inc.	(213) 534 4500
Business Systems International	(818) 998 7227	Ericsson Information Systems	(714) 895 3962
Buttonware Inc.	(201) 746 4296	Esgraph Incorporated	(800) 524 0377
Canon USA Inc., Printer Div.	(516) 488 6700	Expert Technologies	(412) 621 0818
Capital Equipment Co.	(312) 829 6220	Flint Hills Software	(913) 841 4503
Cauzin Systems, Inc.	(203) 573 0150	Form Maker Software, Inc.	(205) 633 3676
Centram Systems West, Inc.	(415) 644 8244	Frost & Sullivan Inc.	(212) 233 1080
CF Inc.	(416) 487 2142	FTL Systems	(416) 487 2142
Chorus Data Systems	(603) 424 2900	Fujitsu America Inc.	(408) 946 8777
Comm Type Interface Typesetting	(213) 938 8973	Future Computing Inc.	(214) 437 2400
Composition Technology Intl.	(818) 848 1010	General Binding Corporation	(312) 272 3700
Compugraphic Corp.	(617) 944 6555	Genesys Systems	(316) 564 3636
CompuNews, Inc.	(509) 826 1110	Genicom Corp.	(703) 949 1188
CompuScan, Inc.	(201) 288 6001	Genoa Systems Corp.	(408) 945 9720
CompuServe	(614) 457 8600	Gnostic Concepts, Inc.	(415) 854 4672
Computer EdiType Systems	(212) 222 8148	Graphic Connections	(206) 251 9750
Computing Software Services Inc.	(212) 432 6077	Graphic Arts Technical Foundation	(412) 621 6941
Concept Technologies, Inc.	(503) 684 3314	Graham Software Corp.	(713) 359 1024

FIGURE 4-95
Newspaper-Style Columns
Newspaper-style or snaking columns are like those you see in newspapers and newsletters. Text flows from the bottom of one column to the top of the next.

NAMES AND ADDRESS

Dennis Hogan	Lakeside Industries 100 Elm Street Westfield, NY 00120	716-555-1212
Nancy Benjamin	Wordcraft, Inc 52 Senaca Road Oakland, CA 10020	403-555-1212
Catherine Rossbach	Real Estate Inc. 1500 Main Street Munsey, IN 10030	313-555-1212

FIGURE 4-96
Parallel-Style Columns
Parallel-style columns are like those you see in tables or where scripts are annotated. Related text is printed side by side.

SUMMARY AND KEY TERMS

- A few programs allow you to print text in more than one **column**.
- In **newspaper-style columns**, text flows from the bottom of one column into the top of the next.
- In **parallel-style columns**, paragraphs are entered side by side.

REVIEW QUESTIONS

1. What are two kinds of columns that can be created on some programs?
2. What is the difference between them?

PRINTING IN COLUMNS

TOPIC 4-22

Combining Graphics with Text

OBJECTIVES

After completing this topic, you will be able to

- Explain how to create graphic images
- Describe how to combine graphics with text

Often, when preparing reports and other kinds of documents, it is necessary to include graphics to illustrate ideas. Traditionally, the graphic illustration was prepared separately and then inserted or pasted in. Now, it is possible to print graphics right in the document (Figure 4-97). To do so, you must first create the image, and then incorporate it into the document.

FIGURE 4-97
Graphics and Text Combined
You can combine graphics with text to illustrate a report or other document. Courtesy of Xerox Corporation

Laser Printers Arrive

Speedier, Less Costly Laser Printers Are Changing the Computer Business

by Mary Smith

Mary Smith pioneered the publishing revolution by being the first to use the phrase Professional-Personal-Desktop-Microcomputer Publishing.

As laser printers gain more attention with lower prices, higher speeds and quality output, high-end dot-matrix printers are starting to lose some of their appeal.

Though PC users are still buying dot-matrix printers, the laser printer is giving them an alternative to think about, according to industry observers.

Laser printers, though relatively expensive, are being used more in networked environments where the distributed use of the printer justifies the expense, several analysts said. The non-impact printers also catch user interest because they are less noisy, offer sharper graphics (commonly 300-by-300 dots per inch) and can produce from eight to 10 pages per minute.

Competing Technologies

- Daisy Wheel
- Dot Matrix
- Laser printers
- Laser printers with white-white engines and copier options, using dry powder toner.

Laser printers still have a few areas that could be improved, according to George Jones, a key industry analyst. He noted that there are no standards in controllers for laser printers and but the cost of using a laser is now less than a dot matrix on a cost-per-copy per minute basis.

The laser printer provides sharper graphic images, Jones noted, and the laser now has the wealth of software support dot-matrix printers have always enjoyed. So, if a user moves to a laser printer from a dot-matrix printer "he can run much of his graphics software and get better graphics resolution," Jones said.

"The next step is developing generic graphics drivers which support lasers at 300-by-300 resolution. That's when you will see a huge impact on dot-matrix printers, both in price and the number of units shipping," he said, adding that it will be a year to 18 months before this happens.

Jones was quick to point out that he never sees dot-matrix printers disappearing. "Multiple-part forms are still important, and an impact printer is needed for that." He also noted that people will always want hard copies for their files or interoffice memos, and the quickest, most cost-efficient way of doing that is through a low-cost dot-matrix printer--without having to wait in line for a share laser printer. Current sales figures seem to bear Jones out. In its June 1985 Store Board Survey, market-research firm Laser Computing of Alamo, Texas, polled over 600 computer specialty stores finding that, while laser-printer sales are up, they have not eclipsed dot-matrix printers.

Laser Computing analyst Todd

This is a liftout. It highlights a key quote or statement in the article.

Wiggins said he expects dot-matrix printers to continue competing with laser printer in the future. He also said the two technologies can work well together. "If you've got a laser

Figure -I-
The Author

shared by six to 10 people, you may still have dot-matrix printers for drafts of your own work. I think there's room for both [type] for a while," he said.

As the prices of laser printers fall, more PC users may choose them over dot-matrix printer. Wiggins said the current value of the laser-printer market is about $450 million, expected to grow to about $2.2 billion by 1990.

Bill James product marketing manager with Acme Hardware which produces impact as well as non-impact printers, said both have a category in which they're most efficiently used.

He said dot-matrix printers are suited for "fast Utility output, like internal documents, and for operational documents such as multi-part forms used with invoices. These are things that you don't need full-font printer for . . . [Dot-matrix printers] are good to have in a manufacturing facility."

As for laser-printer applications, James said they are good in areas "where people don't need multiple-part forms, where they need to output data with high quality and speed--like in a group doing systems

CREATING GRAPHIC IMAGES

There are three ways of creating images to be incorporated into a document and saving them on the disk.

- You can scan the image into the computer.
- You can create the image on the screen with an interactive graphics paint program.
- You can use a memory resident program that captures any image that can be displayed on the screen. You first load the memory resident program and then the program you use to display the image you want to capture. You then display on the screen the graphic you want to include in the document. With the graphic on the screen, you press designated keys to capture the image. Some programs let you specify the size, orientation, and even color of the graphic.

INCORPORATING IMAGES INTO DOCUMENTS

When all the graphics you want to include have been saved in picture files on the disk, you create or retrieve the document file you want to use them in. You insert codes (sometimes called tags) into the document that refer to the names of the picture files on the disk that the graphic images are stored in.

You can then use commands to adjust the size. When you print the document, the picture files that the codes refer to are merged into the document.

TIPS: Combining Graphics with Text

On an IBM PC and compatible computers, you can press the **PrtSc** (Print Screen) key to print whatever is currently displayed on the screen. If you are using a graphics program and display, you can print copies of graphics displayed on the screen if you have loaded the DOS Graphics program. This program is stored on the MS-DOS and PC-DOS program disks. You load it before you load your applications program.

1. Insert the DOS disk into drive A, and then boot the system so that the *A>* prompt is displayed.
2. Type GRAPHICS and then press **Return**.
3. Remove the DOS disk, and then load your applications program.
4. Press **PrtSc** to print an image on the screen.

SUMMARY AND KEY TERMS

- There are three ways to create graphic images. You can scan them into the computer, draw them with a paint program, or capture what is on the screen and store it in a disk file.
- To insert a graphic into a document, you insert a code that shows where it should be printed.

REVIEW QUESTIONS

1. List three ways you can get graphic images into the computer so that you can then combine them with a document.
2. Describe how graphic images can be inserted into a document.

Page Makeup

OBJECTIVE

After completing this topic, you will be able to

- Explain the key concepts in page makeup

Serious desktop publishing requires using a desktop publishing program (also called a page makeup program) that allows you to perform page makeup, a very sophisticated form of formatting. Page makeup programs allow you to design, lay out, and produce professional-looking documents (Figure 4-98). These programs usually have several text-handling and graphics-handling capabilities.

TEXT-HANDLING CAPABILITIES

- You can create text on a word processing program and transfer it into the desktop publishing program so that it flows into predefined columns. Some desktop publishing programs accept only ASCII files, but many now accept formatted (binary) files created on most popular word processing programs.

FIGURE 4-98
Desktop Published Documents
Documents created with a desktop publishing program look as if they were professionally prepared and printed. Courtesy of Aldus Corporation

- You can choose from a wide selection of type fonts.
- You can rotate type to print it in portrait or landscape mode. Some programs allow you to rotate type 360 degrees so that it can be oriented in any direction.
- You can vertically justify text by adding leading, that is, space, between lines so that the first and last lines on each page print in the same position even if the number of lines is different.
- You can hyphenate text based on either a hyphenation dictionary or a hyphenation algorithm, a set of rules stored in the computer's memory.
- You can create multiple columns and justify the text in one or all of them.
- You can print dropout type, white characters against a dark background.

GRAPHICS-HANDLING CAPABILITIES

- You can import graphics and print them side by side with text.
- You can crop, shrink, enlarge, rotate, and move images.
- You can add vertical, horizontal, or diagonal rules of different widths.
- You can use shades of gray to shade boxes or add patterns.
- You can position text and graphics together in boxes.

PAGE AND DOCUMENT DESCRIPTION LANGUAGES

Page makeup programs are the interface between you and the printer. But still another program is between your page makeup program and the printer. This **page** or **document description language** actually controls the printer to obtain the results you want. Research on page description languages began at Xerox Corporation in the mid-1970s. The resulting program, Interpress, was developed from this work. Two members of this original development team left Xerox to form Adobe Systems. Their product, with its roots in the Interpress program, was PostScript, introduced in 1982.

Today, the most popular page description languages are Imagen Corporation's Document Description Language (DDL), Adobe Systems' PostScript, and Xerox Corporation's Interpress. These programs allow page makeup programs to print documents on a variety of printers. A page description language is not something you usually buy separately. Normally, it resides in the printer though some also can be added to the computer by plugging an expansion board into one of its slots.

DESKTOP PUBLISHING SYSTEMS

Although you can desktop publish on almost any microcomputer system, special hardware and software makes the job easier and faster.

A complete desktop publishing system includes several components, some of which are also used for other work on the computer. The best systems allow you to preview the results while working on a document. This ability is called WYSIWYG (pronounced "whizzy-wig"), or "what you see is what you get." Let's look briefly at some of the components of a desktop publishing system.

Computer

Desktop publishing requires a great deal of computer processing power. To work efficiently, the computer must have a powerful microprocessor, a lot of internal memory, and a hard disk drive to store the programs and documents. The new generation of computers meets these requirements, but many earlier models are too limited to effectively run many desktop publishing programs.

Laser Printer

To get the finest printed quality from a desktop publishing system, you need a laser printer. Alternatively, you could print draft copies on a less expensive printer, and then send the disk to an outside service for final printing.

A laser printer normally prints at a resolution of 300 dots per inch (dpi). True typeset quality generally requires 1000 or more dots per inch. To achieve this quality, many desktop publishing programs use a standard coding system that can be read by expensive typesetting equipment. You can send a disk or telecommunicate the document to a typesetter, and they can set your document in type with this extremely high resolution.

To manipulate text, graphics, and fonts, your printer needs a great deal of memory. It takes a megabyte to store a full-page graphic image that is to be printed with a 300-dpi resolution. If your printer has less memory, the graphic must be reduced, or resolution suffers (or worse yet, the entire image is not printed).

High-Quality Display Monitor

Most display screens show only twenty-five lines of text and have a relatively low resolution. This is acceptable for normal word processing, but when you want to work with desktop publishing, a better system is preferable. The ideal system can display a full 8½-by-11-inch page or even two facing pages (Figure 4-99).

The monitor should also be able to display a gray scale, shades of gray ranging from pure white to pure black (see Figure 1-65 in Topic 1-5). The display monitor and its associated hardware and software generate a graphics display (see Figure 1-78 in Topic 1-6). Without this ability, you cannot see how fonts and graphics actually appear until printed.

FIGURE 4-99
Displays
Some monitors can display two facing pages. This is especially useful when you are laying out reports and other documents that will be printed. Courtesy of Aldus Corporation

Graphics-Based Interface

A graphics-based operating system environment, like Windows or GEM, makes it easier to display graphic effects on the screen and operate the printer. These operating system environments contain a set of standard device drivers that allow your printer to duplicate the effects you see on the screen.

Mouse

A mouse is a helpful tool when designing columns, boxes, and other parts of the document. It is also helpful when manipulating images.

Interactive Graphics Program

If you want to create or manipulate images on the screen, you need a program that provides a set of drawing tools. Called painting programs, they allow you to create and edit free-hand line art and to manipulate digitized images that have been scanned into the computer.

Scanner

A scanner allows you to read images like line art, photographs, and signatures into the computer so that they can be combined with text in a document.

SUMMARY AND KEY TERMS

- **Page makeup programs** provide very advanced formatting features.
- **Text-handling capabilities** include a wide selection of fonts and the ability to rotate type, add leading, hyphenate text, and print in columns.
- **Graphics-handling capabilities** include printing graphic images and sizing, rotating, or cropping them. You can also add borders and shading, and you can add text.
- **Document description languages** in your printer make possible sophisticated formats like rotating type and scaling type.
- Desktop publishing systems include a powerful computer, a laser printer, a high-quality display, a graphics-based display, a mouse, and a scanner.

REVIEW QUESTIONS

1. Briefly describe the term *page makeup*.
2. List some ways a page makeup program can manipulate text.
3. List some ways a page makeup program can manipulate graphics.
4. What is a document description language?
5. List and describe some of the elements in a desktop publishing system.

TOPIC 4-24

Glossaries

OBJECTIVE

After completing this topic, you will be able to

- Explain what glossaries are and how to use them

Some programs allocate a small portion of the computer's memory so that you can save repeatedly used sections of text, like the date and closing used on letters. To save text in this area of memory, called a **glossary** (or a *library* or *phrase storage area*), you highlight it in the document, and then execute the *Glossary* command. You then assign the entry a name, usually an abbreviation that you can easily remember.

To copy an entry from the glossary into a file, you move the cursor to where you want the text inserted, execute the *Glossary Retrieve* command, and then specify the name of the entry (Figure 4-100).

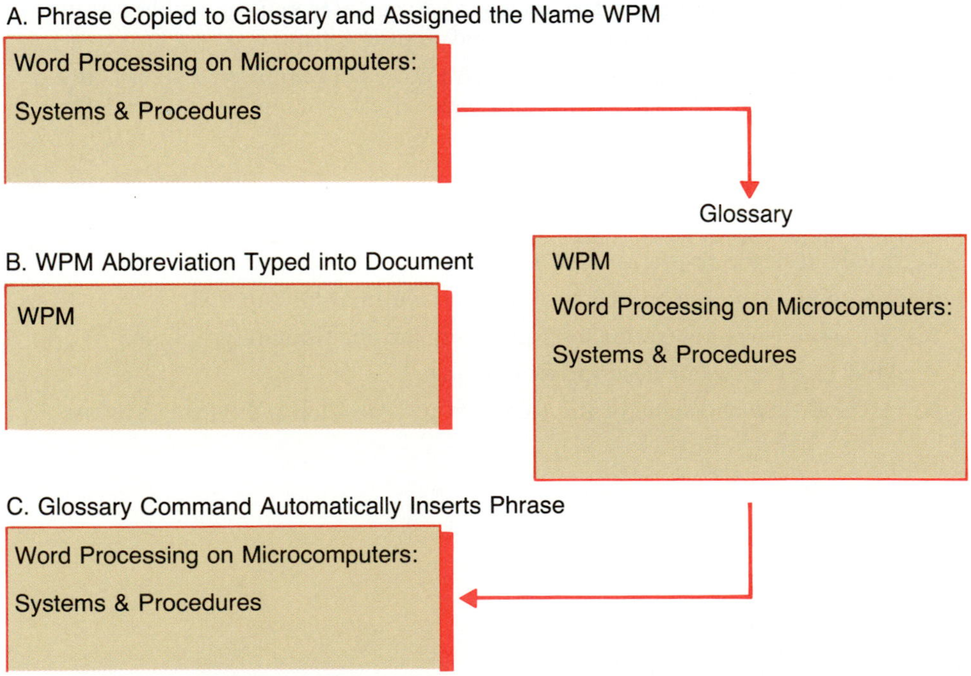

FIGURE 4-100
Glossaries
Glossaries store words, phrases, or other sections of text that you copy to the glossary from a document. First you copy the material to the glossary and assign it a name (a). You then insert the abbreviation into the document (b). When you move the cursor to where you want the text inserted in a document and enter its abbreviation, the text is copied from the glossary into the document (c).

A. Phrase Copied to Glossary and Assigned the Name WPM

Word Processing on Microcomputers:

Systems & Procedures

Glossary

WPM

Word Processing on Microcomputers:

Systems & Procedures

B. WPM Abbreviation Typed into Document

WPM

C. Glossary Command Automatically Inserts Phrase

Word Processing on Microcomputers:

Systems & Procedures

392

Glossaries are great time savers. For example, you can enter the phrase *As soon as possible* and attach it to the abbreviation ASAP. When you type ASAP in the document, the phrase is automatically entered when you use the glossary feature. You can also enter the name and address of someone in the glossary, and then enter it in the document by just typing his or her last name or initials.

After storing text in the glossary, you can generally save it in a file on the disk. This way you can use the glossary with any document by first loading it back into memory or retrieving it from the disk into the current document when needed. Some programs also let you create different glossaries, each for a special purpose. For example, you could have one glossary for customer inquiry letters and another for contracts.

SUMMARY AND KEY TERMS

- A **glossary** is a collection of phrases that you can insert into a document with a few keystrokes.
- Glossaries are normally saved in their own files on the disk so that you can retrieve them in the computer's memory when working on any document.

REVIEW QUESTIONS

1. Describe what a glossary is and when you would use it.
2. Give some examples of when you might use a glossary.

Math

OBJECTIVE

After completing this topic, you will be able to

- Describe the math capabilities available in word processing programs and how to use them

When using a word processing program, you often have columns or lines of numbers that require totals and subtotals. Other times, you have two or more numbers that you want to add, subtract, multiply, or divide. Programs with built-in math functions let you make these calculations on the screen without a separate calculator. Some programs also have advanced math functions that calculate averages or percentages.

CALCULATING NUMBERS IN LINES AND COLUMNS

One math feature automatically totals lines and columns of numbers (Figure 4-101). You enter these numbers in a document, and then tell the program what rows or columns to total and where to place the answer. The procedures you follow vary.

- On some programs, you define columns in the document from a menu, and then enter codes on the rows where you want the answers displayed.

FIGURE 4-101
Adding Rows and Columns
Adding lines and columns calculates and displays the totals in the document.

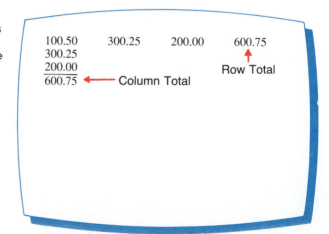

- On other programs, you select a block of numbers, and then select a choice from a menu that adds them. The answer either appears at the cursor's position or is saved in a buffer so that you can insert it anywhere in the document.

CALCULATING FORMULAS

You can also enter numbers into a document, and then add, subtract, multiply, or divide them.

- On some programs, you can point to numbers anywhere in the document one at a time, and then execute the command that adds, subtracts, multiplies, or divides them. For example, to begin, you point to the first number and select *Add* to store it in memory. You then point to the second number and specify if you want to add it to, multiply it by, subtract it from, or divide it into the number in memory. You can continue this for any number of steps, and the result of all calculations is stored in memory as a running total.

- On other programs, you enter the formulas onto a special math screen, and then insert the calculated total into the document by copying it from memory.

To calculate formulas, you should understand two principles: operators and the order of operations.

To calculate formulas with some programs, you enter **operators**, symbols that tell the program what calculations to perform. Along with numbers, operators are used to create formulas. You should be familiar with operators from arithmetic. A typical arithmetic problem might be written as $2+2$. The plus sign is the operator, and it tells you the numbers should be added. You use the same operators with your program, but the symbols are a little different. For example, the division operator is a slash (/), and the multiplication operator is an asterisk (*). Table 4-7 lists typical operators and examples of how they are used. To enter numbers that you want to add, you enter them preceded by a plus sign, or you enter the number by itself. To enter negative numbers or to indicate subtraction, you use the minus sign (the hyphen), or you enclose the number in parentheses.

When constructing formulas that contain more than one operator, another concept, the **order of operations**, becomes important. Every program has a specific order in which operators are calculated. We discuss orders of operation in detail in Topic 5-7.

TABLE 4-7
Word Processing Math Operators

Operation	Operator	Example	Answer
Addition	+ or nothing	100+100 or 100 100	200
Subtraction	− or ( )	200–100 or 200 (100)	100
Multiplication	*	2*2	4
Division	/	4/2	2
Percentage	. or %	.28*100 or 28%*100	28

- Most programs allow you to select a block of numbers on lines and columns and than execute a command that adds them.
- A few programs have the ability to make calculations for you so that you don't have to leave the program to do addition, subtraction, multiplication, and division.
- **Operators** determine the arithmetic that is performed.
- The **order of operations** determines the sequence operations are performed in if more than one operator is used.

REVIEW QUESTIONS

1. What are the two basic ways that you can calculate in a document?
2. What are math operators? List four, and describe what they do.
3. What is the order of operations?

Automatically Generated Lists

OBJECTIVE

After completing this topic, you will be able to

- Explain how lists, tables of contents, and indexes can be automatically generated

When working on a long document with many sections, you often need to prepare a table of contents or an index to help readers find the information they need. Both of these lists refer to subjects in the document and provide page numbers for them. Manually preparing these references takes a great deal of time; moreover, if any revisions are made to the document, all page number references might have to be changed. Many programs now allow you to automatically prepare these lists.

In a program that allows you to automatically create indexes and tables of contents, you first enter codes to indicate which items in the text are to be listed. You then generate and print a table of contents (Figure 4-102), an index (Figure 4-103), or another kind of list, for example, a list of all illustrations or tables in the document. To create automatically generated lists, you normally follow three steps: coding, definition, and generation.

CODING

To specify the entries to appear in the automatically generated list, you must code the appropriate sections in the document. You can specify the level of the heading so that subtopics are listed and indented under topics assigned a higher level; for example, your document may have parts, and each part may have sections. You would specify that the part headings are a level 1 entry, and the section headings are a level 2 entry. When you generate the table of contents or index, the level 2 entries are indented under the level 1 entries.

DEFINITION

To define the automatically generated list, you move the cursor to where you want it to appear in the document. You then specify the type of list it is—a table of contents, an index, or a list. You can also specify how many levels to

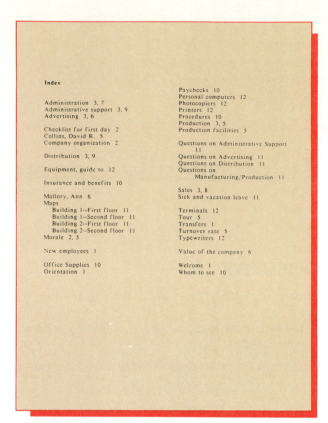

SPECIAL FEATURES

Table of Contents

TOPIC 40 WINDOWS AND SPLIT SCREENS   3

TOPIC 41 KEYBOARD MACROS   4

TOPIC 42 GLOSSARIES   6

TOPIC 43 MATH   8
    CALCULATING NUMBERS IN ROWS AND COLUMNS   8
    CALCULATING FORMULAS   9
        Operators   10
        Order of Operations   11

TOPIC 44 AUTOMATICALLY GENERATED LISTS   13
    CODING   13
    DEFINITION   14
    GENERATION   14

TOPIC 45 FOOTNOTES AND ENDNOTES   16

TOPIC 46 SORTING   18
    THE DATA TO BE SORTED   18
    THE SORT KEYS   18
    THE SORT ORDER   20

TOPIC 47 OUTLINES   22
    OUTLINES   22
    OUTLINERS   23

TOPIC 48 EXCHANGING FILES WITH OTHER PROGRAMS   25

TOPIC 49 USING DOS FUNCTIONS FROM WITHIN THE PROGRAM   29

TOPIC 50 CHANGING DEFAULT SETTINGS   30

FIGURE 4-102
Table of Contents
A table of contents can be automatically generated to show not only the headings in the document but also their level and page numbers.

Index

Administration 3, 7
Administrative support 3, 9
Advertising 3, 6

Checklist for first day 2
Collins, David R. 5
Company organization 2

Distribution 3, 9

Equipment, guide to 12

Insurance and benefits 10

Mallory, Ann 6
Maps
    Building 1--First floor 11
    Building 1--Second floor 11
    Building 2--First floor 11
    Building 2--Second floor 11
Morale 2, 5

New employees 1

Office Supplies 10
Orientation 1

Paychecks 10
Personal computers 12
Photocopiers 12
Printers 12
Procedures 10
Production 3, 5
Production facilities 5

Questions on Administrative Support 11
Questions on Advertising 11
Questions on Distribution 11
Questions on Manufacturing/Production 11

Sales 3, 8
Sick and vacation leave 11

Terminals 12
Tour 5
Transfers 1
Turnover rate 5
Typewriters 12

Value of the company 6

Welcome 1
Whom to see 10

FIGURE 4-103
Index
An index can be automatically generated showing entries in the document and the pages they appear on. Courtesy of Microsoft Corporation

include and whether to indicate page numbers. Some programs automatically generate the table of contents, index, or list at the end of the document.

GENERATION

Once you have defined the list and coded the entries, you execute the command that generates the list. The program then searches through the document for the coded entries, calculates their level and page numbers, and displays the list either where you entered the definition code or at the end of the document.

SUMMARY AND KEY TERMS

- Some programs will automatically create an index or a table of contents for a document.
- Key references are coded, and then the index or table of contents is defined. When you then generate the list, it is inserted at the point of the code, at the end of the document, or in a separate file.

REVIEW QUESTIONS

1. What kinds of lists can some programs automatically generate?
2. List three steps you typically follow to automatically generate these lists.

Footnotes and Endnotes

OBJECTIVE

After completing this topic, you will be able to

■ Describe footnotes and endnotes and how to enter and place them

Footnotes are numbered references printed at the bottom of the page (Figure 4-104). The numbers in the footnotes match the numbers in the text that refer to the footnotes. For example, when you are manually typing a report, your document may cite an author. Immediately following the author's name, you can enter a footnote reference number. At the bottom of

```
You can enter footnotes and endnotes throughout a document. They
are automatically numbered when you enter them and the numbers
change automatically to reflect any new or deleted notes above
them.  When you use the command to edit a footnote or endnote,
the program searches for the next note following the cursor and
asks if you want to edit that note. You can either accept it or
enter a new number[2]. Since the program moves the cursor to the
note, it is usually faster to move the cursor in front of the
note you want to edit before using the edit commands.
```

```
[2]If you enter a new number, the program searches for that
footnote and displays the section of the text that contains the
specified reference number on the screen after you edit the
footnote.
```

FIGURE 4-104
Footnotes
Footnotes appear at the bottoms of the same pages as the references to them in the document.

the same page, you then enter the same number followed by the title of the book, publisher, publication date, and page number cited. **Endnotes** are just like footnotes, but instead of printing at the bottom of the same page as the reference number, they are printed at the end of a section or chapter.

Many programs allow you to enter footnotes and endnotes anyplace in the document. The program then automatically numbers the footnote references in the document and either prints footnotes on the same page as the references to them or prints endnotes at the end of the document.

The procedures for entering footnotes vary. On some programs, you enter the footnote on a specific footnote page, and then enter a code in the document where you want its reference number to appear. On other programs, you position the cursor where you want the footnote reference number to be printed, and then execute the *Footnote* command. A special footnote screen appears on which you type, edit, and format your footnote. When finished, you quit the footnote procedure, and the document reappears on the screen.

When you print the document, the codes entered in the document are converted into sequential numbers, and the footnotes they refer to are printed at the bottom of the same page. To do this, the program must first calculate the length of the footnote, in lines, and then stop printing the text so that enough lines are available to print the footnote.

When you insert new footnotes or delete old ones, all footnote references in the document are automatically renumbered.

SUMMARY AND KEY TERMS

- **Footnotes** are numbered references printed at the bottom of the page.
- **Endnotes** are numbered references printed at the end of the document.
- If you insert or delete footnote or endnote reference numbers in the document, all the following reference numbers automatically adjust.

REVIEW QUESTIONS

1. What is the difference between a footnote and an endnote?
2. What happens to a footnote reference number if you insert a new reference number above it?

Sorting

OBJECTIVE

After completing this topic, you will be able to

■ Describe how to sort lines, paragraphs, or record files

Many programs allow you to **sort**, that is, arrange tables, lists, paragraphs, or record files in a desired order.

DATA TO BE SORTED

To sort a file, you first determine what information to arrange in order. On most programs, you can sort either the entire document or just a specific section, which is similar to selecting a block of text to copy or move it.

SORT KEYS

When you sort a document, you must specify what the program is to use as the basis of the sort. For example, if you want to sort a table that has three columns—name, department, and extension—you can sort it by any column. Perhaps you want the names in alphabetic order to use as a phone directory or the extensions in numeric order for the maintenance department. When you sort, you must tell the program which column you want to sort by. The column you specify is called a **key**. When you select a key and sort the document, it is sorted based on the key, and all lines, paragraphs, or records are rearranged, not just the column that contains the keys. When you sort using a single key, it is the primary key. You can often also specify a secondary key.

The **primary key** is the field the document is first sorted by (Figure 4-105). Ideally, a primary key contains unique information, for example, a drivers license number, an employee number, or a social security number. Sometimes, a unique field does not exist or serve your purpose, for example, when you sort a file by names; then, a perfect sort is not achieved using just a primary key.

A **secondary key** is specified to break ties after the data has been sorted by the primary key (Figure 4-106). For example, if you are sorting a file that contains names, you may have more than one Smith or Jones in the file. If

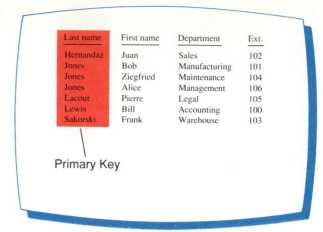

A. Original File

B. Records Sorted on Last Name

Primary Key

FIGURE 4-105
Sorting
Sorting can arrange a file in a specified order. The listings in the original table (a) were entered in a random order. The file was then sorted by specifying the last name as the primary key (b). The sort arranged the last names in ascending alphabetical order, so all the people named Jones are shown below Hernandaz and above Lewis.

you enter their first and last names into separate fields, you can use the secondary key to arrange all the Smiths or Joneses into ascending order using their last names as the primary key and their first names as the secondary key.

Some programs provide for more than one secondary key; if any ties occur in the first two sorts, they can be broken by using a third key.

SORT ORDER

When you sort data, you must specify the order it is to be arranged in. You choose between ascending and descending orders (Figure 4-107). The way data is sorted depends on how the program is set up, but usually the program follows the rules shown in Table 4-8. For example, if you specify an ascending sort, the file is arranged so that any special characters are at the top of the document, followed by numbers arranged from 0 to the highest number, followed by words beginning with uppercase letters from A to Z, followed by words beginning with lowercase letters from a to z. If you specify a descending sort, the order of the file is reversed.

FIGURE 4-106
Secondary Key
A secondary key can break ties in a sort. In the first sort (Figure 4-105), all the last names are in order, but Jones, Ziegfried is listed above Jones, Alice. When the first name is specified as the secondary key, and the names are sorted again, the names are in correct order by both last and first names.

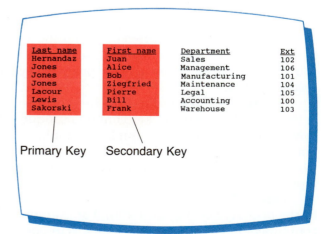

Primary Key   Secondary Key

WORD PROCESSING AND DESKTOP PUBLISHING APPLICATIONS

Before Sort	After Ascending Sort	After Descending Sort
5	#	b
a	4	a
A	5	B
#	A	A
B	B	5
b	a	4
4	b	#

FIGURE 4-107
Sort Order
In an ascending sort, data are arranged in ascending order from the top of the file to the bottom. In a descending sort, data are arranged in descending order from the top to the bottom.

TABLE 4-8
Ascending and Descending Sorts

Characters	Ascending	Descending
Special characters	1 (first)	4 (last)
Numbers	2	3
Uppercase letters	3	2
Lowercase letters	4 (last)	1 (first)

TIPS: Sorting

If your program does not allow you to specify secondary keys, you can achieve the same effect by sorting the data more than once. For example, you might want to sort a list of employees by last name and then by first name. To do this, you sort the table twice. You sort the less important field first, in this case, the first name. You then sort the more important field, in this case, the last name. When both sorts are completed, all employees are listed in order by last name. When two or more employees have the same last name, they are arranged in order by first name.

- **Sorting** is used to arrange tables, lists, paragraphs, or records into a desired order.
- **Sort keys** determine the basis for the sort. The **primary key** specifies what is sorted first. If there are any ties, a **secondary key** can break them.
- When sorting, you can specify if the data is to be sorted into **ascending** or **descending order**.

SUMMARY AND KEY TERMS

1. Why would you want to sort data?
2. What is a sort key? What is the difference between a primary key and a secondary key?
3. What is a sort order? What are the two orders you can use?

REVIEW QUESTIONS

Outlines

OBJECTIVE

After completing this topic, you will be able to

- Describe the differences between outlines and outliners

Programs have two kinds of outlining functions. You use an **outline** function to create standard numbered and indented outlines. You use an **outliner** to organize the text in the document when the headings in the outline and the body text are linked.

OUTLINES

When you want to create a standard outline, you use numbers and indents to identify the levels in the outline. As Figure 4-108 shows, the numbering style can take any one of several forms. Indenting is used to reinforce the numbering system—the lower the level of the outline entry, the more it is indented.

Programs with an outline function automatically number the outline's entries. The level of the number is determined automatically by the number of tab stops it is indented. For example, an entry flush with the left margin may be numbered I, the next entry indented one tab stop may be numbered A, and the next, indented two tab stops, may be numbered 1. If you insert or delete any of the entries, or change the tab stops any of them are aligned with, all the entries below are automatically renumbered. Many programs with this feature allow you to select from various numbering styles.

OUTLINERS

One of the more recent developments in word processing are *outliners*, which allow you to organize your ideas and text before and during writing. Outliners ought not to be confused with outlines that are entered like other documents. Outlines created with an outliner have levels that are automatically numbered and linked to text in the document. The hallmark of an outliner is its ability to display your entire text, **document view**, or just the headings, **outline view** (Figure 4-109). This ability to switch between the headings, which is just like an outline, and the entire document is a powerful feature when you work on long, complicated reports.

A. Standard Outline Numbering

I. THIS IS A LEVEL 1 ENTRY
  A. This is a level 2 Entry
    1. This is a level 3 entry
II. THIS IS ANOTHER LEVEL 1 ENTRY

B. Legal Outline Numbering

1. THIS IS A LEVEL 1 ENTRY
  1.1 This is a level 2 Entry
    1.1.1. This is a level 3 entry
2. THIS IS ANOTHER LEVEL 1 ENTRY

FIGURE 4-108
Outline
Outlines can be numbered in a variety of styles. Here, you see (a) standard outline numbering and (b) legal outline numbering.

- When the document is displayed in its outline view, you can highlight one or more adjacent headings and move, copy, or delete them. When you do this, you also move, copy, or delete the text you have entered under those headings.
- You can analyze on two levels, by content and by organization. When displayed in document view, the text can be entered and edited the same as a normal document. When displayed in outline view, the headings can be moved up or down levels or elsewhere in the outline at the same level. Text can then be entered using the outline as a guide.
- As you get ideas, you can enter them under existing headings, or you can add new headings.

FIGURE 4-109
Outliner
Outliners allow you to view (a) the entire document or (b) only the headings. You can easily switch back and forth between these two views to check both contents and organization.

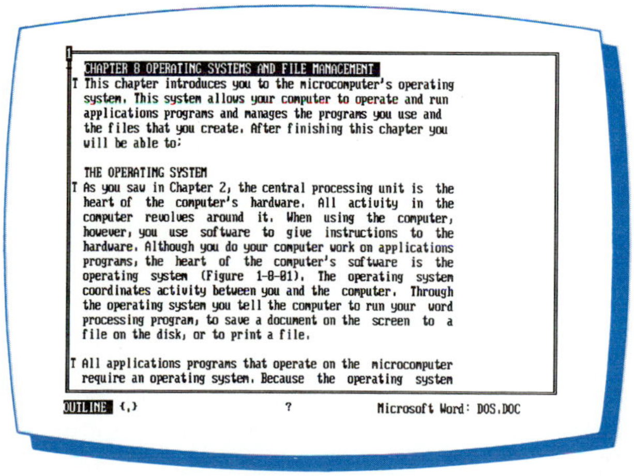

A. Document View

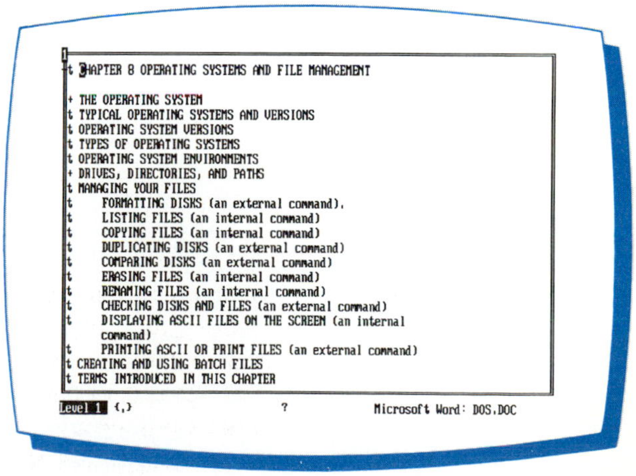

B. Outline View

- You can move around a long document quickly because moving through the outline is faster than moving through the text. You display the document in outline view, move the cursor to the heading of the section you want, and then display the document in document view.

SUMMARY AND KEY TERMS

- Some programs allow you to create **outlines** that are automatically numbered.
- Some programs include **outliners** that allow you to create an outline and use it as the basis for text entry, editing, and reorganization.

REVIEW QUESTIONS

1. What is the primary difference between an outline function and an outliner?
2. When you want more than one level of numbering, how do you control the numbering level assigned to an entry?
3. What are the two views offered by an outliner? How do they differ?

Filling Out Forms

OBJECTIVES

After completing this topic, you will be able to

- Describe how printer advance commands can be used to fill out preprinted forms
- Explain on-screen forms

Many programs now have features that make it easy for you to fill out preprinted forms or to create your own forms and fill them out when needed. There are two ways to do this, with on-screen forms or printer advance commands.

On-screen forms let you duplicate a form on the screen (Figure 4-110). Special commands then automatically move the cursor from blank to blank so that you can fill out the form. When you print the entry, you can print the form headings or only the entries you made into a preprinted form.

Printer advance commands enter codes into a document to vertically advance the printer one or more lines and horizontally advance the printer one or more characters. The entries for each line of the form can be stored together in the document but printed in the desired spaces in the form. (Figure 4-111).

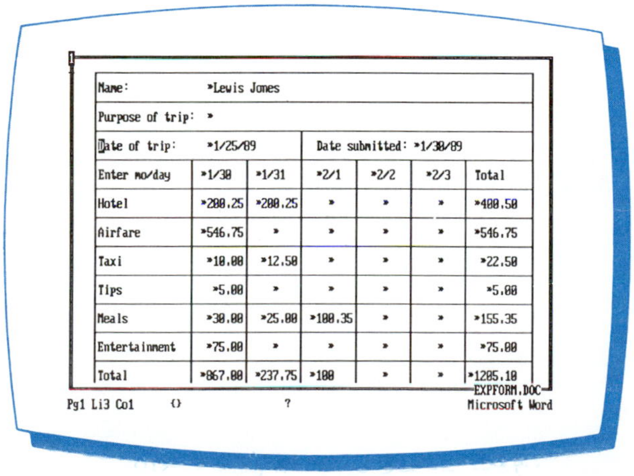

Name:	»Lewis Jones					
Purpose of trip:	»					
Date of trip:	»1/25/89		Date submitted: »1/30/89			
Enter mo/day	»1/30	»1/31	»2/1	»2/2	»2/3	Total
Hotel	»200.25	»200.25	»	»	»	»400.50
Airfare	»546.75	»	»	»	»	»546.75
Taxi	»10.00	»12.50	»	»	»	»22.50
Tips	»5.00	»	»	»	»	»5.00
Meals	»30.00	»25.00	»100.35	»	»	»155.35
Entertainment	»75.00	»	»	»	»	»75.00
Total	»867.00	»237.75	»100	»	»	»1205.10

FIGURE 4-110
On-Screen Form
Some programs allow you to create forms on the screen that you then fill out and print.

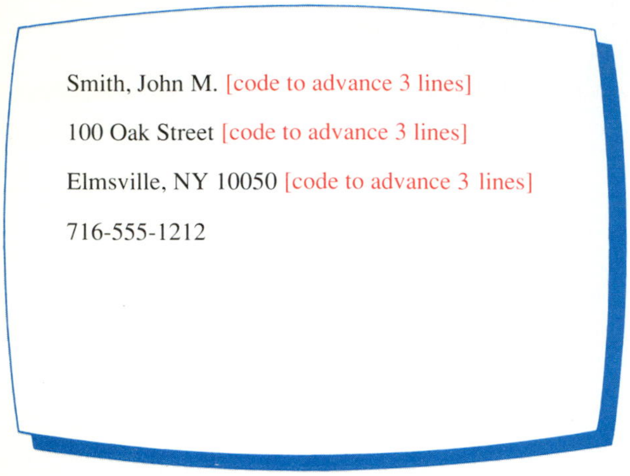

Smith, John M. [code to advance 3 lines]

100 Oak Street [code to advance 3 lines]

Elmsville, NY 10050 [code to advance 3 lines]

716-555-1212

A.

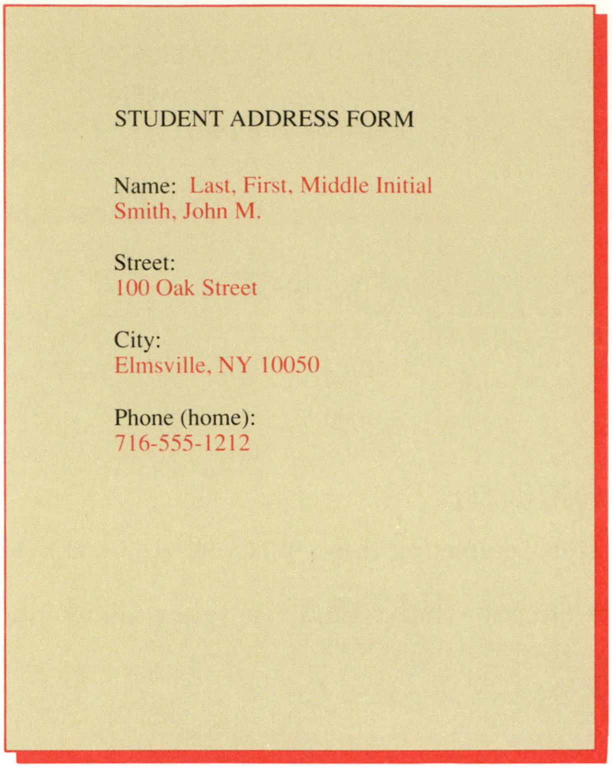

STUDENT ADDRESS FORM

Name: Last, First, Middle Initial
Smith, John M.

Street:
100 Oak Street

City:
Elmsville, NY 10050

Phone (home):
716-555-1212

FIGURE 4-111
Printer Advance
Printer advance can be used to fill out preprinted forms. (a) Here, four lines of text have been entered on the screen. The first three are followed by codes that tell the printer to advance three lines before printing the next line. (b) When the document is printed, the printer fills in the form where the entry spaces are three lines apart.

SUMMARY AND KEY TERMS

- **Printer advance commands** advance the printer up and down or left and right the specified distance.
- **On-screen forms** provide spaces on the screen that match the spaces on a preprinted form.

REVIEW QUESTIONS

1. What is printer advance, and when might you want to use it?
2. What is an on-screen form?

Word Processing Macros

OBJECTIVES

After completing this topic, you will be able to

■ Describe macros and explain what they are used for

■ Explain how you can record and play back macros

Since many of the tasks you perform while word processing are repetitive, you often find yourself pressing the same sequence of keys to save, retrieve, or print files; indent paragraphs; boldface or underline words; and so on. Some programs allow you to use **macros** (also called *keyboard programs*) to automate these repetitive tasks. Macros record a series of keystrokes so that you can then play them back with just a few keystrokes. Recording and playing back keystrokes is easy and can save you a lot of time if you use the same series of keystrokes over and over again.

■ You can record sections of text, just as if they were stored in a glossary or library (see Topic 4-24).

■ You can record and then execute a series of commands. If you have to press five or six keys to execute a command, you can store those keystrokes in a macro and execute it by pressing as few as two keys.

■ Some programs allow you to enter a pause in a macro when you record it. When you play back the macro, it executes all keystrokes up to the pause and then waits for you to enter text or other keystrokes from the keyboard. When you do so and then press **Return**, the macro continues. This is useful when all but a few of the keystrokes are the same. For example, you can record all the keystrokes needed to retrieve a file from the disk but enter a pause so that you can type in the desired file's name.

There are usually four steps to recording keystrokes.

1. You issue a command to tell the program to begin recording keystrokes.
2. You assign the keystrokes to a key on the keyboard, or you assign it a name.
3. You type the keys you want to record.
4. You issue a command to end recording.

When you want to replay the keystrokes (called executing the macro), you usually hold down **Alt** or **Ctrl** while pressing the letter key you assigned it to. If you assigned it a name, you execute the playback command, type the name of the macro, and then press **Return**.

The most powerful word processing programs allow you to retrieve the files macros are stored in so that you can edit them. This way, you can correct any mistakes you may have made or add additional procedures without having to record the keystrokes.

SUMMARY AND KEY TERMS

- **Macros** are used to record and then play back a series of keystrokes. This is useful when entering repetitive text or when formatting several sections using the same series of commands.

- To record a macro, you turn on record mode, type the text or commands to be recorded, turn off record mode, and specify a name for the macro.

REVIEW QUESTIONS

1. Describe the purpose of keyboard macros.
2. List the steps you would follow to record a macro.
3. How do you play back a recorded macro?

Part Five

SPREADSHEET APPLICATIONS

Topic 5-1   Spreadsheet Procedures: An Overview
Topic 5-2   Getting Acquainted with Your Program
Topic 5-3   Typical Spreadsheet Programs
Topic 5-4   Labels and Numbers
Topic 5-5   Ranges
Topic 5-6   Editing Models
Topic 5-7   Formulas
Topic 5-8   Functions
Topic 5-9   Printing Models
Topic 5-10   Changing a Model's Appearance
Topic 5-11   Copying and Moving Data
Topic 5-12   Relative and Absolute Cell References
Case Study   Creating a Five-Year Plan
Topic 5-13   Windows and Fixed Titles
Topic 5-14   Recalculation Methods
Topic 5-15   Lookup Tables
Topic 5-16   Data Tables
Topic 5-17   Date and Time Functions
Topic 5-18   Protection and Security
Topic 5-19   Linking, Combining, and Extracting Files
Topic 5-20   Graphs
Topic 5-21   Data Management
Topic 5-22   Spreadsheet Macros
Topic 5-23   User-Defined Menus
Topic 5-24   Troubleshooting Models

Until recently, accounting, financial analysis, and other mathematical calculations were done by laboriously entering numbers on pages of an accountant's ruled ledger pad, or spreadsheet. The development of spreadsheet applications programs has taken much of the drudgery out of analysis. It may still take as much time to gather the data needed to analyze a situation, but that is where the similarity between the old and new ways ends. You can quickly create a **model** of the financial situation on a spreadsheet program by entering labels, numbers, and formulas. Using the program's built-in functions, you can quickly perform complicated calculations like calculating interest earned and monthly payments on a loan. You can then use the completed model to explore **what-if** questions. If you change any variable—for instance, the price, discount, or sales patterns—the model will recalculate a new result automatically and instantly.

You can save a spreadsheet model and use it again whenever you or others need it. Never again will you forget how a specific analysis was done and have to reconstruct it from scratch the next time you need to use it. Often, when you work with an existing model, you will find ways to make it better and more efficient. Your models will grow in power and simplicity. You can save each revision to provide the base for the next step forward in your understanding and analysis.

Many spreadsheet programs are available, and more are sure to come. But as you will see in this part, many principles are common to all of them. If you understand these principles, you can quickly learn any spreadsheet program.

You may think spreadsheets require a strong background in mathematics; after all, they are primarily used to manipulate numbers. Relax—you could not be further from the truth. Spreadsheets use math, but they do the laborious calculations, not you. Many spreadsheets also contain functions that simplify complex calculations. Spreadsheets allow you to logically approach problems because they make it possible to focus on the problem, not on the calculations. Spreadsheets put tools for analysis and problem solving, once useful only to professionals, within the reach of any interested user.

APPLICATIONS OF SPREADSHEETS

Spreadsheets are used throughout business to analyze almost any type of problem that involves numbers and calculations. Here are some typical business applications they are used for.

Financial Analysis

Any problem that can be quantified can be solved or analyzed with a spreadsheet. In business, spreadsheets analyze the performance of products, sales people, or dealers. They compare costs, prices, and gross margins on individual products in a product line. They also calculate prices, forecast and make budgets for sales, predict expenses and profits, and make cash-flow projections.

■ Analyzing the performance of products, sales people, or dealers. Models can be created to compare sales or expenses by salesperson, sales territory, market, product, or product line. The model can calculate month-to-month results and compare them to previous periods in dollars and as percentages of total amounts.

■ Comparing costs, prices, and gross margins on individual products in a product line. There is a rule that 80 percent of your sales are generated by 20 percent of your products. Spreadsheets provide the perfect tool to identify the strong and weak contributors to your sales. Taking the analysis one step further, comparisons can be made between costs, prices, gross margins, and units to find the major contributors to profits, which may or may not be the same as the major contributors to sales revenues.

- Exploring alternative investments. Using a spreadsheet and its built-in functions to calculate payback periods, returns on investments, and internal rates of returns, you can explore the outcomes under different conditions, for example, changing interest rates.

- Calculating prices. You can explore the results of various approaches such as gross margin and markup over cost to see what your gross margin would be after inventory shrinkage and markdowns.

- Preparing and analyzing monthly financial statements. Models for these statements can be created so that they automatically calculate operating ratios (all expenses shown as a percentage of net sales) and financial ratios, such as the current and quick ratios that reveal your liquidity, and debt-to-equity ratios that show how "leveraged" your firm is. Reducing your raw numbers to ratios like these not only makes your analysis easier but also allows you to compare your results with other firms in the same industry. Many industry associations and financial organizations periodically publish surveys of average industry ratios against which you can compare your own performance.

- Forecasting and budgeting of sales, expenses, or profits. This can be done periodically and compared to actual results so that changes and trends can be seen both in dollars and percentages.

- Projecting cash flow. These projections can be completed in just hours when done regularly with a model customized to your own business. You can see cash shortfalls and surpluses far enough in advance to line up needed financing or take advantage of new investment opportunities.

- Analyzing trends. Raw numbers may not tell the whole story; the real picture may be revealed only through trend analysis. For instance, profits this month may be 10 percent of revenues, which sounds acceptable, but careful analysis may show they were 12 percent in the same period last year and 14 percent the year before.

Downloading from Mainframe or On-Line Computers

Many corporations store large databases of valuable information on mainframe computers. The cost of designing programs that can uniquely analyze this data for departments or individuals usually outweighs the benefits, at least as viewed by top management. But with the right computer system, users can gain access to this information and copy it from the mainframe to their own computers (called downloading), where it can then be analyzed using a spreadsheet. When downloaded, the numbers do not have to be manually entered into the spreadsheet. This saves time and eliminates the possibility of introducing errors.

Outside databases holding vast amounts of information are also available to companies and individuals. All you need to obtain information for analysis is a modem, a communications program, and the willingness to pay the service's usage fees. These services include such well-known ones as Dow Jones News/Retrieval Service and The Source.

Development of Data for Graphs and Charts

Graphs are powerful analytical tools. They can show trends and relationships between series of numbers that would otherwise be missed. For example, a spreadsheet may show sales and costs are both rising. But the relative rates of change are much more obvious on a graph. If sales are rising faster than expenses, profits will increase; if they are rising more slowly, profits will fall. Spreadsheets are an ideal tool to develop the numbers that are then graphed. The spreadsheet-graphics combination is so useful that many spreadsheet programs now come with an integrated graphics capability. This feature makes it so easy to create graphs that they become a valuable tool for exploring what-if analyses, not just for presenting the finished results to others.

Data Management Models

Models for listing, sorting, and extracting any information that can be organized by rows and columns, such as mailing lists, inventory items, and employee payroll records, can be stored in spreadsheet files. Once entered, you can instantly sort data into ascending or descending order. On some programs, you can also extract data that matches a specific criterion. For example, you can list the names and phone extensions of all employees in the marketing department or list all customers in the state of Ohio.

REVIEW QUESTIONS

1. What is what-if analysis? Give an example.
2. Do you have to be skilled at performing arithmetic calculations when using a spreadsheet?
3. What are some common spreadsheet applications?

Spreadsheet Procedures: An Overview

OBJECTIVES

After completing this topic, you will be able to

- Describe the terms *spreadsheet*, *model*, and *template*
- List the steps you follow to create a typical model

One of the primary uses of spreadsheets is to build models to analyze financial or other situations and to explore the effects that changes have on the outcome. You use models to simulate real-world situations. Just as a plastic model of an airplane represents, or simulates, a real plane, a spreadsheet model simulates financial or other situations. When using a spreadsheet, you should understand three basic terms: spreadsheet, model, and template.

A **spreadsheet** (sometimes called a worksheet) is the arrangement of horizontal rows and vertical columns that appears on the screen when you first load the program.

A **model** is the data you enter into the spreadsheet to solve a problem or perform an analysis. To create a model, you use two basic types of entries: labels and values. **Labels** describe or identify parts of the model. **Values** are the numbers to be analyzed and the formulas and built-in functions that perform the analysis.

A **template** is a model all the numbers have been removed from. Since it still retains all the labels, formulas, and functions, you can enter new numbers in the spaces indicated by the labels and the formulas calculate an answer. Mastering a spreadsheet and the business principles needed to analyze a problem takes time. In many firms, people who understand the principles behind an application often collaborate with those who understand a spreadsheet to develop templates of great value to others in the firm. These templates are designed to be used over and over again by anyone who knows how to move the cursor and enter the numbers to be analyzed.

You use spreadsheet models to simulate real-world financial or other situations. Suppose you want to buy a new car and explore how much you can spend while keeping your monthly payments about $170 a month. You probably would not know the actual arithmetic involved, so the first step is to research how monthly payments are calculated. This is the first rule of computer literacy: You cannot use a computer to solve a problem you do not understand.

The principles behind the calculations are quite simple. In this example

- You have between $2,000 and $2,500 for a down payment.
- You know the loan required is the total cost of the car minus the down payment.
- You know the monthly payments are based on the loan amount, interest rate, and term of the loan. These are the numbers you want to explore to see how changes affect the monthly payment. The model you create must have places where you can enter these variables.
- You have discovered that your spreadsheet program has a built-in function that calculates monthly payments if you tell it what amount, interest rate, and period to use.

This is a typical problem that you can quickly solve on a spreadsheet. Now that you know what you want to do, you create the model.

STEP 1: LOAD THE PROGRAM

The first step in creating a model is to load the program so that the spreadsheet is displayed on the screen (Figure 5-1). If you are planning to save your work, you also insert a formatted data disk into drive B, and then close that drive's door.

STEP 2: ENTER LABELS

You enter labels to identify the contents of rows and columns so that you, and others, can understand the model (Figure 5-2). Labels are simply text characters, much like those you would enter on a word processing program.

STEP 3: ENTER NUMBERS

You enter numbers to be used in calculations (Figure 5-3). Numbers can be added, subtracted, multiplied, and divided. You can also format the numbers (and formulas and functions) so that they are displayed with dollar signs, commas, or percent signs.

STEP 4: ENTER FORMULAS

You enter a formula to calculate the amount of the loan required (Figure 5-4). Since you know the cost of the car is $10,000 and your down payment is $2,000, you could subtract the two numbers and enter the result. But if

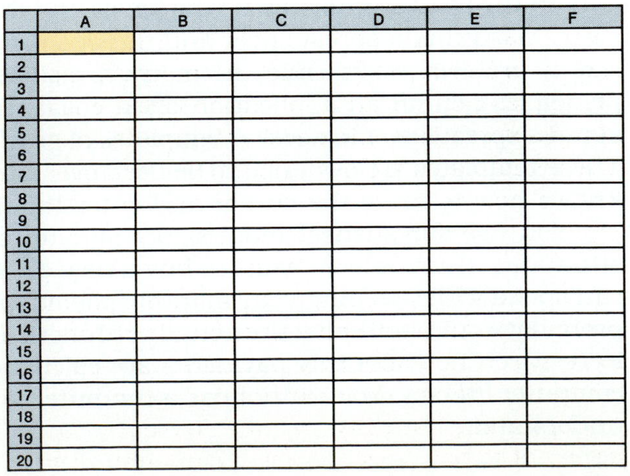

FIGURE 5-1
The Spreadsheet Screen Display
The spreadsheet on the screen is divided into rows and columns much like a ledger pad (see Topic 5-2). Each of the rectangles where rows and columns intersect is a **cell**. It is into these cells that you enter labels, numbers, formulas, and functions.

	A	B	C	D	E	F
1	Cost of car					
2	Down payment					
3	Loan required					
4	Interest rate					
5	Term of loan (in months)					
6	Monthly payment					
7						
8						

FIGURE 5-2
Enter Labels
Labels identify the contents of rows (and columns). Here you enter labels for each row on the auto loan model where you will want to enter numbers, formulas, or functions.

	A	B	C	D	E	F
1	Cost of car	$10,000				
2	Down payment	2,000				
3	Loan required					
4	Interest rate	13%				
5	Term of loan (in months)	36				
6	Monthly payment					
7						
8						

FIGURE 5-3
Enter Numbers
The numbers entered in the model include the cost of the car ($10,000), the down payment ($2,000), the interest rate (13%), and the term of the loan (36 months).

	A	B	C	D	E	F
1	Cost of car	$10,000				
2	Down payment	2,000				
3	Loan required	8,000	← +B1-B2			
4	Interest rate	13%				
5	Term of loan (in months)	36				
6	Monthly payment					
7						
8						

FIGURE 5-4
Enter Formulas
You enter the formula B1-B2 into cell B4. This formula tells the spreadsheet program to subtract the value in cell B2 from the value in cell B1. The result calculated by the formula is 8,000 (10,000 cost in cell B1 minus the 2,000 down payment in cell B2). As you can see, the spreadsheet displays the calculated result, not the formula entered into the cell to calculate it. Moreover, the computer remembers the cells you want subtracted, not their values. This way, if you change the values in either of the cells that the formula refers to, the program automatically calculates a new answer.

you did this, the number would not change if you changed either the cost of the car or the down payment. If you enter a formula that refers to the two cells those numbers are entered in, the loan you require does change if you change the cost of the car or the down payment.

STEP 5: ENTER A FUNCTION

Formulas, like the one that calculates the amount of the loan required, are powerful, but spreadsheets have a special type of formula called a **function** that is even more so. Functions are built into the program and are designed to replace very complicated formulas. In this step, you enter a function that calculates the monthly payment on the loan (Figure 5-5).

STEP 6: EXPLORE WHAT-IFS

So far, the only exciting things you have seen are that formulas and functions perform calculations. Not much to write home about. But now we explore the real power of a spreadsheet—its ability to reflect instantly the changes made in variables (called what-ifs or *sensitivity analysis*).

Since the monthly payment based on the original terms is more than you want to pay, let's see if you can achieve your goal of a payment of about

FIGURE 5-5

Enter Functions
You now enter the program's built-in function that calculates monthly payments into cell B9. The actual function is @PMT(B4,B6/12,B7). You learn about functions in Topic 5-8. For now all you have to understand is that in English, this function reads "calculate and display the monthly payment based on the amount of the loan in cell B4, the annual interest rate in cell B6 (divided by 12 to convert the annual rate into a monthly rate), and the term of the loan in cell B7." The calculated answer is $269.55, way above your goal of $170 a month.

	A	B	C	D	E	F
1	Cost of car	$10,000				
2	Down payment	2,000				
3	Loan required	8,000				
4	Interest rate	13%				
5	Term of loan (in months)	36				
6	Monthly payment	$269.55	← @PMT(B3,B4/12,B5)			
7						
8						

$170 a month. You can easily change the terms of the loan or the price of the car until you find monthly payments that are within a few dollars of your goal. You can also easily explore more what-ifs either to find even lower monthly payments or to compare two or more different deals.

- What if you increase the term of the loan from 36 to 48 months (Figure 5-6)?
- What if you increase the down payment from $2,000 to $2,500 (Figure 5-7)?
- What if you reduce the cost of the car from $10,000 to $9,000 (Figure 5-8)?
- What if you go to a bank that offers a lower interest rate (Figure 5-9)?

STEP 7: PRINT THE MODEL

If you want to share your results with others, or have a copy for your files, you can make a printout. The spreadsheet's *Print* command sends data displayed on the screen to the printer (see Topic 5-9).

STEP 8: SAVE THE MODEL

When creating or entering data into models, be sure to save them often—not just when you finish them. Turning off the computer, power failures, hardware problems, or your own mistakes can cause you to lose files that are in the computer's memory. If you erase the numbers (here, the cost of the car, down payment, interest rate, and term of the loan) and then save the model, you convert the model into a template. Anyone can then retrieve the blank template, enter their own data, and analyze their own car purchase plans.

To save a model, you first assign it a filename acceptable to your computer's operating system, and then execute the program's *Save* command. If the file has already been saved, you have a choice to make. If you save it under the same name, it will overwrite and erase the previous version. You can, however, change the file's name so that a series of versions is saved, which enables you to recall any previous version. Some programs will automatically convert the previous version into a backup copy when a file is saved the second and subsequent times, ensuring that you have the most recent version available if you discover a mistake.

After you save a model, you can retrieve it using the spreadsheet's commands to retrieve files from a disk and load them into memory.

STEP 9: QUIT OR CLEAR THE SCREEN

When you are finished with a model and have saved it, you can work on another model or quit the program.

	A	B	C	D	E	F
1	Cost of car	$10,000				
2	Down payment	2,000				
3	Loan required	8,000				
4	Interest rate	13%				
5	Term of loan (in months)	48				
6	Monthly payment	$214.62				
7						
8						

FIGURE 5-6
What If You Increase the Term of Loan?
To change the term of the loan, you move the cursor to cell B7, type 48 over the current 36 months, and then press **Return**. The function in cell B9 calculates and displays the new monthly payment of $214.62.

	A	B	C	D	E	F
1	Cost of car	$10,000				
2	Down payment	2,500				
3	Loan required	7,500				
4	Interest rate	13%				
5	Term of loan (in months)	48				
6	Monthly payment	$201.21				
7						
8						

FIGURE 5-7
What If You Increase the Down Payment?
If you increase the down payment in cell B2 by $500 (from $2,000 to $2,500), the loan required in cell B3 falls from $8,000 to $7,500. The monthly payment in cell B7 decreases to $201.21.

	A	B	C	D	E	F
1	Cost of car	$9,000				
2	Down payment	2,500				
3	Loan required	6,500				
4	Interest rate	13%				
5	Term of loan (in months)	48				
6	Monthly payment	$174.38				
7						
8						

FIGURE 5-8
What If You Buy a Less Expensive Car?
If you change the cost of the car in cell A1, the loan required in cell B3 falls from $7,500 to $6,500. The monthly payment in cell B7 falls to $174.38.

	A	B	C	D	E	F
1	Cost of car	$9,000				
2	Down payment	2,500				
3	Loan required	6,500				
4	Interest rate	12%				
5	Term of loan (in months)	48				
6	Monthly payment	$171.17				
7						
8						

FIGURE 5-9
What If You Get a Lower Interest Rate?
If you lower the interest rate in cell B4 by 1% (from 13% to 12%), the monthly payment drops to $171.17.

Clearing the Screen

If you want to stay in the program but begin work on a new model, you clear the old model off the spreadsheet using the program's *Clear, Zap,* or *Erase* command. Before you use this command, be sure you have saved the file with the *Save* command. If you erase data from the spreadsheet without first saving it, the data is lost.

If the model you want to work on has already been created and saved on a disk, you use the program's *Retrieve* command. On some programs, retrieving a model from the disk automatically clears the old model from the screen and the computer's memory. On other programs, each model is displayed in its own window, so you have to open new windows for each model and then close them when finished.

Quitting the Program

You quit a program when you want to return to the operating system to quit for the day or perhaps to use another program.

When you are finished with a session, you quit the program with the *Quit* command.

SUMMARY AND KEY TERMS

- After loading the program, you build models by entering labels, numbers, formulas, and functions.
- To explore what-ifs, you change one or more numbers to see how the results calculated by formulas change.

REVIEW QUESTIONS

1. What is the difference between a spreadsheet and a model?
2. What is the difference between a model and a template?
3. What is the purpose of a spreadsheet's functions?
4. What is sensitivity analysis? Give an example.
5. How do you change the data in a cell?
6. What is the model called if you erase all the numbers leaving just the labels, formulas, and functions?
7. When you retrieve a file on some programs, what happens to the currently displayed model?
8. What is the difference between clearing the screen and quitting the program?

Getting Acquainted with Your Program

OBJECTIVES

After completing this topic, you will be able to

- Describe typical spreadsheet screen displays
- Explain how you move around a spreadsheet
- Explain how programs manage their memory
- Describe how you execute commands
- List typical modes, and explain what they mean

To use a spreadsheet, you must understand its screen display, how to move the cursor, and how to execute commands.

THE SPREADSHEET SCREEN DISPLAY

When you load a spreadsheet program, the spreadsheet is usually immediately displayed on the screen. Spreadsheet screen displays have two major areas, the working area and the control area (Figure 5-10).

← A. **FIGURE 5-10**
A Typical Spreadsheet Screen Display
The typical spreadsheet has two areas, the working area (a) and the control panel, which is located at the top or bottom of the screen (b).

- The **working area** (also called the *worksheet*) (Figure 5-11) is a window on the underlying spreadsheet where you create your models. To create models, you can make any of the cell entries described in Table 5-1.
- The **control area** (also called the *control panel* or *status area*) (Figure 5-12) is where menus, prompts, and messages are displayed.

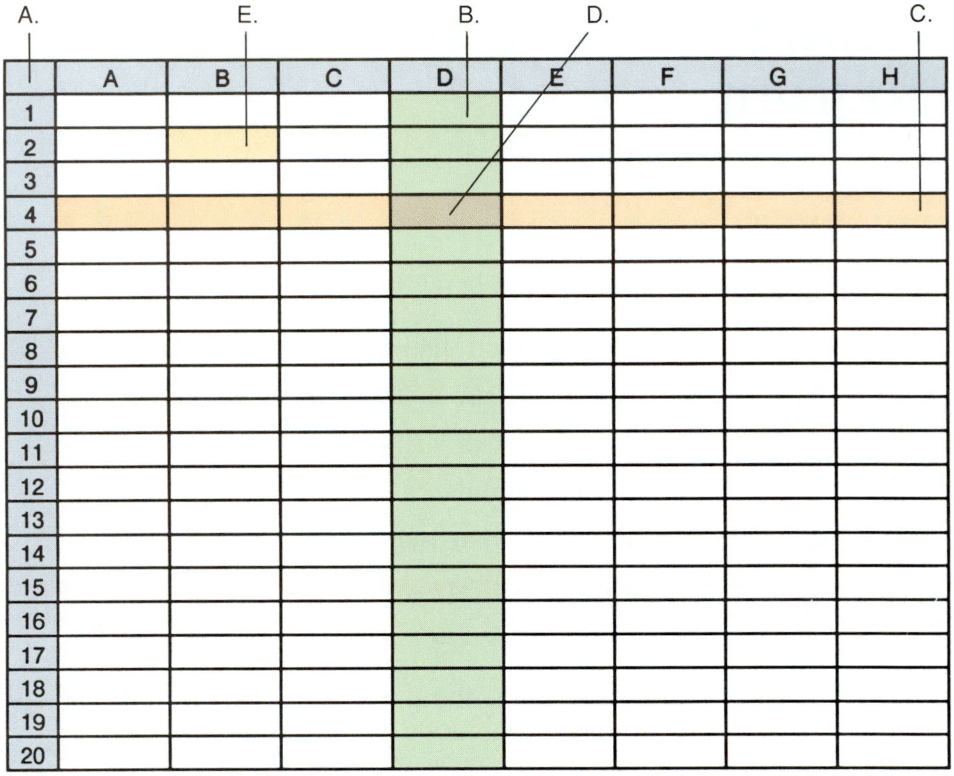

FIGURE 5-11
The Spreadsheet Working Area
The working area of a spreadsheet contains the following elements:

A. A border contains column letters across the top of the spreadsheet and row numbers down the left side. On some programs, these borders can be turned off so that the column and row labels do not appear on the screen. Borders do not usually appear on printouts, but on some programs, you can use a command to have them do so.

B. Columns run vertically down a spreadsheet and are labeled consecutively with letters. The first 26 columns are labeled A to Z, the next 26 are labeled AA to AZ, the next 26 are labeled BA to BZ, and so on.

C. Rows run horizontally across a spreadsheet and are labeled consecutively with numbers, starting with row 1 at the top of the spreadsheet.

D. Cells, the basic working units on a spreadsheet, fall at the intersection of each column and row. They are initially empty when the program is loaded and are referred to by their coordinates, or cell address. Cell addresses are indicated by specifying the column letter(s) followed by the row number.

- The cell at the intersection of column B and row 2 is cell B2.
- The cell at the intersection of column A and row 5 is cell A5.
- The cell at the intersection of column D and row 4 is cell D4.

E. The working area contains a bright reverse video highlight, called the **cursor**, cell pointer, or cell marker. You move this cursor by pressing the cursor movement keys to point to cells when you want to enter, delete, copy, move, or print data. The cell the cursor is positioned in is the active or current cell.

TABLE 5-1
Cell Entries

Entry	Description
Labels and columns of data	Identify models or individual rows
Numbers	Can be used in calculations when referred to by formulas
Formulas and functions	Can calculate numbers entered into the formula itself or into other cells the formula refer to
Formats	Control the way numbers are displayed on the screen and the way labels are aligned in their cells

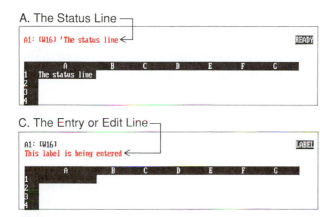

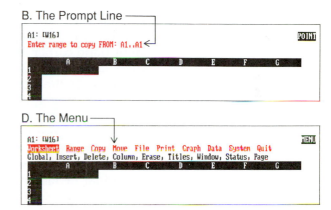

FIGURE 5-12
The Spreadsheet Control Area
The control area is located at the top or bottom of the screen display. The typical control area has three lines, either located together at the top or bottom of the screen. The control panel displays the following information:

A. The **status line** displays information about the cell the cursor is in.

- It indicates the cell's address
- The cell's contents, for example, a label, number, formula, or function. If the cell contains a formula or function, they, and not the calculated result, is displayed.
- The cell's format (for example, dollars, percentages, and so on) and protection status (protected or not protected from your entering new data).

Additional information is displayed on some programs. For example, the status line may display how much memory is left for your model.

B. The **prompt line** displays prompts or messages when the program wants you to provide information. For example, you may be asked to enter the name of the file you want to save or the width you want to set a column to.

C. The **entry** or **edit line** displays the characters that you type as you enter them or when you use the *Edit* command. When you press **Return**, the characters displayed on this line are entered into the cell that contains the cursor. Some programs have a second cursor, called the edit cursor, that appears on this line when you enter and edit data. By positioning it on the line, you can insert or delete characters.

D. The **menu**, or list of commands used to operate the program, is also displayed in this area. On some programs, the menu is displayed all the time; on others, only when a specific key is pressed.

GETTING AROUND A SPREADSHEET

The display screen is just a small window on a large spreadsheet (Figure 5-13), but as you will see, you can scroll it around the underlying spreadsheet with the cursor movement keys. When you want to enter data into cells or execute other commands, you point to cells. The four directional arrow keys move the cursor a cell at a time and repeat if you hold them down. Other keys, or combinations of keys, move the cursor in larger jumps. The larger your models are, the more important these keys and commands become.

For example, the *Goto* command moves the cursor quickly to a specific cell. This command displays a prompt that asks you what cell you want to go to. You just type in the cell coordinates, press **Return**, and the cursor immediately jumps to the specified cell. On many computers, pressing **PgUp** and **PgDn** scrolls you through the spreadsheet a screen page at a time, and pressing **Home** moves the cursor to cell A1 at the upper left-hand corner of the spreadsheet.

Most other commands involve a combination of keys. For example, when using Lotus 1-2-3 on an IBM PC, pressing **Home** moves the cursor to cell A1. But pressing **End** and then **Home** moves the cursor to the lower right-hand corner of the working area of the model. The keys used to make these larger moves depend on the program and computer you are using. Table 5-2 lists the cursor movement keys for Lotus 1-2-3.

Some programs include a search command that allows you to quickly move to a specified label, number, or formula.

As you move the cursor down a column or along a row, it eventually runs into one of the boundaries of the screen display (Figure 5-14). The next time you press the same key, the cursor stays against the edge of the screen (it cannot be moved off the screen), but the screen display scrolls to reveal the next row or column of the spreadsheet. As it does so, the leftmost column or topmost row scrolls off the other side of the screen. You can see this happen if you watch the row and column labels change as you scroll the screen. If the cursor runs into one of the boundaries of the spreadsheet, the computer beeps the next time you press the arrow key that points toward the boundary.

On some programs, you can engage **Scroll Lock** to keep the cursor in

FIGURE 5-13
The Screen Is a Window Onto the Spreadsheet
The display screen is a window onto a large spreadsheet in the computer's memory.

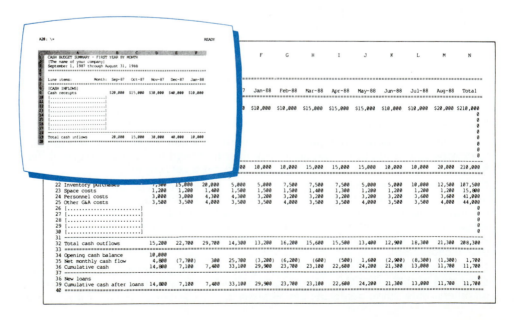

SPREADSHEET APPLICATIONS

TABLE 5-2
Cursor Movement Keys

To Move Cursor	Press	Enter Commands for Your Program
Right or left one column	→ or ←	_____
Up or down one row	↑ or ↓	_____
Right one full screen	**Tab** or **Ctrl-→**	_____
Left one full screen	**Shift-Tab** or **Ctrl-←**	_____
Up or down one full screen	**PgUp** or **PgDn**	_____
To upper left-hand corner (cell A1)	**Home**	_____
To lower right-and corner of working area	**End, Home**	_____
To specified cell	**Goto (F5)**, *cell coordinates*, **Return**	_____

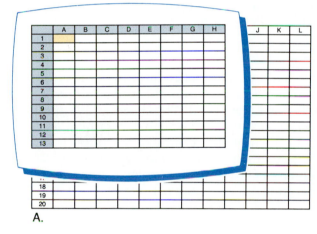

A.

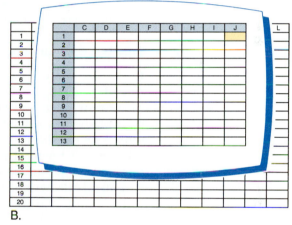

B.

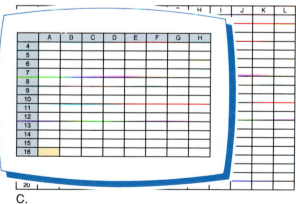

C.

FIGURE 5-14
Scrolling the Screen
Let's see how the screen scrolls:

A. If you position the cursor at the edge of the spreadsheet (called the boundary), pressing cursor movement keys to move it off the spreadsheet causes the cursor to stay where it is and the computer to beep. In this illustration, the cursor is in cell A1, the upper left-hand corner (boundary) of the spreadsheet. Pressing the up or left arrow keys will therefore cause the computer to beep.

B. If the cursor is against the right edge of the screen (but not against the right boundary of the spreadsheet) (A) pressing → causes the screen to scroll to the right (B)—revealing the next column while the column on the other side of the screen scrolls off the screen to make room for it.

C. If the cursor is against the bottom edge of the screen (but not against the bottom boundary of the spreadsheet) (A) pressing the ↓ causes the screen to scroll down (B)—revealing the next row while the row at the top of the screen scrolls off the screen to make room for it.

How Much of a Spreadsheet Can You Use?

The fact that a spreadsheet has a given number of cells doesn't mean you can use them all. The number you can actually use is determined by several factors: the memory your computer has, the shape of the spreadsheet you build, the way the program manages memory, and the data you enter.

For example, in 1987, Lotus published a student edition of their 1-2-3 (Release 2) program. Though the regular edition was priced at $595, the student edition was only $50. There were only a few differences between the student and regular editions, the main ones being file incompatibility and a limit on the number of rows and columns you can use. The student edition was limited to 64 columns and 256 rows, or 16,384 cells. The regular version has 256 columns and 8,192 rows, or 2,097,152 cells.

Some quick comparisons can be made to see just how small the usable capacity of the student edition is compared to the regular version. All these comparisons were made on a typically equipped IBM PC with 512KB of memory. The results might surprise you.

You begin by loading each program, and they leave only 292,400 bytes available for models.

Labels and Numbers

If you use the regular version and enter labels into the cells, you find that a single label, Test, causes the computer to run out of memory when 30,360 cells have been filled. This is only 1.45 percent of the number of cells claimed to be available. Numbers are stored more efficiently, so you can enter a number like 1000 into 73,728 cells before the computer runs out of memory. This is 3.52 percent of the claimed number of cells. On the student version, you can fill all cells without running out of memory. Therefore, you can build a much larger model on the regular version if you use just labels and numbers.

---

the same cell. When you then press the arrow keys, the screen scrolls just as it does when **Scroll Lock** is not engaged, but the cursor does not have to be against the edge of the display to make it do so. When the cursor reaches the edge of the screen, it stays there, and the spreadsheet scrolls under it.

MEMORY MANAGEMENT

If you ever use an accountant's ledger pad for financial analysis, you know that even those with only twenty or so columns can be unwieldy. Spreadsheets come in various sizes, all of them much larger than the largest ledger pads. The number of cells on a spreadsheet can be calculated by multiplying the number of rows by the number of columns. What if some typical spreadsheets were entirely printed out with each cell 1 inch wide and ¼ inch deep? How large would the printouts be? The sizes shown in Table 5-3 may surprise you.

Formulas and Functions

Nobody builds models with just labels and numbers, however; you also use formulas and functions. This is where the surprise comes in. What happens if you enter the simple formula 1+1? On the regular version, you can use only 9,126 cells, or 0.4 percent of its capacity. On the student edition, you can also use 9,126 cells, or 55.7 percent of its capacity. Regardless of the version, you run out of memory long before you run out of cells.

If you use more complicated formulas or functions, things get even worse. For example, here is what happens if you enter the function @IF(A1>1,0,1). On both versions, you can fill only 7,127 cells, 0.3 percent of the regular version's capacity and 43.2 percent of the student edition's.

What if you like complicated formulas, perhaps a payment function nested in an if statement, for *example*, @IF(@PMT (100000),.1,48)—0,1,0))? *On both* versions, you can use only 5,035 cells, 2 percent of the full version's capacity and 30.7 percent of the student edition's.

**Percent of Total Cells Used When
Out of Memory**

Version	Total Cells	Formula	Function	Nested Functions
Regular version	2,097,152	0.4%	0.3%	0.2%
Student edition	16,384	69.4%	54.2%	38.3%

The answer is clear. If you build average-sized models, build models with complex formulas, or don't have the latest add-on memory boards to boost memory above 512KB, you may never even press the limits of the student edition. You most likely will run out of memory before you run out of available cells.

**TABLE 5-3
Spreadsheet Sizes**

Programs	Columns	Rows	Cells	Size If Printed Width (in feet)	Height (in feet)
SuperCalc 3	63	254	16,002	5	5
MultiPlan	63	254	16,002	5	5
Lotus 1-2-3					
Release 1A	256	2,048	524,288	21	43
Release 2	256	8,192	2,097,152	21	171
Microsoft Excel	256	16,384	4,194,304	21	341

Just because a spreadsheet has a given number of cells does not mean you can use them all. The number you can actually use is determined by the memory your computer has, the shape of the spreadsheet you build, and the data you enter.

As you've seen, when you load a spreadsheet program into the computer, the program occupies a certain amount of the available memory. The amount of memory that is then available for you to create models is the difference between the total memory of your computer and the portion of that memory occupied by the program. When you create models, the computer's memory is gradually used up as the model expands in size. The amount of memory you use often depends partly on how you lay out your model (Figures 5-15 through 5-18). No matter where you enter data, most programs store a rectangular area, called the **active area**, in the computer's memory.

To prevent you from running out of memory if you cannot lay out your models as carefully as described, some programs allocate memory based on only the number of cells used. A program using **sparse memory management**, as this technique is called, ignores empty cells in the active area and does not allocate them to memory.

EXECUTING COMMANDS

To execute commands, you use the spreadsheet's menus. On many programs, you press the slash key (/) to display a menu at the top or bottom of the screen. On other programs, a menu bar is always displayed, and you press a key like **Alt** to activate it. One choice in the menu is always highlighted, and a brief description of the highlighted choice is displayed on the line below the menu. You can choose from the menu in one of three ways.

- You can type the first letter in the menu choice's name.
- You can press → or ← to move the highlight (sometimes called a menu pointer) over your choice, and then press **Return**. If you position the highlight over the first or last choice on the menu and then press the arrow key one more time, the highlight wraps around to the other end of the menu. You can quickly move to the first or last menu choice by pressing **Home** or **End**.
- You can point to a menu command with a pointer, and then click one of the buttons on a mouse.

FIGURE 5-15
Direct Entry in Lower Right-Hand Cell
Entering data (or even a format) into cell D4 causes all cells in the rectangular area with cell D4 in the lower right-hand corner to be allocated in memory.

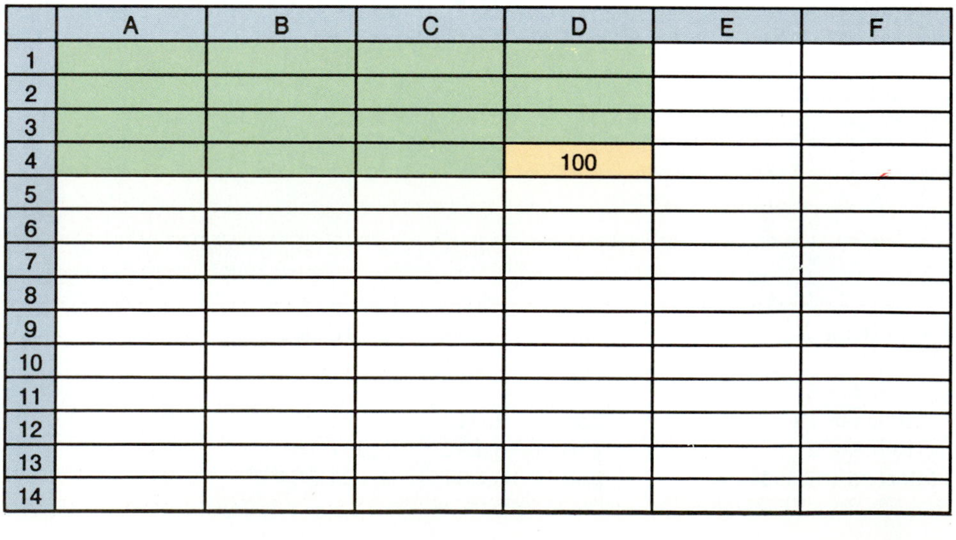

	A	B	C	D	E	F
1						
2						
3						
4				100		
5						
6						
7						
8						
9						
10						
11						
12						
13						
14						

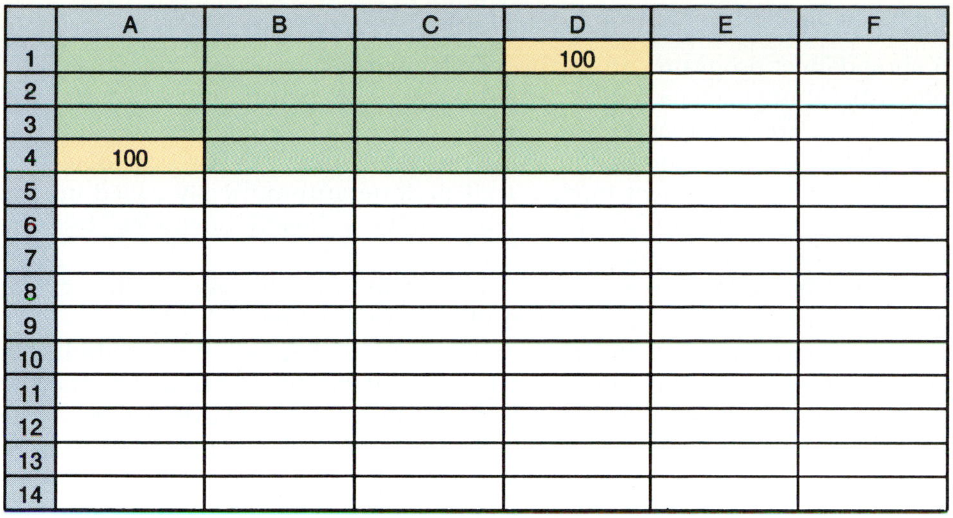

	A	B	C	D	E	F
1				100		
2						
3						
4	100					
5						
6						
7						
8						
9						
10						
11						
12						
13						
14						

FIGURE 5-16
Indirect Entry in Lower Right-Hand Cell
You do not have to enter data or formats into the lower right-hand corner of the active area to have it allocated in memory. If you enter data or formats into cells D1 and A4, it causes the same rectangular area to be allocated. For this reason, models should be kept as square as possible, with the lower right-hand corner as close to the upper left-hand corner as possible especially if memory is limited.

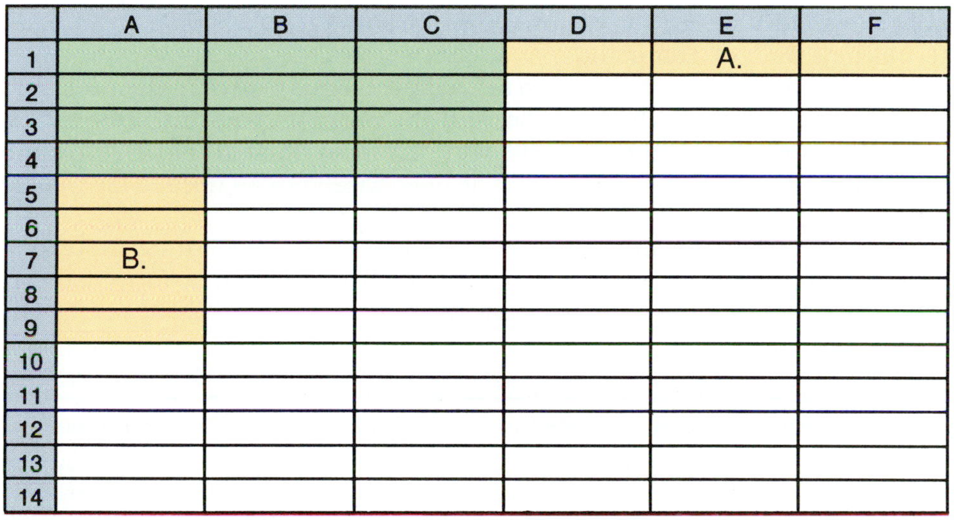

	A	B	C	D	E	F
1					A.	
2						
3						
4						
5						
6						
7	B.					
8						
9						
10						
11						
12						
13						
14						

FIGURE 5-17
Inefficient Layout
In this example, the model has been laid out on the spreadsheet so that the main part of the model occupies a small rectangular area. A few rows are used at the top of the screen (a) and a few columns down the side (b). The result is a rectangle of 54 cells allocated to memory (down to cell C12).

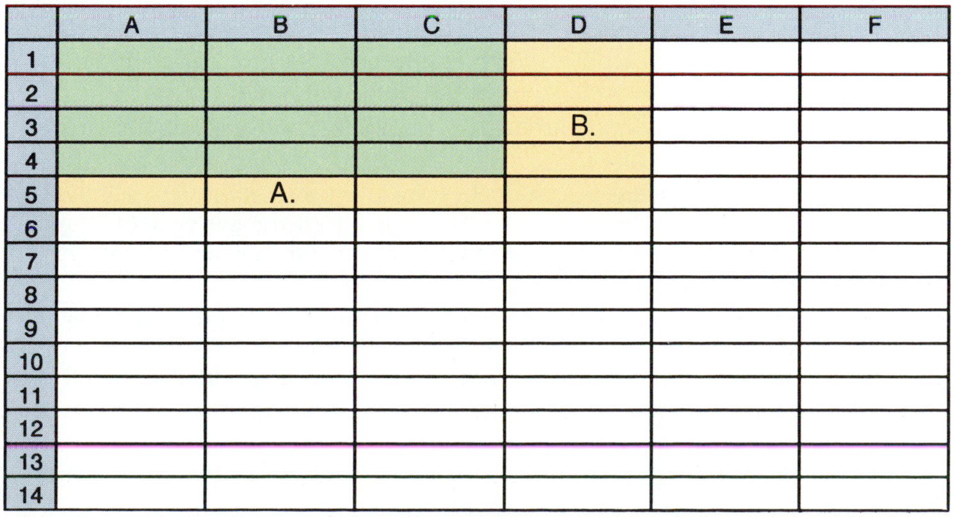

	A	B	C	D	E	F
1						
2						
3				B.		
4						
5		A.				
6						
7						
8						
9						
10						
11						
12						
13						
14						

FIGURE 5-18
Efficient Layout
By rearranging the layout slightly it becomes much more compact; only 20 cells are used, and the model requires less memory.

Mode Indicators

A spreadsheet program can perform only one task at a time. It can accept a new label that you type, but it cannot recalculate, print, or save a file at the same time. For this reason, the current mode is often displayed so that you know what the program is doing or what information it is ready to accept. You do not have to select modes; that is done automatically based on the steps you are performing. All programs have a variety of modes, but the most common are the following:

In **ready mode**, the program is in "neutral" awaiting your instructions, and you can move the cursor around the spreadsheet.

The program goes into **entry mode** when you begin to enter data into a cell. There are two basic kinds of entry mode. If you type a character that the program assumes is a label, it automatically goes into **label mode**. If the first character you type is a value (a number, formula, or function), it goes into **value mode**.

The program goes into **command mode** if you execute a command, for example, copy or move data. When the command is executed, the program goes into wait mode until it is completed. For example, the program goes into **wait mode** when it calculating, printing, or otherwise engaged internally. You have to wait for the program to return to ready mode before entering new data or commands.

If you want to correct or revise the data you have entered into a cell, you can return the data to the edit line, and the program goes into **edit mode**. When the program is in this mode, you can move the edit cursor through the data on the edit line to insert or delete characters as needed (see Topic 5-6).

You can create formulas by pointing to cells with the cursor instead of typing in their cell addresses (see Topic 5-7). When you enter formulas this way, the program goes into **point mode**.

SUMMARY AND KEY TERMS

- The screen display is divided into a working area and a control panel.
- The **working area** contains rows and columns. At the intersection of each row and column is a cell. A cell's address is given by specifying the column letter and row number, for example, cell A1 or cell B20.
- You can enter labels, numbers, formulas, functions, and formats into cells.
- The **control panel** usually contains a status, prompt, and entry or edit line.
- To get around a spreadsheet, you press the arrow keys or **PgUp** and **PgDn**. To move to a specific cell, you use the *Goto* command.
- You can scroll the window around the underlying spreadsheet but cannot move the cursor off it.
- **Memory management** refers to the way the program stores cells with data. The area that is stored in memory is called the **active area**. Some programs use **sparse memory management**, where only the cells that contain data are stored in memory.
- On many programs, you execute commands by pressing the slash key to display a menu. On other programs, a menu bar is always displayed at the top of the screen. To pull down menus, you press a specified key such as **Alt**.

1. What is the purpose of the working area?

2. What is a cell?

3. How are cell addresses given? What is the address of a cell in column 8 and row 30?

4. What is the purpose of the **control area**?

5. The typical spreadsheet program has three lines on the control panel: the status line, the prompt line, and the edit line. What is each line used for?

6. List and briefly describe the four things that you can enter into a cell.

7. What is the purpose of the *Goto* or *Jump* command?

8. Where does **Home** move the cursor on many spreadsheet programs?

9. Where does **End** move the cursor on many spreadsheet programs?

10. What happens when you scroll the screen? Can you move the cursor off the spreadsheet? When you scroll the screen, how do you know where you are?

11. What happens when you scroll the screen with **Scroll Lock** engaged?

12. How do you calculate the number of cells in a spreadsheet?

13. What is a spreadsheet's **active area**?

14. On some programs, when you enter a number into cell D4, what is the active area? If you enter a number into cells D1 and A4, what is the active area?

15. What is **sparse memory management**?

16. What are **modes**? Name and briefly describe a few common spreadsheet modes.

Typical Spreadsheet Programs

OBJECTIVE

After completing this topic, you will be able to

- List and briefly describe some typical spreadsheet programs

There are many spreadsheet programs to choose from. Let's look briefly at the characteristics of a few of the leading spreadsheet programs.

LOTUS 1-2-3, THE TWIN, AND VP PLANNER

Lotus 1-2-3 (Figure 5-19), The TWIN, VP Planner, and similar spreadsheet programs integrate graphics and data management capabilities. These programs also let you write simple programs (called **macros**) that automate many of the commands you use frequently.

FIGURE 5-19
Lotus 1-2-3
Lotus 1-2-3's three-line control panel is located at the top of the screen.

- The first line indicates the cell in which the cursor is positioned and the cell contents, format, and protection status if any (see Topic 5-18). At the far right end of the line is the mode indicator telling you the current state of the program.

- The second line displays cell data as you enter or edit it. When you press the slash key (/) to begin executing commands the menu—a list of keywords—is displayed on this line. Prompts are also displayed on this line.

- The third line displays a brief description of highlighted menu selections when the menu is being used to execute commands.

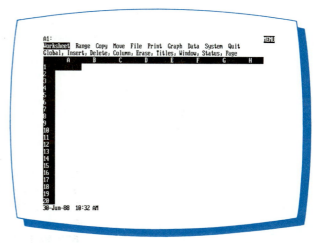

When you press the slash key to execute commands, a menu bar appears at the top of the screen. You can select choices from the menu by using the arrow keys to move a bright highlight, called the menu pointer, along the bar, and then press **Return** to select the highlighted choice. You can also make selections by just typing the first character in the commands name.

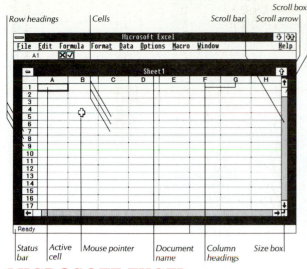

Status bar Active cell Mouse pointer Document name Column headings Size box

FIGURE 5-20
Microsoft Excel
Excel features a menu bar at the top of the screen. You use the computer's mouse to point to choices listed on this bar, and then select them by clicking the button on the mouse. A list of related commands then descends, and you select commands from this menu by pointing and clicking. Courtesy of Microsoft Corporation

MICROSOFT EXCEL

Excel was introduced for the Apple Macintosh and later adapted to run on the IBM PC (Figure 5-20). It is an extremely large spreadsheet with more than 4,000,000 cells. The program uses pull-down menus to execute commands. It also has built-in graphics lets you create macros by recording and then playing back any series of keystrokes. It allows you to create and save your own specialized functions (powerful formulas) so that you can use them again. Excel also has a limited memo-writing capability.

SUPERCALC

SuperCalc is a spreadsheet program that has integrated graphics and data management capabilities (Figure 5-21).

MULTIPLAN

MultiPlan differs in many respects from other programs. It labels both columns and rows with numbers, so cell coordinates are given as R1C1 (intersection of row 1 and column 1), R2C2, and so on (Figure 5-22).

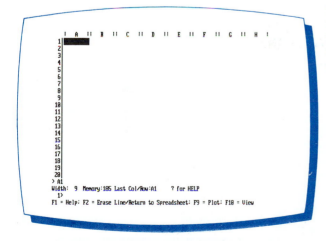

FIGURE 5-21
SuperCalc
SuperCalc is organized with the working area at the top of the screen and the three-line control panel at the bottom.

- The status line indicates the cell in which the cursor is positioned. If that cell contains any data, it is displayed following the cell address.

- The prompt line displays information such as the width of the cell and the memory available in the computer. When executing commands, this line displays prompts listing commands you can choose from.

- The entry or edit line displays cell contents as you enter or edit data. A character count indicator at the left end of the line indicates the current position of the edit cursor. When executing commands, the sequence of commands you have selected appears on this line.

FIGURE 5-22
MultiPlan

MultiPlan's control panel contains four lines displayed at the bottom of the screen.

- The first and second lines are the command lines and display a list of menu commands. You choose a command by typing its first letter or by using a designated key to move the highlight to highlight a command and then pressing **Return**.
- The third line is the message line; it displays error messages and prompts.
- The fourth line, the status line, indicates the address of the cell in which the cursor is positioned, the contents of the cell, the percentage of total memory still available, and the name of the file you are working on.

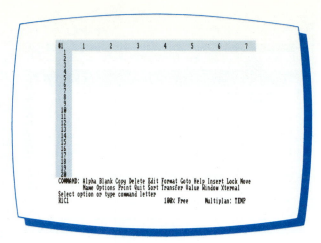

FIGURE 5-23
Quattro

The Quattro spreadsheet allows you to use the same menu commands as Lotus 1-2-3 (a) or its own menus (b). The input line at the top of the screen displays data as you type it until you press **Return** or when you press **Edit** (**F2**) to return to this line for editing. It also displays a description of the commands that can be selected from the highlighted menu command. The two lines at the bottom of the screen are the descriptor line and the status line. The descriptor line displays the contents of the cell containing the cursor. The status line indicates the date and time and the current mode.

QUATTRO

Quattro (Figure 5-23) is a full-featured spreadsheet that allows you to operate the program with its own menu commands or with commands identical to those used by Lotus 1-2-3.

LUCID 3-D

Most spreadsheets are used as standalone programs. Lucid 3D is different; it is a memory resident program (Figure 5-24). This means you can load the program into memory and then load another program like a word processor. When you want to display the spreadsheet, you press **Ctrl-Shift**, and it appears on the screen. To return to your other program, you press **Ctrl-Shift** again.

MICROSOFT WORKS

Besides the standalone programs, spreadsheets are also integrated into almost all integrated programs, including Microsoft Works (Figure 5-25).

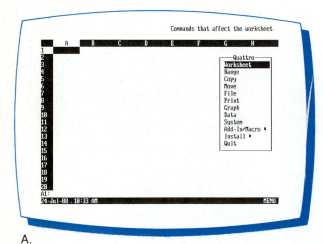

A.

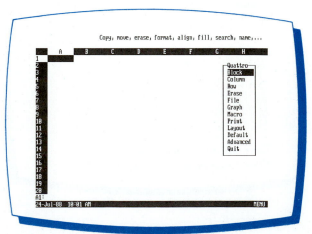

B.

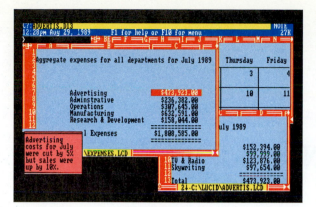

FIGURE 5-24
Lucid 3D
Lucid 3D has an interesting feature in that any cell can display the calculated result from a cell in another model. For example, you can move the cursor to the cell advertising expenses is displayed in and immediately display another model on which these expenses are broken down in detail.

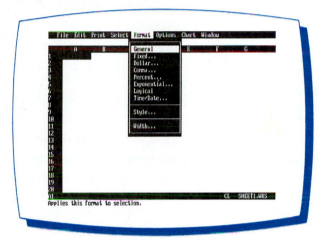

FIGURE 5-25
Microsoft Works
Microsoft Works is operated by pull-down menus and is much like Excel. It is a powerful, easy-to-use spreadsheet built into an integrated program that also contains graphics, word processing, and telecommunications programs.

SUMMARY AND KEY TERMS

- Lotus 1-2-3 integrates graphics and database management capabilities.
- Microsoft Excel uses pull-down menus that list commands. It is an extremely large and powerful spreadsheet.
- SuperCalc also has integrated graphics and database management functions.
- MultiPlan uses a different notation for rows and columns; they are both numbered.
- Quattro allows you to use its own commands or Lotus 1-2-3's.
- Lucid 3-D is a memory resident spreadsheet.
- Microsoft Works is an integrated program that also features graphics, database management, and telecommunications.

REVIEW QUESTIONS

1. List three typical spreadsheet programs.
2. Name one integrated program that contains a spreadsheet as one of its components.
3. What spreadsheet is memory resident?
4. Name two spreadsheets that are clones of Lotus 1-2-3.

Labels and Numbers

OBJECTIVES

After completing this topic, you will be able to

- Describe how you enter labels and numbers
- Describe the Data Fill command and explain what it is used for

You enter data into a spreadsheet by moving the cursor to the cell and then typing in the data. Entries are displayed on the edit line as you type them. When displayed on this line, you press **Backspace** to back over and erase any characters that you have entered incorrectly. You complete the entry by pressing **Return**, which moves the entry from the edit line to the cell the cursor is positioned in. If the cell already contains an entry, you can replace it by typing a new entry over it and then pressing **Return**.

Some programs automatically move the cursor to the next cell on the row or column when you press **Return** to complete an entry. On other programs, you can achieve the same result by pressing one of the cursor movement keys instead of **Return**; this simultaneously completes the entry and moves the cursor to the next cell in the direction of the arrow key you press. For instance, to enter a number into a cell and automatically move down one row, press ↓ instead of **Return** after typing the number. When making several entries along a row or down a column, it is faster to enter data using one of the arrow keys because they enter the data and automatically move the cursor one cell in the direction of the arrow saving you a keystroke each time.

When you enter data, many spreadsheet programs distinguish between labels and values (numbers, formulas, and functions) because they use values but not labels in most calculations. If the first character you type is a letter, most programs assume you are entering a label. If the first character is a number, they assume you are entering a value. For example, Lotus 1-2-3 assumes you are entering a value if you type any of the characters in Table 5-4. If you type any other character, the programs assume you are entering a label.

TABLE 5-4 Characters That Spreadsheets Assume Are Values	
0-9	(numbers)
+	(addition)
-	(subtraction)
*	(multiplication)
—	
$	
#	
@	

ENTERING LABELS

Labels (also called text) are any series of characters, including letters, numbers, and symbols, that you use to describe row and column entries or to provide other descriptive information about the model. To enter a label, you move the cursor to the cell you want to enter it in, type the label, and then press **Return**. This is straightforward with one exception: labels that begin with numbers or certain other characters used in formulas and functions. If the first character you type is one of those listed in Table 5-4, the program assumes you are entering a value. Although this assumption usually saves you time, you sometimes have to override it.

You can override the program's assumptions by typing a designated key or symbol before you type the entry's first character. If you want to enter a label that begins with a number, for example, 100 Elm Street, you first type a **label prefix** such as an apostrophe ('). This puts the program into label mode. You then enter the label by typing it and pressing **Return**. For example, Lotus 1-2-3 has the three label prefix characters that you can use to enter labels beginning with numbers (see Table 5-5). You can also use these label prefixes with labels that begin with letters because they also control the alignment of the label in the cell.

When entering labels, keep the following points in mind:

- Labels can be as long as the program allows. For example, on Lotus 1-2-3, labels can contain up to 240 characters.

- Unless you enter a label prefix, the label is aligned with the default global format setting (see Topic 5-10).

- If a label is longer than its cell is wide, it overflows into the next cell if that cell is empty. If the cell next to it is not empty, the label is **truncated**—that is, only the part that fits in the cell is displayed. Only the display is truncated, not the actual entry. To display the entire label, you can widen the column (see Topic 5-10).

Many spreadsheet programs have a command that lets you repeat a specified character so that it fills the entire width of a cell or row. These commands are ideal for entering ruled lines to separate parts of a model. On Lotus 1-2-3, you press the backslash key (\ ) to repeat the next character you type until the cell is full. For example, pressing \ and then — fills a cell with a single-ruled line. Pressing \ and then ══ fills a cell with a double-ruled line. You can then copy the ruled line to other cells on the row to underline more than one column (see Topic 5-11). The nice thing about repeated labels is that if you change column widths, the labels automatically adjust so that they are always as wide as the columns, no wider or narrower. Table 5-6 illustrates some of the keys you can repeat on Lotus 1-2-3.

ENTERING NUMBERS

You enter numbers just like labels: You move the cursor to the cell where they are to be entered, type them in, and then press **Return** to enter them in the cell. If the first character you type is one of those listed in Table 5-4, entering numbers is automatic because the program recognizes them as values.

Numbers must always begin with a character from 0 to 9 or another designated character such as the plus sign (+) or minus sign (−). They cannot contain spaces, letters, or commas (though commas can be added by formatting as you'll see).

When entering numbers, keep the following points in mind:

- If you enter a number that is too long for the cell, it is displayed as a row of asterisks or other symbols. To display the entire number, you must widen the column or change the number's format (see Topic 5-10).

TABLE 5-5
Label Prefix Characters

Character	Effect on Label
"	Right aligns label
^	Centers label
'	Left aligns label (the default)

TABLE 5-6
Typical Line Patterns

To Enter	Press
-------------	\-
=============	\=
*************	*
....	\.
_____	_

- Numbers are always right aligned on some programs. On these programs, you can change the alignment on a number by entering it as a label, but you cannot then use that number in calculations. On other programs, you can align numbers as well as labels.

- However they are displayed, numbers are always stored in memory with the maximum precision provided by the program, usually up to fifteen digits. For example, you can format the number 1000.1425 so that it is displayed as $1,000, $1,000.14, 1000.142, and so on, but it is always calculated by any formulas that refer to it as 1000.1425 (see Topic 5-7). This is done so that calculations can be as exact as possible. If you want to change the precision of calculation, use the function that rounds numbers (see Topic 5-8).

- Numbers cannot be entered with spaces, commas, or dollar signs. For example, enter one thousand dollars as 1000, not $1,000.00. If you want to format the number, for example, to display dollar signs or commas, use the *Format* commands (see Topic 5-10). These commands can display the number as 1,000, $1,000, or $1,000.00. A few programs also allow you to enter currency as 1,000, $1000, or $1,000.

- Very large and very small numbers can be entered in scientific notation to save space and avoid typing errors. For example, to enter the number 1,000,000, type 1e6 (10 raised to the 6th power). If the column is wide enough, the full number is displayed.

- To enter a percentage, type the number followed by a percent sign, or type in its decimal equivalent. Either way, you must format the cell as a percentage if you want it displayed with the percent sign (see Topic 5-10). When you enter a percentage as a whole number followed by a percent sign, the program automatically converts it into a decimal by dividing the number by 100. For example, entering a percentage as 10% is the same as entering it as 0.1 or 10/100.

USING DATA FILL

The *Data Fill* or *Data Series* command enters an incremented series of numbers in a row, column, or block of cells (Figure 5-26). When using the *Data Fill* command, you specify the range to be filled and what number the series is to start with, the increment to increase or decrease that number by, and what number to stop at. The start, step, and stop values can be positive or negative numbers or formulas.

- The **start value** is the number the series starts with. This number is entered into the first cell in the specified range.

- The **step value** specifies the value each number in the series is to be incremented by. For example, if you start the data series at 1 and specify a step value of 2, the series will be 1, 3, 5, 7, and so on.

- The **stop value** is the number the series ends with. Both the fill range and the stop number you enter determine the results. The *Data Fill* command continues to enter numbers until it reaches the end of the range or the stop number, whichever comes first.

On some programs, you can choose the type of values to enter with this command. The choices include linear, growth, and date.

- **Linear data series** adds the step value to the value in the preceding cell in the series.

	A	B	C
1	Linear	Growth	Date
2	0	1	1-Jan
3	10	2	2-Jan
4	20	4	3-Jan
5	30	8	4-Jan
6	40	16	5-Jan
7	50	32	6-Jan
8	60	64	7-Jan
9	70	128	8-Jan
10	80	256	9-Jan
11	90	512	10-Jan
12	100	1024	11-Jan
13	110	2048	12-Jan
14	120	4096	13-Jan
15	130	8192	14-Jan
16			
17			
18			
19			
20			

FIGURE 5-26
The Data Fill Command
The *Data Fill* or *Data Series* command can be used to quickly enter an evenly incremented series of numbers into a column, row, or block of cells. Here, the data series command has been used to enter three series, linear, growth, and date.

- **Growth data series** multiplies the step value by the value in the preceding cell in the series.
- **Date data series** adds a date period specified as the step value to the date in the previous cell. This is useful when you want to add a series of dates to a model.

- You enter data by moving the cursor to a cell and typing it in. You complete the entry by pressing **Return** or one of the cursor movement keys. Before you press **Return**, you can delete characters with **Backspace**.
- **Text** and **values** (numbers, formulas, and functions) are treated differently since the program can calculate values.
- When entering text that begins with a number, some programs require you to first enter a **label prefix character**.
- Many programs have a command that **repeats** a character a specified number of times.
- **Numbers** always begin with a digit 0-9 or a designated character like a plus or minus sign.
- Numbers are always calculated as they were entered (up to the precision supported by the program) although you can use formats to display them differently.
- Some programs allow you to enter numbers in a variety of ways. For example, percentages can be entered as .1 or 10%, and dollars can be entered as 1000 or $1,000.
- The *Data Fill* or *Data Series* command enters a series of incremented numbers in a row, column, or block of cells. You specify a start, step, and stop value.

1. How do you enter data into a cell?
2. How does a value differ from text?
3. What is a label prefix, and why would you need to use it?
4. How do you enter a label that begins with a number?
5. How would you enter the label 123 Spring Street? The phone number 617-555-1000?
6. How would you enter a label on Lotus 1-2-3 so that it is aligned with the left edge of the cell? So that it is aligned with the right edge? So that it is centered?
7. What is a repeating label? What can they be used for?
8. What do numbers begin with?
9. How would you enter the number $6,580.00?
10. What happens when you enter a number followed by a percent sign?
11. What does the *Data Fill* command do? What values must you specify when using it?

Ranges

OBJECTIVES

After completing this topic, you will be able to

- Describe what a range is
- Explain the difference between global and range commands
- Explain how you select ranges

Many of the commands you use with a spreadsheet affect just single cells, for example, entering numbers, labels, and formulas. Other commands affect all the cells or just those you specify in the command. These are called global and range commands.

GLOBAL COMMANDS

Global commands affect the entire spreadsheet. Some of these commands affect the way information is displayed. For example, there are global commands to set the width of columns, specify how labels are aligned, and control how numbers are displayed. Normally, you specify a global setting based on what works with most of your data. You then override the global setting, as necessary, wherever you want data to look differently from the global format.

RANGE COMMANDS

Other commands, called **range commands** (also called local commands), affect more than one cell. These commands are often used to override the global commands in selected blocks of cells.

When you use range commands, you specify rectangular ranges of cells. A **range** is a group of adjacent cells. Ranges can be as small as a single cell or as large as the entire spreadsheet. The only rule is that the range must be rectangular. There are essentially four rectangular shapes of ranges (Figure 5-27). Understanding ranges is important because you specify them in functions and when formatting, copying, moving, printing, or erasing groups of cells.

When you use range commands, you must specify the range of cells to be affected by the command. On some programs, the sequence is

	A	B	C	D	E	F	G	H
1								
2		A.				B.		
3								
4								
5								
6								
7								
8								
9								
10		C.				D.		
11								
12								
13								
14								
15								
16								
17								
18								
19								
20								

FIGURE 5-27
Ranges
A range is a group of adjacent cells arranged in a rectangular pattern. Ranges can be as small as a single cell and as large as the entire spreadsheet. The only rule is that the range must be rectangular. There are essentially four shapes of ranges.

A. Individual cells, for example, B2.

B. Rows or parts of rows, for example, D2 to G2.

C. Columns or parts of columns, for example, B5 to B17.

D. Blocks (rectangles) of cells, for example, rows 5 through 17 in columns D through G.

1. Initiate the command.

2. Specify the range.

3. Complete the command.

On other programs, you complete the same steps but in a different order; for example, the sequence may be

1. Select (highlight) the range.

2. Execute the command.

You specify or select a range in one of two ways: by typing in the coordinates of the range or by using the cursor or a mouse to point to the cells indicating the range. Figure 5-27 shows the cells that you specify for each type of range in a second color.

■ To select a range by typing, you type two cell addresses that define the range, the upper left-hand and lower right-hand cells in the range (see Figure 5-27). When more than one cell is in the range, you type two cell addresses separated by a delimiter, usually a period or colon. On Lotus 1-2-3, you type A1.C3 to indicate the cells falling in the columns between A and C and the rows 1 and 3. On Excel, you type A1:C1 to indicate the same range.

■ To select a range by using the cursor, you press the arrow keys to point to the upper left-hand and lower right-hand corners of the range. On Lotus 1-2-3, you move the cursor to one of the corners of the range (when the prompt tells you to select the range), and then press the period (.) to anchor that corner of the range. You then use the cursor movement keys to highlight the desired range. On Excel, to select a range by pointing, you use the mouse to point to one corner, hold down one of the buttons, and then drag the highlight over the range.

RANGES   **441**

NAMING RANGES

Some programs allow you to assign names to ranges of cells. Programs that let you name ranges have menu commands that you use to name or remove names from cells. **Range names** are useful because you can refer to the range name and not have to remember or point to its cell coordinates over and over again. Range names are very useful when

- Entering formulas. For example, you can enter a formula like SALES-COSTS if you have assigned those names to ranges of cells.

- Formatting cells. For example, you can specify a currency format for the range of cells named SALES.

- Printing a selected part of the model. For example, you can tell the program to print the range named SUMMARY.

- Copying or moving cells. For example, you can tell the program to copy the range named 1989 to column F.

- Answering the prompt to the *Goto* command. For example, when prompted to enter the cell to go to, you can type SALES, and the cursor jumps to the upper left-hand corner of the range with that name.

SUMMARY AND KEY TERMS

- **Global commands** affect all cells in the spreadsheet.

- **Range commands** affect only specified cells called a range. A **range** is a rectangular group of adjacent cells.

- You select a range by typing or pointing to the cell addresses for its upper left-hand and lower right-hand corners. You separate these cell addresses with a **delimiter**, usually a period or colon. On some programs, you can also select a range by highlighting it with a mouse.

- A few programs allow you to assign **range names** to cells or groups of cells so that those names can be used to create formulas, specify print ranges, and use the *GoTo* command.

REVIEW QUESTIONS

1. What is the difference between a global format and a range or local format?
2. What is a range? Describe some typical shapes of ranges.
3. Describe two ways you specify ranges.
4. What is a delimiter? When is it used? What characters are usually used for delimiters?
5. What are range names? When might you use them?

Editing Models

OBJECTIVES

After completing this topic, you will be able to

- Describe how you edit the contents of cells
- Describe how you erase cell contents
- Explain how you insert and delete rows and columns

If you want to improve or expand a model, you can edit or erase the contents of cells or insert or delete rows and columns.

EDITING CELL CONTENTS

The procedure you use to edit the contents of a cell depends on whether you notice the mistake while entering it or after having entered it.

Editing Data That Is Being Entered

If you notice a mistake while entering data, you generally have four choices.

- You can press **Backspace** to delete one or more characters to the left of the edit cursor. The key repeats if you hold it down so that you can delete characters one after another until you release the key.
- You can press **Esc** to abandon the entry and then correctly reenter it.
- You can press **Return** and then correctly reenter the entry.
- You can press the **Edit** key to enter edit mode, correct the entry, and then press **Return**.

Editing Data That Has Been Entered

After you have pressed **Return** to enter data into a cell, the entry must be returned to the edit line before you can edit it. You first move the cursor to the cell you want to edit, and you then press a designated key. For example, on Lotus 1-2-3 and Excel, you press **Edit** (**F2**). This puts the program into edit mode and displays the cell's contents on the edit line along with a one-character-wide edit cursor. In edit mode, you can freely move the edit cursor through the data and insert or delete characters as needed, much as when you are working on a word processing program. Table 5-7 describes some of

TABLE 5-7
Keys That Move the Edit Cursor and Delete Characters

To Move the Edit Cursor	Press
One character to left or right	← or →
To beginning of line	**Home**
To end of line	End

To Delete	Press
Character to left of cursor	**Backspace**
Character directly over curor	**Del**

the keys you can use on Lotus 1-2-3 and Excel to move the edit cursor and delete characters.

Newer spreadsheet programs, such as Microsoft Excel, also have search and search and replace commands that operate just like those on word processing programs. Using these commands, you can search or search and replace text, formulas, or functions.

ERASING CELL CONTENTS

Most programs have a command you use to erase the contents of one or more cells. This command does not delete the cells themselves, just their contents. To erase the contents of cells, you first select the cells to be erased, and then you execute the *Erase* command (sometimes called the *Blank* command) or specify a range of cells when prompted to do so. For example, on Lotus 1-2-3, you press **/RE** (for *Range, Erase*), and a prompt asks you to specify the range to be erased. When you do so, and then press **Return**, the contents of the cells in the range are erased. The *Erase* command on some programs erases only the labels, numbers, or formulas, not the formats assigned to the cells. On other programs, you can specify what you want erased from the cell. A few programs also let you specify that only numbers be deleted, leaving formulas and labels. This command automatically creates a template that can be used with other data.

INSERTING AND DELETING ROWS AND COLUMNS

One of the advantages of working with spreadsheet models is being able to revise and improve them as you gain more experience with the program and more understanding of an analysis. Most programs let you insert or delete an entire row or column. Others allow you to insert or delete partial rows or columns.

Inserting Rows and Columns

Often, you may find it necessary to insert rows or columns into the middle of an existing model. You can easily do this, and all formulas below the inserted rows, or to the right of the inserted columns, automatically adjust so that they continue to refer to the correct cells (Figure 5-28). When inserting rows and columns, keep the following points in mind:

- Rows are usually inserted above the cursor, and columns are inserted to the left of the cursor.

	A	B	C	D	E	F
1	1	2	3	←SUM(A1..B1)		
2						
3						
4						
5						

A.

	A	B	C	D	E	F
1	1		2	3	←SUM(A1..C1)	
2						
3						
4						
5						

B.

- On programs that insert an entire row or column, the cursor can be in any cell in the row or column you are inserting into. On programs that insert partial rows or columns, you must highlight all the columns you want to insert a row into or all the rows you want to insert a column into.

- If there is data in the last row or column, and you enter a row or column, a message appears telling you the spreadsheet is full.

- You can usually specify a range of adjacent rows or columns so that all of them are set to the same width when inserted.

- If rows or columns are inserted within a print range or a range referred to by a formula, the range expands to include the new rows or columns. If rows or columns are inserted on the edge of the range, they are not included.

Deleting Rows and Columns

Deleting one or more rows and columns has almost the same effect as inserting them. The spreadsheet closes up, and all formulas automatically adjust to refer to the correct cells (Figure 5-29).

However, if you delete any cells that formulas that are not deleted refer to, those formulas will display some form of error message. These messages tell you that the cells they refer to have been deleted. It is therefore wise to save a model before making deletions. After making deletions, be sure to recalculate the spreadsheet to see if any error messages appear in the cells. If you have any doubts, save the model under a new filename so that you do not store it on top of, and erase, the original.

You may also want to convert formulas that refer to parts of the model to be deleted into their currently displayed values before deleting the cells they refer to. Most programs have a special command that converts formulas into their calculated values in situations like this. For example, on Lotus 1-2-3, you can convert formulas into their calculated values so that they do not change during later recalculations if the cells they refer to are changed or deleted. To do this, move the cursor to the cell containing the formula, press the **Edit (F2)** key to move the formula to the edit line, and then press the **Calc (F9)** key. To enter the calculated value into the cell, press **Return**.

When deleting rows and columns, keep the following points in mind:

- You can type in a range of rows or columns to delete or point to them when prompted to enter the range to be deleted.

- If you do not delete the upper left-hand or lower right-hand corner of a range, the range contracts or expands to accommodate the change. If

FIGURE 5-28
Inserting Rows and Columns

A. To insert columns, you first move the cursor to the column to the right of where you want the column inserted. Here it is in column B. Note how the formula in cell C1 is SUM(A1..B1).

B. When you insert a column, as done here with column B, the old column B shifts to the right and becomes column C. Note how the formula has shifted to cell D1 and now reads SUM(A1..C1). It automatically adjusted to include the new column in the range.

FIGURE 5-29
Deleting Rows and Columns

A. To delete columns, you first select them, as done here with column B.

B. When you delete the columns, formulas that refer to cells to the left or right of the deleted column adjust automatically. Those that refer to cells in the deleted column display error messages.

	A	B	C	D	E	F
1	1	10		1	←+A1	
2	2	11		11	←+B2	
3	3	12	5	20	←SUM(A3..C3)	
4	4	13	6	17	←SUM(A4..B4)	
5						

A.

	A	B	C	D	E	F
1	1		1	←+A1		
2	2		ERROR	←+ERROR		
3	3	5	8	←SUM(A3..B3)		
4	4	6	ERROR	←SUM(A4..ERROR)		
5						

B.

these corners are deleted, the range is no longer defined, and formulas referring to it display error messages.

- Rows and columns cannot be deleted when cells in the range are protected (see Topic 5-18).

- On some programs, rows and columns can be deleted to free up memory for new data on a model. After deleting, save the file. When the saved file is retrieved, the available memory increases.

SUMMARY AND KEY TERMS

- When entering data into cells, you can delete characters with **Backspace** until you press **Return**.

- To edit data that has been entered into a cell, you move the cursor to the cell and press the **Edit** key. This returns the data to the edit line where you can edit it much as you would with a word processor. When finished, press **Return** to enter the corrected entry into the cell.

- A few programs give you the ability to search for words or numbers on a model. Some also allow you to search and replace.

- To remove data from the worksheet, you use the program's *Erase* command. This command erases the data in a single cell or any other range you specify.

- You can change the size of a model by inserting or deleting rows and columns. All formulas that do not refer to cells in the deleted rows or columns automatically adjust so that they refer to the correct cells. Those that refer to cells in the deleted rows and columns display error messages.

REVIEW QUESTIONS

1. Explain the two ways of editing the contents of a cell.
2. What command do you use to delete the contents of a range of cells?
3. How do you insert blank rows into a spreadsheet model?
4. What happens when you delete cells that existing formulas refer to?

Formulas

OBJECTIVES

After completing this topic, you will be able to

- Explain what operators are
- Describe a program's order of operations
- Explain the differences between constants and variables
- Describe how you enter formulas by typing or pointing
- Describe strings and what you use them for
- List ways you can annotate formulas

You can enter **formulas** in spreadsheet cells that either calculate numbers directly or refer to cells elsewhere on the spreadsheet into which you enter numbers or other formulas and functions.

When entering formulas, you must understand a few principles, namely, how operators and the order of operations work and the difference between constants and variables. Once you understand these principles, you can enter formulas (and functions) by typing them in or by pointing.

OPERATORS—THE BASIC BUILDING BLOCKS

When you enter formulas, certain keys (and the symbols they generate on the screen) tell the program what calculations to perform. These symbols, or **operators**, are used in conjunction with numbers or cell references to create formulas. Table 5-8 lists typical spreadsheet operators, and Table 5-9 shows how you can use these operators to create formulas.

TABLE 5-8
Spreadsheet Operators

Operator	Use
+	Performs addition
−	Performs subtraction
*	Performs multiplication
/	Performs division
^	Specifies an exponent

447

TABLE 5-9
Spreadsheet Formulas

Formula	Displayed Result
10+10	20
10*4	40
30−5	25
200/5	40
A1+A2	The value in cell A1 plus the value in cell A2
A1*A2	The value in cell A1 multiplied by the value in cell A2
A1−A2	The value in cell A1 minus the value in cell A2
A1/A2	The value in cell A1 divided by the value in cell A2
10+A1	10 plus the value entered in cell A1
2*A1	2 multiplied by the value entered in cell A1
4−A1	4 minus the value entered in cell A1
200/A1	200 divided by the value entered in cell A1
10^2	100; that is, 10 raised to the 2nd power
10^A1	10 raised to the power entered in cell A1

THE ORDER OF OPERATIONS

When you enter formulas that contain more than one operator, another concept, the **order of operations**, becomes important. Every program has a specific order that operators are calculated in. Figure 5-30 shows how the order of operations works in practice.

- Some programs automatically calculate operations from left to right in the order they appear in the formula unless you use parentheses, in which case the numbers in parentheses are calculated first.

- Most programs follow algebra's rules of order of procedure. Operators are assigned a **precedence**, or priority: those with a higher precedence are performed before those with a lower precedence. For example, multiplication and division have equal precedence but a higher precedence than addition and subtraction, which also have equal precedence. Operators with the same level of precedence are calculated from left to right.

Table 5-10 shows the order of operations followed by Lotus 1-2-3. The order ends at level 4 because logical operators have even lower precedence (see Topic 5-8).

You can enter formulas so that operations occur in the desired sequence, but it is usually easier to use parentheses to control the order of calculations regardless of the rules followed by the program. Parentheses control the order of operations regardless of the rules followed by the program. For example, entering the formula as $1+(1/2)$ calculates the correct answer since the operations within the parentheses are always performed first. If parentheses are nested—for example, $1+(1/(1/2))$—the operations are performed from the innermost parentheses outward; in this formula, the answer would be 3.

CONSTANTS AND VARIABLES

When you enter formulas, they can contain both constants and variables.

- **Constants** are numbers you do not expect to change. For example, the formula 5*10 contains only numbers; there are no references to other

FIGURE 5-30
Order of Operations
Suppose you want to add the numbers 1 and 1/2. To do this, you can enter the formula 1 + 1/2. The formula contains two operators, one to add (+) and one to divide (/).

A. If calculations are performed from left to right, the answer is 1. First addition is performed, so 1 + 1 = 2; then division is performed, so 2/2 = 1.

B. If algebra's rules of precedence are followed, the answer is 1.5. First division is performed, so 1/2 = 0.5; then addition, which has a lower precedence, is performed, so 1 + 0.5 = 1.5.

TABLE 5-10
Order of Operations for Arithmetic Operators

Operator	Description	Precedence Level
^	Exponentiation	7
+	Unary plus sign (for example, A1>A4)	6
–	Negation (for example, A1>–A4)	6
*	Multiplication	5
/	Division	5
+	Addition	4
–	Subtraction	4

cells. Numbers contained in formulas are called constants because you can change them only with some difficulty, by reentering or editing the formula, for example, by changing it to 6*10.

- **Variables** are numbers you do expect to change. For example, the formula 6*A1 contains a constant and a cell reference. The number in the cell referred to by the formula can be easily changed and is thus a variable. Numbers like this are called variables because you expect to change them to see what effect different numbers have on the outcome.

When creating a model, you first decide what variables you want to explore, and then structure your models accordingly. Formulas can be all constants (Figure 5-31). But these formulas do not take advantage of a spreadsheet's unique feature to explore what-ifs. To change a formula entered in this way, you must edit or reenter it. You build more powerful models by entering formulas that refer to other cells. This way, you can change the values in the cells the formula refers to, and it calculates them just as if they were part of the formula. For example, formulas can be part constant and part variable (Figure 5-32), or they can be all variables (Figure 5-33).

You should consider almost every number a variable for three reasons.

1. Embedding a number in a formula is making an assumption either that it should not or cannot be changed or that it is unimportant to the outcome of the analysis. When exploring the model, you may find it is very sensitive to changes in that number—a phenomenon you would never discover if the number were embedded in a formula.

2. The next time you use the model, you may forget there is an embedded number and not take it into consideration.

3. Printouts of models generally print out only the displayed values, not the formulas behind them. Anyone else trying to follow your analysis might get lost if too many numbers are embedded in formulas rather than displayed on the printout.

FIGURE 5-31
Formulas That Are All Constants
Formulas with all constants are like those you enter on a calculator. To enter a formula that contains only constants, you might type (1-.2)*10 (100%-20%*$10.00) into cell A1. The formula calculates and displays the number $8. Because the numbers are part of the formula, you cannot change the discount or price to calculate a new result.

	A	B	C	D	E	F
1	$8.00	← (100% - 20%) * 10.00				
2						
3						
4						
5						

	A	B	C	D	E	F
1	List price	$10.00				
2	Discount	20%				
3	Net price	$8.00	← (100%-B2) * B1			
4						
5						

FIGURE 5-32
Formulas That Are Part Constants and Part Variables
To enter a formula that contains constants and variable, you might enter $10.00 into cell B1 and 20% into cell B2. You then enter the formula (100%-B2)*B1 into cell A3. The formula subtracts the percentage in cell B2 from 100% and multiplies the result by the price in cell B1. The numbers in cells B1 and B2 are now variables. You can change them to explore what-ifs.

FIGURE 5-33
Formulas That Are All Variables
To enter a formula that contains only variables, you might add a new line to the model so that you can calculate the discount in dollars. You then enter the formula B2*B1 into cell B3 and the formula B1-B3 into cell B4. Both formulas have variables and no constants.

	A	B	C	D	E	F
1	List price	$10.00				
2	Discount (%)	20%				
3	Discount ($)	$2.00	← B2 * B1			
4	Net price	$8.00	← B1 - B3			
5						

WAYS TO ENTER FORMULAS

There are two ways to enter formulas (and functions): by typing them in or, if they refer to other cells, by pointing with the cursor to the cells referred to.

Typing in Formulas

You can type in a formula that refers to another cell, for example, A1*A2. But this formula begins with a letter, so if you type that letter first, many programs assume you are entering a label. To enter formulas that begin with letters on these programs, you must first type the plus sign (+) to enter the formula as +A1*A2. You can also begin formulas with any of the value characters listed in Table 5-4.

Pointing to Cells

You can use cursor pointing to point to cells referred to in the formula. Pointing is especially useful when you are working on larger spreadsheets where the cells you want to refer to are not displayed on the screen. Experienced users almost always build formulas by pointing because it is faster, more accurate, and easier than typing. Figure 5-34 shows how cursor pointing is used with Lotus 1-2-3 to enter a formula.

When entering formulas, keep the following points in mind:

- Formulas can be as long as the program permits. For example, 1-2-3 allows you to enter up to 240 characters.
- To display a formula on the edit line, move the cursor to the cell that contains the formula. If the formula is too long to be fully displayed, press **Edit** (**F2**), and then use → and ← to move along the line. When you are finished, press **Esc** to return to the spreadsheet and leave the formula unchanged.
- On many programs, when entering formulas that begin with a letter (formulas that refer to other cells, for instance), you must begin the formula with one of the value characters listed in Table 5-4.

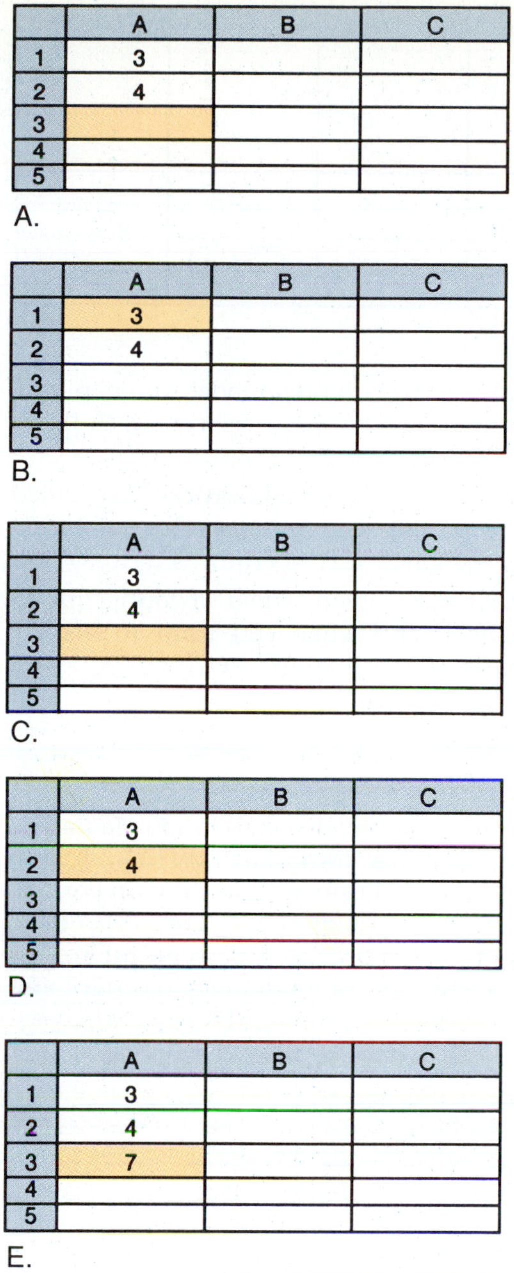

A.

B.

C.

D.

E.

FIGURE 5-34
Using Cursor Pointing to Enter Formulas
The numbers 3 and 4 have been entered into cells A1 and A2. Let's say you want to use cursor pointing to enter a formula into cell A3 that adds the value in cell A2 to the value in cell A1.

A. Move the cursor to cell A3, and then press the plus sign (+) to begin the formula. The formula now reads +.

B. Press ↑ twice to move the cursor to cell A1. The formula now reads +A1.

C. Press the plus sign (+). The formula now reads +A1+.

D. Press ↑ to point to cell A2, the cell you want to add to A1. The formula now reads +A1+A2.

E. Press **Return** to complete the entry, and the formula leaves the edit line and is entered into cell A3. It calculates and displays the result 7.

Correcting Mistakes

If you enter a formula that does not conform to the program's rules, you are automatically placed in edit mode (see Topic 5-6). When this happens, the program moves the cursor to where in the line it thinks the error is. For example, if you try to enter the formula +A1+A and then press **Return**, the computer beeps, the cursor goes to the second A, and you are placed in edit mode. To edit the formula, press → to move the cursor to the right of the A, type 2 and then press **Return**.

STRINGS

Many programs have the ability to handle **strings**, any series of characters used as labels. For example, 100, 100 Elm Street, and John Lewis are all strings. The ability to manipulate strings has several applications.

FIGURE 5-35
Strings
String are entered into cells A1 through A3. references to those cells are then entered into cells A5 through A6. The references carry the strings to the cells they are entered into just as it would carry a value. The advantage of using this approach is not limited to saving time. If the string is changed, all cells referring to it will automatically change, making revision easier and faster.

	A	B	C	D	E	F
1	Sales					
2	Expenses					
3	Profits					
4						
5	Sales	← +A1				
6	Expenses	← +A2				
7	Profits	← +A3				
8						

- If you use the same labels over and over again on a model, you can save time by entering the labels once and then entering references to those cells wherever you want the label to be repeated (Figure 5-35).
- Strings can be joined into longer strings by **concatenation** (also called gluing). To glue strings in this way, the cell references are combined with an ampersand (&) or other specified text operator (Figure 5-36).
- You can include strings in formulas by enclosing them in double quotation marks (Figure 5-37). This is useful when you want to display messages in cells when designated conditions are met.

ENGLISH LANGUAGE FORMULAS

Some programs allow you to enter formulas using English language names instead of cell coordinates. For example, the formula @SUM(B5..B10) – @SUM(B12..B19) is much harder to enter and understand than an equivalent formula entered and displayed as Sales-Expenses. The techniques used for English language formulas vary from program to program. For example, on MultiPlan, Excel, and 1-2-3, you can assign names to ranges and then refer to these names in formulas instead of using the cell addresses.

	A	B	C	D
1	String1	String2	String1	← +A1
2	String1	String2	String1String2	← +A2&B2
3	String1	String2	String1 String2	← +A3& &B3
4	String1	String2	String1 - String2	← +A4& - &B4
5				
6				
7				
8				

FIGURE 5-36
Concatenation
Strings have been entered into columns A and B. The formulas described in column D are then entered into column C.

A. +A1 just copies the string in cell A1 to cell C1.

B. +A2&B2 joins two strings in cell A2 and B2 and displays them as *String 1String 2* in cell C2.

C. To add a space between the strings, you can include the space in the string formula. The formula +A3&" "&B3 (with the space enclosed in double quotes) results in the string *String 1 String 2* being displayed in cell C3.

D. If you include a minus sign (−) inside the double quotes so that the formula reads +A4&" - "&B4, the displayed string is *String 1 - String 2* in cell C4.

	A	B	C	D	E	F
1	Name	Sales	Action			
2	Smith	1000	PROMOTE	← IF(B2 < 10000,"FIRE","PROMOTE")		
3	Jones	9000	FIRE	← IF(B3 < 10000,"FIRE","PROMOTE")		
4	Lewis	12000	PROMOTE	← IF(B4 < 10000,"FIRE","PROMOTE")		
5	Washington	15000	PROMOTE	← IF(B5 < 10000,"FIRE","PROMOTE")		
6	Lee	23000	PROMOTE	← IF(B6 < 10000,"FIRE","PROMOTE")		
7	Gonzales	11000	PROMOTE	← IF(B7 < 10000,"FIRE","PROMOTE")		
8						

FIGURE 5-37
Strings in Formulas
You can create an IF function using strings by entering a formula @IF(B2<10000, "FIRE", "PROMOTE") into cell C2 and then copy it down the column.

This formula reads "If sales in cell B2 are less than \$10,000, then display the string *FIRE*; if they are not less than \$10,000, then display the string *PROMOTE*." If any sales entered into column B are less than \$10,00 the formula in column C displays the string *FIRE*. When the number is \$10,000 or higher, it displays *PROMOTE*.

ANNOTATING FORMULAS

When creating models, some formulas can get quite complicated. When you look at a model a few days later, or when someone else looks at it, the purpose of a formula may not be clear. For this reason, many programs allow you to document your formulas.

- Some programs allow you to attach notes to specific cells. When you use the *Note* command, a window opens. You enter a description of the formula (or data) just as you would on a word processing program. These notes can be displayed on the screen at any time or printed out along with the model.

- A few programs allow you to directly annotate formulas. For example, when using Framework, you can end a formula with a semicolon and then follow it with text describing the formula. On this program, a typical formula and annotation might be +B3-B8;Income minus expenses. All text following the semicolon is ignored when the formula is calculated, but it can be seen when the cursor is positioned in the cell containing the formula.

SUMMARY AND KEY TERMS

- Formulas are created using **operators** that specify what arithmetic operation is to be performed. Typical operators include + (addition) − (subtraction), / (division), and * (multiplication).

- The **order of operations** refers to the sequence operators are calculated in when you use more than one. Those that have a higher **precedence** are calculated first. You can control the order of operations by enclosing parts of a formula in parentheses since operations within parentheses are always calculated first.

- Formulas include constants and variables. **Constants** are numbers entered directly into the formula. **Variables** are references to numbers entered into other cells.

- Some programs allow you to build formulas by **pointing** with the cursor to the cells to be included.

- Many programs allow you to work with **strings**, any series of characters that are otherwise treated as text. You can use cell references to carry strings to other cells or a **text operator** to **concatenate** them (glue them together).

- Some also allow you to enter and display formulas in **English language formulas**. Frequently, it's easier to understand a formula that reads Jan.Sales-Jan.Costs than it is to know what D4-D16 is.

- A few programs allow you to add text at the end of a formula to **annotate** it (describe what it does) or attach **notes** to specific cells. This helps analyze and improve models at a later date.

REVIEW QUESTIONS

1. What are operators? List and describe the functions of four of them.

2. What formula would you enter to multiply the values in cells A1 and C3? To divide A1 by C3? To add them? To subtract A1 from C3?

3. What is the order of operations? If you want to change the order, how can you do so?

4. What is the difference between a constant and a variable?

5. What is a constant? When would you use one?

6. What is a variable? When would you use one?

7. What two ways can you use to enter a formula? Which approach do most experienced users prefer? Why?

8. Why do some programs require you to type a plus sign before entering the first character in a formula, for example, +B2-B3?

9. What is a string? What is the term used to describe gluing two strings together? What type of operator performs this function?

10. What is an English language formula? What is its advantage?

11. What two ways are used to help you understand the purpose of a formula?

TOPIC 5-8

Functions

OBJECTIVES

After completing this topic, you will be able to

- Describe what built-in functions are
- Explain the concepts of syntax
- List and briefly describe typical functions
- Describe logical operators and their uses

All spreadsheet programs contain built-in **functions** designed to perform commonly used calculations. Many of the calculations they can perform are quite complicated, so functions simplify model building by simplifying the formula building you must enter.

Functions have a structure, or **syntax**, that you must follow.

- A **prefix** must begin every function. Frequently, the prefix is an at sign (@) followed by the function's name, usually a contraction of the full name. On some programs, the @ must precede the function's name. On other programs, this is not necessary. For example, a function that sums the values in a series of cells might be called @SUM or SUM, and a function that averages the numbers in a series of cells might be named @AVG or AVG.
- **Arguments** must follow the prefix and be enclosed in parentheses. Arguments can be numbers, cell references, ranges, formulas, or other functions. If the function contains more than one argument, each part is separated from the other by commas or semicolons.

For example, to calculate monthly payments on a loan, the function syntax is @PMT(Principle, Interest, Period). The prefix is @PMT (for **PayMenT**). The arguments are Principle, Interest, and Period and are separated by commas and enclosed in parentheses. If you substitute numbers in the function, for example, the function @PMT(10000,.14,48) calculates and displays monthly payments of $1,402.60.

Instead of entering the values into a function, you can enter them into other cells, and then enter references to those cells into the function (Figure 5-38). The values in these cells are calculated just as if they were a part of the function. Entering the values into their own cells makes them into variables that you can easily change to explore what-ifs. Functions can also be used in combinations (Figure 5-39).

FIGURE 5-38

	A	B	C	D	E	F
1	Principle	$10,000				
2	Interest	14%				
3	Periods	48				
4	Payment	$273.26	← PMT(B1,B2/12,B3)			
5						
6						
7						
8						
9						
10						
11						
12						
13						
14						
15						
16						
17						
18						
19						
20						

FIGURE 5-38
Functions That Refer to Other Cells
The arguments for this function have been entered into cells B1, B2, and B3. The function then includes references to those cells. The references are arranged in the same order as if the values themselves had been entered into the function and are separated by commas. The function calculates the same result as if the values had been embedded, but now you can easily change any of the three arguments, and it calculates a new result.

	A	B	C	D	E
1	Principle	$10,000			
2	Interest	14%			
3	Periods	48			
4	Payment	$273.26			
5	Payment (rounded)	$273.00	← ROUND(PMT(B1,B2/12,B3),0)		
6					
7					
8					
9					
10					
11					
12					
13					
14					
15					
16					
17					
18					
19					
20					

FIGURE 5-39
Functions in Combinations
This figure shows the same function entered in Figure 5-38 nested in another function that rounds the result of the first function's calculation to zero decimal places. The function reads "Round the value of the function @PMT(B1,B2/12,B3) to zero decimal places." The original function calculates the value $273.26, but the new one rounds it to $273.00.

TYPES OF FUNCTIONS

The number and types of functions vary from program to program, as does the exact name of the function and the way its arguments are structured. Functions can usually be grouped into categories such as financial, statistical, and mathematical. Tables 5-11 through 5-16 describe and illustrate some of the functions available on most programs. The actual prefix used to

Entering Functions So That You Can Safely Insert and Delete Columns and Rows

When a function like @SUM totals a range of cells, you can generally delete rows or columns within the range, and the function adjusts automatically. But if you delete the upper left-hand or lower right-hand corner of the range, the cell displays an error message and must be reentered. In these cases, if you move the cursor to the cell containing the error message and look at the formula, it reads something like *@SUM(B3..ERROR)*, indicating which cell in the formula has been deleted.

	A	B	C	D	E	F
1	SALES FORECAST					
2	--------------	-----	-----	-----	-----	------
3	Computers	100	210	441	926	1,945
4	Modems	25	53	110	232	486
5	Printers	50	105	221	463	972
6	Programs	200	420	882	1,852	3,890
7	Manuals	10	21	44	93	194
8	Paper	300	630	1,323	2,778	5,834
9	Diusplays	26	55	115	241	506
10	--------------	-----	-----	-----	-----	------
11	Totals	711	1,493	3,136	6,585	13,828
12						
13						
14						
15						
16						
17						
18						
19						
20						

Ruled Lines

In this figure, ruled lines have been entered on rows 2 and 10. The function @(B2.B10) has been entered into cell B11 and then copied to other columns on the same row. The range refers to the ruled lines, not the rows containing numbers. You can safely insert or delete rows anywhere between the ruled lines without affecting the functions. They will adjust automatically to include the new range.

If you add ruled lines to separate ranges on your models, functions like @SUM that refer to ranges can refer to the lines instead of to the top and bottom rows of numbers in the range. This helps guide you; you can safely insert or delete rows anywhere between the ruled lines without affecting any of the functions.

enter the function is shown in these tables in parentheses. On some programs, the prefix must have an at sign (@). On others, it is not required.

Using range names, you can also define your own functions. For example, to enter a function that calculates the hypotenuse of a triangle, you would normally enter the function @SQRT (A1^2+A2^2) into cell A3. You can then enter the measurements of the two sides of the triangle into cells A1 and A2. Using range names, you would enter the function @SQRT (OPPOSITE^2+ADJACENT^2) and name cell A1 OPPOSITE and cell A2 ADJACENT.

TABLE 5-11
Financial Functions

Present value (@PV) calculates the present value of a series of payments (called an ordinary annuity). Arguments are the payments, interest rate, and period.

	A	B
1	Annual payments	$1,000
2	Rate	8%
3	Periods	20
4	Present value	$9,818.15

← @PV(B1,B2,B3)

Net present value (@NPV) calculates the net present value of an investment. Arguments are the discount rate and future net cash flows.

	A	B
1	Year 1 cash flow	$1,000
2	Year 2 cash flow	2,000
3	Year 3 cash flow	3,000
4	Discount rate	11%
5	Net present value	$4,717.72

← @NPV(B4,B1..B3)

Future value (@FV) calculates the future value of an annuity. Arguments are the regular payment, interest rate, and period.

	A	B
1	Payment	$1,000
2	Rate	10%
3	Periods	25
4	Future value	$98,347.06

← @FV(B1,B2,B3)

Mortgage payments (@PMT) calculates the monthly payments needed to amortize a loan. Arguments are the principle, interest rate, and period.

	A	B
1	Principle	$10,000
2	Interest	12%
3	Periods	48
4	Payment	$1,205.23

← @PMT(B1,B2,B3)

Internal rate of return (@IRR) calculates the internal rate of return of an investment. Arguments are the series of cash flows and the discount rate.

	A	B
1	Payments	Guess
2	($1,000)	14%
3	500	
4	500	IRR
5	500	0.349034419
6	500	

← @IRR(B2,A1..A6)

TABLE 5-12
Statistical Functions

Average (@AVG) calculates the average value of a range of values. Argument is a range of values.

	A
1	1
2	2
3	3
4	4
5	2.5

← @AVG(A1..A4)

Count (@COUNT) calculates the number of nonblank cells in a range. Argument is a range of values

	A
1	1
2	2
3	3
4	4
5	4

← @COUNT(A1..A4)

TABLE 5-12, continued

Maximum (@MAX) calculates the largest value in a range of values. Argument is a range of values.

	A
1	1
2	2
3	3
4	4
5	4

← @MAX(A1..A4)

Minimum (@MIN) calculates the smallest value in the range. Argument is a range of values.

	A
1	1
2	2
3	3
4	4
5	1

← @MIN(A1..A4)

Standard deviation (@STD) calculates the standard deviation of a range of values. Argument is a range of values.

	A
1	1
2	2
3	3
4	4
5	1.118033989

← @STD(A1..A4)

Variance (@VAR) calculates the variance of a range of numbers. Argument is a range of values.

	A
1	1
2	2
3	3
4	4
5	1.25

← @VAR(A1..A4)

TABLE 5-13
Numeric and Mathematical Functions

Sum (@SUM) calculates the total sum of a range of values. Argument is a range of values.

	A
1	1
2	2
3	3
4	4
5	10

← @SUM(A1..A4)

Integer (@INT) calculates the integer part of a number. Argument is a number with at least one decimal place.

	A
1	4.1234
2	4

← @INT(A1)

Round (@ROUND) rounds a number to a specified number of decimal places. Arguments are a number with at least one decimal place and the number of decimal positions you want to round it to.

	A
1	4.1234
2	4.1

← @ROUND(A1,1)

Absolute (@ABS) calculates the "absolute" value of a number—converts negative numbers to positive numbers. Argument is a negative number.

	A
1	-4.1234
2	4.1234

← @ABS(A1)

(continued)

TABLE 5-13, continued

Square root (@SQRT) calculates the square root of a number. Argument is a number.

	A
1	4.1234
2	2.03061567	← @SQRT(A1)

Exponent (@EXP) calculates the base of the natural logarithm (e), that is, (2.7182818) to the power of the argument. Arguments are a number and a power.

	A
1	4.1234
2	61.7688999	← @EXP(A1)

Sine (@SIN) calculates the sine of a radian angle. Argument is a radian angle.

	A
1	4.1234
2	-0.831502746	← @SIN(A1)

Cosine (@COS) calculates the cosine of a number and displays the result as the angle in radians. Argument is a number.

	A
1	4.1234
2	-0.555520641	← @COS(A1)

Tangent (@TAN) calculates the tangent of a radian angle. Argument is a radian angle.

	A
1	4.1234
2	1.49679901	← @TAN(A1)

Arc Sine (@ASIN) calculates the radian angle of a cosine. Argument is a cosine value.

	A
1	0.5
2	0.523598776	← @ASIN(A1)

Arc Cosine (@ACOS) calculates the radian angle of a cosine value. Argument is a cosine value.

	A
1	0.5
2	1.047197551	← @ACOS(A1)

Arc Tangent (@ATAN) calculates the radian angle of a tangent value. Argument is a tangent value.

	A
1	0.5
2	0.463647609	← @ATAN(A1)

TABLE 5-14
Typical Relational Operators

Operator	Description	Operator	Description
=	Tests if values are equal. For example, @IF(A1=1,1,0) displays a 1 if the value in cell A1 is equal to 1, and a 0 if it is not.	>	Tests if one value is greater than another. For example, @IF(A1>1,1,0) displays a 1 if the value in cell A1 is greater than 1, and a 0 if it is equal to or less than 1.
< >	Tests if values are not equal. For example, @IF(A1< >1,1,0) displays a 0 if the value in cell A1 is equal to 1, and a 1 if it is not.	<=	Tests if one value is less than or equal to another. For example, @IF(A1<=1,1,0) displays a 1 if the value in cell A1 is less than or equal to 1, and a 0 if it is greater than 1.
<	Tests if one value is less than another. For example, @IF(A1<1,1,0) displays a 1 if the value in cell A1 is less than 1, and a 0 if it is equal to or greater than 1.	>=	Tests if one value is greater than or equal to another. For example, @IF(A1>=1,1,0) displays a 1 if the value in cell A1 is greater than or equal to 1, and a 0 if it is less than 1.

TABLE 5-15
Typical Logical Operators

Operator	Description
AND	Sets up tests where two or more conditions must be satisfied before a calculation is made. For example, @IF(A1<1#AND#A2>2,1,0) displays a 1 (true) if the value in cell A1 is less than 1 and the value in cell A2 is greater than 2. It displays a 0 (false) if the value in either cell is between 1 and 2.
OR	Sets up tests where one of two or more conditions must be satisfied before a calculation is made. For example, @IF(A1=1#OR#A1=2,1,0) displays a 1 (true) if the value in cell A1 is equal to 1 or 2. It displays a 0 (false) if the value is anything else.
NOT	Sets up tests where one condition must be met and another not. For example, @IF(A1<1#OR##NOT#A2>2 displays a 1 (true) if the value in cell A1 is less than 1 or the value in cell A2 is not greater than 2. It displays a 0 (false) if the value in cell A1 is 1 or more or the value in cell A2 is greater than 2.

TABLE 5-16
Order of Operations for Relational and Logical Operators

Operator	Description	Precedence Level
=	Equal to	3
<	Less than	3
>	Greater than	3
<=	Less than or equal to	3
>=	Greater than or equal to	3
<>	Not equal to	3
NOT	Logical NOT	2
AND	Logical AND	1
OR	Logical OR	1

RELATIONAL AND LOGICAL OPERATORS

When entering functions and formulas, you can use relational and logical operators.

- You use **relational operators** to test if a statement is true or false. For example, the relational operator > (greater than) in the formula A1>1000 calculates TRUE (Lotus 1-2-3 displays a 1 for TRUE) if the value in cell A1 is larger than 1000 and FALSE (Lotus 1-2-3 displays a 0 for FALSE) if it is less than or equal to 1000. Table 5-14 describes some typical relational operators.

- The real power of relational operators is seen when you use them along with **logical operators** in IF statements. You use IF statements to set up tests; for example, if a value is greater than, equal to, or less than another value, one calculation is made; if not, another calculation is

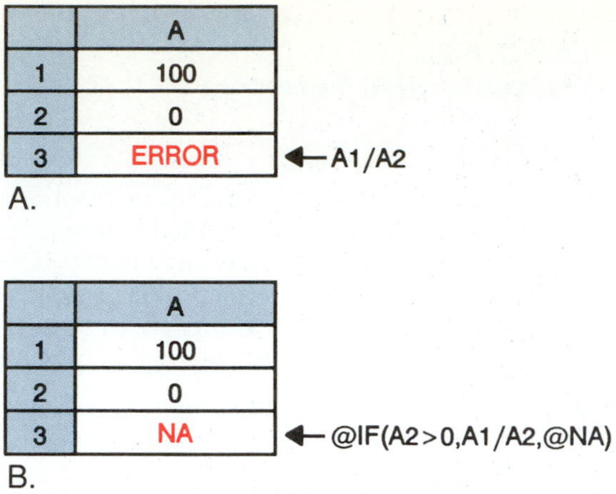

FIGURE 5-40
IF Statements

When you use the division operator (/) in a formula that refers to other cells, an *ERR* or similar message is displayed in the cell containing the formula if the cell referred to in the denominator is blank, as it may be in a template. For example, if you enter the formula A1/A2 into cell A3, it displays an error message if cell A2 is blank (a). To prevent error messages, you can embed the formula in an IF statement. For example, in cell D7 the formula is @IF(A2–0,A1/A2,@NA). This formula now reads "If the value in cell A2 is greater than 0, then divide the value in cell A1 by the value in cell A1; otherwise display an NA (b)."

	A
1	100
2	0
3	ERROR

◀— A1/A2

A.

	A
1	100
2	0
3	NA

◀— @IF(A2>0,A1/A2,@NA)

B.

made. Figure 5-40 shows an example, and Table 5-15 describes some typical logical operators.

Relational operators, like arithmetic operators have orders of precedence.

SUMMARY AND KEY TERMS

- Almost every program contains **functions**, small programs that perform frequently used, and occasionally very complex, calculations.
- Functions have a **syntax** that includes a prefix and arguments. The **prefix** is the name of the function. **Arguments** are the functions to be performed.
- Functions are often grouped by their application. For example, there are financial, statistical, and numeric functions.
- You can use an IF function and **relational operators** to test whether a statement is true or false. Typical relational operators include = (equal to), > (greater than), and < (less than).

REVIEW QUESTIONS

1. What is a function? What are they used for?
2. How would you enter a function to round the value 1.11234? To round the value in cell B4? To round the sum of the values in the range A1..A3?
3. What will the function SUM(B4..B6) do? What is the term SUM called? What is the reference B4..B6 called (other than a range)?
4. How would the formula @IF(A27>0,A1/A2,0) read if you translated it into normal English?
5. List five relational operators, and describe what they are used for.

Printing Models

OBJECTIVES

After completing this topic, you will be able to

- Describe how you print models
- List and briefly describe typical printing options

When you want to print a model, you can print the entire model (Figure 5-41) or a selected range (Figure 5-42). You can also print the file to a printer or to an ASCII text file. Printing to a disk file makes the file usable by other programs or allows you to print it from the operating system. The print file can be retrieved by many word processing programs for editing, formatting, and inclusion in reports. Only the displayed values of the cells are printed to the disk. Since formulas are not printed, the print file cannot be used as a working file. When printing to a disk file, you must specify a name for the file. The program usually adds an extension like .PRT to the file to distinguish it from the original file.

Printing usually involves several steps. For example, when printing a model with 1-2-3, you follow the steps below. On other programs, you follow similar steps, and you choose from similar options.

1. Initiate the *Print* command by pressing **/P** (for *Print*).
2. Specify if the model is to be printed to the disk or to the printer. To print the model to the printer, you press **P** (for *Printer*). To print the model to a file, you press **F** (for *File*). This displays the Print menu (after you specify a filename if printing to the disk). Table 5-17 describes the choices on the Print menu.
3. Select the *Range* command to type in the coordinates of, or use the cursor to point to, the upper left-hand and lower right-hand cells in the

---

TIP: Printing Models

On some programs, you can set a column width to 0 so that its contents do not appear in the printout (see Topic 5-10). On other programs, you can achieve the same effect by hiding the contents of cells (see Topic 5-18).

FIGURE 5-41

Printing the Entire Model
Here the entire model has
been printed. The specified
range was cell A1 as the
upper left-hand corner and
cell G22 as the lower right-
hand corner.

	A	B	C	D	E	F	G	H
1			Jan	Feb	Mar	April	May	
2		ADVERTISING EXPENSES						
3		Journals/Magazines	$2,320	$2,579	$3,187	$3,499	$3,721	
4		Trade Shows	$1,345	$859	$1,639	$2,733	$2,814	
5		Mailing List Purchases	$2,858	$3,143	$3,128	$3,516	$3,671	
6		Catalog- Postage	$3,430	$3,772	$3,754	$4,219	$4,405	
7		Samples	$599	$615	$812	$514	$981	
8		Advertising - Other	$73	$213	$341	$82	$421	
9		TOTALS	$10,625	$11,181	$12,861	$14,563	$16,013	
10		CATALOG INCOME						
11		ski clothing	$11,732	$8,643	$4,692	$2,916	$1,142	
12		bike clothing	$3,251	$9,132	$12,782	$14,297	$16,952	
13		gen. outdoor clothing	$2,163	$5,192	$6,832	$8,645	$7,391	
14		hiking/ski boots	$3,277	$8,527	$7,693	$7,920	$8,153	
15		packs/climbing equipment	$2,116	$5,692	$9,837	$12,321	$13,831	
16		sleeping bags/pads	$4,213	$7,834	$11,651	$14,816	$16,231	
17		tents	$2,788	$7,982	$12,638	$12,156	$14,776	
18		cooking equip/foodstuffs	$2,513	$2,870	$3,988	$4,753	$5,186	
19		bike accessories	$2,488	$2,512	$4,934	$5,329	$7,112	
20		bike/canoe racks	$1,158	$5,837	$7,931	$7,391	$9,128	
21		misc.	$564	$731	$842	$902	$2,768	
22		TOTALS	$36,263	$64,952	$83,820	$91,446	$102,670	

A. Selecting the Range

	Jan	Feb	Mar	April	May
ADVERTISING EXPENSES					
Journals/Magazines	$2,320	$2,579	$3,187	$3,499	$3,721
Trade Shows	$1,345	$859	$1,639	$2,733	$2,814
Mailing List Purchases	$2,858	$3,143	$3,128	$3,516	$3,671
Catalog- Postage	$3,430	$3,772	$3,754	$4,219	$4,405
Samples	$599	$615	$812	$514	$981
Advertising - Other	$73	$213	$341	$82	$421
TOTALS	$10,625	$11,181	$12,861	$14,563	$16,013
CATALOG INCOME					
ski clothing	$11,732	$8,643	$4,692	$2,916	$1,142
bike clothing	$3,251	$9,132	$12,782	$14,297	$16,952
gen. outdoor clothing	$2,163	$5,192	$6,832	$8,645	$7,391
hiking/ski boots	$3,277	$8,527	$7,693	$7,920	$8,153
packs/climbing equipment	$2,116	$5,692	$9,837	$12,321	$13,831
sleeping bags/pads	$4,213	$7,834	$11,651	$14,816	$16,231
tents	$2,788	$7,982	$12,638	$12,156	$14,776
cooking equip/foodstuffs	$2,513	$2,870	$3,988	$4,753	$5,186
bike accessories	$2,488	$2,512	$4,934	$5,329	$7,112
bike/canoe racks	$1,158	$5,837	$7,931	$7,391	$9,128
misc.	$564	$731	$842	$902	$2,768
TOTALS	$36,263	$64,952	$83,820	$91,446	$102,670

B. The Printout

	A	B	C	D	E	F	G	H
1			Jan	Feb	Mar	April	May	
2		ADVERTISING EXPENSES						
3		Journals/Magazines	$2,320	$2,579	$3,187	$3,499	$3,721	
4		Trade Shows	$1,345	$859	$1,639	$2,733	$2,814	
5		Mailing List Purchases	$2,858	$3,143	$3,128	$3,516	$3,671	
6		Catalog- Postage	$3,430	$3,772	$3,754	$4,219	$4,405	
7		Samples	$599	$615	$812	$514	$981	
8		Advertising - Other	$73	$213	$341	$82	$421	
9		TOTALS	$10,625	$11,181	$12,861	$14,563	$16,013	
10		CATALOG INCOME						
11		ski clothing	$11,732	$8,643	$4,692	$2,916	$1,142	
12		bike clothing	$3,251	$9,132	$12,782	$14,297	$16,952	
13		gen. outdoor clothing	$2,163	$5,192	$6,832	$8,645	$7,391	
14		hiking/ski boots	$3,277	$8,527	$7,693	$7,920	$8,153	
15		packs/climbing equipment	$2,116	$5,692	$9,837	$12,321	$13,831	
16		sleeping bags/pads	$4,213	$7,834	$11,651	$14,816	$16,231	
17		tents	$2,788	$7,982	$12,638	$12,156	$14,776	
18		cooking equip/foodstuffs	$2,513	$2,870	$3,988	$4,753	$5,186	
19		bike accessories	$2,488	$2,512	$4,934	$5,329	$7,112	
20		bike/canoe racks	$1,158	$5,837	$7,931	$7,391	$9,128	
21		misc.	$564	$731	$842	$902	$2,768	
22		TOTALS	$36,263	$64,952	$83,820	$91,446	$102,670	

A. Selecting the Range

FIGURE 5-42
Printing a Selected Range
Here only a part of the model, the advertising expenses, has been printed. The specified range was cell A1 as the upper left-hand corner and cell G9 as the lower right-hand corner.

	Jan	Feb	Mar	April	May
ADVERTISING EXPENSES					
Journals/Magazines	$2,320	$2,579	$3,187	$3,499	$3,721
Trade Shows	$1,345	$859	$1,639	$2,733	$2,814
Mailing List Purchases	$2,858	$3,143	$3,128	$3,516	$3,671
Catalog- Postage	$3,430	$3,772	$3,754	$4,219	$4,405
Samples	$599	$615	$812	$514	$981
Advertising - Other	$73	$213	$341	$82	$421
TOTALS	$10,625	$11,181	$12,861	$14,563	$16,013

B. The Printout

TABLE 5-17
Printer Commands

Menu Choice	Description
Range	Specifies the part of the model to be printed.
Line	Advances the paper in the printer one line each time it is selected. If selecting the *Line* command causes the paper to reach the bottom of a page, the paper advances to the top of a new page.
Page	Advances the paper in the printer one full page each time it is selected. This command advances the paper out of the printer and prints a footer at the bottom of the page if you so specified.
Options	Changes the page margins, page length, print font, and several other formats.
Clear	Clears some or all of the print settings previously specified.
Align	Tells the program you have adjusted the paper in the printer, and it is now at the top of the page. When you first load the program, the *Align* command is executed automatically. If you adjust the paper in the printer after beginning a session, be sure to use the *Align* command to reset the top of the page.
Go	Starts printing. On Lotus 1-2-3, this command works only if you have specified a range.
Quit	Leaves the Print menu and returns to ready mode.

range. On some programs, you need not specify a range if you are printing the entire model; on Lotus 1-2-3, you must specify the range.

4. Select the *Options* command to control the layout and appearance. Most programs automatically print on 8½-by-11-inch continuous form paper. Lotus 1-2-3 uses the default settings described in Table 5-18.

5. Select the *Align* command to align the paper in the printer, and then select the *Go* command to begin printing. When you are finished printing, select the *Page* command to advance the paper out of the printer.

TABLE 5-18
Default Printer Settings

Setting	Default
Top margin	Lines 1-2
Header	Line 3
Header margin	Lines 4-5
Lines for model to print on	Line 6-61
Footer margin	Lines 62-63
Footer	Line 64
Bottom margin	Lines 65-66
Paper length	Sixty-six lines
Right margin	Column 4
Left margin	Column 76

OPTIONS

Spreadsheet programs give you a great deal of control over the layout of your printouts. Getting a printout just right can sometimes require some experimenting. After getting the results you want, you should save the model because most programs save the print settings along with the file. The next time you use the model, you do not have to reenter the print settings.

Headers and Footers

Headers and footers can be added to the model to identify it. These may also include page numbers, dates, and times.

Margins

Left, right, top, and bottom margins can be changed. These settings are useful when switching between 8½-by-11-inch and 11-by-14-inch paper. You can tell the program you have changed the paper size or you want to change the layout of a print range by changing the margin settings.

Borders

Borders are used when a model is too wide to print on a single sheet of paper. For example, if you use column 1 for labels and print a wide model, column 1 appears only on the first page of the printout. This makes it hard to identify the contents of the rows on the second and subsequent pages. The same is true if you use row 1 for labels and print a long model. The labels appear only at the top of the first page. In either case, if you specify that these columns or rows be treated as borders, they are printed on each page of the printout. When you set borders, be sure they do not overlap the print range, or duplicate rows and columns will be printed.

On some programs, you can also print the row and column borders or turn them off. When you troubleshoot models, having these borders on a printout lets you annotate formulas to indicate their relationships to other cells. When you then make a final printout, you can turn these border off.

Fonts

On some programs, you can select text and format it so that it prints in a desired font, much as you would do on a word processing program. On other programs, you change fonts by sending setup codes to the printer. Using a small type size lets you print many more characters and lines on a page so that you can squeeze much more data onto a single sheet of paper.

Unfortunately, when using setup strings, different printers use different printer codes. You need to refer to your printer's manual to find the codes used to control printing. You enter setup strings as three-digit decimal ASCII numbers preceded by a backslash (\). For example, on an Epson printer (Table 5-19), the code for compressed print is 015. To use this as a setup string, you would enter \015. If you are entering more than one setup code, enter them one after another. For example, on an Epson printer, the setup string \027\071 turns on doublestrike printing.

Once a setup string is sent to the printer, the printer remains in that mode. To cancel the setup string, turn the printer off and then back on again. On Lotus 1-2-3 Release 2, you can use a pair of split vertical bars (❙ ❙)

TABLE 5-19 Typical Epson Setup Strings	
Print Control	**Setup String**
Compressed print on	\015
Compressed print off	\018
Doublestrike on	\027\071
Doublestrike off	\027\072
Set line spacing to 8 lpi	\0270
Set line spacing to 6 lpi	\0272

to enter setup strings in cells in the worksheet. This allows you to print different sections of the document using different typestyles. For example, on an Epson printer, you can enter ❙❙\015 in a cell to print the first part of a model in compressed type and ❙❙\018 in another cell to print the remainder in normal type.

Orientations and Page Length

You can specify portrait or landscape orientation if your printer offers a choice. The page length can be set to print between twenty and one hundred lines per page. The default length is sixty-six lines on 11-inch paper (six lines per inch). The number of lines from the print range actually printed depends on the top and bottom margins you have set and the space reserved for headers and footers.

Printing Cell Formulas

Normally when you make a printout, it looks the same as when displayed on the screen. But you can also print out the actual contents of cells, not their displayed results. This is especially useful when you want to troubleshoot a model or save a record of its contents.

PRINTING MULTIPAGE MODELS

Some models are simply too large to be printed on a single page. If your document is too wide or long, you may be able to print it out on a single page, or reduce the total number of pages required, by altering the print options.

- If the model is too wide to print on a single page, try making some columns narrower so that more columns fit on the screen and on a printed page. You can reduce the left margin, increase the right margin, or print the model in compressed type. You can also specify several individual ranges to print them on separate pages.
- If the model is too long to print on a single page, you can reduce the top and bottom margins or print the document eight lines per inch. On some programs, you can insert page breaks into the model to indicate sections that are to start on a new page. On other programs, you have to select the ranges for each page one at a time. To speed up the process, you can assign range names to the pages and create a macro to automatically print them in order (see Topic 5-22).

STOPPING THE PRINTER

Different programs offer different commands to stop the printer while it is printing. On some programs, you hold down **Ctrl** while you press **Break**. On other programs, you select *Cancel* from a dialog box. Both commands stop any further text from being sent to the printer. The printer may not stop immediately when you use these commands because some printers have buffers that store sections of the text before they are printed. The text stored in the printer's buffer prints, and then the printer stops. But if you turn off the printer after stopping it, the printer's buffer is cleared.

SUMMARY AND KEY TERMS

- You can send all of a model or just part of it to the printer or to a disk file.
- You can print to the disk when you want to use the model with another program like a word processor. This command prints only the calculated values, not the formulas and functions.
- When printing a model, you can specify options that include headers and footers, margins, borders, fonts, and portrait or landscape orientation.

REVIEW QUESTIONS

1. When making a printout, must you print the entire model?
2. Why might you want to print your model to a file on the disk?
3. What are the advantages of including headers and footers in a printout of a model?
4. What are borders used for?
5. What is a setup string?
6. How do you stop the printer while it is printing? What is a print buffer?

TOPIC 5-10

Changing a Model's Appearance

OBJECTIVES

After completing this topic, you will be able to

- Describe how and why you change column widths
- Explain how you format text and values

When you want your models, whether on the screen or in printouts, to be attractive and easy to read, you use formats to align text and format numbers. When you do this, you can use the global or range format commands.

- A global format affects all cells on the spreadsheet. Generally, you select a global format based on the format that will be used most often in a model and then override it in selected cells to display them as desired.
- To override the global format in selected cells, you use range formats.

Range formats have priority over global formats. For example, if you use a range command to format a group of cells and then change the global format, the format of the cells you formatted with the range command does not change. To make the cells in the range respond again to global commands, you must first reset them to the global format using a command designed for this.

COLUMN WIDTHS

You can change the width of individual columns or of all columns on the spreadsheet, and you can change them before or after you enter data into them. If you use a global command, it changes the width of all columns except those previously changed with a range command.

The width of a column, as measured in characters, determines how many characters can be displayed in cells falling in the column. When you first load a spreadsheet, all columns are usually nine characters wide. You can change the width of any or all columns to between one and the maximum width specified by your program.

Narrow columns let you see more on the screen and squeeze more into a printout, so columns should be as narrow as possible. Some programs even let you set columns widths to 0 so that their contents are hidden on the screen and don't appear in printouts. Since column width is always set for an entire column—it cannot be wider or narrower at the top than at the bottom—a column must be set to the width required by the longest entry in the column.

Column Widths and Text

If you enter text that is longer than the column is wide, the entire text is displayed only if the adjoining cell is empty. If the adjoining cell contains data, the text is truncated. The entire entry appears on the status line if you position the cursor in the cell. If text is too long, you can widen the column, justify the text, or, if the adjoining cell is blank, leave the text as is.

Column Widths and Values

The width of columns also affects whether numbers, entered directly or calculated by formulas, are displayed correctly. If a number is too large to be displayed in a cell, the program might either

- Display it in scientific notation, for example, display 100,000 as 1.00E + 5.
- Fill the cell with symbols, for example, ******, >>>>>>, ######, or !!!!!!.

This does not affect the value of the number, only its display. To properly display the number, change the column width of the cell, or change the format of the number. The column width required to correctly display numbers depends on

- The size of the number. Programs usually require columns to be at least one character wider than the largest value so that there is room to display a negative sign if needed.
- The format used. Formats that display commas or add dollar or percent signs require additional room for these characters.
- The number of decimal places specified when formatting.

For example, the number 12000 needs a column six characters wide, but if formatted as currency to two decimal places, $12,000.00, the same number needs eleven characters. If the number might be displayed as a negative value, the columns widths should each be one character wider; for example, −12000 requires seven characters, and ($12,000.00) requires twelve characters.

FORMATTING TEXT

You can align text (and on some programs, numbers) in cells. They can be aligned with the right or left edge of the cell or centered in the cell. On many programs, you can also justify text. On some programs, you can change the font used for text so that it prints in a different typestyle, in boldfaced or italic type, underlined, or in color.

If you enter text without a label prefix character, some programs align the text based on the global setting (the default setting is usually left aligned) and add the global label prefix character. If you want to change the alignment of text, you can do so as you enter it, or you can use the range and global alignment commands after entering it.

TABLE 5-20 1-2-3 Label Prefixes	
To Align Text	**Press**
With left edge of cell (default)	'(apostrophe)
With right edge of cell (with one-space margin)	"(double quote)
Centered in cell	ˆ(caret)

TABLE 5-21 Lable Prefix Menu Choices	
To Align All Text	**Choose**
With left edge of cells	*Left*
With right edge of cells (with one-space margin)	*Right*
Centered in cells	*Center*

Aligning Text During Entry

You can align text as you enter it by typing a label prefix character before typing the first character in the text. Table 5-20 lists the label alignment characters used by Lotus 1-2-3.

Aligning All Text to Be Entered

You can change the alignment of all text to be entered on the spreadsheet with the global alignment command. For example, on Lotus 1-2-3, you press **/WGL** (for *Worksheet, Global, Label*), and then specify a new default alignment from the menu choices described in Table 5-21. The new alignment affects all text entered after the change is made unless a different label prefix is entered with the text or it is realigned with a *Range* command.

Aligning Previously Entered Text

You can override the global text alignment to realign text in a cell or range of cells. For example, on Lotus 1-2-3, to align previously entered text, you press **/RL** (for *Range, Label*), and then specify that the text be aligned with the left or right edges of the cell or centered between them.

Entering Text That Begins with a Number

As you have seen, many spreadsheet programs use the first character you type to anticipate the kind of information you are entering. If you type a number first, these programs assume the cell is to contain a value. If you type text that begins with a number, one of the label prefixes must be used. If you begin text with a number, or any of the other characters listed in Table 5-4, without first entering a label prefix, the computer beeps, and the program switches to edit mode. The entry is not allowed until you begin it with a label prefix.

Once a number is entered with a label prefix, it cannot be used in mathematical operations. Be careful when entering text that could also be values. Telephone numbers and ZIP codes, in particular, could cause confusion if entered without a label prefix. For example, if you enter the phone number 555–1212, the last digits of the number are subtracted from the first digits, and the result, −657, is displayed. No error message results because the program assumes you are entering a formula.

Justifying Text

Text can be entered and then justified. Unlike word processing, where justifying refers to both margins being even, on spreadsheet programs, **justifying** refers to a command that wraps long sections of text so that it fits within a specified range of cells.

FORMATTING VALUES

Spreadsheet programs provide several formats you can use when formatting values on your spreadsheet. When formatting numbers, you can often specify the number of decimal places to be displayed. Formatting numbers does not affect the way they are used in formulas. Numbers are always accurately calculated up to the number of decimal places offered by the program, usually fifteen or so. For example, you can format the number 1000.1425 so that it is displayed as *$1,000*, *$1,000.14*, *1000.142*, and so on, but it is always calculated by any formulas that refer to it as 1000.1425.

Table 5-22 describes the formats available on 1-2-3. Figure 5-43 illustrates some typical formats. Those offered by other programs are similar although they have different names.

TABLE 5-22
Lotus 1-2-3 Value Formats

Format	Description
Fixed	Displays numbers to a specified number of decimal places.
Scientific	Displays numbers as exponential scientific notation, for example, 1E+01.
Currency	Add a dollar sign ($) before the number, separate thousands with commas, and display negative numbers in parentheses, for example, ($1,000). Some programs also allow you to display foreign currency symbols, for example, Deutsche marks, pounds sterling, and yen, but these may not print out if not supported by your printer.
, (comma)	Separates thousands with commas and displays negative numbers in parentheses, for example, (1,000).
General	Displays numbers to the calculated number of decimal places up to the limit imposed by the program. If the column is not wide enough, numbers are displayed in scientific notation or as an overflow value, for example, *****.
+/−	Displays positive numbers as a row of + and negative numbers as a row of − to create simple bar graphs.
Percent	Displays numbers as percentages followed by a percent sign (%) and multiplies the decimal equivalent by 100 to display the number as a whole number. For example, 10% is displayed as 0.1. When formatted, it is displayed as 10%(0.1*100), but it is still used in formulas as 0.1.
Date	Displays any of three date formats (see Topic 4-13).
Text	Displays formulas as entered instead of as current value. This is helpful when tracing the relationships among cells.
Hidden	Suppresses cell display.
Reset	Resets the range to the global format.

Number in cells | 1.5

FORMAT	DECIMAL PLACES		
	NONE	ONE	TWO
Fixed	2	1.5	1.50
Scientific	2E+00	1.5E+00	1.50E+00
Currency	$2	$1.5	$1.50
, (comma)	2	1.5	1.50
General	1.5	1.5	1.5
Percent	150%	150.0%	150.00%

A.

Number in cells | 100

FORMAT	DECIMAL PLACES		
	NONE	ONE	TWO
Fixed	100	100.0	100.00
Scientific	1E+02	1.0E+02	1.00E+02
Currency	$100	$100.0	$100.00
(comma)	100	100.0	100.00
General	100	100	100
Percent	10000%	10000.0%	10000.00%

B.

Number in cells | 1000

FORMAT	DECIMAL PLACES		
	NONE	ONE	TWO
Fixed	1000	1000.0	1000.00
Scientific	1E+03	1.0E+03	1.00E+03
Currency	$1,000	$1,000.0	$1,000.00
, (comma)	1000	1000.0	1000.00
General	1000	1000	1000
Percent	100000%	100000.0%	100000.00%

C.

FIGURE 5-43
Number Formats
This figure shows some typical formats and how they are displayed when the number of decimal places is changed. The number in the box labeled Number in cells is the number entered into each of the cells in the accompanying table. For example, in (a) the number 1.5 is displayed as 2 when formatted as fixed with no decimal places.

DATA AND LABEL ENTRY SPACES

When creating models to be used over again (sometimes called templates), it helps to indicate where new labels or data should be entered. Parentheses or square brackets can mark the space, and a dollar, number, or percent symbol can be added to identify the kind of data to be entered.

On some programs, you can use these characters anywhere on the spreadsheet. But other programs have the ability to manipulate strings. On some of these programs, functions or formulas that refer to these labels display an error message. Experiment with the data entry and label entry spaces described in Table 5-23.

If you use parentheses in data entry spaces, some programs assume that you are entering a formula unless you first enter a label prefix character. The square brackets ([]) are treated by most programs as text, so no prefix is required unless you want to align the text.

TABLE 5-23
Typical Data Entry and Label Entry Spaces

Numbers	Percentages	Dollars	Labels
(#.....)	(%)	($____)	( )
[#.....]	[%]	[$____]	[ ]
#____	____ %	$____	____

- You change the width of columns individually and in groups.

- If text is too long for a cell, it usually flows into the adjoining cell if that cell is empty.

- If a number is too large to be displayed in a cell with the format assigned to it, it is displayed in scientific notation, or a row of symbols is displayed in the cell. To display the actual number, you change its format or widen the column.

- You format text to align it in a cell. You can do so at the time you enter it or later.

- Justifying text refers to wrapping it so that it fits into a range of cells.

- You format numbers to display them with dollar or percent signs and change the number of decimal places displayed on the screen.

- Newer programs allow you to change fonts or otherwise format words and numbers using boldfacing, italics, or underlining.

1. If you formatted cells with a *Range* command and then change the global format, what happens to the cells formatted with the *Range* command?

2. Why would you want to change the width of a column?

3. What happens if text is too long to fit into a column?

4. What happens if a value is too long to fit into a column? Describe two ways you can correct the problem.

5. What does justify text mean?

6. If a cell displays a row of symbols, for example, ****** or >>>>>>, what is the cause? How do you correct it?

7. If a cell displays a number in scientific notation, for example, 1.00E+5, what is the cause? How do you correct it?

8. List and briefly describe five formats you can use for values.

TOPIC 5-11

Copying and Moving Data

OBJECTIVE

After completing this topic, you will be able to

- Explain how you copy and move data on the spreadsheet

You can copy or move the contents of cells to other locations on a spreadsheet. **Copying** lets you save time by entering a formula once and then copying it as needed. **Moving** lets you reorganize models as you create or revise them. These are two of the most powerful spreadsheet features.

You can also move or copy data from one model to another. On some programs, you open a window for each model, and then copy or move data from one window to the other. On other programs, you copy or move the data to its own file on the disk, and then use the program's commands to combine it with another spreadsheet on the screen (see Topic 5-19).

COPYING DATA

Copying allows you to enter formulas once and then copy them where needed, greatly speeding up the process of model building. For example, you can create a monthly budget by entering the necessary formulas into the first monthly column and then copying them to the other monthly columns.

When you copy a range of cells, a duplicate set of the range's contents and formats is copied from the original cells, called the **source range**, to a new location, called the **target range** (also called the destination range). The data in the cells in the source range is left unchanged (Figure 5-44). If any cells in the target range contain data, it is overwritten by the copied data.

When you copy ranges, you must specify cell addresses that define the source and target ranges (Figure 5-45). When you copy the contents of cells to which formulas in other cells refer, those formulas continue to refer to the original cells, not to the copies. Some programs let you choose whether you want to copy formulas in the source range or their calculated values.

MOVING DATA

When you **move** a range of cells, a duplicate of the cell's contents and formats is moved to the target range, and then the contents of the cells in the source range are automatically deleted (Figure 5-46). If the cells in the target

	A	B	C	D	E	F
1	1	11	21	31		
2	2	12	22	32		
3	3	13	23	33		
4	4	14	24	34		
5	5	15	25	35		
6	6	16	26	36		
7	7	17	27	37		
8	8	18	28	38		
9	9	19	28	38		
10	10	20	30	40		
11						
12						
13		13	23			
14		14	24			
15		15	25			
16		16	26			
17		17	27			
18		18	28			
19						
20						

FIGURE 5-44
Copying a Range
When you copy a range of cells, a duplicate set of the range's contents and formats is copied from the source range to the target or destination range. Data in the cells in the source range is left unchanged

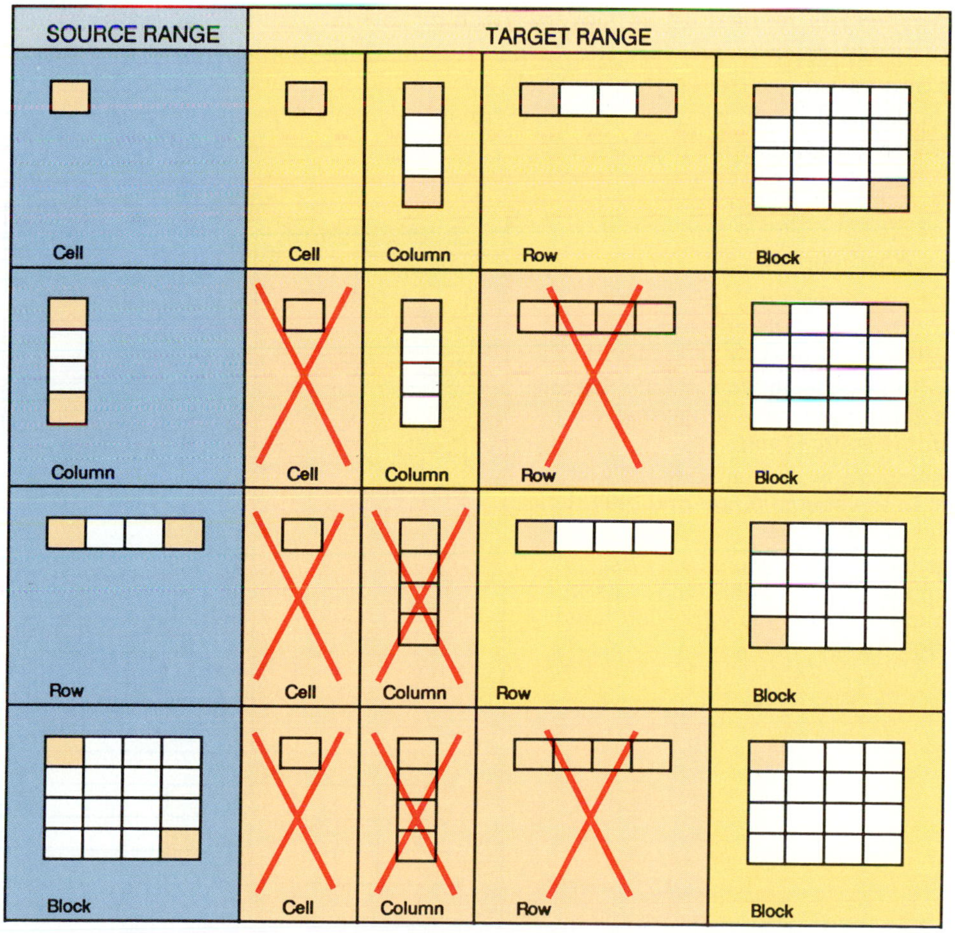

FIGURE 5-45
Specifying Ranges When Copying
The cells you specify as the source and target ranges are shown in a second color. Some combinations of source and target ranges are not possible, for example, copying a column to a cell. These impossible combinations are indicated by being overprinted in color on the figure. (Some programs have a *Transpose* command that allows you to copy data from columns to rows and vice versa.)

	A	B	C	D	E	F
1	1	11	21	31		
2	2	12	22	32		
3	3			33		
4	4			34		
5	5			35		
6	6			36		
7	7			37		
8	8			38		
9	9	19	28	38		
10	10	20	30	40		
11						
12						
13		13	23			
14		14	24			
15		15	25			
16		16	26			
17		17	27			
18		18	28			
19						
20						

FIGURE 5-46
Moving a Range
When you move a range of cells, a duplicate of the cell's contents and formats is moved to the target range, and then the contents of the cells in the source range are automatically deleted.

range contain any data, it is overwritten by the data that is moved in. If any formulas refer to cells in the target range, they display error messages. When you move the contents of cells, you must specify cells that define the source and target ranges. The cells you specify vary depending on the shape of the range (Figure 5-47).

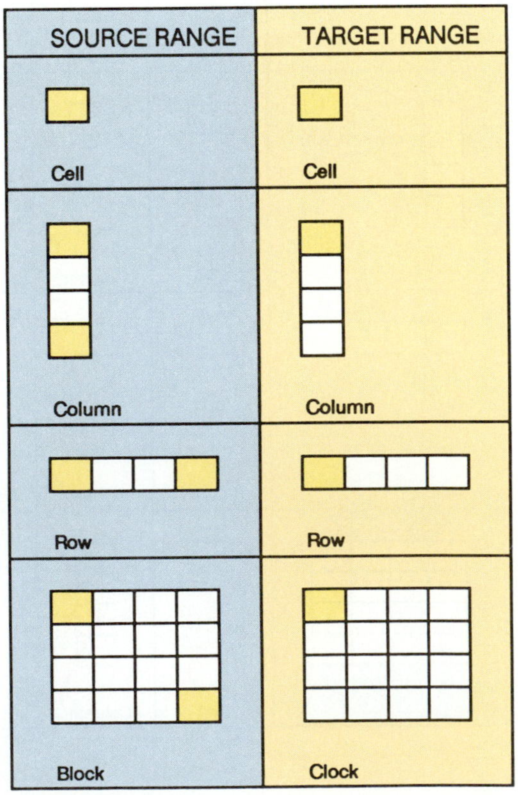

FIGURE 5-47
Specifying Ranges When Moving

- If you are moving a single cell, the source range is the address of that cell, and the target range is the address of the cell you move it to.
- If you are moving a column, you specify the top and bottom cells in the source range and only the top cell in the source range.
- If you are moving a row, you specify the first and last cells in the source range and only the first cell in the target range.
- If you are moving a block, you specify the upper left-hand and lower right-hand cells in the source range and only the upper left-hand cell in the target range.

SOURCE RANGE	TARGET RANGE
Cell	Cell
Column	Column
Row	Row
Block	Clock

	A	B	C	D	E	F
1						
2		100		100	200	300
3		200				
4		300				
5						
6						
7						
8						
9						
10						
11						
12						
13						
14						
15						
16						
17						
18						
19						
20						

FIGURE 5-48
Transposing a Range
Here, the *Transpose* command has been used to copy the numbers in cells B2 through B5 (a column) to cells D2 through G2 (a row).

TRANSPOSING DATA

Some programs have a *Transpose* command that copies or moves the data in cells in a row to a column and from cells on a row to a column—one of the combinations of source and target ranges that isn't possible on many programs (Figure 5-48).

SUMMARY AND KEY TERMS

- When moving or copying data, the **source range** is the range of cells you are copying or moving from. The **target range** is the range you are copying or moving to.
- **Copying** copies data from the source range to the target range. Data in the source range remain unchanged.
- **Moving** copies the data in the source range to the target range and then deletes the data in the source range.
- When copying or moving data, you define the ranges differently depending on the shape of the range being copied or moved.
- You can copy or move a column of data to a row and vice versa with the *Transpose* command.

REVIEW QUESTIONS

1. What is the difference between copying and moving a range?
2. When copying or moving cells, how to you specify the range to be moved?
3. If you copy or move data into a range that already contains data, what happens to the old data?
4. What is the purpose of the *Transpose* command?

TOPIC 5-12

Relative and Absolute Cell References

OBJECTIVES

After completing this topic, you will be able to

- Explain the differences among relative, absolute, and mixed cell references
- Describe how you specify absolute references

If you typed in every formula and function that you needed, you would not have to be concerned about relative and absolute cell references. But they become very important when you enter a formula in one cell and then copy it to others to save time.

RELATIVE REFERENCES

When you create formulas, they often refer to other cells on the spreadsheet. The program does not "remember" the actual cell coordinates (for example, A1); instead, it remembers the position relative to the cell the formula is entered in, for example, one column to the left and two rows up. When you copy the formula to another cell, it refers not to the original cell but to whatever cell is one column to the left and two rows up from the cell you copied it to (Figure 5-49).

This automatic adjustment occurs because the reference to the cell is a **relative reference**; that is, the position of the cell referred to is relative to the position of the formula. The program's default setting is relative references; all formulas have relative references unless you specify otherwise.

ABSOLUTE REFERENCES

You do not always have to keep references to cells relative. You can also make them **absolute references** so that a formula refers to the same cell wherever it is copied on the spreadsheet (Figure 5-50).

MIXED REFERENCES

You can also use **mixed references**, which keep the reference to the row or column relative while making the other reference absolute (Figures 5-51 and 5-52).

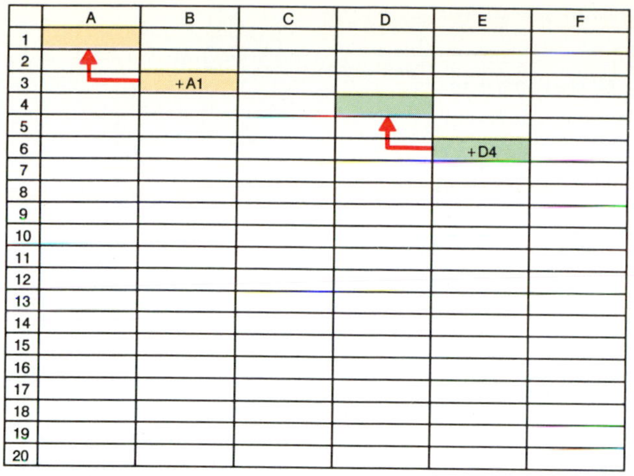

FIGURE 5-49
Copying Relative References
When you enter the cell reference +A1 into cell B3, the value contained in cell A1 is carried to cell B3. But when you copy the formula to cell E6, it no longer refers to cell A1 but to cell D4 because the formula refers to the cell one column over and two rows up.

FIGURE 5-50
Copying Absolute References
When you enter the formula +A1 into cell B3 (the dollar signs indicate both the row and column references are absolute), it has the same result as entering +A1, but it behaves differently when you copy it. It no longer remembers the cell it refers to relative to its position. It remembers the absolute position, in this case, cell A1. When you copy it to another cell, say, cell E6, it still refers to cell A1.

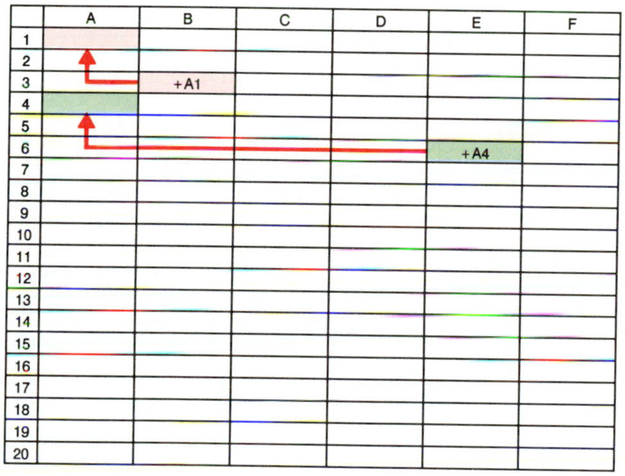

FIGURE 5-51
Copying Absolute Column and Relative Row References
You enter the formula +$A1 (the column reference is absolute, but the row is relative) into cell B3. When you copy the cell reference to cell E6, part of it changes, and part of it does not.

- The column reference, which was made absolute by adding a dollar sign in front of it, does not change when copied. It always refers to column A.

- The row reference, the part of the formula you made relative, does change. It always refers to a cell two rows up, just as it did in the original position.

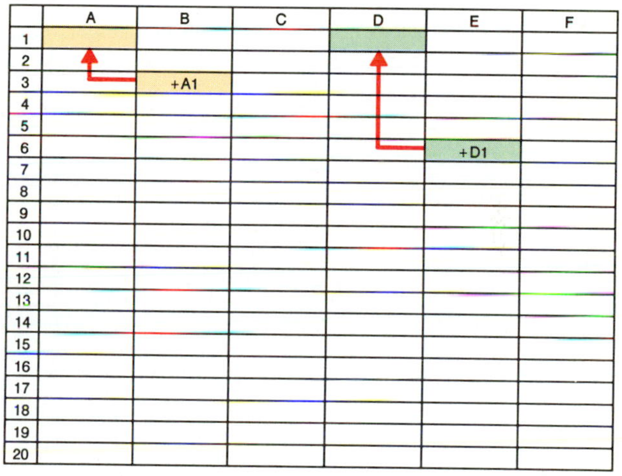

FIGURE 5-52
Copying Relative Column and Absolute Row References
When you enter the formula +A$1 into cell B3 and copy it to another cell, say, cell E6, it always refers to the cell one column to its left (the relative reference) and on the same row as the original position (the absolute reference).

RELATIVE AND ABSOLUTE CELL REFERENCES

481

Cell Reference	Column	Row
A1	Relative	Relative
$A1	Absolute	Relative
A$1	Relative	Absolute
A1	Absolute	Absolute

TABLE 5-24
Absolute and Relative Cell References

Cell Reference	Column	Row
A1	Relative	Relative
$A1	Absolute	Relative
A$1	Relative	Absolute
A1	Absolute	Absolute

SPECIFYING REFERENCES

The way you specify that a cell reference is absolute varies from program to program. On most programs, you specify absolute references by adding dollar signs ($) in front of the column or row references.

Many programs also assign a function key the task of cycling through the four possible combinations so that when you are using cursor pointing to build a formula, you can point to a cell and press the key to select the type of reference you want. When you are pointing to a cell in point mode, the cell reference you are pointing to changes its reference each time you press the specified key. As you cycle through the reference types, the cell reference on the edit line changes. Table 5-24 describes the sequence of available choices.

CASE STUDY
Creating a Five-Year Plan

Creating spreadsheet models is part understanding and part creativity. You have to understand the principles behind the problem you want to solve; no spreadsheet can solve a problem you do not understand. You also have to understand the spreadsheet program because many of the problems you want to solve may require relatively complex models. Finally, you have to know how to structure a model, not just to calculate an answer, but so that it is flexible enough to reveal relationships and answers you may not have expected. The process of building spreadsheet models is like an upward spiral of learning. As you learn more about the program, you tend to learn more about the problem. This encourages you to explore new avenues and to learn even more about the program so that you can execute the analysis you want to perform.

In the topics in this part, we introduce you to the individual procedures you use to create spreadsheet models. In this case study, we look at how you put those individual procedures together to explore a five-year business plan. From this, you should get an overview of how you effectively plan, create, and use models.

Step 1: Planning the Model   The power of a spreadsheet is directly related to your ability to create models that are not only accurate but also flexible and easy to use. First, you should determine what answers you are looking for—perhaps the annual sales, cost of goods sold, and gross margins over a five-year period. Next, you identify the variables, the numbers you want to be able to change to explore their impact on the outcome. This way you can enter formulas that refer to these cells elsewhere on the spreadsheet. When you make a change in any of these variables, all formulas referring to them will recalculate and display new results. Numbers in the cells that these formulas refer to will be treated just as if the numbers were part of the formulas. When creating a model, you have to decide what variables you want to explore. You then structure your models accordingly so that they are listed separately and not embedded in formulas where they can't easily be changed.

In this case study, you want to explore the impact of sales increase and costs of goods on gross margins. Since these are the items you want to explore, your variables are the initial sales, the rate of sales growth, and cost of goods as a percentage of sales.

To plan the model, you begin by drawing a quick sketch, showing where the line items to be included will be located on the spreadsheet (Figure A). You can also briefly annotate the relationship between the elements you will enter.

Step 2: Loading the Program   After you have planned your model, the next step is to load the program if the spreadsheet isn't already on the screen. If you are planning to save your work, you should insert a formatted data disk into drive B, and then close that drive's door.

Step 3: Setting Global Formats   You can display the numbers that you enter into cells in a variety of ways to make them easier to read and to make printouts more attractive and professional looking. You control the way numbers are displayed by changing their format. When you first load a spreadsheet program, one of the program's formats will already be set as the default format. This means any numbers you enter will be displayed in this format. The default format is usually the program's general format. This format displays numbers out to the number of decimal places that are calculated or that you entered.

For example, if you enter the number 1.123400 in a cell, it will be displayed as *1.1234*—only the trailing zeros will be dropped. You can change the default setting to any of the other formats available on the program. Since most of the numbers you will be entering in our model are dollars, you set the format so that all numbers are displayed with no decimal places and with commas separating thousands. Commands like this, that affect the

FIGURE A
The Model's Plan
The plan is simply a sketch of the key features of the model. It indicates the layout and identifies variables and formulas.

	A	B	C	D	E	F
1	PART 1. VARIABLES					
2	Opening Sales					
3	Sales growth rate					
4	Cost of goods sold					
5						
6	PART 2. MODEL					
7	Year					
8	Sales					
9	Cost of goods sold					
10	Gross margin					
11						

FIGURE B
Row Labels
The row labels identify the data that is to be entered into the model.

entire spreadsheet, are called global commands. You select a global format that is best for the greatest number of entries. You can then override this global format as necessary to display the numbers in individual cells, or in groups of cells, in any other format offered by the program. The commands you use to format only a part of the spreadsheet are called range, or local, formats.

Step 4: Entering Labels   Now that you have set the global formats, you can enter labels, numbers, and formulas into any of the spreadsheet's cells. You begin by entering the model's row labels (Figure B).

To enter labels, you use the cursor movement keys to move the cursor to the desired cell. You then type in the label and enter it into the cell by pressing **Return**. (A few programs require you to press a specific key before typing in the label's first character to tell the computer you are entering a label.) As you type in labels (or any other entries), they are displayed on the edit line (sometimes called the entry line). The data appears on the edit line only until you press **Return** to complete the entry. While displayed on the edit line, you can edit the entry to correct mistakes. You press **Backspace** to back over and erase any characters that you have entered incorrectly. If you discover a mistake after pressing **Return**, you can return it to the edit line for editing.

When entering labels, you can change column widths at any time. Since you enter long labels in column A, you must widen it so that the entire labels are displayed. If necessary, you can adjust the width later. To widen a single column, move the cursor to any cell in the column, and then use the program's Column Width command.

Step 5: Entering Numbers   After you have entered labels, you enter the variables used to create and later explore the five-year model (Figure C). You enter the numbers in this example as 1000 (opening sales), . 1 (sales growth rate), and . 56 (cost of goods sold). When you first enter the numbers, they are displayed in the global format you entered earlier—with no decimal places and with commas separating thousands. This global format setting will save time in the long run, but now you can see that the numbers are not displayed as you'd like. The initial sales figure is displayed without a dollar sign, and the two percentages have been rounded off—the sales growth rate entered as .1 has been rounded to 0, and the cost of goods sold percentage entered as .56 has been rounded to 1. To display these numbers the way you want, you have to reformat them with a range format—a format different from the global format you entered earlier.

	A	B	C	D	E	F
1	PART 1. VARIABLES					
2	Opening Sales	1000				
3	Sales growth rate	0.1				
4	Cost of goods sold	0.56				
5						
6	PART 2. MODEL					
7	Year					
8	Sales					
9	Cost of goods sold					
10	Gross margin					
11						

FIGURE C
Variables
The variables are the numbers you want to change to see how they affect the outcome.

Step 6: Formatting Numbers Locally In this step, you use local, or range, formats in those cells that you want to be displayed differently from the global setting. In our model, you format the opening sales number so that it is displayed with a leading dollar sign, and the sales growth rate and cost of goods sold values so that they are displayed as percentages, with no decimal places (Figure D).

Numbers formatted with the program's range format commands are displayed differently from the way you entered them. You do not enter the commas, dollar signs, or percent signs; these were added by the format commands. But no matter how the numbers are formatted and displayed, they are used in calculations just as they were entered. For example, a number entered as 10.12345 and then formatted to be displayed as $10.12 will still be calculated by any formulas referring to it as 10.12345.

Step 7: Entering the First Year's Formulas Now that you have entered the variables, you create the five-year plan. Begin by entering the formulas that calculate the first year of the forecast. You can enter formulas into spreadsheet cells either to calculate numbers directly, like a calculator, or to refer to values that you enter into other cells.

You know that when you use a calculator you must follow certain rules when entering formulas so that you get the correct result. For example, on a calculator, specific keys have been assigned the task of performing specific calculations like addition, subtraction, multiplication, and division. You must enter numbers and press these keys in a certain sequence to get the correct result. The same basic rules apply when you enter formulas into spreadsheet cells. If you make a mistake and incorrectly enter a formula, the

	A	B	C	D	E	F
1	PART 1. VARIABLES					
2	Opening Sales	$1,000				
3	Sales growth rate	10%				
4	Cost of goods sold	56%				
5						
6	PART 2. MODEL					
7	Year					
8	Sales					
9	Cost of goods sold					
10	Gross margin					
11						

FIGURE D
Range Formats
Formats change the way the numbers are displayed but not the way they are calculated by formulas.

FIGURE E
First Year's Formulas
The first year's formulas carry down the sales from cell B2 and then calculate cost of goods and gross margin for those sales.

	A	B	C	D	E	F
1	PART 1. VARIABLES					
2	Opening Sales	$1,000				
3	Sales growth rate	10%				
4	Cost of goods sold	56%				
5						
6	PART 2. MODEL					
7	Year	1989				
8	Sales	1,000	← B2			
9	Cost of goods sold	560	← B4*B8			
10	Gross margin	440	← B8-B9			
11						

FIGURE F
Second Year's Formulas
The second year's formulas calculate sales based on the previous year's sales and the growth rate in cell B3. They also calculate cost of goods and gross margin for the sales.

	A	B	C	D	E	F
1	PART 1. VARIABLES					
2	Opening Sales	$1,000				
3	Sales growth rate	10%				
4	Cost of goods sold	56%				
5						
6	PART 2. MODEL					
7	Year	1989	1990	← B7+1		
8	Sales	1,000	1,100	← B8+($B3*C8)		
9	Cost of goods sold	560	616	← $B4*C8		
10	Gross margin	440	484	← C8-C9		
11						

computer will usually beep and display an error message in the cell. A few programs will also place the cell contents onto the edit line and put the program into edit mode so that you can correct the mistake.

When you enter formulas on a spreadsheet, only their calculated result is displayed in the cell, not the formula itself. To see the formula, you move the cursor to the cell into which the formula has been entered to display it on the status line. Figures E and F show the displayed results and the formulas that calculate them. To enter the formulas, follow these instructions.

Year (Cell B7)

Move the cursor to cell B7, and enter a date identifying the first year's column. You could enter this date as a label, but enter it as the number 1989 so that you can use it in the next step as the basis for a formula to date the other annual columns. You have to reformat the number because the global format displays it as 1,989 (with a comma separating thousands), and you want it displayed as a fixed number.

Sales (Cell B8)

Now enter a formula that carries down the opening sales from cell B2 by entering a reference to that cell into cell B8. The way you enter this cell reference varies from program to program. On some programs, you enter the reference B2 into cell B8, and then any value entered into cell B2 is automatically carried to cell B8. On other programs, if you enter the reference as B2, it will appear in the cell as a label that cannot be used in calculations. On these programs, you tell the program you are entering a formula by typing the plus sign (+) before typing the letter B. Therefore, the formula you enter in cell B8 on these programs is +B2.

If you change the number in cell B2, the number in cell B8 changes automatically. Notice how the number carried down from cell B2, and not the cell reference B2, is displayed in cell B8. Also notice that the cell reference carries down only the value, not the format. The number in cell B8 does not have the leading dollar sign.

Cost of Goods Sold (Cell B9)

The cost of goods sold is initially 56 percent of sales, so you could enter the formula .56*1000 into cell B8, which would calculate $560. But if you then change the opening sales in cell B2 or the cost of goods percentage in cell B4, the cost of goods in this cell would not change; you would have to edit or reenter the formula to reflect the change. A better approach is to enter the formula using cell references instead of the numbers themselves. This way, if the numbers in any of the cells to which the formula refers are changed, the formula will recalculate and display a new result. The formula we enter, B4*B8, multiplies the contents of cell B4 (the cost of goods sold percentage of 56 percent) by the contents of cell B8 (this year's sales of $1,000). The result is 560.

Gross Margin (Cell B11)

Gross margin is sales (cell B8) minus cost of goods sold (cell B9). You type the formula B8–B9 into cell B11, and then press Return to enter it. The displayed result is 440 (1000 - 560).

Step 8: Entering the Second Year's Formulas   The formulas you enter for the second year are similar to those you entered into the first year's column except for one significant difference: You enter them so that you can copy them and still have them refer to the correct cells. This way you can instantly make a two-year plan into a three-, four-, five-, or fifty-year plan just by copying the formulas (Figure G).

Year (Cell C7)

You enter the formula +B7+1 into cell C7 to date the second year's column. The displayed result is 1,990 (1989 + 1) until you reformat it. Now you see why you did not enter the date into the first column as a label. If you had,

	A	B	C	D	E	F
1	PART 1. VARIABLES					
2	Opening Sales	$1,000				
3	Sales growth rate	10%				
4	Cost of goods sold	56%				
5						
6	PART 2. MODEL					
7	Year	1989	B7+1	C7+1	D7+1	E7+1
8	Sales	1,000	B8 + ($B8*B8)	C8 + ($B8*C8)	D8 + ($B8*D8)	E8 + ($B8*E8)
9	Cost of goods sold	560	$B4*C8	$B4*D8	$B4*E8	$B4*F8
10	Gross margin	440	C8-C9	D8-D9	E8-E9	F8-F9
11						

FIGURE G
Copied Formulas
The copied formulas refer to the cells specified by the absolute and relative references.

you couldn't create additional dates just by adding the number 1 to the previous year. In the next step, you see what happens to this formula when you copy it to the other annual columns.

Sales (Cell C8)

Sales in the second year are based on the previous year's sales and the sales growth rate in cell B3. Initially, they will be 10 percent greater than they were in the first year. The formula you enter to calculate this growth is last year's sales + 10 percent of last year's sales, or B8+(B3*8).

Since you will copy the formula that you enter into this column to the other annual columns, it must meet two conditions when copied.

- The part of the formula referring to cell B3 (the sales growth rate) must refer to that cell regardless of the column you copy it to. This is called an absolute reference because it refers to the same cell wherever it is copied.
- The part of the formula referring to the previous year's column must always refer to the column to it's immediate left regardless of the column you copy it to. This is called a relative reference because it refers to cells that are relative to its position.

Relative references are the program's default reference, and all references are relative unless you specify otherwise. The way you do this varies from program to program, but with many programs, you type a dollar sign ($) before a cell reference to indicate that the cell it refers to shouldn't change when the formula is copied. The formula you enter into cell C8 using this method is B8+(B8*$B3). It calculates the result 1,100 (1,000+(1000*.1)).

Cost of Goods Sold (Cell C9)

Cost of goods sold is calculated by a formula that multiplies the cost of goods percentage figure in cell B4 by sales in this column. Again, this formula will be copied to other columns, and you want it to refer to cell B4 regardless of the column you copy it to. To do this, the reference to cell B4 must be an absolute reference. You therefore enter the formula $B4*C8 into cell C9, and the displayed result is 616 (.56*1100).

Gross Margin (Cell C11)

Gross margin is calculated by a formula identical to that entered into the first annual column except it refers to the sales and cost of goods calculated in this column. You can just copy the formula entered into the previous column. You entered it into that column as B8-B9, but since both references are relative, the formula becomes C8-C9 when you copy it to column C.

Step 9: Copying the Second Year's Formulas   You can now copy the formulas you entered into column C to as many annual columns as you like, and all values will be calculated correctly. (If any of these formulas are to be formatted with local formats, you should do so before copying them since formats are copied along with formulas.) To copy the formulas, you initiate the copy command, and then answer two prompts.

- The range to be copied from
- The range to be copied to

	A	B	C	D	E	F
1	PART 1. VARIABLES					
2	Opening Sales	$1,000				
3	Sales growth rate	10%				
4	Cost of goods sold	56%				
5						
6	PART 2. MODEL					
7	Year	1989	1990	1991	1992	1993
8	Sales	1,000	1,100	1,210	1,331	1,464
9	Cost of goods sold	560	616	678	745	820
10	Gross margin	440	484	532	586	644
11						

FIGURE H
Copied Results
The calculated results show how sales increase at 10 percent a year for a five-year period.

Here you copy the contents of the cells located between rows 7 and 11 in column C to the same rows in columns D, E, and F. Let's look at how the formulas behave when you copy them to these columns (Figure H).

Row 7   Year

The formula you entered as B7+1 into column C appears as C7+1, D7+1, and E7+1 in columns D through F. The formula always adds 1 to the calculated value in the column to its left, resulting in dates from 1989 to 1993.

Row 8   Sales

The formulas on row 8 contain both relative and absolute cell references, so let's carefully look at them to see how they behave when you copy them.

The relative references to cell B8 in the original formula always refer to sales in the column to its left despite which cell it was copied to on the same row. For example, the original formula in column C has two references to column B. When copied to column D, these references refer to column C; in column E, they refer to column D; and so on.

The absolute reference to cell B3, however, remains the same regardless of the column you copy it to. Thus the formula always calculates sales that are 10 percent greater than the previous year.

Row 9   Cost of Goods Sold

The formula you entered to calculate cost of goods also contains an absolute reference. When you copy it, the formula always multiplies the contents of cell B4 (the absolute reference) by the sales in the column it's copied to (the relative reference). The result is that each year's cost of goods is 56 percent of the current year's sales.

Row 11   Gross Margin

The formula you entered to calculate gross margin contains only relative references, so when you copy it to other columns, it always subtracts the current year's cost of goods from the current year's sales.

Step 10: Exploring What-Ifs   Once you have created a model and calculated some initial results, you do not stop. The purpose of the model is to explore what-ifs, to see how results change under varying conditions. When exploring what-ifs, you can do so in one of two ways: individually or cumulatively.

- When you explore what-ifs individually, you restore any previous changes to their original values before you explore a new change.
- When you explore what-ifs cumulatively, you leave any previous changes as is and introduce new changes.

The advantage of exploring what-ifs individually is that you can see the relationship between causes and effects more easily because any effects can be traced to a single cause. The reason you explore what-ifs sequentially is that few solutions to business problems can be achieved by making a single change. Multiple changes are almost always required to obtain a desired result. Sequential changes let you experiment with several changes at the same time so that the best combination of changes can be identified.

What If the Sales Growth Rate Increases from 10 to 15 Percent?

Let's see what happens when you change one of your assumptions and increase the annual sales growth rate from 10 to 15 percent. To make a change of this kind, you move the cursor to the cell containing the sales growth rate, type a new entry over the old, and then press **Return**. The new value replaces the old one, and when the spreadsheet is recalculated, it is used by formulas that refer directly or indirectly to the cell you entered the change into. All such formulas automatically recalculate and display new results. Let's look at what happens when you increase the sales growth rate (cell B3) from 10 to 15 percent (Figure I).

Sales (Row 8)

Sales increase in all but the first year by 15 percent instead of the original 10 percent.

Cost of Goods Sold (Row 9)

Cost of goods sold also increases but remains a constant 56 percent of sales.

Gross Margin (Row 11)

Gross margins increase because sales are increasing faster than cost of goods sold.

What If the Cost of Goods Sold Increases from 56 to 60 Percent?

In this what-if, let's leave the previous change as is, and then increase cost of goods sold from 56 to 60 percent of sales (Figure J).

FIGURE I
What-If Sales Growth Rate Increases
When you increase the sales growth rate variable, sales increase more rapidly.

	A	B	C	D	E	F
1	PART 1. VARIABLES					
2	Opening Sales	$1,000				
3	Sales growth rate	15%				
4	Cost of goods sold	56%				
5						
6	PART 2. MODEL					
7	Year	1989	1990	1991	1992	1993
8	Sales	1,000	1,150	1,323	1,521	1,749
9	Cost of goods sold	560	644	741	852	979
10	Gross margin	440	506	582	669	770
11						

	A	B	C	D	E	F
1	PART 1. VARIABLES					
2	Opening Sales	$1,000				
3	Sales growth rate	15%				
4	Cost of goods sold	60%				
5						
6	PART 2. MODEL					
7	Year	1989	1990	1991	1992	1993
8	Sales	1,000	1,150	1,323	1,521	1,749
9	Cost of goods sold	600	690	794	913	1,049
10	Gross margin	400	460	529	608	700
11						

FIGURE J
What-If Cost of Goods Sold Increases
When you change the cost of goods variable, cost of goods increases faster than sales.

Sales (Row 8)

Sales stay the same as in the previous what-if but are still higher than in the original example in all but the opening year, where they remain unchanged.

Cost of Goods Sold (Row 9)

Cost of goods sold also increases from the previous what-if and is higher than the original example because it is now 60 percent instead of 56 percent of sales.

Gross Margin (Row 11)

Gross margins are lower than in the previous what-if but are higher than in the original example. If your goal is to obtain higher gross margins when cost of goods sold is increased (perhaps because of increased prices), you have discovered the way you can achieve this—increase sales sufficiently to achieve the increase in gross margins despite the increased cost of goods.

Step 11: Creating Graphs Many spreadsheet programs have a built-in graphics capability. Since this option is becoming increasingly common, let's see how you would use graphs. Figure K shows two graphs: one using the original sales growth rate of 10 percent and one with the rate changed to 15 percent. They both plot the values calculated on rows 8 (sales), 9 (cost of goods sold), and 11 (gross margin) over the five-year period covered by the plan. A quick comparison of the two graphs makes the relative rates of growth in sales, cost of goods sold, and gross margins much clearer. The value of graphs is that they show relationships and trends like these much better than numbers do.

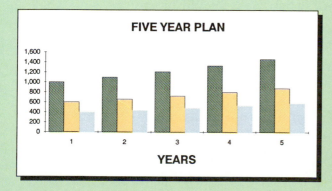

FIGURE K
Graph
A graph shows the results at a glance.

Creating Models

When you first learn to use a spreadsheet, the basic rule is keep your models simple. Take the time to label all values and formulas so that you know what they are the next time you use the model. Take the time to lay out the model on the screen so that it's clear what is to be entered where and what results are being calculated by formulas. The little extra time it takes to document your models is always worth the effort, especially if you plan to use the model again or expect someone else to be able to understand a printout or to use the models themselves. Here are some points to keep in mind when creating a spreadsheet model.

- Start small and expand the models gradually. Models that start out large and complex tend to be difficult to understand, troubleshoot, and audit.
- Identify variables, those numbers you will want to change, to see their effect on the model.
- Save time by entering formulas once and then copying them where needed. For example, if you are building a monthly budget, enter the necessary formulas in the first column, and then copy that column to the other eleven monthly columns.
- Save your work frequently. A power failure, brownout, or a serious mistake could cause you to lose a lot of work.
- Test and audit your results before you rely on them for major decisions. It may seem atavistic, but you should check all calculated results using a pencil and paper so that you can be sure your mechanical calculations match your electronic ones. The ease with which you can create formulas on a spreadsheet is matched only by the ease with which you can enter, copy, or move them incorrectly.
- You may want to create supplemental models to break down some line items in even more detail. Although an analysis of gross sales may show a steady increase, a breakdown of those sales by market may reveal that sales are increasing dramatically in one market while falling off in another. Making decisions based on just the gross figure would prevent you from addressing the problems associated with the declining segment of the market.

- Explore what-ifs extensively. Look for the variables the model is most sensitive to. For example, one user was analyzing a direct mail campaign to see how many units would have to be sold to break even. Several variables were involved, including the cost of the mailing piece and the cost of the product being sold. To the user's surprise, the model was much more sensitive to changes in the unit mailing cost than it was to the cost of the unit being sold. On reflection, the reason was simple. The cost of the mailing piece was multiplied by the number mailed. The cost of the product was multiplied by the number sold. With a 2 percent response rate expected, a 1 cent cost in the mailing piece was equivalent to a 50 cent rise in the cost of the product. Without having explored a series of what-if questions, this "principle" would have gone unrecognized.
- Save the finished work. You can use it again and improve it as you understand more about the principles behind the problem and learn how to use the program better.
- Document the model. At the time you create a model, you usually understand what each of the formulas does. But the next time you use it you may forget some of the assumptions you built into it. Thus you should document all models—especially by labeling all items on the model. You should also make a printout of the model as it appears on the screen and another printout of the cell formulas. You can then write explanatory notes on these printouts so that you'll understand the model later. If other people use the model as a template, the documentation has to be even better. A brief description of what the model does, where data should be entered, and what calculations are made should be clearly explained. If you have built any assumptions into the model, you should also document them so that others know about them. For example, a model using a tax table may be quickly dated. If other users are unaware of the source of the tax rates the model is based on, they might assume the model is still accurate.

- Relative references in formulas don't refer to a specific cell when copied. They always refer to a relative position, such as two columns to the left and one row up.

- Absolute references always refer to the same cell regardless of where they are copied to.

- Mixed references combine absolute and relative references.

- On most programs, you enter a dollar sign in front of a row or column reference to make it absolute. Many programs provide a function key that cycles you through the four possible combinations, A1, $A1, A$1, and A1.

1. What is the difference between a relative and an absolute cell reference?

2. What are mixed references?

3. How do you specify absolute references in Lotus 1-2-3?

4. What key do you use in Lotus 1-2-3 to cycle through the four possible combinations of cell references?

5. If you enter the formula B3 into cell D4 and then copy it to cell G6, what cell will it refer to in its new position?

6. If you enter the formula B3 (the $ indicates an absolute reference) into cell D4 and then copy it to cell G6, what cell will it refer to in its new position?

7. If you enter the formula $B3 (the $ indicates an absolute reference) into cell D4 and then copy it to cell G6, what cell will it refer to in its new position?

8. If you enter the formula B$3 into cell D4 and then copy it to cell G6, what cell will it refer to in its new position?

Windows and Fixed Titles

OBJECTIVES

After completing this topic, you will be able to

- Describe the differences between windows and split screens
- Explain why you use fixed titles

There are times when you want to work with more than one model at the same time. Other times, a model is too large to see all of it on the screen. Some programs allow you to open multiple windows on the screen. When a model is too large to be displayed on the screen, some programs allow you to split the screen. You can also use fixed titles to view widely separated parts of a model at the same time.

WINDOWS

The newest spreadsheet programs allow you to have more than one model on the screen at the same time (Figure 5-53). Each model is displayed in its own **window**. When more than one model is displayed in this way, it is easy to compare them or to copy and move data between them.

Many older programs allow you to split the screen horizontally or vertically so that you can display widely separated sections of the spreadsheet on the screen at the same time (Figure 5-54). The two parts of the spreadsheet displayed in the split screen's windows can be scrolled together (called **synched**) or separately (called **unsynched**) so that you can bring together the sections of the model you want to compare on the screen at the same time. Split screens are especially effective if you want to explore what-if situations. For example, to see the effect of changes in sales and expenses on profits, you can split the screen and then scroll it so that you can see both the cells you want to change and the cells you want to watch to see the effects of the changes. When using split screens, keep the following points in mind:

- Entering data in either part of the split screen affects the underlying spreadsheet as a whole.
- Titles, column widths, global formats, and label prefixes can be set differently in each part of the split screen. When the windows are cleared, the format of the upper or left window becomes the format for the entire spreadsheet.

494

	WINDOW 1			
	A	B	C	D
1	Cost of car	$12,000		
2	Down payment	2,000		
3	Loan required	10,000		
4	Interest rate	13%		
5	Term of loan (in months)	48		
6	Monthly payment	$268.27		
7				
8				
9				
10				

	WINDOW 2			
	A	B	C	D
1	Cost of car	$12,000		
2	Down payment	2,000		
3	Loan required	10,000		
4	Interest rate	13%		
5	Term of loan (in months)	48		
6	Monthly payment	$268.27		
7				
8				
9				
10				

FIGURE 5-53
Multiple Windows
Newer programs allow you to open multiple windows on the screen. Each window contains its own model.

	A	B		C	D	E	F
1	PART 1. VARIABLES		1				
2	Opening Sales	$1,000	2				
3	Sales growth rate	15%	3				
4	Cost of goods sold	56%	4				
5			5				
6	PART 2. MODEL		6				
7	Year	1989	7	1990	1991	1992	1993
8	Sales	1,000	8	1,150	1,323	1,521	1,749
9	Cost of goods sold	600	9	690	794	913	1,049
10	Gross margin	400	10	460	529	608	700
11			11				
12			12				
13			13				
14			14				

FIGURE 5-54
Split Screens
When the screen is split, you press the Window key to move the cursor between them. The same parts of the model can be displayed in both windows, but one can be formatted to display the calculated results of formulas and the other the formulas themselves.

FIXED TITLES

Since the topmost rows and leftmost columns are often used for labels identifying the contents of rows and columns, scrolling can make them temporarily disappear from the screen. Many programs allow you to prevent this by **fixing** (also called *locking*) these titles into position so that the rest of the model scrolls under them (Figure 5-55). Some programs allow you to fix any rows and columns on the screen; others fix only column A and row 1. Generally, you are offered four choices.

- Fix rows
- Fix columns
- Fix both rows and columns
- Clear, or unfix, rows and columns

	A	B	C	D	E
1	Part 1. Variables:				
2	Initial sales	1,000			
3	Sales growth rate	10%			
4	Cost of goods sold	56%			
5					
6	Part 2. Model:				
7	Year	1988	1989	1990	1991
8	Sales	1,000	1,100	1,210	1,331
9	Cost of goods sold	560	616	678	745
10	Gross margin	440	484	532	586
11					
12					
13					

A.

FIGURE 5-55
Fixed Titles
In this illustration, columns A and B have been fixed.

A. When you position the cursor in the rightmost column of the screen, columns A through E are displayed.

B. When you press the right arrow key, the spreadsheet scrolls to the left to bring columns F through H into view. Notice how columns A and B have not scrolled off the other side of the screen, but columns C, D, and E have scrolled under the fixed column and are no longer visible.

	A	B	F	G	H
1	Part 1. Variables:				
2	Initial sales	1,000			
3	Sales growth rate	10%			
4	Cost of goods sold	56%			
5					
6	Part 2. Model:				
7	Year	1988	1464		
8	Sales	1,000	820		
9	Cost of goods sold	560	820		
10	Gross margin	440	644		
11					
12					
13					

B.

SUMMARY AND KEY TERMS

- **Windows** allow you to load more than one model at the same time.
- Older programs allow you to **split the screen** so that you can view the same file through two or more windows. When split, you can scroll the two windows together (**synched**) or separately (**unsynched**).
- You **fix titles** to keep the topmost rows and leftmost columns locked in position so that they won't scroll off the screen.

REVIEW QUESTIONS

1. What are windows? What are they used for?
2. How does a split screen differ from windows?
3. What does the *Sync* command do? The *Unsync* command?
4. When you split the screen and then format two windows differently, what happens when you clear the screen? Which window's formatting remains in effect if you had two horizontal windows? If you had two vertical windows?
5. What are fixed titles? What are they used for? List three ways can you fix titles.

Recalculation Methods

OBJECTIVES

After completing this topic, you will be able to

- Describe how programs recalculate formulas and functions
- Describe when recalculation occurs and the order formulas are recalculated in
- Describe forward and circular references

Recalculation occurs when you change numbers in a model and want all formulas updated to reflect the change. Recalculation commands control when recalculation occurs and the order formulas are recalculated in.

WHAT CELLS ARE RECALCULATED

Programs vary in the way they recalculate a spreadsheet. Most spreadsheets automatically recalculate all the formulas in your model every time you enter a new formula or value so that any cells referring to a new or changed value display correct results. The larger your model becomes, the longer it takes to recalculate it. Two approaches have been introduced into newer programs to speed up recalculation: background and minimal recalculation.

- Some programs recalculate the formulas in cells on the screen first so that your display is updated. The rest of the cells are then recalculated while you continue to work on the model. This is called **background recalculation**.
- Some programs recalculate only those cells that refer to cells where numbers have been changed. This is called **minimal recalculation**.

WHEN RECALCULATION OCCURS

You can usually specify when a spreadsheet recalculates and the number of times it does so. The choices offered include automatic, manual, and iteration.

- *Automatic* recalculates the entire model every time any data is entered in a cell.

- *Manual* recalculation occurs only when you press the specified recalculation key. Since the time required to recalculate a model depends on the model's size and the number and complexity of its formulas, you can use manual recalculation to speed up your work. This mode prevents recalculation from occurring every time you enter a number or formula. You recalculate the spreadsheet only when you want to check the results so far. Programs usually display an indicator telling you when the spreadsheet needs to be recalculated to display the correct current values in cells containing formulas.
- *Iteration* determines the number of times the recalculation cycle is repeated. When a model has circular or forward references, the iteration setting is used to recalculate the model the necessary number of times.

Since recalculation can take a long time on large models, some programs have a command that recalculates only a single formula. For example, on Lotus 1-2-3, you move the cursor to the cell containing the correct formula, press **F2**, and then press **Return**.

ORDER OF RECALCULATION

In addition to controlling when the model recalculates, you can control the order in which formulas are recalculated.

Natural first recalculates all formulas to which a formula refers before recalculating the formula. Forward references can be used in models when the spreadsheets is set to this mode without having to recalculate the spreadsheet more than once to calculate the correct result.

Columnwise begins in cell A1, recalculates column A, then goes to B1, recalculates column B, and so on (Figure 5-56). Use columnwise recalculation only when you need to explicitly control the order of recalculation (if there is a circular reference in your model, for example).

Rowwise begins in cell A1, recalculates row 1, then goes to A2, recalculates row 2, and so on (Figure 5-57). Use rowwise recalculation only when you need to explicitly control the order of recalculation.

FORWARD REFERENCES

When a formula refers to a cell in any column to its right or on any row below it, it is a **forward reference**. When a spreadsheet is set to some types of recalculation, a correct answer is not calculated because the formula refers forward to a cell that has not yet been recalculated. To display the correct result, the spreadsheet may have to be recalculated a second time.

	A	B	C	D	E	F
1	1	9	103	111	119	
2	2	10	104	112	120	
3	3	11	105	113	121	
4	4	12	106	114	122	
5	5	13	107	115	123	
6	6	100	108	116	124	
7	7	101	109	117	125	
8	8	102	110	118	126	
9						
10						

FIGURE 5-56
Columwise Recalculation
Columnwise recalculation begins in cell A1, recalculates column A, then goes to B1, recalculates column B, and so on.

	A	B	C	D	E	F
1	1	2	3	4	5	
2	6	7	8	9	10	
3	11	12	13	100	101	
4	102	103	104	105	106	
5	107	108	109	110	111	
6	112	113	114	115	116	
7	117	118	119	120	121	
8	122	123	124	125	126	
9						
10						

FIGURE 5-57
Rowwise Recalculation
Rowwise recalculation begins in cell A1, recalculates row 1, then goes to A2, recalculates row 2, and so on.

CIRCULAR REFERENCES

Circular references occur when a formula refers either directly or indirectly to itself. Some programs display an indicator if the model contains one or more circular references to warn you they exist. If they do exist, you must recalculate the spreadsheet more than once to get the correct result, and even then, a correct result may not be possible.

Circular references that eventually give a correct result are said to converge. Unfortunately, some circular references diverge; that is, each time the spreadsheet is recalculated, the answer is further from the correct result. For example, if you enter the formula $1 + A1$ into cell A1 it refers to itself, so it is a circular reference. Each time you recalculate the spreadsheet, the formula adds 1 to the currently displayed value—essentially acting as a counter displaying the number of times the spreadsheet is recalculated. Other kinds of circular references continue to display new values each time the spreadsheet is recalculated or toggle between two results and never reach a correct calculation. Some of these toggle between two states, and others diverge from the correct answer.

- When you change a number in a spreadsheet, formulas display the new results only when the spreadsheet is **recalculated**.
- Recalculation controls what cells are recalculated, when they are recalculated, and in what order.
- When the program recalculates the formulas on the screen first, it is called **background recalculation** because other cells are recalculated while you continue working.
- If the program recalculates only those formulas that are affected by a change you make, it is called **minimal recalculation**.
- Most programs offer recalculation that is manual or automatic. **Manual recalculation** requires you to press a key to recalculate the model. **Automatic recalculation** recalculates it each time you enter a number or make a change.
- Iteration controls the number of times a spreadsheet is recalculated.
- Recalculation is normally set to **natural** so that all formulas to which a given formula refers are recalculated first. You can also set recalculation **by row** or **by column** in specific circumstances.
- **Forward references** are cell references that refer to cells below a formula or to its right.
- **Circular references** are cell references in a formula that refer directly or indirectly to the cell it has been entered into.

SUMMARY AND KEY TERMS

1. When you change a number in a model, what must occur before formulas reflect the change?
2. What does background recalculation mean?
3. What does minimal recalculation mean?
4. What is the difference between manual and automatic recalculation?
5. What does iteration refer to?
6. List and briefly describe three orders formulas can be recalculated in.
7. What is natural recalculation?
8. What is the difference between columnwise and rowwise recalculation?
9. What are forward references? Circular references?

REVIEW QUESTIONS

TOPIC 5-15

Lookup Tables

OBJECTIVES

After completing this topic, you will be able to

- Describe the purpose of lookup tables
- Explain the differences between horizontal and vertical lookup tables
- Describe how the offset determines the value selected from the table

What if you are calculating taxes due, and the tax rate varies depending on the net income earned? Do you have to enter the tax rate manually after calculating the tax rate? The answer is no if your program has the ability to use **lookup tables**. The function of these tables is quite simple; you use them to look up a value on a table. A lookup function

- Looks for a specified value on a row or column of the table
- Selects a corresponding value in an adjoining row or column

Spreadsheet programs have two kinds of lookup tables: vertical and horizontal. Figure 5-58 shows how you would create a vertical lookup table. Figures 5-59 and 5-60 show what happens when you use the vertical lookup table to explore what-ifs. Horizontal lookup tables (Figure 5-61) work the same way as vertical lookup tables, but the lookup function looks up a value on one row of a table and then selects values in the same column on adjoining rows. Figures 5-62 and 5-63 show what happens when you use the horizontal lookup table to explore what-ifs.

On a lookup table, you specify which row or column the value is selected from by specifying an **offset**. For example, if the offset is 1, the value on the row or column next to the value being looked up is selected. If the offset is 2, the value on the second row or column is selected.

	A	B	C	D	E	F
1	TAX CALCULATION MODEL			TAX RATE LOOKUP TABLE		
2	Net income	$7,500		Income	US rate	UK rate
3	Tax rate (US)	10%		$0	0%	0%
4	Tax rate (UK)	15%		$1,000	10%	15%
5	Taxes due (US)	$750		$10,000	20%	25%
6	Taxes due (UK)	$1,125				
7						
8						
9						
10						
11						

FIGURE 5-58
Vertical Lookup Table
The model above has two parts, the tax calculation model (columns A and B) and the tax rate lookup table (columns D through F). To use the model, you enter a net income value into cell B2. The model contains two lookup functions, in cells B3 and B4, that then look up the net income you entered on the lookup table (cells D3 through F5). These lookup functions carry the corresponding tax rates for the amount you enter for both the United States (US) and United Kingdom (UK) from the table to cells B3 and B4. Formulas in cells B5 and B6 will multiply the respective tax rates by the net income in cell B1 to calculate taxes due.
Let's look at the function entered into cell B3. The actual function is @VLOOKUP(B2,D3.F5,1). The function may look complicated, but it has only three simple arguments, separated from one another by commas. When the function is calculated, here is what happens.

- B2 is a reference to cell B2, into which you enter the net income. This is the value the function will look for on the lookup table.

- D3.F5 is the next argument. It tells the function that the table is located in the range with D3 as the upper left-hand corner and F5 as the lower right-hand corner. The table is arranged vertically, so it will look in the leftmost column (D) of the table for a value equal to the value in cell B2. All lookup functions assume the search range is in ascending order, so it looks at the values from the top of the range down.

- 1 is the **offset**. When the function finds the value, in this case $1,000 in cell D4, the offset tells the function to select the corresponding value from the cell one column to the right, in this case the 10% in cell E4.

The function you enter into cell B4 is identical to the one you entered into cell B3—with one exception. Its offset is 2, not 1. The lookup function therefore finds the same value as the lookup function in cell B3 ($1,000) but returns the value in the cell two columns to its right (F4).

	A	B	C	D	E	F
1	TAX CALCULATION MODEL			TAX RATE LOOKUP TABLE		
2	Net income	$10,000		Income	US rate	UK rate
3	Tax rate (US)	20%		$0	0%	0%
4	Tax rate (UK)	25%		$1,000	10%	15%
5	Taxes due (US)	$2,000		$10,000	20%	25%
6	Taxes due (UK)	$2,500				
7						
8						
9						
10						
11						

FIGURE 5-59
Exploring What-If 1
When you change net income to $10,000, the lookup functions find a matching value in cell D5 and select the values 20% (when the offset is 1) and 25% (when the offset is 2).

FIGURE 5-60

Exploring What-If 2
When you enter a value that doesn't match one of those listed on the lookup table, the function will find the value equal to OR less than the value being looked up. If you enter a net income of $7,500 into cell B2, the function will return the values of 10% and 15% because the closest value equal to, or less than, itself, is $1,000.

	A	B	C	D	E	F
1	TAX CALCULATION MODEL			TAX RATE LOOKUP TABLE		
2	Net income	$7,500		Income	US rate	UK rate
3	Tax rate (US)	10%		$0	0%	0%
4	Tax rate (UK)	15%		$1,000	10%	15%
5	Taxes due (US)	$750		$10,000	20%	25%
6	Taxes due (UK)	$1,125				
7						
8						
9						
10						
11						

	A	B	C	D	E	F
1	Quantity	1		LIST PRICE LOOKUP TABLE		
2	Item Number	1		1	2	3
3	List price	$8.95		$8.95	$15.95	$24.95
4	Discount	0%				
5	Net Price (unit)	$8.95		DISCOUNT LOOKUP TABLE		
6	Total Due	$8.95		1	100	500
7				0%	10%	25%
8						
9						
10						
11						

FIGURE 5-61

Horizontal Lookup Table
Let's say you have a mail order business where customers call to place orders. The person that answers the phone asks for the quantity and item number and enters them into a model. The model then uses two horizontal lookup tables to look up the list price based on the item number and discount based on the quantity. Other formulas calculate the next price and total due.

Here, the model is designed so that you enter the quantity into cell B1 and the item number into cell B3. A lookup function in cell B3 then looks up the item number on the list price lookup table and returns the appropriate list price. A similar lookup function in cell B4 looks up the quantity entered into cell B1 on the discount lookup table and returns the discount.

Let's look at the function entered into cell B3. The actual function is @HLOOKUP(B2,D2.F3,1).

- B2 is a reference to cell B2, into which you enter the item number. This is the value the function looks for on the lookup table.

- D2.F3 is the next argument. It tells the function the table is located in the range with D2 as the upper left-hand corner and F3 as the lower right-hand corner. The table is arranged horizontally, so it looks in the leftmost column (D) of the table for a value equal to the value in cell B2. All lookup functions assume the search range is in ascending order, so it looks at the values from the left to right on row 3.

- 1 is the offset. When the function finds the value in the lookup table, in this case the 1 in cell D2, the offset tells the function to select the corresponding value from the cell one row down, here, the $8.95 in cell D3.

	A	B	C	D	E	F
1	Quantity	100		LIST PRICE LOOKUP TABLE		
2	Item Number	1		1	2	3
3	List price	$8.95		$8.95	$15.95	$24.95
4	Discount	10%				
5	Net Price (unit)	$8.06		DISCOUNT LOOKUP TABLE		
6	Total Due	$805.50		1	100	500
7				0%	10%	25%
8						
9						
10						
11						

FIGURE 5-62
Exploring What-If 1
When you change the quantity to 100, the lookup function automatically looks up that quantity on the discount lookup table and changes the discount to 10%.

	A	B	C	D	E	F
1	Quantity	100		LIST PRICE LOOKUP TABLE		
2	Item Number	3		1	2	3
3	List price	$24.95		$8.95	$15.95	$24.95
4	Discount	10%				
5	Net Price (unit)	$22.46		DISCOUNT LOOKUP TABLE		
6	Total Due	$2,245.50		1	100	500
7				0%	10%	25%
8						
9						
10						
11						

FIGURE 5-63
Exploring What-If 2
When you change the item number to 3, the lookup function automatically looks up that item number on the list price lookup table and changes the list price to $24.95.

■ **Lookup tables** are functions that look up a value in a table and select a value in an adjoining row or column.

■ Lookup tables can be arranged either **horizontally** or **vertically**.

■ The row or column from which the value on the table is selected is determined by the **offset** you specify in the lookup function.

SUMMARY AND KEY TERMS

REVIEW QUESTIONS

1. What is a lookup table? Describe briefly how they work, and list some examples of where they might be used.

2. List two ways lookup tables can be arranged in.

3. What does the offset that you enter in the lookup function determine?

TOPIC 5-16

Data Tables

OBJECTIVES

After completing this topic, you will be able to

- Describe the purpose of data tables
- Explain the difference between one-input and two-input data tables

Data tables speed up the process of exploring what-ifs. They allow you to run a series of values through a cell in a model and capture the output from one or more other cells. Most programs have two kinds of data tables: one input and two input.

The one-input (also called *Data Table 1*) command runs a series of values through a single input cell on the model and captures the output from as many output cells as the program allows. One-input data tables have the following elements (Figure 5-64):

- A model that has both numbers and formulas. One of the cells is designated as the **input cell**. One or more cells are designated as the **output cells**. Each output cell must contain a formula that refers directly or indirectly to the input cell. You know if it does when a change in the number in the input cell changes the number calculated in the output cell.

- A series of values arranged in a column. These are the **input values** that are to be run through the model's input cell.

- One or more columns adjacent to the one containing the input values with formulas above them that refer to the output cell. The formula can be a simple reference to the output cell or a formula that refers directly or indirectly to the output cell.

When you run the data table command, the program runs each of the input values through the input cell. It then calculates and captures the value for the output cells and lists them on the same row as the input value that caused them.

The two-input (also called *Data Table 2*) command runs two series of numbers through two different input cells and captures the output from a single cell (Figure 5-65). Two-input data tables have the following elements:

	A	B	C	D	E	F
1	Cost of car	$10,000			B6	B5*B6
2	Down payment	$2,000		1%	$225.66	$8,124
3	Loan required	$8,000		2%	$229.14	$8,249
4	Interest rate	13%		3%	$232.65	$8,375
5	Term of loan (in months)	36		4%	$236.19	$8,503
6	Monthly payment	$269.55		5%	$239.77	$8,632
7				6%	$243.38	$8,762
8				7%	$247.02	$8,893
9				8%	$250.69	$9,025
10				9%	$254.40	$9,158
11				10%	$258.14	$9,293
12				11%	$261.91	$9,429
13				12%	$265.71	$9,566
14				13%	$269.55	$9,704
15				14%	$273.42	$9,843
16				15%	$277.32	$9,984
17						
18						
19						
20						

FIGURE 5-64

One-Input Data Table

In this one-input table, you have a model that calculates monthly payments on a loan. The model has one input cell (B4) and one output cell (B6). The data table (D1..F16) includes is series of input values (column D) and two formulas (E1 and F1) that directly or indirectly refer to the output cell on the model (B6).

When you run the data table, you specify the table range and input cell. The table range must include both the column of input values and the output formulas. To do this, the range includes all cells between D1 and F16. The input cell is the cell the values are run through, in this case, the interest rate cell (B4). When you run the data table, the series of interest rates in column D is run through cell B4 one at a time. The program then captures the output of cell B6 and puts the value on the same row as the input amount that caused it. If you look at the AUTOLOAN model itself, you see that when the interest rate in cell B4 is 13%, the monthly payment in cell B6 is $269.55. On the data table, the interest rate of 13% in cell D14 has the same monthly payment on the same row in the next column. Also, the formula in cell F1 multiplies the term of the loan in cell B5 by the value in cell B6 so that column F lists total payments for all interest rates.

- A model that contains two input cells and one output cell. The output cell must contain a formula that refers directly or indirectly to the input cell

- Two series of values that are to be run through the two input cells. One series is on a row, and one is on a column.

- A cell at the intersection of the row and column of input values that contains a formula. The formula can be a simple reference to the output cell or a formula that refers directly or indirectly to the output cell.

When you run the data table command, the program runs pairs of input values through the input cells. It then calculates and captures the value for the output cell and lists it in the cell on the same column and row as the two input values that caused it.

	A	B	C	D	E	F
1	Cost of car	$10,000				
2	Down payment	2,000.00				
3	Loan required	8,000.00				
4	Interest rate	10%				
5	Term of loan (in months)	36				
6	Monthly payment	$258.14				
7						
8						
9		B6	12	24	36	48
10		1%	$670.28	$336.82	$225.66	$170.09
11		2%	$673.91	$340.32	$229.14	$173.56
12		3%	$677.55	$343.85	$232.65	$177.07
13		4%	$681.20	$347.40	$236.19	$180.63
14		5%	$684.86	$350.97	$239.77	$184.23
15		6%	$688.53	$354.56	$243.38	$187.88
16		7%	$692.21	$358.18	$247.02	$191.57
17		8%	$695.91	$361.82	$250.69	$195.30
18		9%	$699.61	$365.48	$254.40	$199.08
19		10%	$703.33	$369.16	$258.14	$202.90
20						

FIGURE 5-65

Two-Input Data Table

You use a two-input table to run two series of input values through two input cells and capture a single output. Here, the model has two input cells (B4 and B5) and one output cell (B6). The data table includes two series of input values (row 9 and column B) and one formula that directly or indirectly refers to the output cell on the model (B9). When you run the data table, you specify the table range and the two input cells. The program runs the two series of input values through the input cells, and the table is filled with values showing how the monthly payments are affected by changes in interest rates and loan periods.

SUMMARY AND KEY TERMS

- Data tables speed up the exploration of what-ifs. They run a series of values through one of more cells and capture the output from one or more specified cells.

- A one-input table runs a series of values through one cell in the model and captures the output from the number of cells allowed by the program. The output can be either from a cell on the model or calculated by a formula on the table that directly or indirectly refers to the input cell.

- A two-input table runs two series of values through two cells in the model and captures the output from a single cell. The output can be either from a cell on the model or calculated by a formula on the table that directly or indirectly refers to one of the input cells.

REVIEW QUESTIONS

1. What is the purpose of data tables?
2. What is the difference between a one-input table and a two-input table?
3. When you run a data table for the first time, what information must you specify?
4. What is the table range? The input cell?
5. What is the output cell?
6. Try to think of three practical uses for data tables.

Date and Time Functions

OBJECTIVES

After completing this topic, you will be able to

- Describe the purpose of date and time functions
- Explain how you can use date and time arithmetic

Most programs provide functions that display dates and times as **serial numbers**. The serial number can be formatted so that the data and time are displayed in a variety of other formats. Figure 5-66 shows the results of formatting dates calculated with date functions.

The serial numbers can also be added and subtracted, for example, to find the number of days between two dates or the numbers of hours, minutes, and seconds between two times (Figure 5-67). The serial numbers are usually calculated by counting from a date at the turn of the century. (For example, Lotus 1-2-3 counts from December 31, 1899; Excel from January 1, 1900; and SuperCalc from March 1, 1900.)

The number of date and time functions available varies from program to program, as does their syntax. Table 5-25 describes some of the date and time functions available on Lotus 1-2-3.

	A	B	C	D	E	F
1			DATE FORMAT			
2	FUNCTION	NONE	DD-MMM-YY	DD-MM	MMM-YY	
3	DATE(70,1,11)	25579	11-Jan-70	11-Jan	Jan-70	
4	DATE(89,3,12)	32579	12-Mar-89	12-Mar	Mar-89	
5	DATE(45,3,20)	16516	20-Mar-45	20-Mar	Mar-45	
6						
7						
8			TIME FORMAT			
9	FUNCTION	NONE	H.MM	H.MM.SS	H:M AM/PM	
10	TIME(12,1,45)	0.501215278	12:01	12:01:45	12:01 PM	
11	TIME(10,10,10)	0.423726852	10:10	10:10:10	10:10 AM	
12	TIME(18,50,45)	0.785243056	18:50	18:50:45	6:50 PM	
13						
14						
15						

FIGURE 5-66
Date and Time Formats
All columns on rows 2 through 5 have the same date functions. In column A, they are displayed as text. In column B, they are displayed unformatted. The numbers indicate the number of days since the turn of the century. The next three columns show how they are displayed when formatted with one of the programs date formats. The same description applies to the time functions on rows 10 through 12.

	A	B	C	D	E	F
1		Unformatted	Formatted			
2	Date of birth	25598	30-Jan-70	← @DATE(70,1,30)		
3	Current date	32813	1-Nov-89	← @DATE(89,1,11)		
4	Number of days	7215	7215	← B3-B2		
5	Number of years	19.76712329	19.76712329	← B4/365		
6						
7						
8						
9						
10						

FIGURE 5-67
Date Arithmetic

What if you were born on June 1, 1970, and wanted to find out how many days you have lived through November 1, 1989? You would enter these two dates, and then subtract the earliest from the latest to calculate the number of days. You enter the function @DATE(70,1,30) into cell B2 and the function @DATE(89,10,1) into cell B3. Their arguments are (Year,Month,Day). You then format the dates so that they are displayed in the format DD-MMM-YY. The formula B3-B2 in cell B4 calculates the number of days between the two dates—in effect, how many days you have lived. The formula B4/365 in cell B5 calculates the number of years you have lived.

TABLE 5-25
Date and Time Functions

Function	Description
@NOW	Calculates the current date or time if it was entered into the computer system's clock when starting up.
@DATE (YEAR, MONTH, DAY)	Calculates the serial number for the specified date. For example, @DATE (89,1,30) calculates the serial number 32509 on Lotus 1-2-3.
@TIME (HOUR, MINUTE, SECOND)	Calculates the serial number for the specified time. For example, @TIME(12,0,0) calculates the serial number .5007060185 on Lotus 1-2-3.

SUMMARY AND KEY TERMS

- Most programs allow you to enter dates and times using functions.
- You can format the function to change the way the dates and times are displayed.
- Dates and times entered with function calculate **serial numbers** that can be manipulated with formulas. For example, you can find the number of days between two dates or the number of hours or minutes between two times.

REVIEW QUESTIONS

1. What is a date function?
2. What is date arithmetic?
3. What are the three date and time functions? When would you use them?
4. Describe the model you would build to calculate the number of days you have been at college so far.

Protection and Security

OBJECTIVES

After completing this topic, you will be able to

- Describe how you can protect cells on a model
- Explain how you can hide cells and windows
- Describe the purpose of passwords

Many spreadsheet programs provide several options you can use to ensure the integrity and security of your models.

CELL PROTECTION

When you initially create a model, none of the spreadsheet's cells are protected so that you can enter data into them. As you have seen, entering data into a cell deletes any data that was there. If you enter a number or label into a cell containing a formula, the formula is deleted. This can seriously damage a template.

After you have completed a model, you can protect or lock part or all of it so that you (or another user) cannot inadvertently delete, change, or enter data. You can protect cells so that they cannot be edited, overwritten with new data (by typing, copying, or moving cells into their range), or deleted unless you first remove their protection. If you are planning to use the

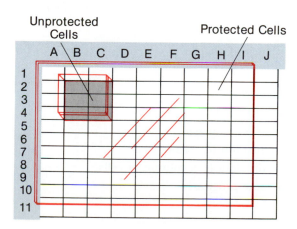

Unprotected Cells

Protected Cells

FIGURE 5-68
Protection
Over those cells where you still allow data to be entered or changed, "holes" open up in this shield.

model as a template, shared by other users, protection is especially important. Others may be less familiar with the model or unfamiliar with the program, thus increasing the likelihood of mistakes.

Protecting cells is like placing a protective shield over the model (Figure 5-68). Many programs display unprotected cells in a different intensity or color so that you can distinguish them from protected cells.

Programs use two different approaches to protect cells.

- Some programs are set up so that all cells are unprotected unless you use a command to protect them.

- Other programs use a two-step process: All cells are protected, but you can turn protection on and off. When protection is off, changes can be made anywhere on the spreadsheet. When protection is on, changes can be made only in those cells you have specifically designated as unprotected.

HIDING CELLS OR WINDOWS

Occasionally, you work at display terminals that people can see as they walk by, or you make printouts that are to be widely circulated, or you share your models with other users. What if sensitive data is on the model, perhaps a list of salaries? You can hide this data from other users by hiding the cells or windows the data is displayed in. The simplest way of doing this is to set the column width to zero so that the data is not displayed on the screen or in printouts. Some programs also allow you to hide ranges of cells. Hidden cells cannot be seen or printed unless you first unhide them.

PASSWORDS

Protecting and hiding cells does not provide absolute security. Experienced users can often easily disable protection or unhide the data. Some programs provide a higher level of security by letting you assign **passwords**. Without the password, cell protection cannot be disabled, and hidden cells cannot be unhidden. If you assign a password and then forget it, you cannot see data or remove protection, so be sure to use passwords you will remember.

SUMMARY AND KEY TERMS

- Most spreadsheets allow you to protect the contents of selected cells that you don't want to inadvertently delete, overwrite, or otherwise destroy.

- Some programs also allow you to hide data or require a password to view or change a file.

- Some programs allow you to assign passwords to prevent some cells from being seen on the screen or in printouts. Other allow you to assign passwords so that protection cannot be turned off.

REVIEW QUESTIONS

1. In what circumstances is cell protection useful?
2. How does cell protection affect your model?
3. Give two ways in which cell protection may work.
4. What two ways are there to hide the data in cells?
5. What is the simplest way to hide the data in a column of cells?
6. What is a password used for on some programs?

Linking, Combining, and Extracting Files

OBJECTIVES

After completing this topic, you will be able to

- Describe how models can be linked
- Explain how the data in one model can be combined with another
- Explain how data in one model can be extracted to its own file

Most spreadsheet programs allow you to combine all or part of one model with another. There are two ways of doing this: by establishing direct links between two or more files or by copying data between them. Both approaches are useful when you want to consolidate budgets or speed up model building.

LINKING MODELS

Some programs allow you to design models so that one **dependent model** (also called a *master model* or *summary model*) summarizes the results of several **supporting models** (also called *supplemental models* or *detailed models*). These supporting models contain detailed breakdowns of the items summarized on the dependent model.

For example, you might have a dependent model that lists the monthly sales of each product in a store and totals them. If you then create an income statement (the master model), the cell for monthly sales can be linked to the cell in the dependent model that totals the sales of individual products. If you change any of the product sales figures on the dependent model, the sales on the master model change automatically.

Although creating models this way keeps models to a manageable size, it also creates problems. A change on any of the supporting models must be transferred to the dependent model because each model is in a separate file. A few programs allow you to link models so that this data is transferred automatically. To do so, you enter remote references into the dependent model that specify the name of the supporting model and the cell addresses on that model you want data to be transferred from (Figure 5-69).

When you link models in this way, the order you update and retrieve them in becomes important on many programs if the program does not allow you to retrieve all of them at the same time. For example, what if you

511

	A	B	C	D	E	F
1	Sales	$21,000				
2	Cost of Goods	$12,600				
3	Expenses	$8,400				
4						
5						
6						
7						
8						
9						
10						

A. The Dependent Model

	A	B	C	D	E	F
1	Computers	$10,000				
2	Printers	$3,000				
3	Software	$5,000				
4	Display screens	$1,000				
5	Hard disk drives	$2,000				
6	Total sales	$21,000				
7						
8						
9						
10						

B. The Supportive Model

FIGURE 5-69
Linking Models
A dependent model contains references to cells on one or more supporting models. If any changes are made on the supporting models, the dependent model reflects those changes.

linked three models so that model 1 is linked to model 2 and model 2 is linked to model 3? If you make a change to model 3, save it, and then retrieve model 1, it won't be updated. To update it, you first must retrieve model 2 so that it becomes updated. You then save model 2 and retrieve model 1. When retrieving models and changing data, always follow these two steps.

1. Retrieve the supporting models, and make the changes.
2. Retrieve the dependent model. When it is retrieved from the disk, the program checks to see if it contains any references to cells in other files. If it does, it updates the cells containing those references using the current calculated values in the cells on the model that it refers to.

COMBINING FILES

To combine files, you use a command to copy a file, or part of a file, on the disk to a model that is displayed on the screen. When you do this, for example, to consolidate budgets, the models you want to combine must be designed so that the combined data appears in the right place on the model on the screen. You can do this by creating a template and making copies for others to use. To combine the files

1. Save the file you are working on. This way if anything goes wrong, you can retrieve the model and try again.
2. Move the cursor to the upper left-hand cell where the data is to be combined. The data that is combined overwrites and erases any data in the range of cells it is combined in, so the position of the cursor and the design of the models is important.
3. Execute the *File Combine* commands. (Table 5-26 describes Lotus 1-2-3's.)
4. Answer any prompts that appear on the screen.

SPREADSHEET APPLICATIONS

TABLE 5-26
Combine Command Menu Choices

Menu Choice	Description
Copy	Copies the contents of the file on the disk to the file on the screen; you may be offered the option to copy the formulas or just their calculated values
Add	Copies only the calculated values from the file on the disk and adds them to the values in the cells they are copied to; normally does not copy labels from the file on the disk, just the values
Subtract	Copies only the calculated values from the file on the disk and subtracts them to the values in the cells they are copied to; normally does not copy labels from the file on the disk, just the values

EXTRACTING FILES

The program's *Extract* command copies a part of a model to its own file on a disk. You can then combine this extracted file with any other model or retrieve it directly. You may be offered the option of extracting the formulas in the range you are extracting or just their calculated values. If you extract any formulas that refer to cells that are not also extracted, these formulas refer to empty cells when the extracted file is retrieved.

SUMMARY AND KEY TERMS

- A few programs allow you to **link** separate files so that a change in one spreadsheet is automatically reflected in another. The model that contains the references to other models is called the **dependent model**. The models it refers to are called the **supporting models**.

- When models are linked, the order you retrieve them in is important unless you can retrieve them all on the screen at one time. You should always retrieve the dependent model only after you have made changes to the supporting models.

- Some programs allow you to **combine files** to copy data into a model or to add or subtract models.

- You can **extract** part of a model to its own file on the disk.

REVIEW QUESTIONS

1. What is the disadvantage of using supplemental models?
2. What does it mean to link files?
3. If you link models, why is the order they are updated and retrieved in so important on some programs?
4. When updating linked models, what order must you follow?
5. Why might you want to combine files?
6. What are the four basic steps in combining files?
7. If you combined two files and wanted to add the values, how would you do it?
8. If you wanted to copy part of a model to its own file on the disk, what command would you use?

Graphs

OBJECTIVES

After completing this topic, you will be able to

- Explain why graphics programs are integrated into spreadsheets
- Briefly describe how you create a graph

Charts and graphs created on business graphics programs can be used to analyze financial and statistical data. For example, you can use graphs to find trends and relationships between sets of numbers like sales, expenses, and profits over a period. The results can then be printed out for distribution to others or for inclusion in a report.

Graphics for analysis programs are integrated into most spreadsheet programs so that data generated on the program can be quickly and easily displayed as a graph. This integration increases the speed with which you can generate graphs and allows the graph to be automatically updated when data in the spreadsheet changes. Thus you can use graphs as analytical tools for viewing the results of different scenarios. We discuss graphics in detail in Part Seven.

The power of graphs is that they graph ranges of cells and not just actual values. When any of the values in those cells are changed, the graphs immediately and automatically reflect those changes. Graphs are easy to create. For example, to create a graph with Lotus 1-2-3, there are only five steps.

1. Display the Graph menu. Table 5-27 describes the choices on Lotus 1-2-3's Graph menu.
2. Specify the range of cells to be used for the X axis.
3. Specify the range of cells to be used for at least one data range.
4. Select a graph type.
5. Display the graph (Figure 5-70).

TABLE 5-27
Lotus 1-2-3's Graph Menu Commands

Menu Choice	Description	Menu Choice	Description
Type	Selects one of the five graph types: Line, Bar, XY, Stacked-Bar, and Pie	Save	Saves the current graph in a file so that you can print it
X (range)	Sets the X-axis range, the range all other ranges are plotted against	Options	Specifies various options for enhancing the graph, including legends, formats, titles, and scaling
A-F	Specifies as many as six data ranges plotted against the X range	Name	Names a graph so that it can be viewed at a later time
Reset	Cancels all graph settings for the current graph	Quit	Exits from the Graph menu and returns to ready mode
View	Displays the current graph		

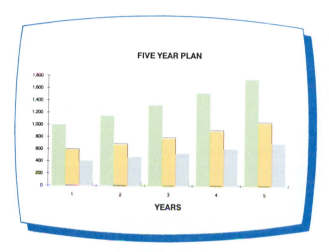

FIGURE 5-70
Graph
A graph can plot the data on a spreadsheet. When you change the data, the graph changes automatically.

SUMMARY AND KEY TERMS

- Most spreadsheets have integrated graphics that allow you to graph key items in models.
- Graphs are automatically updated whenever a number in the model is changed.
- When you create more than one graph of the same model, you can name the graphs and save them along with the model. That way, you can use graphs to look at more than one aspect of a model.

REVIEW QUESTIONS

1. What is the main advantage of creating graphs with a spreadsheet?
2. What are the five basic steps in creating a graph?
3. What is the Lotus 1-2-3 command for displaying the current graph?
4. What are the Lotus 1-2-3 commands for specifying data ranges?
5. What types of graphs can you create in Lotus 1-2-3?

TOPIC 5-21

Data Management

OBJECTIVES

After completing this topic, you will be able to

- Explain the purpose of database functions
- Describe how you sort a database
- Explain how you query a database to find, extract, and delete information

Spreadsheets have limited built-in database capabilities. This feature is ideal for organizing and analyzing tables containing sales figures, inventory, mailing or distribution lists, customer accounts, check registers, or any other data that needs to be collected, sorted, and analyzed. Databases are created with most of the same commands used to create a model. In fact, a **database** is just a model organized into fields and records (see Figure 5-71). On a spreadsheet, records are entered into rows, with one field in each column.

SORTING A DATABASE

Databases can be quickly sorted into ascending or descending order. You can specify which columns are to be used as the primary and secondary keys. The **secondary key** is specified when there is a possibility of duplicate data in the **primary key**. For example, if you were sorting a database by name, you would want to use the Lastname field as the primary key and the Firstname field as the secondary key. When the data is sorted, any records with the same last name are subsorted by first name.

When you use primary and secondary keys, select the keys in descending order of importance. The primary key should be the more important field, and the secondary key should be the less important field. For example, to sort a database by state and name, specify the state as the primary key if that is the more important field.

To sort a database, you need to specify only the range to be sorted. When specifying the range to sort, include only the data records. Do not include field names, or they will be sorted along with the data.

	A	B	C	D	E	F	
1	FST_NAME	SCD_NAME	STREET	CITY	ZIP	PHONE ←	— Field name
2	John	Williams	100 Elm	Chicago	10001	617-555-1212	
3	Bill	Washington	200 Main	New York	10500	413-555-1212	
4	Mary	Gonzales	125 Oak	Los Angeles	60030	201-555-1212 ←	— Record
5	Alex	Chang	1000 First	Dallas	81987	512-555-1212	
6	Jose	Moriety	23 Mill	Portland	21876	306-555-1212	
7							
8							
9			↑				
10							
11			Field				
12							
13							
14							
15							
16							
17							
18							
19							
20							

FIGURE 5-71
A Spreadsheet Database
A spreadsheet database is a range of cells containing one or more columns and at least two rows. It has the following parts:

A. Field names are placed on the first row and are used to label the columns where data is entered.

B. Records are entered on the second and subsequent rows. Records are sets of related data, much like Rolodex™ cards that contain a person's name, address, and phone number.

C. Fields are the columns of information that make up a record. A record consists of the information contained within the fields of the database. For example, on a Rolodex card, the fields might be the person's name, street address, city, state, ZIP code, and phone number. A record includes the data for all these fields that pertains to one person.

QUERYING THE DATABASE

You can use a spreadsheet database as a major record keeping and analysis tool. The *Data Query* commands can be used to

- Find records meeting specified criteria
- Delete records meeting specified criteria
- Delete duplicate records
- Create a new database containing only selected records or fields

To use *Data Query* commands, you must first specify an input or database range, a criterion or criteria range, and an output or extract range (Figure 5-72).

Finding Records in a Database

The *Find* command highlights selected records in the input range that meet the requirements specified in the criterion range. If more than one record meets the requirements specified in the criterion range, it is highlighted one at a time. Press the arrow keys to move the highlight to subsequent records.

	A	B	C	D	E	F
1	INPUT RANGE:					
2	Dept.	Course	Instructor	Day	Time	Bldg.
3	Math	136	Davis	T,T	9:00	Stoner
4	Math	200	Davis	M,W,F	9:00	Widner
5	English	124	Jones	T,T	12:00	Drew
6	Biology	101	Smith	M,W,F	10:00	Hayes
7						
8	CRITERION RANGE:					
9	Dept.	Course	Instructor	Day	Time	Bldg.
10			Jones			
11			Davis			
12						
13	OUTPUT RANGE:					
14	Dept.	Course	Instructor	Day	Time	Bldg.
15	Math	136	Davis	T,T	9:00	Stoner
16	Math	200	Davis	M,W,F	9:00	Widner
17	English	124	Jones	T,T	12:00	Drew
18						
19						
20						

FIGURE 5-72

The Input, Criterion, and Output Ranges

A. The **input range** specifies the range of cells the program looks in during a data query. The input range is either the database itself or some portion of it.

B. The **criterion range** specifies the range where the query specifications are listed. The criterion range must be at least two rows. The first row contains some or all of the database's field names; the remaining rows are used to enter criteria to be used in the query.

- If you enter more than one criterion on the same row, matches occur only if **all** criteria are met.
- If you enter criteria on adjacent rows, records are found if **any** criterion is met.
- Blank rows in the criterion range cause all records to be found.

You can use the wildcard symbols to find records containing labels. The asterisk substitutes for any characters from the position of the asterisk to the end of the label. For example, the entry John* in the criterion range would find any records that contained John as the first four letters in the appropriate field, including John, Johnny, and John Jacob. The ? stands for any single character. For example, h?t would find hut, hat, hot, and hit.

C. The **output range** specifies where data extracted during a query is stored. An output range is necessary only if you are using the *Extract* or *Unique* command from the Query menu.

Extracting Records from a Database

The *Extract* command copies records in the input range that meet selected criteria from the criterion range to the output range. You can use the *Extract* command to copy selected parts of a database to another range in the spreadsheet. That range can then be printed or saved as a separate model.

Extracting Only Unique Records

The *Unique* command extracts records that meet selected criteria into the output range. If duplicate records exist, only the first one is extracted. You can use the *Unique* command as a fast way of deleting all duplicate records from a database. Using the *Unique* command with a blank line in the criterion range copies all records to the output range, but it copies only one copy of those that are duplicated, leaving the other copies behind. You can copy the output range to a new file and use it as the new database.

Deleting Unneeded Records

The *Delete* command deletes records from the input range that meet the requirements specified in the criterion range. *Delete* "closes up" the database, deleting empty rows. Each time you try a delete, you are given the choice to cancel the command or continue. If you continue, the records are permanently deleted. Before you use the delete option, extract the records you are considering deleting. This gives you the opportunity of checking the records before erasing them. It also gives you a temporary backup copy of the records in the output range. The output range can be copied to another file for later reference, or it can be erased.

USING CRITERION FORMULAS IN A DATABASE

When entering criteria in a database, you can enter logical operators to show relationships (Table 5-28). Criterion formulas are recalculated once for each record in the database. If the formula evaluates as true (not equal to zero) for a record, that record is accepted as a match.

USING DATABASE STATISTICAL FUNCTIONS

The database statistical functions (Table 5-29) are similar to the regular statistical functions except that they are used specifically with a database. Database statistical functions are entered in the form @FUNCTION(INPUT RANGE, OFFSET, CRITERION RANGE).

- The input and criterion ranges are the same as those used in the Query commands.
- The offset is the number of the field (column) in the database that contains the specified data. To calculate the offset number, start at the leftmost column in the database and count across, beginning with zero. For example, if your three fields in a database were Name, Price, and Sales, the offset number of the first field (Name) would be 0, the next field would be 1, and the last field 2.

TABLE 5-28
Operators Used in a Criterion Formula

Operator	Description	Precedence
<	Less than	3
<=	Less than or equal to	3
>	Greater than	3
>=	Greater than or equal to	3
=	Equal to	3
< >	Not equal to	3
#AND#	Logical AND	1
#OR#	Logical OR	1
#NOT#	Logical NOT	2

TABLE 5-29
Database Statistical Functions

Function	Description
@DAVG	Averages the values in the selected field that match the specified criteria
@DCOUNT	Counts all nonblank cells of records in the selected field that match the specified criteria
@DMAX	Selects the largest value in the selected field that matches the specified criteria
@DMIN	Selects the smallest value in the selected field that matches the specified criteria
@DSTD	Finds the standard deviation of the selected field that matches the specified criteria
@DSUM	Totals the values in the selected field that match the specified criteria
@DVAR	Finds the variance in the selected field that matches the specified criteria

Select a cell or cells where you want to store the values generated by the functions. Do not use cells included in a data output range because they would be overwritten by any *Extract* commands.

SUMMARY AND KEY TERMS

- A **spreadsheet database** is data organized into columns and rows. Each column is a **field**, and each row is a **record**.

- **Sorting** is used to arrange rows of data into ascending or descending order. The **primary key** determines the column the data is sorted by. The **secondary key** specifies a second column to use when breaking any ties in the primary sort.

- You can also **query** the database to find or delete records. To do so, you enter **database** or **input range, criterion**, and **output ranges**. You can then enter criterion in the criterion range, and all matching records in the database are copied to the output range.

- **Database statistical functions** are similar to regular statistical functions but are designed to be used specifically with databases. Their arguments are the input range, the offset, and the criterion range.

REVIEW QUESTIONS

1. List some reasons for organizing data in a spreadsheet database?
2. Where are field names entered on a database? Where are records entered?
3. What is a primary key? A secondary key?
4. What does *Query* command allow you to do?
5. What are the three key parts of a database?
6. What does the input range specify? The criterion range? The output range?
7. When must you use an output range?
8. What are the three arguments in a database statistical function?
9. List and briefly describe three database statistical functions.

TOPIC 5-22

Spreadsheet Macros

OBJECTIVES

After completing this topic, you will be able to

- Describe the purpose of macros
- Explain how you record macros or create them with a macro language

Macros are simply a way to store keystrokes so that they can be played back later. They can save you from having to rekey repetitive data or commands. It is like making a piano into a player piano; the only difference is the computer's keys do not move up and down—it is all done electronically. Macros are created in two ways: by recording them or by using a macro language.

RECORDING MACROS

Recording macros is usually a two-step process.

1. Record keystrokes. You execute a command to begin recording keystrokes. On some programs, this is called **learn mode**. You then enter the data or commands you want to use again. The keystrokes are automatically recorded as you run through the sequence of commands or characters you want to record.
2. Attach the keystrokes to a key. After the keystrokes are recorded, you are prompted to select a key they will be attached to. You then turn off the record mode.

Whenever you want to play back the recorded keystrokes, you hold down one of the special keys on the keyboard (usually **Alt**), and then press the key you attached the macro to. The entire sequence of keystrokes will be automatically replayed.

MACRO LANGUAGES

On some programs, you can also enter macros by typing them in, assigning names to them, and then executing them. When entering them like this, you are actually using a **macro language**. You then enter the keystrokes needed as a label and name the label. The language contains **keywords** used to indicate keys on the keyboard (see Table 5-30). Until you have all com-

TABLE 5-30
Lotus 1-2-3's Macro Keywords

Macro	Keyword Equivalent	Macro	Keyword Equivalent
Function Keys		**Other Keys**	
Edit (F2)	{edit}	←	{left}
Name (F3)	{name}	→	{right}
Abs (F4)	{abs}	↑	{up}
Goto(F5)	{goto}	↓	{down}
Window (F6)	{window}	**Home**	{home}
Query (F7)	{query}	**End**	{end}
Table (F8)	{table}	**Backspace**	{bs}
Calc (F9)	{calc}	**Del**	{del}
Graph (F10)	{graph}	**Esc**	{esc}
		Return	˜ (the tilde)

mands memorized, the best way to create a macro is to enter the entire command keystroke by keystroke, noting on a sheet of paper the keys you press.

Let's look at an example. To print a worksheet on Lotus 1-2-3, you must press the slash key (/), and then select *Print, Printer, Align, Go, Page,* and *Quit.* But you can create a macro so that this same series of commands is executed when you hold down **Alt** and press the letter **P** (or any other key you assign the series of keystrokes to). This macro would be written as {HOME}/ppagpq.

- {HOME}, enclosed in braces, tells the program to move the cursor to cell A1.
- The slash (/) calls up the Main menu.
- The sequence of letters (ppagpq) is the same sequence you would type to print the model from the keyboard.

After entering the macro, you assign it a name; in this example, you name it so that it is executed when you hold down **Alt** and press **P.**

When entering macros, keep the following points in mind:

- You must enter macros as labels. Some keys like the slash key (/) must be preceded by a label prefix character if they are the first character on a line. Lotus 1-2-3 ignores the label prefix character when it reads the contents of the cell. If you want a label prefix character to be used at the beginning of a line, you must enter two prefixes; the first converts the second into a label.
- Macros are easier to read and understand if you selectively use uppercase and lowercase letters. For example, put all keystrokes in lowercase, and all range names, cell contents, and cell coordinates in uppercase. A macro that prints a range named page1 is easier to read when entered as '/pprPAGE1~agpq than when entered as '/PPRPAGE1~AGPQ.
- Macros usually should not refer to cell coordinates because inserting or deleting rows and columns can change those coordinates and confuse the macro. Use range names to refer to blocks of cells.
- Macros with an appropriate name are automatically executed when the model is retrieved.
- Macros containing cursor movement keywords ({right}, {left}, and so on) may not work the same when **Scroll Lock** is engaged. Always be

sure **Scroll Lock** is not engaged before executing a macro containing these commands.

- Always save a file after creating a macro. If a file is not saved after the macro has been created, the macro is not saved.

- Always save a file before executing a new macro. That way if anything changes as a result of the macro (intentionally or not), you have a copy of the original file.

- Most programs offer a **step mode** so that you can work your way through a macro one step at a time. In this mode, you must press a key to execute the next keystroke in the macro. Using this mode, you can easily analyze or troubleshoot a macro.

USING OPERATOR INPUT

Macros can be made to pause during execution and accept operator input. For example, on Lotus 1-2-3, you use the {?}~ command to pause the macro for operator input. The macro continues only after you press **Return**. The {?} command is followed by a tilde (~) since pressing **Return** once completes the entry but does not resume the macro. You can use this pause command with one of the /X commands described in Table 5-31.

BRANCHING MACRO COMMANDS

Macros can be made to continue reading macro keystrokes at other locations on a spreadsheet. This is called **branching**, and it is useful when using macros to create menus (see Topic 4-18). Table 5-32 describes Lotus 1-2-3's branching commands.

TABLE 5-31
Macro Commands That Pause for Operator Input

Command	Description
/XL (message)˜(location)˜	Displays a message of up to thirty-nine characters on the second line of the control panel and pauses so that you can enter a label. After pressing **Return**, the label typed is entered in the location cell using a left-aligned prefix character.
/XN (message)˜(location)˜	Displays a message of up to thirty-nine characters on the second line of the control panel and pauses so that you can enter a number, formula, range name, or function. After pressing **Return**, the numeric value of the entry is stored at the location.

TABLE 5-32
Branching Macro Commands

Command	Description
/XG (location)˜	The macro jumps to the specified location and continues reading keystrokes.
/XC (location)˜	The macro jumps to the specified location and continues reading keystrokes, remembering where it left off. When a XR command is encountered, the macro returns to where it left off. The subroutines can be nested up to sixteen levels deep.
/XR	If a macro branched as a result of a /XC command, it returns to where it left off when /XR is encountered.
/XI (formula)	If the formula is TRUE (not zero), the macro continues reading keystrokes in the same cell; otherwise, it reads the keystrokes in the cell below.
/XM (menu name)˜	The macro jumps to the cell containing the menu name and displays the menu on the screen.

Fourth-Generation Programming Languages

Until recently, most applications programs were written for specific purposes by individual users and companies. To write these programs, developers used programming languages. These languages, like hardware, are considered to have generations.

First-generation programming languages were called machine languages. Second-generation languages were called assembly languages. Third-generation languages were high-level languages like BASIC, COBOL, and FORTRAN.

The widespread adoption of microcomputers and widely available applications programs have almost eliminated the need for users and developers to use these programs. The reason is that many applications programs have a built-in programming capability. If the program has to be customized for a specific use, the user or developer can use these built-in languages to do the customizing. These new programming languages are called *fourth-generation languages.*

One of the first programs to give developers this ability was dBASE II which had a very powerful, but somewhat complicated, programming language. When Lotus 1-2-3 was introduced, it simplified programming by introducing macros, a way to write short programs that automated the spreadsheet. The final breakthrough was the introduction of the record ability. This feature allowed users to turn on record mode, execute the keystrokes they wanted to capture, and then play them back whenever they were needed. The latest development is to combine record and programming so that you can record and then edit macros.

- **Macros** store keystrokes so that you can play them back later without entering them from the keyboard.

- You can record keystrokes in **learn mode**. To do so, you turn on learn mode, execute the keys, and then assign them a name or attach them to a key on the keyboard.

- You can use a **macro language** to write macros, just as a programmer would write a program. **Keywords** specified by the program are used to indicate what keys on the keyboard should be executed.

- You can enter commands into a macro that pause the macro for input from the keyboard.

- When writing macros, you can use commands that make them **branch**. For example, if one condition is met, they branch to one macro, and if another condition is met, they branch to a second.

- Macros, and other programming languages that users have access to when running an applications programs, are called **fourth-generation languages**.

1. What is a macro?
2. What are two ways you can create macros?
3. List the three steps you follow to record a macro.
4. When using a macro language to write a macro, what are the special terms called that you enter to indicate what keys should be executed?
5. What is the macro command for pressing **Return**?
6. What kind of data must macros be entered as?
7. Why should you selectively use uppercase and lowercase letters when entering macros?
8. Do macros often refer to cell coordinates? Why or why not?
9. It is important to save a file both after creating a macro and before executing a macro. Why is this?
10. How do you work through a macro a step at a time?
11. Describe the macro command {?}.
12. What are branching macro commands used for?
13. What is a fourth-generation programming language?

TOPIC 5-23

User-Defined Menus

OBJECTIVE

After completing this topic, you will be able to

■ Describe how you create user-defined menus

Programs that provide you with a macro language also allow you to create your own menus. These **user-defined menus** (Figure 5-73) can be displayed and executed just like the menus built into the spreadsheet program. They are useful additions for models used over and over again or by many people. For example, you can create a menu that lists commands to print the model, display graphs, or even display areas of the spreadsheet where you have entered text describing the model.

Menus need at least two names. The cell containing the /XM command must be attached to a keystroke, and the name following the /XM command must be assigned to the first cell in the actual menu.

The basic steps in creating a user-defined menu on Lotus 1-2-3 are as follows (Figure 5-73):

1. **Create the macro that calls up the menu.** The /XM (menu name) ~ command is used to call up a menu. The cell containing the command is named following the rules for naming a macro—a backslash (\) followed by a letter or a zero. The first cell in the list of menu selections is named using the same name used in the /XM command. When the macro is executed, the menu is displayed on the second line of the screen.

2. **Enter the menu selections and their descriptions.** The first row of the menu contains the main selections (up to eight). The second row contains an extended description of each selection.
   ■ There cannot be blank cells between menu selections.

   ■ The cell after the last menu selection must be empty. If that cell contains data, an error message is displayed.

   ■ Begin each menu item with a different letter. Macro menus work the same way Lotus 1-2-3's built-in menus do. You can select the menu option desired by pointing to it and pressing **Return** or by typing the first letter of the option. If the macro menu has two options beginning with the same letter, typing that letter executes the leftmost entry.

	QUIT-MENU	SAVE	PRINT	LINE	BAR
	Return to model				
	O	P	Q	R	S
1	/xmMENU~ ←—A.				
2					
3					
4	B.				
5	QUIT-MENU	SAVE	PRINT	LINE	BAR ←—C.
6	Return to model	Save as 5YRPLAN	Print the model	Display line graph	Display bar graph —D.
7		/fs5YRPLAN~r	pprA1.F10~agpg	/gnuLINE~vq	/gnuBAR~vq ←—E.
8		/xmMENU~	/xmMENU~	/xmMENU~	/xmMENU~ ←—F.
9					
10					

FIGURE 5-73
User-Defined Menus
User-defined menus can be displayed and executed just like the menus built into the spreadsheet program.

A. The /XM(menu name) ~ command is used to call up a menu. You name this cell with a backslash and a letter so that you can display the menu by holding down Alt while pressing the letter you used to name it.

B. The first cell in the list of menu selections is named using the same name used in the /XM command. When the macro is executed, the menu is displayed on the second line of the screen.

C. The first row of the menu contains the main selections (as many as eight).

D. The second row contains an extended description of each selection.

E. The macros begin on the third row of the menu, immediately under the extended description.

F. The /XM MENU~ commands redisplay the menu whenever one of the actions listed on the menu has been completed.

■ Since all menu selections are displayed on the screen at once, the length of the menu selection names is important. If the total length of the combined names does not fit on the control panel, an error message is displayed.

3. **Name the macro that calls up the menu.** You use a backslash and a letter so that you can display the menu by holding down Alt while pressing the letter you used to name it.

4. **Name the menu.** The /XM command that displays the menu refers to a menu name. You assign that name to the leftmost entry in the menu.

5. **Create the macros that perform each separate menu selection.** The macros begin on the third row of the menu, immediately under the extended description. To return to the menu after finishing an option, copy the /XM command to the last cell in each menu macro entry.

■ On programs that provide a macro language, you can create menus that operate just like the programs. These are called **user-defined menus**.

■ In Lotus 1-2-3, there are five steps in creating a menu. You create the macro that calls up the menu, enter the menu names and their descriptions, name the macro that calls up the menu, name the menu, and then enter the macro keystrokes that each menu selection performs.

REVIEW QUESTIONS

1. Why might you want to create a user-defined menu?
2. What are the five basic steps in creating a 1-2-3 menu?
3. 1-2-3 macro menus need at least two names. What are they?
4. Which 1-2-3 branching macro command is used to call up a menu?

TOPIC 5-24

Troubleshooting Models

OBJECTIVES

After completing this topic, you will be able to

- Describe some typical problems you encounter when creating models
- Describe some techniques you can use to troubleshoot models

When entering or testing models, you may occasionally encounter problems or get unexpected results. If so, you have to do some troubleshooting. The first step is to identify the problem; then you correct it.

COMMON PROBLEMS

Here are some common problems you might encounter.

- The computer beeps when data is entered. This tells you something is wrong. Use the edit commands to correct the entry.
- A row of asterisks or other symbols is displayed in a cell. This is caused by a column's being too narrow to display them properly. Change the size of a number, the format, the number of decimal places, or the column width.
- An error message is displayed in a cell. This is commonly caused by entering a formula that divides by 0 or by deleting a row or column containing a cell to which a formula refers.
- Recalculation is not performed. If recalculation is set to manual, you must press the recalculation key to recalculate the spreadsheet after making changes so that the changes are reflected in formulas.

TROUBLESHOOTING ON THE SCREEN

Relationships can be traced throughout a model by using the @NA function if it's available on your program. If you enter the @NA function in any cell containing a value, all formulas referring to that cell, either directly or indirectly, will display an *NA* in their cells when the spreadsheet is recalculated. This is an excellent way to find what formulas are referring to a particular cell, especially before deleting rows and columns.

Some programs allow you to display the contents of cells rather than their calculated results. This is an ideal way to check the relationships among cells. You may also be able to split the screen and then format one part of the screen to show the formulas and the other part to show the calculated results.

Newer programs have a *Trace* command that allows you to display the relationship between cells (Figure 5-74). You can position the cursor in any cell, and then use the command to highlight the cells that are precedent or dependent.

- **Precedent cells** are those cells whose values are used by the formula in the highlighted cell.
- **Dependent cells** are those cells whose formulas use the value entered or calculated in the highlighted cell.

PRINTING OUT DIAGNOSTIC TOOLS

Large models can be checked faster if you have a printout of the model with row and column labels matching the screen display (Figure 5-75). To do this, print out the borders (column letters and row numbers) if your program allows you to do this. If not, you can achieve the same result by adding a column of numbers to the right of and a row of column labels below the model. Print out these labels along with the model.

	A	B	C	D	E	F
1	PART 1. VARIABLES					
2	Opening Sales	$1,000				
3	Sales growth rate	15%				
4	Cost of goods sold	60%				
5						
6	PART 2. MODEL					
7	Year	1989	1990	1991	1992	1993
8	Sales	1,000	1,150	1,323	1,521	1,749
9	Cost of goods sold	600	690	794	913	1,049
10	Gross margin	400	460	529	608	700
11						
12						
13						

FIGURE 5-74
Trace Command
Here, the cursor was positioned in cell B4, and the command was used to trace dependent cells. The cells on row 9 were highlighted because their result depends on the value entered into cell B9.

	A	B	C
1	Cost of car	$10,000	
2	Down payment	2,000	
3	Loan required	B1-B2	
4	Interest rate	13%	
5	Term of loan (in months)	36	
6	Monthly payment	ABS(PMPT(B4/12,B5,B3))	
7			
8			
9			
10			
11			
12			
13			

FIGURE 5-75
Printed Diagnostic Tools
A printout of all the model's formulas makes the relationships among cells easier to trace. Most programs have a print option that allows you to send cell contents, such as formulas, to the printer instead of the displayed results.

SUMMARY AND KEY TERMS

- When you encounter problems with a model, you can enter the NA function into a cell and see what other cells display NA. Those that do, directly or indirectly refer to the cell you entered the function into.

- Many programs allow you to display formulas on the screen.

- Newer programs have a *Trace* command that shows what cells refer to the cell containing the cursor. Those that do are called **dependent cells**. You can also use the command to indicate what cells the cell containing the formula refers to. These are called **precedent cells.**

- You can print out cell formulas instead of their contents to make a record of a model or to find out how formulas relate to each other.

- A few programs allow you to print out the row and column labels so that you can refer to the printout when checking the relationships between cells.

REVIEW QUESTIONS

1. List four problems that you might encounter when entering models.

2. If a cell displays a row of symbols, for example, ****** or >>>>>>, what is the cause? How do you correct it?

3. If a cell displays a number in scientific notation, for example, 1.00E + 5, what is the cause? How do you correct it?

4. Why would you enter the NA function into a cell?

5. If you use the *Trace* command, what is a dependent cell? A precedent cell?

Part Six

DATABASE MANAGEMENT APPLICATIONS

Topic 6-1   Record Management and Database Management
Topic 6-2   Database Management Procedures: An Overview
Topic 6-3   Typical Record and Database Management
                 Programs
Topic 6-4   Getting Acquainted with Your Program
Topic 6-5   Defining a Database File
Topic 6-6   Entering Records
Topic 6-7   Displaying Records
Case Study   1 Creating a Database of Names and Addresses
Topic 6-8   Query Languages
Topic 6-9   Using Criteria to Display Records
Topic 6-10   Adding, Updating, and Deleting Records
Case Study   2 Using Queries and Updating Records
Topic 6-11   Sorting Records
Topic 6-12   Indexing Records
Case Study   3 Sorting and Indexing Files
Topic 6-13   Printing Reports
Case Study   4 Printing Reports
Topic 6-14   Restructuring the Database
Topic 6-15   Making New Databases from Existing Files
Case Study   5 Joining Files
Topic 6-16   Writing Programs
Case Study   6 Writing Programs
Topic 6-17   Data Security
Topic 6-18   Hypermedia

The concept behind database management programs is simple. They allow you to store information in your computer, retrieve it when you need it, and update it when necessary. You can store large amounts of information like mailing lists, inventory records, or billing and collection information in files. You can then manipulate the information in these files with the database management program. For example, you can

- Add new information
- Find specific information
- Update information that has changed
- Sort the information into a specified order
- Delete information that is no longer needed
- Print out reports containing all or some of the information contained in the file(s)

Because of the power and flexibility of these programs, the applications are almost endless.

- You can maintain mailing lists for sales and marketing purposes. Names and addresses stored using a database management program can be easily kept up to date. The data can also be used to automatically print letters, envelopes, and mailing labels.

- You can manage inventory by recording products or supplies moving into and out of a business. The program can give you answers to questions like, "How many parts are left in inventory?" or "How many were shipped this month?"

- You can manage assets like stock portfolios so that you always know what stocks you have and what their value is. You can ask the program questions like, "What IBM stocks do I have?" "What stocks have increased in value since I bought them?" or "What stocks have I sold this year?"

- You can maintain a file of frequently used names, addresses, and phone numbers. You can then ask the program questions like, "What phone numbers are listed for SMITH?" or "What phone numbers are listed in area code 617?"

- You can maintain checking accounts so that you can ask questions like, "What checks have been written to Dr. Smart?"

- You can store and retrieve illustrations like photographs or line drawings. The illustrations are first scanned into the computer and then labeled or described with text. You locate a specific illustration by searching for one or more words used in its label or description.

The applications of database management programs in specific businesses and industries are also widespread.

- In the construction industry, they are used for construction estimating, job costing, project management, and bid management.

- In finance, they are used for accounting, cash management, financial reports, fixed asset management, lease management, and inventory control.

- In medical offices, they are used for office management and administration, nursing management, medical records systems, and pharmacy management.

- In scientific labs, they are used for statistical computations and data analysis.
- In sports, they are used to analyze performance statistics.
- In real estate, they are used for property management, escrow accounting, mobile park management, property listing, and real estate investment trust management.

1. List three things you can do with the information stored in a database.
2. List and briefly describe some typical database applications.

Record Management and Database Management

OBJECTIVES

After completing this topic, you will be able to

- Understand the difference between a record management program and a database management system

- Understand the concept of a relational database

The management of databases is one of the most important applications of microcomputers. A **database** is simply one or more files that contains an organized body of information. The database exists but doesn't actually do anything itself. To create, maintain, and use a database, you use a **database management program**. (When reading about databases, you will often find the terms spelled as database or data base. There is no difference between the two terms; the spelling just hasn't been standardized.)

RECORD MANAGEMENT PROGRAMS

In the early days of business computing, separate programs were created for each application. For example, the payroll department would have a program that created and maintained a file containing names, addresses, and payroll information of employees. The personnel department would use a different program that maintained a separate file containing names, addresses, hiring dates, insurance policies, and vacation schedules. Whenever a new application was needed, a new program was written, and the data needed for that application was entered and maintained. The data in the payroll department's file could not be used by the personnel department's program. Each of the files the information was stored in could be used only by the program that created it. If an employee changed her name or left the firm, several files would have to be updated.

Record management programs (sometimes called *file management* or *flat file database programs*), including those integrated into word processing and spreadsheet programs, store, maintain, and use data stored in single files (Figure 6-1). If you use a record management program to store data on various aspects of a business, you must store the data for different applications in separate files. If you want to make changes, you must make them in each file when information is duplicated. Let's say you have one file

534

FLIGHT	TO	FROM	DEPART	ARRIVE
AA100	Boston	Los Angele	10:00	14:00
AA200	Boston	Chicago	11:00	15:00
AA300	Boston	NY	12:00	16:00
UA100	Los Angele	Chicago	13:00	17:00
UA200	Chicago	NY	14:00	18:00
UA300	Atlanta	NY	15:00	19:00
PANAM1	NY	London	16:00	20:00
PANAM2	NY	Paris	17:00	21:00
PANAM3	NY	Toronto	18:00	22:00

RECORD MANAGEMENT PROGRAM

FIGURE 6-1
Record Management Programs
Record management programs can address only one file at a time. To manage information in another file, you must clear the first file from memory and retrieve the new one.

for names, addresses, and phone numbers and another file for payroll information. If a person's name occurs in both files, the name must be separately entered into each file. If the name must be changed or deleted later, it must be separately changed in or deleted from each file.

DATABASE MANAGEMENT PROGRAMS

As the amount of information being processed increases, the record management method of using separate files to store information becomes cumbersome because information must be extensively duplicated. An employee's name might appear in several different files, for example, payroll, vacation, and expense accounts. There are disadvantages to this duplication.

- It increases the risk of errors in the information. Since a person's name would have to be entered more than once, any changes in status would have to be made in different files, perhaps by different people. Over time, the data's accuracy deteriorates. For example, changes might be made in some files and not in others, or some data might be entered correctly into one file and incorrectly into another.

- It increases the amount of data entry since some information must be entered more than once.

- It requires more storage space, which causes problems when the database is large.

The concept of a database, introduced in the early 1970s, eliminates these problems. In a database, the data is stored so that there is no duplication of data. For example, a person's name can appear in the database only once, so a change must be made only once. **Database management programs** (also called data base management systems, or DBMS) are used to manage these databases. They can do everything a record management program can do, but they can also do much more. The main difference is that a database management program can use interrelated data stored in one or more files (Figure 6-2), thus eliminating the duplication of data and the need to enter updates more than once into different files.

There are many database management programs now on the market that let you create small-scale versions of relatively large databases like those used in corporations. These database management programs can create and use a database consisting of one or more files.

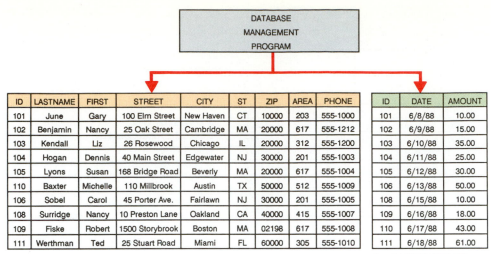

FIGURE 6-2
Database Management Programs
Database management programs can manage the data in more than one file.

A. NAMELIST File

ID	LASTNAME	FIRST	STREET	CITY	ST	ZIP	AREA	PHONE
101	June	Gary	100 Elm Street	New Haven	CT	10000	203	555-1000
102	Benjamin	Nancy	25 Oak Street	Cambridge	MA	20000	617	555-1212
103	Kendall	Liz	26 Rosewood	Chicago	IL	20000	312	555-1200
104	Hogan	Dennis	40 Main Street	Edgewater	NJ	30000	201	555-1003
105	Lyons	Susan	168 Bridge Road	Beverly	MA	20000	617	555-1004
110	Baxter	Michelle	110 Millbrook	Austin	TX	50000	512	555-1009
106	Sobel	Carol	45 Porter Ave.	Fairlawn	NJ	30000	201	555-1005
108	Surridge	Nancy	10 Preston Lane	Oakland	CA	40000	415	555-1007
109	Fiske	Robert	1500 Storybrook	Boston	MA	02198	617	555-1008
111	Werthman	Ted	25 Stuart Road	Miami	FL	60000	305	555-1010

B. AMOUNTS File

ID	DATE	AMOUNT
101	6/8/88	10.00
102	6/9/88	15.00
103	6/10/88	35.00
104	6/11/88	25.00
105	6/12/88	30.00
106	6/13/88	50.00
108	6/15/88	10.00
109	6/16/88	18.00
110	6/17/88	43.00
111	6/18/88	61.00

Database management programs are more powerful than record management programs because they allow you to create and access multiple, interrelated files, whereas record management programs can work with only one file at a time. Database management programs, therefore, have a major advantage since many applications they are used for require more than one file. For example, the accounting process requires separate files for the general ledger, accounts receivable, and accounts payable. A program that can work with more than one file eliminates the need for duplicating information in separate files and reduces the task of updating the information. Moreover, because data is entered only once, the accuracy of the information is much improved.

RECORD MANAGEMENT VERSUS DATABASE MANAGEMENT

Users often misunderstand the differences between record management programs and database management programs, and advertisers often misrepresent them. Almost all data management programs for microcomputers are called database management programs, but many are actually record management programs because the program can work with only one file at a time. Although record management programs are easy to learn and use, their one-file limitation makes them unsuitable for many applications. Database management programs, however, are harder to learn and operate than record management programs because they are much more powerful. The application you plan for the program, not the advertiser's claims, should determine which type of program you use. Using a database management program simply to maintain a mailing list would not make sense. But trying to create a customized, full-featured accounting system using a record management program would be equally inappropriate.

DATABASE MODELS

When you enter information into a database, the information is stored on the disk in one or more files. This is the **physical storage** of the information. Programs that update and manipulate the information in the database handle all aspects of the physical storage so that you do not have to. Al-

ID	LASTNAME	FIRST	STREET	CITY	ST	ZIP	AREA	PHONE
101	June	Gary	100 Elm Street	New Haven	CT	10000	203	555-1000
102	Benjamin	Nancy	25 Oak Street	Cambridge	MA	20000	617	555-1212
103	Kendall	Liz	26 Rosewood	Chicago	IL	20000	312	555-1200
104	Hogan	Dennis	40 Main Street	Edgewater	NJ	30000	201	555-1003
105	Lyons	Susan	168 Bridge Road	Beverly	MA	20000	617	555-1004
106	Baxter	Michelle	110 Millbrook	Austin	TX	50000	512	555-1009
107	Sobel	Carol	45 Porter Ave.	Fairlawn	NJ	30000	201	555-1005
108	Surridge	Nancy	10 Preston Lane	Oakland	CA	40000	415	555-1007
109	Fiske	Robert	1500 Storybrook	Boston	MA	02198	617	555-1008
110	Werthman	Ted	25 Stuart Road	Miami	FL	60000	305	555-1010

← A. Field Name

} B. Rows of Data

FIGURE 6-3
Relational Database
A relational database table contains rows and columns much like a spreadsheet.

A. The columns are fields, and the labels at the top of each field are the field names. Each column on the table has a fixed length.

B. There is one or more rows of data, and each row is a record.

though the physical storage is not important to you, the way you view the data, its **logical storage**, is. Logical storage refers to the way the information in different files can be related.

The logical arrangement of files is called the **database model** (or database schema). Three typical models are **network**, **hierarchical**, and **relational**. Almost all microcomputer database management systems use the relational model, so this is the only model we discuss in this part.

The concept behind relational databases was developed around 1970 by E.F. Codd at IBM. To understand a relational database, imagine a drawer in a filing cabinet. Information is stored in folders and inserted into the drawer. In a record management system, each set of folders stands alone; thus to find a specific letter, you select the most likely folder and look in it. If the letter is not there, you try again. But in a relational database, each folder is cross-referenced to other folders in the file. If the letter is not in the first folder, there will be cross-references suggesting other files you should look in. In a database, these cross-references are called **relationships**.

A relational database consists of one or more tables, called **relations**. You see the information arranged as tables, not the way it is stored on the disk. A relational database table contains rows and columns much like a spreadsheet (Figure 6-3).

ID	LASTNAME	FIRST	STREET	CITY	ST	ZIP	AREA	PHONE
101	June	Gary	100 Elm Street	New Haven	CT	10000	203	555-1000
102	Benjamin	Nancy	25 Oak Street	Cambridge	MA	20000	617	555-1212
103	Kendall	Liz	26 Rosewood	Chicago	IL	20000	312	555-1200
104	Hogan	Dennis	40 Main Street	Edgewater	NJ	30000	201	555-1003
105	Lyons	Susan	168 Bridge Road	Beverly	MA	20000	617	555-1004
106	Baxter	Michelle	110 Millbrook	Austin	TX	50000	512	555-1009
107	Sobel	Carol	45 Porter Ave.	Fairlawn	NJ	30000	201	555-1005
108	Surridge	Nancy	10 Preston Lane	Oakland	CA	40000	415	555-1007
109	Fiske	Robert	1500 Storybrook	Boston	MA	02198	617	555-1008
110	Werthman	Ted	25 Stuart Road	Miami	FL	60000	305	555-1010

A.

ID	DATE	AMOUNT
101	6/8/88	10.00
102	6/9/88	15.00
103	6/10/88	35.00
104	6/11/88	25.00
105	6/12/88	30.00
106	6/13/88	50.00
107	6/15/88	10.00
108	6/16/88	18.00
109	6/17/88	43.00
110	6/18/88	61.00

B.

FIGURE 6-4
Linked Database Tables
This database contains two tables. The first table (a) is used to store customer names, addresses, and phone numbers. The second table (b) is used to store any charges the customers make and the date they made them. When more than one table is used, they are linked using a common field that contains unique data, in this case, the customer's ID number.

Since a database can contain more than one table, the tables can be linked to one another, as Figure 6-4 shows. As you see later, you manipulate the data in these tables to enter, update, and find information stored in the database. You can also combine two or more files into a new file.

SUMMARY AND KEY TERMS

- A **database** is one or more files that contains an organized body of information.
- To create and use databases, you use a **record management program** or a **database management program**. Record management programs can work with only single files. Database management programs can work with one or more files at the same time.
- The way a database management program stores information on the disk is called the **physical storage**. The **logical storage** refers to the way you view the data in the database.
- The logical storage of files is called the **database model**. There are three common types of database models: **network**, **hierarchical**, and **relational**.
- A relational database model, the kind most often used in microcomputer database management programs, organizes data into tables, called **relations**.

REVIEW QUESTIONS

1. What is a database?
2. What is the difference between a record management program and a database management program?
3. What are two or three disadvantages to duplicating information when using a record management program?
4. What is the difference between physical storage and logical storage?
5. What is a database model? List three types of models. Which model is most frequently used for programs that run on microcomputers?
6. How is information stored logically in a relational database?
7. What are columns and rows known as when discussed in the context of a relational database table?
8. When do you use a program's query language?

Database Management Procedures: An Overview

OBJECTIVE

After completing this topic, you will be able to

- Briefly describe the steps you follow to create and use a database

Before discussing database management in detail, we look briefly at the procedures you would follow to create and use a database file that contains names and addresses. We discuss all the procedures introduced here in greater detail in the following topics, but this overview should give you a feel for how these programs work and how you can use them.

STEP 1: PLANNING THE DATABASE

You want to keep track of names and addresses, so you must first plan exactly what information is to be included in the database. This planning is important because the way the information is broken down determines how you can access it later. You begin by listing the information you want to store.

- Name and ID number
- Street
- City
- State and ZIP code
- Phone number

After thinking about the information, you realize you may want to sort it later by last name, ZIP code, or area code. To do so, you need to break down the list still further.

- ID number
- Last name
- First name
- Street
- City
- State
- ZIP code
- Area code
- Phone number

ID	LASTNAME	FIRST	STREET	CITY	ST	ZIP	AREA	PHONE
101	June	Gary	100 Elm Street	New Haven	CT	10000	203	555-1000
102	Benjamin	Nancy	25 Oak Street	Cambridge	MA	20000	617	555-1212
103	Kendall	Liz	26 Rosewood	Chicago	IL	20000	312	555-1200
104	Hogan	Dennis	40 Main Street	Edgewater	NJ	30000	201	555-1003
105	Lyons	Susan	168 Bridge Road	Beverly	MA	20000	617	555-1004
106	Baxter	Michelle	110 Millbrook	Austin	TX	50000	512	555-1009
107	Sobel	Carol	45 Porter Ave.	Fairlawn	NJ	30000	201	555-1005
108	Surridge	Nancy	10 Preston Lane	Oakland	CA	40000	415	555-1007
109	Fiske	Robert	1500 Storybrook	Boston	MA	02198	617	555-1008
110	Werthman	Ted	25 Stuart Road	Miami	FL	60000	305	555-1010

B.

C.

A.

FIGURE 6-5
Fields and Records
Databases are organized into fields (a), each of which has a name (b) and records (c).

STEP 2: DEFINING THE DATABASE

Once you have a list of the information that you want to store, you create a database file to store it in. This information is not stored randomly in a file; it must be stored in a highly organized way so that the program can find it later. The way data is organized in a database is really quite simple. It is always organized into fields and records (Figure 6-5).

- A **record** is a description of a person, thing, or activity. In this example, a record is the complete name, address, and phone number for a person.
- A **field** is one part of the description stored in the record. In our file, the fields are those you broke down in Step 1.

When you first create a database file, you have to tell the program what fields you plan on storing so that it can allocate room for them. This step is called defining the database. When you define a database, you describe each field by specifying its name, length, and the type of data to be stored, for example, text, dates, or numbers that can be calculated. You enter these descriptions using the program's create database or define database screen (Figure 6-6).

STEP 3: ENTERING DATA

Once you have defined the database file, you can enter data for each person. Many programs display forms on the screen that display the field names you

FIGURE 6-6
Defining a Database
When you execute the dBASE command that creates a new database file, the screen where you define fields is displayed. You move the cursor from field to field, and enter each field's name, type, and width. If the field is numeric, you can also specify the number of decimal places.

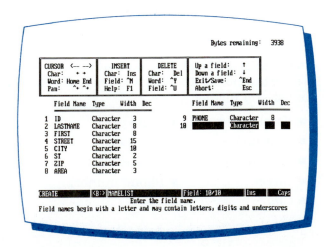

DATABASE MANAGEMENT APPLICATIONS

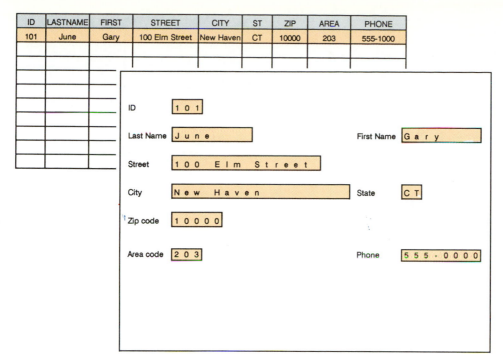

ID	LASTNAME	FIRST	STREET	CITY	ST	ZIP	AREA	PHONE
101	June	Gary	100 Elm Street	New Haven	CT	10000	203	555-1000

ID [1 0 1]

Last Name [J u n e]   First Name [G a r y]

Street [1 0 0   E l m   S t r e e t]

City [N e w   H a v e n]   State [C T]

Zip code [1 0 0 0 0]

Area code [2 0 3]   Phone [5 5 5 - 0 0 0 0]

FIGURE 6-7
Entering Data
As you enter data, the information is stored in a table in memory and on the disk. Each fill-in blank is a field, and all the fields make up a record.

ID	LASTNAME	FIRST	STREET	CITY	ST	ZIP	AREA	PHONE
101	June	Gary	200 End Street	Oakland	CT	45678	415	555-2222
102	Benjamin	Nancy	25 Oak Street	Cambridge	MA	20000	617	555-1212
103	Kendall	Liz	26 Rosewood	Chicago	IL	30000	312	555-1200
104	Hogan	Denni						
105	Lyons	Susa						
106	Baxter	Michel						
107	Sobel	Caro						
108	Surridge	Nanc						
109	Fiske	Robe						
110	Werthman	Ted						

ID [1 0 1]

Last Name [J u n e]   First Name [G a r y]

Street [2 0 0   E n d   S t r e e t]

City [O a k l a n d]   State [C A]

Zip code [4 5 6 7 8]

Area code [4 1 5]   Phone [5 5 5 - 2 2 2 2]

FIGURE 6-8
Updating the Database
To change data in a database, you display the record you want to change, and enter the new data into the appropriate fields. The data in the database is then changed.

assigned. To enter data, you move the cursor from field name to field name and type in the data. The data you enter into the form is automatically entered into the database (Figure 6-7).

STEP 4: UPDATING THE DATABASE

Whenever persons in your database move or change their names, their records must be updated to reflect the changes. To make these changes, the necessary files are opened, commands are used to locate the records, and the new data are entered in place of the old (Figure 6-8).

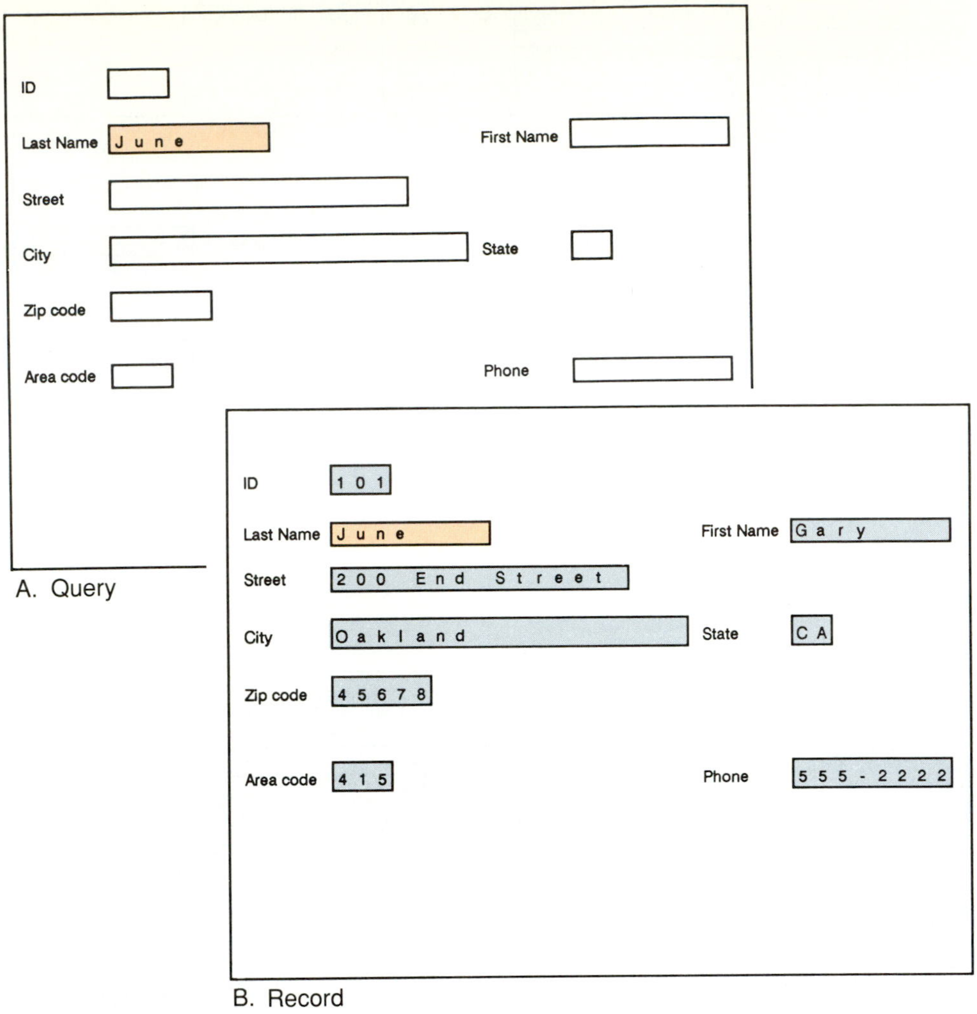

ID		
Last Name	June	First Name
Street		
City		State
Zip code		
Area code		Phone

A. Query

ID	1 0 1	
Last Name	June	First Name	Gary
Street	2 0 0 E n d S t r e e t	
City	Oakland	State	C A
Zip code	4 5 6 7 8	
Area code	4 1 5	Phone	5 5 5 - 2 2 2 2

B. Record

FIGURE 6-9
Querying the Database
To find a specific record,
you query the database.
Here the name June has
been entered in the
LASTNAME field of the
query screen (a), and the
record with that name in
that field is displayed (b).

STEP 5: QUERYING THE DATABASE

What if you want to call Gary June, whose name and address have been entered into your database. To do so, you can **query** the database for all records where the last name is June. When you execute the command, the record for any person whose last name is June is displayed on the screen. If there is more than one June, the first record for that name is displayed, and then you can scroll though all other records that have June in them until you find the correct record (Figure 6-9).

STEP 6: PRINTING REPORTS

One of the most valuable features of a database management program is its ability to generate reports. **Reports** are simply selected parts of the database displayed on the screen or printed out in a specified way. For example, using our database, you can print a report that lists just names, phone numbers, and amounts due (Figure 6-10) or mailing labels that include complete addresses (Figure 6-11).

FIGURE 6-10
Printing Reports<Amounts
Due
Reports can be
comprehensive, even
calculating totals and
subtotals.

Page No.   1

11/03/89

AMOUNTS DUE

First Name	Last Name	Area Code	Phone Number	Amount Due
** Amounts due from state: CA				
James	Poe	415	555-1007	10.00
** Subtotal **				
				10.00
** Amounts due from state: CT				
Tina	Culman	203	555-1000	10.00
** Subtotal **				
				10.00
** Amounts due from state: FL				
Jose	Alverez	305	555-1010	61.00
** Subtotal **				
				61.00
** Amounts due from state: IL				
Liz	Kendall	312	555-1200	35.00
John	Davis	312	555-1020	75.00
** Subtotal **				
				110.00
** Amounts due from state: MA				
Nancy	Benjamin	617	555-1212	15.00
Daphne	Swabey	617	555-1004	30.00
Robert	Fiske	617	555-1008	18.00
** Subtotal **				
				63.00
** Amounts due from state: NJ				
Dennis	Hogan	201	555-1003	25.00
Carol	Sobel	201	555-1005	50.00
** Subtotal **				
				75.00
** Amounts due from state: TX				
Lars	Porsena	512	555-1009	43.00
** Subtotal **				
				43.00
*** Total ***				
				372.00

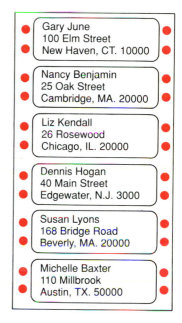

FIGURE 6-11
Printing Reports—Mailing
Labels
The same database can
also be used to print
simpler reports, like
mailing labels.

SUMMARY AND KEY TERMS

- **Fields** are individual pieces of information like a phone number, a first name, a street address, or a price.
- **Records** are collections of fields that describe a person, thing, or activity.
- The first step in creating a database is defining the database. In this step, you specify what fields are to be in each record and describe the kind of information each field is to hold.
- When you enter data into the database, you often fill in a form that is displayed on the screen.
- When you want to change information in a database, you **update** records.
- When you want to find information in a database, you **query** the database.
- You can print out information in the database. The printouts are called **reports**.

REVIEW QUESTIONS

1. What is a field? A record? Give examples of each.

2. What is the first step in creating a new database file? What do you do in this step?

3. What appears on the screen when you enter data into the database?

4. What is it called when you change information in the database?

5. What is it called when you look for data in the database?

6. What is a printout of information in the database called?

DATABASE MANAGEMENT APPLICATIONS

Typical Record and Database Management Programs

OBJECTIVE

After completing this topic, you will be able to

- Describe some typical record and database management programs

Database management programs are available in several versions, including

- Standalone programs, like Ashton-Tate's dBASE, are designed to be used independently.
- Applications programs, like word processors and spreadsheets, frequently have record management capabilities built in, as you saw in Parts Four and Five.
- Integrated programs almost always have a record management program as one of their components.

Here, we look at some examples of each of these types of programs. One, dBASE, is a true relational database management system, so it can work with more than one file. All the others are record management programs that can work with only one file at a time.

dBASE

dBASE is a standalone relational database program and, for years, has had the largest share of the market. It was originally published as dBASE II and has been revised several times. Each version has improved on previous ones by making the program easier to use. On dBASE II, only a dot appeared on the screen, and all commands had to be typed. The latest version is much simpler because it includes easy-to-use menus (Figure 6-12).

SPREADSHEETS

Many spreadsheets like Excel, VP Planner, and Lotus 1-2-3 contain limited record management capabilities. Using the program, you can sort, find, and extract records. A database is created right on the spreadsheet. A row is

FIGURE 6-12
dBASE III Plus

The dBASE screen display has the following elements:

A. A menu bar at the top of the screen contains a series of menus that can be pulled down.

B. The status bar displays the command in progress, the current default drive, the name of the current file, and the number of records. It also indicates if **Caps Lock** and **Num Lock** are engaged or not.

C. The navigation line, just below the status bar, displays messages listing the keys and commands you can use.

D. The message line, the bottom line on the screen, displays messages when the program wants you to enter information. When the menu bar is displayed, this line briefly describes the highlighted menu choice.

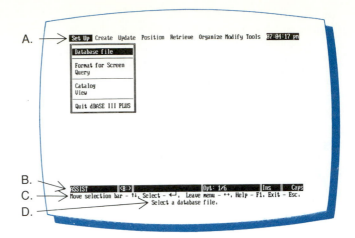

used for headings indicating the contents of each column (field names). Cells (fields) on rows below these headings (records) can then be filled in with specific information (Figure 6-13). You can then sort the data or extract selected records.

WORDPERFECT

WordPerfect (Figure 6-14), like many other word processing programs, includes a record management capability. This built-in database is used to maintain lists of names and address and other information to be inserted into primary documents during merge printing.

FIGURE 6-13
Spreadsheets

On this spreadsheet, records are entered on rows and fields are entered into columns. The column headings are used for the field names. At any time you can sort the data into ascending or descending order based on the contents of any column. For example, you can sort it into alphabetical order by last names or by city. You can also quickly find a specific record or extract records in whole or in part from the database. For example, you could extract all records with MA in the ST field.

	A	B	C	D	E	F	G	H	I
1	INPUT RANGE:								
2	ID	LASTNAME	FIRST	STREET	CITY	ST	ZIP	AREA	PHONE
3	101	June	Gary	200 End Street	Oakland	CA	45658	415	555-2222
4	102	Benjamin	Nancy	25 Oak Street	Cambridge	MA	20000	617	555-1212
5	103	Kendall	Liz	26 Rosewood	Chicago	IL	20000	312	555-1200
6	104	Hogan	Dennis	40 Main Street	Edgewater	NJ	30000	201	555-1003
7	105	Lyons	Susan	168 Bridge Road	Beverly	MA	20000	617	555-1004
8	106	Baxter	Miclelle	110 Millbrook	Austin	TX	50000	512	555-1009
9	107	Sobel	Carol	45 Porter Ave.	Fairlawn	NJ	30000	201	555-1005
10	108	Surridge	Nancy	10 Preston Lane	Oakland	CA	40000	415	555-1007
11	109	Fiske	Robert	1500 Storybrook	Boston	MA	02198	617	555-1008
12	110	Werthman	Ted	25 Stuart Road	Miami	FL	60000	305	555-1010
13									
14	CRITERION RANGE:								
15		Dept.	Course	Instructor	Day	Time	Bldg.		
16		June							
17									
18	OUTPUT RANGE:								
19		Dept.	Course	Instructor	Day	Time	Bldg.		
20	101	June	Gary	200 End Street	Oakland	CA	45658	415	555-2222

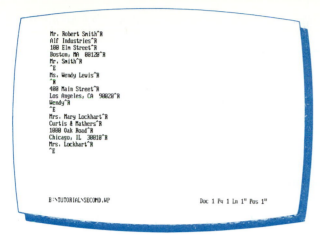

FIGURE 6-14
WordPerfect
WordPerfect database files use special characters to end fields and records. The ^R indicates the end of a field, and the ^E indicates the end of a record.

FIGURE 6-15
Microsoft Works
When you display the database function on Microsoft Works, a blank screen appears. You then enter field names to lay out an on-screen form. When completed, you use the form to enter data into the database file.

MICROSOFT WORKS

Microsoft Works is an integrated program that includes spreadsheet, word processing, record management, and telecommunications functions. When you select the database function from the Main menu, you can create forms on the screen that you then use to enter data into the database file (Figure 6-15).

- WordPerfect has built-in database management capabilities that are used primarily for merge printing.
- Microsoft Works is an integrated program with a built-in database function.

REVIEW QUESTIONS

1. List three types of database management programs.
2. Name one program that is a relational database program.
3. When database capabilities are built into applications programs, are they relational database programs?

Getting Acquainted with Your Program

OBJECTIVES

After completing this topic, you will be able to

- Explain how you enter commands by typing them or selecting them from a menu
- Explain the importance of correctly quitting a database program

When you load a database management program, it displays a command line or menus. A few programs offer you both options. For example, on dBASE, you can execute all commands just by typing them from the dot prompt. On later versions, many commands are also listed on menus if you use the program's assist mode or Control Center. Both sets of commands have the same effect. But choosing commands from a menu is easier than remembering the commands, and typing is faster than pulling down menus. You can use both approaches as you work with the program.

ON-LINE HELP

To help with commands, most database management programs provide extensive on-line help. You can obtain help through a menu or display help information about a specific command (Figure 6-16).

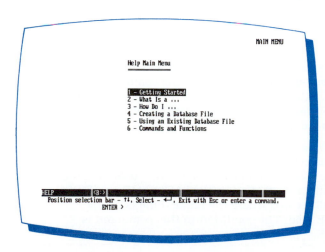

FIGURE 6-16
On-Line Help
On dBASE, you type HELP and then press **Return** to display the Help Main menu. You can also type HELP <COMMAND> and then press **Return** to display help on a specific command. For example, to display help on the *Assist* command, type HELP ASSIST and then press **Return**.

COMMAND LINE PROGRAMS

Some programs are operated by typing commands. These commands are much like sentences but in a highly stylized form understandable to the program. If you make a typo while entering a command, press **Backspace** to delete characters, and then retype them correctly. If you incorrectly enter a command, the program displays an error message, and some programs ask if you want help displayed.

The commands that you enter must follow the structure, or syntax, required by the program. If a command is not structured properly, the program cannot understand it. For example, to display help on the DISPLAY command when using dBASE, you type HELP DISPLAY, not HELP ON DIS-PLAY. Table 6-1 describes how you structure commands when using dBASE. Not all commands include all four parts, but all commands must include the name of the command, called the verb.

In addition to the structure of commands, there are usually other rules you must follow. Table 6-2 describes those required by dBASE.

Entering commands is time consuming, and it is easy to make errors. To speed up the process, many programs assign the most frequently used commands to function keys. dBASE also has a *History* command that stores the commands you type in a buffer so that you can display them again without having to retype them each time you use them. Whenever the command line is displayed, you can press the up arrow key to display the last command you entered. If you press the key repeatedly, you cycle through several of the previous commands.

TABLE 6-1
dBASE Command Parts

Part	Description
Verb	The first part of every command must begin with the command's name, for example, DISPLAY, LIST, CLEAR, HELP. This tells the program the action you want performed.
Scope	An optional part of many commands specifies what part of the file you want the action performed on. For example, LIST ALL tells the program to display all records. LIST 5 tells it to display just record number 5. The scopes in these commands are ALL and 5.
Noun	The noun specifies the object of the command, for example, a file, field, or variable. For example, the command LIST LASTNAME, FIRST tells the program to display just the contents of the LASTNAME and FIRST fields. The nouns in this command are LASTNAME and FIRST.
Condition	In many commands, you enter conditions that specify the nouns to be acted on. For example, the command LIST LASTNAME, FIRST FOR LASTNAME="June" tells the program to display the information in the LASTNAME and FIRST fields for all records where the name June is in the LASTNAME field. The condition in this command is LASTNAME="June".

TABLE 6-2
dBASE Rules for Entering Commands

Item	Description
Case	You can type commands in uppercase letters, lowercase letters, or any combination of both. For example, to quit the program, you can type QUIT, quit, or Quit.
Length	Commands can be as long as 254 characters (including spaces).
Spaces	Words within a command can be separated by one or more blank spaces.
Shorthand	When typing longer commands, you must type only the first four characters. For example, typing DISPLAY STRUCTURE and DISP STRU give the same result.

MENU PROGRAMS

You can execute many commands by selecting choices from menus (Figure 6-17). This greatly reduces the number of rules you have to remember when entering commands.

COMMANDS VS. MENUS

dBASE now offers users a choice between commands and menus. Each option has advantages and disadvantages. Using commands, the steps to change the default drive to drive B and then display a list of files on that drive are as follows:

1. Press **Esc** to remove the menu bar and display the dot prompt.
2. Type SET DEFAULT TO B: and then press **Return**.
3. Type DIR *.* and then press **Return**.

Now let's see how you use dBASE's menus. When you first load dBASE III Plus, the help menus are displayed at the top of the screen. If the menu bar is not at the top of the screen, you can type a command to display it.

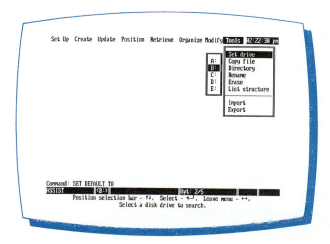

FIGURE 6-17
The dBASE Menus
The dBASE program has an assist mode that allows you to execute commands by selecting choices from pull-down menus.

1. Type `ASSIST` and then press **Return** to display the menu bar.
2. Press T to pull down the Tools menu and highlight *Set drive*.
3. Press **Return** to select *Set drive*.
4. Highlight *B:* on the menu, and then press **Return**.
5. Highlight *Directory*, and then press **Return** to display a submenu listing your computer's disk drives.
6. Highlight *B:*, and then press **Return**.
7. Highlight *.* All Files*, and then press **Return** to display a list of all files on drive B.
8. Press any key to return to the menu bar.

When you are familiar with the program, typing the commands is much faster than using the menus. The menus, however, free you from having to remember the commands; you just select choices from menus that are displayed one after another.

CLEARING OR QUITTING

When you work on a database program, the program opens files that you must close before quitting the program or working on another project. If you turn off or reboot the computer without quitting properly, the files you have been working on may be damaged, and data may be lost. There are usually two commands you can use to protect your files.

- One command closes all open files and returns you to the command line or menus so that you can work on another file. For example, on dBASE, you type `CLEAR ALL` and then press **Return** to clear all open files from memory.

- Another command closes all open files and returns you to the operating system so that you can run another program or quit for the day. For example, on dBASE, you type `QUIT` and then press **Return** to quit the program and return to the operating system.

SUMMARY AND KEY TERMS

- Some programs have on-line help that is available by pressing a specified key or typing a command.
- Some programs are command-line programs and require that you type commands in response to prompts that appear on the screen. The commands that you type must follow the program's rules. dBASE has a *History* command that displays commands that were entered previously so that you can scroll though them instead of retyping them.
- The easiest-to-use programs are those operated by selecting choices from menus.
- When you work with a database management program, it opens temporary files on the disk that are closed automatically when you close the files or correctly quit the program.

REVIEW QUESTIONS

1. What is the advantage of menu-operated programs?
2. What purpose does dBASE's assist mode serve?
3. What is the purpose of dBASE's *History* command?
4. List five rules for entering commands on dBASE.
5. Why should you correctly quit a database program?

Defining a Database File

OBJECTIVES

After completing this topic, you will be able to

- Describe entities and attributes
- Describe how data is organized into fields, records, and files
- Explain how you plan a database
- Describe how database files are defined, and briefly describe field names, types, and lengths
- Explain why you would want to display a dictionary or a file's structure

The first step in using a database management program is to define the database file you want to store data in. To define a database, you must know how the program stores the data that you plan on entering. Moreover, since databases are hard to revise after you have entered data into them, you should know how to carefully plan a database before you actually define it with the database management program.

THE ORGANIZATION OF A DATABASE

When you enter information into a database management program, it is stored in a file. The information you enter must be organized so that the program can easily manipulate it. To understand how a program manages information, you must first understand the five levels of organization used to store and manipulate data (Figure 6-18).

ENTITIES AND ATTRIBUTES

Every database is created using entities. An **entity** is the subject of a record that is created, for example, a customer. To describe an entity, for example, a specific customer, you must decide what facts describe it and differentiate it from all other entities. These facts are called **attributes** and are used as the database's fields. Attributes for a customer could be the customer's ID, last name, first name, street address, city, ZIP code, area code, and phone number. The attributes you select determine what fields each record in the database will contain.

553

A.

ID	LASTNAME	FIRST	STREET	CITY	ST	ZIP	AREA	PHONE
1								

B.

ID	LASTNAME	FIRST	STREET	CITY	ST	ZIP	AREA	PHONE
101								

C.

ID	LASTNAME	FIRST	STREET	CITY	ST	ZIP	AREA	PHONE
101	June	Gary	100 Elm Street	New Haven	CT	10000	203	555-1000

D.

ID	LASTNAME	FIRST	STREET	CITY	ST	ZIP	AREA	PHONE
101	June	Gary	100 Elm Street	New Haven	CT	10000	203	555-1000
102	Benjamin	Nancy	25 Oak Street	Cambridge	MA	20000	617	555-1212

E.

ID	LASTNAME	FIRST	STREET	CITY	ST	ZIP	AREA	PHONE
101	June	Gary	100 Elm Street	New Haven	CT	10000	203	555-1000
102	Benjamin	Nancy	25 Oak Street	Cambridge	MA	20000	617	555-1212

ID	DATE	AMOUNT
101	6/8/88	10.00
102	6/9/88	15.00

FIGURE 6-18
Levels of Data Organization
When you enter data into a record management program, you enter records and fields. A record is like an index card; it contains all the information about a product, person, or other item. A field is a piece of the information in a record, for example, a name, an address, a phone number, or a price.

A. When you enter information into a computer, you type it in from the keyboard. The first level of organization is, therefore, the alphanumeric characters you type, for example, numbers and letters.

B. You use one or more characters to enter fields, for example, a person's ID or name. Fields can be numbers (101), names (June), names and numbers (100 Elm Street), or formulas (100*3).

C. Related fields are stored together as records, for example, a person's ID, last name, first name, street, city, state, ZIP code, area code, and phone number.

D. Related records are stored together as files, for example, a list or customers.

E. Related files are stored together as a database. The database contains interrelated files that can be combined or from which information can be drawn.

As you have seen, relational databases can be thought of as interrelated tables of information. Each table should have a field containing key attributes that uniquely identify the records in the table. The field containing these key attributes is used to link the files in the database. There are many kinds of key attributes. For example, those used to uniquely identify persons include

- Social security numbers
- Vehicle license numbers
- Driver's license numbers
- Bank account numbers
- Employee serial numbers
- Purchase order numbers
- Telephone numbers
- Credit card numbers
- Policy numbers
- Dates and times
- Account numbers

PLANNING YOUR DATABASE FILES

When you design a database, it is important to follow these three steps.

1. Determine what entities to include. These entities will become the records in the database.

2. Choose attributes that can describe each entity. Be sure that at least one attribute is unique so that entities can be differentiated from one another. This unique attribute is called the **key attribute**.

3. Determine the way each attribute is entered, including the type of data (for example, text, dates, or numbers) and the length of each field.

When you first create a database, you must tell the program what information you are going to keep. This is not as straightforward as you might think. When asked what information they need, many managers will say "everything." But it is usually impossible to include everything because of the limited availability of the information, the cost of collecting the information if it is available, and the cost of recording and holding the information if it can be collected. Therefore, when deciding what information to keep, you should spend some time thinking about what type of questions you wish to ask and have answered by the data. This, in turn, will tell you what data you need to keep.

As you compile a list of the data you want to store, you can sketch it out, specifying the attributes each entity is to contain, assigning field names to the attributes, and specifying the type and length of the data to be entered into each field. While planning a database, you must also consider the limitations of the program you are using. Programs differ in the types of fields they provide, the number of fields allowed per record, the length of fields, and the length of records. You should also be sure to break down the attributes so that you can later access and manipulate the data.

The number of fields you set up depends on the amount of information you want to store. In some cases, you might divide certain basic information into more than one field so that you can manipulate it more easily. The fields you use to sort the file and find specific records are called **key fields**. For example, if you used only one field for both the persons' first and last names, and then entered names like John Smith, Betty Lewis, and Roger Wentworth, your file would be limited. You could not sort names based on the persons' last names. You also might not be able to find the record. To sort the persons' names, you set up two fields, one for the first name and one for the last name. The same is true of addresses. For example, if you do not enter ZIP codes into a separate field, you will not be able to sort the records by ZIP codes. Your decision on what fields to set up will be influenced by the field types provided by your program.

Designing a relational database requires very careful planning because more than one file can be involved. Not only does each file need to be well planned, but the relationships between files must also be carefully thought through. Figure 6-19 shows the plan for a database that contains two files, one to manage a list of customer names and addresses and the other to manage charges that they make and the dates they were made.

DEFINING A FILE

When you define a database file, you specify the fields it contains and provide information about each field. For example, you specify

- The names of the fields to be included in the file

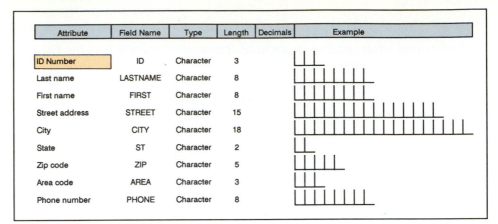

FILE: NAMELIST

Attribute	Field Name	Type	Length	Decimals	Example
ID Number	ID	Character	3		
Last name	LASTNAME	Character	8		
First name	FIRST	Character	8		
Street address	STREET	Character	15		
City	CITY	Character	18		
State	ST	Character	2		
Zip code	ZIP	Character	5		
Area code	AREA	Character	3		
Phone number	PHONE	Character	8		

FILE: AMOUNTS

Attribute	Field Name	Type	Length	Decimals	Example
ID Number	ID	Character	3		
Date of purchase	DATE	Date	8		
Amount purchased	AMOUNT	Numeric	6	2	

FIGURE 6-19
Planning a Database
When planning a database, you list the attributes you want to include for each entity. You then plan the name of each field, its type, and its length. If you want to be able to link the tables, one of the attributes must be common to both files. For example, in this database, we plan to have two files, one to list customer names, addresses, and phone numbers. The other lists customer charges and the dates they were made. The common field, or key attribute, that links both files in the database is the ID field.

- The type of data to be entered into each field
- The length of each field
- The validity checks, if any, that you want to use to ensure that data is correctly entered into a field

When you execute the program's command that defines, or creates, new database files, a definition screen appears (Figure 6-20). You enter the definition of each field into the form using the cursor movement keys to move from field to field. If you make any mistakes, you can correct them with **Backspace** or **Del**. When finished defining the file, you use the program's command that saves the definition.

Field Names

When naming fields, you always use unique field names. The same field name cannot be used more than once in the same file. Typical field names might be LASTNAME, FIRST, STREET, CITY, STATE, ZIP, AREA, and PHONE. Besides being unique, field names must follow other rules required by the program. Table 6-3 describes the field name rules that dBASE observes.

Field Types

Your decision about what fields to set up will be influenced by the field types provided by your program. All programs let you store characters and numbers, but some also let you store dates, times, or comments. Some even let you create fields that calculate an answer based on the entries in other fields. Typical fields types include

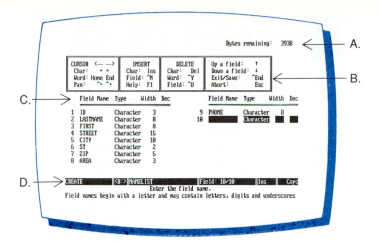

FIGURE 6-20
Database Definition Screen Display
The dBASE screen used to define a file has several elements.

A. In the upper right-hand corner, an indicator shows how many bytes of memory are available for your file.

B. Below the bytes-remaining indicator is a help screen that lists the commands you can use to move the cursor; insert characters and fields; display help; delete words, characters, and fields; and either save and exit the defined file or abort the procedure.

C. Across the center of the screen are two sets of four columns with headings used to define fields. The cursor is blinking in the first column labeled Field Name.

D. The status bar at the bottom of the screen displays the current command (*CREATE*), the default drive, the name of the file you are creating, and the position of the cursor by field and record.

When you start, the cursor is in the left of the column with the *Field Name* highlight. The number (*1*) at the far left indicates which field you are defining. To enter field definitions, enter the field name, and then press End to move the cursor to the next description for the field. When you press Return after entering the field width, a new blank field appears.

TABLE 6-3
Field Name Rules

Length	Must be between one and ten characters long.
First character	Must start with a letter and contain only letters, numbers, and underscores.
Spaces	Must not have blank spaces, but you can substitute underscores. For example, you cannot enter the field name LAST NAME, but you can enter LAST_NAME.

■ **Character fields** (also called *text fields*) store all characters you can enter from the keyboard, including letters, numbers, symbols, and spaces. When numbers are entered into these fields, for example, ZIP codes, they are treated as text, not values. Numbers entered into these fields cannot be used in calculations.

- **Numeric fields** store values, including numbers, signs, and decimals. There are two kinds of numeric fields, integers (numbers without decimal places) and decimals. Numbers entered into these fields can be used in calculations.

- **Calculating fields** are used to make calculations entered into other numeric fields. For example, if you are tracking a student's progress through college, you would want to store all of his or her courses and corresponding grades. Since many student activities, like joining a sports team or earning a scholarship, depend on grade point averages, one field can be designated to automatically calculate these for each course.

- **Logical fields** (sometimes called Boolean fields) are used to enter only true or false notations. For example, on dBASE, you enter true as T, t, Y, or y and false as F, f, N, or n.

- **Date fields** store dates, which you can display in several formats. When dates are entered into these fields, they can usually be used in calculations. Dates can be added and subtracted, or numbers can be added to or subtracted from them. This allows you to get answers to questions like, "What is the average number of days between orders?"

- **Time fields** operate just like date fields but are used to enter hours and minutes instead of days.

- **Memo fields** are used to enter descriptive text, much as you would enter notes to yourself into a notebook. They are similar to character fields, but they generally hold more text and are not used in some operations. Though all other fields are used for specific information, these fields are for general information. You can enter notes about any of the other fields into the record, for example, a note that a price or address is expected to change and the date this is expected to happen. To preserve memory, a memo field often has a variable field length. As you enter text, the size of the field and the amount of memory or data storage space used increases automatically.

Field Lengths

When planning the file, you need to decide how many characters long each field has to be. The program specifies how long the field length can be. Table 6-4 describes the field lengths that dBASE allows. Deciding field lengths ought not to be taken lightly. If you make the field too short, you will lose information. For instance, if you allowed only seven characters for the name, you could enter the name Smith but not the name Hamilton. But if you make the field too long, you waste memory and space on the disk used to store the file, limiting the number of fields in the record or the number of records in the file. Therefore, you need to balance the amount of information held with the space required to hold that information.

The length of the field specifies the number of characters allowed. If the field is numeric, you must specify the total number of digits in the number and the number of decimal places. The program needs to know this so that it can store the values entered into these fields in a way that you can use them in calculations. When designating the length of numeric fields, include room for a minus sign, the total number of characters, and a decimal point. For example, if you specify the field is five characters long with two digits to the right of the decimal point, you can enter values from -9.99 to 99.99. You cannot enter numbers lower than -9.99 (for example, -10.00) and greater than 99.99 (for example, 100.00) because they contain six characters.

TABLE 6-4
dBASE III Plus Field Lengths

Field Type	Length (in characters)
Character fields	1-254
Numeric fields	1-19 (including 0-15 decimal places)
Logical fields	1 (set automatically)
Date fields	8 (set automatically)
Memo fields	1-5000 (set automatically)

Validity Checks

Validity checks (also called *editing checks*) are provided by some programs to help prevent you from making mistakes when you enter data. For example, you can specify that only text of a certain length or numbers entered in a specific way can be entered into a given field. Specifying the largest value that can be entered into a payroll field will prevent your writing a paycheck for $3000.50 when it was meant to be $300.50. If you enter data that violates the rules you specify, it will not be accepted, and the computer will beep, or a prompt will appear telling you to reenter the data.

DATABASE DICTIONARIES

A desirable feature of a database management program is a dictionary (also called a *catalog* or *directory*). When you create a new database file, you make an entry into this dictionary. The dictionary is a separate file containing descriptive, specific information about each file in the database. For example, a typical dictionary entry will include

- The name (or number) of each data field
- The field type, whether a text field, numeric field, date or time field, or another field type provided by the program
- The length of each field and, if the field is numeric, the number of decimal places
- The validity checks that are assigned to ensure that data is entered correctly

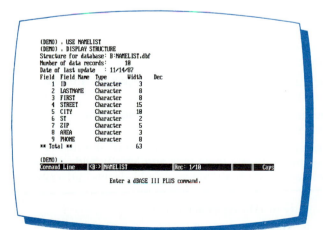

FIGURE 6-21
Database Structure
On dBASE, you type DISPLAY STRUCTURE and then press **Return** to display the program's structure. This command lists the field names, field types, and field widths used to define the current file.

Some programs also allow you to display this information for individual files. For example, dBASE has a command that displays the file's structure (Figure 6-21).

SUMMARY AND KEY TERMS

- Data in a database has five levels: characters, fields, records, files, and databases.
- Planning a database is important since you want to be able to easily enter and find data.
- Databases contain entities and attributes. **Entities** are the subjects of records. **Attributes** are the facts (fields) included in each record.
- **Key attributes** are key fields that uniquely identify records.
- When you **define a file**, you indicate the name of the field, the type of data to be entered, its length, and validity checks, if any.
- **Field types** include character (text), numeric, calculating (where a result in one field can be calculated using entries in other fields), logical, date, time, and memo.
- **Memo fields** have a variable field length so that it expands to fit the data you enter.
- **Field names** must be unique. The same field name cannot be used more than once in a file.
- The maximum record length, number of fields, and field lengths are limited by most programs. This may affect your ability to create the kind of file you want.
- Some programs allow you to specify **validity checks** so that inaccurate information cannot be entered into the input form. For example, a validity check can protect you against having numbers entered into a text field or visa versa.
- **Database dictionaries** contain descriptive data about each database file.

REVIEW QUESTIONS

1. List the five levels of data in a database.
2. Why would you not be able to sort names based on last names if you entered both first and last names into one field?
3. Sketch out a database file you would use to maintain a file containing your friends' names, addresses, and telephone numbers. Assume you want to be able to sort the file by last name and ZIP code.
4. What is an entity? List a few.
5. What are attributes? List some for each entity you listed in question 3.
6. What is a key attribute? Why are they important?
7. Briefly describe each of the following types of fields:

Character	Logical	Memo
Numeric	Date	

8. What length would you specify for a field into which the largest number you were going to enter was 100.00? 10.00? 1000.00?
9. Why not specify the maximum length available for each field so that you do not have to plan field lengths so carefully?
10. Plan a database that you would use to catalog all of your record albums. List the field names you would use, and indicate their type and length fields. What do you think would be the best key attribute so that you could always find a specific song?
11. What is the purpose of validity or editing checks?
12. What is the purpose of a database dictionary?

Entering Records

OBJECTIVE

After completing this topic, you will be able to

■ Describe the different types of methods used to enter data

Once you have defined a database file, you can enter data into it. If you have just defined the database, the program's input form is displayed on the screen. If you are entering data into a database that was defined earlier, you must first retrieve (or *open*) the file.

You can enter records in any order you want. There is no need to worry about the order because you can sort the file into any desired order after you enter the records. The number of records you can enter is determined by the size of each record and the program's limitations. Generally, programs that create disk-based data files can store more records because the number is limited only by the available disk space. Programs that create memory-based data files are limited by the amount of memory in your computer.

Depending on the program you are using, the screen that is displayed when you enter records can include any of the following:

■ A record number is displayed on the screen (Figure 6-22).

■ A list of field names is displayed on the screen (Figure 6-23).

■ Prompts are displayed on the screen one after another to guide you when entering data (Figure 6-24). The prompts can specify the type and format of data you will enter. For example, a prompt could read *Enter phone number:* or *Enter phone number in the format 000-0000:*.

■ A blank form appears on the screen (Figure 6-25).

When a record is completed, the program usually asks if the data was entered correctly. If you respond *No*, you can return to fields to edit them and make corrections. If you respond *Yes*, the data is recorded in the file and automatically saved onto the disk. Only the data you entered into the form is saved in the file. The prompts or on-screen form are only a guide to help you enter information correctly.

All programs automatically design an input form for you, but some let you modify it so that it is more useful. On-screen forms (also called *input screens* or *views*) are an extension of prompts. Some programs allow you to

FIGURE 6-22
Record Number
On programs that display just a record number, you enter fields one after another, separating them with delimiters, usually commas or colons. When you press **Return**, the next record number appears.

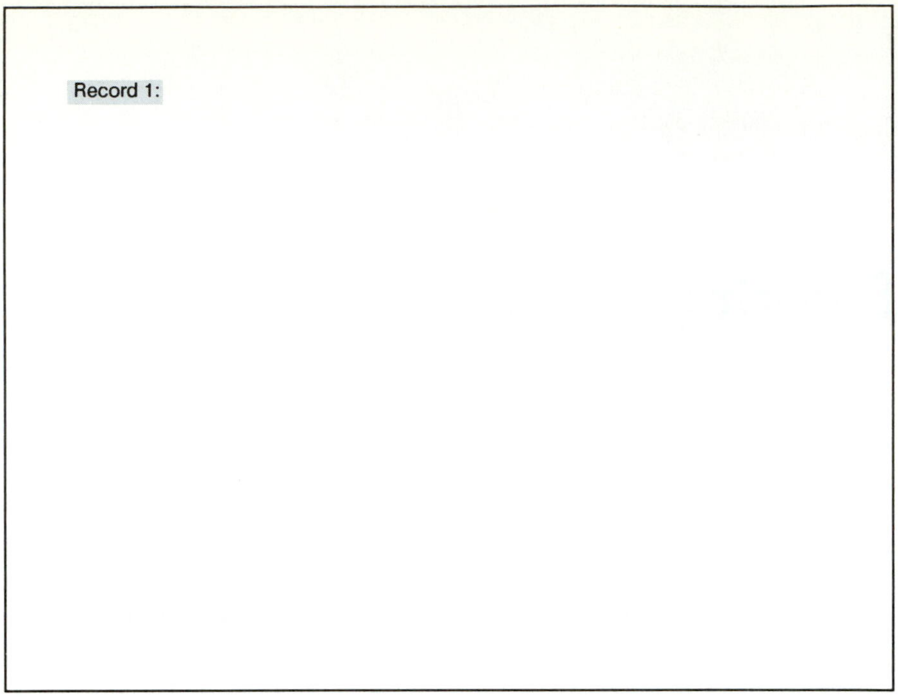

Record 1:

A. Blank Form

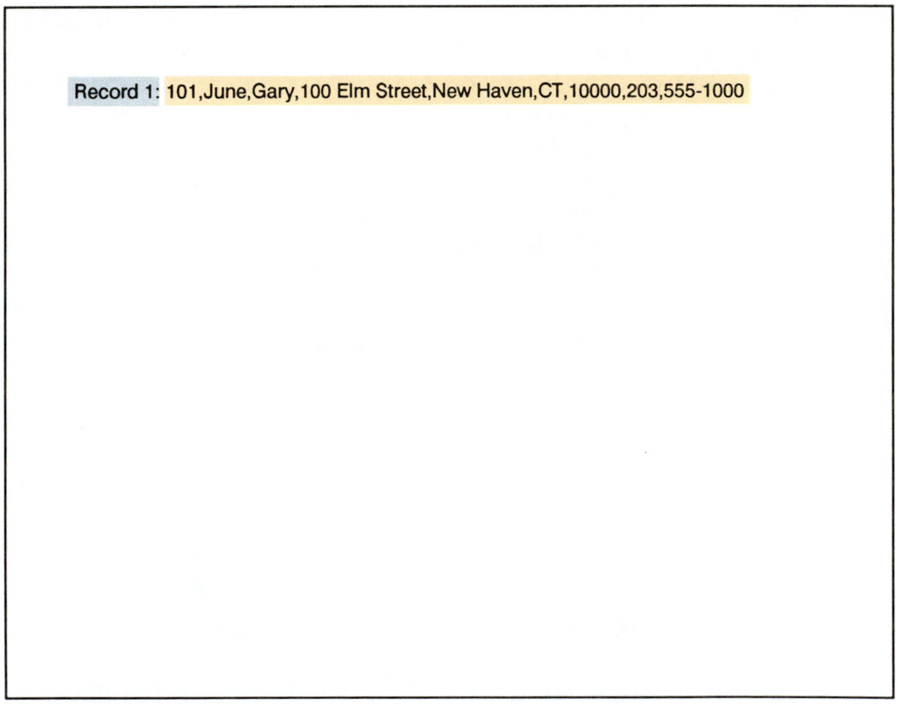

Record 1: 101,June,Gary,100 Elm Street,New Haven,CT,10000,203,555-1000

B. Completed Form

design forms on the screen, which look like familiar preprinted forms. On these programs, you create a form by "drawing" it on your screen using the cursor to point to positions on the screen, typing in a prompt, and then specifying the type and length of the field. Since the prompt is meaningful

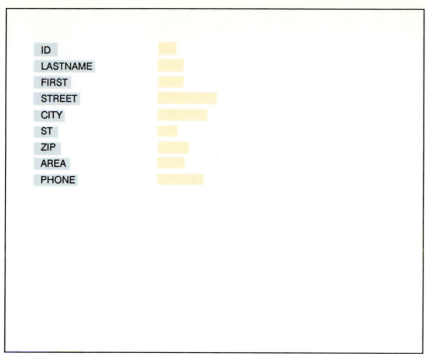

A. Blank Form

FIGURE 6-23
List of Field Names
On programs that display
a list of field names on the
screen, you move the
cursor to each field and
enter data into the spaces
provided. The length of the
field is indicated by the
length of the space. When
finished, you press a
specified key to display the
same list again to enter
the next record.

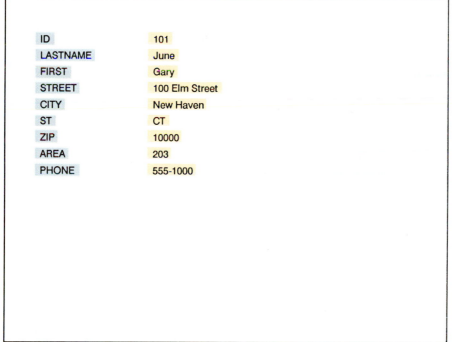

B. Completed Form

to the user, but may not be meaningful to the program, you must indicate
the relationship between it and a corresponding field in the record file. For
example, a prompt may read *Enter last name:*, and the field in the record
file that the data you enter is stored to may be named LASTNAME. You must

FIGURE 6-24
Prompts

On programs that display prompts, you enter fields as each prompt appears and then press a designated key to enter the information and display the next prompt. Although the actual field names do not appear on the screen, the prompts are linked to specific fields. Any data you enter in response to a prompt is entered into the field it is linked to.

Enter ID number:

A. Blank Form

Enter ID number: 101
Enter last name: June
Enter first name: Gary
Enter street address: 100 Elm Street
Enter city: New Haven
Enter state: CT
Enter zip code: 10000
Enter area code: 203
Enter phone number: 555-1000

B. Completed Form

tell the program that data entered in response to this prompt is to be stored in that field in the record.

When creating an on-screen form, be sure to consider the form you receive the information in, and plan for the most efficient movement of the

FIGURE 6-25

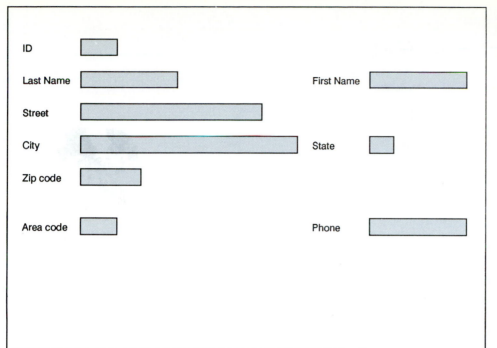

A. Blank Form

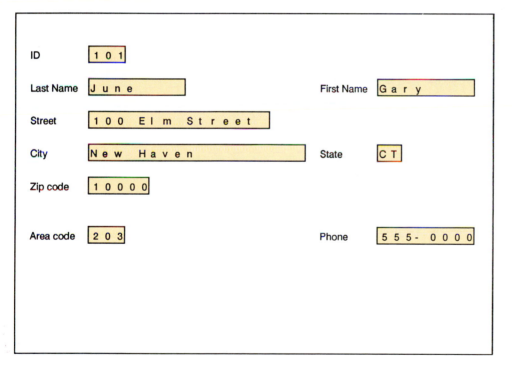

B. Completed Form

cursor from one field to the next during the entry of information. For example, if you are transferring data from customer purchase orders into a file, your on-screen form should parallel the structure of the purchase order forms as closely as possible.

FIGURE 6-26
Multiple-Form Programs
In some cases, all people with access to the database are not allowed to see all the field. In (a), the user can see the name and address but not the phone number. In (b), another user, authorized to see all the information, can see all the fields.

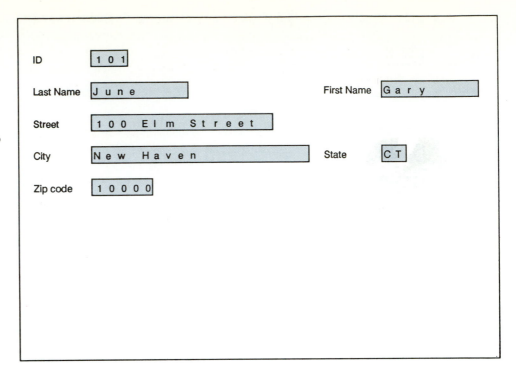

A. Without Phone Number

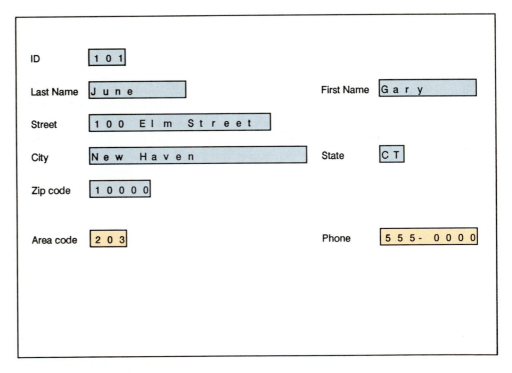

B. With Phone Number

The form used for entering data is not always the best form for other purposes. For example, an accountant might want to view the information differently from the person who enters order information. Thus some programs allow you to create more than one form, or view, for each record file

(Figure 6-26). These forms can make the record files easier to use by excluding unneeded information from the screen. They can also prevent information from appearing in certain forms so that unauthorized users cannot see certain data. Other forms can be designated as "read only" so that users can view but cannot enter or change data.

- To enter records into a database file, you must **open** (retrieve) the file.
- The maximum number of records that can be entered into a single file varies from program to program. A program's limit should not exceed the number of records in the largest file you anticipate using.
- You enter records in response to a record number, a list of field names, prompts, or on-screen forms.
- **Multiple on-screen forms** can be used to view the data in the file in more than one way. They also provide basic security by restricting some views so that sensitive information does not appear on the screen.

1. In what order do you enter records?
2. List four ways the screen is displayed when you enter records.
3. What is an on-screen form? Why do some programs offer more than one type?
4. When you fill out an on-screen form is the form and the data saved to the disk or just the data?

TOPIC 6-7 Displaying Records

Displaying Records

OBJECTIVES

After completing this topic, you will be able to

■ Describe how you can display one or more records

■ Describe what a record pointer is

FIGURE 6-27
Displaying Individual Records
On dBASE, if you type DISPLAY 5 and then press **Return**, record number 5 is displayed on the screen.

FIGURE 6-28
Displaying Groups of Records
On dBASE, if you type BROWSE and then press **Return**, a list of records is displayed on the screen.

Once data has been entered into a database file, you generally work with specific records. For example, you may want to look up the phone number of Gary June, change the address of someone who has moved, or delete a record for someone who has been dropped from your customer list. To do this, you use commands that display only a selected record on the screen (Figure 6-27), or you use designated keys to scroll through groups of records contained in the file (Figure 6-28), much as you would flip through the cards in an index card file. If the file has just been created, the records will appear in the order they were entered in. If the file has been sorted, the records will appear in the order they were sorted into.

Many of the commands you use to display records move a **record pointer** within the file. This record pointer, which is not displayed, makes

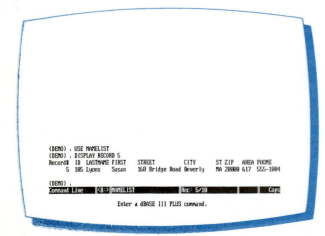

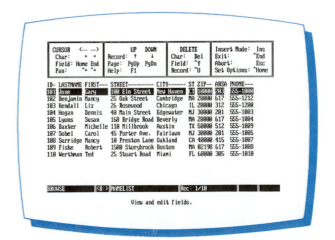

568

ID	LASTNAME	FIRST	STREET	CITY	ST	ZIP	AREA	PHONE
101	June	Gary	100 Elm Street	New Haven	CT	10000	203	555-1000
102	Benjamin	Nancy	25 Oak Street	Cambridge	MA	20000	617	555-1212
103	Kendall	Liz	26 Rosewood	Chicago	IL	20000	312	555-1200
104	Hogan	Dennis	40 Main Street	Edgewater	NJ	30000	201	555-1003
105	Lyons	Susan	168 Bridge Road	Beverly	MA	20000	617	555-1004
106	Baxter	Michelle	110 Millbrook	Austin	TX	50000	512	555-1009
107	Sobel	Carol	45 Porter Ave.	Fairlawn	NJ	30000	201	555-1005
108	Surridge	Nancy	10 Preston Lane	Oakland	CA	40000	415	555-1007
109	Fiske	Robert	1500 Storybrook	Boston	MA	02198	617	555-1008
110	Werthman	Ted	25 Stuart Road	Miami	FL	60000	305	555-1010

A. GOTO 5

ID	LASTNAME	FIRST	STREET	CITY	ST	ZIP	AREA	PHONE
105	Lyons	Susan	168 Bridge Road	Beverly	MA	20000	617	555-1004
106	Baxter	Michelle	110 Millbrook	Austin	TX	50000	512	555-1009
107	Sobel	Carol	45 Porter Ave.	Fairlawn	NJ	30000	201	555-1005
108	Surridge	Nancy	10 Preston Lane	Oakland	CA	40000	415	555-1007
109	Fiske	Robert	1500 Storybrook	Boston	MA	02198	617	555-1008
110	Werthman	Ted	25 Stuart Road	Miami	FL	60000	305	555-1010

B. BROWSE

FIGURE 6-29
The Record Pointer
On dBASE, if you type
GOTO 5 and then press
Return, the record pointer
moves to record 5. If you
then type BROWSE and then
press **Return**, files are
listed on the screen
beginning with record 5.

the file it points to the **current record** (Figure 6-29). Subsequent commands then start from, or apply to, the current record.

Programs usually have more than one command to display records or move the record pointer. For example, Table 6-5 describes the dBASE commands that display records.

TABLE 6-5
dBASE Commands That Display Records

Command	Description
DISPLAY	Displays specific records. For example, DISPLAY ALL displays all records, DISPLAY ALL FIRST displays all entries in the field named FIRST, and DISPLAY NEXT 5 FIRST displays the contents of the FIRST field in the next five records.
LIST	Displays specific records, but unlike DISPLAY, if the list is longer than the screen, the display does not pause when the screen is full. You can press **Ctrl-S** to stop and restart the scrolling for a large file.
BROWSE	Displays as many as seventeen records at a time on the screen. When in browse mode, you can press **Ctrl-Home** to display a menu of GOTO options.
GOTO	Specifies the record to go to when typed from the dot prompt before entering a BROWSE command. You can specify a specific record number or the options TOP or BOTTOM. For example, GOTO 5 displays record number 5, GOTO TOP displays the first record, and GOTO BOTTOM displays the last record when you then use the BROWSE command.
SKIP	Moves the record pointer ahead the specified number of records. For example, if you use the command GOTO TOP and then the command SKIP 5 when you specify the BROWSE command, it displays all records beginning with record 6.

CASE STUDY 1
Creating a Database of Names and Addresses

In this case study, you use dBASE to create the database file of names and addresses illustrated throughout the topics in this part. When creating the file and entering records, you type commands rather than use the menus provided by dBASE's assist mode. You begin by loading the program.

Step 1: Defining a Data File   Before you can enter data into the file, you must define it by specifying field names, types, and lengths. To do so, you type CREATE NAMELIST and then press **Return**. The drive spins, and in a moment, the screen used to define a file appears (Figure A).

To enter field definitions, you press **End** and **Home** to move the cursor between the fields. First enter the field name, then the field type, and finally the field length. When you press **End** or **Return** after entering the field width, a new blank field appears. When you have finished entering all the fields, press **Ctrl-End**, and the prompt reads *Press ENTER to confirm. Any other key to resume.* Press **Return** to save the file definition on the disk. In a moment, the prompt reads *Input data records now? (Y/N).* You can either press **Y** and begin entering data or press **N**, and the dot prompt reappears. Here, you press **N** to return to the dot prompt.

Step 2: Displaying a File's Structure   Now, type LIST STRUCTURE and then press **Return** to display a file's structure (Figure B). The information on the screen gives you the number of records in the file, the date it was last updated, a description of each field, and the total width of all fields.

Step 3: Entering Records   To enter records, type APPEND and then press **Return**. The screen displays a help menu below which are the fields you enter data into (Figure C). These are the field names you entered when you defined the file. Next to each field name are highlights indicating the field's length. The current field, the one you enter data into when you type, contains the cursor. When entering records, they are automatically saved onto the disk when you move to the next record. However, to be sure the last record is saved, when you have finished making corrections, save the file and return to the dot prompt. Press **Ctrl-End**, and the dot prompt reappears.

FIGURE A (below left)
Defining the Database
The CREATE command displays the database definition screen (a). As you enter the description for each field in the file, the descriptions are listed one after another (b).

FIGURE B (below right)
Displaying the File's Structure
The DISPLAY STRUCTURE command displays the file's structure.

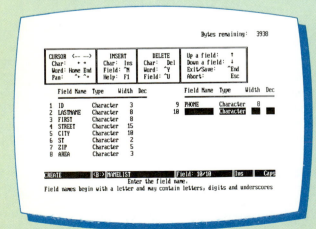

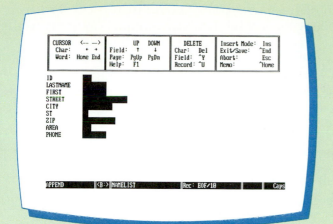

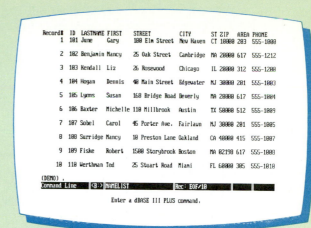

Step 4: Listing Records   To list the records that you added, type LIST and then press **Return**. A list of all the records is displayed, and the dot prompt reappears (Figure D).

Step 5: Browsing Records   Use the BROWSE command to display records. The BROWSE command works just like the LIST command, but BROWSE displays seventeen records at a time. Before using the command, type GOTO TOP and then press **Return** to move the menu pointer to the top of the file. Then type BROWSE and press **Return**. A help menu and a list of all the records is displayed on the screen (Figure E). When you are finished looking at the records, press **Esc** to leave browse mode and return to the dot prompt.

Step 6: Displaying Records   On dBASE, you display specific records with the DISPLAY command. You can qualify the command by specifying a scope. For example, to display record 1 by number, type DISPLAY RECORD 1 (or just DISPLAY), and then press **Return**.

To display record 3, type SKIP and then press **Return**. A message *Record No. 3* indicates you have skipped to record 3. Now, type DISPLAY and then press **Return**. The SKIP command moves the record pointer to the next record in the file. When you then use the DISPLAY command, the record to which the record pointer points is the one that is displayed.

FIGURE C (above left)
Entering Records
The APPEND command displays a form into which you enter data into fields.

FIGURE D (above right)
Listing Records
The LIST command displays a list of the records in the database.

FIGURE E (below left)
Browsing Records
The BROWSE command displays a list of the records in the database.

FIGURE F (below right)
Displaying Records
The DISPLAY ALL command displays a list of the records in the database.

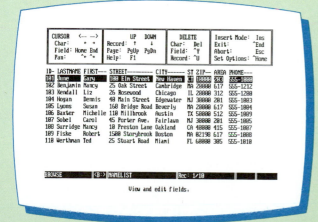

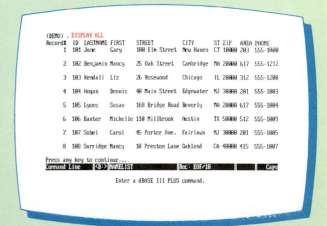

DISPLAYING RECORDS   571

To display all the records, type DISPLAY ALL and then press **Return**. This is like the LIST command, but if your database contains too many records to fit on the screen, it displays those that do fit and then pauses until you press a designated key to continue. Here, the first eight records are displayed (Figure F). Press any key to display the rest of the records and return to the dot prompt.

SUMMARY AND KEY TERMS

- You can display individual records on the screen or display a list of them and then and scroll through them.
- When you display a specific record, you move the **record pointer** to it. This pointer always points to the **current record**.

REVIEW QUESTIONS

1. Why might you want to display specific records?

2. What is a record pointer?

3. List and briefly describe some of the dBase commands that display files.

TOPIC 6-8

Query Languages

OBJECTIVES

After completing this topic, you will be able to

- Describe the purpose of a query language
- List and briefly describe the most common types of query languages

Scrolling through a file to look at records one after another in the order they are stored or sorted can take a long time if the file has many records. What if a customer calls about his or her account and wants to know what date a purchase was made? Using the customer ID number and the amount of the purchase, you can immediately locate the date of the purchase by asking the program to display any charges to the customer's account for the specified amount. Questions like this, when addressed to a database, are called **queries**. You can use queries to display, update, delete, and insert records into a database file. The records, or specified fields from the records, can be displayed on the screen or printed out in a report.

The way you propose queries varies from program to program, but there are essentially two ways to so, with a query language or a query-by-example form.

QUERY LANGUAGES

Query languages are special languages you use to ask questions and execute commands. Query languages can be simple or complex. On powerful database management programs, they are similar to programming languages. For example, the can contain functions that calculate sums; count records; or indicate maximum, minimum, and average values in an entire file. They can also contain arithmetical operators like +, −, *, or / and relational and logical operators (see Topic 6-9).

Most users never learn how to use complex query languages. Instead, companies hire developers who use the language to write custom applications that are then used by operators who have a limited understanding of the program. Newer programs are trying to make query languages easier to use and more standardized. The query language you use depends on your program.

Program-Specific Languages

Some programs have query languages that are specific to only that program. When using one of these query languages, your queries must follow the rules specified by the program. For example, the rules you must follow when working with dBASE include those described in Topic 6-4. Since these queries can become quite complex, you can usually store them in a special query file for use later.

Structured Query Language

Program-specific languages have drawbacks. For example, user's familiar with one program cannot operate another without first learning a new language. For this reason, a standard query language is desirable. Though there is no such thing as a standard query language, IBM's **structured query language** (**SQL**—pronounced "sequel") comes fairly close. Introduced by IBM in the 1970s for use on large computers, SQL is now being widely implemented on microcomputers.

Natural Languages

Since query languages can be intimidating to users, some programs use **natural language** queries. Queries in a natural language program are much closer to how you would ask a question in English. Natural language queries, like English questions, have rules that must be followed. For example, you use keywords so that the program can understand the query, and the order of the question is important. A typical query might read "Display all records with June in the LASTNAME field."

Many of the words you enter are ignored by the program; they are more for your benefit than for the program's. For example, if you want to find a specific record, you can ask the question in several ways as long as you include the keywords *Display, all, June,* and *LASTNAME*. For example, you could pose the same question as "Please display a list of all the people whose last name is June in the LASTNAME field in the file."

Natural language queries have one major advantage: They appear more like English to the user. But this user-friendliness has a price. Natural language queries are usually longer than the cryptic commands used by traditional systems, which means more typing, a nuisance to experienced users. The increased length also introduces the possibility of typing errors.

QUERY BY EXAMPLE

Writing queries is difficult and requires an understanding of the program's query language. Many of the newer programs have adopted an approach that simplifies working with the database. This process, called **query by example** (**QBE**), uses fill-in forms. When you want to query the database, you make a selection from a menu, and a form appears on the screen. This form lists all the fields in the file. Using this form, you pose queries and enter any conditions such as the files to be used and the records to be included.

- **Query languages** allow you to locate specific records based on the data they contain.
- Query languages include program-specific languages, structured query language, natural languages, and query by example.
- **Program-specific query languages** are used only with the program they accompany.
- The **structured query language** is a standard language incorporated into many programs.
- **Natural-language** programs allow you to use English-like commands.
- **Query-by-example** programs allow you to enter queries by filling out a form on the screen.

1. What is a query language, and what are four operations that it is used for?
2. List and briefly describe four types of query languages?
3. What is a natural language? What is its major advantage? Does it have any disadvantages?

TOPIC 6-9

Using Criteria to Display Records

OBJECTIVES

After completing this topic, you will be able to

- Describe how you establish search criteria
- Explain how you use relational and logical operators

In Topic 6-8, we introduced you to query languages. When using queries, you often specify **criteria**, the rules the program follows to select the records or fields that are to be displayed. Using these languages, you can find one or more records by specifying criteria. Only those records that match the criteria are then displayed. To find a specific record, you generally follow these steps.

1. Execute the program's *Display*, *Locate*, *Search*, or *Find* command. Depending on the program, you do this by typing a command, pressing a function key, or making a selection from a menu.
2. Enter the criteria to be used in the search.
3. Begin the search.
4. View the displayed record or print, update, or delete it.
5. Continue searching for other records that meet the criteria.
6. Exit from the command.

CRITERIA

Criteria are used to specify the record or records you want to find. You do this by specifying a field to look in and a value to look for. The value can be a text string or a number. Ideally, the field you use to search the file contains unique values. Unique values, such as a driver's license number, an employee number, or a social security number, are unlikely to be duplicated in more than one record. In some cases, you may have trouble identifying a field where all the data would be unique. For example, if your file contains names, addresses, and phone numbers, the only unique field is likely to be the phone number. If that is what you are looking for, it is unlikely you would want to look it up in the phone book and then search the file for the number that you now already know. In these situations, you have to be creative when first designing the database. For example, if you store first names in one field and last names in another, you can search the file using both of these fields as keys or search fields. This way, the program will find a specific record where the first name is Dennis and the last name is Hogan.

After specifying the fields to be searched and the criteria to be used, the program searches the specified field in all the records in the file. If it finds a match, it displays the entire record on the screen. If more than one record meets the criteria, you execute the programs command that displays the next record. When the records are displayed, you can update or delete them.

In addition to displaying selected records, you can display selected fields from those records. For example, if your database has names, addresses, and phone numbers, and you are interested only in the last name and phone number, you can display just fields that contain those elements.

RELATIONAL OPERATORS

When searching numeric, date, or time fields, you can use the relational operators less than, greater than, equal to, and not equal to. For example, when searching for text strings, you can look for records that meet equal or nonequal criteria. In a search using an equal criteria, the search will look for all records that match the criteria you specify. For example, you can ask the program to find a record with June in the field named LASTNAME. Any record with June in this field will be displayed. In a search using an unequal criteria, all records but the one you specify will be displayed. For example, you can ask the program to find all records that do not have June in the LASTNAME field. Figure 6-30 shows how an equal criteria is entered as a query language, and Figure 6-31 shows how it is entered as a query by example. Table 6-6 describes relational operators you can use to specify criteria.

LOGICAL OPERATORS

Sometimes, you want to find a record, or a group of records, that meet more than one criteria. To do so, most programs let you construct a search condition that contains several criteria using logical operators. You usually specify if one or all of the criteria are to be met by connecting the condi-

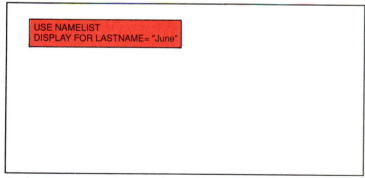

A. Query

ID	LASTNAME	FIRST	STREET	CITY	ST	ZIP	AREA	PHONE
101	June	Gary	100 Elm Street	New Haven	CT	10000	203	555-1004

B. Record Displayed

FIGURE 6-30
Equal Criteria Entered with a Query Language
In this query, the file NAMELIST is first retrieved or opened with the USE command. The query then asks the database to display any record with LASTNAME equal to June (a), and that record is displayed (b).

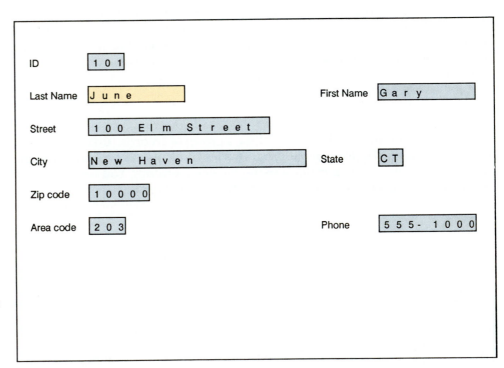

A. Query

FIGURE 6-31
Equal Criteria Entered as a Query by Example
The name June entered in the LASTNAME field (a) results in the record with that name in that field being displayed (b).

B. Record Displayed

tions with logical operators and connectors. For example, Figure 6-32 shows how two fields are used and two criteria are met for a query language, and Figure 6-33 shows how two fields are used and two criteria are met for a query by example. Table 6-7 describes logical operators you can use to specify criteria.

TABLE 6-6
Relational Operators

Operator	Description
>	Finds all records greater than the criteria you specify. For example, AMOUNT>10.00 finds all records where the AMOUNT is more than 10.00; DATE>1/10/89 finds all records where the DATE is later than January 10, 1989; and NAME>"June" displays all records alphabetically after June.
<	Finds all records less than the criteria you specify. For example, AMOUNT<10.00 finds all records where the AMOUNT is less than 10.00; DATE<1/10/89 finds all records where the DATE is earlier than January 10, 1989; and NAME<"June" displays all records alphabetically before June.
=	Finds all records equal to the criteria you specify. For example, LASTNAME="June" finds all records with June in the field named LASTNAME; AMOUNT=10.00 finds all records where the AMOUNT is 10.00; and DATE=1/10/89 finds all records where the DATE is January 10, 1989.
>=	Finds all records greater than or equal to the criteria you specify. For example, LASTNAME>="June" finds all records with June or any name alphabetically later in the field named LASTNAME; AMOUNT>=10.00 finds all records where the AMOUNT is 10.00 or more; and DATE>=1/10/89 finds all records where the DATE is January 10, 1989, or later.
<=	Finds all records less than or equal to the criteria you specify. For example, LASTNAME<="June" finds all records with June or any name alphabetically earlier in the field named LASTNAME; AMOUNT<=10.00 finds all records where the AMOUNT is 10.00 or less; and DATE<=1/10/89 finds all records where the DATE is January 10, 1989, or earlier.
<>	Finds all records not equal to the criteria you specify. For example, LASTNAME<>"June" finds all records except those with June in the LASTNAME field, and DATE<>1/10/89 finds all records not dated January 10, 1989.

TABLE 6-7
Logical Operators

Operator	Description
.AND.	Two or more conditions must be met. For example, AMOUNT=10.00.AND.NAME="June" finds all records where the AMOUNT is 10.00 and the name is June.
.OR.	One or another condition must be met. For example, AMOUNT=10.00.OR.NAME="June" finds all records where the AMOUNT is 10.00 or the name is June.
.NOT.	Condition must not be met. For example, AMOUNT=10.00.NOT.NAME="June" finds all records where the AMOUNT is 10.00 and the name is not June.

FIGURE 6-32
Multiple Criteria as a Query Language
In this query, the file NAMELIST is first retrieved or opened with the USE command. The query then asks the database to display any record with LASTNAME equal to June and ST equal to MA (a), and that record is displayed (b).

```
USE NAMELIST
DISPLAY FOR FIRST NAME = "Nancy" .AND.ST = "MA"
```

A. Query

ID	LASTNAME	FIRST	STREET	CITY	ST	ZIP	AREA	PHONE
102	Benjamin	Nancy	25 Oak Street	Cambridge	MA	20000	617	555-1212

B. Record Displayed

FIGURE 6-33
Multiple Criteria as a Query by Example
In this query, the data Nancy has been entered into the FIRSTNAME field and MA into the STATE field (a). This causes the record with both of those entries to be displayed (b).

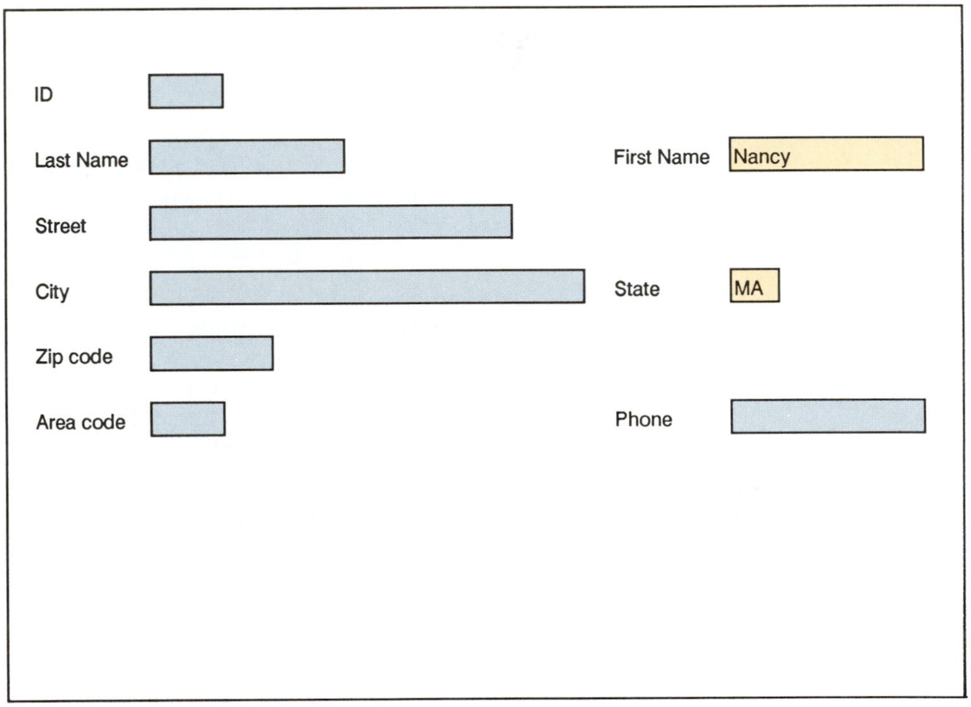

ID

Last Name   First Name   Nancy

Street

City   State   MA

Zip code

Area code   Phone

A. Query

MAKING CALCULATIONS

With many programs, you can enter queries that calculate selected fields in one or more records. To do so, you enter functions into the queries. For example, to sum the numbers in the AMOUNT field, you enter the command SUM AMOUNT. You can also sum selected records. For example, the command SUM AMOUNT FOR ST="MA" sums only the numbers in the AMOUNT fields in records that have MA in the ST field. Table 6-8 describes three functions that can be used with dBASE.

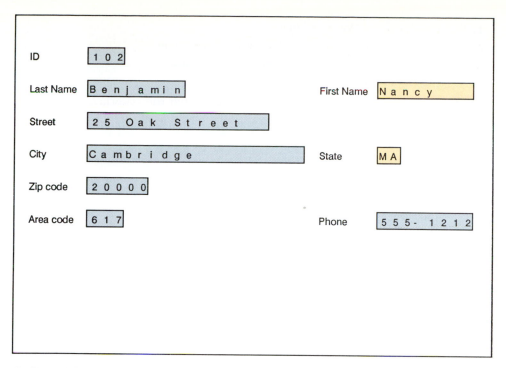

B. Record Displayed

TABLE 6-8 **Statistical Functions**	
Function	**Description**
AVERAGE	Calculates the average in a specified numeric field
SUM	Calculates the total in a specified numeric field
COUNT	Counts the number of records that meet a specified criterion

SUMMARY AND KEY TERMS

- Queries contain **criteria** that specify which records are to be displayed.
- Queries can contain **relational operators** that qualify criteria. For example, you can look for records that are equal to, greater than, or lesser than the specified criteria.
- Queries can contain **logical operators** that join two or more criteria. Typical logical operators specify if all criteria, some criteria, or no criterion should be met. Only the records that match the criteria are displayed.
- Some programs allow you to use **wildcards** to stand for one or more characters in a criterion.
- Queries can be written so that they not only display selected records but also display only selected fields from those records.
- Many programs contain **functions** that perform calculations. Typical functions are those used to perform mathematical and statistical calculations.

1. What are criteria? What do they do?

2. What are relational operators? List and describe some.

3. What are logical operators? List and describe some.

4. What is the purpose of a wildcard?

5. Do all queries display complete records that match the criteria?

6. Assume you have a list of customers in the following file structure:

   Last name:
   First name:
   Company:
   Phone:
   Last contact:
   Last sale:
   Items purchased:

   How would you set up search criteria to find all customers named Jones? To find all customers to whom you made a last sale after January 1, 1985? To find all customers named Jones who bought a book?

7. If you had a field with part numbers 1000 through 9999, what wildcard would you use to display part numbers 1000, 2000, 3000, and so on? What wildcard would you use to display part numbers 1011, 1111, 1211, 1311, and so on?

8. If you want to perform a calculation, can you do so?

9. What three calculations can you perform with dBASE using functions?

TOPIC 6-10

Adding, Updating, and Deleting Records

OBJECTIVE

After completing this topic, you will be able to

■ Describe how you add, insert, update, and delete records

Besides death and taxes there is at least one other certainty in life. The sooner you collect all the information you need, the sooner it will be outdated and require modifications to make it up to date. With card files, this is quite straightforward. All you have to do is to read through a card file until you find the card that is in error, and then replace it with a corrected card. Though straightforward, finding the card is not necessarily fast. Think of the problem of updating a card file with 500 cards in it, even if they are in alphabetical order. To update the file, you would have to sort through all 500 cards each time you wanted to find the one to update. A database management program lets you update your records much more easily. You can just edit the information in fields, or add or delete complete records.

ADDING RECORDS

When you want to add new records to a file, you display a blank record on the screen and then type in a new record, just as you entered the initial records into the file. Unlike a card index file, where you would want to insert the card in the proper order, the database management program will generally add it to the end of the file or insert it into a space where you have previously deleted a record (Figure 6-34). New records can be added one after an-

Rec #	ID	LASTNAME	FIRST	STREET	CITY	ST	ZIP	AREA	PHONE
1	101	June	Gary	100 Elm Street	New Haven	CT	10000	203	555-1000
2	102	Benjamin	Nancy	25 Oak Street	Cambridge	MA	20000	617	555-1212
3	103	Kendall	Liz	26 Rosewood	Chicago	IL	20000	312	555-1200
4	104	Hogan	Dennis	40 Main Street	Edgewater	NJ	30000	201	555-1003
5	105	Lyons	Susan	168 Bridge Road	Beverly	MA	20000	617	555-1004
6	106	Baxter	Michelle	110 Millbrook	Austin	TX	50000	512	555-1009
7	107	Sobel	Carol	45 Porter Ave.	Fairlawn	NJ	30000	201	555-1005
8	108	Surridge	Nancy	10 Preston Lane	Oakland	CA	40000	415	555-1007
9	109	Fiske	Robert	1500 Storybrook	Boston	MA	02198	617	555-1008
10	110	Werthman	Ted	25 Stuart Road	Miami	FL	60000	305	555-1010
11	111	Edwards	Jim	50 Locust St	Teaneck	NJ	30000	201	555-1111

← Added Record

FIGURE 6-34
Adding Records
When you add records, they are added at the end of the file.

FIGURE 6-35
Inserting Records
When you insert records,
they are entered into the
specified position in the
file, and all the following
records are renumbered.

Rec #	ID	LASTNAME	FIRST	STREET	CITY	ST	ZIP	AREA	PHONE
1	101	June	Gary	100 Elm Street	New Haven	CT	10000	203	555-1000
2	102	Benjamin	Nancy	25 Oak Street	Cambridge	MA	20000	617	555-1212
3	103	Kendall	Liz	26 Rosewood	Chicago	IL	20000	312	555-1200
4	104	Hogan	Dennis	40 Main Street	Edgewater	NJ	30000	201	555-1003
5	105	Lyons	Susan	168 Bridge Road	Beverly	MA	20000	617	555-1004
6	106	Baxter	Michelle	110 Millbrook	Austin	TX	50000	512	555-1009
7	111	Edwards	Jim	50 Locust St	Teaneck	NJ	30000	201	555-1111
8	107	Sobel	Carol	45 Porter Ave.	Fairlawn	NJ	30000	201	555-1005
9	108	Surridge	Nancy	10 Preston Lane	Oakland	CA	40000	415	555-1007
10	109	Fiske	Robert	1500 Storybrook	Boston	MA	02198	617	555-1008
11	110	Werthman	Ted	25 Stuart Road	Miami	FL	60000	305	555-1010

← Inserted Record

other without worrying about the order they are added in or where they are inserted into the file. After they have been entered, they can easily be sorted into any desired order.

INSERTING RECORDS

Some programs let you insert a record into a file at a specific point. First you display the record that you want the new record to be inserted below, and then you use the INSERT command to enter the new record. Inserting records takes more time than adding them to the file because the program must make room for them between already existing files (Figure 6-35). It is like trying to squeeze one more person into a crowded elevator—the new file has to elbow its way in. To make room for the new record, the file must be resorted by the program, and this takes time.

UPDATING RECORDS

It is often necessary to update records in a database file; for example, when customers change addresses, their records must be updated. To do this, you first use the command to find the specific record to be updated and display it on the screen. You then revise the contents of the appropriate fields. You can also use a command that updates all the records in a file. For example, you can add a number to all the numbers in a numeric field or change all the dates in a date field. When combined with query commands that establish criteria, this command can update groups of records that match the specified criteria.

DELETING RECORDS

If a customer no longer buys from the company, a product is no longer manufactured, or an item is no longer in inventory, its record in a database file is no longer needed. These unwanted records should be deleted from the file. To do this, you first use the command to find the specific record to be updated or deleted and display it on the screen. You then revise the contents of appropriate fields, or delete the entire record. Some programs do not immediately delete records from the disk when you specify that they be deleted. The deleted record is just marked with an electronic flag. These **flagged records** are ignored when other file operations are used, and they can often be recovered if needed and if another record has not been added in their place. Usually, they can be permanently removed by an operation called **packing**.

CASE STUDY 2
Using Queries and Updating Records

In this case study, you look for records in the NAMELIST file and then make changes to selected records. You can look for a group of records that match specific criteria, for example, using a FOR clause to search for character strings like the state of MA. The character string must be enclosed in double quotation marks. When using this command, the case you use for characters is also important; if a field has been entered as MA, lowercase ma will not display any records.

Before completing procedures like those described here, you must always load the program. You then open the file you want to work on. To do so in this case study, you type USE NAMELIST and then press **Return**.

Step 1: Displaying Records That Match a Single Criterion Here you enter criteria that specify which records and which fields are to be displayed (Figure A).

To display all fields in records, type DISPLAY FOR ST="MA" and then press **Return**. (The quotation marks are entered on either side of the MA to indicate it is text.) The three records with MA in the ST field are entirely displayed.

To display only one field in the same records, type DISPLAY LASTNAME FOR ST="MA" and then press **Return**. The same three records are displayed but only the specified LASTNAME field.

To display selected fields in the same records, type DISPLAY ID, LASTNAME, FIRST, AREA, PHONE FOR ST="MA" and then press **Return**. Again, the same three records are displayed but only the specified fields.

Step 2: Displaying Records That Match Two Criteria In this step, you display records that match multiple criteria (Figure B).

To display records that are equal to one value OR another, type DISPLAY LASTNAME FOR ST="MA". OR. ST="NJ" and then press **Return**. The LASTNAME fields for the five records that match the criteria are displayed.

Now, display the ID, LASTNAME, and ST fields for all customers who live in Massachusetts OR whose IDs are greater than 108. To display records greater than 108, type DISPLAY ID, LASTNAME, ST FOR

FIGURE A (below left)
Displaying Records with a Single Criteria
The DISPLAY command can be qualified so that it displays all fields in records for ST="MA" and so that it displays selected fields for the same criteria.

FIGURE B (below right)
Displaying Records with Multiple Criteria
The DISPLAY command can be used in conjunction with logical operators so that records must meet one criterion OR the other.

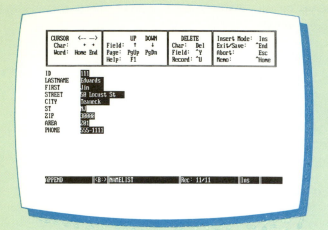

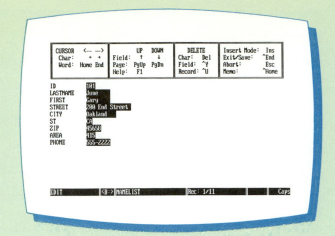

FIGURE C (above left)
Adding Records
When you add records, an on-screen form appears on the screen. You enter a new record just as you entered the original records.

FIGURE D (above right)
Editing Records
The EDIT command displays the specified record on the screen so that you can change the data in its fields.

ST="MA". OR. ID>"108" and then press **Return**. The specified fields of the four records that have either MA in their ST field or an ID greater than 108 are displayed.

Step 3: **Adding Records** Now, use dBase III's APPEND command to add records to the end of a file. Type APPEND and then press **Return**. A blank record appears on the screen, and the status bar indicates it is at the end of the file (*EOF*). Enter the record shown in Figure C. When you enter the last field of the record, a new blank record is displayed. Press **PgUp** to return to the record you just added. When you are finished, press **Ctrl-End** to save the file and return to the dot prompt.

Step 4: **Editing a Record** To edit a record, you simply display the record, and then you edit it. Here you change the address and phone number of someone who has moved. To edit a specific record, type EDIT 1 and then press **Return**. The record is displayed on the screen. You want to change it so that it matches Figure D. To do so, move the cursor to the *STREET* field, and then press **Ctrl-Y** to delete the field's contents. Type 200 End Street and then press ↓ to move to the *PHONE* field. Type in the new phone number. Move the cursor to the other fields you want to make changes in, and type them in. When you fill in the last field, a new blank record is displayed. Press **PgUp** to return to the record you edited, and then check it. Press **Ctrl-End** to exit and save the change.

To see the changes, type BROWSE and then press **Return**. Press **PgUp** once to display all the records.

Step 5: **Deleting Records** When records are no longer needed, you can delete them from the file. This is a two-step process: First you flag them, and then you delete them. To delete a record, type DELETE RECORD 11 and then press **Return**. The prompt *1 record deleted* appears. But the record has not actually been deleted; it has simply been flagged for deletion. To see this, type LIST and then press **Return** (Figure E). Record 11 has been marked with an asterisk to indicate it has been flagged for deletion.

To delete the record from the file, type PACK and then press **Return**. The message *10 records copied* indicates the record has been deleted, and only ten of the original eleven records remain. To see this, type LIST and then press **Return**. Record 11 is no longer in the file.

FIGURE E
Deleting Records
When you delete a record, it is actually just flagged for deletion as the asterisk flagging record 11 shows.

SUMMARY AND KEY TERMS

- When you add records to a file, they are added to the end of the file.
- When you insert a record, it is inserted below the record that you specify.
- When you update records, you change the information in its fields. Some programs provide global search and replace that changes duplicated data in a record file.
- When records are no longer needed, you delete them. On some programs, the records are not actually deleted; they are just **flagged** for deletion. To actually delete them, you must **pack** the file.

REVIEW QUESTIONS

1. When you add new records to a file, where are they stored in the file?
2. What is the difference between inserting a record and adding one?
3. Why does inserting a record take longer than adding one to the end of the file?
4. When you delete a record, what does the program do before permanently deleting the record? How do you permanently delete them?

TOPIC 6-11

Sorting Records

OBJECTIVES

After completing this topic, you will be able to

- Describe how you sort database files on primary and secondary keys
- Explain how characters are sequenced when you sort a file

Sorting a file rearranges the records into a specified order. Since the file is actually rearranged on the disk, sorting a large file can take a great deal of time. To sort a file, you first determine what information is to be arranged in order. Since this data is stored in fields, you specify what field is to be reordered and in what order its data is to be sorted. For example, you can sort the file so that the names are arranged alphabetically, or you can sort it so that a given set of numbers is arranged in ascending or descending order. When the file is sorted based on a specific field, all the records are copied to a new file where they are rearranged. When you specify the field to be used, you are designating it as the key. You can often specify more than one key— one primary key and one or more secondary keys. When you sort a file based on the specified keys, complete records, not just the fields containing the keys, are sorted.

PRIMARY KEYS

The **primary key** is the field that is sorted first. If you are sorting a list of names in the original file, the primary key will sort it so that all the names are in ascending alphabetical order (Figure 6-36). Ideally, a primary key contains unique information, for example, a driver's license number, an employee number, or a social security number.

SECONDARY KEYS

Sometimes, a unique field does not exist or serve your purpose, for example, when you sort a file by last names and more than one last name is spelled the same way. In these cases, a perfect sort is not achieved using just a primary key; a secondary key, such as the first name, must be used to break ties. In Figure 6-36, which was sorted using last names as the primary key, all the Joneses and Smiths are together, but neither group is in the correct

588

#	LASTNAME	FIRSTNAME
1	Smith	Vance
2	Jones	Marie
3	Lewis	John
4	Jones	Stuart
5	Curtin	Dennis
6	Smith	Adam
7	Stanford	David
8	Smith	Robert
9	Benjamin	Nancy
10	Swabey	Daphne
11	Vogel	Terry
12	Smith	Frank
13	Jones	Lewis

A. Original Order

#	LASTNAME	FIRSTNAME
9	Benjamin	Nancy
5	Curtin	Dennis
2	Jones	Marie
4	Jones	Stuart
13	Jones	Lewis
3	Lewis	John
1	Smith	Vance
6	Smith	Adam
8	Smith	Robert
12	Smith	Frank
7	Stanford	David
10	Swabey	Daphne
11	Vogel	Terry

B. Primary Key Is LASTNAME

FIGURE 6-36
Sorting a File on a Primary Key
When you sort a file, you specify a primary key that is to be used as the basis of the sort. Here, the original file (a) shows the order in which the file was originally arranged. After sorting using the LASTNAME field as the primary key, the file is sorted in ascending order by last name. But note how the primary key did not perform a complete sort. The files are not organized correctly by first name. For example, Jones, Stuart is listed before Jones, Lewis.

order by first name. Secondary keys are used to break ties in the file after it has been sorted by the primary key (Figure 6-37). The number of secondary keys that are allowed varies from program to program. The more that are allowed, the more accurately complicated files can be sorted.

SORT ORDERS

When you sort a file, you can specify that it be sorted into ascending or descending order. Figure 6-38 shows a file sorted by number.

When you sort numbers, this is straightforward. If you sort the numbers 0 to 9 in ascending order, they are arranged from 0 to 9; in descending order, they are arranged from 9 to 0. But the way letters and other symbols are arranged can vary depending on the procedure used by the program. Figure 6-39 lists the order into which characters are sorted by dBASE and Excel.

#	LASTNAME	FIRSTNAME
1	Smith	Vance
2	Jones	Marie
3	Lewis	John
4	Jones	Stuart
5	Curtin	Dennis
6	Smith	Adam
7	Stanford	David
8	Smith	Robert
9	Benjamin	Nancy
10	Swabey	Daphne
11	Vogel	Terry
12	Smith	Frank
13	Jones	Lewis

A. Original Order

#	LASTNAME	FIRSTNAME
9	Benjamin	Nancy
5	Curtin	Dennis
2	Jones	Marie
4	Jones	Stuart
13	Jones	Lewis
3	Lewis	John
1	Smith	Vance
6	Smith	Adam
8	Smith	Robert
12	Smith	Frank
7	Stanford	David
10	Swabey	Daphne
11	Vogel	Terry

B. Primary Key Is LASTNAME

#	LASTNAME	FIRSTNAME
9	Benjamin	Nancy
5	Curtin	Dennis
13	Jones	Lewis
2	Jones	Marie
4	Jones	Stuart
3	Lewis	John
6	Smith	Adam
12	Smith	Frank
8	Smith	Robert
1	Smith	Vance
7	Stanford	David
10	Swabey	Daphne
11	Vogel	Terry

C. Primary Key Is LASTNAME and Secondary Key Is FIRSTNAME

FIGURE 6-37
Sorting a File on a Secondary Key
By specifying the same primary key, and then specifying that the FIRSTNAME field be used as a secondary key, the file is correctly sorted (c).

FIGURE 6-38
Sort Orders

Here is the same file sorted by number into ascending (a) and descending orders (b). Notice how the name fields are rearranged so that they stay on the same line as the number they are associated with.

#	LASTNAME	FIRSTNAME
1	Smith	Vance
2	Jones	Marie
3	Lewis	John
4	Jones	Stuart
5	Curtin	Dennis
6	Smith	Adam
7	Stanford	David
8	Smith	Robert
9	Benjamin	Nancy
10	Swabey	Daphne
11	Vogel	Terry
12	Smith	Frank
13	Jones	Lewis

#	LASTNAME	FIRSTNAME
13	Jones	Lewis
12	Smith	Frank
11	Vogel	Terry
10	Swabey	Daphne
9	Benjamin	Nancy
8	Smith	Robert
7	Stanford	David
6	Smith	Adam
5	Curtin	Dennis
4	Jones	Stuart
3	Lewis	John
2	Jones	Marie
1	Smith	Vance

A. Ascending Order   B. Descending Order

FIGURE 6-39
Sort Sequence

The sequence into which characters are sorted is based on the procedures used by the program. Excel assigns a lower place in the sequence to numbers than dBase does. dBase sequences the uppercase letters A through Z above the lowercase letters a through z. Excel sequences them as A a, B b, C c, and so on.

d BASE	Excel
(space)	0
!	1
"	2
#	3
$	4
%	5
&	6
'	7
(	8
)	9
*	(space)
+	!
,	"
-	#
.	$
/	%
0	&
1	'
2	(
3	)
4	*
5	+
6	,

d BASE	Excel
7	-
8	.
9	/
:	:
;	;
<	<
=	=
>	>
?	?
@	@
A	A a
Z	Z z
[	[
\	\
]	]
^	^
_	_
a	{
z		
{	{
>		

SUMMARY AND KEY TERMS

- Sorting a file arranges it in a specified order.
- The file is sorted first by the primary key and then by one or more secondary keys. All programs have one primary key, but the number of secondary keys varies. The more secondary keys you have, the closer to perfect are the sorts you can achieve.
- You can sort a file into ascending or descending order.

REVIEW QUESTIONS

1. Why might you want to sort a file?
2. Explain the purpose of a key field.
3. What is the purpose of a primary key? A secondary key?
4. What is a tie in a sort?
5. Into what orders can you sort a file?

Indexing Records

OBJECTIVE

After completing this topic, you will be able to

- Describe the difference between sequential and indexed database files

Sorting is not always the best way to arrange a list.

- It can take a long time to sort an entire file if the list is long.
- A file can be sorted in only one order at a time. For example, a name and address file used for mailings might be sorted by last name to produce a reference list. It would then be sorted by ZIP code for printing mailing labels because the post office gives reduced rates for mailings that are presorted by ZIP code. To maintain lists like these in more than one order, you would need separate files, each sorted differently.
- Some commands, like FIND, work only on indexed fields. Searching the entire database for a string would take a very long time. Searching for the string in the index, and then displaying the matching record, is much faster.

To overcome these problems, some database management programs, have an index capability. To understand the difference between sorting and indexing, let's look at how a database management program finds a specific record without, and then with, an index.

SEQUENTIAL FILES

Records are physically stored in a file on the disk much like pages are organized in a book. When you search a **sequential file** for a specific record, the program begins at the beginning of the file and reads each record until it finds the one you want. If you create a file with many records, the data cannot all fit in the computer's memory at the same time. Much of it will be stored on one or more disks and read into memory as needed. When the program tries to sequentially find a file, it begins to read these records into memory in batches, looking for the record it wants. If it does not find the record, it replaces the first batch of records in memory with others from the disk and continues to look. Retrieving data from disks is slow compared to the speed of processing the records once they are in memory. It can take a long time just to find a specific record. If the program is also sorting the file into a specific order, it can go on for hours rearranging the records a few at a time.

Suppose your file has 10,000 records in it, and you want to find a specific record. Sequentially finding this record would be time consuming, especially if it were near the end of the file. As often as not, the program would have to read half the file, 5000 records, before it found the record you wanted. Sequential file scans are fine if you always need to look at or process all the records in a file. But if you want to find only specific records, this method may be unsatisfactory. The solution to this problem is to have the program index the file.

INDEXED FILES

Indexed files were developed to overcome the problems of using sequential files. The idea behind an indexed file is similar to that of an index at the back of a book. The index lets you look up a term and go directly to where it is discussed. This is called **direct access**. Then you can sequentially search from there to find the exact place on the page. This combination of direct access and sequential search is called the **index-sequential method**.

As you enter records into a file, the program sequentially numbers them. These numbers represent the order in which they are physically stored in the file. This order is usually the one the records were entered in unless the entire file has been sorted.

To index a file, you select the field you want it indexed by. Ideally, this field contains unique values. Once you specify the field, the program creates a shorter companion file for the index. The index contains only the record numbers assigned by the program and the contents of the field that the file has been indexed on (Figure 6-40). The field contents are sorted into ascending or descending order.

When you use an index to find a particular record, you specify the value to be looked for in the indexed field. The program first reads the index file and scans the records there. Since the index is generally much smaller than the file, this can be done quickly. When it finds a record that matches the search criteria you entered, it looks for its record number, or record pointer, and goes directly to where that record is stored on the disk. The computer then starts reading data records from that point until it finds the record it is looking for or one that has a higher key. If it finds a higher key, it knows the record it is looking for does not exist.

Indexes allow you to keep a file in order by several primary keys without having to physically resort it each time or maintain duplicate files. For example, the original file can have two indexes, one sorting it by department

FIGURE 6-40
An Indexed File
Here, a database file (a) has been indexed by LASTNAME (b). The file remains in its original order, but the index is arranged alphabetically by last name. When searching for a record, the program searches the index file and then uses the record pointer to find the matching record in the database. These pointers give the physical location of the records stored in the file on the disk.

Record #	ID	LASTNAME	FIRST	STREET	CITY	ST	ZIP	AREA	PHONE
1	101	June	Gary	100 Elm Street	New Haven	CT	10000	203	555-1000
2	102	Benjamin	Nancy	25 Oak Street	Cambridge	MA	20000	617	555-1212
3	103	Kendall	Liz	26 Rosewood	Chicago	IL	20000	312	555-1200
4	104	Hogan	Dennis	40 Main Street	Edgewater	NJ	30000	201	555-1003
5	105	Lyons	Susan	168 Bridge Road	Beverly	MA	20000	617	555-1004
6	106	Baxter	Michelle	110 Millbrook	Austin	TX	50000	512	555-1009
7	107	Sobel	Carol	45 Porter Ave.	Fairlawn	NJ	30000	201	555-1005
8	108	Surridge	Nancy	10 Preston Lane	Oakland	CA	40000	415	555-1007
9	109	Fiske	Robert	1500 Storybrook	Boston	MA	02198	617	555-1008
10	110	Werthman	Ted	25 Stuart Road	Miami	FL	60000	305	555-1010

A. Database File

Record #	LASTNAME
6	Baxter
2	Benjamin
9	Fiske
4	Hogan
1	June
3	Kendall
5	Lyons
7	Sobel
8	Surridge
10	Werthman

B. Indexed on LASTNAME

DATABASE MANAGEMENT APPLICATIONS

Record #	ID	LASTNAME	FIRST	STREET	CITY	ST	ZIP	AREA	PHONE
1	101	June	Gary	100 Elm Street	New Haven	CT	10000	203	555-1000
2	102	Benjamin	Nancy	25 Oak Street	Cambridge	MA	20000	617	555-1212
3	103	Kendall	Liz	26 Rosewood	Chicago	IL	20000	312	555-1200
4	104	Hogan	Dennis	40 Main Street	Edgewater	NJ	30000	201	555-1003
5	105	Lyons	Susan	168 Bridge Road	Beverly	MA	20000	617	555-1004
6	106	Baxter	Michelle	110 Millbrook	Austin	TX	50000	512	555-1009
7	107	Sobel	Carol	45 Porter Ave.	Fairlawn	NJ	30000	201	555-1005
8	108	Surridge	Nancy	10 Preston Lane	Oakland	CA	40000	415	555-1007
9	109	Fiske	Robert	1500 Storybrook	Boston	MA	02198	617	555-1008
10	110	Werthman	Ted	25 Stuart Road	Miami	FL	60000	305	555-1010

A. Database File

Record #	LASTNAME
6	Baxter
2	Benjamin
9	Fiske
4	Hogan
1	June
3	Kendall
5	Lyons
7	Sobel
8	Surridge
10	Werthman

B. Indexed on LASTNAME

Record #	ST
8	CA
1	CT
10	FL
3	IL
2	MA
5	MA
9	MA
4	NJ
7	NJ
6	TX

C. Indexed on ST

FIGURE 6-41
A File with Multiple Indexes
You can create indexes for more than one field name so that you can quickly access records using either field as the basis for a query. Here the database file has been indexed on both the LASTNAME and ST fields.

Record #	ID	LASTNAME	FIRST	STREET	CITY	ST	ZIP	AREA	PHONE
1	101	June	Gary	100 Elm Street	New Haven	CT	10000	203	555-1000
2	102	Benjamin	Nancy	25 Oak Street	Cambridge	MA	20000	617	555-1212
3	103	Kendall	Liz	26 Rosewood	Chicago	IL	20000	312	555-1200
4	104	Hogan	Dennis	40 Main Street	Edgewater	NJ	30000	201	555-1003
5	105	Lyons	Susan	168 Bridge Road	Beverly	MA	20000	617	555-1004
6	106	Baxter		110 Millbrook	Austin	TX	50000	512	555-1009
7	107	Sobel		45 Porter Ave.	Fairlawn	NJ	30000	201	555-1005
8	108	Surridge		10 Preston Lane	Oakland	CA	40000	415	555-1007
9	109	Fiske		1500 Storybrook	Boston	MA	02198	617	555-1008
10	110	Werthman		25 Stuart Road	Miami	FL	60000	305	555-1010

A. Database File

Record #	LASTNAME + FIRST
6	Baxter Michelle
2	Benjamin Nancy
9	Fiske Robert
4	Hogan Dennis
1	June Gary
3	Kendall Liz
5	Lyons Susan
7	Sobel Carol
8	Surridge Nancy
10	Werthman Ted

B. Indexed on LASTNAME

FIGURE 6-42
A File Indexed on More Than One Field
You can index a file on more than one field name so that you can access records in an order similar to that provided by a sort on a primary and secondary field. Here the database file has been indexed on both the LASTNAME and FIRST fields. Notice how the index concatenated the two fields into one.

and another by phone number (Figure 6-41). You can also index a file on more than one field. This is similar to sorting a file using a primary and secondary key. The index can be compiled by concatenating two or more fields, for example, to index a file by both first and last names (Figure 6-42).

Once you have created an index, some programs automatically maintain it. If you add, insert, or delete records in the file, these programs automatically update the index. Some programs also allow you to index large indexes so that they can be scanned faster. This breaks a search into two steps. The program uses the first index to find a record in the second index and, from there, finds its location in the file.

Indexes do have drawbacks. Since they are automatically updated, making a small change in a field takes longer than it would without the index. You can have more than one index for each file, so changes can take a long time. And indexes are like any other file; they take up disk storage space.

CASE STUDY 3
Sorting and Indexing Files

In this case study, you sort and then index the NAMELIST file that you created in Case Study 1. Figure A shows the original file.

Step 1: Sorting a File   A file can be easily sorted on any field. Let's sort the file alphabetically by LASTNAME. To retrieve the file from the disk in drive B, type USE NAMELIST and then press **Return**. The disk spins as the file is loaded into the computer's memory, and then the dot prompt appears.

When sorting files, you do not sort the original file; you create and name a new file that the sorted file is stored in. To sort the file, type SORT ON LASTNAME TO TEMP and then press **Return**.

The drive spins as the file NAMELIST is written to a new file TEMP, where it is sorted alphabetically by LASTNAME. In a moment, the message *100% Sorted 10 Records sorted* appears along with the dot prompt. To see the new file, type USE TEMP and then press **Return**. Then, type BROWSE and press **Return**. The file (Figure B) is sorted so that all records are arranged by last name in ascending order. Press **Esc** to return to the dot prompt. If you were to retrieve the original NAMELIST file, you would find it unsorted and still in its original order.

Step 2: Indexing a File   dBASE III allows you to index a file, a fast and versatile way to arrange files in order. Indexing must also be done before you can use commands like FIND that locate specific records. To begin, type USE NAMELIST and then press **Return**.

To index the file, type INDEX ON LASTNAME TO LAST and then press **Return.** In a moment, the message reads *100% indexed 10 Records indexed*, and the dot prompt reappears.

To see the results, type SET INDEX TO LAST and then press **Return**. Type BROWSE and then press **Return**. The original file (Figure C) now appears in sorted order although the records in the file have not been physically sorted.

Step 3: Using Multiple Indexes   One of the advantages of indexes is that a file can be kept in more than one order. To do this, you create additional indexes. Let's create a new index based on the ST field and then look at the file using this new index and the LAST index created previously.

To create a second index, type INDEX ON ST TO STATE and then press **Return**. In a moment, the message reads *100% indexed 10 Records indexed*, and the dot prompt reappears. Let's use the new index to view the file.

To see the results, type SET INDEX TO STATE and then press **Return**. Type BROWSE and then press **Return**. The file (Figure D) now appears sorted by state. Press **Esc** to return to the dot prompt. Let's look at the file indexed by last name. To do this, you first must specify the index.

To see the file indexed by LASTNAME, type SET INDEX TO LAST and then press **Return**. Type BROWSE and then press **Return**. The file appears sorted by last name just as it did in Step 3. Press **Esc** to return to the dot prompt.

Step 4: Finding a Specific Record   dBASE III finds specific records using the FIND command. This command (like many others) works only on in-

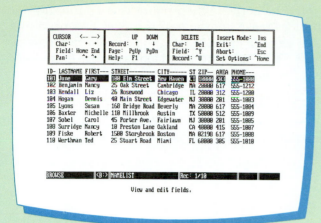

FIGURE A
The Original File
The original NAMELIST file has the records arranged in the order they were entered.

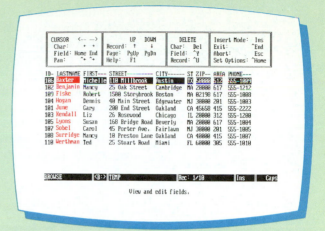

FIGURE B
The Sorted File
The TEMP file to which NEWFILE was sorted has the records arranged alphabetically by LASTNAME.

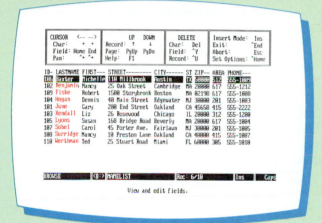

FIGURE C
The File Indexed on LASTNAME
The original NAMELIST file is displayed sorted by LASTNAME when indexed on that field.

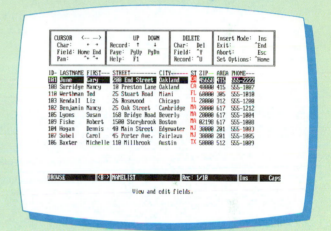

FIGURE D
The File Indexed on ST
The NAMELIST file is displayed sorted by ST when indexed on that field.

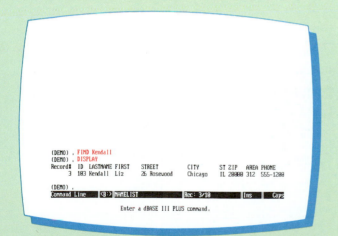

FIGURE E
Finding a Record
The FIND command looks up a string in the index, and the DISPLAY command then displays the record that contains the string.

dexed files, and the index must be active. When using this command, be careful about uppercase and lowercase characters. If a field has been entered as Kendall, trying to find kendall or KENDALL will cause the program to display the message *No find*. The FIND command looks for the first characters you specify in the field. You can enter either a complete name or a partial name.

To display the record for Kendall, type SET INDEX TO LAST and then press **Return**. Type FIND Kendall and then press **Return**. Type DISPLAY and then press **Return**. The record with Kendall in the index is displayed on the screen (Figure E).

SUMMARY AND KEY TERMS

- Searching though a file one record at a time is called a **sequential search**. These are time consuming.

- **Indexing** creates a file that contains only the contents of a specified field and **pointers** from those contents to the full record that contains them. When you use an index to find a particular record, you specify the contents of the indexed field that you are looking for. The program then searches the index for that contents and uses the pointer to locate the complete record in the database file.

REVIEW QUESTIONS

1. Under what conditions can you use the FIND command, and what does it do?
2. What are two major advantages of using indexes? What is the primary disadvantage?
3. What is the difference between sorting and indexing a file?
4. Describe direct access.

Printing Reports

OBJECTIVES

After completing this topic, you will be able to

- Explain the parts of a typical report
- List the steps you follow to print a report

There are usually several ways to print out the information in a database file. For example, many of the commands you have learned about display information on the screen. On most programs, you can also direct this information to the printer so that you have a copy for reference. For example, when using dBASE, whenever you want a printed record of your work, you can use the SET PRINT ON command to toggle the printer on. When finished, you can then use the SET PRINT OFF command to toggle it off.

Most businesspeople do not actually use the database file itself. Generally, they use reports created from part of the information stored in the file. The file might contain information about all aspects of the business. Reports are then designed to organize specific information needed by different people such as the sales manager, the president, or the finance department. Each report provides only the information needed by those it is printed for. Reports are not always complicated. For example, checks prepared on computers are reports. Reports consist of selected fields from selected records.

Reports are usually in tabular form, with information arranged in rows and columns. The typical report contains the information shown in Figure 6-43. Reports are created in five basic steps and then printed.

1. Decide what fields are to be included in the report. A report does not have to print out all the data contained in a database file. Selected fields can be printed so that the report is customized for the use it is being put to. For example, you might have a file that contains names, addresses, and items purchased. When you print a report, you might want to list only the names and addresses of your customers. You can also concatenate fields in a report. For example, on dBASE, you can specify the field as FIRST+LASTNAME to join two fields. The name in the two fields is then printed as Gary June, not June in one field and Gary in another.

AMOUNTS DUE

First Name	Last Name	Area Code	Phone Number	Amount Due
** Amounts due from state: CA				
James	Poe	415	555-1007	10.00
** Subtotal **				10.00
** Amounts due from state: CT				
Tina	Culman	203	555-1000	10.00
** Subtotal **				10.00
** Amounts due from state: FL				
Jose	Alverez	305	555-1010	61.00
** Subtotal **				61.00
** Amounts due from state: IL				
Liz	Kendall	312	555-1200	35.00
John	Davis	312	555-1020	75.00
** Subtotal **				110.00
** Amounts due from state: MA				
Nancy	Benjamin	617	555-1212	15.00
Daphne	Swabey	617	555-1004	30.00
Robert	Fiske	617	555-1008	18.00
** Subtotal **				63.00
** Amounts due from state: NJ				
Dennis	Hogan	201	555-1003	25.00
Carol	Sobel	201	555-1005	50.00
** Subtotal **				75.00
** Amounts due from state: TX				
Lars	Porsena	512	555-1009	43.00
** Subtotal **				43.00
*** Total ***				372.00

FIGURE 6-43
Typical Report

A. A heading that identifies the report.

B. A heading for each column.

C. The columns that contain data from selected fields.

D. Totals and subtotals (for groups of records), which can be printed by entering "report breaks" to indicate what records are to be included.

2. Lay out the order the fields are printed in. Reports are arranged in rows and columns much like a table. But you can specify the order the columns are arranged in.

3. Sort or index the file so that it will print data in a desired order (Figure 6-44).

4. Specify the criteria, if any (see Topic 6-5). This allows you to print selected records and selected fields from those records.

5. Specify if there are to be totals or subtotals calculated for numeric fields. To do this, you specify the field that will be totaled. This field is not the field that contains the numbers to be totaled but any field that contains duplicate data. For example, in the report shown in Figure

```
Page No.        1
08/16/88
                              AMOUNTS DUE

    FIRST NAME    LAST NAME    AREA CODE  PHONE #     AMOUNT DUE


** AMOUNTS DUE FROM: NJ
   Dennis        Hogan        201        555-1003        25.00
** Subtotal **
                                                         25.00


** AMOUNTS DUE FROM: FL
   Ted           Werthman     305        555-1010        43.00
** Subtotal **
                                                         43.00


** AMOUNTS DUE FROM: IL
   Liz           Kendall      312        555-1200        35.00
** Subtotal **
                                                         35.00


** AMOUNTS DUE FROM: CA
   Gary          June         415        555-2222        10.00
   Gary          June         415        555-2222        40.00
   Gary          June         415        555-2222        50.00
   Nancy         Surridge     415        555-1007        10.00
** Subtotal **
                                                        110.00


** AMOUNTS DUE FROM: TX
   Michelle      Baxter       512        555-1009        50.00
** Subtotal **
                                                         50.00


** AMOUNTS DUE FROM: MA
   Nancy         Benjamin     617        555-1212        15.00
   Susan         Lyons        617        555-1004        30.00
   Robert        Fiske        617        555-1008        18.00
** Subtotal **
                                                         63.00

*** Total ***
                                                        326.00
```

FIGURE 6-44
Report Breaks for Totals
After you format a report,
you can sort or index the
file to change the order in
which records appear.
Here, (a) has the records
organized by state and (b)
by area code (see next
page).

6-43, the file contains a field named ST (for state) and a field named AMOUNT. To prepare a report that subtotaled amounts by state, it would be sorted or indexed so that all identical items are listed together, and then the ST field would be specified as the criterion for subtotals to generate the report shown. Some programs let you create subtotals at various levels.

How reports are formatted varies from program to program. Generally, the approach used to specify what data is to be printed and how it is to be arranged is similar to that used to create input forms. On some programs, you define the report by entering field names and other specifications in response to prompts or field names (Figure 6-45). On others, you create print forms similar to those used to enter data. Some programs even allow you to change the layout of your reports, perhaps so that you can print selected fields in specific locations to fill in a preprinted form. These on-screen forms are used to specify what fields and records are to be printed by entering cri-

FIGURE 6-44b

```
Page No.         1
08/16/88
                                        PHONE NUMBERS

First              Last            Area        Phone           Amount
Name               Name            Code        Number          Due


** AMOUNTS DUE FROM: 201
  Dennis           Hogan           201         555-1003         25.00
** Subtotal **
                                                                25.00


** AMOUNTS DUE FROM: 305
  Ted              Werthman        305         555-1010         43.00
** Subtotal **
                                                                43.00


** AMOUNTS DUE FROM: 312
  Liz              Kendall         312         555-1200         35.00
** Subtotal **
                                                                35.00


** AMOUNTS DUE FROM: 415
  Gary             June            415         555-2222         10.00
  Gary             June            415         555-2222         40.00
  Gary             June            415         555-2222         50.00
  Nancy            Surridge        415         555-1007         10.00
** Subtotal **
                                                               110.00


** AMOUNTS DUE FROM: 512
  Michelle         Baxter          512         555-1009         50.00
** Subtotal **
                                                                50.00


** AMOUNTS DUE FROM: 617
  Nancy            Benjamin        617         555-1212         15.00
  Susan            Lyons           617         555-1004         30.00
  Robert           Fiske           617         555-1008         18.00
** Subtotal **
                                                                63.00

*** Total ***
                                                               326.00
```

FIGURE 6-45
Report-Form Screen
The report-form screen lists
menu choices you use to
define a report format.

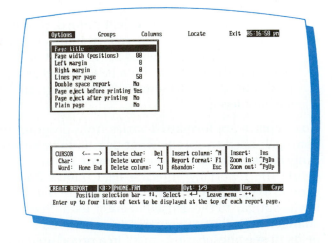

teria into the appropriate fields, much as when the form is used to find a specific record.

Since it takes time to lay out a report, most programs let you save the **report formats** you create so that they can be used again. You assign each format a name, and then save it onto the disk so that it can be retrieved.

CASE STUDY 4
Printing Reports

In this case study, you open the NEWFILE1 file you created by joining the NAMELIST and AMOUNTS files. You then create and print a variety of reports. Once you have created a database file, you can generate a variety of reports that display the information in the file on the screen or in a printout. These reports can include all fields and records or selected fields and records.

Here, you first display and then print a report that contains only the first name, last name, area code, and phone number fields from all records. You then modify the report to add the AMOUNT field and calculate subtotals.

Step 1: Defining the Report Format   To retrieve a file from the disk in drive B, type USE NEWFILE1 and then press **Return**. To name the file the report format will be saved in, type CREATE REPORT and then press **Return**. The prompt reads *Enter report file name:*. Type PHONE and then press **Return** to display the Options menu.

To add a heading, press **Return** to select *Page title*. Type PHONE NUMBERS in the page heading area. Press **Ctrl-End** to save the title.

Now, to specify the first field to be printed and a heading for the column it prints in, press **C** to pull down the Columns menu (Figure A). Press **Return** to select *Contents*, press **F10** to display a list of field names, highlight *FIRST*, and then press **Return** two times. Highlight *Heading*, and then press **Return**. Type First press **Return**, and then type NAME. To return to the menu, press **Ctrl-End**. Highlight *Width*, press **Return**, type 11 and then press **Return**.

To specify the second field and heading, press **PgDn** to display a new column form. Use the same commands described for the first field, but set the *Contents* to *LASTNAME*, enter Last Name for the heading, and set the width to 11. When finished, press **PgDn** to display a new column form. To specify the third field, set the *Contents* to *AREA*, enter Area Code for the heading, and set the width to 9. When finished, press **PgDn** to display a new column form. Finally, for the fourth field, set the *Contents* to *phone*, enter Phone Number for the heading, and set the width to 9.

To save the report form, press **E** to pull down the Exit menu. Press **Return** to select *Save*.

Step 2: Display the Report on the Screen   To display the report on the screen, type USE NEWFILE1 INDEX LAST and then press **Return**. Type REPORT FORM PHONE and then press **Return**. The report scrolls onto the screen (Figure B). All eleven records are listed but only four of the original eight fields. The address, date, and amount information are not included. And the order of the fields is different from how it appears in the file. First names

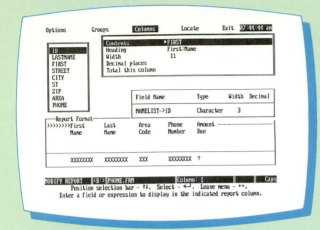

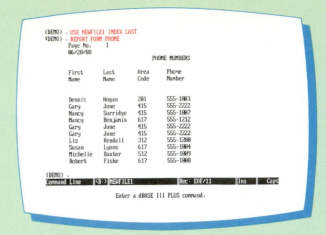

are now listed before last names. The files are arranged by state, a field that has not been displayed. Let's change the order by creating a new index.

Step 3: Change the Order of the Records To change the order in which records appear in the report, type INDEX ON AREA TO AREA and then press **Return**. Type SET INDEX TO AREA and then press **Return**. Type REPORT FORM PHONE and then press **Return**. The report scrolls onto the screen (Figure C). The report is now in order by area code. After creating a report, you can change how information in it is arranged by using a new index, as you did here.

Step 4: Print the Report To print the report, type SET PRINT ON and then press **Return**. Type REPORT FORM PHONE and then press **Return**. The report scrolls onto the screen and prints on the printer. To turn the printer off, type SET PRINT OFF and then press **Return**.

Step 5: Modify the Report Form to Print Subtotals Now, modify the report format so that it prints subtotals for states. To begin, type MODIFY REPORT PHONE and then press **Return** to display the Options menu.

First, add a new column for the amounts field. To begin, press C to pull down the Columns menu. Press **PgDn** to scroll though the existing column definitions until you display a new blank column form. Press **Return** to select *Contents*, press **F10** to display a list of field names, highlight *AMOUNT*, and then press **Return** two times. Highlight *Heading*, and then press **Return**. Type Amount press **Return**, type Due and then press **Ctrl-End**. Highlight *Width*, press **Return**, type 6 and then press **Return**. Highlight *Decimal*, press **Return**, type 2 and then press **Return**.

Now, specify the field on which subtotals will be grouped. Press G to pull down the Groups menu. Press **Return** to select *Group on expression*, press **F10** to display a list of field names, highlight *ST*, and then press **Return** two times. Highlight *Group heading*, press **Return**, type AMOUNTS DUE FROM: and then press **Return**.

To save the report form, press E to pull down the Exit menu. Press **Return** to select *Save*.

Step 6: Display and Print the Report To display the report on the screen, Type USE NEWFILE1 and then press **Return**. Type SET INDEX TO STATE and then press **Return**. Type REPORT FORM PHONE and then press **Return**.

```
▼DEMO) , REPORT FORM PHONE
        Page No.    1
        06/28/88
                              PHONE NUMBERS

        First       Last       Area     Phone
        Name        Name       Code     Number


        Dennis      Hogan      201      555-1003
        Ted         Werthman   305      555-1010
        Liz         Kendall    312      555-1200
        Gary        June       415      555-2222
        Gary        June       415      555-2222
        Gary        June       415      555-2222
        Nancy       Surridge   415      555-1007
        Michelle    Baxter     512      555-1009
        Nancy       Benjamin   617      555-1212
        Susan       Lyons      617      555-1004
        Robert      Fiske      617      555-1008

(DEMO) ,
Command Line   <B:> NEWFILE1          Rec: EOF/11     Ins   Caps

        Enter a dBASE III PLUS command.
```

```
                                          35.00
        ** AMOUNTS DUE FROM: MA
        Nancy       Benjamin   617      555-1212   15.00
        Susan       Lyons      617      555-1004   30.00
        Robert      Fiske      617      555-1008   18.00
        ** Subtotal **
                                          63.00

        ** AMOUNTS DUE FROM: NJ
        Dennis      Hogan      201      555-1003   25.00
        ** Subtotal **
                                          25.00

        ** AMOUNTS DUE FROM: TX
        Michelle    Baxter     512      555-1009   50.00
        ** Subtotal **
                                          50.00

        *** Total ***
                                         326.00

(DEMO) ,
Command Line   <B:> NEWFILE1          Rec: EOF/11     Ins   Caps

        Enter a dBASE III PLUS command.
```

FIGURE C (above left)
The Report Order Changed
Here, the index has been changed to AREA, so the report is now organized by area code.

FIGURE D (above right)
Report with Subtotals on Screen
The report now shows subtotals for each state, and a total appears at the bottom of the screen.

FIGURE E (left)
Printed Report with Subtotals
The printed report shows all the records and subtotals.

```
Page No.      1
08/16/88
                          AMOUNTS DUE

    FIRST NAME   LAST NAME     AREA CODE PHONE #    AMOUNT DUE

** AMOUNTS DUE FROM: 201
 Dennis        Hogan        201      555-1003      25.00
** Subtotal **
                                                   25.00

** AMOUNTS DUE FROM: 305
 Ted           Werthman     305      555-1010      43.00
** Subtotal **
                                                   43.00

** AMOUNTS DUE FROM: 312
 Liz           Kendall      312      555-1200      35.00
** Subtotal **
                                                   35.00

** AMOUNTS DUE FROM: 415
 Gary          June         415      555-2222      10.00
 Gary          June         415      555-2222      40.00
 Gary          June         415      555-2222      50.00
 Nancy         Surridge     415      555-1007      10.00
** Subtotal **
                                                  110.00

** AMOUNTS DUE FROM: 512
 Michelle      Baxter       512      555-1009      50.00
** Subtotal **
                                                   50.00

** AMOUNTS DUE FROM: 617
 Nancy         Benjamin     617      555-1212      15.00
 Susan         Lyons        617      555-1004      30.00
 Robert        Fiske        617      555-1008      18.00
** Subtotal **
                                                   63.00

*** Total ***
                                                  326.00
```

The report scrolls onto the screen (Figure D). All eleven records are listed but only four of the original eight fields. The records are grouped by state, and subtotals are calculated for each state. The total appears at the bottom of the report.

To send the report to the printer, type REPORT FORM PHONE TO PRINT and then press **Return**.

The selected fields are printed on the printer along with subtotals (Figure E). The command to print is different from the one you used in Step 4. This form does not require that you set the printer to off when the command is completed. The printer is automatically turned off.

SUMMARY AND KEY TERMS

- When you print out data in a database it is called a **report**. A report is usually in tabular form.
- Reports can contain headers or titles, fields, and subtotals and totals.
- Some programs have a limited number of predetermined **report formats**. Others allow you to customize your own. A few allow you to create an on-screen form that shows exactly what the report will look like when printed. This lets you design a report that can fill in preprinted forms available on continuous form paper, like invoices or paychecks.
- Most programs allow you to save your report formats so that you can use them again.

REVIEW QUESTIONS

1. Define a report, and compare it to a database file.
2. What information does a typical report contain?
3. What are the five basic steps to create reports?
4. If you had a database file with a field named ITEMS that contained item numbers and a field named AMOUNT that contained the number of each item in inventory, what field would you specify that subtotals be grouped on?
5. What dBASE command do you use to rearrange information in a report after you have created its format?

TOPIC 6-14

Restructuring the Database

OBJECTIVE

After completing this topic, you will be able to

■ Explain how you modify the structure of a database file

There are times when a database has to be changed after it has been created. Changes might include adding new fields or modifying the definition of existing ones. For example, what if one field contains ZIP codes, and the characteristics of ZIP codes change (as they recently did). The ZIP code field was initially five characters long. But the new ZIP code field might have to be ten characters long.

If a change like this is necessary, the file can be restructured. This is usually done by copying the file's contents to a temporary file while the original file is being restructured. On most programs, this is done automatically. You then either specify new fields or change the definitions of existing fields. When the restructuring is complete, the contents are copied from the temporary file back into the restructured file.

When restructuring files, keep the following points in mind:

■ If the restructuring adds new fields, those fields are blank.

■ You may not be able to make two changes at the same time, for example, changing the name of the field and the length of the field. If you do, the field may be left blank.

■ If a numeric field is redefined as a character field, or other field type, it will be left blank.

■ Restructuring files after they are created allows you to add or change fields without having to reconstruct a new file.

■ When you restructure a database, the program copies the data to a temporary file and then copies it back into the restructured file.

SUMMARY AND KEY TERMS

1. How is a database restructured, and why is this done?
2. What happens if you restructure a file and you add new fields?
3. What happens if you restructure a file and you redefine a numeric field as another field type?

REVIEW QUESTIONS

Making New Databases from Existing Files

OBJECTIVES

After completing this topic, you will be able to

- Explain how multiple files are joined into new tables
- Describe how records and fields can be selected and projected to new files

Since data in a relational database is stored independently from how it is viewed, you can change your view of the data at any time. This is done by creating new tables from existing tables in different combinations. The result of combining tables is always another table. In many ways, this is much like a cut-and-paste operation where rows or columns are cut from different tables and combined into a new table.

To work with more than one file, you must load them all into memory. To do so, database management programs let you divide the computer's available memory into independent work areas. You specify the areas, and which files are opened in them, with the SELECT command.

JOINING TABLES

If you have two files with a common field, you can join them into a third table (Figure 6-46). The JOIN command constructs a new table by combining fields in one table with fields in another table, provided both tables have the same value in a specified common field. All records that fail to have the same value in the common field are deleted from the new table.

Although data is entered only once into each file, you can view all the data in the database in different ways. For example, you can join the customer names in one file with the amounts they owe in another to create a new table. At the end of each month, the AMOUNTS file can be joined with the NAMELIST file to prepare a complete file from which reports and bills can be prepared. When the two files are joined, the customer's ID number, which appears in both files, is used as the identifying, or key, field. A typical join command might be written as

```
SELECT 1
USE AMOUNTS
SELECT 2
USE NAME LIST
JOIN WITH AMOUNTS TO NEW FILE 1 FOR I=AMOUNTS->ID
USE NEW FILE 1
LIST
```

ID	LASTNAME	FIRST	STREET	CITY	ST	ZIP	AREA	PHONE
101	June	Gary	100 Elm Street	New Haven	CT	10000	203	555-1000
102	Benjamin	Nancy	25 Oak Street	Cambridge	MA	20000	617	555-1212
103	Kendall	Liz	26 Rosewood	Chicago	IL	20000	312	555-1200
104	Hogan	Dennis	40 Main Street	Edgewater	NJ	30000	201	555-1003
105	Lyons	Susan	168 Bridge Road	Beverly	MA	20000	617	555-1004
106	Sobel	Carol	45 Porter Ave.	Fairlawn	NJ	30000	201	555-1005
107	Surridge	Nancy	10 Preston Lane	Oakland	CA	40000	415	555-1007
108	Fiske	Robert	1500 Storybrook	Boston	MA	02198	617	555-1008
109	Baxter	Michelle	110 Millbrook	Austin	TX	50000	512	555-1009
110	Werthman	Ted	25 Stuart Road	Miami	FL	60000	305	555-1010

A. NAMELIST Database File

ID	DATE	AMOUNT
101	6/8/89	10.00
102	6/9/89	15.00
103	6/10/89	35.00
104	6/11/89	25.00
105	6/12/89	30.00
106	6/13/89	50.00
107	6/15/89	10.00
108	6/16/89	18.00
109	6/17/89	43.00
110	6/18/89	61.00
101	6/18/89	30.00
101	6/19/89	45.00

B. AMOUNTS Database File

ID	LASTNAME	FIRST	STREET	CITY	ST	ZIP	AREA	PHONE	DATE	AMOUNT
101	June	Gary	100 Elm Street	New Haven	CT	10000	203	555-1000	6/8/89	10.00
101	June	Gary	100 Elm Street	New Haven	CT	10000	203	555-1000	6/18/89	30.00
101	June	Gary	100 Elm Street	New Haven	CT	10000	203	555-1000	6/19/89	45.00
102	Benjamin	Nancy	25 Oak Street	Cambridge	MA	20000	617	555-1212	6/9/89	15.00
103	Kendall	Liz	26 Rosewood	Chicago	IL	20000	312	555-1200	6/10/89	35.00
104	Hogan	Dennis	40 Main Street	Edgewater	NJ	30000	201	555-1003	6/11/89	25.00
105	Lyons	Susan	168 Bridge Road	Beverly	MA	20000	617	555-1004	6/12/89	30.00
106	Sobel	Carol	45 Porter Ave.	Fairlawn	NJ	30000	201	555-1005	6/13/89	50.00
107	Surridge	Nancy	10 Preston Lane	Oakland	CA	40000	415	555-1007	6/15/89	10.00
108	Fiske	Robert	1500 Storybrook	Boston	MA	02198	617	555-1008	6/16/89	18.00
109	Baxter	Michelle	110 Millbrook	Austin	TX	50000	512	555-1009	6/17/89	43.00
110	Werthman	Ted	25 Stuart Road	Miami	FL	60000	305	555-1010	6/18/89	61.00

C. Tables Joined on ID to Create New File

FIGURE 6-46
Joining Tables
Here, the NAMELIST and AMOUNTS files contain a common ID field (a) that can be used to join them into a new table (c). All records that fail to have the same value in the common field are deleted from the new table.

SELECT 1 selects memory area 1, and USE AMOUNTS opens the AMOUNTS file in that memory area.

SELECT 2 selects memory area 2, and USE NAMELIST opens the NAMELIST file in that memory area.

JOIN specifies that the NAMELIST file in the current memory area is to be joined with the AMOUNTS file and the new file is to be named NEWFILE1. The FOR part of the command specifies that the common field is the ID field. The AMOUNTS–> part of the command specifies that the ID field can be found in the AMOUNTS file. This does not have to be specified for the NAMELIST file because that is the active file since you USEd it last. When the JOIN command is executed, a new table is created. The JOIN command automatically deletes duplicate data.

SELECTING TABLES

The SELECT operation extracts records from a table to create a new table (Figure 6-47). The records, and the fields within the records, contained in the new table are determined by the criteria you have established.

A. Database File

ID	LASTNAME	FIRST	STREET	CITY	ST	ZIP	AREA	PHONE	DATE	AMOUNT
101	June	Gary	100 Elm Street	New Haven	CT	10000	203	555-1000	6/8/89	10.00
101	June	Gary	100 Elm Street	New Haven	CT	10000	203	555-1000	6/18/89	30.00
101	June	Gary	100 Elm Street	New Haven	CT	10000	203	555-1000	6/19/89	45.00
102	Benjamin	Nancy	25 Oak Street	Cambridge	MA	20000	617	555-1212	6/9/89	15.00
103	Kendall	Liz	26 Rosewood	Chicago	IL	20000	312	555-1200	6/10/89	35.00
104	Hogan	Dennis	40 Main Street	Edgewater	NJ	30000	201	555-1003	6/11/89	25.00
105	Lyons	Susan	168 Bridge Road	Beverly	MA	20000	617	555-1004	6/12/89	30.00
106	Sobel	Carol	45 Porter Ave.	Fairlawn	NJ	30000	201	555-1005	6/13/89	50.00
107	Surridge	Nancy	10 Preston Lane	Oakland	CA	40000	415	555-1007	6/15/89	10.00
108	Fiske	Robert	1500 Storybrook	Boston	MA	02198	617	555-1008	6/16/89	18.00
109	Baxter	Michelle	110 Millbrook	Austin	TX	50000	512	555-1009	6/17/89	43.00
110	Werthman	Ted	25 Stuart Road	Miami	FL	60000	305	555-1010	6/18/89	61.00

A. Database File

ID	LASTNAME	FIRST	AREA	PHONE	DATE	AMOUNT
101	June	Gary	203	555-1000	6/8/89	10.00
101	June	Gary	203	555-1000	6/18/89	30.00
101	June	Gary	203	555-1000	6/19/89	45.00
102	Benjamin	Nancy	617	555-1212	6/9/89	15.00
103	Kendall	Liz	312	555-1200	6/10/89	35.00
104	Hogan	Dennis	201	555-1003	6/11/89	25.00
105	Lyons	Susan	617	555-1004	6/12/89	30.00
106	Sobel	Carol	201	555-1005	6/13/89	50.00
107	Surridge	Nancy	415	555-1007	6/15/89	10.00
108	Fiske	Robert	617	555-1008	6/16/89	18.00
109	Baxter	Michelle	512	555-1009	6/17/89	43.00
110	Werthman	Ted	305	555-1010	6/18/89	61.00

B. Table Selected with Just Selected Fields

FIGURE 6-47
Selecting Tables
The SELECT operation extracts records from one table (a) into another file (b).

PROJECTING TABLES

The PROJECT operation extracts COLUMNS (fields) from a table to create a new table (Figure 6-48). The fields contained in the new table are determined by the criteria you have established.

FIGURE 6-48
Projecting Tables
The PROJECT operation extracts fields from one table (a) into another field (b).

ID	LASTNAME	FIRST	STREET	CITY	ST	ZIP	AREA	PHONE	DATE	AMOUNT
101	June	Gary	100 Elm Street	New Haven	CT	10000	203	555-1000	6/8/89	10.00
101	June	Gary	100 Elm Street	New Haven	CT	10000	203	555-1000	6/18/89	30.00
101	June	Gary	100 Elm Street	New Haven	CT	10000	203	555-1000	6/19/89	45.00
102	Benjamin	Nancy	25 Oak Street	Cambridge	MA	20000	617	555-1212	6/9/89	15.00
103	Kendall	Liz	26 Rosewood	Chicago	IL	20000	312	555-1200	6/10/89	35.00
104	Hogan	Dennis	40 Main Street	Edgewater	NJ	30000	201	555-1003	6/11/89	25.00
105	Lyons	Susan	168 Bridge Road	Beverly	MA	20000	617	555-1004	6/12/89	30.00
106	Sobel	Carol	45 Porter Ave.	Fairlawn	NJ	30000	201	555-1005	6/13/89	50.00
108	Surridge	Nancy	10 Preston Lane	Oakland	CA	40000	415	555-1007	6/15/89	10.00
109	Fiske	Robert	1500 Storybrook	Boston	MA	02198	617	555-1008	6/16/89	18.00
110	Baxter	Michelle	110 Millbrook	Austin	TX	50000	512	555-1009	6/17/89	43.00
111	Werthman	Ted	25 Stuart Road	Miami	FL	60000	305	555-1010	6/18/89	61.00

A Database File

ID	LASTNAME	FIRST	STREET	CITY	ST	ZIP	AREA	PHONE	DATE	AMOUNT
101	June	Gary	100 Elm Street	New Haven	CT	10000	203	555-1000	6/8/89	10.00
101	June	Gary	100 Elm Street	New Haven	CT	10000	203	555-1000	6/18/89	30.00
101	June	Gary	100 Elm Street	New Haven	CT	10000	203	555-1000	6/19/89	45.00

B. Table Projected with Just the Records for "June"

DATABASE MANAGEMENT APPLICATIONS

CASE STUDY 5
Joining Files

In this case study, you use dBase to join the NAMELIST and AMOUNTS files shown in Figure A.

Step 1: Joining Complete Files   You can select more than one area in memory to open database files in. Here, you open two memory areas and then open the NAMELIST and AMOUNTS files in them. (If the menu is displayed, press **Esc** to display the dot prompt.) To select the first memory area and assign a file to it, type SELECT 1 and then press **Return**. Type USE AMOUNTS and then press **Return**. To select the second memory area and assign a file to it, type SELECT 2 and then press **Return**. Type USE NAMELIST and then press **Return**. Both files are now open in memory.

Step 2: Join All Fields in the Files   Now, join all fields from both files so that you have a new file that contains all the data from each file. To do so, type JOIN WITH AMOUNTS TO NEWFILE1 FOR ID=AMOUNTS-->ID and then press **Return**. The drive spins, and in a moment, the message reads *10 records* joined, and the dot prompt reappears.

To display the new file, type USE NEWFILE1 and then press **Return**. Type BROWSE and then press **Return**. The new file appears on the screen and looks just like the original NAMELIST file (Figure B). But the two fields combined from the AMOUNTS file are at the right-hand side of the screen. To

ID	LASTNAME	FIRST	STREET	CITY	ST	ZIP	AREA	PHONE
101	June	Gary	100 Elm Street	New Haven	CT	10000	203	555-1000
102	Benjamin	Nancy	25 Oak Street	Cambridge	MA	20000	617	555-1212
103	Kendall	Liz	26 Rosewood	Chicago	IL	20000	312	555-1200
104	Hogan	Dennis	40 Main Street	Edgewater	NJ	30000	201	555-1003
105	Lyons	Susan	168 Bridge Road	Beverly	MA	20000	617	555-1004
110	Baxter	Michelle	110 Millbrook	Austin	TX	50000	512	555-1009
106	Sobel	Carol	45 Porter Ave.	Fairlawn	NJ	30000	201	555-1005
108	Surridge	Nancy	10 Preston Lane	Oakland	CA	40000	415	555-1007
109	Fiske	Robert	1500 Storybrook	Boston	MA	02198	617	555-1008
111	Werthman	Ted	25 Stuart Road	Miami	FL	60000	305	555-1010

A. NAMELIST

ID	DATE	AMOUNT
101	6/8/88	10.00
102	6/9/88	15.00
103	6/10/88	35.00
104	6/11/88	25.00
105	6/12/88	30.00
106	6/13/88	50.00
108	6/15/88	10.00
109	6/16/88	18.00
110	6/17/88	43.00
111	6/18/88	61.00

B. AMOUNTS

FIGURE A
The NAMELIST and AMOUNTS Files
The NAMELIST and AMOUNTS files can be joined on the common ID field.

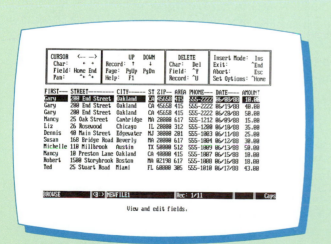

FIGURE B
The Joined File
The JOIN command joins all records in the two files into a new file.

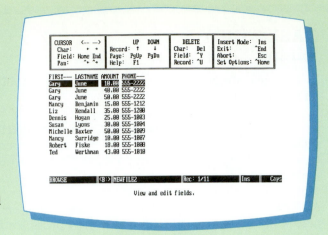

FIGURE C
Selected Fields Joined
You can specify selected fields in the JOIN command so that only those fields are joined into a new file.

```
┌─────────────────┬──────────────────┬──────────────────┬──────────────────────┐
│ CURSOR  <─ ─>   │         UP  DOWN │ DELETE           │ Insert Mode: Ins     │
│ Char:    ← →    │ Record:  ↑    ↓  │ Char:    Del     │ Exit:        ^End    │
│ Field: Home End │ Page:  PgUp PgDn │ Field:    ^Y     │ Abort:       Esc     │
│ Pan:     ^← ^→  │ Help:     F1     │ Record:   ^U     │ Set Options: ^Home   │
└─────────────────┴──────────────────┴──────────────────┴──────────────────────┘

FIRST─── LASTNAME AMOUNT PHONE───
Gary     June      10.00 555-2222
Gary     June      40.00 555-2222
Gary     June      50.00 555-2222
Nancy    Benjamin  15.00 555-1212
Liz      Kendall   35.00 555-1200
Dennis   Hogan     25.00 555-1003
Susan    Lyons     30.00 555-1004
Michelle Baxter    50.00 555-1009
Nancy    Surridge  10.00 555-1007
Robert   Fiske     10.00 555-1008
Ted      Werthman  43.00 555-1010

BROWSE       <B:> NEWFILE2            Rec: 1/11        Ins    Caps
                          View and edit fields.
```

pan the screen back and forth, press **Ctrl-→** a few times to pan the file to the left. The new database file now contains DATE and AMOUNT fields. Press **Ctrl-←** a few times to pan the file to the right. Press **Esc** to leave browse mode and return to the dot prompt.

Step 3: Join Selected Fields   When you join two files, you need not combine all the fields. You can specify that selected fields be combined to form a new table. For example, suppose you want to know the names and phone numbers of people who have outstanding charges so that you can call them.

To begin, first type USE NAMELIST and then press **Return**. You have to do this because you loaded NEWFILE1 into the current memory area in Step 2. Now, to join only selected fields into a new file, type JOIN WITH AMOUNTS TO NEWFILE2 FOR ID=AMOUNTS-->ID FIELDS FIRST, LASTNAME, AMOUNT, PHONE and then press **Return**.

To display the new file, type USE NEWFILE2 and then press **Return**. Type BROWSE and then press Return. The new file (Figure C) contains the first and last names and phone numbers from the NAMELIST file and the amounts from the AMOUNTS file. Press **Esc** to leave browse mode and return to the dot prompt.

SUMMARY AND KEY TERMS

- You can create new database files from existing files.
- The JOIN operation creates a new file by joining fields from two files. The fields are joined using a key field that contains unique data.
- The SELECT operation extracts records from a file into a new file.
- The PROJECT operation extracts fields from a file into a new file.

REVIEW QUESTIONS

1. Explain what the JOIN operation does.
2. When joining two existing tables, what conditions must be met?
3. Explain what the SELECT operation does.
4. Explain what the PROJECT operation does.

TOPIC 6-16

Writing Programs

OBJECTIVES

After completing this topic, you will be able to

- Explain how you write programs that automate databases
- Describe how you can run database programs you write without running the database management program they were written on

Until now, you have entered commands one at a time. But dBASE III allows you to write and save programs. This saves you time when you use the same commands over and over again and makes the program easier to operate for people with little or no experience. For example, you can write a program that displays menus that other users then make choices from so that they do not have to know the program's commands. You can also design and display forms on the screen so that users can more easily enter data. You can also ensure that they enter the desired data, for example, amounts neither larger nor smaller than a given value.

To write a program, you generally follow these steps.

1. Determine what you want the program to do.
2. Design the specific steps the program will follow.
3. Write the actual program (called the **code**). On dBASE, you execute the MODIFY COMMAND command, which puts the program into text edit mode. This mode is much like a word processing program. You can type and edit commands and then save them in their own file on the disk. For example, to write or edit a program named MENU, you type MODIFY COMMAND MENU. If you are writing the program file, the text edit screen appears blank. If the file already exists, it is displayed on the screen. You do not have to specify an extension for the file the program is stored in, but dBASE III Plus automatically adds the extension .PRG to all program files.

   You can display the commands stored in a program file with the TYPE command. When using the TYPE command, you must specify the file's extension. For example, to display the contents of a program file named MENU, you type TYPE MENU.PRG and then press **Return** to display the program on the screen.

4. Test the program, and fix any mistakes. After writing or editing a program, you execute it with the DO command. For example, to execute a program named MENU, you type DO MENU and then press **Return**. The commands stored in the program file are then automatically executed.

5. Write a description of the program (called the **documentation**).

DEVELOPING APPLICATIONS

When specialists write programs that automate a database so that others can easily use it, they frequently use special programs, called **applications generators**. These applications generators partially automate the process of writing code so that programs can be written faster and with fewer errors. Since many applications are very complex, like accounting and inventory systems, applications generators can save a great deal of time and money. After developing applications, every user does not have to use the database program to run them. To eliminate this need, applications can be either compiled programs or run-time versions of the programs.

Complied Programs

A database application can be compiled with a compiler. The resulting program runs just like any other applications program.

Run-Time Versions of Programs

A run-time version of a program is similar to a compiled program, but you need a copy of the run-time version to run the application. This run-time version has many of the features of the original database management program used to operate the program, but it does not have the features used to create applications.

■ The indents specify the level of nesting for the commands. Text edit mode has tab stops set every five characters. To indent a line, press **Tab.** These indents are important. The program executes a command and then looks to see if any commands are indented under it. If commands are indented, it executes those before returning to commands at the same indent level.
When finished adding the commands, press **Ctrl-W** to save it and return to the dot prompt.

CASE STUDY 6
Writing Programs

In this case study, you write a program that displays a menu on the screen so that you can make choices to add records or browse through the records in the NAMELIST and AMOUNTS files.

Step 1: Enter Text Edit Mode To write a program, you first enter the program's text edit mode, and then specify the name of the file the program will be saved in. Here, let's specify that the program be stored in a file named MENU. (If the menu is displayed, press Esc to display the dot prompt.)

To enter text edit mode, type MODIFY COMMAND MENU and then press **Return**.

Step 2: Enter the Menu Screen Display Let's begin by writing that part of the program that displays a list of menu choices on the screen. Enter the commands shown in Figure A. The first line beginning with * (asterisk) is a comment line. The asterisk tells dBase not to execute what follows it when you run the program. The CLEAR command clears the screen before the menu is displayed. The SET BELL OFF command turns off the computer's speaker so that a beep does not sound when you enter a menu choice. The lines beginning with @ (at sign) display text on the screen. The numbers following the @ specify the row and column the text begins in. The SAY command tells the program to display the text that follows on the screen in the specified position. The text to be displayed must be enclosed in double quotation marks as shown.

Now that you have written the program, save it and return to the dot prompt. Then display the contents of the program file on the screen. To save the program, press **Ctrl-W**.

Step 3: Run the Program To run the program, type DO MENU and then press **Return**. The menu is displayed on the screen, and the dot prompt reappears (Figure B). You cannot make choices from the menu yet because no commands have been added to the menu choices.

Step 4: Adding the Menu Choices Now, enter the commands that execute the choice you make from the menu.

FIGURE A (below left)
Writing a Program
This program displays a list of menu choices on the screen.

FIGURE B (below right)
Run the Program
When you run the program, the menu choices appear on the screen.

```
* MENU.PRG
CLEAR
SET BELL OFF
@ 2,33 SAY "MAIN MENU"
@ 4,25 SAY "1. ADD NAMES TO NAMELIST FILE"
@ 5,25 SAY "2. BROWSE NAMELIST FILE"
@ 6,25 SAY "3. ADD CREDITS TO AMOUNTS FILE"
@ 7,25 SAY "4. BROWSE AMOUNTS FILE"
@ 8,25 SAY "5. EXIT"
@ 10,25 SAY "ENTER CHOICE (1 - 4):"
```

```
                    MAIN MENU

            1. ADD NAMES TO NAMELIST FILE
            2. BROWSE NAMELIST FILE
            3. ADD CREDITS TO AMOUNTS FILE
            4. BROWSE AMOUNTS FILE
            5. EXIT

            ENTER CHOICE (1 - 4): █




Command        <B:> NAMELIST          Rec: 1/10
            Enter a dBASE III PLUS command.
```

FIGURE C
Writing a Program
The boldface code lists the
commands that are
executed when you make
one of the program's menu
selections.

```
* MENU.PRG
CLEAR
SET BELL OFF
@ 2,33 SAY "MAIN MENU"
@ 4,25 SAY "1. ADD NAMES TO NAMELIST FILE"
@ 5,25 SAY "2. BROWSE NAMELIST FILE"
@ 6,25 SAY "3. ADD CREDITS TO AMOUNTS FILE"
@ 7,25 SAY "4. BROWSE AMOUNTS FILE"
@ 8,25 SAY "5. EXIT"
@ 10,25 SAY "ENTER CHOICE (1 - 4):"
ANS=" "
@ 10,47 GET ANS PICTURE "9"
READ
IF ANS="1"
        USE NAMELIST
        APPEND
        DO MENU
ELSE
        IF ANS="2"
            USE NAMELIST
            BROWSE
            DO MENU
        ELSE
            IF ANS="3"
                USE AMOUNTS
                APPEND
                DO MENU
            ELSE
                IF ANS="4"
                    USE AMOUNTS
                    BROWSE
                    DO MENU
                ELSE
                    IF ANS="5"
                        CLEAR
                        CANCEL
                    ENDIF 5
                ENDIF 4
            ENDIF 3
        ENDIF 2
ENDIF 1
```

Step 5: Run the Program To run the program, type DO MENU and then press **Return**. The menu appears as before, but now a highlight follows the make selection line. This is where your selection is entered.

Step 6: Use the Menu To make selections from the menu, press 1 to display a new, blank record for the NAMELIST file. Press **Esc** to return to the menu. A blank record from the NAMELIST file should be displayed on the screen. Press **Esc** to cancel the command and return to the menu. Continue making choices, and then press **Esc** to return to the menu. When finished, press 5 for *Exit* to return to the dot prompt.

To revise the MENU.PRG command file, type MODIFY COMMAND MENU and then press **Return**. The program appears on the screen in edit mode so that you can add to it.

Enter the commands shown in boldfaced in Figure C.

- The first command creates the memory variable ANS and specifies that it can store a single character.

- The second command tells the program to store any menu choice entered in row 10 on column 47 in the memory variable named ANS. The PICTURE "9" part of the command specifies that only a number from 0 to 9 can be stored in that memory variable.

- The READ command tells the program to read the number stored in the memory variable.
- The commands beginning with IF tell the program what to do when you enter a menu choice. For example, if you type 1 to make a selection from the menu, the commands USE NAMELIST and APPEND are immediately executed. When you are finished adding records, the DO MENU command displays the menu again so that you can make another choice. Since you can make any one of five choices from the menu, the following ELSE and IF statements execute other commands.

SUMMARY AND KEY TERMS

- Most database management programs have **command languages** that can be used to develop custom applications.
- Once applications are written, they can be distributed to other users as compiled programs or run-time programs. **Compiled programs** can be run without having the actual database management program used to create them. They run just like any other applications program. **Run-time programs** are similar but must include a run-time version of the program used to create them.

REVIEW QUESTIONS

1. What five steps do you follow when writing a program?
2. What dBASE command do you use to begin writing a program?
3. What dBASE command do you execute to display the contents of a program file?
4. What dBASE command do you execute to run a program file?
5. What is a complied program? A run-time program?
6. What is a memory variable?

TOPIC 6-17

Data Security

OBJECTIVES

After completing this topic, you will be able to

- Describe why and how information in the database should be protected

- Explain how multiple users can share a database and the issues that arise

The information stored in a database is often valuable. If the database is used by only one person, the database can be protected from unauthorized users by keeping the floppy disks it is stored on under lock and key. If the computer has a hard disk drive, a power switch lock or keyboard lock can be added so that a key is required to turn on and use the computer. You can also use an all-or-nothing password to prevent others from seeing the database. If you know the password, you can use the database; if you don't, you can't.

If users share the database, additional security measures are needed to make sure the information is not modified or viewed by unauthorized users.

PASSWORDS

On a multiple-user database, **passwords** can be used to provide different types of access. Some users can be given just read-only access, whereas others can be allowed to enter and update the files. This prevents unauthorized users from entering data into the database. One person is usually designated as the database administrator. The administrator assigns operating authority to other users.

DATA ENCRYPTION

Data encryption stores data on a disk in a scrambled form so that if data is accessed with a program other than the authorized one, it appears unintelligible on the screen.

616

AUDIT TRAILS

No security system is perfect; when data is extremely sensitive, an **audit trail** is essential. An audit trail is a record of insertions, deletions, modifications, and restorations performed on a file. A typical entry on the audit trail may include

- The operation that was performed
- The computer it was done from
- The identification of the user who performed it
- The date and time it was done
- The database, table, record, and field that were affected
- The original entry of the changed fields
- The new entry of the changed fields

DATA INTEGRITY

The true value of a database depends entirely on the accuracy, or **integrity**, of the information stored in it. Often, when you complain about an error in a computer-produced bill and are told it was a computer error, the real reason is either sloppy recording of the transaction or errors in entering the data into the database. The computer is innocent. Accuracy can be affected in several ways.

1. Data can be entered or updated incorrectly.
2. Data modification can produce invalid results.
3. Hardware or software can malfunction.

Data Entry

One way to control the accuracy of data is to prevent unauthorized users from making any entries into the database. Another way is to use the DBMS to check entered data.

- **Format checking.** The computer can automatically check the format of an entry to ensure conformity with a specific pattern. For example, the program can check that the entry has a specific number of characters or contains only letters or only numbers.
- **Range checking.** The computer can check the entered values to make certain they are within an expected range or match a previously defined set of values.
- **Accuracy checking.** The computer can check to make sure an item entered actually exists. If it does exist, the computer can automatically provide the correct price for the item and any other relevant information. For example, if a clerk enters a sales invoice, the computer checks to see if the customer exists in the billing file. If the customer does exist, the computer automatically enters the customer's address. The check both ensures accuracy and saves the clerk from having to enter this information. The opportunities are almost limitless.

Data Modifications

To limit the likelihood of modifications that affect the accuracy of the information in the system, only skilled operators can be permitted to modify the system.

Hardware or Software Malfunctions

If serious damage is done to a database, it should be possible to reconstruct it. This is done by frequently backing up the files on a separate disk or disks and storing them in a safe place. These disks can then be used to recover damaged files.

MULTIUSER DATABASES

As networks and microcomputer-mainframe links are more widely used, the issues that arise with multiuser large systems become important for microcomputer users. In a shared environment, security and data integrity become critical. Moreover, the problem of simultaneous access to files and records by two or more users must be solved.

When the information in a database is being updated, two or more users may try to make a change to the same data at the same time. For example, suppose only one unit of a particular inventory item is in stock, and two order-entry people try to accept an order for it at the same time. If this is not controlled by the program, one of these updates will be lost, and one customer will be left with an unfilled order. To prevent this from happening, **file locking** (also called record locking) is used. When the first user selects a file or record for updating, the system locks that file or record to prevent access by other users until it is released, in its updated form, by the first user.

SUMMARY AND KEY TERMS

- Some programs allow you to specify **passwords** so that files cannot be seen without entering the correct password.
- **Data encryption** scrambles data on the disk so that it cannot be read by unauthorized users.
- **Audit trails** are useful when several users share the program so that you can tell who did what with the database.
- **Data integrity** refers to the accuracy of the data it contains.
- Since database management programs are generally used for important files, it is vital that the files be backed up so that they can be reconstructed in case of a problem. Since making back ups can be time consuming, a good program will make it as easy and foolproof as possible.
- When a multiuser database is being used, it contains **file locking** so that two users cannot change a file or record at the same time.

REVIEW QUESTIONS

1. What are passwords used for?
2. What does data encryption do?
3. What are audit trails, and why are they important?
4. What are some of the ways the integrity of data in a database can be ensured?
5. What are some important issues when a database is shared by users?

Hypermedia

OBJECTIVES

After completing this topic, you will be able to

- Explain what hypermedia is
- Describe some typical hypermedia programs
- Explain what stackware is and how it can be used

Computers have been widely used for processing numbers, but applications for processing words and graphics have been relatively limited. This is all changing as new ways of dealing with text and graphics are developed. One of the most exciting concepts related to databases is **hypertext**, a term coined by Ted Nelson in the 1960s. This concept allows you to directly link information in a much less structured way than traditional database programs. An extension of the concept, **hypermedia**, refers to the same way of handling words, sounds, graphics, animation, and video. Users can organize information in the way they think—by association. Its unique navigational methods allow users to browse and quickly search through large bodies of information. This is extremely useful with mass storage optical media. For example, a CD-ROM disk with 500MB can store up to sixteen million cards.

All hypermedia-based programs use a graphical display to represent cards, cells, and windows that are dynamically linked. Links (buttons, arrows, or text) embedded in areas of each card connect it to other cards so that you can easily move from one card to another related card. For example, you can design a series of cards, called a **stack**, illustrating and describing the history of technology. You could then paste a button from the menu onto each wheel in each illustration that links all wheels appearing in the stack. When you then display any of the cards with wheels, you can scroll through all other cards with wheels just by clicking on the wheel button.

Using a hypermedia stack, an auto mechanic could point to the engine on a car and then point to a part on the engine. The program would then display the technical specifications, supplier, and price of the part.

TYPICAL HYPERMEDIA PROGRAMS

The first microcomputer hypermedia program was Owl International's Guide, but the one that first found widespread application was Apple's HyperCard.

The first widely distributed microcomputer program to use this concept was HyperCard, written by Bill Atkinson for the Apple Macintosh. This program allows you to store up to 32KB of data on index-sized cards. The data on any card can be directly linked to data on any other card. The devices you use to do this are called buttons. Owl International's Guide program does not limit the amount of text as does HyperCard.

STACKWARE

The introduction of HyperCard made applications development much easier for most users. **Stackware** is the name coined by Apple for the applications written for HyperCard. Many of these applications are written by users and widely distributed free to other users. Typical applications are reference materials and training courses. Since the program can also execute commands indicated on cards, it is also used as a front end to other applications. For example, dialing a phone number on the computer usually requires an understanding of a telecommunications program. If someone stored the commands that make calls on a card, you could dial a number just by pointing and clicking. Stacks have been developed for retail sale and for in-house use by corporations.

Business Class is an electronic travel planning system that provides thousands of facts about travel, including currency exchange rates, travel schedules, and local customs.

Colophone Incorporated used HyperCard to develop interactive museum displays. Using high-resolution video displays, laser discs, and a Macintosh computer, museum visitors can locate information by pointing to icons and images on the screen.

Dialog Information Services is an on-line information service that supplies more than 300 databases covering a wide range of subjects. Using HyperCard, subscribers can easily access this information without threading their way through menus. HyperCard is like a card catalog that lets users find information in the database much as they would in a library.

The Perseus Project at Boston College, Harvard, and other major universities is using HyperCard to organize 100MB of text and 10,000 images related to classical Greek civilization. With the information stored on optical disks, users can easily browse though the text and images to find what they are looking for.

The Point Foundation has developed a HyperCard stack that contains the entire *Whole Earth Catalog*. Users can browse through the stack or search for specific topics.

PROGRAMMING

Hypertalk, HyperCard's programming language, is used to write **scripts**, programs or macros that automate the program for you and that are executed by HyperCard. This program contains graphics, sound effects, and animation routines.

- **Hypertext** is a subset of **hypermedia**, and it allows you to access information by association.
- Data in a hypermedia program are organized in **stacks** like a stack of 3-by-5-inch cards.
- Data on cards are related to data on other cards by **threads**. These threads are attached to **buttons**. When you click with a mouse on a button, other cards connected to that button by a thread are displayed.
- Stacks that have been developed by other users and are distributed are called **stackware**.
- Most hypermedia programs include a programming or **script language** that lets you automate the program.

REVIEW QUESTIONS

1. What is the difference between hypertext and hypermedia?.
2. What is a stack? Stackware?
3. How are data in a stack related?
4. What is a script language used for?

Part Seven

GRAPHICS APPLICATIONS

Topic 7-1   Business Graphics
Topic 7-2   Types of Business Graphs
Topic 7-3   Analyzing Data Graphically
Topic 7-4   Graph Options
Case Study   Creating a Graph with Lotus 1-2-3
Topic 7-5   Interactive Graphics
Topic 7-6   Computer-Aided Design
Topic 7-7   Displaying and Printing Graphics
Topic 7-8   Graphics Standards
Topic 7-9   Audiovisual Presentations

The adage that a picture is worth a thousand words appropriately applies to computer graphics. In a single glance, graphics can convey information that would be difficult or even impossible to put into words—and you can use your microcomputer to generate graphics very easily.

There are two basic kinds of computer graphics programs.

1. Business graphics programs that you use to create charts and graphs that represent numeric data.

2. Interactive graphics programs that you use for computer-aided design and to generate original, free-form art and designs on the screen. They are called interactive because you create, edit, and manipulate the images directly on the screen.

In this part, we look at both types of graphics programs and the principles behind them. We also introduce you to many graphics applications including the following:

- You can create charts and graphs with business graphics programs to analyze financial and statistical data. For example, you can use graphs to find trends and relationships between sets of numbers like sales, expenses, and profits over a period. You can then print out the final results for distribution to others or for inclusion in a report.

- You can use slide show programs to store a series of graphic images so that you can display them one after another on your computer's screen (or project them onto a larger screen) to support an audiovisual presentation. You can control how long each graph stays displayed on the screen by using the program's automatic advance feature, or you can manually advance the graphs.

- You can create and edit art and illustrations quickly and easily using an interactive graphics painting program.

- You can create and edit designs for printed materials, products, and even buildings using computer-aided design programs.

- You can scan illustrations into the computer's memory and then manipulate them with an interactive graphics program.

- You can photograph graphics that are displayed on the screen and then use the resulting prints or slides in an audiovisual presentation.

- You can use education and entertainment programs that make extensive use of on-screen graphics. Creating them, however, requires extensive programming experience.

REVIEW QUESTIONS

1. What are the two types of graphics programs? What is each used for?
2. List and briefly describe some graphics applications.

Business Graphics

OBJECTIVES

After completing this topic, you will be able to

- Briefly describe the two major types of business graphics programs
- Give examples that demonstrate the usefulness of business graphics

The use of business graphics is greatly expanding. Instead of a calculator, a drafting table, and an artist, today's businesses produce graphics with microcomputers, graphics programs, and graphics printers. The modern method is fast. You can work out a detailed business plan with a spreadsheet, graph the data with the spreadsheet's integrated graphics functions, and plot the results as bar graphs or pie charts in a matter of minutes. The finished graphs can then be transferred

- to a program that enhances them, for example, to add text, select from a variety of typefaces, add boxes around them, and add shades or colors
- to a slide program designed to polish and present them in sequence
- to a desktop publishing program where they can be incorporated into a document

Graphs are important tools in business because managers and analysts often need to find or illustrate patterns in sets of numbers. Many people who do not like interpreting tables of numbers find that business graphs can provide the same information more quickly and efficiently.

For instance, if your profits increased from $5000 to $25,000, this would seem to be a successful trend. But if sales increased from $25,000 to $500,000 over the same period, the growth in profits wouldn't seem nearly as impressive. Obviously, a single set of numbers by themselves tells only part of the story; their relationship to other sets of numbers tells another. How then can numbers be easily related and compared? One way is to present the numbers as graphs that pictorially represent the relationship. When you create graphs, the trend in profits looks great until you plot them to show their relationship to sales (Figure 7-1).

The three examples shown in Figure 7-2 illustrate how valuable graphics can be as a communication tool. The first example presents information in words, the second relies on numbers, and the third presents the information in graphic form. All three presentations give the same information, but there are significant differences in the time it takes you to understand the

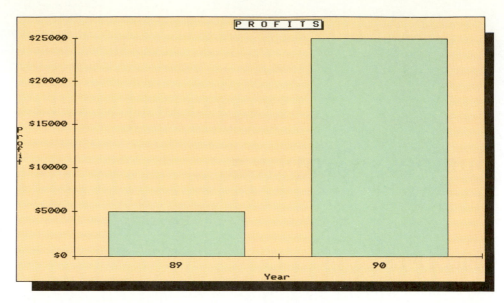

A.

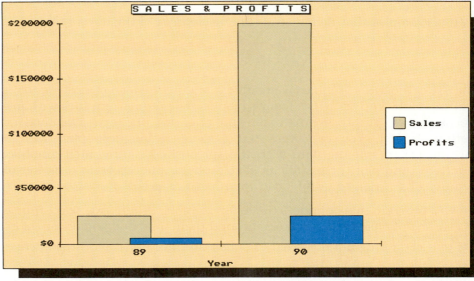

B.

FIGURE 7-1
Trend in Profits
Graphs can reveal
relationships between sets
of numbers. In graph (a),
just the company's profits
have been plotted. The
increase looks dramatic. In
graph (b), the profits have
been plotted against sales.
Now it becomes obvious
that there is a problem.
The company's growth in
profits is lagging behind
its growth in sales.

trends and relationships. Although there has been growth in both sales and the number of stores as the first example explains, it's apparent from the graphs that BBCC's position may not be as strong as Mr. Almost would like you to think. The graphs reveal a disturbing trend. The number of stores has increased dramatically, but the sales of computers have grown only slightly. If prices have not risen substantially during this period, the income of each store must be down considerably.

There are two types of business graphics programs, although the distinctions between them are narrowing: programs that create graphs for analysis and programs that create graphs for presentation to others.

Graphics for analysis programs are integrated into spreadsheet, database, and statistics programs so that data generated on the program can be quickly and easily displayed as a graph (Figure 7-3). This integration increases the speed with which you can generate graphs and also allows the graph to be automatically updated when data in the spreadsheet or database changes. Thus you can use graphs as analytical tools, viewing the results of different scenarios rather than just presenting final results to others.

Byer Beware Computer Corporation reports that its phenomenal growth has continued during the past year. Marvin B. Almost, the chairman, is pleased to announce that sales of computers, BBCC's primary product, have continued their healthy trend. Sales have increased from 3000 computers to 3122 computers over the past five years. Mr. Almost is also pleased to announce that the number of stores in the chain also increased dramatically over the same period from 1000 to more than 3000. This is just another sign of the health and vitality of the Byer Beware Computer Corporation under the leadership of Mr. Almost.

Numeric Description		
Year	Stores	Sales
1988	1000	3000
1989	1300	3030
1990	1690	3060
1991	2197	3091
1992	2856	3122

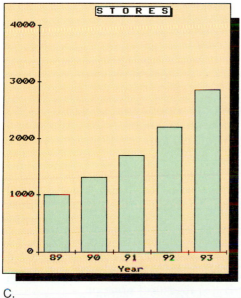 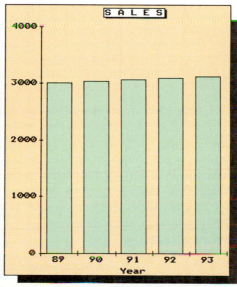

C.

FIGURE 7-2
The Power of Graphics
These three example show how much more descriptive graphics are than words or numbers.

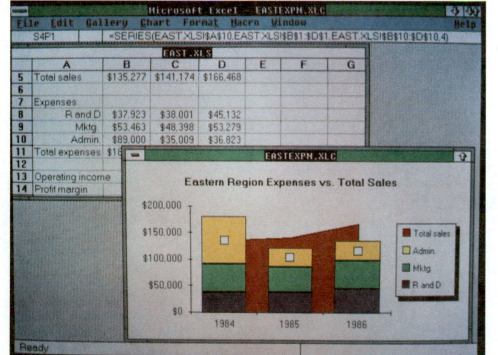

FIGURE 7-3
Graphics for Analysis Programs
Many spreadsheet programs have built-in graphics functions. These graphics programs make it possible to quickly and easily create graphs of the data in your models.
Courtesy of Microsoft® Excel

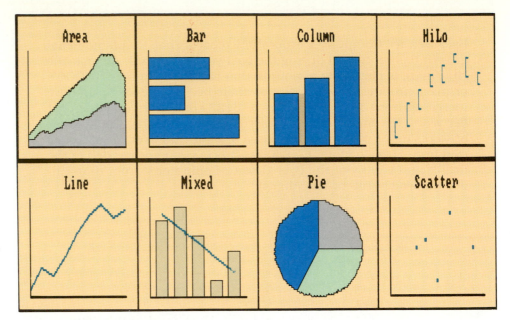

FIGURE 7-4
Presentation Graphics
Presentation graphics programs generally offer a wide selection of graph types and type sizes and typestyles for labels. Microsoft's Chart offers the eight basic graph types shown. Each of these graph types is also available in several versions.

Graphics for presentation programs are standalone programs. They are more powerful than the integrated analysis packages in that they offer a wider variety of controls over the way the graph appears (Figure 7-4). The problem with these programs is that you have to enter the data into the graphics program by keying it in or by transferring it from another program. If you change data in the underlying model, the graph will not reflect the change unless you transfer the new data to the graphics program. These additional steps take time and may discourage you from using the graphs as analytical tools.

SUMMARY AND KEY TERMS

- Graphs can be quickly created using a spreadsheet program.
- Graphs can be transferred to another program to enhance them, to a slide program that presents them in sequence, or incorporated into a document.
- There are two types of **business graphics programs**, those that create graphs used for analysis and those that create graphs for presentation.

REVIEW QUESTIONS

1. List three programs to which you can transfer a graph you created on a spreadsheet.
2. List and briefly describe the two types of business graphics programs.

Types of Business Graphs

OBJECTIVES

After completing this topic, you will be able to

- Describe the differences between discrete and continuous data
- List and describe the different types of business graphs and when to use them

When creating a business graph, first you gather the data and organize it, and then you create the graph for viewing or printing. When creating the graph, you select the type of graph that best illustrates the data. When doing so, most programs allow you to instantly change the type of graph without reentering the data. You can experiment with several graph types to find the one that best illustrates the data. For example, when creating graphs, you are usually graphing discrete or continuous data.

Discrete data consists of values measured at a series of selected points. When plotted on a graph, all data between those points is meaningless. Graphs of this kind are frequently called **time-series graphs** and are used in business to plot sales, profits, inventory, and other important financial values (Figure 7-5).

Continuous data occurs when measurements have been sampled to de-

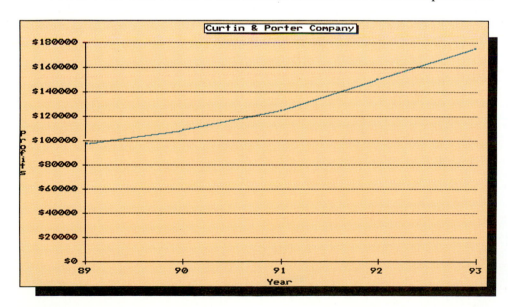

FIGURE 7-5
Discrete Data
Discrete data is a set of values representing specific periods of time or other units. For example, the profits from five annual income statements can be plotted to show trends. If you pick a point on the X axis (the horizontal axis) that falls between periods and read it up to the line connecting data points and then across to the Y axis (the vertical axis), you will not locate the results at that point in time. For example, profits were not $140,000 midway through 1990.

629

FIGURE 7-6
Continuous Data
Continuous data is a set of values that represent an unbroken range of values. For example, an oceanographer can measure the temperature of the water at various depths in the ocean. If samples are measured at increments of 100 feet from the surface down to 1000 feet, a graph can be plotted using the available data points. When the graph is completed, temperatures can be estimated for any depth by reading up from the X axis, which shows depth, and across to the Y axis, which shows temperature.

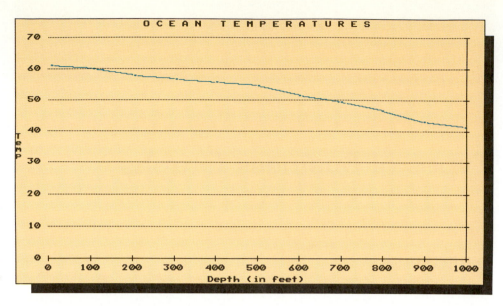

termine a trend. Although each data point is a discrete value, the points are sampled so that when plotted, values between the measured data points can be estimated from the graph (Figure 7-6). This estimation of values falling between data points that were actually measured and plotted is called **interpolation**. When graphing continuous data, a general rule is that the more data points you have measured and plotted, the more accurate the graph is.

Let's look at some examples to see how you would select graphs that illustrate the five-year plan described in Part Five (Figure 7-7).

LINE GRAPHS

A **line graph** (Figure 7-8) plots a series of values, called the data set (or data range), against the X axis (the horizontal axis) and can be used to plot discrete and continuous data.

SCATTER GRAPHS

Scatter graphs plot ranges with symbols that are not connected by lines (Figure 7-9). The sole function of the lines in the line graph is to indicate trends and make the graph easier to read. The scatter graph, though without the lines, contains all the actual data. Whether you use line graphs or scatter graphs is a matter of personal taste.

FIGURE 7-7
Five-Year Plan
The five-year plan illustrates the company's expected sales, costs of goods, and gross margins over a five-year period.

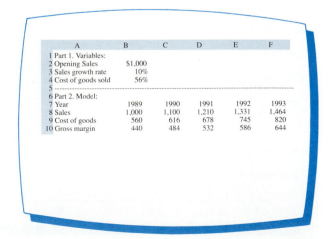

	A	B	C	D	E	F
1	Part 1. Variables:					
2	Opening Sales	$1,000				
3	Sales growth rate	10%				
4	Cost of goods sold	56%				
5	---------------------					
6	Part 2. Model:					
7	Year	1989	1990	1991	1992	1993
8	Sales	1,000	1,100	1,210	1,331	1,464
9	Cost of goods	560	616	678	745	820
10	Gross margin	440	484	532	586	644

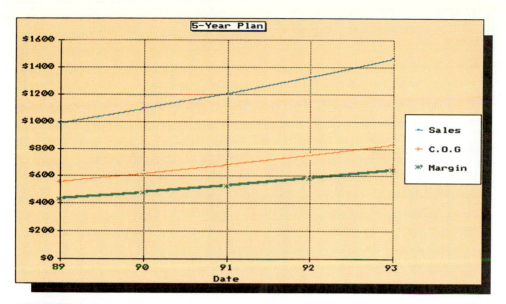

FIGURE 7-8
Line Graph
On a line graph, the X axis contains a series of descriptive labels with no numeric value—here, the annual periods covered by the five-year plan. The data points plotted against these periods are indicated by symbols connected by lines. The three data sets from rows 8, 9, and 10 of the model are plotted against the X axis. The legends at the right-hand side of the graph identify each data set with a label and the same symbol used to plot it on the graph. For example, sales are indicated by dots, cost of goods sold by plus signs, and gross margins by stars. Each of these symbols on the graph represents actual data points from the model. For example, 1988 sales on the model are $1,000. This value can be seen on the graph by reading up from the 88 label on the graph's X axis to the sales line and then reading across to the Y axis to find the value.

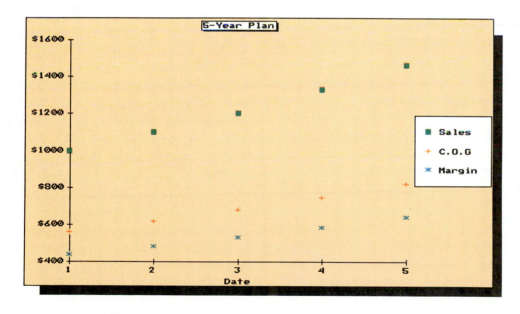

FIGURE 7-9
Scatter Graph
This scatter graph plots the same information as the line graph in Figure 7-8, but the lines connecting the symbols have been removed. The lines connecting the symbols on the line graph did not provide meaningful information—no sales or gross margins were achieved, and no expenses were incurred between the periods.

BAR GRAPHS

Bar graphs are like a series of snapshots taken at intervals. When the bars on the graph are lined up in some meaningful order, they show relationships, changes, and trends. All bars on a bar graph start at the zero line.

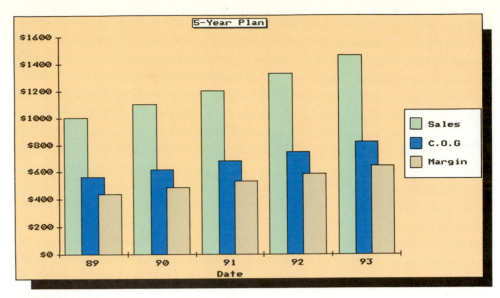

FIGURE 7-10
Bar Graph
This bar graph was created using the same X axis and data sets as those used for the line graph in Figure 7-8. On this graph, however, the values are represented by bars rather than by points connected by lines. Since three data sets were plotted, there are three bars for each period on the graph. The legends used to identify each bar have also changed; instead of symbols, patterns are now used. Each bar represents an actual value on the model. As this graph illustrates, the primary purpose of graphs is to reveal trends and relationships. In most cases, it is difficult to determine exact values by reading a graph. If you read across the tops of the three bars for 1989 to the Y axis, you can see that in this period, sales were $1,000, cost of goods sold was about $550 (actually $560 if you look at the number on the model itself), and the gross margin was about $400 (actually $440). The trends over the five years can be seen by noting the change in sizes for matching bars for each period.

Positive values are indicated by bars that extend up from this base line; negative values, by bars that extend down. Bar graphs are particularly appropriate for discrete data, for example, if you want to graph the sales of several divisions within a company or make a comparison of sales by product (Figure 7-10).

STACKED-BAR GRAPHS

Stacked-bar graphs are similar to bar graphs, but instead of the bars being arranged side by side, they are stacked on top of each other. A stacked-bar graph can show several sets of data at the same time (Figure 7-11).

XY GRAPHS

At first glance, **XY graphs** can look like line graphs, and under some circumstances, the two are identical. But because the XY graph uses values instead of labels on the X axis, it can do much more than a line graph. For example, XY graphs can be used to find correlations between two or more sets of data. Whereas a line graph might show you the increase in a line item over time, an XY graph could show how that increase is related to another line item, such as net sales or profits (Figure 7-12). Table 7-1 shows the pairs plotted on the graph. The data points are located above the appropriate values on the scaled X axis.

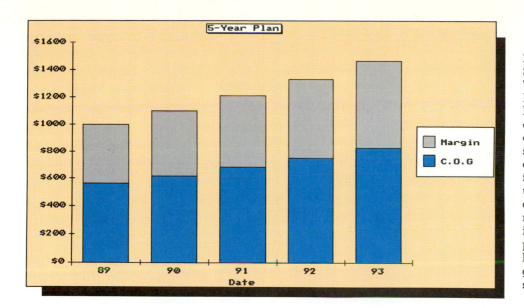

FIGURE 7-11
Stacked-Bar Graph
The stacked-bar graph
looks like the bar graph in
Figure 7-10, but the values
are stacked on top of each
other instead of side by
side. The total height of
each bar is equal to sales
for the period and is made
up of two components—
cost of goods and gross
margins. If sales were
included, the graph would
plot twice its actual values
because cost of goods and
gross margins are equal to
sales.

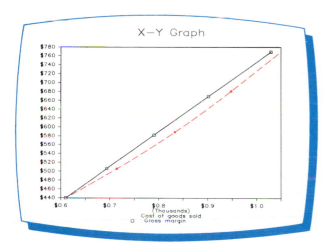

FIGURE 7-12
XY Graph
In this *XY* graph, the *X* axis has been changed from
the periods used in the previous examples. Instead,
it uses the values for cost of goods sold on row 9 so
that gross margins are now plotted against cost of
goods rather than over a period of time. The
resulting graph has taken on a new appearance.
First of all, the *X* axis is scaled just like the *Y* axis;
its smallest and largest values are determined by
the data being plotted. The values on the graph are
read as pairs of values. Cost of goods sold values
are paired against the corresponding gross margin
values. For example, when cost of goods sold are
$560, gross margins are $440.

TABLE 7-1
Values Plotted on XY Graph

Cost of Goods Sold	Gross Margins
$560	$440
644	506
741	582
852	669
979	770

PIE CHARTS

A **pie chart** is like a single bar on a stacked-bar graph; it can show only one
set of data at a time. To compare different sets of data (for example, changes
between one period and another), you must create and compare more than

TYPES OF BUSINESS GRAPHS

633

FIGURE 7-13
Pie Chart
Since pie charts can plot
only one set of values, the
data sets from the model
used to create the pie chart
here include the cost of
goods and gross margins
for the first year. The pie
chart is shown as they
normally appear (a) and
with one slice "exploded"
to emphasize it (b). In both
cases, the entire pie
represents sales, and each
slice indicates the relative
size of the two
components.

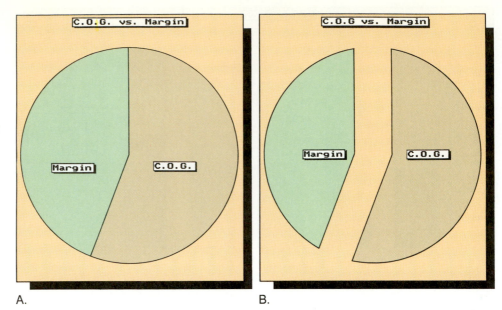

A.

B.

one pie chart. Pie charts are generally used to illustrate relationships such
as sales of various products in a product line and market shares. The pie
represents the "whole" or 100 percent, and the individual slices represent
parts of the whole. The relative sizes of the parts are indicated by the size of
the pie slices (Figure 7-13).

AREA GRAPHS

Area graphs (also called surface graphs or stacked-line graphs) have some of
the characteristics of both stacked-bar and line graphs. Like stacked-bar
graphs, they stack the values on top of each other. But instead of representing values with bars, they represent them with lines (Figure 7-14).

FIGURE 7-14
Area Graph
Here, the same two data
ranges used for the
stacked-bar graph in
Figure 7-11 are plotted as
an area graph.

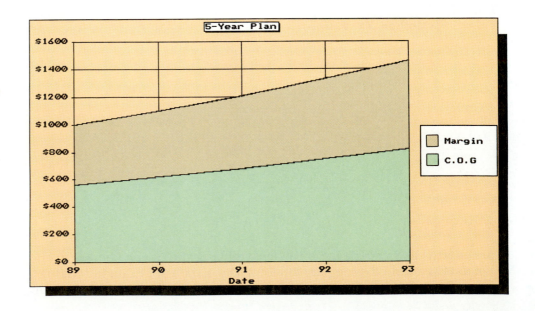

GRAPHICS APPLICATIONS

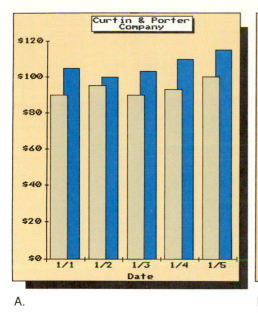

A.

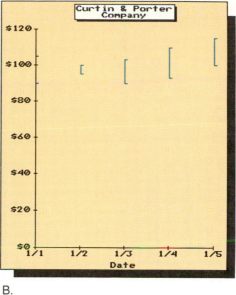

B.

FIGURE 7-15
Hi-Lo Graph
FIGURE 7-15
Hi-Lo Graph
Here are two graphs. One
(a) is a bar graph plotting
stock prices over a five-day
period. The other (b) is a
hi-lo graph that shows the
same information in an
easier-to-read format. The
bars are compressed to a
single line with their
values indicated by tic
marks.

HI-LO GRAPHS

Hi-lo graphs are similar to bar graphs except that they use vertical lines
with tic marks to indicate more than one value for each period. They are
widely used to plot data such as the high, low, opening, and closing prices of
stocks (Figure 7-15).

COMBINATION GRAPHS

Combination graphs display one or more data sets as one type of graph, perhaps a bar graph, and other sets of data as another type, usually a line or
area graph (Figure 7-16). Using combination graphs like this is one way to
emphasize one set of data while still showing its relationship to other sets of
data.

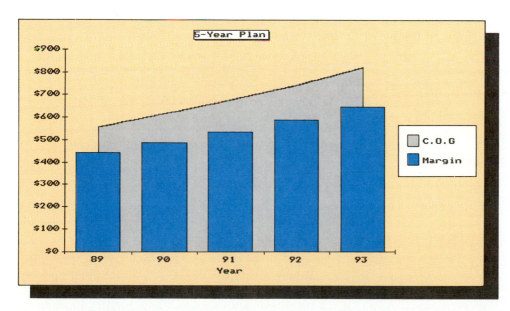

FIGURE 7-16
Combination Graph
This combination graph
plots the same data as the
stacked-bar in Figure 7-11.
Here, the data for gross
margins is plotted as a bar
graph, and the data for
cost of goods is plotted as
an area graph. The bars
representing margins
stand out from the other
data on the graph.

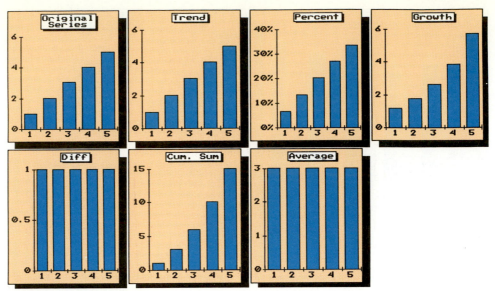

FIGURE 7-17
Statistical Techniques

Microsoft's Chart will take your original data set and create a new data set that you can graph using one of the following statistical techniques:

Original series shows the original series of values 1 through 5 entered as data to be analyzed.

Trend calculates a new series using the least squares approximation technique.

Percentage calculates each value in the series as a percentage of the total series.

Growth calculates a new series as an exponential growth curve.

Difference subtracts subsequent values to show the differences between the original data points.

Cumulative sum makes the first value in the new series the same as the first value of the original series and then adds the second value to it to create a new second value.

Average calculates the sum of the values in the series and divides it by the number of data points in the series.

STATISTICAL GRAPHS

Some programs allow you to enter your data once and then use the graphics program to analyze it using statistical techniques (Figure 7-17).

SUMMARY AND KEY TERMS

- Graphs represent two types of data: **discrete** and **continuous**.
- Typical graph types include line, scatter, bar, stacked-bar, *XY*, pie, area, and hi-lo. Some programs allow you to combine graph types on the same graph, for example, lines and bars or bars and areas. Other programs will automatically perform and graph a statistical analysis of your data.

REVIEW QUESTIONS

1. How does discrete data differ from continuous data? What types of graphs or charts would you use for each?

2. What is interpolation?

3. List four basic graph types, and discuss briefly what each type is used for.

4. If you were going to plot monthly sales and expenses for a twelve-month period, which type of graph(s) would best represent this data?

5. Under what conditions would an *XY* graph be more helpful than a line graph?

GRAPHICS APPLICATIONS

Analyzing Data Graphically

OBJECTIVES

After completing this topic, you will be able to

- Describe how to use graphs to analyze data
- List and describe several graph dos and don'ts

When using graphs to present and analyze data, you should understand a few principles about how to plot and read the graphs. It is especially important to know how graphs can be misleading if the data is not properly presented. Here is a list of things to consider when graphing information.

- Keep in mind that the point of charts and graphs is to communicate.
- Before creating a graph, consider carefully what point you want to make, and then select the data and graph type that best illustrates that point.
- Do not plot too many data sets, or the graph will be hard to read. There is a tendency to plot all the available data when a selective approach might make the point better.
- Do not plot ranges of small values on the same graph with large values. The expanded Y axis needed to accommodate the larger values will flatten and distort the smaller values against the X axis.
- Graphics programs automatically create graphs using the data sets you supply. To do so, they take the smallest and largest values in the sets and scale the Y axis so that both extremes fit onto the graph. Automatic scaling has advantages and disadvantages (Figures 7-18).
- When comparing two or more graphs, make sure their scales are the same. What may seem to be parallel trends might actually be taking place on two very different levels. For example, be sure you consider the Y-axis scales on your graphs. Figure 7-19 illustrates how easily distortions can be introduced into graphics. Unless you take the time to read and understand the graph scales used, you can be misled or mislead others.
- Be sure the X-axis data points actually represent the data (Figure 7-20). What seems to represent minor variations in data could really be major swings, or vice versa. The slope of a plotted line has no real meaning until it is measured against a scale.

FIGURE 7-18
Automatic Scaling
When automatic scaling is used to create two or more graphs that are to be compared, each graph may have a different Y- axis scale (a). This makes a comparison of graphs very difficult. If you didn't read them carefully, you would think that Actual results were almost identical to Projected results. A careful reading, however, would reveal that the Y axis is different on the two graphs. Values on the Projected graph range from 0 to $500, whereas values on the Actual graph range from 0 to $400.
Most programs allow you to manually scale graphs so that you can specify the upper and lower ranges to be plotted on the Y axis (b). When the same two graphs are scaled manually, the Y axes are made identical. Notice how much easier it is to compare values on the two graphs now that they have the same scale.

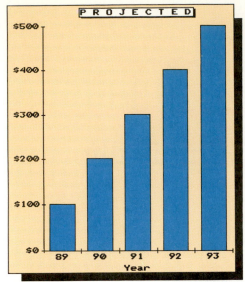
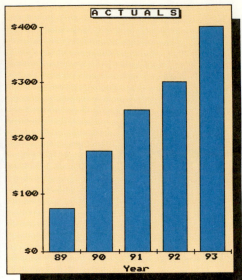

A.

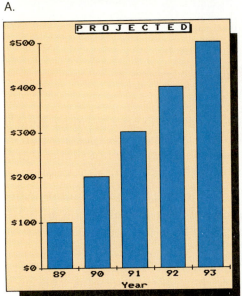
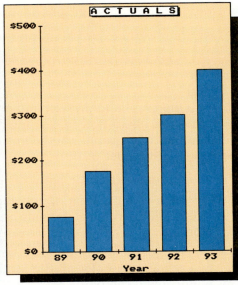

B.

FIGURE 7-19
Different Y-axis Scales
These two graphs showing imaginary inflation rates for the years 1985 through 1994 have identical data plotted, but they use different scales on the Y axis. Even though the data are identical, the choice of scales might lead the careless viewer to two different conclusions. Although both graphs show the consumer price index rising from 300 to 390, the graph on the left suggests that inflation is raging, whereas the graph on the right suggests it is rising gradually.

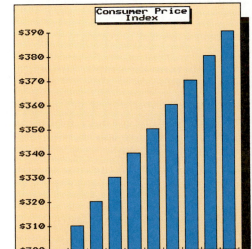
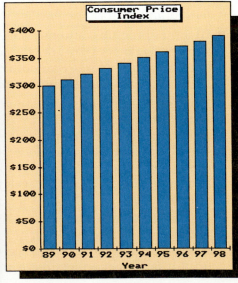

GRAPHICS APPLICATIONS

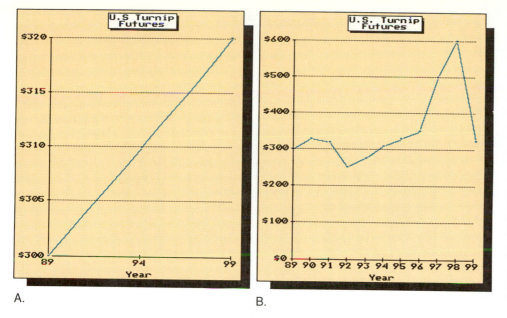

A.

B.

FIGURE 7-20
Different X-axis Scales
If you choose data points that are too far apart, you may miss short-term changes. One graph shows a steady rise in the value of turnip futures (a). The other graph shows that there have been major short-term swings in their value (b). Neither graph's data is incorrect, but again, each graph can lead to a different conclusion. Sometimes it is helpful to intentionally suppress short-term swings to detect or illustrate a possible long-term trend. But it is never helpful to do this unintentionally.

- When creating area graphs, plot them so that irregularities in one data set do not distort the data plotted above it (Figure 7-21).

- One problem with stacked-bar graphs is that the data ranges you plot may not add up to a meaningful total (Figure 7-22).

- There are two things to avoid when creating pie charts: The data ranges may not add up to a meaningful whole, and cramming too many segments into the same pie chart makes it difficult to read and interpret (Figure 7-23).

- When using many graphics functions integrated into spreadsheet programs, make sure the data ranges exactly parallel the X axis. If the X axis uses labels or values from a row of cells, the data ranges should be rows of cells. For example, if the X axis is the range of cells between columns A and F, the data ranges should be the same.

FIGURE 7-21
Area Graph Distortions
The same two data ranges are plotted on these area graphs. Here, one graph (a) plots a data set with significant variations below another data set without variations. The wide variations in the lower data set are reflected in the other range, which is plotted on top of it. The graph makes it look as if there have been major changes in both sets of data during the period. In the other graph (b), the order of the ranges is reversed, and the graph reflects the data more accurately. You can clearly see that only one set of data changed, whereas the other remained unchanged.

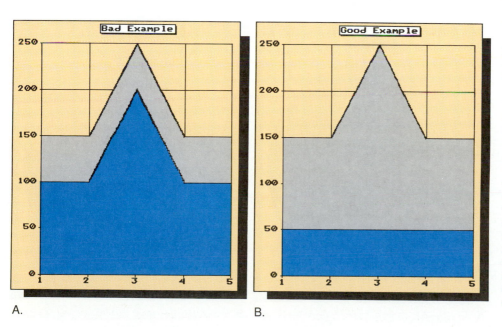

A.

B.

FIGURE 7-22
Stacked-Bar Graph Distortions

Sales have been plotted along with the cost of goods sold and gross margins (a). Since sales equals cost of goods sold plus gross margins, the graph is misleading. For this reason, when creating stacked-bar graphs, make sure your data ranges are components of a total that has some significance to you. If you plot parts of the whole as percentages instead of plotting the actual values (b), the bars will all total 100 percent and fill the graph from top to bottom. This makes it easy to compare the sizes of different components in relation to the whole. Although the stacked-bar graph in Figure 7-11 makes it appear that cost of goods and margins have been growing, this graph shows that their relationship, as a percentage of sales, has remained relatively constant over the five-year period.

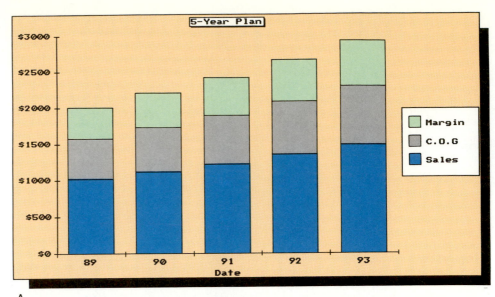

A.

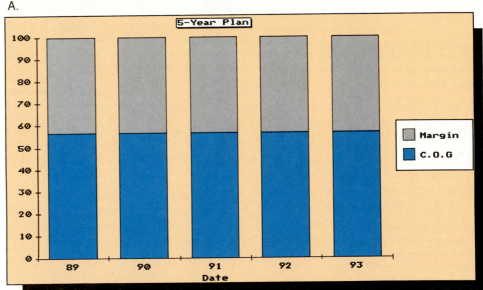

B.

FIGURE 7-23
Pie Chart Distortions

If net sales had been included in the pie chart, you would have the same problem as you have with bar graphs if the total does not add up to a meaningful figure (a). Here, net sales take up half the pie, and its two components, cost of goods and gross margins, take up the other half. Cramming too many segments into the same pie chart makes it very difficult to read and interpret (b).

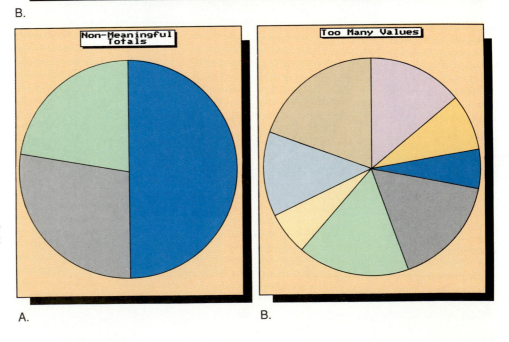

A.

B.

GRAPHICS APPLICATIONS

- If you can control the graph's **aspect ratio** (the ratio between its width and height), do not stretch it out until it is too wide and narrow or too tall and narrow since either will distort data plotted on the graph.

- Don't jump to any conclusions about trends. For example, with just a few data points, a line graph will show an even line or curve that might have nothing to do with the real situation. Study your data carefully, and remember, the more data you have in the data sets, the more accurate your analysis is likely to be.

SUMMARY AND KEY TERMS

- Graphs can be misleading if you do not plot your data correctly.
- Be careful when setting or reading the Y axis on graphs. If the scales do not match on two graphs, it is more difficult to compare them.
- Be careful when setting or reading the X axis. If the graph does not have enough data points, the data could be misleading.
- On stacked-bar graphs and pie charts, make sure the data sets add up to some meaningful total. Do not plot any data that is part of any other data being plotted. For example, do not plot both total sales and the sales of an individual item on the same graph.

REVIEW QUESTIONS

1. Graphs can be misleading for several reasons. List some graph types and ways distortions of the data can be introduced and prevented.

2. What problems are caused when someone tries to compare two graphs with different Y-axis scales?

3. What problem can occur when too few data points are plotted?

TOPIC 7-4

Graph Options

OBJECTIVE

After completing this topic, you will be able to

- List and briefly describe the types of options available to make business graphs more effective

Business graphics programs generally offer you a lot of control over the way your data is presented on a graph or chart. Here are some of the many options available on most graphics programs.

- One or two lines at the top of the graph are used to enter the graph title or heading.
- The X-axis title describes the range of labels or values against which data is being plotted.
- The Y-axis title describes the data ranges being plotted.
- Data labels are inserted inside the graph area to describe data ranges.
- Legends identify the symbols or patterns used to plot graphs so that data ranges can be distinguished from one another.
- Data ranges are the series of numbers that you plot.
- Grid lines can be displayed vertically, horizontally, or both vertically and horizontally to make data points easier to read across or down to the values on the axes.
- Automatic scaling is normally the default setting. The Y axis expands to include the largest and smallest data point being plotted. If you generate a series of graphs by changing data in the model, the scale on each may be different.
- Manual scaling can be used to override the program's automatic scaling of the Y axis. On XY graphs, the X axis can also be manually scaled.
- Scale formats can be used to control the way numbers on the axes are displayed.
- Choice of type (fonts and sizes) is available on some programs to format legends, titles, and other text on the graph.
- Line thickness can be varied to emphasize or deemphasize selected data ranges.

642

- Lines and symbols can be varied on line graphs and *XY* graphs. The data points can be represented by symbols by themselves or connected with lines. When data labels are used, the symbols and lines can both be suppressed so that data points are indicated only by the data labels.

- Colors can be specified so that each range of data on the graph is displayed in a different color.

- Patterns used to differentiate data ranges on bar graphs and pie charts can be changed on black-and-white displays to distinguish them more easily.

- Overlays allow you to superimpose data ranges—perhaps a line graph of sales on top of a bar graph of profits.

- Skip is used when the *X* axis gets crowded with a series of long numbers or dates like January 1987 through December 1989. Sometimes, the labels will even overlap. To prevent this, some programs let you "skip" some labels, for example, so that only every other label is displayed.

- Often there are times when you want to create more than one graph of the same data. When you do this, there must be a provision to save graph descriptions in a library so that you can recall them later. Programs do this by letting you name the graph or save the graph description.

- Comment and note blocks provide a few lines where you can enter comments on the graph.

- A slide show feature allows you to display a series of graphs on the screen in any order you want and to control how long they are on the screen.

- Print density controls can be used to print graphs on a dot-matrix printer in one or more densities. Each option makes the indicated number of passes over the characters, slightly offsetting the dots each time to create a darker, denser image.

CASE STUDY
Creating a Graph with Lotus 1-2-3

Let's see, step by step, how you use Lotus 1-2-3 to graph the five-year plan that we discussed in the case study in Part Five (Figure A).

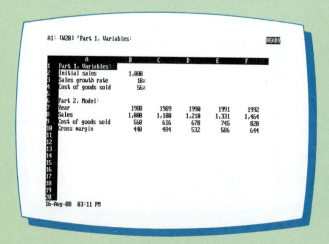

FIGURE A
The Five-Year Plan Model
The five-year plan calculates sales, costs of goods sold, and gross margins for a five-year period.

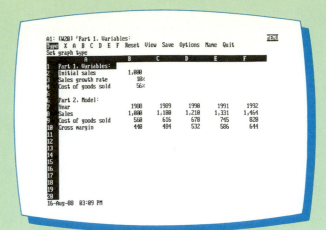

FIGURE B
The Main Graph Menu
The Lotus 1-2-3 Main Graph menu lists all the basic commands you use to create, view, and save graphs.

Step 1. Display the Graph Menu You begin by creating or retrieving the model you want to graph. To create a graph of the model, you press /G (for *Graph*) to display the Main Graph menu on the screen. Many of the graph commands are entered from this menu or from the Graph Options menu.

Step 2. Make Basic Selections from the Main Graph Menu You use the Main Graph menu to select the type of graph you want to use and to set both the X axis and the data ranges. You also choose commands from this menu for both viewing and saving graphs (Figure B).

Step 3. Use the Graph Options Menu When you want to add various refinements to your graph, such as adding titles or formatting the numbers used to label the X and Y axes, you use the Graph Options menu (Figure C). You select this menu from the Main Graph menu. Here are some of the choices from the Graph Options menu and how they affect the graph.

- *Legend* adds legends to the bottom of the graph.
- *Format* selects symbols, lines, or both at or between data points on the graph.
- *Titles* adds titles to the top of the graph (up to two lines) and to the X and Y axes.
- *Grid* adds horizontal or vertical grid lines, or both, on the graph.

FIGURE C
The Graph Options Menu
The Lotus 1-2-3 Graph Options menu lists all the commands you use to fine-tune your graph. For example, you can control scales, add legends and titles, and select colors for the data ranges.

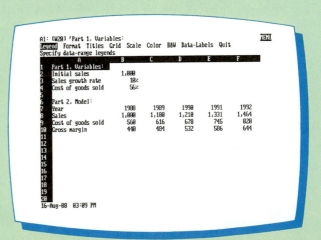

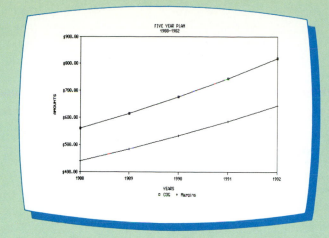

FIGURE D
The Graph
A graph created on Lotus 1-2-3 is suitable for analysis and changes whenever the data in the model changes.

- *Scale* formats the numbers displayed on the X and Y axes.
- *Color* displays the graph in color. (This option works only if you have a color display.)
- *Quit* returns you to the Main Graph menu, from which you can view or save the graph.

Step 4. View the Graph After specifying the options for the graph, you select *Quit* from the Graph Options menu to return to the Main Graph menu. You then select *View* from that menu to display the graph (Figure D).

- Graphics programs provide many options. Typical options include titles, data labels, legends, grid lines, automatic or manual scaling, scale formats, colors, and graph type.

SUMMARY AND KEY TERMS

1. What is a data label? A legend?
2. What is the difference between manual and automatic scaling?
3. If your graph has labels that overlap on the X axis, what option would you use to correct the problem?

REVIEW QUESTIONS

Interactive Graphics

OBJECTIVE

After completing this topic, you will be able to

■ Describe interactive graphics programs and what they are used for

The business graphics we have so far discussed have all been created by the program based on the data you supply. But another family of graphics software allows you to directly interact with the screen using a mouse, light pen, or graphics tablet to draw or modify images on the screen. These images can be created entirely on the screen, or you can scan them into the computer and then refine them. New hardware also lets you enter images into the computer using a video camera. With this equipment, you can even capture images from TV broadcasts.

Though some limited work had already been done on using computers for graphics, in 1962, Ivan Sutherland, a graduate student at MIT, published his doctoral dissertation "Sketchpad: A Man-Machine Graphical Communication System," and this laid the groundwork for later developments in the field. Sutherland wrote

I think of a computer display as a window on Alice's Wonderland in which a programmer can depict either objects that obey well-known natural laws or purely imaginary objects that follow laws he has written into his program. Through computer displays I have landed an airplane on the deck of a moving carrier, observed a nuclear particle hit a potential wall, flown in a rocket at nearly the speed of light and watched a computer reveal its innermost workings.[1]

Painting and drawing programs that let you create free-form illustrations on the screen have gained increasing popularity with many users. Most of these programs provide a set of tools and patterns that are used to create images.

Architects, draftspeople, engineers, and designers are all moving toward the use of interactive graphics to increase their productivity. And the technology needed to support these complicated and powerful programs on microcomputers is rapidly being developed.

---

[1]Ivan Sutherland, *Scientific American*, June 1970.

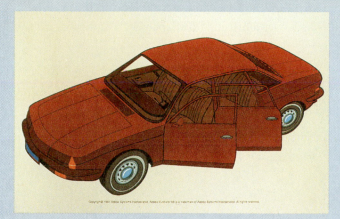

INTERACTIVE GRAPHICS

Interactive graphics program, in the hands of skilled artists, can create exceptionally high quality images.

This automobile was drawn using an interactive graphics program. It would be ideal for a book or magazine illustration. Courtesy of Adobe Systems

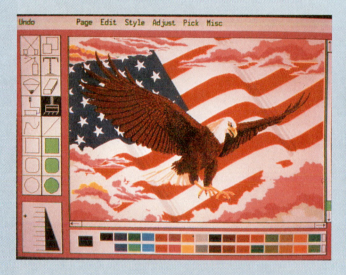

Most graphics programs have menus that display icons for the tools and picture elements the artist has to choose from. Courtesy of ZSoft

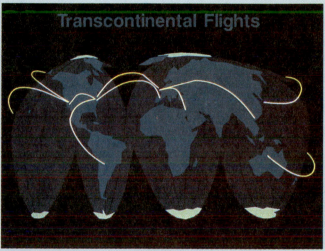

Graphics can be created directly on the screen and diplayed there for others to look at or analyze. Courtesy of IBM Corporation.

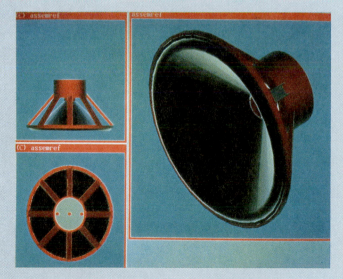

Technical illustrations can be prepared that show the design of products. Courtesy of AutoDesk

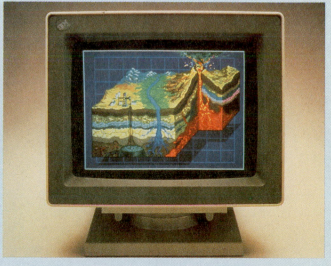

Graphics can be created that convey ideas like this map of the world illustrating the routes for transcontinental flights. Courtesy of Software Publishing Corporation

SUMMARY AND KEY TERMS

- **Interactive graphics programs** allow you to draw directly on the screen.
- These programs are used by architects, draftspeople, engineers, and designers.

REVIEW QUESTIONS

1. What hardware devices can you use to create drawings on the screen?
2. List two ways images can be entered into the computer rather than drawn on the screen.

Computer-Aided Design

OBJECTIVE

After completing this topic, you will be able to

■ Describe the types of programs used in computer-aided design

Computers and new programs are revolutionizing the way design, engineering, and manufacturing are done. The advantage of these programs is that they can create and store large numbers of elements—called **boilerplate**—that can be used as building blocks. For example, a designer sitting at a drafting table uses a T square, triangles, and other drawing aids to create a drawing a line at a time. On the computer, the designer uses the keyboard, a light pen, or a digitizing tablet to create the drawing on the screen. Elements like lines, boxes, circles, and patterns can be selected from a library of stored elements and positioned on the screen. Any of the elements can be easily resized, moved, or copied elsewhere on the drawing. Another advantage is that the program will zoom any small section up to a full-screen view so that the designer can add fine details.

When a designer works on paper, the scale of the drawing is determined before the first line is drawn. On a computer, the design is created on the screen, so the scale can be decided, and changed, when the final drawing is printed out on a printer or plotter.

The availability of these tools doesn't eliminate the subjective decisions the designer has to make. They just make completing the working drawings faster and easier.

Architects, engineers, and draftspeople use **computer-aided design** (**CAD**) and **computer-aided design and drafting** (**CADD**) programs to greatly speed up the conceptualization of designs and their conversion into working drawings. They can create scaled models on the screen, rotate them in two or three dimensions, and revise them with these programs.

Computer-aided design programs are designed to work with two-dimensional and three-dimensional drawings. Two-dimensional programs are used for architectural drafting, organizational charts, flow diagrams, and electrical circuit drawings. Some two-dimensional programs offer you **plan views** and **elevation views** so that you can see three-dimensional objects in all three dimensions (Figure 7-24). Three-dimensional programs are used in architecture and for interior drawings and to model other three-dimensional objects. These programs can create drawings identical to those created on a two-dimensional program but also offer additional views including **perspective views** and **wire-frame views** (Figure 7-25).

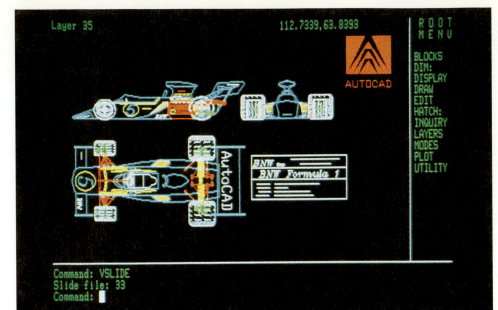

FIGURE 7-24
Two-Dimensional Programs
On two-dimension
programs, the plan view
(a) shows the object as
viewed from above. The
elevation view (b) shows
the object from four sides
as if you were walking
around it to view each side
face on. Courtesy of
Autocad

FIGURE 7-25
Three-Dimensional Programs
On three dimensional programs, the perspective
view (a) shows lines converging toward a vanishing
point, just like railroad tracks seem to converge
toward the horizon. Courtesy of AutoDesk. The wire-
frame view (b) shows an outline of the object. These
wire-frame views can be rotated on the screen, and
some programs allow you to change the wire-frame
view into another view by removing hidden lines
and then filling in solid areas with shadings. You
can also place "lights" in the image, and the
program automatically calculates highlights and
shadows. Courtesy of Autocad

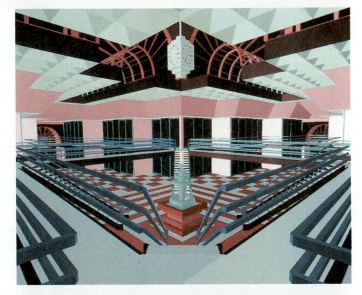

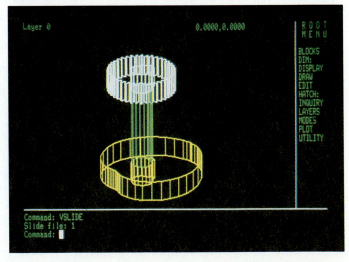

Computer-Aided Engineering and Manufacturing

Besides computer-aided design programs, engineers use **computer-aided engineering** (**CAE**) programs to perform analysis. For example, these programs tell engineers if the beam they have specified can withstand the loads it will have to carry. When the design is completed, utility programs can be used to generate related documents like a parts list (called a bill of materials) that itemizes all the elements used in the design. When the designs are finished, **computer-aided manufacturing** (**CAM**) programs can be used to produce the instructions for the computers that control the machinery that produces the product.

SUMMARY AND KEY TERMS

- Architects and others use **computer-aided design** programs to create detailed drawings.

- These programs allow users to create and save **boilerplate**, elements that can be retrieved and used over and over again.

- These programs can work with two-dimensional or three-dimensional drawings.

REVIEW QUESTIONS

1. What views can be created and displayed by a two-dimensional computer-aided design program?

2. What additional views can be created and displayed by three-dimensional programs?

Displaying and Printing Graphics

OBJECTIVES

After completing this topic, you will be able to

- Describe the basic types of graphic displays

- Explain how graphic images are displayed on the screen

- Describe typical graphic input devices

- Describe the types of devices used to print graphic images

FIGURE 7-26
Cathode Ray Tube
A CRT contains three key elements: an electron gun, deflection plates, and a phosphorous screen. The electron gun emits a stream of electrons, and a focusing system focuses this electron stream onto the screen. Monochrome displays have one electron gun, and color monitors have three—one for each of the primary colors red, green, and blue. The CRT contains two sets of deflection plates or coils. When charged with electricity, these move the beam of electrons horizontally and vertically. One set sweeps the beam from left to right across the screen. The other moves it up and down the screen. As the moving electron beam sweeps across the screen, it "paints" an image on the photosensitive phosphorus surface.

When creating graphic images, you want to be able to display them on the screen and then print them out. We introduced the hardware and techniques used to do this in Part One. In this topic, we look at some of these devices and techniques in greater detail.

GRAPHICS DISPLAYS

The type of display screen you use determines the kind of graphics you can display. All displays used for detailed graphics use a cathode ray tube (CRT) similar to the one in your TV set (Figure 7-26). Most color displays also use CRTs to create the image (Figure 7-27). These CRT displays fall into one of two categories, digital or analog.

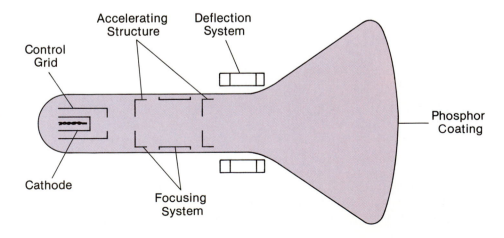

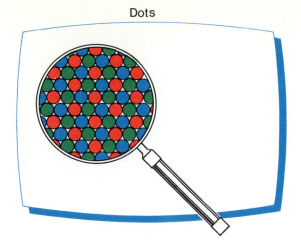

Dots

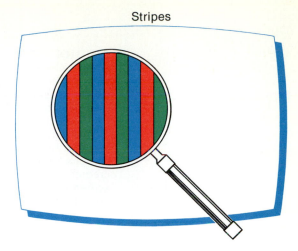

Stripes

Digital Displays

Digital displays are those that follow the standards introduced with the original IBM PC computers. They use a color graphics adapter (CGA) or an enhanced color graphics adapter (EGA) to create an image on the screen. Each of these adapters has its own **scanning rate**, the frequency at which the signal is sent to the display. For example, a CGA adapter has a horizontal scanning rate of 15.75 kilohertz (thousands of cycles per second), and an EGA adapter has a scanning rate of 21.85 kilohertz. A display must match the adapter's scanning rate, or problems occur. Until recently, you had to buy a new display screen when you changed adapters. This problem has been solved with the introduction of **multisync monitors** (also called multiscan monitors). These displays analyze the frequency of the signal coming from the adapter and adjust automatically.

Analog Displays

Analog displays were introduced with IBM's PS/2 computer line. Unlike digital displays where each pixel can be on or off or display only a few colors, analog technology makes many more colors possible. Analog displays can display any set of 256 colors at one time, chosen from more than 262,000 colors.

FIGURE 7-27
Color CRT
Color screens are coated with three different types of phosphor arranged in a pattern of small dots, rectangles, or stripes. One kind glows red when hit by the electron beam, one glows blue, and the other glows green. A mask between the electron guns and the screen allows each of the three electron guns to illuminate only the phosphorus matching its color. The relative intensities of the three beams produce the range of colors on the screen.

HOW IMAGES ARE CREATED ON THE SCREEN

Graphic images are painted onto the screen by an electron gun. Two techniques are used to paint these images on the screen, vector graphics and raster graphics.

Vector Graphics

Vector graphics displays (also called stroke or calligraphic displays) move the electron beam so that it draws straight lines between points on the screen, like a connect-the-dots puzzle. The programmer has only to tell the computer where each line should begin and end (Figure 7-28). Vector graphics displays are fast and create crisp images, two of the reasons they are widely used for computer-aided design and arcade video games. Their major disadvantage is that they cannot fill in solid spaces with color; they can create only line drawings. A vector graphics display creates a circle by

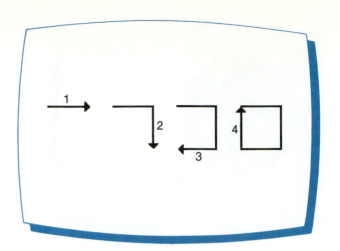

FIGURE 7-28
Images Created with a Vector Graphic Display
When an image is created using vector graphics, the CRT's electron beam moves between points to create a line. For example, a vector graphics display creates a square on the screen by moving the electron beam from one corner to the next as it draws four straight lines.

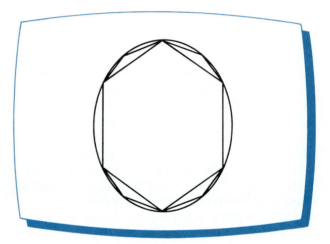

FIGURE 7-29
Images Created with a Vector Graphic Display
On a vector graphics display, the more straight lines used to construct a circle, the higher the resolution and the truer the circle.

drawing a polygon. The resolution, or degree of detail and sharpness, of a vector graphics display is determined by the number of straight lines it uses to create circles and curved lines (Figure 7-29).

Raster Graphics

Raster graphics displays are the most common display found in microcomputer systems. These displays do not create images by moving the electron beam between specified points on the screen. Instead, they sweep the beam across and down the screen in a regular, unchanging pattern, much as your eyes do as they read this page (Figure 7-30). Figure 7-31 shows the way a raster display creates squares and circles.

Some raster displays draw alternating lines on the screen. On the first pass, they paint every other line. On the next pass, they fill in the alternate lines left blank on the first pass. Displays that use this approach are called **interlaced displays**. Displays that fill in each line without skipping alternate lines are called **noninterlaced displays**.

The number of pixels, and hence the screen's resolution, is determined by the number of rows and columns the screen is divided into and the size of each pixel. The aspect ratio, the ratio of rows to columns, determines the shape of the pixels. An aspect ratio other than 1 may cause some distortion of circles and diagonal lines.

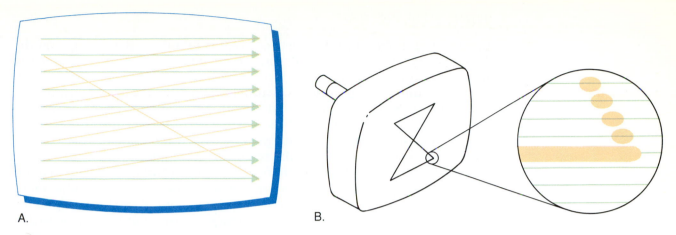

A.   B.

FIGURE 7-30
Raster Graphics Display Sweep Pattern
On a raster graphics display, the electron beam begins its first sweep in the
upper left-hand corner of the screen. The horizontal deflection plates or coils, to
which a voltage is applied, sweep the beam horizontally across the screen (a).
When it reaches the end of the line, a change in voltage returns the beam to the
left side of the screen, and the vertical deflection plates move it down where it
begins its next horizontal sweep. The intensity of the electron beam is greatly
reduced during the backward sweep (called the retrace), so no image is painted
on the screen. After the beam sweeps across the last line on the screen, it returns
to the upper left-hand corner to begin again. This entire process is called a raster
scan, and the entire screen is painted fifteen to thirty times per second to refresh
the image so that it does not fade. As the beam sweeps across the screen, it is
turned on and off to create lines and dots on the screen (b).

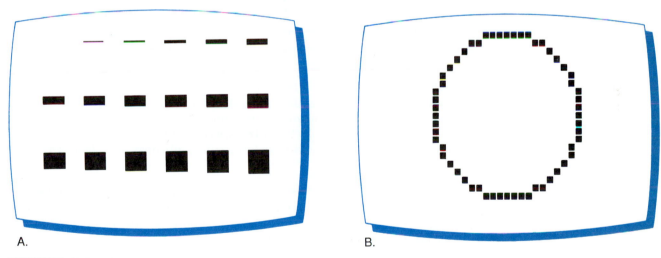

A.   B.

FIGURE 7-31
Images Created with a Raster Graphics Display
To create a square, a raster graphics display paints the square one line at a time
(a). As a result, the image can be filled in rather than just appear as a line
drawing. A raster graphics display uses dots to draw a circle (b). The the size of
the dots and the spacing between them determine the display's resolution.

INPUT DEVICES

Interactive graphics programs let you create and manipulate images on the screen. As you saw in Topic 1-6, you can create images on the screen using light pens, mice, or graphics tablets. You can also read them into the computer's memory using graphics scanners. Graphics scanners convert images printed on paper into a digital form that can be used by the computer. They divide the image into pixels, and while scanning the image one line at a time, they measure the brightness level (called the gray level) or color of each pixel in the image. When the scanning is completed, the entire image is stored in the computer's memory as a series of numeric values, one for the level of brightness of each pixel in the image and one for the color. Once the image has been stored in the computer's memory, it can be manipulated by a program designed to work with images of this kind. When it is displayed on the screen, the digitizing process is reversed—the numeric value of each pixel in the original image controls the brightness or color of its corresponding pixel on the display screen.

When an image is converted, its content is ignored; it doesn't matter if the image is text, numbers, or an illustration. None of the characters has been converted into the ASCII value needed to manipulate the text with a word processing system. Graphics scanners have five major elements.

- A light source to illuminate the image.
- A sampling aperture to focus the scanner on just a single pixel in the image.
- A scanning mechanism to move the sampling aperture across and down the image so that each pixel can be sampled in sequence. On some graphics scanners, the image to be scanned is mounted on a drum, and the sampling aperture is moved back and forth across the drum as it revolves the image.
- A sensor to measure the brightness of the pixel being sampled. The sensor converts the brightness into an electrical voltage.
- A quantitizer (called an analog-to-digital converter) to convert the electrical voltage from the sensor into an integer value. Inexpensive graphics scanners for microcomputers generally use only two values on the gray scale, white and black. More expensive graphics scanners can assign up to 256 values so that levels of brightness and colors can be recorded.

Once you have created graphs on the screen, you can use them to communicate important information to others. There are two ways to do this: printing out graphs for distribution or using the computer to organize and even present an audiovisual presentation.

PRINTING GRAPHS

In addition to output devices like laser printers (see Topic 1-6), many graphics are printed on **plotters**. Plotters come in a variety of configurations, but all use pens (as many as eight colors) to draw an image. The printer stops automatically at certain points so that you can change pens to change colors, or the pens are changed automatically. The most common kind of plotter is a flat-bed plotter (Figure 7-32), so named because it keeps the paper stationary on the bed of the plotter. A movable arm mounted across the bed above the paper can move in one direction. A pen mounted on the arm can move in the other direction (Figure 7-33). Other plotters move the paper

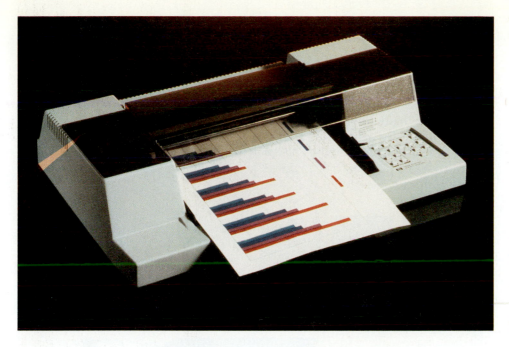

FIGURE 7-32
Flat-Bed Plotter
Flat-bed plotters hold the paper in a fixed position while the image is drawn by a pen mounted on a moving arm. Courtesy of Hewlett-Packard

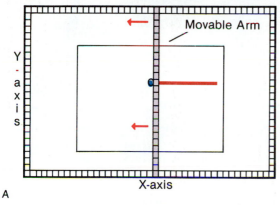

A

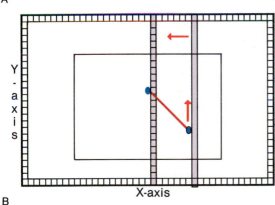

B

FIGURE 7-33
How a Flat-Bed Plotter Draws an Image
On a flat-bed plotter, if just the arm or the pen moves, the result is a straight vertical or horizontal line (a). If both the arm and the pen move (b), the result is a diagonal line or curve, depending on the relative speed and direction of the movement of the arm and the pen.

along one axis while the pen moves along another, and some mount the paper on a drum that revolves under the pen. If the pen is stationary while the drum moves, a straight line is drawn down the length of the paper. If the drum remains stationary while the pen moves, a straight line is drawn across the paper. If both the pen and drum move at the same time, either a diagonal line or a curve will be drawn depending on the relative speed of the two components.

Dot-Matrix Graphics

Since graphics are displayed on a screen and stored in memory in a similar grid, it's a simple matter to transfer images from memory to paper. Whenever the value stored in memory is a 1, the dot is printed in the corresponding position on the paper. Whenever the value in memory is a 0, the corresponding position on the paper is left blank. By controlling the position dots are printed in, an illusion of brightness can be conveyed (a). The ability to convey brightness allows dot-matrix printers to print realistic, almost photographic, images (b).

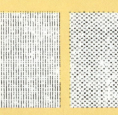

A.

B.

Reprinted with permission of Epson America, Inc., from the RX-80 Printer User's Manual, copyright 1983.

SUMMARY AND KEY TERMS

- Most high-quality graphics displays are based on cathode ray tubes. These displays are either **digital** or **analog**.
- Images are created on the screen with vector or raster graphics. **Vector graphics displays** draw straight lines between specified points. **Raster graphics displays** repeatedly sweep across and down the screen, painting images as it does so.
- You can use graphics scanners to get graphic images into the computer.
- **Plotters** can be used to print graphics. They draw images using pens attached to moveable arms.

REVIEW QUESTIONS

1. What are the major elements that make up a CRT, and what does each do?
2. What is the major difference between a vector graphics display and a raster graphics display?
3. How do plotters work?

TOPIC 7-8

Graphics Standards

OBJECTIVE

After completing this topic, you will be able to

- Briefly describe the problems encountered using graphic files with other applications programs

When you create graphics images and then print or save them, they are printed or saved in a format determined by your hardware and the program.

HARDWARE

Graphic images are created on the screen, and the image you see is determined by the type of display you are using. If you are using a color graphics adapter, the resolution is lower than if you are using an enhanced graphics adapter or a video graphics array. When you send the image to the printer, many programs print it using the same resolution displayed on the screen. Other, more sophisticated programs, convert it into the maximum resolution available in the printer.

FILE FORMATS

When you save a graphic file, it is saved in the format determined by the program you are using. Since there are no established standards for file formats, you can have problems when trying to use an image created on one program with another program. You may encounter this problem often, for example, when merging a graphic image into a document with a desktop publishing program or when trying to display a graphic created on one system on another system. This problem is being addressed in two ways: by the adoption of standards and the development of conversion utilities.

Standards

Many programs are now supporting **Tagged-Image-File-Format** (**TIFF**), a file format developed by Aldus and Microsoft. This standard allows graphics programs and scanners to reproduce images in a format that is usable by any desktop publishing program.

Conversion Utilities

Since many programs still have their own unique file formats, conversion programs have been introduced to convert one format into another. For example, Hijack converts files created on the following systems into any of the other listed formats:

- Amiga (IFF files)
- CompuServe Image Format (GIF files)
- HP Laserjet (HPC files)
- Lotus (PIC files)
- Macintosh (MacPaint files)
- PC Paintbrush (PCX files)
- PostScript (PSC files)
- Scanner (TIFF files)
- Text (TXT files)

To convert a file from one of the formats into another, you simply specify the source and target file formats, and the program automatically converts the file so that you can use it on the specified program.

SUMMARY AND KEY TERMS

- When you create graphic images, they are saved in a format that is determined by your hardware and program.
- Some programs save and print graphics using the same resolution as the screen. Others print it at the maximum resolution offered by the printer.
- Programs have different formats for the files that they create. This prevents you from using a graphic created on one program with another program. Many programs now support a common format so that you do not have this problem. The format is called the **Tagged-Image-File-Format (TIFF)**.
- If your program uses a nonstandard file format, you can use a program to convert it into the format of the program you want to transfer it to.

REVIEW QUESTIONS

1. If you wanted to print draft copies of a graphic on your low-cost printer, and then send it to an outside service to prepare it for publications, what should you be sure your program supports?
2. Why is it sometimes difficult to use a file created on a graphics program with another applications program?
3. What is the Tagged-Image-File-Format (TIFF)?

Audiovisual Presentations

OBJECTIVES

After completing this topic, you will be able to

- Explain how you create slide shows
- Describe other ways to present audiovisual presentations

Graphics do not always have to be printed to be useful. Many times, you want to share them with a group during a discussion or presentation. A family of programs has been developed so that you can do so. These programs make it easy to capture images on the screen and present them like a slide show.

CREATING SLIDE SHOWS

Slide show programs use images from the screen. To prepare a show, you follow three steps: create the images, edit the images, and sequence the images.

Creating Images

The first step is to get the images into the computer. You do this by scanning them in or creating them with another applications program. For example, you can scan in a picture of a business's headquarters and use a spreadsheet to create a graph of the company's annual sales and then display them on the screen one after another. When displayed, you use the program's capture feature to store the screen image in a file on the disk. To do so, you first load the capture program and then the images. When the image is displayed, you press **Shift-PrtSc** or other designated keys. The program asks you for a filename, and when you provide it and press **Return**, the image is saved.

Editing Images

Once the images are in the computer, you can use the programs edit features to add text and boxes, crop the image (blow up a part of it), or modify tones or colors.

Sequencing Images

When the images are completed, you use the program's script commands to sequence the show. In this step, you specify the order the images should be displayed in (or whether they should change only when you press a key). You can also specify special effects. For example, you can have one image dissolve into another so that there isn't an abrupt change between images. You can also have one image fade before the next appears.

Presenting the Images

Once the images have been sequenced, you can share them with others. For example, you can present the slide show to a small group gathered around the computer or to a larger group by projecting the images onto a larger screen using a projector connected to the computer (Figure 7-34).

OTHER FORMS OF PRESENTATION

You don't have to use slide show programs to present finished graphics. If you want to present the images using more traditional approaches, you can print them out as overhead transparency masters or convert them into slides.

- Overhead transparencies can be created by printing the graphs on clear acetate or mylar. These transparency masters can then be projected onto a wall or screen using an overhead projector. To do this, you need a printer that can print on single sheets of acetate.

FIGURE 7-34
Projector Connected to Computer
A special projector can be connected to the computer and laid on top of an overhead projector. It then projects an image onto the wall or a screen so that a large group can see the screen display. Courtesy of Kodak, Inc.

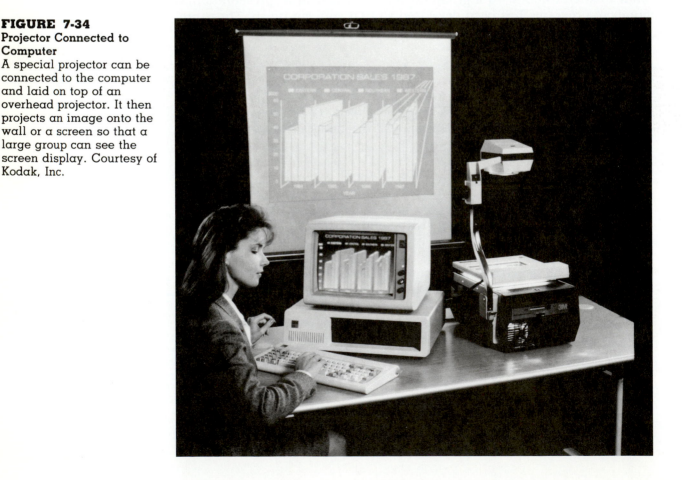

GRAPHICS APPLICATIONS

■ Cameras can also be used to capture the screen image on film so that it can be presented as a print or slide. For example, graphics programs used in conjunction with the Polaroid Palette (Figure 7-35) or similar products can be used to generate 35 mm slides or instant images. The Polaroid Palette also allows you to add colors to images created on a black-and-white display monitor.

SUMMARY AND KEY TERMS

■ Slide show programs organize images so that they can be presented to groups.

■ You can create images or scan them into the computer and then capture the image on the screen. When you capture an image, it is stored on the disk in its own file.

■ You can edit captured images and then use the program to write a script that sequences them. You can also specify special effects.

■ You can play back the presentation on a computer screen or use a projection device to project it onto a screen or wall.

■ Besides slide shows, you can print out overhead transparencies and photograph the image on the screen.

REVIEW QUESTIONS

1. What does a capture program do?
2. List two things you can do to images when you edit them.
3. What are scripts? What do you do with them?
4. List two special effects you can use in a slide show.
5. What device would you use to present a slide show to a large group?

Part Eight

COMMUNICATIONS APPLICATIONS

Topic 8-1   Local Area Networks
Topic 8-2   Wide Area Networks
Topic 8-3   Telecommunications Equipment
Topic 8-4   Communications Programs
Topic 8-5   Communications Settings
Topic 8-6   Transferring Files
Case Study   Calling a Bulletin Board
Topic 8-7   Telecommunications Principles

Computers are useful by themselves, but their power increases when they are connected to other computers and other users. There are two ways to connect computers. One way is for computers located on the same campus or in the same building to be wired together into a local area network. The other way is for computers anywhere in the world to be connected into wide area networks using the regular telephone lines. In either case, the computers you are connected to can be other microcomputers or a mainframe. Connecting computers to local or wide area networks allows them to communicate or telecommunicate. Using computer communications, you can send and receive electronic mail, bank by phone, get the latest stock quotes, and tie into information services like The Source and CompuServe.

When connected to other computers, you can

- Exchange electronic mail with other users.
- Transfer free, public-domain software from another computer onto one of your own disks so that you can run those programs on your computer.
- Call up commercial databases or information services like The Source and other, more specialized services like Dow-Jones News Retrieval.
- Hold conferences with one or more other users.

REVIEW QUESTIONS

1. What is the difference between a local area network and a wide area network?
2. List four things you can do when connected to other computers.

TOPIC 8-1

Local Area Networks

OBJECTIVES

After completing this topic, you will be able to

- Describe why computers are connected into networks
- Describe typical network architectures
- Explain how signals are sent along a network
- Describe how traffic is controlled on a network

There is a saying that "The whole is greater than the sum of its parts." This is certainly true of microcomputers. Individually, they are useful, but when linked into a **local area network** (**LAN**), they become even more so. Local area networks can connect computers within a single building or in several nearby buildings, on a college campus, for instance. It is estimated that almost six million computers are already connected into local area networks, and that number is growing. There are two primary reasons for connecting computers into local area networks.

- The computers can share expensive peripherals like plotters, laser printers, and hard disk drives. Where there are only a few computers this can also be accomplished by switches that switch a printer or other device between the computers (Figure 8-1).
- The computers can communicate with each other, and users can exchange information and electronic mail.

Local area networks are created by connecting microcomputers, printers, and hard disks with wires or cables. Microcomputers connected into a network operate together as equals. Each microcomputer has its own computational ability, so it can function either alone or as part of the network. LANs differ from multiuser systems where dumb terminals, or microcomputers that act like dumb terminals, are connected to a central computer. In a multiuser system, the dumb terminal can draw only on the resources in the main computer; it cannot run its own programs. In a LAN, the computers can be regular microcomputers or **diskless workstations**, which are microcomputers without disk drives. All the programs it runs and all the data files it saves are stored on the network's hard disk drive. Diskless workstations are more secure than computers with disk drives. For example, users

667

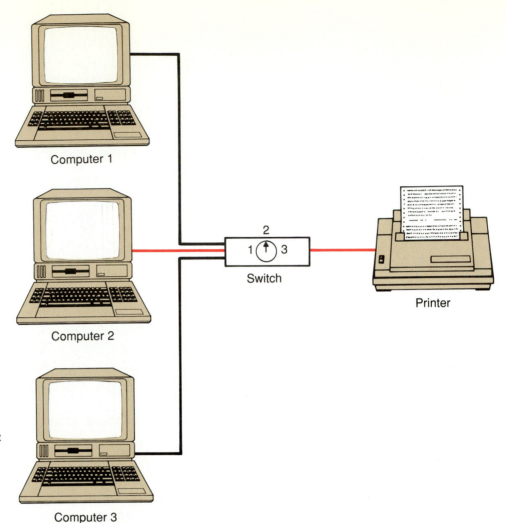

Computer 1

Computer 2

2
1 ① 3

Switch

Printer

Computer 3

FIGURE 8-1
Switches
Switches that connect
computers to devices like
printers and modems are
like a simple network.
Mechanical switches
require you to turn a
selector knob and can print
the output from only one
computer at a time.
Electronic switches
automatically route print
jobs from any of the
connected computers.

cannot illegally copy program or data files that are stored on the network's
hard disk.

Several networks are available that connect microcomputers and their
peripherals. In this topic, we explore the basic concepts of local area
networks.

NETWORK ARCHITECTURE

Microcomputers can be arranged to form a network in several ways. This
layout is called **network architecture** (or topology). All network architectures include hardware, called **nodes**, and wires or cables over which data is
sent between the nodes. A node is a single, addressable device, for example,
a microcomputer or printer. A network's architecture refers to the way the
data flows between nodes, not to the way they are physically arranged in an
office.

Bus Architecture

Bus architecture (Figure 8-2) connects all nodes to a single bus, much as
the components are organized within the computer. In a bus arrangement,
a signal addressed to another node is sent from a microcomputer to the bus.

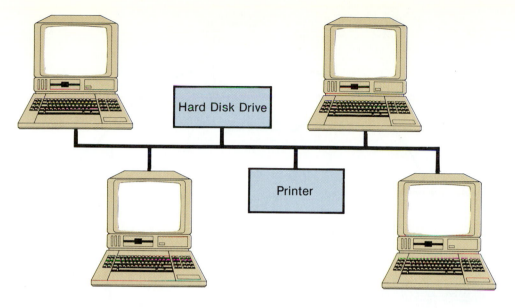

FIGURE 8-2
Bus Architecture
In a system designed around a bus, all components are connected to the same set of wires or cables. Each computer operates independently of the others.

All other nodes on the network, which are also connected to the same bus, examine the signal. If the signal is addressed to them, they accept it. If it is not, they ignore it. Since each node is separately connected to the network, any node can break down without affecting other nodes. This feature makes bus architecture one of the most popular arrangements for networks.

Ring Architecture

Ring architecture (Figure 8-3) arranges the nodes on the network in a circle. When one of the microcomputers on the network sends a signal, it passes it to the next node on the network. If it is not addressed to that node, it is retransmitted to the next node and so on around the circle until it reaches the node it is addressed to. Because each node on the network retransmits any signal that is not addressed to it, if one node breaks down, the entire network breaks down. Unlike the other two systems, where new equipment can be plugged into the bus or host computer, a ring network requires rewiring when new equipment is added. To insert a new node, the connection between two existing nodes must be broken. The new node is then installed and wired to the two adjacent nodes.

Star Architecture

Star architecture (Figure 8-4) has the nodes connected to a central, or host, computer. When one of the microcomputers on the network sends a signal, it is sent to the host, which routes it to the node it's addressed to. There are no direct connections between the nodes on the network except through the host computer. If the host breaks down, so does the network. But if one of the other microcomputers breaks down, no harm is done. The others continue to function.

Network Servers

When printers, modems, and hard disk drives are connected into a network, additional hardware, called **network servers**, is required to allow these nodes to be shared by all the microcomputers on the network. There are four basic kinds of servers.

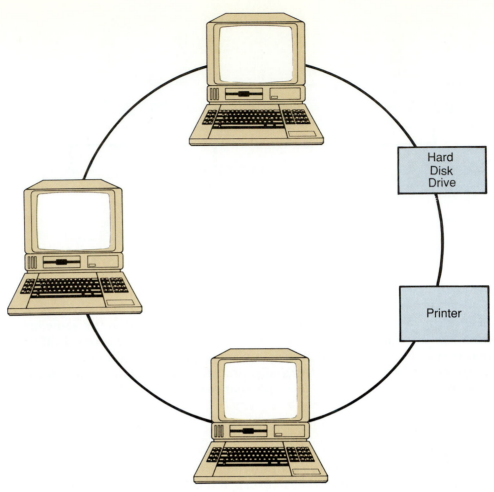

FIGURE 8-3
Ring Architecture
In a system designed around a ring, each computer routes data from the computers on either side.

- **Print servers** allow all computers on the network to use the same printer.
- **File servers** allow all computers on the network to use the same hard disk drive.
- **Routing servers** connect two or more networks with the same architecture. Generally, the networks must be supplied by the same vendor or be otherwise compatible. For example, a routing server can connect an IBM LAN to another IBM LAN if the IBM LANs are compatible.
- **Gateway servers** connect two or more different types of networks. These gateways simplify the network and reduce network expenses. For example, if each computer in a network had direct access to a mainframe, each would require a special add-on board. But when a gateway server is used, only the computer that acts as the gateway requires the add-on board. All the other computers in the network access the mainframe through that board.

NETWORK CONNECTIONS AND SIGNALS

When signals are sent through a network, they are sent between nodes along a common set of wires. Microcomputers and their peripherals that are organized in a network must be connected by hardware, which includes both the add-on cards that plug into each node's expansion slots and the cables that connect them. Three types of cables are used to connect the computers in the network: **twisted pair**, **coaxial**, and **fiber optic** (Figure 8-5).

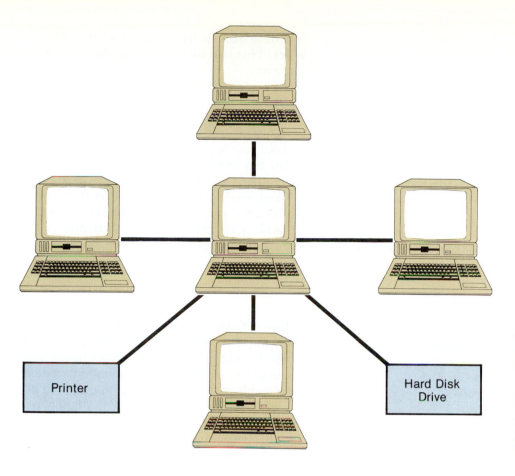

FIGURE 8-4
Star Architecture
In a system designed around a star, all the computers are connected to a central computer. All traffic on the network passes though this central computer.

A.

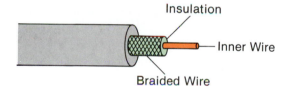

Insulation

Inner Wire

Braided Wire

B.

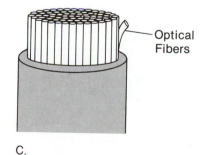

Optical Fibers

C.

FIGURE 8-5
Network Wiring
Three types of wires or cables are used to connect computers in a local area network.

A. Twisted-pair wires are just like telephone wires. They are the least expensive way to connect computers because the wire is cheap and easy to install. Their disadvantages are a relatively slow speed and a tendency to pick up electrical interference that can cause high error rates.

B. Coaxial cables are layered. An inner wire is surrounded by an insulating material that is, in turn, surrounded by a braided wire. This braided wire shields the inner wire from any noise or other signals in the environment that can affect the quality of the transmission. Coaxial cables are reliable and have a wide bandwidth, so they can transmit data much faster than twisted-pair wires.

C. Fiber-optic cables are made of plastic or glass fibers covered with an opaque sheath that keeps light from entering or escaping. The digital data signals from a microcomputer, or other node, are used to modulate a light beam to convert it into pulses. These light pulses are sent along the optical fibers and are unmodulated at the receiving end. Fiber optics are fast and reliable, as well as small and light. They also have an extremely wide bandwidth, so a large number of signals can be sent simultaneously.

Since several nodes may be sending data at the same time, the signals must be kept separated on the wires. This can be done by sending them at different times or different frequencies.

Baseband

When the signals are sent at different times, the network is called **baseband**. Figure 8-6 shows two computers sending signals, and each is unaware of the other's presence on the network. The baseband network merges the signals so that those from the two computers are sent along the network one at a time, separated from each other by time. Baseband networks operate at medium speed. Because they use unmodulated signals, modems are unnecessary. Baseband networks can also transmit voice messages in digitized form that can be stored and played back when desired.

Broadband

When the signals are sent at different frequencies, the network is called **broadband** (Figure 8-7). Unlike baseband networks, where only one signal is sent at a time, a broadband network can simultaneously carry many signals. To send data at different frequencies, a number of carrier frequencies are used to electronically divide the cable into a number of **channels**. The digital data from the computer must be modulated onto these higher frequency carrier waves using the same principles discussed in Topic 8-7. To do this, modems are required at all nodes to convert digital signals into analog signals and then back again. A major advantage of a broadband network is that it can carry audio, video, and digital data at the same time. Each device on the network uses its own channel to transmit and receive data.

Communications Interface Units

All the computers, printers, and other hardware are connected to the network though a **communications interface unit** (**CIU**). The type of CIU required depends on what signal is used in the network. In a broadband net-

FIGURE 8-6
Baseband Signals
In a baseband network, signals are sent at different times.

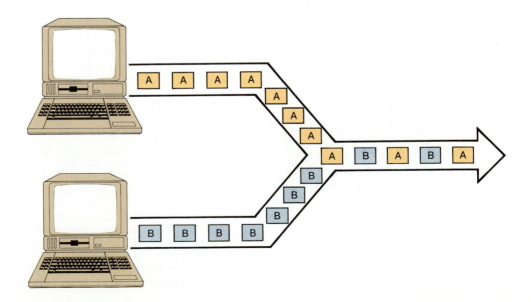

COMMUNICATIONS APPLICATIONS

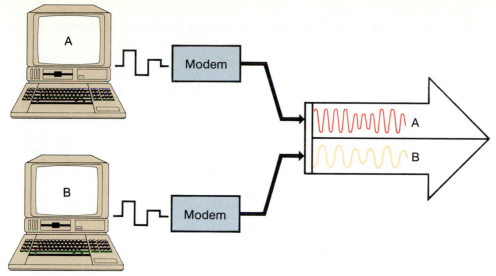

FIGURE 8-7
Broadband Signals
In a broadband network, computers send signals onto the network at the same time but at different frequencies.

work, where the sending node modulates the signal, and the receiving node demodulates it, the CIU is a modem. On a baseband network, where unmodulated digital signals are sent along the network, the CIU is a **transceiver** (a combination *trans*mitter and re*ceiver*). In either case, the CIU performs several functions.

- Monitors the traffic on the network to see when the hardware connected to it can send a message.

- Checks traffic on the network to see if a message is addressed to its node and, if so, accepts it.

- Retransmits or repeats messages if the message is not addressed to its node. This is done only in a ring network since bus and star networks do not require signals to be retransmitted from node to node.

- Converts signals from the network into a form acceptable to its node and vice versa. For example, on a broadband network, it converts digital signals into analog signals when sending data and converts analog signals into digital signals when receiving data. If necessary, it converts parallel signals into serial signals and vice versa, for example, when its node is a serial printer.

- Detects errors in messages addressed to its node and, if found, requests that the sending node retransmit the data.

NETWORK TRAFFIC CONTROL

The nodes connected to a network are each assigned a unique address. When a node wants to communicate with another node (either computers or peripherals), it adds its address to the message it is sending. Since several computers may be sending messages, two or more may try to send signals at the same time. If this happens, the messages will not get through. Two common methods of solving this problem are collision detection and token passing.

Collision Detection

In a network using **collision detection**, none of the computer's nodes are aware of the others. Each node transmits data whenever it wishes. If no other computer is sending data, the message is received by the device it was addressed to, and acknowledgment is sent back to the sending node. But if two computers transmit at the same time, their messages collide, and neither gets through. Since no acknowledgment is sent to the sending computers, both computers have to retransmit. To prevent the messages from colliding on the next try, the computers randomly generate a pause before another attempt is made. Since both computers randomly time their pauses, they most likely will make their next attempts at different times. Because the number of collisions increases as the number of computers using the line increases, a heavily used network that uses collision detection may operate slowly.

Token Passing

Token passing is a more sophisticated way to time signals so that they do not collide with each other. A single encoded signal, called the token, is sent around the network (Figure 8-8). Any node can let it pass or choose to grab it. The node holding the token is the only one allowed to transmit data on the network. An analogy is a group of people passing a tape recorder around a conference table. Any person can choose to speak into it or pass it to the next person. In the network, a node holding the token sends data addressed to another node. All the other nodes look at the message as it goes around the network to see if the message is addressed to it. If the message is not addressed to it, the node passes it along to the next node on the network. When the message has been received by the node it is addressed to, the receiving node sends back an acknowledgement that the data was received. The token is then put back into circulation. Since there is only one token in circulation, no collisions can occur. Because no single computer can use it twice in a row, other computers have fair access to it.

FIGURE 8-8
Token Passing
In a network using token passing, a single token circulates around the network. The node holding the token is the only one allowed to transmit data on the network. Since there is only one token in circulation, no collisions can occur.

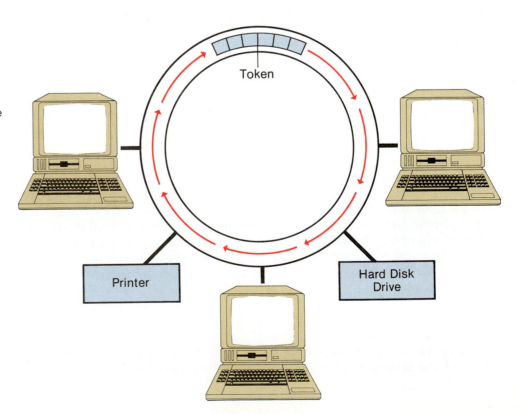

Token

Printer

Hard Disk Drive

COMMUNICATIONS APPLICATIONS

NETWORK SOFTWARE

Networks are managed by **network management programs** that route messages and allow computers to be connected and disconnected. These programs should be as transparent, or invisible, to the user as possible. When fully transparent, the user does not even know they are connected to a network. Each computer operates just as it does when disconnected from the network. Unfortunately, this goal has not yet be achieved, and network management software adds another level of knowledge required by the user. Eventually, this problem will be solved, and computers on a network will operate as simply as telephones, which though connected to an extremely complicated and immense network, operate as very simple devices.

Moreover, operating systems and applications programs used on a network must be modified. For example, most programs are designed for standalone computers. A user on a standalone can use these programs to retrieve or save files as he or she wishes. But when these programs are used on a network, these operations must be regulated because two or more users may want to work on the same file at the same time. To prevent this from happening, applications programs, or the operating system, must be able to lock files that are currently being used so that other users cannot retrieve and modify them. When the first user saves or quits the file, it is then automatically unlocked so that another user can retrieve it. Many of the security problems discussed on multiuser database management programs also apply to networks (see Topic 6-17).

SUMMARY AND KEY TERMS

- Computers can be connected by wires and cables into **local area networks**. The computers in a network can be regular microcomputers or **diskless workstations**.

- The hardware connected to a network is called a **node**. The ways nodes are connected to each other is called the network's **architecture**. Typical architectures include **bus**, **ring**, and **star**.

- Networks are either baseband or broadband. **Baseband** networks send signals from different nodes at different times. **Broadband** networks send signals from many nodes at the same time but at different frequencies. Each frequency is called a **channel**.

- Traffic on a network is controlled by **collision detection** or **token passing**. On a collision detection network, if signals collide and do not get through, they are retransmitted. On a token ring network, a token continually circulates, and only the node that grabs the token can send a message.

REVIEW QUESTIONS

1. What does the acronym LAN stand for?
2. What are the advantages of having computers and other hardware connected to a network?
3. What is a diskless workstation? Why are they more secure?
4. What is a node?
5. Describe the three ways that computers can be organized in a network's architecture. What is one advantage and one disadvantage of each arrangement?
6. What is the difference between a baseband and a broadband network? Can you think of one advantage and one disadvantage of each?
7. What is the purpose of a communications interface unit?
8. Describe two ways networks keep signals from interfering with each other when they are being sent over a network.

TOPIC 8-2

Wide Area Networks

OBJECTIVES

After completing this topic, you will be able to

- Describe wide area networks
- List and briefly describe computers that you can call
- Explain the purpose of packet-switching networks

Many users call computers that are not connected into a network. To do so, they dial up these computers using their modems, which are connected to the telephone lines. These telephone lines are also referred to as the **Public Switched Telephone Network** (**PSTN**) or **wide area network**. Using this network, you can call other computers, information services like CompuServe, or bulletin boards set up by companies or individual users. The computer that you call is the **host computer**. The host computer can be the computer that runs the information service, a mainframe or minicomputer, a PC running a bulletin board, or another computer running a communications program.

You can communicate with thousands of computers through telecommunications. They fall into four classes.

- Information services offer a variety of databases and other services. You must subscribe to the service and are then billed for the time you are connected to the service.
- Electronic mail services are available for sending messages and mail. Your message is stored by the computer and then forwarded to the person it is addressed to when he or she logs on (signs on) to the service.
- Bulletin boards are set up by individuals or groups. You can call them without charge.
- Private wide area networks set up by corporations are open only to members of the company.

CALLING OTHER COMPUTERS

You can call any other computer that is also equipped with a modem. To do so, the computer you are calling must be on, running a communications software program, and set to **answer mode**. Besides calling other computers, you can use your computer to answer incoming calls. This is handy if, for instance, you want to set up your own bulletin board or you are not sure when your branch office will call for this month's income statement and you want to go to lunch.

To use your computer to answer and record incoming calls, you need an auto-answer modem; most auto-dial modems can answer the phone as well. If your modem allows you to set the number of rings before it answers the phone, you may have to adjust this setting. Some communications programs let you assign passwords. Callers are prompted to enter the password and are usually given three tries to get it right. If they enter the correct password, communications continue. If not, the modem disconnects and hangs up the phone.

Remote Computing

What if you are at home and you want to find a file on your computer in the office? You can do so by using **remote computing**. With remote computing, your home computer can call the office computer, which must be running a remote computing program or a regular communications program set to **host mode**, to search for files and even run applications programs. The keys you press on your keyboard in this mode do not affect your computer; rather, they control the computer you are connected to. The information displayed on your screen is the same information displayed on the remote computer's screen. These programs were originally developed by support services that wanted to be able to check a user's computer from a distance. The usefulness of these programs has led to their being made available as standalone programs and incorporated into many communications programs.

Because you can access files and programs on the remote computer, most programs of this kind are designed so that you can protect your computer from unwanted intruders by assigning passwords. Users without the correct password cannot gain access to the computer.

Hard-Wired Computers

You can also wire two computers together so that they act just like a wide area network. This is useful when you want to exchange files between two computers that are not part of a network and are located close to each other. To do this, you use a special cable called a **null-modem cable** to connect the two computers. This cable is just like the one you use to connect a standalone modem to your computer, but two wires have been reversed. When calling a computer connected in this way, you follow all the same procedures you use to call one over the phone lines, but you don't enter a phone number. The other computer answers automatically when you select it for a call.

CALLING INFORMATION SERVICES

There are many commercial information services that you can subscribe to. For example, CompuServe, established in 1979, is a typical information service. Some of the services it offers are

- News bulletins from AP and *The Washington Post*
- Weather reports for any area of the country
- Sports scores

- An electronic encyclopedia
- Electronic mail
- Home shopping and banking
- Discussion forums on various topics
- Computer games
- Home management programs (for example, Balancing Your Checkbook)
- Travel reservations
- Business news
- Stock quotations
- Standard & Poor's analysis
- Brokerage service
- Electronic conferencing
- A business reference library
- Personal finance programs (for example, Calculating Your Next Raise)
- Forums for personal computer users
- Services for professionals in aviation, legal, medical, engineering, etc.

CALLING ELECTRONIC MAIL SERVICES

One of the major uses of wide area networks is the distribution of **electronic mail** (also called E-mail). E-mail services are provided by both commercial and private networks. MCI is typical of the commercial electronic mail services available to microcomputer users. MCI offers various ways for you to send mail.

- An Instant Letter is used to send a letter to another subscriber. It is immediately available for retrieval by the person it is addressed to.
- An MCI Letter is sent to the computer just like an Instant Letter, but MCI transmits it to the MCI postal center closest to the person it is addressed to, prints it, and then gives it to the U.S. Postal Service for delivery.
- Overnight Letters and Four-Hour letters are similar but are delivered by courier.

MCI Mail also lets you use your computer as a Telex station to connect with more than one million other Telex users around the world. Moreover, MCI lets you broadcast your mail to a mailing list that you store on the service. When you send the message to the service, it routes it to everyone on the specified list. Several private E-mail services also exist for special uses.

- Bitnet connects many colleges and universities.
- Arpanet connects government researchers in colleges and industry.
- BIX connects serious computer users.

Using these networks, users can **teleconference**. They can leave messages for each other to be read later, or if two users call at the same time, they can type messages back and forth.

CALLING BULLETIN BOARDS

Bulletin board systems (**BBS**) (also called public access message systems) are set up by firms or individuals. For example, Figures 8-9 and 8-10 show the opening menus of two different bulletin boards of this kind. Many of

COMMUNICATIONS APPLICATIONS

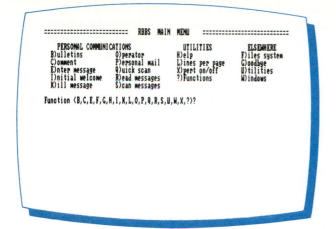

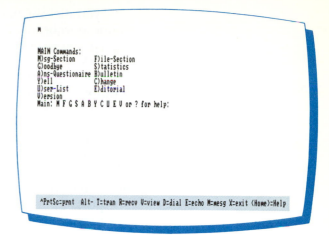

these bulletin boards are run by an intriguing assortment of people whose interests include exchanging computer know-how, arranging dating services, exchanging gossip, and sharing programs and games that you can transfer to your own disk. Many bulletin boards also have a public message base where you, or any other caller, can write anything your heart desires (unless you break the law) and which any other caller can read. Many also provide electronic mail services that allow you to assign a password to a message so that it can be read only by the person it is addressed to. These messages can also be read by the **system operator** (**SYSOP**), the person who runs the system. This person can see everything on the bulletin board. Most systems also have a **chat mode** so that you can exchange messages in real time with the SYSOP or with other users if the bulletin board accepts calls on more than one line.

Locating the first bulletin board to call is the hardest part. You can often get numbers from magazines, users' groups, and friends. Since most bulletin boards list other bulletin boards, you will soon be aware of hundreds. If you call one, though, do not be surprised to find that the number is no longer in service. Since most of these boards are operated by individuals, they open as people become interested and close when they lose interest or run out of money to support the cost of maintaining the system. Many software companies also run bulletin boards. Users can call in to get the latest information from the company, exchange ideas with other users, and download programs.

One of the most popular bulletin board programs is Fido, written by Tom Jennings. The interesting thing about bulletin boards based on this program is that they act like a wide area network. You can call a local Fido BBS, called a node, and leave a message addressed to any other node on the network. In the early morning hours, when phone charges are lowest, each node on the network dials the nodes messages have been addressed to and sends the messages. The recipients can then call in to their local node the next day and read their messages.

PACKET-SWITCHING NETWORKS

When you call an outside service like CompuServe, you do not have to pay a long-distance rate if you use a service like TeleNet or Tymnet. These services, called **packet-switching networks**, are designed to connect computers around the country. They have **access points** (also called nodes or ports) in hundreds of cities throughout the world. For example, Tymnet has more than 10,000 access points in 500 cities and 67 countries. To use the ser-

FIGURE 8-9 (above left)
The Boston Computer Society Opening Menu
The Boston Computer Society offers a bulletin board for its members. The service is used to exchange messages between members and to list announcements about upcoming events.

FIGURE 8-10 (above right)
The Fido Network Opening Menu
The Fido Network is the only bulletin board system where local bulletin boards are connected into a network. Messages posted on a local Fido bulletin board are automatically sent to any other specified Fido bulletin board during the early morning hours. This way, long-distance users can exchange messages for the cost of a local phone call.

vice, you dial the phone number of the local access point using a local telephone number. If your town does not have one, you may have to place a long- distance call to the nearest town that does. When you connect with the network, you indicate the service you are calling. The network then takes your local call and sends it to that service. These services work only if the computer you are calling is also on the system.

Packet-switching networks transmit digital data (Figure 8-11). Since they pack a lot more data onto the same lines, they are generally cheaper than placing a long-distance call directly to the computer over any available phone line. When you are connected to a phone line, you use only a small part of its capacity, and much of the time you are connected, no data is being sent or received. Packet-switching networks use the same kinds of lines but package your data along with that of other users. By time sharing the lines, more data can be sent, and the lines are used more efficiently, which lowers the cost for all users. Moreover, the networks charge you based on the amount of data you transmit rather than the time you are connected.

Since packet-switching networks generally connect fixed points at the host end, packet-switching companies have introduced a type of service that lets you connect with any phone number in a given area. These services, like TeleNet's PC Pursuit and Tymnet's Outdial, allow you to dial a local number to access the network. You then dial the area code you want to call, and you are connected to a modem at that end from which you can dial any number in the remote city. These systems are widely used to connect with out-of-town BBSs that are not fixed nodes on the network.

FIGURE 8-11
A Typical Packet
A typical packet sent over a packet-switching network is bundled. The first bits in the packet contain identifying information, including the receiving and sending addresses. Following this identifying information is the actual data you are sending. The packet ends with additional identifying data required by the network.

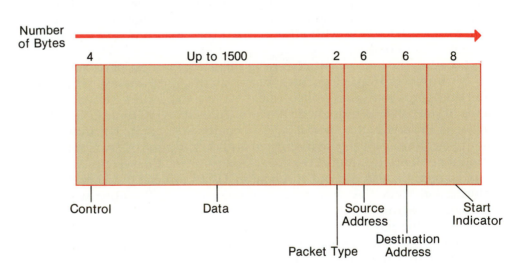

SUMMARY AND KEY TERMS

- Computers connected over the telephone lines are called a wide area network. The computer that you call over these lines is called the **host** computer, and it must be set to **answer mode**.

- You can call commercial information services, electronic mail services, bulletin boards, and private networks.

- If you are at one computer, and control another computer over the telephone lines, it is called **remote computing**.

- You can connect two computers using a **null-modem cable**.

- When you call many commercial services, you call a local **access point** on a **packet-switching network**.

1. What is the computer that you call called? What mode must it be set to?
2. List five types of computers that you can call.
3. What is remote computing?
4. What is a null-modem cable used for?
5. What is E-mail?
6. What is a bulletin board? What is chat mode?
7. What is the advantage of using a packet-switching network? How does it work?

Telecommunications Equipment

OBJECTIVES

After completing this topic, you will be able to

- Explain the differences between dumb and smart modems
- Distinguish among various types of communications standards

To telecommunicate with another computer, you need a modem and a communications program. A modem lets your computer transmit information over a cable or telephone line. You will need a serial port, which is frequently built in to the computer, and a cable to connect it to the modem. You will also need a wire to connect the modem to the phone line. We introduced you to modems in Topic 1-8, but here, we look at them in more detail.

THE LIGHTS ON YOUR MODEM

Most standalone modems have a series of lights that are used to tell you the status of the modem. They are usually labeled with initials (Figure 8-12).

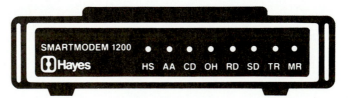

FIGURE 8-12
Modem Lights
Standalone modems usually have lights that indicate the current status of the communications session. The lights on the Hayes Smartmodem 1200 include

HS (High Speed) lights up when the modem is transmitting at 1200 baud.
AA (Auto-Answer) lights up when the modem is set to answer the phone to receive messages from other computers.
CD (Carrier Detect) lights up when the modem recognizes a signal from the computer you are calling. If you are calling a service or using long-distance lines, you are being billed whenever this light is on.
OH (Off Hook) lights up when the modem is actually using the telephone line.
RD (Receiving Data) lights up when the modem is receiving data from the computer you are calling.
SD (Sending Data) lights up when data is being sent from your computer.
TR (Terminal Ready) lights up when there is power to both the computer and the modem.
MR (Modem Ready) lights up when the power is turned on and the modem is ready.
Courtesy of Hayes Microcomputer Products Inc.

DUMB AND SMART MODEMS

Modems are classified as dumb or smart, perhaps better referred to as manual or automatic. With a **dumb modem**, you must use the phone to dial the number you want to reach. When you hear a screech, indicating you are connected to another computer, you either plug the telephone handset into the modem (if it is an acoustic coupler) or throw a switch to connect the modem to the line. For the modem to answer a call, you must answer the phone and then turn the modem on.

With a **smart modem**, you can dial the phone directly from the keyboard; a phone need not even be nearby. You can also store phone numbers in a directory so that you can place calls with a few simple keystrokes. This is called **auto-dial**. Smart modems can also be used to transmit log-on procedures needed to gain access to computers that require passwords and other identifying information. With a smart modem, you enter this information once. Then you can call, and log on to the computer by typing only a few keystrokes.

Most smart modems can also be set to **auto-answer**. In this mode, the modem detects any incoming calls, answers the phone, and establishes communications. When the call is completed and the other computer hangs up, the auto-answer modem also disconnects and hangs up.

COMMUNICATIONS STANDARDS

Since the phone companies own many of the telecommunications lines over which data is transmitted in this country, they have been very influential in setting standards for equipment connected to these lines. The standards are generally followed by modem manufacturers to ensure that their equipment is compatible with that of the telephone companies. Some modems use only one of these standards, which means you cannot connect to computers that do not use the same standard. Other modems allow you to switch manually or automatically between standards. Thus you can change the settings to match those of the computer you are communicating with.

High-speed modems that transmit 9600 bits per second have not yet agreed to a standard. As a result, you usually must buy modems for both ends of the connection from the same manufacturer.

- Bell 103A is the standard for full-duplex (see Topic 8-4), asynchronous 300-bits-per-second modems.
- Bell 212A is the standard for full-duplex, asynchronous/synchronous 1200-bits-per-second modems.
- CCITT V.22 is the standard for full-duplex, asynchronous/synchronous 2400-bits-per-second modems.
- V.32 is the standard for full-duplex 9600-bits-per-second modems connected to PSTN dial-up lines.
- V.29 is the standard for 9600-bits-per-second modems connected to two-wire PSTN lines or four-wire leased lines. On PSTN lines, it runs at half-duplex, and on leased lines, it runs at full-duplex.

SETTING UP A MODEM

Most modems have a series of switches, called **DIP switches**, that you must set in a certain sequence to use the modem with a communications program (Figure 8-13). Often, these switches have been preset at the factory,

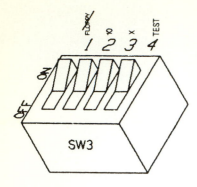

FIGURE 8-13
DIP Switches
Modems usually contain
DIP switches. Each dip
switch has two positions:
up and down. The manual
accompanying the
communications program
should tell you what these
settings should be. If the
manual does not mention
them, you can assume that
you do not have to change
the default settings.
Courtesy of
Hewlett-Packard

but these default settings may not work with your program. To make things even more complicated, you frequently cannot even see these switches unless you remove the modem's cover.

Integrated Services Digital Network

The **Integrated Services Digital Network (ISDN)** is the latest development in telephone communications. This proposed network will gradually replace the traditional telephone wires that you use whenever you make a phone call. The ISDN international standards allow users to simultaneously send voice, data, and video over local, national, and international telephone networks. Since this network is digital, and not analog like the current system, modems are not required. Data can be sent directly from the computer at up to 64 kilobits per second, which is much faster than today's modems can send data.

SUMMARY AND KEY TERMS

- To telecommunicate you need a modem. Modems are either dumb or smart. A smart modem does not require a phone to work. They can also be used with programs that store phone numbers and **auto-dial**.
- The communications standards that modems support are usually set by telephone companies or international organizations. There are separate standards for each of the most common transmission speeds.
- To set up a modem for use with your system, you may have to set **DIP switches** to specified settings.

REVIEW QUESTIONS

1. What equipment do you need to telecommunicate?
2. What function does the modem serve?
3. List three of the lights on a modem, and briefly describe what they indicate.
4. What is the basic difference between a dumb modem and a smart modem?
5. List the communications standards used by 300- and 1200-baud modems.
6. How do you set up a modem for use with your system?

Communications Programs

OBJECTIVES

After completing this topic, you will be able to

- Describe the principles of communications programs
- List and briefly describe some typical communications programs

When you use a modem to call other computers, you use a communications program. Here we introduce you to the principles behind these programs and some popular communications programs.

INTRODUCTION TO COMMUNICATIONS PROGRAMS

When you use a communications program with a modem, most of the process is automated for you.

Command Sets

Most modems use commands that are based on those developed by Hayes, a major manufacturer of modems. Modems that use this command set are called **Hayes compatible**. Typical Hayes commands include the prefix AT (for Attention) followed by special characters that stand for commands. For example, since phones are either tone or pulse, ATDT (Attention, Dial, Tone) tells the modem to dial a number using tone mode. ATDP (Attention, Dial, Pulse) tells the computer to dial the number using pulse mode. ATH (Attention, Hangup) tells the computer to break the connection and hang up the phone.

Dialing Directories

If you often call the same computers, you can enter their names and addresses into the programs **dialing directory** along with other information such as the communication parameters the system uses (see Topic 8-5). When you want to call the computer, you retrieve the dialing directory file and select the number to be called. The number is then dialed automatically using the communications parameters you specified in the file.

Auto Redial

Many programs have an **auto-redial** feature. If you get a busy signal on the first try, you can use this to automatically redial the number at specified periods until a connection is made. When the computer is reached, the computer beeps to signal you that a connection has been made. Some programs allow you to specify a list of numbers to be dialed in sequence. If the first number is busy, the program automatically dials the second. This process is repeated until a connection is made with one of the numbers.

Script Languages

Most communications programs have **script languages** that allow you to automate many operations. Script languages are similar to macros in word processing and spreadsheet programs. You can either write a small program or record your keystrokes for playback later. One of the most common uses for these script languages is to automate dial-up and log-on sequences when calling information utilities. If you enter and save these sequences, you can automatically dial and be logged on to the system when you call it. To protect yourself, you should not include your password in these saved sequences if others have access to your program disk. Programs that allow you to write scripts are more powerful. For example, you can write a script that dials a number at a specified time, logs on, checks for mail, downloads it to your computer, and then logs off. Since the entire process is automated, and done when phone charges are lowest, this automation can save you a good deal of money.

TYPICAL COMMUNICATIONS PROGRAMS

Many communications programs are available. Here is a brief description of some of the most widely used.

FIGURE 8-14
PC Talk
PC-Talk (a) runs on the IBM PC and compatibles and contains a dialing directory (b) where you can store sixty separate names, numbers, and communications settings for people or services you call.

PC-Talk

PC-Talk is one of the most widely used communications programs for microcomputers. It and the distribution concept behind it were developed by Andrew Fluegelman when he was editor of *PC World* magazine. Fluegelman developed a unique concept called **Freeware**™. Freeware programs are distributed at no cost or for a modest duplication fee. If users like them, they send a contribution to the developer (Figure 8-14). PC-Talk was the first Freeware program. Because Fluegelman trademarked the term *Freeware*,

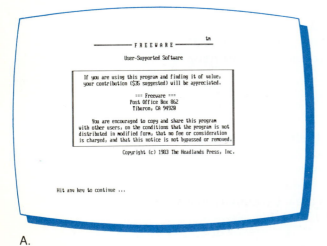

A.

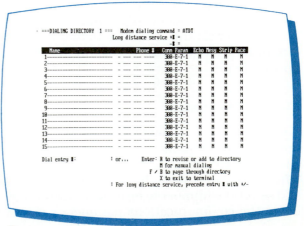

B.

COMMUNICATIONS APPLICATIONS

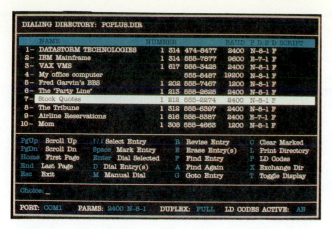

FIGURE 8-15
PROCOMM PLUS
PROCOMM PLUS is a very powerful shareware communications program that includes a dialing directory and script language that you can use to automate your telecommunications procedures.

other programs that are distributed using this concept are called shareware programs.

PROCOMM PLUS

PROCOMM PLUS is a powerful, full-featured, shareware communications program (Figure 8-15). It includes a dialing directory, several error-correcting file transfer protocols, and a script language you can use to automate the program. It has built-in context-sensitive help screens that guide you though its operation.

Crosstalk

Crosstalk is another popular communications program. When loaded, it displays a status screen listing the name and communications settings for a computer you want to call (Figure 8-16). You can create files for each service you call and store them in their own files. When you want to make a call, you load the file you created for that service, type DIAL, and then press **Return** to make the call. The latest version is also fully menu operated, but you can also use the same commands introduced in earlier versions.

Microsoft Works

Microsoft Works, an integrated program, includes telecommunications as one of its features (Figure 8-17). It allows you to store dialing information in files that you then retrieve when you want to call another computer. It is operated with pull-down menus that list all the program's commands.

FIGURE 8-16 (below left)
Crosstalk
The Crosstalk Status Screen lists all the communications settings. The *Command?* prompt at the bottom of the screen is where you enter commands.

FIGURE 8-17
Microsoft Works (below right)
Microsoft Works includes a menu-driven telecommunications program.

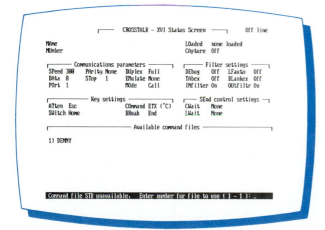

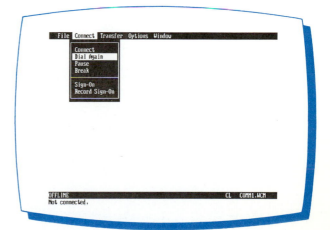

SUMMARY AND KEY TERMS

- **Communications programs** are required for wide area communications. When using them, you enter commands from the modem's **command set**. Most command sets are **Hayes compatible**.

- Communications programs include **dialing directories** that store phone numbers and other information about the computers you call. They also have **auto-redial** capability so that you can keep trying one or more numbers until you get through.

- **Script languages** are used to write programs that automate your communications sessions.

- Typical communications programs include PC-Talk, PROCOMM PLUS, Crosstalk, and Microsoft Works.

REVIEW QUESTIONS

1. What is the purpose of a communications program?
2. What is a commands set? What does it mean to say it is Hayes compatible?
3. What is the purpose of a dialing directory? An auto-redial feature?
4. What is a script language used for?
5. List three typical communications programs.

Communications Settings

OBJECTIVES

After completing this topic, you will be able to

- List and describe communications settings
- Describe communications parameters
- Explain the differences among simplex, half-duplex, and full-duplex transmissions
- Explain echoing

When you use a modem to communicate with other computers, you must be sure both computers are using the same communications settings. Typical settings that you must enter before making a call include

- Phone number
- Modem setup string
- Dial type (prefix)
- Baud rate
- Communications parameters
- Data flow control
- Terminal emulation
- Echoing
- Duplex

Many of the settings that we discuss in this topic may have been made for you. If so, all you have to do is enter the phone number you want to call, dial it, and then log on. Even if you have to make all the settings, you have to do it only once. After you make the initial settings, you can save them and can use them again.

PHONE NUMBER

The phone number is the number of the computer that you want to call. If you want to dial the number from the office, you specify that the 9 be dialed before the number. When calling from home, you specify the MCI number.

The phone number you enter and the way you enter it depend on where you are calling from, where you are calling to, and the long-distance service you use.

If you are calling from your home phone, you enter a phone number the way you would dial it, for example, 555-5555. Some programs let you enter the dashes in phone numbers to make them easier to read. Others do not allow this, so the number must be entered as 5555555.

Sometimes you will be calling from a business phone that requires you to dial a prefix like 9 to get an outside line, and sometimes you will be using a long-distance service that requires you to call a local access number and then enter your identification number and the number you are calling. In either case, you have to dial a number, wait for a dial tone, and then dial the rest of the number. For example, you might have to dial 9, wait for the dial tone, and then dial 555-1212. You must tell the program to pause and wait for the dial tone at the appropriate point in the number and then, when it hears the dial tone, resume dialing. To tell the program to pause, you enter a designated symbol in the phone number, usually a comma, where you want it to pause, for example, 9,5551212. Some programs interpret the comma as an instruction to pause for a specified length of time; others pause until they sense the dial tone. For programs that pause for a given length of time, you can enter more than one comma to lengthen the pause, for example, 9,,,,555-1212. That way if the dial tone takes a long time, the program will still be waiting rather than dialing without the dial tone.

If you are using the program to call the same number through a switchboard or using a special phone service, many programs allow you to store a number of long-distance or other numbers that are dialed before the phone number. For example, you might enter a 9 in one of these settings and your MCI access number in another.

MODEM SETUP STRINGS

Many modems require you to send them a **setup string** (also called an *initialization string* or *dial prefix* code) before you send a phone number to dial. Since these numbers are used with every call, you have to enter them only once. The modem setup string sends a series of commands to your modem before you dial a number. The command, if Hayes compatible, begins with AT followed by specific commands. For example, to lower the speaker volume, you enter LI, and to display the message BUSY when it encounters a busy signal, you enter X3. The complete command is entered as ATLIX3. To dial a pulse phone, you enter ATDP. To dial a tone phone, you enter ATDT.

BAUD RATES

A modem's speed is measured in **baud rate**, or bits per second. Generally, modems are classified as low, medium, or high speed. Low-speed modems transmit 300 bits per second. Since each character you send contains 10 bits, a low-speed modem transmits or receives about 30 characters per second. Medium-speed modems transmit 1200 bits per second (about 120 characters) or 2400 bits per second (about 240 characters). A high-speed modem transmits 9600 or more bits per second (960 or more characters). The terms *bits per second* and *baud rate* are often used interchangeably although this is not exactly correct. Whether they are identical depends on the way the modem's signal is coded. For example, the Hayes SmartModem 1200 actually operates at 600 baud, but it uses a coding and modulation technique to squeeze 2 bits into the space normally occupied by 1 bit. Thus it transmits 1200 bits per second.

The speed a modem can transmit and receive data in is often important. The faster it operates, the shorter the time you are connected to the phone circuit and the service you are calling. Although most services charge a higher fee for a faster connection, you can still save money by using a faster modem. When you are connected to long-distance lines and are being billed by the minute, the costs of transmitting a file depend on the speed it is transmitted at. For example, a 300-baud modem takes about 64 seconds to transmit the 1920 characters in a normal computer screen display. A 1200-baud modem can send the same information in 12.8 seconds, and a 2400-baud modem, in 6.4 seconds.

Your computer is able to send information much faster than it can be transmitted over the phone lines because phone lines are designed for relatively low-frequency voice communications. Normal telephone lines are reliable up to about 2400 baud. Using them to transmit data at high speeds often causes errors. New technology is already addressing this problem and can handle transmissions of 9600 bits per second. For example, many high-speed modems automatically check the error rate and change the transmission speed if necessary. If a high error rate is encountered, it slows down the transmission speed, and when errors are reduced, it speeds back up. Some modems step up and down in increments when they encounter problems, for example, from 9600 to 4800 to 2400 and then to 1200. Others have sharper changes in transmission speeds. For example, if problems are encountered at 9600 baud, they drop to 1200. The smaller increments are preferable because average transmission speeds are kept as high as possible.

COMMUNICATIONS PARAMETERS

If data were sent over the phone lines using parallel communications, it would be easy for the receiving computer to know where each byte started and stopped. But since data is sent serially, a bit at a time, a procedure has to be used that tells the receiving computer where each byte begins and ends. To do this, date is usually sent in packages containing 10 bits. Figure 8-18 shows the 10 bits that are used to transmit the letter *a* as they would appear before they were modulated. These 10 bits contain all the information needed to send a single character. You can designate how these 10 bits are used by specifying the **communications parameters**.

When data is transmitted by your modem, you always have 1 start bit and 1 stop bit. However, you can change the parity and the number of data bits that are sent. The setting you use depends on the type of files you are planning to send and receive.

The **data bits** can be set to either 7 or 8 bits. These bits contain the ASCII code of the character being transmitted. The number of bits sent is called the **data word length**. If a word length of 7 bits is used, you can send the 127 standard ASCII characters. A word length of 8 bits allows you to send the 255 characters in the extended ASCII character set. You can use 7 bits when transmitting ASCII text files that contain only the first 127 characters in the ASCII character set. But to send binary files that contain the extended character set, you must use all 8 bits.

Parity can be set to odd, even, or none. When set to odd or even, a single bit checks for errors in the data bits during transmission. This digit is a function of the number of bits in the character being sent. When the number of bits in the character and the parity bit are added, the result can be

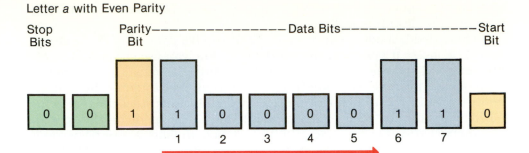

Letter *a* with Even Parity

Stop Bits — Parity Bit — Data Bits — Start Bit

| 0 | 0 | 1 | 1 | 0 | 0 | 0 | 0 | 1 | 1 | 0 |

1 2 3 4 5 6 7

Direction of Transmission

FIGURE 8-18
Communications Parameters
When data is transmitted by your modem the following occurs:

1. The sequence begins with the telephone line in a neutral state.
2. The first transmitted bit is called the start bit. You cannot change this setting, and its value is always 0.
3. The next set of bits is either 7 or 8 bits long and contains the ASCII digital equivalent of the character being transmitted. The least significant bit is sent first.
4. The next bit sent is called the parity bit. This is a single bit that checks for errors during transmission. This digit is a function of the number of bits in the character being sent. When the number of bits in the character and the parity bit are added, the result can be odd or even parity.
5. Finally, one or more stop bits are sent to end each data word. They always have a value of 0. They inform the receiving computer that the complete character has been transmitted and return the line to its neutral state for transmission of the next character.

odd or even parity. For example, the letter *a* is defined by 7 bits, which read 1100001. If you add the values of these 7 bits, the total is 3. If parity is set to even, the parity bit will be 1 so that the total increases to 4, an even number. If parity is set to odd, the parity bit will be 0 so that the total remains 3, an odd number. If the receiving computer finds that the total is not even or odd when it should be, it is called a **parity error**. The receiving computer then automatically requests that the data be retransmitted. You can use parity only when sending or receiving 7 data bits. Table 8-1 lists and describes the parameters that you can use to send various types of files.

If you specify 8 data bits so that you can send the complete 256 ASCII character set, there is no room for a parity bit, so parity is set to none. In this situation, errors are checked for by the communications protocols discussed in Topic 8-6. If you are using 8 data bits and no parity, and strings of unintelligible characters are displayed on your screen when you connect with another computer, switch to 7 data bits and even parity.

TABLE 8-1
Communication Parameters

Parity	Data	Stop	Used For
Even	7	1	ASCII text files
Odd	7	1	ASCII text files
None	8	1	Binary and program files

DATA FLOW CONTROL

When you send data to another computer, it is sent as a stream. At certain points, the receiving computer must acknowledge receipt of the information and let the sending computer know if the information was received correctly or not. But sometimes data may be transmitted faster than it can be received. To prevent this, some form of **flow control** is required. There are usually two possible settings for flow control.

Xon/Xoff is a form of flow control built into the communications software. If the receiving computer has a buffer, your data is stored in that buffer until it can be processed. If the buffer becomes full, the receiving computer sends an Xoff signal to the transmitting computer to tell it to temporarily stop the transmission. When the receiving computer catches up, it sends the transmitting computer an Xon signal to tell it to resume the transmission.

Hardware flow control specifies that flow control is handled at the hardware level. This type of flow control is useful when using a high-speed modem.

TERMINAL EMULATION

When you use a communications program to call another computer, your computer becomes a dumb terminal. A variety of terminal types are on the market, and the type of terminal that your computer becomes is called its **terminal emulation**. You must tell your program what kind of terminal you want to emulate so that you match the computer you are calling. Among the terminals that can be supported by a communications program are the following:

- TTY is a basic emulation that supports only **Tab**, **Backspace**, **Return**, and line feeds.
- VT52 emulates the Digital Equipment Corporation VT 52 terminal.
- VT102 emulates the Digital Equipment Corporation VT102 terminal.
- ANSI emulates the DOS 3.0 ANSI.SYS device driver and is frequently used by bulletin boards.
- IBM 3101 emulates the IBM 3101 terminal.

SIMPLEX, HALF-DUPLEX, AND FULL-DUPLEX

When data is sent between computers over wires, several techniques keep messages from interfering with each other on the lines. The techniques are classified by the way data moves over the lines.

Simplex

When data is sent in only one direction, for example, from your computer to your printer, the process is called **simplex**. Television and radio also use simplex communications. Because you can receive but not send (or send but not receive), simplex is rarely used in telecommunications.

Half-Duplex

When data flows in both directions over a line but in opposite directions at different times (like a ping-pong ball), it is called **half-duplex**. A typical example of half-duplex is a CB radio because when you press a button to talk, you can't hear the other party. With half-duplex, when a computer transmits data, the sending computer seizes the line. When the transmission is completed, the receiving computer turns the line around and becomes the sending station. This form of transmission is slower because it takes time for the message to be sent and received and for the line to be turned around. You will notice a delay when using a half-duplex mode. It is generally used only in older, less sophisticated equipment or when high-speed modems need to use the entire bandwidth of the wire.

Full-Duplex

When data is sent in both directions over a line at the same time, it is called **full-duplex** (also called echoplex or just duplex). A typical example of full-duplex is a telephone because both persons can talk and be heard at the same time. Microcomputers using asynchronous communications (see Topic 8-7) generally operate in full-duplex mode. In this mode, the wire is divided into two separate bandwidths with separate carrier frequencies, one to transmit and one to receive. Table 8-2 lists sample frequencies for full-duplex mode.

ECHOING

Echoing determines whether or not your computer will echo the keys you type on the screen at the same time they are sent to the other computer. When you type characters on your computer's keyboard, they are echoed on the screen so that you can see what you have typed. This echoing can be set to local or remote (Figure 8-19). When you are using full-duplex communications, the echo is set to remote so that the receiving computer can echo them to you as a form of error checking. When you are using half-duplex communications, the echo is set to local because the remote computer does not send them back to you. You can encounter errors if your settings do not match. If either of the following occurs, change your setting.

- If your computer is set to half-duplex and remote echoing, the receiving computer doesn't echo, so nothing that you type will appear on your screen.

- If your computer is set to full-duplex and local echoing, both the characters that you type and those echoed by the remote computer are displayed on your screen, so each character that you type appears twice.

TABLE 8-2
PSTN Frequencies

	Send	Receive
Carrier	1170 hertz	2125 hertz
Digital 0 (off)	1270 hertz	2225 hertz
Digital 1 (on)	1070 hertz	2025 hertz

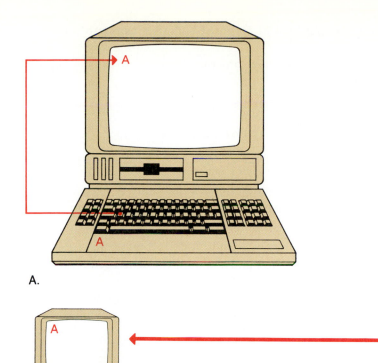

A.

B.

FIGURE 8-19
Local and Remote Echoing
Local echoing (a) sends a signal directly from your keyboard to the screen. Remote echoing (b) is one form of error checking. Each time you type a character on your keyboard, it is sent to the receiving computer, which accepts it and then sends it back to your computer to be displayed on the screen. This lets you monitor the results. If the character that appears on the screen is not the one you typed, an error has occurred in the transmission. If this happens, you can backspace over the incorrect character and retype it.

- When you call another computer, both computers must be using the same settings.

- When you enter phone numbers to call, you can enter special characters that cause the program to pause and wait for a dial tone before continuing to dial.

- Modem **setup strings** must be sent to the modem to set it up before a number is dialed. These setup strings are from the modem's command set.

- **Baud rates** measure how many bits are transmitted per second.

- **Communications parameters** determine how data is sent and can perform simple **error checking**. All data is transmitted with one **start bit** and one **stop bit**, but you can send 7 or 8 **data bits**. If you send 7 data bits, you can send a **parity bit** that determines if the 7 data bits were sent correctly. If you send 8 data bits, you cannot use parity checking.

- **Data flow control** prevents data from being sent faster than it can be received. The most common is **Xon/Xoff**.

- Your computer must **emulate** a specific terminal type when telecommunicating.

- When data is sent over the phone lines, it is sent in one of two ways. **Half-duplex** means the data flows in two directions at different times. **Full-duplex** means it flows in both directions at the same time but at different frequencies.

- **Echoing** can be set to either **local** or **remote**. When set to local echoing, keys you press are sent directly from your computer to your screen. When set to remote echoing, the characters you type are sent to the other computers and then sent back to your screen.

SUMMARY AND KEY TERMS

1. When you call another computer, can they use different communications settings?

2. Why would you want a communications program to pause when dialing a phone number?

3. What are setup strings used for?

4. How is the baud rate calculated?

5. How many start bits do you always use? How many stop bits?

6. What function does parity serve?

7. If you send 8 data bits, what must parity be set to?

8. What is the most common form of data flow control?

9. What is terminal emulation? What terminal must you emulate?

10. What is the difference between half- and full-duplex?

11. Describe the main difference between local and remote echoing.

12. If you are connected to another computer and keys you type do not send characters to your screen, what is wrong?

13. If you are connected to another computer and keys you type appear twice on your screen, what is wrong?

TOPIC 8-6

Transferring Files

OBJECTIVES

After completing this topic, you will be able to

- Describe the types of files you can send and receive
- Explain the purpose of communications protocols

When transmitting files, you can type them from the keyboard, and when receiving them, you can view them on the screen. But these methods are not always suitable. For example, you may want to send a message after you have carefully written and revised it. You might also want to transmit or receive more complicated documents like programs or spreadsheet files. To do this, you can create and edit the files on regular applications programs and then transmit them to the other computer. When you send or transmit a file to another computer, it is called **uploading**. When you receive a file from another computer, is called **downloading**.

Before uploading or downloading files, you have to understand the two kinds of files you can send or receive: text and binary. As you saw in Topic 3-8, text files are files that have been saved in an ASCII format. Many applications programs have a command that saves files in this format. The command generally includes the expression *Text file* or *ASCII file*. You can also create these files using an applications program's command to print to the disk.

Binary files include two basic types of files.

- Executable program files like BASIC programs, which can usually be identified by their .EXE or .COM extensions
- Encoded (formatted) files like those produced on WordPerfect, dBASE, Lotus 1-2-3, and other applications programs

Binary files require a more sophisticated transmission procedure because, unlike text files, a single missing or incorrect bit can make them unusable. To transmit or receive these files, you must use 8 data bits with no parity and the XMODEM error checking protocol.

DISPLAYING INFORMATION ON THE SCREEN

When your computer is connected to another computer, you can scroll through messages or download ASCII text files so that they are displayed on your screen. You can also route copies of these files either to your printer or to a file on a disk. This is called **text capture**, and no error checking is done by the program.

Most programs provide two ways to send the data to the printer. You can send just what is currently on the screen, or you can send anything that appears on the screen during a session. To do either, you press specified keys on the keyboard or make menu selections. You use the same keys or menu choices to turn the printing off. Continuously sending data to the printer slows you down because the printer prints more slowly than you can receive.

Since large files take a long time to read on the screen or print out, it is usually faster to store them in a file on the disk so that you can read them or print them out later. To do so, you execute the program's file save commands and specify a filename. Anything that appears on your screen, whether originating from your keyboard or the remote computer, will be stored in the specified file. The data received from the other computer will also be displayed on your screen unless you are using a communications protocol that displays messages that tell you which block is being received and verifies its receipt.

UPLOADING AND DOWNLOADING FILES

One way to communicate with another computer is to send and receive program and data files that are stored on a disk. For example, a software company can send you an update to their program, or a sales manager can send a sales report to the home office. To send or receive files, you must use the communication program's command to upload or download a file, and then specify both the name of the file to be uploaded or downloaded and the communications protocol to be used in the file transfer.

Many files that are exchanged over the phone lines are **compressed** by the sender so that they can be transmitted more quickly. The recipient then uses a program to **uncompress** the files once they are received. Depending on the type of files being sent, compression can save a great deal of time and dramatically lower phone costs. For example, a graphics file that might normally take 20 minutes to transmit can be transmitted in 5 minutes if it is first compressed. Programs that compress and uncompress files are found on many bulletin boards. The most popular program of this kind is a shareware program called ARC. If you like it, you send the developers a small fee.

There is a cliche that if anything can go wrong, it will. This certainly applies to the high-speed transmission of digital data over telephone lines that are designed to carry voice communications. If even 1 bit of data is received incorrectly, all the following data may be garbled. It's like a high-speed train hitting a bump in the track and derailing. Until phone circuits are improved for digital data, **communications protocols** (also called link protocols) are used to check for errors and correct them during transmission. We have already discussed the parity bit and echoing, which are simple but limited forms of error checking. Their major problem is that two errors in the same character can cancel each other out, and the character is then accepted as correct when it is not. More sophisticated protocols establish rules the computers must follow when exchanging information. To use any of these protocols, both the transmitting and receiving computers must be able to support it. Protocols establish the following:

- Block size is the number of bits in each block of data sent at a time.
- Duplex is the sequence data exchange occurs in. It can be either half-duplex or full-duplex.

- **Handshaking** is the method used to respond to the receipt of data either correctly or incorrectly received.

- Error detection is the procedure used to detect errors in the data received by the remote computer.

- Error correction is the procedure followed when an error is detected. The procedure can be either a request that the block be retransmitted or a determination that the transfer be aborted.

XMODEM

One popular, and sophisticated, error checking scheme is XMODEM, written by Ward Christianson of Chicago. This is a public-domain program, essentially a gift to the computing community. This program uses a simple technique. To use XMODEM, communications parameters must be set to no parity and 8 data bits.

1. It sends data in blocks of 128 bytes. The data is not displayed on the screen as it is being sent or received.

2. Each of the bytes contains an ASCII character, which is identified by its ASCII number. For example, the letter A is ASCII 01000001, B is 01000010, and so on.

3. The program adds the values of all the ASCII characters in the block and sends the ASCII character for that value last. This value is called the checksum character.

4. The receiving end adds the values of all ASCII characters in the block it receives and checks it against the checksum character to see if they match.

5. If they match, the receiving computer sends an acknowledgment back to the transmitting computer, which then sends the next block. If it detects an error, the receiving computer requests that the block be retransmitted.

Kermit

The XMODEM protocol requires 8 bits of data, and some computers can accept only 7. Other computers that can accept 8 bits cannot accept control characters and deletes. To overcome these problems, Frank de Cruz at Columbia University developed the public-domain program Kermit. This protocol can handle either 7 or 8 bits and automatically converts the 8th bit when necessary so that it can be understood by the remote computer. Kermit is used extensively to communicate with mainframe computers. One of its advantages is that it error checks commands you type as well as files you upload and download.

YMODEM

YMODEM, developed by Chuck Forsberg, is similar to XMODEM but sends data in 1024-bit packets instead of 128-bit packets. Another version, called YMODEM BATCH, allows for the transfer to multiple files.

CompuServe B

CompuServe B (also called CIS B) is used on the CompuServe Information Service.

High-Speed Modem Protocols

As modem speeds increase to 9600 bits per second and higher, it becomes increasing difficult to maintain a connection and accurate data transfer over telephone lines. Although XMODEM is currently the most widely used error checking protocol, faster transmission speeds require more sophisticated error checking. Today, several new protocols are vying for acceptance. Since both sending and receiving modems must use the same protocol, it will simplify things if one becomes the standard. Until there is an accepted standard, users should buy modems for both ends of a connection from the same manufacturer, or they may be unable to talk to each other.

Two protocols contending for an industrywide standard, are asymmetrical and pseudo full-duplex.

- **Asymmetrical** protocols split the phone line into two channels. One is used to send data at a high speed. The other is used to send confirmation and slow-speed data in the opposite direction.

- **Pseudo full-duplex** protocols are like half-duplex; that is, they send data in one direction, and then the line reverses so that confirmation can be sent in the other.

Two implementations of these standards are X.25 (or X.PC) and Microcom Networking Protocol (MNP). At the moment, MNP is the leading contender to become the industry standard.

CASE STUDY
Calling a Bulletin Board

Many users of modems and communications programs use them to call public or corporate bulletin boards. In this case, we introduce you to how you call the bulletin board used by people who test software for the WordPerfect Corporation. We use PROCOMM PLUS, one of the leading communications programs. These steps are almost identical to those you would use to dial into an information service like CompuServe.

Step 1: Load the Program Insert the PROCOMM program disk into drive A, and then close the disk drive door. From the *A>* system prompt, type PCPLUS and then press **Return**. In a moment, an opening message is displayed (Figure A), and then the terminal mode screen appears (Figure B).

Step 2: Display the Dialing Directory Press **Alt-D** to display the dialing directory, and a blank dialing directory appears on the screen (Figure C). The dialing directory lists spaces for 200 entries, 10 of which are displayed on the screen at one time. Each line contains spaces where you can enter a name and phone number. The directory also lists the default communications parameters that will be used to make a call unless you change them. The listed settings are the ones most commonly used when communicating with other microcomputers.

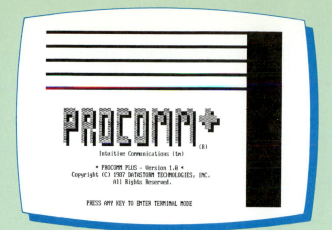

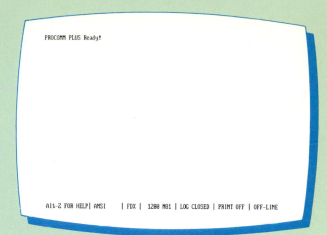

Step 3: Enter the Phone Number and Communications Parameters

Highlight the entry that you want to enter or revise, and then press **R** to display the entry listing (Figure D). Enter the name, phone number, and communications parameters and file exchange protocols (Figure E). When finished, a series of prompts asks if you want to accept the entry and save it to the disk (Figure F).

Step 4: Call the Bulletin Board

After you enter the necessary information the first time, you make a call by answering this prompt by pressing **D** for *Dial Entry(s)*, and then the prompt reads *Entry(s) to dial* (Figure G). Press **1** and then press **Return** to dial the computer listed in entry 1 on the dialing directory.

You hear a high-pitched squeal as the number is dialed, and then the phone rings at the other end (unless the number is busy). The other computer's high-pitched screech indicates you have connected to the computer, and the carrier detect light on your modem (if it has one) lights up, also indicating you have connected. Often you have to press **Return** a couple of times before you get a sign-on notice. This allows the other computer to determine the baud rate you are using so that it can adjust its own.

When you are connected, you are asked to enter you name and a password. If you do this correctly, the bulletin board's Main menu appears (Figure H).

FIGURE A (above left)
The Copyright Screen
The PROCOMM copyright screen appears when you first load the program.

FIGURE B (above right)
The Terminal Mode Screen
The terminal mode screen is displayed when you are ready to enter commands.

FIGURE C (below left)
The Dialing Directory
The dialing directory displays up to ten phone numbers per screen.

FIGURE D (below right)
The Entry Listing
When you edit or revise a listing in the dialing directory, an entry screen is displayed.

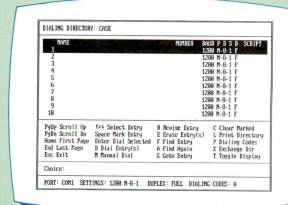

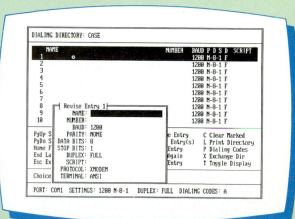

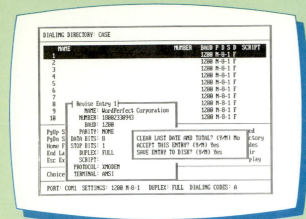

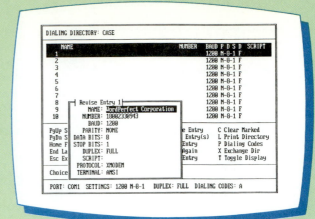

FIGURE E (above left)
The Entry
When you enter or revise a listing, the entries are displayed as you enter them.

FIGURE F (above right)
Prompts When Finished
When finished entering or revising a listing, a series of prompts is displayed.

FIGURE G (below left)
The Dialing Prompt
When you press **D** for *Dial Entry(s)*, a prompt asks you which listing you want to dial.

FIGURE H (below right)
The Bulletin Board Main Menu
When you connect with a bulletin board, the Main menu is displayed. This menu lists all the boards commands.

Step 5: Read Messages To read messages, you press **R** for *Read Messages*, and a prompt asks you if you want to read a specific message or all of them. Responding to either prompt displays messages on your screen that were entered by other users (Figure I).

Step 6: Enter a Message To leave a message of your own, you press **E** for *Enter a new message* from the Main menu, and a text editing screen is displayed. You type your message, and then press **Return** twice. A prompt then asks if you want to save the message, edit it, or abandon it.

Step 7: Upload a File To upload a file, you press **U** for *Upload a file* from the Main menu. A prompt asks you to enter the name of the file. When you do so, and specify the file transfer protocols you are using, the file is uploaded to the bulletin board's hard disk drive.

Step 8: Download a File To download a file, you press **D** for *Download a file* from the Main menu. A prompt asks you to enter the name of the file. When you do so, and specify the link protocols you are using, the file is downloaded from the bulletin board to your disk drive.

Step 9: Hanging Up Although you can disconnect from a bulletin board or other service by turning off the modem, it is discourteous to do so. You should always use the bulletin board's command to log off the service so that you don't create problems on the computer you are connected to.

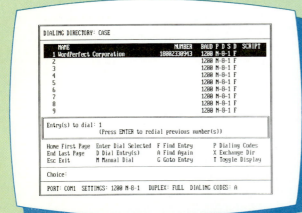

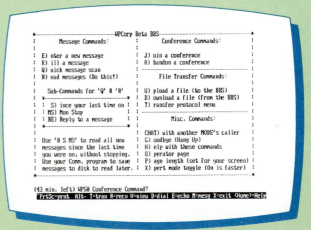

```
Date: 02-10-88 (08:18)          Number: 115
  To: DURK MERRELL              Refer#: NONE
From: SHERMAN ROBINSON           Read: NO
Subj: EPSON FX-286             Status: PUBLIC MESSAGE

   On installation, I have basically succeeded in getting the program
loaded on my machines, with problems as noted earlier. When can I
bypass the WP.FIL? Is it for installation only? As noted earlier,
I get asked to insert the WP-2 disk when I load up. Hitting F7 makes
the message go away, and the machine starts properly. After that, it
appears to load normally, with no further requests for the WP-2 disk.
   On printers, I still cannot get the Epson FX-286 to work properly.
It still advances about 1/4 page after every page of printing,
throwing everything off. I will have to put the Epson back into
IBM Proprinter emulation mode, or try the Epson FX-86e driver.
What do you folks suggest??
   On usage, I have started using the program on a paper. One
funny thing happened when I saved it. One time, when I hit F10
and tried to save to the default file name, I was informed that
the file was "locked". I saved to a different name successfully,
exited, restarted WP, and could not replicate the problem.

More: (Y)es, (N)o, (NS)non-stop, (T)hread, (#), (RE)ply?
PrtSc=prnt  Alt- T=tran R=recv V=view D=dial E=echo M=mesg X=exit <Home>=Help
```

FIGURE I
A Message
You can display messages that have been left by previous users.

Things That Can Go Wrong

The most common problems users have when calling other computers are the use of incorrect cables or incorrect switch settings in the modem. If nothing happens when you dial the number, the problem is probably in one of these areas though other problems can also occur.

- You hear a busy signal. Hang up and dial again.

- You get connected, but illegible characters appear on your screen. Your parameter settings do not match the computer you called. Find out what the correct settings should be, and set yours to match the computer you are calling.

- You do not hear the modem dialing the number. Either your modem is not connected correctly or its switches have not been set properly.

- The connection is fine, but when you type, either no characters appear on the screen or two characters appear for every one you type. This means your echo setting does not match the other computer's. Turn echo on if you do not see any characters, or turn it off if you see two for every one you type.

SUMMARY AND KEY TERMS

- Sending files to another computer is called **uploading**. Receiving files from another computer is called **downloading**.
- You can upload and download ASCII text files or binary files.
- When connected to another computer, you can display messages and ASCII text files on your screen. You can **capture** this text that appears on your screen and send it to a disk file.
- When you want to transfer a file from one computer's disk to another's, you can upload or download it. Some files are **compressed** to reduce transmission time.
- When you transfer a file, both computers must use the same communications protocols to ensure the file is transferred without errors. Some popular protocols include XMODEM, Kermit, and YMODEM.

REVIEW QUESTIONS

1. What do downloading and uploading refer to?

2. What two types of files can you transfer between computers?

3. When text is displayed on your screen, what is it called when you save it in a disk file?

4. Why are files compressed before they are transferred?

5. What are communications protocols, and what role do they play in telecommunications? Name two.

Telecommunications Principles

OBJECTIVES

After completing this topic, you will be able to

- Describe the types of signals that can be used to communicate
- Describe the ways signals can be modulated
- Describe the importance of bandwidth
- Explain the difference between asynchronous and synchronous communications

Some of the principles at work behind telecommunications are quite technical. You do not have to understand these principles to telecommunicate, but you should know something about them so that you can follow new developments and evaluate new products.

COMMUNICATION SIGNALS

All electronic data is transmitted by using a transmitter to send electrical voltages that periodically change in form. A receiver then interprets, or decodes, these changing voltages to reconstruct the original message. Messages can be sent in either digital or analog form.

Digital Signals

A simple example of digital signaling is the telegraph. An operator at one end presses a key, closing a circuit and sending a pulse of electricity over the telegraph line. A receiver connected to the other end of the line receives this pulse and emits a click. By varying the time between keystrokes, the sender conveys a message to the listener at the other end of the line who knows how to interpret the clicks. In a computer, as you saw in Topic 1-0, the changes in voltage are digital in nature, just as they are in the telegraph. In a computer, digital 0s and 1s are transmitted as low and high voltages (Figure 8-20).

FIGURE 8-20
Digital Signals
Data is sent out of the computer as digital signals.

Analog Signals

Other than the computer and the telegraph, most communications are analog in nature. For example, when you say hello to a friend, your voice generates analog sound waves that the listener hears and interprets.

Analog waves have a smooth, sinusoidal shape that varies in frequency, amplitude, and phase (Figures 8-21 and 8-22).

MODULATION

When the telephone and radio were being developed, it was discovered that high frequencies could be transmitted more effectively than low frequencies. Since most of the information transmitted over the telephone and radio, such as voices and music, have relatively low frequencies, **modulation** is used to transmit the signals more efficiently. Modulation is a process whereby the signal (the information) is superimposed onto a higher frequency, called the **carrier wave**. When computer data is sent over phone lines, it sounds like a high-pitched screech if you pick up a phone tied into the transmission. This screech, which is being transmitted too fast for you to interpret, is the carrier wave.

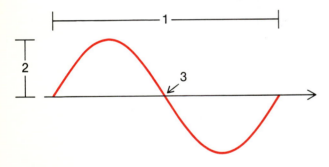

FIGURE 8-21
Analog Signals
Analog waves are used to transmit voice and data over the telephone lines.

1. The frequency is the distance between peaks on the wave. From the top or bottom of one wave to the top or bottom of the next is called a cycle. The shorter the distance between peaks, the higher the frequency—the number of complete cycles transmitted in a given period. Frequency is measured in cycles per second (CPS) or hertz (Hz). One cycle per second is 1 hertz, 1000 per second is 1 kilohertz, and 1 million cycles per second is 1 megahertz.

2. As the analog wave is transmitted, its voltage rises and falls. The distance between the zero baseline and the maximum voltage is called the amplitude.

3. The point at which an analog wave meets the zero line, or any other point on its curve, is called its phase.

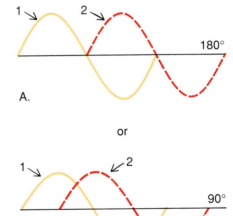

FIGURE 8-22
Phases
The phase of a signal is easier to see if two waves are superimposed. In (a) the first wave (1) has already reached its highest point when the second wave (2) is at its low point. These waves have different phases, exactly 180 degrees apart. In (b) the first wave (1) is at its highest point when the second wave (2) is at zero. These waves are exactly 90 degrees apart.

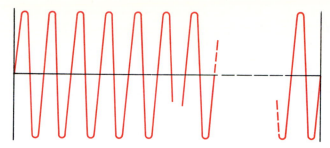

FIGURE 8-23
Unmodulated Carrier Wave
A carrier wave is an unmodulated analog signal transmitted at a high frequency.

Carrier waves are also used in the radio industry. A transmitter at the studio uses the low-frequency voice and music signals to modulate a high-frequency carrier wave. At the receiving end, a radio tuned to the carrier wave frequency demodulates the signal. It does this by separating the low-frequency voice or music from the high-frequency carrier wave. It then sends this low-frequency demodulated signal to the speakers, which reproduce the sound in its original form so that you can hear it. In this way, music with a frequency range of 0-15,000 cycles per second can be transmitted on the much higher frequencies you pick up on your radio receiver.

An unmodulated carrier wave (Figure 8-23) looks just like the analog wave in Figure 8-21, the only difference being that it usually has a much higher frequency. Household electricity is a typical unmodulated analog carrier wave. It has a frequency of 60 cycles per second or hertz and an amplitude of 110 volts. Some household intercom and alarm systems can be plugged into electrical outlets to carry messages on the household wiring. They just modulate their signal on top of the existing carrier wave, eliminating the need for additional wiring.

Three common forms of modulation are used with modems and other forms of electronic transmissions.

- **Amplitude modulation (AM)**, which is also used to transmit AM radio broadcasts and television pictures. Amplitude modulation changes the amplitude of the cycles in the carrier wave (Figure 8-24).

- **Frequency modulation (FM)**, which is also used to transmit FM radio broadcasts, television sound, and telephone conversations. A form of this modulation, called **frequency shift keying (FSK)**, is used by low-speed modems to transmit digital data over analog telephone circuits (Figure 8-25).

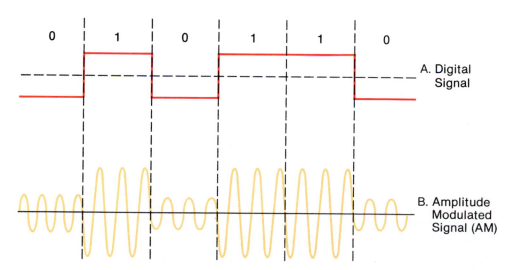

A. Digital Signal

B. Amplitude Modulated Signal (AM)

FIGURE 8-24
Amplitude Modulation
This figure shows a digital signal that is to be transmitted (a) and how the signal is used to modulate the carrier by varying its amplitude (b). You can clearly see the shape of the original signal reflected in the amplitude of the carrier wave. The transmitter superimposes (modulates) the signal on the carrier wave, and the receiver separates (demodulates) the two signals.

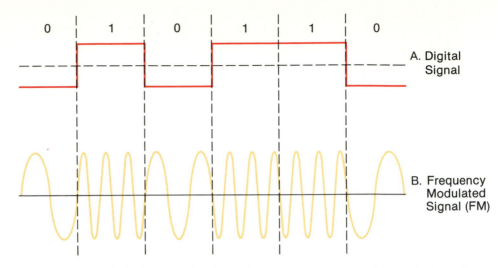

FIGURE 8-25
Frequency Modulation
This figure shows the same signal as Figure 8-24 (a), but it is now modulated using frequency modulation (b). Instead of changing the amplitude of the carrier, this modulation process changes its frequency at key points. Digital 0s and 1s are represented by shifting the frequency of the carrier wave to a slightly higher or lower frequency. For example, if the carrier wave frequency is 1170 hertz, a 0 is conveyed by increasing the frequency to 1270 hertz, and a 1, by lowering it to 1070 hertz.

A. Digital Signal

B. Frequency Modulated Signal (FM)

■ **Phase modulation** (**PM**), which is used in more sophisticated modems to increase the amount of information that can be sent (Figure 8-26).

BANDWIDTH, CODING, AND MODULATION

One of the key limits on the amount of data that can be transmitted is **bandwidth**, a measurement of the range of frequencies that can be sent. This range determines the amount of data that can be conveyed. For example, the phone system is designed to carry a range of frequencies from 300 to 3400 hertz, a bandwidth of 3100 hertz (3400-300). Since telephone lines have a relatively narrow bandwidth, special techniques must be used to send data faster. Four-level **phase shift keying** (**PSK**) is used to send more than 1 bit per baud. The popular Hayes Smartmodem 1200, for example, uses this form of modulation because the telephone wire does not have a bandwidth wide enough to carry a 1200-baud signal. PSK modulation encodes 2 bits per baud, so the modem transmitting at 600 baud is actually transmitting 1200 bits per second.

ASYNCHRONOUS AND SYNCHRONOUS

Data is usually transmitted either asynchronously or synchronously over the phone line. The method used determines the timing and the amount of data sent in a single operation.

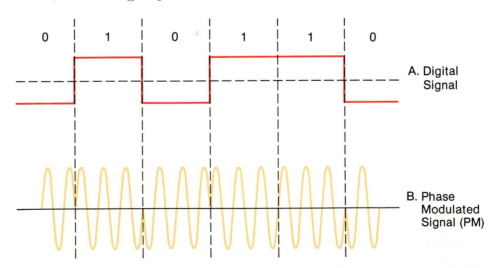

FIGURE 8-26
Phase Modulation
Phase modulation conveys data by changing the starting point of the cycles in the analog carrier wave. This figure shows the same signal as Figures 8-24 and 8-25 (a), but these are now shown modulated using phase shifting (b). As you can see, the starting point of the waves is changed to shift between digital 0s and 1s. A 1 is indicated by no shift, and a 0 is indicated by a 180-degree shift.

A. Digital Signal

B. Phase Modulated Signal (PM)

Asynchronous data transmission sends characters one at a time. The timing between the bits in a given character is always precise, but the timing between different characters is random. The timing of the sending and receiving computers does not have to be synchronized, hence the term *asynchronous*, which means not synchronized. This form of data transmission is often used when the timing between characters is determined by an operator who is typing data on a keyboard.

Synchronous data transmission is faster because it sends groups of characters called blocks or packets at specific intervals, which are timed by a clock. Both the timing within the character and between characters is precise. The sending and receiving computers must have their timing synchronized, hence the term *synchronous*, which means synchronized. This form of data transmission is widely used in communications between mainframes or from a mainframe to its terminals. The Hayes Smartmodem 1200 and other modems using PSK modulation also use synchronous transmission to send signals over the phone lines.

SUMMARY AND KEY TERMS

- The signals sent from your computer are digital signals and must be converted into analog signals for transmission over the phone lines.

- To convert digital signals into analog signals, an analog **carrier wave** is **modulated** by the digital signal. There are three basic ways to modulate a signal: **amplitude modulation**, **frequency modulation**, and **phase modulation**.

- One of the key limits on how much data can be transferred in a given period is **bandwidth**.

- When data is sent, it can be sent asynchronously or synchronously. **Asynchronous** transmission sends one character at a time, and the timing between characters can be random. **Synchronous** transmission sends groups of characters, and the timing between characters is precise.

REVIEW QUESTIONS

1. What is the difference between analog and digital signals?
2. What is a carrier wave? What is it used for?
3. Describe three common forms of modulation.
4. How does asynchronous data transmission differ from synchronous data transmission?

Part Nine

OTHER APPLICATIONS

Topic 9-1   Project Management Programs
Topic 9-2   Idea and Outline Processors
Topic 9-3   Desktop and Personal Information Managers
Topic 9-4   Accounting Programs
Topic 9-5   Utility Programs
Topic 9-6   Expert Systems

There are many specialized applications programs that enhance other programs or are versions of other programs adapted to serve specific functions. For example, idea processors gather and organize ideas so that proposals, plans, and strategies are more carefully developed. Accounting programs are really powerful applications of database programs designed to handle a specific aspect of a firm's business. Utility programs are simple, inexpensive programs that modify the computer, programs, or files. Expert systems are the first step in the development of programs that incorporate artificial intelligence. Finally, vertical applications programs are tailored for specific industries. In this part, we explore some examples of these useful and popular programs that expand the applications of computers. You can choose from many such applications programs. Broadly, they are classified into vertical and horizontal applications programs.

Vertical applications programs are those designed for a specific purpose in a specific industry. For example, a loan officer in a bank or an investment counselor might use a program designed specifically to analyze an investment opportunity. Even some word processing programs have been developed for vertical markets. For example, technical word processing programs have been developed for technical writers and others who work on complicated documents containing mathematical formulas, footnotes, and illustrations.

Horizontal applications programs are those designed for many users in a wide variety of businesses. These programs are designed to be flexible enough so that they can be applied to various tasks. For example, a typical horizontal applications programs is a word processing program that you can use to write a memo, a report, a book, or even another program. Another is a spreadsheet program that you can use to analyze an investment or calculate the payments on a new car.

REVIEW QUESTIONS

1. What is a horizontal applications program?
2. What is a vertical applications program?

Project Management Programs

OBJECTIVE

After completing this topic, you will be able to

- Explain the principles of project management and how project management programs work

Directing the orderly progression of a project so that it is completed both on schedule and on budget is called **project management**. Whatever the project, from marketing campaigns to construction projects, you ask the same questions.

- What is the earliest the project can be completed?
- What would it cost to do it faster?
- What is the best way to organize both the steps in the project and the staff needed to complete those steps?
- How soon does each step have to be started, and when does it have to be completed?
- What is the last date final decisions have to be made about particular aspects of the project?
- How will the timing of various steps in the project affect cash flow?
- What staff is required, and when are they needed?

These questions can be difficult to answer, especially when the project is complicated or when other projects are running simultaneously.

Sophisticated analytical techniques to help gather, organize, and manipulate project management data have always been used in the construction and defense industries. These industries undertake many large projects where the sequence, timing, and costs of thousands of individual steps require coordination and control. Common expressions associated with these techniques include critical paths, crashing schedules, PERT (program evaluation and review) charts, and Gantt charts. Because these techniques demanded extensive experience and resources (including mainframe computers), they were used only on the most complicated and expensive projects.

New software applications programs are now making the same tools accessible to microcomputer users with limited or no project management experience. Expertise in the techniques that underlie the programs is often unnecessary.

THE PRINCIPLES OF PROJECT MANAGEMENT

Project managers are concerned with three main variables. First, they break the project down into steps or tasks and key events or milestones. Every project has several tasks and at least two milestones—a beginning and an end. Next, the steps are organized into some logical sequence, with a starting date and duration determined for each step. Finally, costs are calculated; these are frequently related to when tasks are done and how long they take. Relating these three variables traditionally has been time consuming and expensive, especially when managers want to optimize a schedule or explore what-if questions. When scheduling a project, it is helpful to ask the following questions and to know immediately what the impact would be on the budget and completion date of the project:

- What if some steps can be completed faster?
- What if some steps take longer than expected?
- What if the budget is cut for some of the project?

Optimizing a project schedule and exploring what-ifs require a minimal understanding of the critical path and crashing schedules, both of which concern improving a project schedule.

The Critical Path

If you know the sequence that tasks must be completed in and how long each takes, you can find a series of tasks that are sequential and interdependent. Each subsequent task cannot be begun until the previous one is completed. For example, a roof cannot be put on a house until the walls are up, and the walls cannot be built until the foundation is completed.

When these dependent tasks are laid out end to end, they form the project's **critical path**. Any delays in the tasks on this path delay the entire project. Tasks not on the critical path—for example, paving the driveway—do not affect the project's completion date.

Crashing Schedules

Speeding up a project, called **crashing the schedule**, can be done only by changing the dates on the critical path. But to complicate matters, the critical path is not fixed. Changing some dates on the existing critical path may result in another path's becoming critical, so further improvements in the schedule require speeding up the completion of tasks on the new critical path. Dates can sometimes be improved by spending more money on certain tasks, which may save money on others.

Because the order, timing, and costs of the individual tasks are interrelated, they all affect the total cost of the project and its completion date. To minimize the times and costs associated with a project requires a careful analysis of each step in the process.

PROJECT MANAGEMENT GRAPHICS

Graphics are often used to show the complicated relationships in the timing and sequence of a project. Most project management programs generate two types of graphics after the manager has entered the beginning dates and duration of all tasks: **PERT charts** (Figure 9-1) and **Gantt charts** (Figure 9-2).

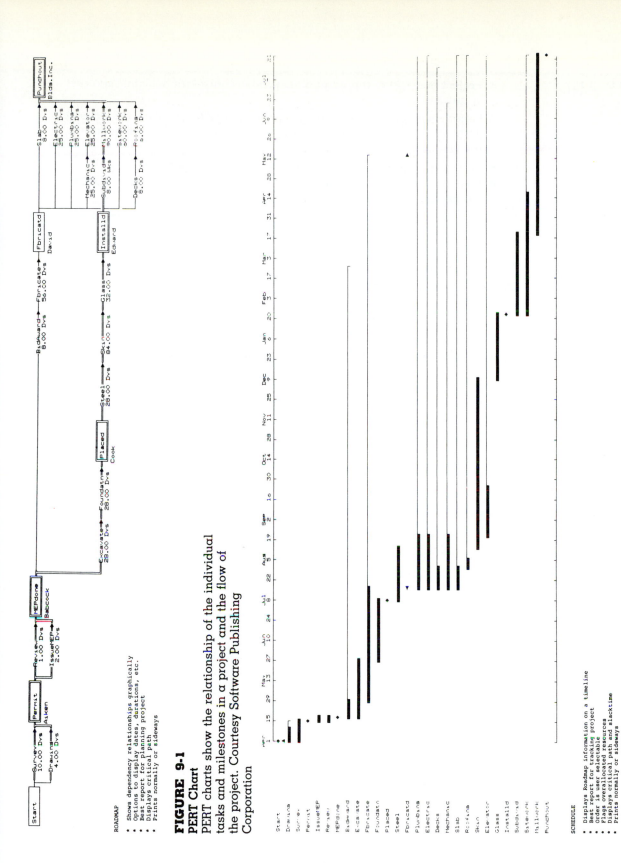

ROADMAP

- Shows dependency relationships graphically
- Options to display dates, durations, etc.
- Best report for planning project
- Displays critical path
- Prints normally or sideways

FIGURE 9-1
PERT Chart
PERT charts show the relationship of the individual tasks and milestones in a project and the flow of the project. Courtesy Software Publishing Corporation

SCHEDULE

- Displays Roadmap information on a timeline
- Best report for tracking project
- Order is user selectable
- Flags overallocated resources
- Displays critical path and slacktime
- Prints normally or sideways

FIGURE 9-2
Gantt Chart
Gantt charts use bars and a time line to illustrate the beginning and ending dates of each task making up the project. Courtesy Software Publishing Corporation

SUMMARY AND KEY TERMS

- **Project management programs** are used to control the schedule and cost of projects.
- Project management programs can automatically calculate the **critical path**, the sequence of tasks whose schedule must be improved to improve the overall schedule.
- Speeding up a project is called **crashing the schedule**.
- Project management programs provide two types of graphics: **PERT charts** and **Gantt charts**.

REVIEW QUESTIONS

1. Describe some of the answers you can get with a project management program?
2. What is the name of the path that must be improved to improve a project's overall schedule?
3. What is it called when you speed up a project?
4. What is a PERT chart? What information does it provide?
5. What is a Gantt chart? What information does it provide?

TOPIC 9-2

Idea and Outline Processors

OBJECTIVE

After completing this topic, you will be able to

- Describe idea and outline processors and what you use them for

Idea and outline processing programs are very useful when you are preparing plans and reports. Although these programs are increasingly being integrated into word processing programs, some are available as standalone programs.

IDEA PROCESSORS

Idea processors like ThinkTank (Figure 9-3) help you gather and organize ideas. When addressing a new problem, most people jot down notes and ideas as they come to mind. They are often written on note pads, restaurant napkins, business cards, and almost every other conceivable place. As the ideas are generated, people collect and organize them, generally by breaking them down into steps or topics. An idea processor automates this process for you and gives you additional advantages as well.

- You can quickly reorganize ideas and topics.
- You can easily add new topics and delete unnecessary ones.

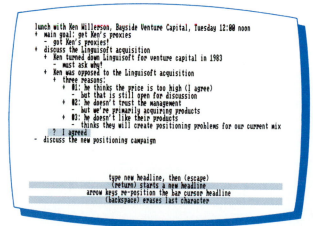

FIGURE 9-3
ThinkTank
ThinkTank was the first idea processor. Ideas can be entered, moved, and inserted to organize them in outline form. You can organize and reorganize frames in an outline. As you get new ideas, you can enter them under an existing heading or create a new heading for them.

717

- You can combine related topics.
- You can break up large topics into subtopics.

FIGURE 9-4
Outline Programs
You can view the entire document, or you can close it up so that you see just the outline's headings. This not only lets you see both the overall structure of the document and the details in each section, it also lets you move quickly through a long document. You display the document in outline view, highlight the heading of the section you want to move to, and open that section to see the text it contains.

OUTLINE PROGRAMS

Outline programs were initially designed as utility programs but are now often integrated into word processing programs. These programs allow you to enter headings much as you do when manually preparing an outline. But outline programs automatically number the headings and indent subheadings to indicate their level. If you insert or delete an entry, the program automatically renumbers all the headings that follow the revision. Many of these programs also allow you to enter text linked to a specific heading. If you copy, move, or delete a heading, all text associated with it is also copied, moved, or deleted. These programs also let you look at your document in document or outline view (Figure 9-4).

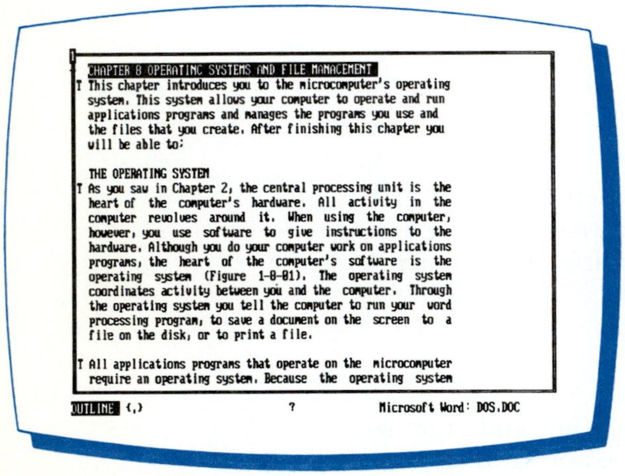

A. Document View

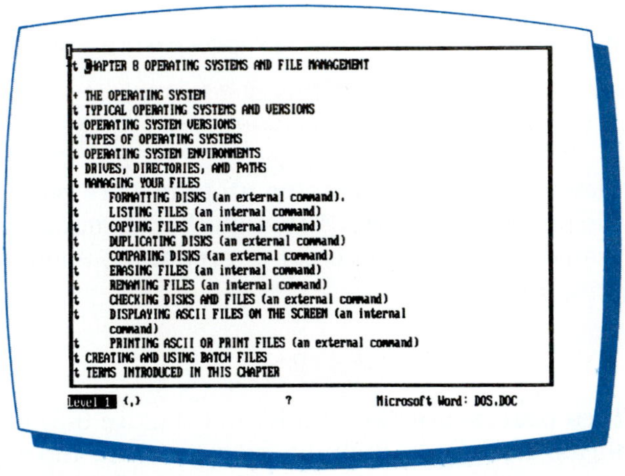

B. Outline View

SUMMARY AND KEY TERMS

- **Idea processors** are used to organize ideas in steps.
- **Outline programs** attach body text to headings so that if you copy, delete, or move the heading, the body text is also copied, moved, or deleted. They also let you look at the document in two ways. You can use outline view to display just the headings and document view to display the headings and body text.

REVIEW QUESTIONS

1. List four things you can do with an idea processor.
2. What is the key feature of an outline program? What two views can you use to look at your information?

Desktop and Personal Information Managers

OBJECTIVE

After completing this topic, you will be able to

- Describe desktop and personal information manager programs and what you use them for

Several programs have been developed to ease your work on a computer. These programs fall into two classes, desktop managers and personal information managers.

DESKTOP MANAGERS

Often when working on a computer, you must change programs to change tasks. This is not a serious problem when you spend a lot of time on each task and have to interrupt your work only occasionally to change programs. But there are some tasks that you need access to all the time, for example, keeping an appointment schedule or automatically dialing your phone. To quit a spreadsheet program and load a phone dialing program to make a call probably takes more time than looking up the number and dialing it yourself.

Several programs, called **desktop managers**, have been introduced that solve this problem (Figure 9-5). You load these programs into the computer before any applications programs so that even when you are working on your word processing or spreadsheet program, the desktop manager can be displayed on the screen (usually in a window) simply by pressing a few keys. When you call up the desktop manager, the applications program is suspended. When you press another key, the desktop manager is gone, and you are returned to the applications program you were working on. Desktop managers are really integrated programs since they combine different functions.

PERSONAL INFORMATION MANAGERS

Throughout any business day, you jot down notes on paper, make appointments on calendars, and enter phone numbers into phone directories. Most people also make to-do lists to keep their work organized and assign priori-

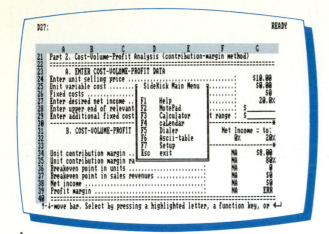

A.

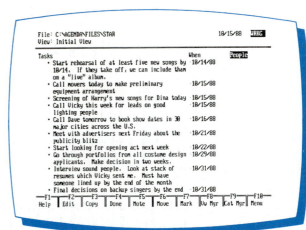

B.

FIGURE 9-5 (above)
Sidekick
When Sidekick is loaded into the computer's memory, its menu can be displayed by just pressing two keys as shown here when working on Lotus 1-2-3 (a). The menu lists available functions: a calculator, note pad, auto dialer (used in conjunction with a Hayes Smartmodem or compatible modem), appointment calendar, phone directory, and ASCII table. Any of these can be displayed by highlighting them on the menu and then pressing **Return**. Data can be moved between other programs you are using by first copying it from one program to the note pad (b), and then copying it from the note pad to the other program.

FIGURE 9-6 (right)
Agenda
Lotus's Agenda lets you access your information in any of three ways: by when a task is due, by the person responsible, or by priority.

ties. A new class of programs, called **personal information managers**, has been developed to make these tasks easier. Generally these programs let you enter data and then view it in several ways. For example, you can enter data and assign it to categories like calls to make or memos to write. You can also assign multiple categories to tasks so that you can find them later from different perspectives. Lotus's Agenda is typical of these kind of programs (Figure 9-6).

SUMMARY AND KEY TERMS

- **Desktop managers** provide several tools useful to business people. For example, they usually contain appointment calendars, phone dialers, and calculators.

- **Personal information managers** allow you to enter information and then look at it from more than one viewpoint.

REVIEW QUESTIONS

1. What is a desktop manager program? Why can it be used while working on another program?

2. What is the purpose of a personal information manager? What is its unique feature?

Accounting Programs

OBJECTIVES

After completing this topic, you will be able to

- Explain how computerized accounting systems work
- Describe typical reports that accounting programs generate

The dream of every bookkeeper and accountant is a single-entry system where data is entered only once and is automatically transferred to the appropriate accounting ledgers and reports. For example, when a sale is entered, the item is automatically deducted from inventory, the income and cost are posted to the general ledger, and if the sale was on credit, the money due is added to the accounts receivable ledger.

Accounting programs have long been available to large companies using mainframes and custom software. They now are available to smaller firms with access to microcomputers. These programs not only reduce the amount of data that must be entered but also automatically prepare numerous management reports, such as income statements and balance sheets.

Many of these programs are available as modules that can be integrated into a complete system. These modules can be bought separately, one for each aspect of accounting. Many firms begin by computerizing one part of their accounting process, perhaps the general ledger. Later, when the first program is running smoothly, they introduce a new module, perhaps accounts payable, accounts receivable, or a payroll program. In this way, a manual system can be gradually converted into a fully automated one.

Almost all accounting programs store the data you enter into a database. In this sense, they are specialized database management applications programs. As you saw in Part Six, a database management program lets you work on more than one file at the same time. A few accounting programs use a record management system, so each file must be independently created and maintained. Accounting programs based on database management, because of their complexity, work best on hard disk drives where all the necessary files and programs are available simultaneously. When you use them on microcomputers having floppy disk drives, you must frequently change disks to make the necessary data available.

Accounting programs do not replace the need for good accountants—they just make their jobs more productive. Accounting software is actually bookkeeping software. An accountant makes decisions that influence what data is kept and in what form and then analyzes the results. Accounting programs simply remove the drudgery of the accounting process; they put information into the correct slots. For these reasons, accountants should be involved when the program is set up to ensure that the assumptions entered into it are correct. Accountants should also then review all reports for accuracy and make important decisions about the final financial statements.

HOW AN ACCOUNTING SYSTEM WORKS

Computerized accounting systems follow the same basic rules as manual systems. To understand how the computerized versions work, we first review how the manual systems work.

Journals and the General Ledger

In a manual bookkeeping system, you enter debits and credits as they occur into a series of books called **journals**. The journal entries are later copied, or posted, to another book called the **general ledger**.

Most bookkeeping systems have at least three journals: one for payroll, one for accounts receivable (money owed the business), and one for accounts payable (money owed by the business). When a transaction occurs, it is immediately entered into one of these journals. The journal entries are classified using a **chart of accounts**—a numbered listing of each account the firm uses. This numbered approach ensures a standardized breakdown of all possible categories and eliminates the need to use long labels to describe every entry. For example, when an employee submits an expense voucher for a car rental, the accounting department may classify it as account number 5130.

Periodically, the entries made in the journals are posted to the general ledger. Here they are entered on separate pages, each one devoted to an account. The general ledger tells the bookkeeper which accounts are to be debited and which are to be credited. For example, when the employee expense voucher is processed, the amount entered in account 5130 in the appropriate journal is transferred as a debit to a page in the ledger labeled 5130—Auto Expenses. When the check is drawn, it is credited to the cash account, which is on another page in the ledger. Each debit is thus matched by an equal and opposite credit in another account. This double-entry system ensures that the ledger remains in balance.

Reports

With journals and the general ledger, a bookkeeper can prepare reports for management, including an income statement, a balance sheet, aged accounts receivables, and so on. These reports are used to determine the financial condition of the firm and to make decisions that affect profitability and growth.

THE COMPUTERIZED ACCOUNTING SYSTEM

As you can see, much of the work in a manual system involves entering data, adding and subtracting again and again, and copying data from journals to the ledger and to reports. A computerized version is like the manual system with one exception. Data is entered only once, and all calculations are made automatically. Data is entered into the appropriate journal, and it is automatically posted to the general ledger. Reports summarizing the results can also be produced automatically, without the additional transfer of figures. This reduces the possibility of introducing errors when copying figures and greatly speeds up the process.

When a firm's accounting system is computerized, it is usually done in parts. As each part is converted from a manual into a computerized system, both are used in parallel for a time to make sure results match. During this period, the manual system also provides a backup if problems should arise with the computerized version. Computerized accounting programs have three stages: setup, data entry and maintenance, and analysis of reports.

Setup

Although all accounting programs follow similar principles, every business using them is unique. One company's breakdown of accounting items (chart of accounts), customers, and suppliers is different from that of another firm. For this reason, a program straight from the dealer must be set up, or customized, for each business. This process is time consuming and requires careful planning because revising an accounting system is difficult once it is up and running. Setup involves several different steps depending on which part of the system is being computerized, but it always includes the following:

- Developing a chart of accounts
- Entering all vendors' names, addresses, telephone numbers, IDs, and credit terms
- Entering all customers' names, addresses, telephone numbers, IDs, and credit terms

Data Entry and Maintenance

Once a system is set up, it is put into use. As a business grows, its customer and vendor base changes, so the program requires periodic maintenance to keep the information current. Some of the entry and maintenance procedures include

- Entering transactions
- Posting journal entries to the general ledger
- Printing reports
- Adding and deleting vendors and customers
- Revising credit terms
- Voiding transactions

Analysis of Reports

One major advantage of a computerized accounting system is its currency. If transactions are entered as they occur, up-to-date management reports, including cash requirement reports, income statements, and balance sheets, are available at any time.

Just as the system will not replace the need for a good accountant, it will also not replace the need for management involvement. In fact, the number of available reports will generally far exceed the information supplied with a manual system—and offer the manager more opportunities for analysis and action. For example, aging accounts receivables will reveal which customers pay on time and which do not. Identifying these delinquent accounts and speeding up their payments will reduce costs and increase profitability.

COMPONENTS OF A COMPUTERIZED ACCOUNTING SYSTEM

Here are some of the components that make up accounting programs and the management reports that they generate.

Chart of Accounts

All accounting systems begin with a chart of accounts that lists all asset, liability, equity, revenue, and expense categories. Account category numbers are assigned in ranges so that related accounts can be grouped together. Figure 9-7 shows a typical chart of accounts. These numbered accounts allow for accurate entry and posting of numbers in the system without having to use longer labels. The system uses the numbers when it posts journal entries to the general ledger and prepares reports.

General Ledger Programs

The general ledger program is the heart of an automated accounting system. It is the part of the program into which all other components feed their data, and it represents all accounts and their transactions for the period. From it are produced the two major financial statements used by managers to monitor the financial condition and performance of the firm: the balance sheet and the income statement.

The Balance Sheet

The balance sheet (Figure 9-8) is appropriately named; it must always balance. The balance sheet is a snapshot of a firm's condition at a given point in time, such as the end of the month, quarter, or year. In simple terms, a balance sheet is a record of what the company has done with its income and the money provided by creditors, lenders, and stockholders. Managers and

FIGURE 9-7
Chart of Accounts
The order of the categories is significant. For instance, assets are listed in descending order according to their ability to be converted into cash. Money market funds appear higher on the list because they can be converted into cash by making a phone call. Inventory, on the other hand, must be sold before receipts can be collected.

Account type	Account Category	Account	Account #
Assets			1000–1999
	Current assets		1000–1499
		Cash	1000
		Money Market	1001
		Inventory	1002
	Fixed assets		1500–1799
	Other assets		1800–1999
Liabilities			2000–2999
	Current liabilities		2000–2599
	Long-term liabilities		2600–2999
Equity			3000–3999
	Paid-in capital		3000–3500
	Retained earnings		3501–3999
Revenue			4000–4999
	Sales revenue		4000–4500
	Service revenue		4501–4999
Cost of sales			5000–5999
	Merchandise purchases		5000–5500
	Freight-in		5501–5999
Expenses			6000–7999

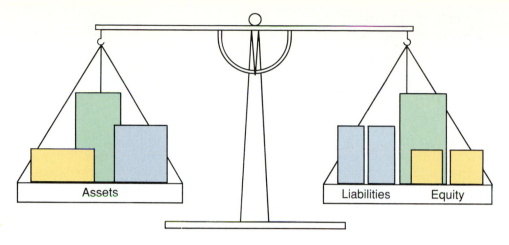

FIGURE 9-8
The Balance Sheet
There are two sections of the balance sheet. The left-hand side shows the firm's assets (what the firm owns). The right-hand side shows the liabilities (what the firm owes) and the owner equity, which together represent the claims against the assets or how the firm paid for its assets.

owners use the balance sheet not only for evaluating financial conditions but also for setting management and company goals. The balance sheet is also a window through which bankers, creditors, stockholders, and others can look at a company.

The Income Statement

Business owners and managers must have a way to measure the success or failure of their business or department and to show the net results of subtracting expenses from sales or revenues. The income, or profit-and-loss, statement is the gauge most often used to determine profitability. Unlike the balance sheet, which shows the financial condition of a company at a given point in time, the income statement (Figure 9-9) shows the profit or loss over a period, usually a month, quarter, or year.

Other General Ledger Reports

The other reports supplied by a general ledger program vary from program to program but typically include a trial balance. This is simply a list of all account balances and totals for all credits and debits and is used to check that the ledger is in balance and to provide a breakdown of data for an accountant. Other reports might include

- Cash disbursements journal
- Cash receipts journal

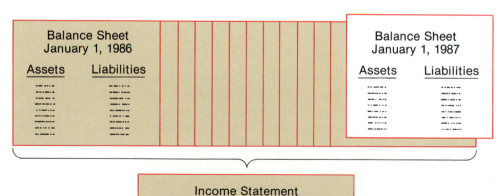

FIGURE 9-9
The Income Statement
The income statement shows the profitability of the firm over a period.

- Cash sales journal
- Account activity report
- Cash reconciliation form
- Check register

Accounts Payable Programs

An accounts payable program is used to record a firm's purchases and liabilities and the payments made against them. The individual transactions are maintained in vendor records until the end of the month, or other period, when they are totaled and posted to the general ledger. Typical reports prepared by an accounts payable program include

- Payables (transaction) ledger
- Payables detailed general ledger
- Open invoice register
- Cash requirements report
- Payables chart of accounts
- Vendor list
- Checks, check stubs, and check register
- Aging report

Accounts Receivable Programs

Accounts receivable programs record what customers owe the company. The balance in the accounts receivable is adjusted for bad debts. Typical reports prepared by an accounts receivable program include

- Customer master list
- Payments (transactions) journal
- Aging report
- Statements (invoices)
- Detailed accounts receivable ledger
- Accounts receivable summary
- Sales journal
- Customer reference list
- Finance charges journal

Payroll Programs

Payroll programs have four separate functions: data entry, tax calculations, check printing, and preparation of management reports. They maintain employee payroll records, perform all calculations, and print payroll checks. They also automatically keep track of all information required by federal, state, and local governments. Some programs will even automatically prepare payroll documents like W-2 forms. Typical reports generated by a payroll program include

- Attendance report
- Check register
- Quarterly earnings report

OTHER APPLICATIONS

- Federal, state and local W-2 forms
- Union reports
- Employee report

Other Accounting Programs

- Inventory accounting programs are designed for either manufacturers or retailers. They keep track of inventory items in stock, out of stock, on order, and on back order. Prices, costs, discounts, and reorder points are flagged. These programs print complete inventory lists, inventory valuations, price lists, and inventory checklists. They also record part numbers, part names, reorder points, preferred inventory levels, and reorder lead times.

- Job costing programs are used to track labor, equipment, subcontractor, and overhead costs for small companies providing products and services.

- Order processing programs are used to enter and track sales from when they are made until they are shipped and billed. They can be used to prepare the necessary invoices and mailing labels.

- Fixed assets programs are used to computerize depreciation of fixed assets. They also keep track of the location, custodian, class, price, date purchased, investment tax credits, estimated life, disposal method, and gains and losses on a sale.

SUMMARY AND KEY TERMS

- Accounting programs are actually bookkeeping programs. They allow you to enter your business accounts and automatically post it to the correct accounts.

- Accounting programs contain **journals** and a **general ledger**. Accounts are broken down on a **chart of accounts**. When you make entries in a journal, the program automatically posts them to the general ledger.

- Accounting programs automatically prepare reports like the balance sheet and income statement.

REVIEW QUESTIONS

1. What are accounting programs used for?
2. Name and briefly describe three components of an accounting system that can be computerized.
3. What are accounting reports? What are the two principle reports generated by a general ledger program?

Utility Programs

OBJECTIVE

After completing this topic, you will be able to

- Describe the purpose of utility programs and give some examples

Utility programs are small, generally inexpensive, single-task programs that perform various useful functions. They generally make the computer work faster or more efficiently.

PRINT SPOOLERS

Because the computer is generally tied up while the printer is printing, you lose time when you print out files, especially if the files are long. Print spoolers provide a partial solution to this problem. They designate a part of the computer's memory as a buffer (you specify the size), and when you issue a print command, the data is printed to this area of memory. The computer then sends this data to the printer and returns the rest of memory to the computer's control so that you can work on other files. In effect, the computer does two things at the same time: It prints the data in the background while you work on another file in the foreground. But when you execute a command (for example, to move the cursor from the beginning to the end of the file you are working on), the computer may take more time than usual because it must wait for the CPU to be temporarily freed from printing.

RAM DISKS

RAM disks, or electronic disks, are software programs that set aside a part of the computer's memory for the storage of programs and data files. This area is assigned a disk drive name; for example, on a system with two floppy disks, A and B, the memory is called C. The program treats this area of memory as if it were a third disk drive. Unlike with a regular disk drive, data stored in this area will be lost when the power is turned off unless it is first copied onto a floppy or hard disk. However, since a RAM disk is electronic and has no moving parts like a typical disk drive, data can be stored and retrieved more quickly. This makes it ideal for certain applications.

As you have seen, some programs are disk based—that is, only the core of the program is in memory all the time, and it goes to the disk for overlays when needed. Whenever it needs an overlay, the program stops momentarily, and the disk drive spins while the overlay is moved from the disk into memory. Since the computer can access information from memory faster than it can access it from a disk, the speed of this type of program is increased with RAM disks.

Some programs also save parts of long files on the disk and keep only the part you are currently working on in memory. When you scroll to a distant part of the document, the computer has to store the part on which you are working on the disk and retrieve the part to which you are moving—greatly slowing down the program. When working on programs of this kind, you can save the file in an electronic disk while you are working on it to speed up the program's operation. But to keep it permanently, you must save it on a floppy or hard disk since any data saved in the electronic disk is lost when the computer is turned off.

HARD DISK BACKUP PROGRAMS

When backing up hard disk files onto floppy disks, you can spend as much as an hour or two swapping disks and copying files. **Hard disk backup programs** are designed to reduce the time required to back up a disk; sometimes, it may take no more than a few minutes. These programs also allow you to optimize a hard disk drive. After you have repeatedly saved files on the disk, the files are scattered all over the disk. This means the read/write head has to move frequently when saving or retrieving the file, which slows down the hard disk. By optimizing the hard disk drive, the files are arranged on the disk in order, with all parts of the same file located next to one another. This allows you to save and retrieve files much more quickly.

KEYBOARD ENHANCERS

Keyboard enhancer programs (also called keyboard processors and macro processors) are used to customize the computer keyboard.

Redefining Keys

You can redefine the meaning of keys on the keyboard with a keyboard enhancer. When you press the redefined key, the program intercepts the signal, converts it into the signal for the newly assigned meaning of the key, and sends that signal to the computer. You can even go so far as to redefine all the keys, converting the typical QWERTY keyboard into a Dvorak keyboard.

Creating Keyboard Macros

You can also assign a series of keystrokes to a single key to save time. For example, you can attach the series of keystrokes needed to save a file to a single key, perhaps the letter S. Then, when that key is pressed while holding down another key like **Alt** or **Ctrl**, the file will be saved. Some programs allow you to save definitions in their own files, so a series of definitions can be assigned for different programs.

OTHER UTILITY PROGRAMS

- **File encryption programs** like Superkey can encrypt data stored on disks or transmitted over telephone lines so that it cannot be retrieved by users without a password. This is especially important on hard disk systems and on networks where several people have access to data files. Many encryption schemes are in use; some are hardware based, some are software based, and some use a combination of hardware and software. One frequently used encryption standard is the U.S. government's **Data Encryption Standard** (**DES**), which is used on mainframe computers and on some microcomputer systems.

- **File conversion programs** convert files created on one program or operating system so that they can be run on another.

- **File indexers** are used to print out lists of files stored on disks. These programs list files in a sorted order, with comments added, the file size, and the date files were created.

- **File recovery programs** can restore files that have been inadvertently deleted from a disk. When you execute an *Erase* command on most computers, all it does is delete the first character in the filename from the disk directory. All other data is left intact on the disk until you save another file on top of it. If you discover the mistake in time, you can use one of these programs to restore the filename to the directory so that you can retrieve the file. You can recover the file provided you do not store any other files on the disk since these would overwrite the file.

- **Copy-protection programs** allow you to ensure that your disks cannot be copied by other users.

DEMO PROGRAMS

What if you want someone to design a program for you? How do you tell them what it would look like and the commands it should offer? This was a major problem until Dan Bricklin (one of the developers of VisiCalc) introduced his program, Dan Bricklin's Demo Program. With this program, you can create screen images and save them on disk files. You can then play them back in any desired sequence to demonstrate how a program should look and operate. At this stage, the program is only simulated; it doesn't actually work. But it is easy to get feedback from potential users since they are given the feel of a real program. Once the design of the screens has been completed, someone can write the actual program to make it a real program.

SUMMARY AND KEY TERMS

- **Utility programs** are used to perform useful but limited tasks.
- Typical utilities create print spoolers and RAM disks, back up hard disk drives, and redefine the keyboard.

REVIEW QUESTIONS

1. What is the purpose of a utility program?
2. List four typical utility programs, and describe the function of each.

Expert Systems

OBJECTIVE

After completing this topic, you will be able to

- Describe the principles behind expert systems

Expert systems (also called knowledge-based systems) are designed to simulate the human reasoning processes on a particular subject. For example, an experienced mechanic asked to fix a car that does not start, approaches the problem systematically. This approach can be illustrated on a flow chart, troubleshooting chart, or decision tree.

Figure 9-10 shows a typical troubleshooting chart used to describe the procedures to check out a car that does not start. The mechanic runs through this sequence of branching steps mentally while working on the problem.

Expert systems are essentially similar to the troubleshooting chart. An expert works with a programmer to develop a sophisticated, computerized, branching program that works through the same reasoning process the expert uses to solve the problem. When the program is in use, the screen displays a series of questions. The user enters an answer, and the program branches automatically to the next question based on that answer. As the user works through the program, supplying answers and running suggested tests, he or she will eventually reach the correct solution to the problem. For example, the dialogue between the user and the computer might go like this.

Computer: What's the problem?

Operator: Car won't start.

Computer: Will the engine turn over?

Operator: No.

Computer: Turn on the headlights.

Operator: Ok.

Computer: Do they work?

Operator: No.

Computer: Check the battery charge and main fuse.

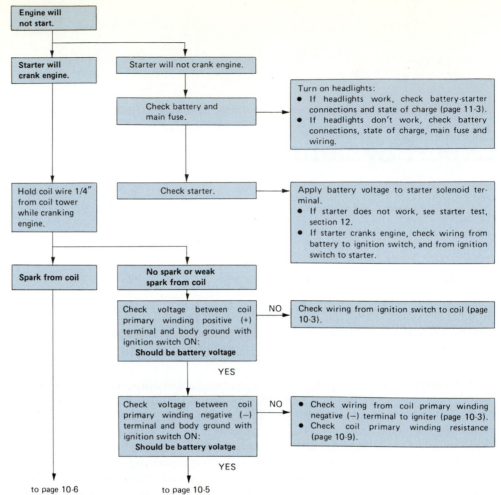

FIGURE 9-10
Troubleshooting Chart
A troubleshooting chart is a branching list of questions. Depending on the answer you give to any questions, you take one or another branch. ©1979 Honda Motor Co., Ltd.

The chart contains the following boxes:

Engine will not start.

Starter will crank engine.

Starter will not crank engine.

Check battery and main fuse.

Turn on headlights:
- If headlights work, check battery-starter connections and state of charge (page 11-3).
- If headlights don't work, check battery connections, state of charge, main fuse and wiring.

Hold coil wire 1/4" from coil tower while cranking engine.

Check starter.

Apply battery voltage to starter solenoid terminal.
- If starter does not work, see starter test, section 12.
- If starter cranks engine, check wiring from battery to ignition switch, and from ignition switch to starter.

Spark from coil

No spark or weak spark from coil

Check voltage between coil primary winding positive (+) terminal and body ground with ignition switch ON:
Should be battery voltage

NO → Check wiring from ignition switch to coil (page 10-3).

YES

Check voltage between coil primary winding negative (−) terminal and body ground with ignition switch ON:
Should be battery volatge

NO →
- Check wiring from coil primary winding negative (−) terminal to igniter (page 10-3).
- Check coil primary winding resistance (page 10-9).

YES

to page 10-6   to page 10-5

Expert systems for microcomputers have been developed for financial and medical users, among others, but they are still in the early stage of their development. The difference between human reasoning and expert systems is the computer's inability to produce human insights. If a special situation has not been encountered by the expert involved in the program's development, it will not be included in the program, and the expert system will not know how to handle it.

SUMMARY AND KEY TERMS

- **Expert systems** consist of a database of information about a subject.
- The information in an expert system is stored on a decision tree so that as you enter responses, the program branches to the next appropriate question.

REVIEW QUESTIONS

1. What is an expert system?
2. Describe briefly how one operates.

Glossary

A

A>. The DOS system prompt that indicates the A drive is the current default drive.

Absolute reference. A spreadsheet reference that specifies a formula which, when copied elsewhere on the spreadsheet, continues to refer to the same cell. Absolute references are frequently specified with dollar signs ($), for example, A1, or when replicating by specifying no change. See Relative reference.

Absolute value. The numerical value of a real number.

Accelerator boards. Add-on boards that can be inserted into a computer's expansion slot to add a faster microprocessor to the computer.

Access. The process of locating information stored in memory or on a disk.

Access points. The local phone number that you dial to connect your computer into a network.

Access time. The time a disk drive takes to locate information stored on a disk.

Accounting programs. Applications programs designed for bookkeeping purposes.

Acoustic coupler modem. An inexpensive modem that has two rubber cups into which you press a telephone handset to make a connection between the computer and the telephone line.

Active area. The area of the spreadsheet that is stored in the computer's memory.

Active cell. The cell on a spreadsheet in which the cursor is currently positioned.

Active window. The window (when there are several on a spreadsheet) in which the cursor is currently positioned.

Add-on boards. Boards containing electronic circuits that are inserted into the computer's expansion slots to expand its capacity or improve its performance. Also referred to as cards, boards, or expansion boards.

Address (n). A "name" assigned to a memory location, or peripheral, so data can be sent to it.

Address (v). When one component sends a signal to another component that tells the component that it wants its attention.

Address bus. The communications path between the CPU and the computer's internal memory used to specify locations in memory where data is to be stored to or retrieved from. See Data bus.

Algorithm. A set of rules in a program that define for the computer how to solve a specific problem. Algorithms are frequently used in word processing hyphenation programs.

All points addressable (APA). The ability of a printer to print dots anywhere on a page, allowing it to print graphics. Also, the ability of a computer screen to display dots in any position, allowing it to display graphics.

Alphabetic keys. The keys on the computer's keyboard that are arranged just as they are on a typewriter keyboard. If you press the **Shift** or **Caps Lock** key you will get uppercase letters. Also see Dvorak keyboard and Qwerty keyboard.

Alphanumeric. Any combination of letters, numbers, symbols, and spaces.

Alt key. A special purpose key that is usually held down while pressing another key to execute a command.

Amplitude. The measurement of voltage on an electrical wave, from the zero base line to the top of the wave.

Amplitude modulation (AM). The transmission of data via a signal that contains information which varies the amplitude of a high frequency carrier wave. See Frequency modulation and Phase modulation.

Analog display. A display that accepts analog video signals.

Analog signal. A signal that conveys information by varying in amplitude, frequency, and phase. Analog waves have a smooth, sinusoidal shape. Also see Digital signal.

Analog waves. Transmission waves that are sinusoidal in shape.

ANSI. American National Standards Institute.

Answer mode. A setting on modems and/or communications programs that tells the computer to answer the phone when it rings.

Application. A specific task to which a computer is put, for example, word processing, financial analysis, or record management.

Applications generator. A program that partially automates the process of writing applications programs.

Applications program. A program designed to turn the computer into a tool for a specific application, such as word processing.

Architecture. The internal design of a computer that includes the busses along which signals travel between components.

Area graph. A graph that plots data much like a stacked bar-graph.

Argument. Part of the syntax of a spreadsheet function. Arguments can be values, cell references, ranges, other functions, or other cells.

Artificial intelligence (AI). The ability of a computer to simulate human reasoning.

Ascending order. A method of sorting documents and files beginning with A (or 0) up through Z (or 10).

ASCII. Acronym for American Standard Code for Information Interchange. This group sets standards for the codes that represent characters in the computer field.

ASCII text files. Files saved in a format specified by the American Standard

Code for Information Interchange. Files saved in this format often can be used by other programs or transmitted by modem because they have a standard format.

Aspect ratio. The ratio between the height and width of a graph or pixels on the display screen.

Asymmetrical protocols. A high-speed modem error-checking protocol that splits the line into two channels, one for data and one for error checking and other messages.

Asynchronous. A method of transmitting data where the timing between the bits in a byte of data are timed precisely but the timing between bytes is random. See Synchronous.

Attributes. In a database, the facts that describe an entity. For example, if the entity is an employee, the attributes might be name, phone number, and salary.

Audit trail. A record of the users who have accessed files and any changes that have been made.

Authorized user. Any person authorized to work with a computer, program, or file. Authorization is usually granted by the Management Information Systems Department or a network or department manager.

Auto-answer. A modem or communications program setting that tells the modem to answer the phone automatically when it rings.

Auto-dial. A feature of smart modems that allows you to dial a number from the communications program rather than manually dialing the phone.

AUTOEXEC.BAT file. A DOS batch file that automatically provides instructions to the computer when you first turn it on, for example, to set the clock and then load a program.

Automated attendant. A front end to a voice mail system that directs you to the person you are trying to reach.

Automatic paragraph reforming. A feature that automatically aligns text with the left and right margins when text is inserted or deleted.

Automatic scaling. A graphics program feature that automatically calculates the scale of the Y axis based on the range of numbers in the data being plotted.

Automation. The process of using machines and other devices to perform manual tasks.

Auto-redial. A modem or communications program setting that has the modem redial phones numbers when busy signals are encountered.

Autorepeat feature. Any key that, when held down, will continue to enter the character or function until it is released.

Auxiliary storage. See Disk.

B

B>. The DOS system prompt that indicates the B drive is the current default drive.

Back copy. An earlier version of a file that is saved if extensive revisions or changes are being made. Some programs automatically save a back copy.

Back copy file. See Backup copy

Background. The program not currently being used when two or more programs are simultaneously being run on the computer.

Background recalculation. When a spreadsheet first recalculates the cells that are displayed on the screen and then recalculates other cells when the microprocessor isn't busy with other tasks.

Backspace key. The key used most frequently to correct errors. The **Backspace** key moves the cursor to the left and deletes incorrect characters as it moves back through the line of characters.

Backtab key. The key that moves the cursor from right to left between tab stops. Usually the same as the **Tab** key but pressed while holding down **Shift**. Also see Tab key.

Backup copy. A duplicate of a file saved onto a separate disk in case the original disk is damaged.

Bandwidth. The size of the transmission channel. The bandwidth determines how much, and how fast, data is transmitted.

Bank-memory switching. A way of expanding memory by using the microprocessor's address space as a window into a larger area of memory that cannot be addressed directly.

Bar code scanner. A device that can read the universal product codes on packages and convert them into electronic signals that the computer can understand.

Bar graph. A graph that plots the size of values using bars.

Baseband. When signals from more than one computer are sent along the same wire at different times. See Broadband.

BASIC. An easy to learn computer programming language that is available on almost all microcomputers.

Batch file. A file that contains commands, for example, the names of programs to be executed, to accomplish a specific task.

Baud rate. A measurement of the speed of transmission when telecommunication or sending data over circuits.

Bin. A holder, attached to a printer, used to hold a stack of single sheets of paper.

Binary digit. See Bit.

Binary file. A file created with an applications program that contains non-ASCII codes specific to that program.

Binary system. A number system that presents all numbers as combinations of 0s and 1s.

Bin selection. A printing option, offered by some programs, that gives you a choice of paper on which to print.

BIOS (basic input-output system). The system through which data enters and leaves the computer, for example, so it can be displayed on the screen.

Bit. The smallest unit of data stored in (or communicated) to a computer. A bit is a digital signal consisting of two possible states, 0 and 1. Bit is a contraction of the words *binary* and *digit*.

Bit mapping. See Memory mapping.

Block. Any series of adjacent characters, words, sentences, or paragraphs.

Board. See Add-on boards.

Boilerplate. The text in a primary file that is to appear in all copies of a document when it is merge-printed.

Boldface. A character enhancement that makes the letter or word appear darker when printed out.

Boolean algebra. A system of symbolic logic that reduces statements to symbols, and manipulates them by means of algebraic formulas to determine certain "truths."

Boot. To load a program into the computer's memory.

Border. The surrounding edge of a spreadsheet which contains column and row labels.

Boundary. The outer limits of the spreadsheet beyond which you can't move the cursor or enter data.

Branching. The process by which the computer makes a decision on what to do next based on a calculation or other preexisting condition.

Broadband. When signals from more than one computer are sent along the same wire at different frequencies. See Baseband.

Broadcast. To transmit copies of your document to several recipients at the same time via electronic mail service.

Bubble memory. Internal memory stored using a technology that is nonvolatile; it is not lost if the computer is turned off.

Buffer. A part of the computer's memory where keystrokes or sections of deleted text are stored temporarily. The keystrokes stored in a buffer can be replayed and the deleted text stored there can be copied back into the document. Also known as a clipboard, scrapbook, or scrap.

Bug. The common term for any computer error that causes unexpected results when the program is used.

Bulletin board system (BBS). A computer you can call (usually for free) to send and read messages. Also called public access message system.

Bus. See Data bus, Address bus.

Bus architecture. The design of the bus (circuits) along which signals are sent between components in the computer.

Business graphics programs. Programs that create graphs of business data for analysis or presentation.

Byte. A unit containing 8 or 9 bits. Each byte contains the information necessary for identifying a single character.

C

C>. The DOS system prompt that indicates the C drive is the current default drive.

Cache. An area in memory where the most recently used data is stored in case it is needed again.

CAD. Acronym for Computer Aided Design.

Calculating fields. Fields in a database that can calculate numbers that are entered into other fields.

Camera-ready copy. Manuscript from which the printer can make plates used to print multiple copies on a printing press.

Caps Lock key. The key that switches the other keys between entering uppercase or lowercase letters.

Card. See Add-on boards.

Carriage return. A signal sent to the printer telling it to move the print head down one line and back to the left margin. Entered by pressing **Return** on most programs.

Carrier wave. A high frequency wave onto which lower frequency messages can be modulated.

Cathode ray tube (CRT). A display tube used in many desktop computer displays.

CD-ROM disk. Information stored on a laser disk and read into the computer from a CD-ROM disk drive.

Cell. The basic working unit on a spreadsheet. A cell falls at the intersection of a column and a row.

Cell address. The cell's coordinates that give it its location on the spreadsheet screen. A cell address is usually given as the column label followed by the row number, e.g. A1, B1.

Cell pointer. See Cursor.

Cell protection. The prevention of data from being entered into cells on a spreadsheet. Data in protected cells cannot be changed unless the cells are first unprotected.

Centered text. Text that is centered midway between the left and right margins or the left and right edges of a spreadsheet cell.

Central processing unit (CPU). The part of the computer that performs calculations and other functions.

Centralized. Any process or organization that is grouped together into a single unit. Also see Decentralized.

Centronics interface. See Parallel port.

Channels. The division of a single wire into separate communications pathways by transmitting information at different frequencies.

Character display. A display screen that can only display characters and not graphics. Also see Graphics display and All points addressable.

Character fields. Fields in a database where you enter text. If you enter numbers, like phone numbers, they cannot be calculated.

Character format. A type of emphasis, such as underline, italic, or boldface, that you can give to various sections of your text so that they will be highlighted. Also known as a character attribute.

Character generator. A ROM chip that creates characters that are then displayed on the screen.

Characters. Any letter, number, or symbol.

Characters per second (CPS). The measurement used to state the speed of a printer.

Chart. A visual layout of information that lets you analyze a situation in terms of relationships. The pie chart is probably the most common type.

Chart of accounts. A listing of all income and expense categories to which accounting charges can be made.

Chat mode. A mode where people at connected computers can type messages back and forth.

Chip. A small piece of silicon on which numerous electronic components and an electronic circuit are etched. Chips are used in computers for microprocessors and for internal memory.

CHKDSK command. The DOS command that you use to find out if all of the files stored on a disk are in contiguous sectors. This command also tells you how much total memory there is in the computer and on a disk and how much remains unused and available for other programs, documents, or other files.

Circular reference. A spreadsheet formula that may refer either directly or indirectly to itself. See Absolute reference and Relative reference.

Clipboard. See Buffer.

Clock rate. The rate at which signals and data are sent between elements in the computer.

Clone. A software or hardware product that acts much like another product.

Closed architecture. A computer designed in such a way that devices cannot be plugged directly into its bus to expand the computer's capabilities.

CMOS chip. Complementary-metal-oxide-semiconductor chip used for memory. This chip has low power requirements so it is frequently used in laptop and other portable computers.

Coaxial cable. A cable composed of one inner wire surrounded by an insulating material and an outer braided wire which protects it from noise.

Code. An agreed-upon meaning assigned to signals or symbols so that they can be interpreted and understood by others.

Cold boot. Starting the computer by turning it on.

Collision detection. A method used to prevent signals on a network from interfering with each other.

Color graphics adapter (CGA). An early standard that allows graphics to be displayed on a computer screen when an add-on card and display screen using the standard were added to the computer.

Column (spreadsheets). The vertical cells on a spreadsheet (as opposed to the horizontal ones). Usually, columns are labeled with letters or numbers across the top of the screen.

Column (word processors). On word processing programs, columns are one character wide and are specified when you set margins or tabs.

Column mode. A function that allows you to move, copy, delete, or format columns of text rather than lines.

Combination graph. A graph that combines more than one graph type, for example, lines and bars.

Command. Any instruction that you give to the computer to tell it what to do.

Command-driven program. A program that operates when you type commands from the keyboard. See Menu-driven program.

Command mode. The mode the computer enters when a spreadsheet menu is displayed.

Command processor. One of the functions of an operating system that interprets commands entered on the keyboard and converted to signals understandable to the microprocessor.

Communications interface unit (CIU). A device used to connect hardware to a network.

Communications parameters. The method used to allocate the bits sent over a phone line for each character in a message or file. Bits can be either start, parity, data, or stop bits.

Communications programs. Programs that allow the communications between computers over telephone lines.

Communications protocols. The method used to ensure that the messages and files exchanged between computers are accurately received.

Compatibility. A measurement of a computer's or program's ability to act just like another.

Compatibility box. The area of OS/2 that lets you run programs written for DOS.

Complete instruction set chips (CISC). Microprocessors that have extensive built-in commands. See Reduced instruction set chips.

Composite color display. An inexpensive color display to which colors are fed on a single wire along with the image. Also see RGB color display.

Compress. A procedure that removes unnecessary bytes from a file so it takes up less room on a disk or can be transmitted more quickly.

Computer. A device that makes calculations.

Computer-aided design (CAD). Using a computer instead of a drafting board to create engineering and other designs.

Computer-aided design and drafting (CADD). Using a computer to prepare detailed working drawings.

Computer-aided engineering (CAE). Using a computer to perform engineering analysis.

Computer-aided manufacturing (CAM). Using a computer to control manufacturing processes.

Computer compatibility. The ability of a computer to run the same software as the computer with which it's compatible.

Computer literacy. A user's level of understanding of, and familiarity with, the principles of computer hardware and software.

Concatenate. To join (glue) two or more strings together.

Concurrent processing. See Multitasking.

Conditional page break. A page format command that moves a specified number of lines to the next page if they won't all fit on the current page when a document is being printed.

Configuration file. A file that a program looks to for special instructions when you first load it. Configuration files normally contain the default settings that the program uses.

Constants. Numbers that are contained (embedded) in formulas, instead of being entered in cells to which formulas refer.

Context sensitive. A help system that displays help based on the command you are using at the moment.

Continuous data. The data (in graphics) that is sampled and measured to determine a trend. The values between the measured data points can be estimated. See Discrete data.

Continuous form paper. Individual sheets of paper connected together, usually with perforations between them. Also called fan-fold.

Control area. The area of a spreadsheet screen display where menus are displayed.

Control bus. The wires within a computer to send messages between components telling those components what function to perform.

Control code. A command that you enter by holding down the **Ctrl** key and pressing another key at the same time. Frequently control codes are used to format documents. The symbol ^ often indicates the **Ctrl** key, for example ^A tells you to hold down **Ctrl** while you press the letter A.

Control key. See **Ctrl** key.

Control panel. An area of the spreadsheet screen that is reserved for showing commands, menus, prompts, messages, and for displaying the contents of the cell you are entering.

Conventional memory. The first 640K of memory that is directly addressable by DOS.

Co-processors. Special purpose microprocessors used to relieve the computer's CPU of time consuming chores that would slow it down. Typical co-processors are used to perform math calculations, and handle updating of graphics on the screen.

Copy. To duplicate any form of data or files.

Copy command. The command used to copy text in a document.

Copy edit. To correct spelling, punctuation and grammar and to make other minor corrections to a manuscript.

Copying. Making a duplicate copy.

Copy protection. A technique that prevents users from making copies of disks.

Copy protection program. A program that prevents a disk from being copied.

Core. The part of a disk-based program that resides in the computer's memory and retrieves overlay files from the disk when needed. Also known as the kernel. Also see Disk-based program.

CP/M. Acronym for Control Program for Microcomputers, a popular operating system for personal computers, especially early 8-bit models.

CPS. Abbreviation for Characters Per Second. The measurement for data transmission.

CPU. Abbreviation for central processing unit. The CPU is the heart of the microcomputer and is composed of integrated circuits etched into a silicon chip.

Crashing the schedule. Shortening the completion time of tasks that fall on a project's critical path.

Criteria. The conditions that you want met when the computer performs a specific task.

Critical path. The sequence of tasks in a project where each task can only be started when the prior task is completed.

CRT. Abbreviation for Cathode Ray Tube. CRTs are used in many display monitors to create the image you see on the screen.

Ctrl key. The key you use to enter commands. You hold the **Ctrl** key down while you press other keys.

Current record. The record in a database that is marked by the record pointer.

Cursor. A bright underscore character, one-character-wide highlight, or one-cell wide highlight, that you move with cursor movement keys to enter, delete, or select text in a document or spreadsheet on the screen.

Cursor movement keys. The specified keys on the keyboard, including the four directional arrow keys, used to move the cursor.

Cut. To move part of a file on which you are working to a buffer.

Cut and paste. To move or copy blocks from one file to another or from one section of a document to another.

D

Daisy wheel printer. A fully-formed character printer whose print element is shaped like the head of a daisy with each character on a petal.

Data. Any alphanumeric input or output from the computer. It also refers to any collection of information stored in the computer's memory.

Database. Information stored in one or more files and organized into fields and records.

Database management program. A program that organizes, manipulates, and retrieves information from one or more database files.

Database model. The structure of a database. The relational model is the one most frequently found in microcomputer databases.

Data bits. Those bits sent over a phone line that contain the character being sent.

Data bus. The circuit along which data travels between all of the computer's internal components. See Address bus.

Data encryption. A process that secures data so it cannot be read by unauthorized users.

Data Encryption Standard (DES). An encryption method used to protect data.

Data file. Any computer file that contains information entered by a user.

Data processing. The processing of company data with a computer.

Data processing (DP) department. A centralized department in a company that performs corporate-level computer tasks.

Data transfer rate. The rate at which data in the external storage device is transferred into memory.

Data word length. The number of bits sent in parallel in a computer.

Date fields. Fields in a database where you enter dates.

Decentralized. Computers or procedures that are scattered through a company.

Decimal system. A math system based on the number 10.

Decimal tab. A special tab stop used to enter numbers in columns so that their decimal points are aligned in the same column.

Dedicated word processor. The requirement that a computer or other device perform a single task, for example, word processing.

Default drive. The drive the computer will automatically look to when a command is issued, unless a different drive is specified in the command.

Default format. The format in which your document is printed unless you specify otherwise.

Default settings. The settings entered into a program by its designers with the expectation that they will satisfy most users most of the time. Examples are margin settings, page size, text alignment, and the number of lines printed per inch. Generally, the default settings can be changed by the user.

DEL command. A DOS command that erases files from the disk.

Delete. To erase or remove from a document and the computer's memory.

Delimiter. A symbol (frequently a comma or colon) that separates two fields in a record file or two cell coordinates in a spreadsheet formula or function.

Demodulation. The retrieval of a signal from a modulated carrier wave. See Modulation.

Density. The quality of printed characters. Density is controlled by the number of times the print head strikes the character in the same position or by the thickness of the character on the type element. Determines the amount of data that can be stored on a disk.

Dependent cells. The cells in a spreadsheet where formulas refer to the cell being examined.

Dependent model. A spreadsheet file that contains formulas that refer to another file.

Desktop manager. A program that contains several useful utilities such as a calendar, notebook, and appointment manager.

Desktop publishing. The process of preparing high-quality printed documents with a microcomputer and laser printer.

Desktop publishing program. A program that is used in desktop publishing.

Destination range. See Target range.

Destructive backspace. A term used to describe a **Backspace** key that deletes characters to its left when pressed.

Diacriticals. Symbols used to indicate that a letter has a particular sound.

Digraphs. A pair of letters indicating a specific sound.

Dialing directory. A list of phone numbers and communications settings stored in a communications program.

Dialog box. A list of prompts that appears on the screen when you are executing commands.

Dictionary. A database file that lists and describes all of the related database files.

Digital. Representing data with the digits 0 and 1.

Digital display. A display screen that receives signals in digital form.

Digital processing. Processing digital data in a computer.

Digital signal. A signal that is transmitted via electrical pulses. In a computer, the digital 0's and 1's are transmitted as low and high voltages. See Analog signal.

Digitize. To translate information into digital signals, for example, into a series of 0's and 1's, so that a computer can understand them. Also see Graphics scanner.

Digitizing tablet. See Graphics tablet.

DIP switches. Small on/off switches within many computer hardware components that allow you to change default settings.

DIR command. The DOS command that displays a list of the files on a disk.

Direct access. The ability of the computer to locate data in a file directly, without having to search though all of the data in the file.

Direct connect modem. A modem that connects to the computer with a wire or cable. See Acoustic coupler modem.

Directional arrow keys. The four arrow keys on the keyboard that move the cursor around the screen a character or line at a time.

Directory. A list of the files stored on a disk. Also called a catalog.

Discrete data. Data (in a graphics program) that consists of values measured at a series of selected points. The data between these selected points is meaningless. See Continuous data.

Disk. The magnetic media on which the computer records information. Disks represent the most common form of computer storage. Also known as a floppy, a floppy disk, and a diskette. Also see Hard disk.

Disk-based program. Programs that store parts of large documents on which you are working on the disk. This allows you to create large documents that would be too big to fit in the computer's memory. It also refers to programs that are only partially loaded into memory and that call in other parts of the program when needed. See Core and Overlay file.

Disk cache. An area in a computer's memory reserved for storing data that was most recently retrieved from the disk in the event it is needed again.

DISKCOMP command. A DOS command that compares two disks to see if they are the same.

DISKCOPY command. A DOS command that makes an exact duplicate copy of a disk.

Disk drive. The device on the computer into which you insert the floppy disk(s). The disk drive can store to, or retrieve programs and data from, these disks.

Diskless workstation. A computer without disk drives that is connected into a network.

Disk operating system. See DOS and Operating system.

Display screen. The computer's screen. The screen gives you instant feedback by displaying whatever input you have entered. Also known as a monitor or display monitor.

Distributed logic. A term used to describe a dedicated word processing system where each workstation can process data.

Distribution device. A device, like a modem, that can exchange information between computers.

Dithering. A process that allows printers to simulate half-tone images like photographs while actually printing only black dots.

Document (n). Any file containing text created on a word processor.

Document (v). To label items on spreadsheet and database models so that you will not forget built-in assumptions and will be able to understand these models at some future date.

Documentation. Written information describing hardware or software.

Document compare feature. A feature that allows you to see the differences between two versions of the same document.

Document Content Architecture. (DCA). A standard that makes it possible to exchange files between programs and computers.

Document description language. Programs that communicate between a desktop publishing program and a printer.

Document-oriented program. A word processing program that displays a document as one continuous strip.

Document screen. The screen display that appears on a word processing program when you enter or edit a document.

Document view. The way you normally view a document on the screen. See also Outline view.

DOS. Abbreviation for disk operating system. DOS is the interface between you and your personal computer. All applications programs require that you first load the disk operating system before you load the programs. DOS also includes several utility programs that you use to format disks, copy, delete, and rename files, and so on.

Dot-matrix printer. A printer that creates characters or images from a pattern of dots. Some dot-matrix printers use a type element with pins arranged in a matrix; others use heat, a laser, or diodes to create the images. A dot-matrix printer is more flexible than a fully formed character printer, and offers a wider range of type styles.

Dot stream. The signals sent to the display screen indicating that indicate the data to be displayed.

Double-density disk. A disk that has 48 tracks per inch.

Double-sided disk. A disk on which both sides have been certified for storing data.

Download. To retrieve data from another computer into a computer's memory or onto a disk. Also refers to copying fonts from a disk into a laser printer's memory.

Downloadable fonts. See Soft font.

Draft. An early version of a document.

Driver. A small program that runs between an application program and the hardware so that they will work together.

Dropout type. Light characters printed against a dark background.

Dumb modem. A modem that cannot dial a phone number from a communications program. Phone numbers must be manually dialed on a connected phone.

Dumb terminal. A computer terminal that consists of a keyboard and screen. It is limited to displaying input and transmitting codes to the computer. It does not have the ability to process information or run its own programs.

Dump. Sending the data on the screen to the printer.

Duplex. See Full duplex.

Duplex printing. Printing on both sides of a sheet of paper.

Dvorak keyboard. A layout of alphabetic keys on the keyboard designed for greater speed and efficiency. See also QWERTY keyboard.

Dynamic page display. A method of displaying on the screen where pages will break when they are printed. To be dynamic, the display must automatically change when adding or deleting text changes the place where pages will break.

Dynamic RAM (DRAM) chip. A chip used for a computer's memory. The data stored in the chip must be periodically refreshed.

E

EBCDIC. A code that assigns characters to specific binary numbers. Used primarily on large mainframe computers.

Echoing. Sending data to the screen at the same time it is sent elsewhere so that you can monitor the results.

Edit. To correct errors in word processing documents, spreadsheet cells, or database records.

Edit cursor. The cursor that appears and which you use to insert and delete characters when you use the edit command to move the contents of a spreadsheet cell to the edit line or when answering prompts.

Edit mode. The mode a spreadsheet enters when you edit the entry in a cell.

Electroluminescent display. A display screen made from small diodes that light up to form characters and graphics.

Electron gun. The element in a CRT that emits a stream of electrons that "paints" the image on the phosphor screen.

Electronic. Devices that operate with electrons in a vacuum, gas, or semiconductor solids.

Electronic digital computer. A device that processes data in a digital form using electronic devices.

Electronic mail. Mail sent directly from one computer to another using a network or a modem connected to the telephone line.

Electronic spreadsheet program. See Spreadsheet.

Electrostatic printer. A printer that transfers characters to paper by applying an electrical charge that attracts toner.

Elevation view. A side view of a three-dimensional object.

Emulate. To act the same as or be like something else.

Encrypt. To code data in such a way that an unauthorized user cannot see or use it.

Encryption program. A program that encrypts data.

Endnotes. Notes printed at the end of a document that are referred to from reference numbers within the document. See Footnotes.

Enhanced color graphics adapter (EGA). A graphics add-in card that improves the display of graphics on the screen.

Enter key. See Return key.

Entity. The subject of a record in a database.

Entry/edit line. The line on which you enter information (on a spreadsheet program), when prompted to do so. Also displayed on the edit/entry line are the contents of cells as you enter or edit them.

Entry mode. The mode that a spreadsheet enters while you enter data into a cell.

Enumerations. Indented numbered entries.

Erasable optical disk. In optical disk that data can be erased from to make room for new data.

ERASE command. A DOS command that erases files from a disk.

Ergonomics. The study of the interaction of people and machines so the machine is designed to accommodate the needs of the user.

Error message. A message that appears when you make a mistake.

Esc key. A key frequently used to cancel commands.

Expanded memory. Memory in a computer that cannot be addressed directly by the operating system.

Expanded memory scheme (EMS). A method used to address memory that cannot be addressed directly.

Expansion board. See Add-on boards.

Expansion slot. An electrical connection inside the computer's cabinet into which you can plug add-on boards or boards and peripherals and thereby expand the computer's functions.

Expert system. A program that contains facts and a system of rules that emulates an experts reasoning process.

Extended memory. Memory in a computer using an 80286 or 80386 chip between 1M to 16M that can be addressed by OS/2.

Extension. A file suffix composed of a period (.) followed by one to three characters. The extension is frequently added automatically by a program so that you can identify which program was used to create it, for example, Word adds .DOC to the files it creates. Extensions also identify file types, for example, .EXE for executable program files, and .TXT for ASCII text files.

External commands. DOS commands that are not automatically loaded into the computer along with the operating system. To use external commands, their files must be on a disk in one of the disk drives. See also Internal commands.

External storage. Information that is stored outside of the computer's memory (RAM).

External storage device. A device used to store information outside the computer, generally on hard or floppy disks, or on a cassette tape.

F

Facsimile machine. A machine that can send a copy of a printed document to another facsimile machine over the telephone lines.

Fiber-optic cable. A cable used in networks where the signals are sent by modulating a light beam.

Field. Any individual item that makes up a record in a record file or a database file.

File. Associated data in the computer's memory or saved onto a disk. This may be a program, data for a database, a spreadsheet model, or a letter created by your word processor.

File compression. The process of compressing a file so it takes up less room on the disk. Compressed files can be stored more easily or transmitted more quickly.

File conversion program. A program that converts a data file created with one program so that it can be used by another.

File encryption program. A program that encrypts data so it cannot be read by unauthorized users.

File locking. Preventing two users from accessing and changing the same file at the same time.

File management. The process of managing files on your disks. It includes saving, retrieving, erasing, copying, and renaming files. It also is sometimes used as a synonym for record management, as in "I use a file management program."

Filename. The name you assign to a file when you save it onto a disk, so that you can retrieve it later. The computer's operating system determines the length of file name, as well as the characters you can use in it.

File recovery program. A utility program that allows you to recover programs that you have deleted with the DOS ERASE command.

File server. A hard disk drive used to store program and data files so that they can be accessed by all computers on a network.

Final-form text (FFT). A document saved in IBM's Document Content Architecture format so it can be printed on other equipment using a program that utilizes the same format.

Fixed pitch. When characters are printed without taking their width into consideration. Each character occupies the same space. Also see Proportional spacing and Kerning.

Fixed titles. One or more rows or columns that are "fixed" in position on the screen so they will remain displayed as you scroll data. Also called locked titles.

Flagged record. A database record that has been marked for deletion but not yet actually deleted.

Flat-panel display. A display screen that is thin so it can be easily carried. Usually found on portable computers.

Floppy disk. A round disk covered by a magnetic material and enclosed in a plastic cover. Used to store program and data files.

Floppy disk drive. A disk drive that saves files to, and retrieves them from, floppy disks.

Flow control. A process of controlling data being transmitted so it is not sent faster than it can be received.

Flush left. Text aligned with the left margin or left edge of a spreadsheet cell.

Flush right. Text aligned with the right margin or right edge of a spreadsheet cell.

Font. A complete set of characters in one typeface, style and size, for example, Courier, bold, 12 point.

Font cartridge. A cartridge that contains fonts which you plug into a printer.

Font server. A hard disk drive on which fonts are stored so they can be used by the printer when needed.

Footer. The line or lines of text that can be printed in the bottom margin of one or more pages of a document. A footer may contain the page number, date, time, and so on.

Footnotes. Notes printed at the end of a page that are referred to from reference numbers on the same page. See Endnotes.

Forced upgrade. A procedure whereby the publisher of a program makes minor changes while making previous versions of the program incompatible with the new one.

Foreground. The program currently being used when two or more programs are being run on the computer simultaneously. See Background.

Format (spreadsheets). A command you execute to control the way numbers are displayed on the screen. Format also refers to commands used to align labels in their cells.

Format (word processors). The arrangement or layout of lines of text on a page and the typefaces and styles used to print them. Formats include page breaks, text alignment, margins, and boldfacing or underlining.

FORMAT command. The command you use with new disks to prepare them for use on your computer. The format command magnetically divides a disk into tracks and sectors used by the computer to find information stored on the disk.

Format line. The line at the top of (or within) a word processing document which, on some programs, controls the format, such as margins, text alignment, and tab stops. Also called a ruler line.

Formatted disk. A disk that has been coded with 0s and 1s with the operating system's format command so it can store digital data from the computer.

Formatting. The process of putting a series of 0s and 1s onto a blank disk with the operating system's format command so that it can receive digital information.

Form document. See Primary document.

Formula. A group of symbols (in a spreadsheet program) that expresses a calculation. Formulas can contain constants (4*3) or can refer to variables entered in other cells (4*A1). Operators, such as +, −, *, and /, in the formula indicate the arithmetic calculations to be performed.

Forward reference. A situation in which a formula in a spreadsheet cell refers to a cell below it, or to its right that also contains a formula. Depending on how recalculation is performed, the first formula can be recalculated before the cell to which it refers has been and thereby display an incorrect result unless the spreadsheet is recalculated a second time.

Fragmented files. Files on the disk that are not stored in adjacent sectors.

Freeware. A trade name for a concept developed by Andrew Fluggelman whereby software is distributed free, or for a modest duplication fee, and then paid for if the user likes it.

Frequency modulation (FM). A process of transmitting information via a signal that contains data which varies the frequency of a high frequency carrier wave.

Frequency shift keying (FSK). A form of frequency modulation used by many modems.

Full duplex. A method of sending data over a line in both directions at the same time. See Half duplex.

Fully formed character printer. A printer that creates characters on the paper by striking a metal or plastic character against an inked ribbon much like a typewriter.

Function. A small program built into a spreadsheet program to calculate complicated calculations like interest due, averages, and present value.

Function key. Any of several specific keys on the keyboard that makes the computer execute a particular function. The specific function one of these keys performs is generally assigned by the programmer who develops the pro-

gram. For example, on the IBM PC, the F1 key will frequently display a help screen if you are running an applications program.

G

Gantt chart. A chart used in project management that indicates when tasks begin and end.

Gas plasma display. A display screen that displays images by illumination small dotlike bubbles of gas.

Gateway server. A device that connects two or more different types of networks so they can communicate.

General ledger. A component of an accounting system.

Gigabyte (GB). A storage capacity of roughly one billion (10 raised to the power of 9) characters.

GKS. Abbreviation for Graphics Kernal System. A standard for graphics.

Global command. Any command that affects the entire spreadsheet or the entire document.

Global format. A format that affects the entire document or spreadsheet.

Glossary. Those sections of the computer's memory or a file on the disk where you can save sections of text so that it can be quickly inserted over and over again with only a few keystrokes. Also known as a library or phrase storage area.

Goto. A key or command used to move the cursor to a designated cell rather than move there using the cursor movement keys. Also called jump.

Graph. A visual representation of verbal or numeric information. Various types of graphs include line graphs, scatter graphs, bar graphs, stacked-bar graphs and X-Y graphs.

Graphics. Images comprised of more than characters.

Graphics display. The process by which each dot (pixel) on the display screen is given a corresponding bit in the computer's memory. Also known as bit-mapping or all points addressable (APA).

Graphics for analysis programs. Programs that automatically change a graph when you change the data on which it is based. Frequently integrated into spreadsheet programs.

Graphics for presentation programs. Graphics programs that provide a wide range of graph types and options so you can create more attractive graphs.

Graphics processing. The computer's ability to create and manipulate graphic images.

Graphics program. A program that allows you to create or manipulate graphic images in a computer.

Graphics scanner. A scanner that converts images on paper into a digital form that can be displayed and processed by a computer.

Graphics tablet. A device on which you draw with a stylus to enter graphics into a computer.

Gray scale. A range of tones from pure white to pure black in a series of steps, each of which is increasingly darker.

Gutter margin. A special margin on alternate pages of a document which is to be printed on both sides of the page. The wider gutter margin accommodates a binding.

H

Hacker. A computer buff who has a technical background and approach to the field.

Half-duplex. A method of transmitting data that allows data to be sent in both directions but at different times. See also Full duplex and Simplex.

Handshaking. A procedure that allows two computers to know they are connected and communicating correctly.

Hanging indent. A type of indent that places the first line of a paragraph at the left margin, and subsequent lines at a specified tab stop. Also known as reverse indent or outdent.

Hard carriage return. A return that you enter at the end of a paragraph by pressing the **Return** key. You can remove it only by using the program's delete command. Also known as a required carriage return.

Hard copy. The printed output from a computer.

Hard disk. A hard, magnetic disk on which data is stored. The hard disk can store much more data than the floppy disk.

Hard disk backup program. A program that copies files from a hard disk drive to a backup medium like floppy disks or tape drive.

Hard disk drive. See Hard disk.

Hard hyphen. A hyphen that you enter manually using the hyphen key. This hyphen prints out regardless of where it appears in the paragraph. Two words connected by a hard hyphen will not split at the right margin; the two words and connecting hard hyphen wrap to the next line.

Hard page break. A page break that you force by entering a command. A hard page break is not moved when you add or delete text above it or repaginate the document. The only way to delete it is with the program's delete command.

Hard sectored disk. A disk with more than one sector hole punched in it.

Hard space. Two words or characters connected by a hard space will not split at the right margin; the two words or characters and connecting hard space wrap to the next line.

Hardware. The physical equipment that makes up a computer system.

Hardware flow control. Using hardware instead of software to control data being transmitted so it is not sent faster than it can be received.

Hayes compatible. Modems that use the same set of instructions developed for Hayes modems.

Head crash. A damaging collision of the hard disk's read/write head with the spinning disk. Head crashes occur due to power failures when the disk is operating or other malfunctions.

Header. A line or lines of text printed in the top margin of each page of a document. A header may contain the page number, date, time, and so on.

Help key. The key designated to display help screens when you press it.

Hertz (Hz). A frequency measurement. One hertz (hz) equals one cycle per second (CPS).

Hierarchical database. One of several possible logical arrangements of data in a database.

Highlighting. To emphasize text on the screen by displaying it in reverse video (dark characters against a light background) or in a color different from the display's regular color.

Hi-lo graph. Graphs which are similar to bar charts, except they use vertical lines with tic marks to indicate two (or sometimes four) values on each line. Also called Hi-lo-open-close graphs.

Home key. One of the keys on the keyboard that moves the cursor usually to the top of the screen, the top of the document, or the left end of a line. On a spreadsheet it returns the cursor to the top left position of the spreadsheet.

Horizontal applications program. A program with applications in almost any business.

Horizontal scrolling. The shifting of the screen sideways so that documents wider than the screen can be seen. See also Vertical scrolling.

Host computer. The controlling computer that one or more other computers are connected to.

Host mode. When a computer is set to control other computers.

Hypermedia. A method of linking and relating words, sounds, graphics, and video in an unstructured way.

Hypertext. A method of linking and relating words in an unstructured way.

Hyphenation algorithms. Rules built into a program that help it determine where to place hyphens when you hyphenate a document.

Hyphenation dictionaries. A list of words containing hyphenation points used by the program that help it determine where to place hyphens when you hyphenate a document.

Hyphenation zone. The zone on either side of the right margin in which words are hyphenated.

I

Icon. A visual representation of a command that is displayed on the screen, such as a wastebasket or a file. To execute the command you point to the icon and press a designated key or click one of the buttons on a mouse.

Idea processor. A software program especially designed so you can easily enter and organize ideas for plans, tasks, proposals and reports.

IF statement. A logical statement that is designed to determine the next step based on a previous calculation. For example, IF X then Y otherwise Z.

Illegal character. A character that cannot be used for a filename.

Image digitizer. See Scanner.

Impact printer. A printer that transfers characters to paper by striking an inked ribbon against the paper.

Indent. Any measurement in from the margin of a text. An indent often marks the beginning of a paragraph, column, or new subheading. See also Hanging indent.

Indexed file. A file that is sorted quickly by means of an index rather than sorting the files physically on the disk.

Index-sequential method. A method of finding data in a database using an index to narrow the search and then using sequential access to find the specific information.

Information center (IC). A department in many companies that performs computer functions.

Information processing. The processing of words, numbers, and graphics with a computer.

Information processing cycle. The five stages in processing words, graphics, and data: input, processing, output, storage and retrieval, and distribution and communications.

Initialize. See Formatting.

Ink-jet printer. A printer that creates characters by spraying ink through nozzles.

Input. To enter data into a computer's CPU for processing or storing in memory.

Input cell. The cell in a spreadsheet model when a data table substitutes a series of numbers.

Input device. Any device used to enter information into the computer. Input devices include program disks, keyboards, light pens, voice recognition systems, and graphics tablets.

Input/output manager. The part of DOS that controls the exchange of information between the computer and peripherals like the keyboard, printers, and display screens.

Input values. The numbers in a spreadsheet data table that are run through the input cell one after another.

Insert mode. A mode where typing new text into existing text causes the existing text to the right of and below to move aside or down to make room for the new text.

Install. The process of preparing an applications program disk so that it can communicate with the hardware. Also includes changing any system default settings such as margins, drives or directories, and so on.

Installation program. The program that is used to install an applications program. It installs the necessary drivers and DOS files.

Instruction set. The rules built into a microprocessor that enables it to perform its activities.

Integrated circuit (IC). A solid-state circuit containing electronic devices like transistors.

Integrated program. A program that includes several applications such as word processing, spreadsheet, and graphics so that you can switch quickly back and forth between them and transfer data.

Integrated Services Digital Network (ISDN). The digital telephone network being installed world-wide to replace the existing analog network. This network enables the transmission of voice, data, and video without modulation.

Integrity. The accuracy of the data in a database.

Intelligent computer. A computer that contains a microprocessor and is capable of processing data.

Interactive. Any graphics program that allows you to change the image on the screen.

Interactive graphics programs. Graphics programs whose images can be directly manipulated on the screen.

Interface. The point at which two different elements meet; for example, the connection between a computer and a modem, a user and a computer, or a computer and a printer. See Port.

Interlaced display. A display where every other line is painted on each sweep of the electron beam.

Internal commands. DOS commands that are always available when the system prompt A>, B>, or C> is on the screen. See also External commands.

Internal fonts. Fonts that are built into a printer so they are available at all times.

Internal memory. That part of the computer that stores data while the computer is in use. Generally divided into random access memory (RAM) and read-only memory (ROM).

Interpolation. Determining a value from the values on either side. For example, if it was 70° at 10 AM and 80° at 11 AM, you can interpolate that it was 75° at 10:30 AM.

Interpreter (DOS). For a computer to execute a program, it must first be translated from the language the programmer used to one the computer can work with. Programs that do this are called interpreters.

Inverse video. When text is highlighted on the screen by reversing the normal colors. For example, if the screen normally displays black characters against a white background, inverse video displays characters as white characters against a black background.

Invisible soft hyphen. A hyphen that appears and prints only when it falls at the end of a line.

I/O port. Abbreviation for Input/Output port. This port connects the computer to external peripherals.

Italics. A character format that emphasizes text by slanting it when printed.

Iteration. A method of controlling the number of times spreadsheet formulas are recalculated.

J

Journals. Components of an accounting system.

Joystick. An input device that directs the cursor's movements by moving a movable stick.

Jump. See Goto.

Justified (spreadsheets). Aligning cell contents with the left or right edges of the cell or centered between them.

Justified text (word processors). Text that has both right and left margins evenly aligned.

K

Kernal. See Core.

Kerning. A way of spacing printed characters so that they are closer together.

Key. Used to specify the information on which a file will be sorted. For example, you can specify that a file be sorted in alphabetic order by name and the name is then the key. Also see Primary key and Secondary key.

Key attribute. The attribute in a database that uniquely identifies records.

Keyboard. The input device from which you type information into the computer. Keyboards generally have alphanumeric keys, function keys, special keys, and many have a numeric keypad.

Keyboard enhancer program. A program that allows you to redefine the functions assigned to the keys on your keyboard.

Keyboard program. See Macro.

Keyboard template. A plastic card that fits on or over the keyboard to guide you when using a program.

Key field. The field in a database that contains key attributes.

Key word. A word in a macro language that represents one of the keys on the keyboard.

Kilo (K). A suffix (abbreviated to K) whose value equals 1000, for example, 128K is 128,000.

Kilobit. A measurement for memory storage equivalent to 1024 bits.

Kilobyte (KB). A measurement of memory storage equivalent to 1024 characters or bytes.

Kilohertz (KHz). A frequency measurement. One kilohertz equals one thousand cycles per second.

L

Label. An alphanumeric entry, as opposed to a numerical one on a spreadsheet. Most programs assign labels a numeric value or zero. Others treat them as strings that can be manipulated with formulas just as numbers can be.

Label mode. The mode a spreadsheet enters while you enter text.

Label prefix. The character you type on a spreadsheet before entering a label that begins with a number or when you want to align the label in the cell.

LAN. See Local area network.

Landscape mode. Printing a page so the printed text or image is aligned with the long axis of the paper. Also see Portrait mode.

Large scale integration (LSI). The process of incorporating many computer components onto a single chip.

Laser disk. An external storage device that can store vast amounts of data. A typical 12-inch laser disk can store the equivalent of 1 million typewritten pages. Also known as optical disk or CD ROM.

Laser printer. A dot-matrix printer that uses a laser beam and revolving drum to create high resolution images.

LCD. See Liquid Crystal Display

Leading. The space between printed lines of text.

Learn mode. The mode used to record keystrokes so you can play them back. Used to automate procedures when working with applications programs.

LED. See Light-emitting diode display.

LED printer. A printer that creates an image on paper using light emitting diodes (LEDs).

Legal characters. Characters that are acceptable to the computer for specific purposes.

Letter quality. Generally refers to a print quality of typed documents comparable to that provided by a regular typewriter.

Library. See Glossary.

License. What you actually buy when you purchase a computer program. You do not own the program, you just purchase the license to use it.

Light-emitting diode (LED) display. A display screen that creates the image with light-emitting diodes.

Light pen. A hand-held device that allows you to draw directly on the screen, or make choices from menus.

Line. A horizontal division on the screen or page. On a standard display screen there are 24 lines. On a standard 8½-by-11 inch page there are 66 lines for text and margins.

Line graph. A graph using lines to connect the points in a set of data to indicate trends.

Line length. The maximum number of characters displayed on the screen or printed on each line. On word processing programs, this is usually the result of the left and right margin settings.

Line printer. A printer that prints one line of text at a time.

Liquid crystal display (LCD). A display screen that creates an image with liquid crystals.

Literal dictionary. A dictionary that looks up prefixes and suffixes as well as a word's root.

Load. The process of copying a program or data from a disk into the computer's memory.

Local area network (LAN). A method of connecting computers and peripherals, in a relatively small area, so that they can communicate with one another and exchange data. Also known as LANs.

Local command. A command that affects only a selected portion of the spreadsheet. Also called a Range command.

Local format. A format that only affects one part of the document, or one cell on a spreadsheet. Also called a Range format.

Locked title. See Fixed titles.

Logical fields. Fields you enter data into where you want to specify a Yes/No answer.

Logical operator. A mathematical calculation that tests the truth or falseness of a statement. For example, =, <>, <, >, <=, are logical operators.

Logical storage. The way a program shows a user how data in memory and on the disk is organized. See Physical storage.

Log on/off. To connect up with (or exit from) the service with which the computer telecommunicates.

Lookup table. A table containing data (such as tax rates) that spreadsheet functions can use to find a corresponding value.

M

Macro. A sequence of keystrokes that are stored so they can then be executed with one key, or with a combination of a few keys.

Macro language. Key words and other elements that allow you to create macros.

Main memory. See Random-access memory.

Main menu. The first menu that appears on the screen when you first load some word processing programs. It contains the basic commands that you use to open and print files and perform other procedures.

Mainframe computer. A large computer.

Management information systems (MIS) department. A department in many companies that is responsible for the procedures and equipment used to process information.

Manual. A book that describes how to use a computer or program.

Margin. The space on either side of a page and at the top and bottom of the page. Margins can be adjusted to suit your document.

Margin release. A command that allows you to enter text to the left of the left margin.

Master document. See Primary document.

Math mode. A mode in which a word processing program can add numbers and calculate formulas.

Media. The magnetic material on which computer information is stored. Usually a floppy disk, a hard disk, or tape.

Megabyte (MB). One million bytes.

Megahertz (MHz). A frequency measurement. One megahertz equals one million cycles-per-second.

Memo fields. Fields in a database into which you can enter notes or comments. These fields are not as highly structured as are others.

Memory. See Random-access memory and Read-only memory.

Memory-based program. Programs that store the entire document on which you are working on in memory. Memory based also refers to those programs that load completely into memory.

Memory cache. An area of memory where the most recently used data is stored in case it is needed again.

Memory management. The way you (or the program) store data in the computer's memory.

Memory mapping. The process by which each dot (pixel) on the display screen is given a corresponding bit in the computer's memory.

Memory resident programs. A program that is always in memory in case you need it when you are working on another program. Also called terminate and stay resident (TSR) programs.

Menu. A list of choices displayed on the screen from which you can select a command.

Menu-driven program. A method of operating a program by selecting commands from a menu. See Command driven program.

Menu pointer. A bright highlight moved by the directional arrow keys to point to or highlight a choice on the menu.

Menu tree. An arrangement of menu commands similar to a family tree.

Each branch of the menu tree sends you along a particular avenue of operation.

Merge printing. Inserting variables into a primary document to produce a number of customized documents. Variables can be entered from the keyboard or stored in a secondary file from which they are automatically merged into the form document while it is being merge-printed.

Message area. The space (at the top or bottom of the screen) where messages and prompts are displayed when you are executing commands.

Micro channel architecture (MCA). The bus design introduced by IBM when they introduced their PS/2 series of computers.

Microcomputer. A computer built around a microprocessor and designed for nontechnical users. Also known as a personal computer or desktop computer.

Microprocessor. A chip containing thousands of circuits that allow it to process data. Used as the central element of a microcomputer (often abbreviated to CPU) and as co-processors.

Microspace justification. Justification which is obtained by inserting spaces as small as 1/120th of an inch between words and letters.

Minimal recalculation. A spreadsheet feature where only those cells that are affected by changes are recalculated.

Mixed reference. A cell reference in a spreadsheet which is part relative and part absolute.

Mode. Any of several states of operation that the computer adopts in order to perform certain functions. For example, on a spreadsheet the program is in label mode when text is being entered, value mode when numbers or formulas are being entered, or command mode when commands are being executed. On a word processing program you switch to insert mode when you want to insert characters into existing text, and to typeover mode when you want to type over and replace existing characters.

Model. A simulation of a real situation. Spreadsheet models are created by entering numbers, labels, and formulas.

Modem. A piece of hardware which converts computer-generated signals into those which can be transmitted by telephone.

Modulation. The process of converting digital signals to analog signals so they can be transferred over telephone wires. See Demodulation.

Monitor. See Display screen.

Monochrome display screen. A display screen that uses only a single color. Text is usually displayed on the screens as light characters against a green, black, or amber background.

MOS chip. A metal-oxide-semiconductor chip commonly used for a computer's memory.

Mouse. A hand-held, movable device that directs the cursor's movements.

Moving. Copying data to a new location and then deleting it in the original location.

MS-DOS. Abbreviation for Microsoft disk operating system. This operating system, a variation of PC-DOS, is generally required on IBM PC compatible computers.

Multilevel menus. See Nested menus.

Multisync monitor. A display that accepts two or more input signal frequencies.

Multitasking. The ability of a computer to run more than one program at the same time.

Multiuser computer system. A system of microcomputers or dumb terminals that are hooked up to a central computer and use its computational power.

N

NAPLPS. Abbreviation for North American Presentation Level Protocol Syntax. This is the ANSCII standard for the transmission of graphics and text over telephone wires.

Natural language. A language that makes it easier to manipulate a database because the commands are more like normal speech and less like cryptic commands.

Natural recalculation. An order of recalculation which directs that the cells to which a formula refers be calculated first, before the formula is recalculated.

Near-letter-quality (NLQ). A term used to describe the output of some high quality printers when it isn't as high as letter quality. See Letter quality.

Nested menus. A way of arranging menu commands so that making a selection from a menu displays another menu. Each succeeding level of menus offers more specific choices. Also known as Multilevel menu.

Nested parenthesis. Parenthesis which is embedded in another parenthesis, e.g., $1+(1/(1/2))$. An operation will always be performed from the innermost parenthesis outward.

Nesting. Inserting a command or calculation within another command or calculation so it is executed at the appropriate time.

Network. Two or more computers connected together with cables so they can exchange files and share resources like printers and hard disk drives.

Network architecture. The design of a network.

Network database. A database designed to be accessed by multiple users at the same time.

Network management programs. Programs that supervise and control a network.

Network manager. The person assigned the responsibility of resolving any problems with a network or the people who use it.

Network server. Any device designed to be accessed by all of the computers connected to a network.

Newspaper-style columns. Columns of text that flow from the bottom of one column to the top of the next.

Node. A connection to a network, where a computer or peripheral can be connected, so they can send and receive data over the network.

Noncontiguous sectors. Parts of a file on a disk that are stored in sectors that are not adjacent to each other.

Nonimpact printer. Printers that form characters without striking an inked ribbon against the paper.

Noninterlaced display. A display where each line is painted in sequence.

Nonvolatile. Memory that does not lose data when the power is turned off.

Null-modem cable. A cable used to directly connect the serial ports on two computers so they can exchange data.

Numeric fields. Database fields into which you enter numbers that you want to be able to calculate.

Numeric keypad. Number keys arranged like those on a calculator.

Numeric keys. The keys located above the alphabetic keys on the keyboard. When you hold down the **Shift** key, the symbols above the numbers appear on the screen.

Num Lock key. The key that activates the numbers on the numeric keypad when these keys also double as cursor movement keys. You must engage the Num Lock key to enter numbers and disengage it to move the cursor.

O

OEM. An original equipment manufacturer who buys equipment, supplies,

or program, from other companies and then sells it under its own name.

Offset. See Page offset.

On-screen forms. Forms that are displayed on the screen so you can easily enter data.

Open architecture. A computer designed so that boards can be plugged into a slot connected directly to the computer's bus so that the computer's capabilities can be expanded.

Open codes. Formatting codes that override default formats from the point at which they are entered to the end of the document or to the next code of the same type.

Open look. The user interface developed to make the UNIX operating system easier to use.

Operating system. The program that controls the computer's hardware.

Operating System/2 (OS/2). The operating system developed by IBM and Microsoft to replace DOS.

Operating system environment. A more sophisticated version of an operating system that allows more than one program to be run, more than one file to be displayed on the screen, and allows the user to execute most commands from menus.

Operator. A symbol used in a formula that tells the spreadsheet program what calculation to perform. The + operator, for example, tells the program to perform addition.

Optical character recognition (OCR). The process of converting printed characters to computer data with an optical device.

Optical disk. See Laser disk.

Optional hyphen. See Soft hyphen.

Order of operations. The sequence in which a formula is calculated. Every program has a specific sequence to follow.

Original equipment manufacturer (OEM). See OEM.

Orphan. The first line of a paragraph that, when printed out, appears as the bottom line of the page.

Outline. A numbered and indented list of headings that shows the organization and relative importance of the topics.

Outline program. A program that automatically indents and numbers headings in an outline.

Outliner. A program that links headings and body text so moving, copying, or deleting a heading also moves, copies, or deletes the associated text. Also allows you to collapse the document so you see just headings (outline view) or expand it so you see both headings and text (document view).

Outline view. A view of a document in outline mode so the body text is collapsed and only the headings are displayed. See Outliner and Document view.

Output cell. The spreadsheet cells from which the results are stored on a data table when a series of numbers are run through the input cell.

Output device. Any device used to get data out of a computer. Typical output devices are the display screen, printers, plotters, and modems.

Overlay file. The part of the program stored on the disk until needed when it is called into memory by the program's core.

Overprint. To have the printer type over a character with another character, for example, to print an accent or a symbol not on the keyboard.

Override. To modify or change a default setting.

Overtyping. Typing new text over existing text so previously entered characters are replaced by the new characters.

Overwrite. To save the latest version of a file when both files have the same filename. The old file is erased, and the new one replaces it.

P

Packet switching. The process of transmission whereby data is transmitted in blocks along lines that are also shared by other transmitters. Data is sent more cheaply this way since users are charged only for the amount of data transmitted, not the amount of time used.

Packet-switching networks. Networks that send data from more than one user at the same time.

Packing. An operation that permanently removes deleted records from a database file.

Page break. The point at which one page ends, and the printer advances to the top of the next sheet when printing.

Page description language. See Document description language.

Page makeup. See Desktop publishing program.

Page offset. The distance, measured in characters, from the left edge of the paper to where the text is printed.

Page-oriented program. A word processing program that breaks a document into pages and does not allow you to see the bottom of one page and the top of the next on the screen at the same time.

Page printer. A printer, like a laser printer, that forms an entire page in its memory before it begins printing it.

Pagination. The process of breaking a document into pages.

Paging. Breaking a document into pages.

Paired codes. Formatting codes that are entered in pairs. The first code begins a format and the second ends it.

Paragraph reform. Realignment of text, after insertions or deletions, so that it realigns with the margins. Also called line adjust, paragraph aligning, or rewrite.

Parallel port. A port that carries data 8 bits at a time on parallel paths. Frequently used for printers and connections to networks. Also known as a Centronics interface.

Parallel-style columns. Columns arranged side by side.

Parity. A method of checking data transmission for errors. Parity bits are added to the data as odd or even bits.

Parity bit. A single bit that checks to see if any errors have occurred during transmission. The receiving computer checks parity and if it doesn't match, the computer asks that the data be retransmitted.

Parity error. An error that occurs when data is not sent correctly.

Park program. A utility program that moves a hard disk drive head to an unused area of the disk so that banging the computer does not damage data.

Pascaline. The name given to the mechanical calculating mechanism that Pascal devised for adding and subtracting.

Password. A form of protection that allows access only to users who know the assigned password.

Paste. Moving something that has been copied or cut from a document to another place in the document or to another document.

Path. A way of specifying the location of a file on a hard disk drive when saving or retrieving. A path begins from the root directory and narrows down to the specific file you are looking for. For example, C:\LETTERS\1987 specifies that the file 1987 is in the directory LETTERS on drive C.

PC. Abbreviation for personal computer.

PC-DOS. A version of the MS-DOS operating system that runs on IBM PCs and compatible computers.

Peripheral. Any standalone addressable device like a printer or modem, connected to a computer using cables.

Personal computer. See Microcomputer.

Personal information manager. Programs designed to allow you to view your data in more than one way.

Perspective view. A view of a three-dimensional object where the size of objects depends on their distance from the viewer.

PERT chart. A chart created with a project management program that graphically shows the organization of tasks.

PgDn key. A key that scrolls the screen down one screenful or one page.

PgUp key. A key that scrolls the screen up one screenful or one page.

Phase modulation (PM). A type of modulation that conveys data by changing the starting point of the cycles in the analog carrier wave.

Phase shift keying (PSK). A form of modulation used in telecommunications.

Phrase storage area. See Glossary.

Physical storage. The way data, like that stored in a database, is magnetically stored on the disk. See Logical storage.

Picture element. See Pixel.

Pie chart. A chart that illustrates relationships of parts to the whole. The pie (or circle) represents the whole, and the segments within the circle represent various parts.

Pin feed. The pins built into a printer to engage the holes in continuous form paper.

Piracy. The act of copying a copyrighted program for sale or use by others without the permission of the copyright holder.

Pitch. The number of characters printed per inch. The most frequently used pitches are 10 pitch (pica) and 12 pitch (elite). There are either 10 or 12 characters to the inch.

Pixel. A dot on the screen illuminated to create an image.

Plan view. A view from above of a three-dimensional object.

Plotter. A device that draws images by moving a pen across the paper.

Plug compatibility. The ability to connect devices to a computer's ports.

Point mode. The mode a spreadsheet enters while you are creating formulas or functions by pointing to cells with the cursor.

Points. A unit of measure for type. Approximately 1/72 of an inch.

Pop-up menu. A list of commands that pop up on the screen.

Port. An electrical connection on the computer into which a cable can be plugged so the computer can communicate with another device such as a printer or modem.

Portable operating system. An operating system that can be run on more than one type of computer with minimal changes.

Portrait mode. Printing a page so the printed text or image is aligned with the short axis of the paper. Also see Landscape mode.

Precedence. See Order of operations.

Precedent cells. Spreadsheet cells that contain values referred to by the formula in the cell being examined.

Presentation Manager. The graphic user interface for OS/2 that allows you to load programs and execute operating system commands by pointing and clicking with a mouse.

Primary document. The document used in merge printing that contains the text to appear in all copies and the codes that instruct the program what data to insert during merge printing and where to insert it.

Primary key. The key by which a file is sorted first.

Primary memory. See Random-access memory.

Print. To send a document that is in the computer's memory to a printer to be printed out.

Print buffer. A buffer into which some programs print a file so it can then be printed from the buffer and you can continue editing.

PRINT command. A DOS command that sends a text or print file to the printer.

Printer. The device that prints out a document. Popular printers include laser printers, dot-matrix printers, and ink-jet printers.

Printer advance. A code that advances the printer a specified distance.

Printer control codes. Codes entered into a document to send a command to the printer to control its operation. Typical applications are to change type sizes and character attributes. Printer command codes are specific to a printer and are listed in the accompanying manual.

Printer set-up codes. A command sent to the printer to control its operation. Typical applications are to change type sizes and character attributes. Set up codes are specific to a printer and are listed in the accompanying manual.

Print file. A file that sends a file to a disk instead of to a printer. A print file serves as a preview of the printout because all format commands, like top and bottom margins and headers and footers, are interpreted so that it prints on the screen disk just as it

would on the printout. A print file can be printed or displayed on the screen directly from DOS.

Printhead. The element in a printer that forms the printed image on the paper.

Printout. The paper output from the printer.

Print queue. One or more files waiting to be printed.

Print server. A device that connects the computers on a network to a printer.

Print wheel. A type element. See also Daisy wheel printer.

Program (n). A set of instructions that tells the computer what to do and when to do it. Programs are subdivided into systems programs, like the operating system, and applications programs used for word processing, spreadsheets, or graphics.

Program (v). To write a set of instructions that will run on a computer.

Programmer. A person who writes computer programs including those you use to process words and information.

Project management. The process of managing the costs and schedules associated with projects.

Prompt. A screen request that asks you for more information before executing a command. Prompts are answered by typing a reply and pressing the **Return** key.

Prompt line. The line on which a prompt appears.

Proportional spacing. A method of assigning more or less space to characters based on their width. For example, an *m* is given more space than an *i* when it is printed out on a printer.

Proprietary operating system. An operating system sold by a single company.

Protected mode. The mode used by OS/2 to keep applications programs from interfering with each other's areas of memory.

PSK. Abbreviation for Phase Shift Keying, a form of phase modulation used by some modems.

Public Switched Telephone Network (PSTN). The telephone network that you use when you make a phone call.

Pull-down menu. A list of commands pulled down from the top of the screen with a command or by pointing to it with a mouse. The pulled-down menu lists other choices.

Punched card. A cardboard card in which holes (representing data) are punched. It is fed into a card reader

that converts the data to bits which are then transferred to the computer for processing.

Q

Quad-density disk. A disk with 96 tracks per inch.

Query. A question posed to a database.

Query by example. A form displayed on the screen so you can enter queries to a database by filling out the appropriate spaces.

Query language. A language used to pose queries to a database.

Queue. To specify the sequence in which a number of files are automatically printed.

Quick reference card. A card that comes with many programs and that summarizes all of their commands.

Quit. To leave the program and return to the computer's operating system.

QWERTY keyboard. The standard arrangement of keys on the keyboard. Named after the arrangement of the first six keys on the top row.

R

Ragged left. Text that has an even right margin and a ragged left margin.

Ragged right. Text that has an even left margin and a ragged right margin.

Random-access memory (RAM). That part of memory that holds the programs and data currently in use.

Range. A group of cells on a spreadsheet program that are selected for an operation.

Range command. See Local command.

Range format. See Local format.

Range name. The name assigned to a range of cells on a spreadsheet.

Raster graphics display. A graphics screen display that is produced by the electron gun sweeping across and down the screen in a regular, unchanging pattern, much as eyes read a page.

Read. To insert text from another file into the document you are currently working on.

Reading a file. To insert text from another file into the document you are currently working on.

Read-only memory (ROM). ROM holds the instructions that the computer needs in order to function when it is first turned on. The information in

ROM is not lost when the power is turned off.

Read/write slot. The oblong opening in the outer plastic jacket of a floppy disk through which the drive's read/write head comes in contact with the magnetic disk.

Ready mode. The mode a spreadsheet enters when it is waiting for your next instruction.

Real mode. The mode in an 80286 chip that allows you to run programs that were written for earlier chips like the 8086 and 8088.

Reboot. See Boot.

Record. A group of related fields such as names and addresses that make up a record file.

Record management programs. A program that manages information like a database management program but which isn't as powerful.

Record pointer. An invisible pointer in a database that indicates the current record.

Redlining. A format assigned to text that is inserted into a document so that others can easily see the changes. See Strikeout.

Reduced instruction set chips (RISC). A microprocessor that contains fewer built-in instructions or functions allowing it to operate more quickly. See Complete instruction set chips.

Reinkers. A device that applies more ink on a used ribbon.

Relational database. A database where data is organized into tables.

Relational operator. Operators that indicate relationships such as equal to, greater then, or less than.

Relations. The formal name for the files in a relational database that contain data.

Relationships. The cross-references between two or more files in a relational database.

Relative reference. A spreadsheet formula reference to another cell that refers to its position relative to the cell containing the formula, e.g., 2 rows up and one column over. When the formula is copied it will refer to a cell in the same relative position to the cell to which it is copied. See also Absolute reference.

Remote computing. Operating a computer from a remote site.

RENAME command. A DOS command that changes the name of a file using a modem and the telephone lines.

Repagination. A command used on a page-oriented program when changes are made to a document that affect its length. The command ensures that all text falls on the appropriate page of the printed document.

Repeat command. A command that repeats previously entered keystrokes.

Replacement mode. See Typeover.

Report. A printed document containing the contents of a record file or database. The report can include all of the data or just the data in selected fields and selected records.

Report format. The design specifications for a printed database report.

Required carriage return. See Hard carriage return.

Required hyphen. See Hard hyphen.

Required space. See Hard space.

Resolution. An indication of the sharpness of characters or images on a printout or the display screen.

Retrieve. To transfer a file from a disk into the computer's memory.

Return key. Frequently the final keystroke; for example when entering data into spreadsheet cells, ending paragraphs in documents, or executing commands. Also known as the Enter key.

Reverse video. A reversal of the screen's usual brightness. For example, if you work on a screen that shows green characters on a black screen, reverse video will give you black characters on a green screen.

Revisable-form text (RFT). A document saved in IBM's Document Content Architecture format so it can be edited or printed on other equipment using a program that utilizes the same format.

RGB color display. A high-quality color monitor to which the three primary signals—red, green, and blue—are fed to it on separate wires.

Ribbon. A length of inked cloth inserted in a cartridge and used in a printer to transfer characters to the paper.

Ring architecture. When the computers in a network are connected along a single path so that messages can flow from the starting point, through the other computers, and then back to the starting point in a loop.

ROM. See Read-only memory.

Root directory. The one directory on a disk that is created when the disk is first formatted. The root directory can be subdivided into additional subdirectories, so files can be organized more efficiently.

Root-word dictionary. A dictionary that checks root words and ignores prefixes or suffixes.

Routing server. Devices that connect two or more networks that have the same architecture.

Row. The horizontal line of cells on of a spreadsheet that intersect with a column. Rows are usually numbered down the left side of the screen with row one at the top.

RS-232-C port. See Serial port.

Ruler line. A line at the top or bottom of the screen that displays margins and tab stops.

Running feet. Footers that print on two or more consecutive pages. See Footer.

Running heads. Headers that print on two or more consecutive pages. See Header.

S

Save. To copy a file from the computer's memory onto a disk.

Scale. To change the range covered by the Y-axis on a graph. Scaling can be done either manually or automatically.

Scanner. An input device that reads information from hard copy and transmits it to the computer. There are currently three kinds of scanners: character recognition scanners, bar-code readers, and bit-image converters (digitizers).

Scatter graph. A graph that plots data with dots or other symbols.

Scrap. See Buffer.

Scrapbook. See Buffer.

Script languages. A programming language built into applications programs so users can automate procedures.

Scroll bar. The bar on the right side of some screens which contains the scroll box.

Scroll box. A small box on the side of the screen which indicates what part of the document is currently displayed on the screen.

Scrolling. To move text vertically or horizontally on the screen in order to see different parts.

Search. To look for a string throughout the document.

Search and replace. To look for a string throughout the document or other file and replace it with another string.

Secondary file. A file that stores variables to be merged into a primary file while merge printing to create a number of customized documents. Secondary files are organized in fields and records. Also known as a data file, database, record file, or variable file.

Secondary key. A key that breaks ties when a file is sorted by the primary key.

Secondary storage. See External storage.

Sector. A portion of the floppy or hard disk onto which data is written, or read from. The space on a formatted disk is divided into tracks and sectors so data can be located easily.

Sector hole. The hole in a disk (and the disk's outer envelope) which the drive uses to determine the orientation of the disk when it is spinning.

Select. To choose a block of text by highlighting it so that it can be copied, moved, deleted, or formatted.

Self-booting. See System disk.

Sensitivity analysis. See What-ifs.

Serial. A method of transmission that sends data one bit at a time. Also called serial transmission.

Serial port. A port that transmits information one character at a time, as opposed to a parallel port that transmits several bits of data at a time. Also known as RS-232-C.

Settings form. See Dialog box.

Settings sheet. See Dialog box.

Setup string. A string of characters that is sent to the printer to set the mode it uses to print a document.

Set variable. A merge code in a primary file that specifies the data to be inserted in place of another merge code.

Shared logic. Interconnected computers that are able to process information by themselves when they are no longer connected to the system or network to which they are attached.

Shareware. See Freeware.

Sheet feeder. A mechanical device that automatically feeds cut sheets of paper to a printer.

Shell. A menu-driven user-friendly interface that makes operating system commands easier to use.

Shell document. See Primary document.

Silicon chip. A small electronic device made from silicon, on which electronic circuits and devices are etched or deposited.

Simplex. A method of transmitting data that allows transmission in only one direction, for example, a radio station. See Duplex and Half duplex.

Single-density disk. A floppy disk on which data is stored on 48 tracks.

Single-sided disk. A magnetic disk on which data is stored on only one side.

Singletasking operating system. The ability of an operating system to run only one program at a time.

Singletasking. The ability of a computer to run only one program at a time.

Site license. A license from a publisher that allows you to make copies of their program for use at a specific site, or to run their program on a network used by more than one user.

Slot. See Expansion slot.

Smart modem. A modem that allows you to dial phone numbers from the keyboard or communications program.

Soft carriage return. A return that the computer automatically enters when it wraps words to the next line as text is entered.

Soft font. A font supplied on a floppy disk so you can download it to the printer when needed.

Soft hyphen. A hyphen that only appears in the word (on the printout) if, when a paragraph is reformed before printing, it is required. Also known as a syllable, optional, normal, or ghost hyphen.

Soft page break. A page break that the program inserts automatically when the maximum number of lines on a page is reached. If data is added or deleted so that the number of lines change, a soft page break adjusts automatically.

Soft-sectored disk. A floppy disk on which sectors are specified when the disk is formatted for use with a particular operating system.

Soft space. Spaces that are inserted between words when you press the Spacebar.

Software. A general term that refers to programs saved onto a magnetic medium.

Solid state. Electronic components made from solid materials as opposed to vacuum and gas tubes.

Sort. To arrange a file into a desired order using keys. For example, a mailing list can be sorted by descending numeric order by zip codes, or in ascending alphabetical order by last name.

Soundproof enclosure. A device that fits over a printer to reduce the amount of noise that escapes into the office.

Source disk. The disk that holds data destined to be transfered to a target disk.

Source range. The cells containing data that is to be copied or moved to another range. See Target range.

Spacebar. The key that inserts spaces when entering data.

Sparse memory management. A spreadsheet program technique where memory is allocated only to those cells where data has been entered.

Spelling checker. A program containing a dictionary that checks the spelling of any word or words in the document.

Split screen. A divided screen which allows the user to look at two or more parts of the same file at the same time.

Spreadsheet. An arrangement of columns and rows into which data is entered for analysis.

Spreadsheet program. A program that allows you to enter labels, numbers, formulas, and functions into cells to calculate and organize information.

Stack. The method used to organize data with a hypermedia program.

Stacked bar graph. A graph that has values stacked on top of each other as opposed to side-by-side.

Stackware. The organized information developed by users of hypertext programs.

Standalone microcomputer. A computer system that is not connected to other computers.

Standalone program. Any program that is not integrated into another program.

Star architecture. A network where all of the computers are connected to a central computer.

Start value. The first number entered by a data fill command.

Startup drive. The drive to which the computer looks for programs when you first turn it on. The startup drive is almost always drive A.

Static RAM chip. A memory chip that does not have to be refreshed as frequently as a dynamic RAM chip.

Status area. See Status line.

Status line. The line at the top or bottom of the screen which provides important information. For example, on a word processing program it gives the current page, line and column in which the cursor is positioned. On spreadsheet programs the current cell, its contents, and its format is generally given.

Step mode. A mode that allows you to execute a macro one command at a time to see how it runs and makes it easier to find any problems.

Step value. The value that a data fill command increments each successive number.

Sticky menu. A menu from which you cannot exit without selecting a quit or exit choice on the menu. Unlike a regular menu, it does not disappear automatically when a command is executed.

Stop codes. Codes that tell the printer to pause until a specified key is pressed.

Stop merge. A merge code that tells a merge print to end.

Stop value. The value at which a data fill command stops entering numbers.

Storage capacity. The amount of information that can be stored in a computer on magnetic media.

Storage device. See External storage device.

Stored program. The concept where a program is stored in the computer's memory along with the data that it is to process.

Strikeout. A format assigned to text in a document that is proposed for deletion. See Redlining.

String. One or more characters, e.g. any character, number, word, phrase, sentence, or paragraph, that appear in sequence, and can be considered as a group.

Style and grammar checker. A program that compares the user's style to conventional stylistic rules and flags any variation.

Style sheets. Lists of previously defined formats that can be quickly assigned to the parts of a document.

Subdirectory. One of several other directories you create from the main root directory. See Root directory.

Submenu. See Nested menus.

Subscript. A number, word, or phrase positioned below the rest of the line.

Superscript. A number, word, or phrase positioned above the rest of the line.

Support. The help, education, and assistance provided to users by the companies that sell them products.

Supporting model. A spreadsheet model that contains cells that are referred to by a master model.

Syllable hyphen. See Soft hyphen.

Symbolic referencing. A feature where a code in one page of a document refers to a page or other number elsewhere in the document. The code always correctly displays the number to which it refers even if that number is changed.

Synched. When a spreadsheet screen display is divided into two windows that are then scrolled together. See Unsynched.

Synchronous. A method of transmission where the timing between the bits in a byte of data and the timing between bytes are both timed precisely. See Asynchronous.

Syntax. The rules that must be followed when entering a function or query.

System. Any collection of elements designed to work together to perform a task.

System defaults. The settings entered into a program by its designers. These can usually be changed by the user.

System disk. A disk that contains the operating system so that the operating system and the applications program can be loaded from it.

System operator (SYSOP). The person who manages and operates a bulletin board.

System prompt. The prompt that is displayed on the screen when the operating system is running and no applications programs have been loaded.

System software. Operating system software like PC DOS, MS DOS, CP/M, and UNIX that controls the computer. Also includes a variety of utility programs.

T

Tab key. The key that moves the cursor from left to right between tab stops. See also Backtab key.

Tab stop. The stop or stops that provide alignment points across the page so that columns and indents can be created.

Tagged-Image-File-Format (TIFF). A standard that defines a format in which graphic images are stored on the disk.

Target disk. The disk that receives data transferred from the source disk.

Target range. The cells specified as the new location for the contents of cells in the source range when they are moved or copied. Also called the destination range.

Telecommunication. A method of communicating between computers using telephone lines and a modem.

Teleconference. Exchanging messages with other computer users over the phone lines.

Template (spreadsheets). A model which is designed to be used over and over again. It contains all of the necessary labels and formulas used in a spreadsheet and can be used by anyone who knows how to move the cursor and enter numbers.

Template (word processors). See Primary document.

Terminal emulation. Setting up a computer so it acts just like a dumb terminal.

Text. Any words or numbers that make up a document.

Text capture. Capturing in a disk file the text that appears on your screen when in telecommunication with other computers.

Thermal printer. A printer that creates characters on paper with heat.

Thesaurus. An editing aide that allows you to highlight a word and request that a list of synonyms be displayed.

Thimble. A type element used in some fully formed character printers.

Time fields. Fields in a database where you enter only times.

Toggle. To switch between two states. Many computer commands toggle, that is, they either turn a mode on or off or switch back and forth between two states.

Token. The electronic signal circulated in a network using token passing to prevent messages from interfering with each other. Only the device holding the token can transmit data.

Token passing. A traffic control method used in a network to prevent two or more devices from transmitting data at the same time.

Toner. The chemical in a laser printer that is fused to paper to create an image.

Touch screen. A screen sensitive to the finger touch so that the user's finger can select menu commands or move the cursor.

Trackballs. A device where spinning a ball moves the cursor on the screen.

Tracks. The concentric paths around a disk on which data is stored.

Tracks per inch (TPI). The number of tracks per inch on a disk. The higher the TPI, the more data the disk can store.

Tractor feed. An accessory device used on many printers to feed continuous form paper to the printer.

Transceiver. A device used to connect computers to a baseband network.

Transistor. A precursor of the integrated circuit, the transistor was the first solid state electronic device.

Trojan horse. A program in which someone has planted a virus in the hopes that when you run the program, the virus damages your data.

Truncate. Shorten to fit.

Twisted-pair cable. Cables used in networks that contain pairs of wires twisted around each other like telephone wire.

TYPE command. The DOS command that displays ASCII files on the screen.

Typeface. A specific type design, for example, Courier or Times Roman.

Typeover mode. A mode where data being entered types over and replaces existing text. Also known as replace, strikeover, overtype, or insert off mode.

Typesetter. A person who sets type so it can be printed.

Typesetting. The process of setting type.

Type size. The size of a printed character, usually specified in points.

Typestyle. A version of a typeface, for example, bold or italic.

Typewriter mode. A mode where characters typed on the keyboard are printed on the printer when you press the **Return** key to end a line or paragraph.

U

Uncompress. Expanding a file that has been compressed so that it can be read by the program for which it was designed.

Undelete command. The command that restores text deleted by mistake.

Underline. A format used to emphasize text by underlining it when printed out. Also called underscoring.

Underscore. See Underline.

Undo command. A command on some programs that reverses the results of the previous command in case it was mistakenly entered.

Universal product code (UPC). The code assigned to bar codes to give them meaning.

UNIX. A popular operating system.

Unsynched. When a spreadsheet screen display is divided into two windows that are then scrolled independently of each other. See Synched.

Updates. New releases of existing programs that correct problems in the previous version or which contain improvements.

Upload. To send a file to a mainframe or other microcomputer.

User. Anyone who operates a computer.

User-defined menus. Menus created by users of applications programs rather than by the program's authors.

User memory. See Random-access memory.

Utility program. Any program that allows you to perform a single task more easily.

V

Vacuum tubes. One of the earliest electronic devices that was replaced by the transistor.

Validity check. A method of checking database input data for accuracy. For example, you might specify that only text of a certain length can be entered in a field.

Value. A number, formula, or function that is used in calculations.

Value mode. The mode a spreadsheet enters when you are entering numbers, formulas, or functions.

Vaporware. A derogatory term applied to programs that are long promoted but never introduced.

Variable (spreadsheets). Any data entered into a model's cell, to which formulas in other cells refer. It's called a variable because it can easily be changed (varied) during a sensitivity analysis.

Variable (word processors). Personalized data which is inserted into a form letter in order to customize it.

Variable name. A code inserted into a primary document that specifies what information is to be inserted from the keyboard or from a secondary file. When the primary document is merge printed, the variable name code is replaced with data entered manually from the keyboard or automatically from the secondary file.

Variables. Data that is inserted into copies in place of variable names when a primary document is merge printed.

Variables file. See Secondary file.

Vector graphics display. A graphics display that moves the CRT's electron beam between points on the screen to draw straight lines.

Vertical applications programs. Applications programs designed for narrow market segments.

Vertical scrolling. Moving the document up and down on the screen so you can read or edit it.

Video display. See Display screen.

Video display terminal (VDT). See Display screen.

Video graphics array (VGA). A high-resolution graphics standard for display screens.

Virtual memory. A procedure where the hard disk is treated just like RAM when operating systems or applications programs need more storage space.

Virtual 8086 mode. An extension of real mode on computers with 80286 and 80386 chips.

Virus. A program designed to reproduce itself onto other magnetic media with the goal of destroying a user's data.

Visible soft hyphen. A hyphen that splits a word when the word will not fit on the end of a line.

Voice input device. An input device that recognizes the human voice and converts it into computer code.

Voice mail. The digital storage and routing of phone messages.

Voice template. An electronic pattern for individual spoken words that allows a computer to recognize speech.

Volatile memory. Memory which will be lost if the power fails. RAM, for instance, is volatile.

W

Wait mode. A spreadsheet mode that tells you wait because the program is busy performing a task like recalculation.

Wait states. The missed cycles that occur when a microprocessor has to wait for information to be fed to it from memory.

Wand. A hand-held device used to read bar codes.

Warm boot. Restarting the computer by pressing designated keys instead of turning it off and back on. On the IBM PC, you warm boot by pressing **Ctrl-Alt-Del**.

What-ifs. The process of changing a value in a spreadsheet to see how the results are affected.

Wide area network. Computers equipped with modems and connected together by telephone lines.

Widow. A short line ending a paragraph and appearing by itself at the top of a printed page.

Wildcard. A characters used in search and replace operations to stand for one or more characters in the same position in the string.

Window. The area created on a split screen that displays different parts of the same file (or different files). See Split screen.

Wire-frame view. A view of a three-dimensional object that removes solid areas so you can see the structure.

Word processing. Entering, editing, storing, distributing, and printing words with a computer.

Word processing program. An applications program designed specifically to handle the creation of written documents such as memos, letters, reports, articles, and books.

Word wrap. The ability of the word processing program to calculate whether the word being entered will fit onto the end of the line. If not, the word is automatically moved to the next line.

Working area. The area of a spreadsheet that contains the cells you enter data into.

Worksheet. See Spreadsheet.

Workstation. A computer or terminal connected to a central computer or network. Also known as node.

WORM disk. An optical disk on which you can store information once, write once, read many times.

Write-protected. A disk on which the write-protect notch has been covered to prevent files from being stored on it, or which doesn't have a write protect notch.

Write-protect notch. The notch on a floppy disk that allows you to store, erase, and rename files on the disk when it is uncovered but prevents you from doing so when covered.

Writing blocks. To move or copy a selected block from the document on which you are working to its own file on the disk.

WYSIWYG. The acronym for "what you see (on the screen) is what you get (on the printout)".

X

X-Modem. A popular error checking protocol used when uploading and downloading files over the telephone lines.

Xon/Xoff. A software-based flow control that prevents data from being sent between computers faster than it can be received.

XY graphs. Graphs with values on both the X-axis and the Y-axis.

Z

Zap. To erase data on a spreadsheet.

Index

Abacus, 17–18
ABC computer, 24, 25 (fig.)
Absolute references, 480, 481 (fig.), 482, 489, 493
Accelerator boards, 67
Access points, 679–680
Access time, 115
Accounting programs, 721–727
  applications of, 721–722
  components of, 724–727
  manual accounting systems and, 722
  operation of, 722–724
Accounts payable programs, 726
Accounts receivable programs, 726
Accuracy checking, 617
Acoustic coupler modems, 128, 130
Active area, in spreadsheets, 428, 430
Ada, 23
Adapter Definition File (ADF), 67
Add-on boards, 54 (fig.), 66–67, 71
  accelerator boards, 67
  multifunction boards, 66–67
Address bus, 65, 71
Adobe Systems, 389
Aiken, Howard, 24
AIX, 148
Aldus Corporation, 38
Algorithms
  fonts, 343
  hyphenation, 334, 335
Allen, Paul, 36
All points addressable (APA) printing, 99. See also Bit mapping
Altair, 30
Alt (Alternate) key, 79, 225
Alternate format lines. See Format lines
American National Standards Institute code. See ANSI code
American Standard Code for Information Interchange. See ASCII code
Amplitude modulation (AM), 707
Analog graphics displays, 653
Analog signals, 706
  modems and, 127
Analog-to-digital converters, 656
Analytical engine, 20–21

Annotation, of formulas, 453
ANSI code, 46, 47
Answer mode, 676–677, 680
Append command, 586
Apple computers, 30–31, 32–33 (figs.)
  Dvorak keyboards for, 77
  first logo, 32 (fig.)
Apple DOS, 148
Apple I, 30–31, 32 (fig.)
Apple II, 30-31, 33 (fig.), 39
  address bus for, 65
Apple LaserWriter printer, 31, 38
Apple Macintosh, 31, 33 (fig.), 620
  address bus for, 65
  data bus for, 64
  operating system, 140, 148
  ROM, 58
Applications generators, 612
Applications programs, 12, 16, 210.
      See also specific programs
  bugs in, 263
  clones of, 262–263, 265
  command-driven, 228
  copy protection and, 259–260, 265
  data files and, 252–258
  disk-based, 253–254, 258
  documentation for, 260–261, 265
  formatting system disks for, 182–184
  horizontal, 712
  installing, 249–251
  introduction to, 211–217
  issues related to, 259–265
  licensing, 260, 261 (fig.), 265
  loading, 218–220, 222
  memory-based, 252, 253 (fig.), 258
  menu-driven, 226
  operating systems and, 140
  piracy and, 260, 265
  program disks, 249
  quitting, 220–221, 222
  self-booting, 218, 222
  site licensing and, 260, 265
  support for, 261, 265
  training in, 261
  updates of, 262, 265
  using operating system functions within, 257–258

vertical, 712
viruses and, 263–264, 265
ARC, 698
Architecture, 64–66, 71
  bus, 668–669
  closed, 66
  micro channel, 65, 67
  network, 668–670
  open, 66
  ring, 669, 670 (fig.)
  star, 669, 671 (fig.)
Area graphs, 634, 639 (fig.)
Arguments, for functions, 455, 462
Arithmometer, 20
Arpanet, 678
Artifical intelligence (AI), 29
ASCII code, 46–47, 52
  OCR devices and, 81
  typing, 383
ASCII text files, 256, 258, 697, 703
  displaying, 200–201
  file exchange and, 25
  printing, 200–201
  transmission of, 697, 703
Ashton-Tate, 37
Aspect ratios
  of graphs, 641
  of raster displays, 654
Assembly languages, 524
Asterisk (*) wildcard, 176–178
Asymmetrical modem protocols, 700
Asynchronous data transmission, 708–709
AT&T Unix, 148
Atanasoff, John, 24
Atanasoff-Berry Computer (ABC), 24, 25 (fig.)
Atkinson, Bill, 620
Attributes, 553, 560
  key, 555
Audiovisual presentations, 661–663
Audit trails, 617
Auto-answer modems, 677, 683
AUTOEXEC.BAT, 154, 204–206
Automated attendant, 130
Automatic paragraph reforming, 300
Automatic recalculation, 497, 499

Automatic referencing. *See* Symbolic referencing

Automatic scaling, of graphs, 637, 638 (fig.)

Automatic Typewriter Company, 271

Automation, 17

Auto-redial programs, 686

Autorepeat feature, on keyboards, 73

Auto-Typist, 271

A/UX, 148

Auxiliary storage. *See* External storage

Babbage, Charles, 20–21

Background, 150

Background recalculation, 497, 499

Backspace key, 78, 294, 298
   correcting mistakes with, 289

Backtab key, 79, 352

Backup copies, 119, 249

Balance sheet, 724–725

Bandwidth, 708, 709

Bank-memory switching. *See* Paging

Bar codes, 80

Bar code scanners, 80, 88

Bardeen, John, 49

Bar graphs, 631–632
   stacked, 632, 640 (fig.)

Barnaby, John, 37

Barometers, 18

Baseband networks, 672

Base memory. *See* Conventional memory

BASIC, Microsoft, 36

Batch files, 154, 204–206

Baud rates, 690–691

Bell Labs, 28, 49

Bernoulli box, 119

Berry, Clifford, 24

Billings, John, 24

Binary digits. *See* Bits

Binary files, 255, 258
   transmission of, 697, 703

Binary numbers, 41–42

Binary system, 41–42

Bin selection, 243

BIOS, 144

Bit mapping, 95, 106

Bitnet, 678

Bits, 44, 52, 55–56

Bits per second, 690–691

BIX, 678

Blocks. *See also* Documents; Text
   column, 304
   copying, 306, 307 (fig.), 310
   copying to disk file, 308–309
   defined, 295, 303–305
   deleting, 307, 309 (fig.), 310
   line, 303–304
   moving, 306, 398, 310
   moving to disk file, 308–309
   rectangular, 304–305
   selecting, 305–306, 310

Block size, 698

Boards. *See* Add-on boards

Boilerplate, 270
   computer-aided design and, 649, 651

Boldfacing, 337

Bookkeeping software. *See* Accounting programs

Boole, George, 23

Boolean algebra, 23

Booting, 153, 161

Borders, in spreadsheets, 422 (fig.), 467

Boxes, drawing, 380–381

Brainard, Paul, 38

Branching, in macros, 523–524, 525

Brattair, Walter, 49

Bricklin, Dan, 36–37, 730

Broadband networks, 672, 673 (fig.)

Broadcasting, 270

Browse command, 571

Bubble memory, 60

Buffers, 61, 71
   undo, 298

Bugs, in applications programs, 263

Bulletin boards, 700–703

Bulletin board systems (BBSs), 678–679

Bureau of the Census, U.S., 23

Bus architecture, 668–669

Buses, 54 (fig.)
   address, 65, 71
   control, 65
   data, 64–65, 71
   defined, 64, 71

Business
   computer impact on, 5–6
   microcomputers in, 10–15
   organization of computers in, 123–125

Business Class, 620

Business graphics, 624. *See also* Graphics
   for analysis, 626–627, 637–640
   applications of, 625–626
   as communication, 625–626
   defined, 213
   options available in, 642–645
   overview of, 628
   for presentations, 628

Business graphs, 629–630. *See also* Graphs

Buttons, 619, 621

Bytes, 44, 50, 51, 52

Byte Shop, 33 (fig.)

Cables
   coaxial, 670–672
   fiber optic, 670–672
   twisted pair, 670–672

Caches, 71

CAD. *See* Computer-aided design

CADD. *See* Computer-aided design and drafting

CAE. *See* Computer-aided engineering

Calculating fields, 558

Calculation capabilities
   in database management programs, 580, 581
   in word processing programs, 394–396

Calculators
   Arithmometer, 20
   early, 20
   Pascaline, 18, 19 (fig.)

CAM. *See* Computer-aided manufacturing

Capacitive screens, 88

Caps Lock key, 74, 75

Carriage returns, 286–287, 293
   hard, 200, 286–287
   joining text separated by, 299–300
   soft, 286

Carrier waves, 706–707, 709

Case, changing, 301

Cathode ray tubes (CRTs), 91, 106, 652–653
   analog displays, 653
   digital displays, 653

CD-ROM disks, 116–118, 122

CD-THOR disks, 118

Cell contents
   displaying, 529, 530
   editing, 443–444, 446
   erasing, 444

Cell formulas. *See* Formulas

Cell marker. *See* Cursor, in spreadsheets

Cell pointer. *See* Cursor, in spreadsheets

Cell protection, 509–511

Cell references
   absolute, 480, 481 (fig.), 493
   mixed, 480, 493
   relative, 480, 481 (fig.), 493
   specifying, 482

Cells, 422 (fig.)

Census Bureau, U. S., 26

Centered alignment, 331

Centralized information processing, 123–125

Central processing unit (CPU), 53–57, 66, 71

Centronics interfaces. *See* Parallel ports

Channels, in broadband networks, 672

Character displays, 96–97, 106

Character fields, 557

Character formats, 320

Characters, 46–47
   transposing, 301, 302 (fig.)

Character sets, 106

Characters per second (CPS), 102

Chart of accounts, 722, 724

Chat mode, 679

CHKDSK command, 194–196

Christianson, Ward, 699

Circuit boards, 49

Circular references, 499

CIS B, 699

CISC chips, 57, 71

Clearing the screen, in spreadsheets, 419–420

Clipboard, 307 (fig.). *See also* Buffers

Clock, 67, 71

Clock rate, 65–66

Clones, of applications programs, 262–263, 265

Closed architecture, 66
CLS command, 161
Clusters, 195, 196
CMOS chips, 60
Coaxial cables, 670–672
Codd, E.F., 537
Codes. *See* Control codes
Cold boot, 153, 161
Colleges, microcomputers in, 14 (fig.)
Collision detection, 673–674, 675
Colophone Inc., 620
Color displays, 92–93
Color graphics adapters (CGA), 96, 653
Color printing
 ink-jet printers, 102
 in word processing, 337
Column blocks, 304
Column mode, 304, 310
Columns (word processing)
 newspaper-style, 384–385
 parallel-style, 384–385
 printing in, 384–385
Columns (spreadsheets), 422 (fig.)
 changing width of, 470–471
 deleting, 445–446, 457
 inserting, 444–445, 446, 457
Columnwise recalculation, 498, 499
Combination graphs, 635
COMMAND.COM, 154
Command-driven programs, 228
Command language, 611–612
Command line programs, 550
Command lines, 281 (fig.)
Command mode, 430
Command processor, 141–142, 142
Commands
 canceling, 229
 executing, 223–229, 229, 428–430
 vs. menus, 228
Comments, about files, 235
Communications interface units (CIUs), 672–673
Communications parameters, 691–692
Communications programs, 10, 216, 685–688
 applications of, 658
 auto-redial feature, 686
 command sets, 685
 defined, 217
 dialing directories, 685, 688
 typical, 686–687
Communications protocols, 698–699
Communications settings, 689–695
 baud rates, 690–691
 data flow control, 693, 695
 echoing, 694, 695
 full-duplex transmission, 694, 698
 half-duplex transmission, 693–694, 698
 modem setup strings, 690
 parameters, 691–692, 695
 phone number, 689–690
 simplex transmission, 693
 terminal emulation, 693
Communications signals, 705–706
 analog, 127, 706

digital, 127, 705
Compatibility, 135–136, 137
 operating systems and, 207
Compatibility box, 147
Compiled programs, 612, 615
Complementary-metal-oxide semiconductor (CMOS) chips, 60
Complete instruction set chips (CISC), 57, 71
Compose command, 383–383
Composite color displays, 93
Composite screens, 106
Compressed files, 698
CompuServe, 676, 677–678
CompuServe B, 699
Computer-aided design and drafting (CADD), 649
Computer-aided design (CAD), 649–651
Computer-aided engineering (CAE), 651
Computer-aided manufacturing (CAM), 651
Computer chips. *See* Microprocessors
Computer compatibility, 135–136, 137
Computerized typesetting, 270
Computer literacy, 6, 15
Computers. *See also* Microcomputers
 electronic digital, 24–29, 39
 fifth generation, 29
 first generation, 26–27
 fourth generation, 29
 generations of, 26
 history of, 17–39
 household uses of, 48
 mainframe, 125–127
 mechanical, 17–24
 second generation, 28
 third generation, 28–29
Computer systems, 4
Computing devices, history of, 49–50
Computing-Tabulating-Recording Company, 24
Concatenation, joining strings by, 452
Concurrent processing. *See* Multitasking
Conditional page breaks, 327
Configuration files, 236
Constants, in formulas, 448–449, 453
Context sensitive help screens, 223, 229
Continuous data, business graphs and, 629–630
Continuous form paper, 104, 240 (fig.)
Control area, of spreadsheet, 421, 422, 423
Control bus, 65
Control codes
 displaying, 297–298
 for fonts, 342–343
 for formatting, 247, 248, 321–322
 inserting, 321–322
 for merge printing, 371–372
 for selecting a block, 306
 in word processing programs, 281 (fig.)
Control panel, in spreadsheets, 430
Conventional memory, 207

Conversion utilities, for graphics programs, 660
Co-processors, 57, 71
COPY command, 185–186, 306
 vs. DISKCOPY command, 187
 renaming files with, 191
COPY CON command, 205, 206
Copying
 blocks, 306, 307 (fig.), 310
 blocks to disk file, 308–309
 data, in spreadsheets, 476, 477 (fig.), 479
Copy protection, 249, 259–260, 265
Copy-protection programs, 730
Core, 254
CP/M, 36, 144
CPU. *See* Central processing unit
Crashing the schedule, 714, 716
Criteria, displaying records with, 576–581, 585–586
Criterion formulas, 519
Criterion range, 518 (fig.), 519, 520
Critical path, 714, 716
Crosstalk, 687
Ctrl (Control) key, 79, 225
Ctrl-Alt-Del command, 154
Ctrl-C command, 161
Ctrl-PrtSc command, 160–161
Current record, 569
Cursor, 78
 in spreadsheets, 422 (fig.), 424–426, 430, 450–451
 in word processing, 281 (fig.), 284, 285, 295–297, 302, 304 (fig.)
Cursor pointing, entering formulas by, 450–451
Cutting, blocks, 306. *See also* Moving

Dashes, indicating with hyphens, 288
Data, 7
 analysis of, with graphs, 637–640
 copying, 476, 477 (fig.)
 moving, 476–478, 479
 transposing, 479
Database dictionaries, 559–560
Database management programs, 7, 611–615
 advantages of, 535–536
 applications of, 532–533
 applications generators for, 612
 audit trails in, 617
 command language, 611–612
 command line programs, 550–552
 compiled, 612, 615
 data encryption in, 616
 data integrity in, 617–618
 defined, 214–215, 217, 534, 538
 development of, 535–536
 first, 37
 integrated, 545
 menu programs, 551–552
 multiuser, 618
 on-line help, 549
 in other applications programs, 545
 overview of, 532–533, 549–552

Database management programs (*cont.*)
  passwords in, 616
  procedures for, 539–543
  quitting (clearing), 552
  vs. record management programs, 535–536
  run-time versions of, 612, 615
  security of, 616–618
  spreadsheets as, 414, 516–520
  standalone, 545
  typical, 545–548
Database models, 536–538
  hierarchical, 537
  network, 537
  relational, 537–538
Database reports. *See* Reports
Databases, 214, 534
  attributes in, 553
  browsing records in, 571
  creating, 570–571, 606–610
  criterion formulas in, 519
  defined, 214, 534
  defining, 540, 543, 553–560, 570
  displaying records in, 568–572
  displaying structure, 570
  entering data into, 540–541, 543, 561–567, 570
  entities in, 553
  listing records, 571
  multiuser, 618
  organization of, 553–554
  planning, 539, 555, 556 (fig.)
  printing reports from, 542
  querying, 517–519, 520, 542, 543
  restructuring, 605
  sorting, 516–517, 520
  in spreadsheets, 507–508, 516–520, 545–546
  statistical functions in, 519–520
  updating, 541, 543
Database tables
  joining, 606–607, 609–610
  linked, 537 (fig.)
  projecting, 608
  selecting, 607–608
Data bits, 691, 695
Data bus, 64–65, 71
Data disks, formatting, 179–181. *See also* Floppy disks
Data encryption, 616
Data Encryption Standard (DES), 730
Data entry spaces, 474
Data files
  applications programs and, 252–258
  disk-based, 255, 258
  memory and, 254–255
  memory-based, 254, 258
Data Fill command, 438–439
Data flow control, 693, 695
Data integrity, 617–618
Data processing, 7, 8
  cycle, 15
  departments, 10, 11 (fig.), 15, 123
Data Query command, 517
Data Series command, 438–439
Data tables, 504–506

Data transfer rate, 116
Data word length, 691, 695
Date, automatic entry of, 293, 294, 360
DATE command, 161
Date data series, 439
Date fields, 558
dBASE, 558, 568 (fig.), 569 (fig.), 597
  commands, 550–551
  creating a database in, 570–571
  record display commands, 568 (fig.), 569 (fig.)
  structure, 559 (fig.), 560
dBASE II, 37, 39, 524, 545
dBASE III Plus, 611, 546 (fig.), 559 (fig.)
DBMS. *See* Database management programs
Decentralized information processing, 123, 124–125
Decimal system, 41
Decimal tabs, 353–354, 357
Decision trees, 731–732
de Cruz, Frank, 699
Dedicated word processors, 268
Default alignment, 332–333
Default drives, 163–164, 235
Default formats, 320–324, 324
Default settings
  changing, 246, 247–248, 639, 640 (fig.)
  defined, 246, 248
  overriding, 246–247
  system, 247–248
  word processing programs and, 276
Delete (DEL) command, 192, 193, 294, 298, 299 (fig.), 586
  in database management programs, 584, 587
  in spreadsheet databases, 519
Deleting
  blocks, 307, 309 (fig.), 310
  columns, 445–446, 457
  destructive backspace for, 78, 289, 294
  rows, 445–446, 457
Delimiters
  in merge printing, 374
  in ranges, 441, 442
Demo programs, 730
Density
  of dot-matrix printer characters, 98
  of fully formed character printers, 102
Dependent cells, 529, 530
Dependent models, 511, 513
Desktop computers, 53. *See also* Microcomputers
Desktop managers, 719, 720
Desktop publishing, 30, 31, 56. *See also* Page makeup programs
  defined, 211, 217
  development of, 270–272
  full-page displays and, 91
  graphics scanners and, 82
  word processing programs and, 211–212, 271–272

Desktop publishing systems, 389–391
  display monitor, 390
  graphics-based interface, 391
  interactive graphics program, 391
  laser printer, 390
  microprocessor, 390
  mouse, 391
DESQview, 150
Destructive backspace, 78, 289, 294
Detailed models. *See* Supporting models
Diacriticals, 382
Diagnostic tools, printing, 529, 530
Dialing directories, 685, 688, 700
Dialog boxes, 228, 229
Dialog Information Systems, 620
Dictionaries. *See also* Spelling
  adding to, 316
  database, 559–560
  hyphenation, 334, 335
  literal, 316
  maintenance of, 317
  root word, 316
  supplemental, 317, 319
Difference engine, 20
Digital Equipment Corp., 29, 271
Digital graphics displays, 653
Digital processing, 41–42, 52
Digital Research, 36, 37
  GEM, 150
Digital signals, 44–47, 127, 705
Digital tablets. *See* Graphics tablets
Digits, 41
Digraphs, 382
DIP switches, 67
  on modems, 683–684
DIR command, 172–174, 175
Direct access, to indexed files, 592
Direct-connect modems, 128, 130
Directional arrow keys, 78 (fig.)
  in spreadsheets, 424–426
  in word processing, 295–296
Directories, 165–170
  changing, 167
  creating, 197–199
  moving among, 167 (fig.)–168 (fig.)
  printing listings of, 174
  removing, 197–199
  root, 165–170
  specifying, 235–236
  storing listings of, 174
DIR/P command, 173, 175
DIR/W command, 173, 175
Discrete data, business graphs and, 629
Disk-based data files, 255, 258
Disk-based program, 253–254, 258
Disk caches, 61–62
DISKCOMP command, 189–190
DISKCOPY command, 187–188
Disk drives. *See* Floppy disk drives; Hard disk drives
Disk files. *See also* Files
  copying or moving a block to, 308–308
  printing to 241

Diskless workstations, 667–668, 675
Disks. *See* Data disks; Floppy Disks;
    Hard Disks; System disks
Display command, 568–572, 585–586
Display screens, 90–97, 106
    cathode ray tube (CRT), 91, 106,
       652–653
    character displays, 96–97
    color, 92–93
    for desktop publishing, 390
    emulation of, 251
    flat-panel displays, 91–92
    graphics, 95–96, 652–655
    how images are displayed on, 93–96
    monochrome, 92
    types of, 90–93
Distribution devices, 2, 123–130
Dithering, 84
Division lines. *See* Format lines
Documentation, 260–261, 265, 612
Document compare command, 318
Document description languages, 391.
    See also Page description
    languages
Document-oriented programs, 291, 292
    (fig.), 294, 328
Document preview, 323, 324 (fig.)
Documents. *See also* Blocks; Text
    assembling on screen, 377–378
    assembling while printing, 378–379
    editing, 273–274, 275, 295–302
    entering, 274, 285–294
    formatting, 276
    naming, 273–274
    opening, 273–274
    printing, 276–277
    retrieving, 274
    revising, 275
    saving, 276
    with text and graphics combined,
      386–387
Document screens, 279, 281 (fig.)–284
    (fig.)
Document view, in outliners, 404–406
DOS, 144–146. *See also* MS-DOS;
    PC-DOS
    commands, 156–161
    loading, 155
    shells, 144, 145 (fig.), 157
    utility programs, 158–160
    versions, 149
DOS 4.0, 144, 145 (fig.)
    CHKDSK command in, 195–196
    DOS Utilities screen, 181, 184
    executing commands in, 157–158
    file display in, 174
DOS 4.0 Shell
    comparing disks in, 189
    copying files in, 186
    duplicating disks with, 187
    menus, 157
    renaming files in, 191
Dot-matrix printers, 98–100, 102, 106
    density of, 102
    fonts and, 342
    interactive graphics on, 658

operation of, 100–101
Dot stream, 93
Double-density disks, 112
Doublestriking, 337
Downloadable fonts, 105, 342
Downloading, 126, 697, 413, 698–699,
    703
Draft quality printing, 102
DRAM chips, 59-60, 71
Drexon Laser Card, 120 (fig.)
Drivers, 250
Drives. *See* Floppy disk drives
Dropdown insertion, 297
Dumb modems, 683
Dumb terminals, 123, 124, 130, 667
Duplex printing, 104
Dvorak, August, 75, 76–77
Dvorak keyboard, 75, 76–77, 729
Dynamic page break display, 326, 329
Dynamic RAM. *See* DRAM

Eames, Office of Charles and Ray, 50
EBCDIC code, 46
Echoing, 694, 695
Eckert, J. Presper, 24, 26
Eckert-Mauchly Computer Corporation,
    26
Economist, The, 86
Edison, Thomas, 263
Edit cursor, 423 (fig.). *See also* Cursors
Editing
    cell contents, 443–444, 446
    defined, 295
    documents, 273–274, 275, 295–302
    records, 586
    spreadsheet models, 443–446
    vs. revising, 295
Editing aids, 315–319
Editing checks. *See* Validity checks
Edit key, 443, 446
Edit line. *See* Entry line
Edit mode, 430
EDVAC, 25, 27
Electroluminescent displays, 92
Electronic Control Company, 26
Electronic digital computers, 24–29
Electronic mail, 270, 678
Electrostatic printers, 104
Elevation views, in CAD, 649
E-mail. *See* Electronic mail
Emulation, 251
Encryption programs, 118
End key, 295
Endnotes, 399–400
Engelbart, Doug, 31
English language formulas, 452, 453
Enhanced color graphics adaptors
    (EGA), 96, 653
ENIAC, 24–26, 27
Entering
    documents, 274, 285–294
    formulas, 485–488
    functions, 417, 418 (fig.), 457
    labels, 484
    numbers, 484
Enter key, 78

Entities, 553, 555, 560
Entry line, 423 (fig.)
Entry mode, 430
Enumerations, 354
Envelopes, merge printing, 375
EPROMs, 59
Erasable optical disks, 116, 118
ERASE command, 192–193, 730
Erasing
    cell contents, 444
    files, 192–193
Ergonomics, 76, 132–133, 137
Errors. *See also* Mistakes
    correction, 699
    detection, 699
    messages, 229, 528
    in programming, 263
Esc (Escape) key, 78, 226, 229
Esteridge, Phillip, 31
Excel, 507, 545
Expanded memory, 207–208
Expanded memory scheme (EMS), 208
Expansion slots, 54 (fig.), 66, 71
Expert systems, 731–732
Extended Binary Coded Decimal
    Interchange Code. *See* EBCDIC
    code
Extended memory, 207–208
External commands,
    DOS, 161
    operating systems, 156
External storage, 2, 107–122
Extract command, 513, 518

Facsimile (fax) machines, 128–129, 130
Factories, microcomputers in, 15 (fig.)
Fiber optic cables, 670–672
Field lengths, 558, 560
Field names, 556–557, 560
Fields
    calculating, 558
    character, 557
    in database management programs,
      540, 554, 555
    date, 558
    defined, 543
    joining, 609–610
    key, 555
    logical, 558
    memo, 558
    in merge printing, 373–374
    numeric, 558
    in spreadsheet databases, 516, 520
    time, 558
    types of, 556–558, 560
Fifth generation computers, 29
File Combine command, 512–513
File compression, 84
File conversion, 257, 258, 730
File encryption programs, 729–730
File folder systems, 233
File formats, 257
File indexers, 730
File locking, 618
File management programs. *See* Record
    management programs

Filename extensions, 171–172, 232, 237
Filenames
  assigning, 171–172
  defined, 175
  long, systems for recognizing, 233
  tips for selecting, 236–237
File recovery programs, 730
Files
  ASCII, 256
  binary, 255
  combining, 512–513
  converting to other format, 257
  copying, 185–186
  erasing, 192–193
  exchanging between programs, 256–257
  extracting, 513
  fragmented, 194
  keeping track of, 236–237
  listing, 172–174
  naming, 232–233
  print, 256
  printing, 239–245
  protecting, 118–119
  recovering, 192, 193
  renaming, 191
  retrieving, 233–234
  saving, 231–232, 237
  specifying more than one, 176–178
  transferring, 697–703
  types of, 255–256
File servers, 670
File types, 255–256
Financial analysis, 412–413
Financial functions, 458
Find command, 517, 591, 594–596
First generation computers, 26–27
Fixed asset programs, 727
Fixed drives. See Hard disk drives
Fixed pitch, 341, 343
Fixed titles, 495–496
Flagged records, 584, 587
Flat file database programs. See Record management programs
Flat-panel displays, 91–92, 106
Floppy disk drives, 108–110
  data transfer rate of, 116
  default, 163–164
  drive light, 111
  electronic circuits, 110
  loading an applications program from, 219
  photoelectric cell, 110–111
  read-write heads, 110
  slot, 111
  source, 158
  specifying, 163–165, 235–236
  storage capacity, 115
  target, 158
Floppy disks, 108–110
  backup copies, 119
  care of, 119, 121–122
  center hole, 110
  characteristics of, 108–109, 110
  checking, 194–196
  comparing, 189–190

data storage and retrieval, 115–116
density, 112
duplicating, 187–188
formatting, 179–184
hard-sectored, 112
labeling, 180, 181
magnetic recording surface, 110
plastic jacket for, 109
read/write slot, 109
sector hole, 110
sectors, 112
security and, 118–119
self-booting, 182, 184
sides, 111–112
sizes of, 108, 112
soft-sectored, 112
source, 158
storage capacity, 111–112
storage envelope for, 109
storing, 112–113
target, 158
tracks, 112
write-protecting, 186
write-protect notch, 109, 110
Fluegelman, Andrew, 686
Flush left alignment, 330
Flush right alignment, 330
Flystra, Dan, 36, 38
Fonts, 99 (fig.), 105, 240, 339–343
  algorithms, 343
  cartridges, 342
  changing, 342–343
  defined, 339
  display screens and, 96
  downloadable, 105
  editing, 343
  internal, 342
  screen display of, 343
  soft, 343
  in spreadsheets, 467–468
  stop codes for, 343
Font servers, 342, 343
Footers, 358–360, 467
Footnotes, 399–400
Forced upgrades, 262, 265
Foreground, 150
FORMAT/4 command, 180, 181
Format checking, 617
Format codes, 321 (fig.). See also Control codes
  default settings and, 247
  inserting, 321–322
FORMAT command, 179–181, 183
Format lines, 281 (fig.), 322
Formats
  default, 320–324
  global, 483–484
  levels of, 324
  spreadsheets, 423 (fig.)
FORMAT/S command, 182, 184
Format style sheets, 361–369. See also Style sheets
Formatting, 112
  disks, 112, 179–181, 183
  documents, 276
  levels of, 320
  numbers, locally, 485

text, in spreadsheets, 471–472
values, 473
FORMAT/V command, 180, 181
Form documents, 270
Form feed, 240
Form letters, 376
Forms, filling out, 407–408
Formulas, 423 (fig.), 447–454
  annotating, 453
  constants in, 448–449, 453
  copying, 476, 477 (fig.), 479, 487 (fig.), 488
  correcting mistakes in, 452
  deleting rows and columns in, 445–446
  displaying on screen, 529, 530
  English language, 452, 453
  entering, 416–417, 450–451, 453, 485–488
  extract command and, 513
  moving, 476–478, 479
  order of operations in, 448
  printing, 468
  typing in, 450
  variables in, 449–450, 453
  in word processing programs, 395–396
Forsberg, Chuck, 699
Forward references, 498, 499
Fourth-generation computers, 29
Fourth-generation programming languages, 524, 525
Fragmented files, 194
Frankston, Bob, 36–37
Freeware, 686–687
Frequency modulation (FM), 707, 708 (fig.)
Frequency shift keying (FSK), 707
Full-duplex transmission, 694, 698
Full-page displays, 91
Fully formed character printers, 98, 106
  density of characters, 102
  operation of, 100, 101 (fig.)
Function keys, 79, 224–225
Functions, 423 (fig.)
  entering, 417, 418 (fig.), 457
  financial, 458
  numeric and mathematical, 459–460
  in spreadsheets, 455–462
  statistical, 458–459
  syntax of, 455, 462
  types of, 456–460

Gantt charts, 714, 715 (fig.)
Gas plasma displays, 92
Gates, Bill, 36, 37, 38, 144
Gateway servers, 670
GEM, 150
General ledger, 722
General ledger programs, 724–726
Gigabyte, 45, 50, 51, 52
Global commands, 440
Global formats, 470, 483–484
Glossaries, 392–393
Gluing. See Concatenation, joining strings by

GOTO command, 424
Grammar checkers. *See* Style and
	grammar checkers
Graphics, 8
	combining with text, 386–387
	creating, 387
	file formats, 659–660
	hardware, 659
	incorporating into documents, 387
	input devices, 81–85
	integrated, 514–515
	printing, on dot-matrix printer, 99
		(fig.)
	printing from screen, 160
	in project management programs,
		714–716
	in spreadsheets, 491
Graphics add-on boards, 96
Graphics-based interface, for desktop
	publishing, 391
Graphics cards, 106
Graphics displays, 95–96, 106,
	652–655
Graphics files
	conversion utilities for, 660
	standards for, 659, 660
Graphics pad. *See* Graphics tablets
Graphics processing, 8
Graphics programs. *See also* Business
	graphics; Interactive graphics
	applications of, 624
	business, 213
	defined, 213, 217
	interactive, 213
	types of, 624
Graphics scanners, 82–84, 88, 656
Graphics standards, 659–660
Graphics tablets, 84–85
Graphs. *See* Business graphs
	area, 634, 639 (fig.)
	aspect ratios of, 641
	automatic scaling of, 637, 638 (fig.)
	bar, 631–632, 640 (fig.)
	combination, 635
	data analysis with, 637–640
	distortions in, 637–640
	hi-lo, 635
	line, 630, 631 (fig.)
	options for, 642–645
	pie charts, 633–634, 247–248, 639,
		640 (fig.)
	scatter, 630–631
	spreadsheets and, 414, 514–515
	stacked-bar, 632, 640 (fig.)
	statistical, 636
	time-series, 629
	XY, 632–633
Gray level, 656
Gray scale, 84
Growth data series, 439
Gutter margins, 346, 351

Hackers, 31
Half-duplex transmission, 693–694,
	698
Handshaking, 699
Hanging indents, 355 (fig.)

Hard carriage returns, 200, 286–287
Hard disk drives, 60, 108, 113–114
	back-up copies, 119
	backup programs, 729
	care of, 119, 121
	data transfer rate of, 116
	head crash, 114
	loading an applications program
		from, 220
	organization of, 165–170
	park program for, 114, 122
	removing directories from, 197–199
	security and, 118–119
	storage capacity of, 114, 115
	with removable media, 114, 118–119
Hard hyphens, 288, 294, 298
Hard page breaks, 327
Hard spaces, 288, 294
Hardware flow control, 693
Hardware, 2–3, 4, 30–35
Hard-wired computers, 677
Harvard Mark I, 24, 25 (fig.)
Harvard University Instructional
	Laboratories, 77
Hayes-compatible modem command
	sets, 685, 688
Hayes Smartmodem, 690–691
Head crash, 114
Headers, 358–360, 467
Heath, Chet, 67
Help
	key, 223
	on-line, 229, 549
	screens, 223–224, 229
Hidden characters, 297–298
Hidden codes, 302, 322
Hiding data, in spreadsheets, 510
Hierarchical database models, 537
High-capacity disks, 112
High-capacity drives, 180, 181
High-level languages, 524
Highlighting. *See* Selecting blocks
Hijack, 660
Hi-lo graphs, 635
History command, 550, 552
Hoerni, Jean, 50
Hoff, Marcian E. (Ted), 30, 55
Hollerith, Herman, 23–24
Homebrew Computer Club, 30
Home key, 295, 424
Homes, microcomputers in, 14 (fig.)
Hopper, Grace, 263
Horizontal alignment, 330–332
Horizontal applications programs, 712
Horizontal motion index. *See*
	Microspace justification
Horizontal page layout, 344–347
Host computers, 676
Host mode, 677
HyperCard, 620
Hypermedia, 619–623
Hypertext, 619, 621
Hyphenation, 333–335
	algorithms, 334, 335
	command, 333–335, 335
	dictionaries, 334, 335
	zone, 333, 334, 335

Hyphens, 288, 294
	hard, 288, 298
	indicating dashes with, 288
	soft, 288, 298, 333

IBM computers, 24, 31, 34–35 (figs.)
	1401, 28
	360 series, 29
	700 series, 27
	Intel microprocessors for, 55, 56
	operating system, 37–38, 140,
		143–147
IBM AT, 10, 35 (fig.)
	address bus for, 65
	keyboard, 73, 74 (fig.)
	microprocessor for, 56
IBM Automatic Sequence-Controlled
	Calculator, 24
IBM character set, 383
IBM MC/ST, 271
IBM MT/ST, 271
IBM PC, 31, 35 (fig.)
	address bus for, 65
	data bus for, 64–65
	keyboard, 73, 74 (fig.)
	microprocessor for, 56
IBM PS/2, 35 (fig.)
	address bus for, 65
	analog displays, 653
	compatibility and, 136
	data bus for, 65
	micro channel architecture, 67
	microprocessor for, 56
	video graphics display, 96
IBM XT, 114
Icons, 148
Idea processors, 709–710
IF statements
	in spreadsheets, 461–462
	in merge printing, 372
Illegal characters, 175
Illegal file names, 232
Image digitizers. *See* Graphics
	scanners
Impact printers, 100–101, 106, 337
Income statement, 725
Indents, 354, 355 (fig.). *See also* Tabs
Indexes, 591–596
	advanages of, 592–593
	automatically generated, 397–398
	drawbacks of, 592
	examples, 594–596
	multiple, 592–593, 594
	vs. sorting, 591, 594–595
Indexing systems, for long file names,
	233
Index-sequential search, 592
Information centers (ICs), 133
Information processing, 4–16
	centralized, 123–124, 125
	cycle, 8–10
	decentralized, 124
	types of, 6–8, 9 (fig.)
Information services, 677–678
Information theory, 23
Infrared screens, 88
Ingalls, Dan, 31

Ink-jet printers, 102
Input cells, for data tables, 504–506
Input devices, 73–88
  defined, 2, 73
  graphics, 81–85, 656
  joysticks, 87
  mice, 87
  text, 73–81
  touch screens, 87–88
  trackballs, 87
  voice, 85–87
Input/output (I/O) manager, 141, 142
Input range, 518 (fig.), 519, 520
Input screens. See On-screen forms
Input stage, of information processing, 8
Input values, for data tables, 504–506
Insert command, in database management programs, 584
Inserting
  columns, 444–445, 446, 457
  rows, 444–445, 446, 457
  text, 297
Insert (Ins) key, 297
Insert mode, 297, 302
  spacebar in, 287–288
Insert-off mode. See Typeover mode
Installation programs, 249–251
Instruction sets, 56–57, 71
Integrated circuits (ICs), 28–29, 39
  defined, 54
  history of, 50, 69 (fig.)
  single-function vs. multi-function, 54–55
Integrated programs, 216, 217, 512–513
Integrated Services Digital Network (ISDN), 684
Intel microprocessors, 50, 55, 56. See also Microprocessors
  CISC chip, 57
  8008, 30
  80286, 146
  80386, 70 (fig.), 146
Interactive graphics, 624, 646–648. See also Graphics
  defined, 213
  for desktop publishing, 391
  displays for, 652–655
  dot-matrix printers for, 658
  input devices for, 656
  plotters for, 656–657
  printing, 656–657
  for slide shows, 661–662
Interlaced displays, 654
Internal commands
  DOS, 161
  operating systems, 156
Internal fonts, 342
Internal memory, 57–58, 71
International Business Machines Corp. See IBM
International Dvorak Federation, 77
Interpolation, business graphs and, 630
Interpress, 389
Inventory accounting programs, 727

Invisible soft hyphens, 288
Iowa State University, 24
Iteration, 498, 499

Jacquard, Joseph Marie, 22
Jacquard-loom, 21, 22
Jet Propulsion Laboratory, 37
Job costing programs, 727
Jobs, Steve, 30–31, 32 (fig.)
JOIN command, 606–607, 609–610
Journals (accounting), 722
Joysticks, 87
Justified text, 331–332, 335
  in spreadsheet models, 472

Kapor, Mitch, 38
Kemeny, John, 36
Kermit, 699, 703
Kerning, 341, 342 (fig.), 343
Key attributes, 555
Keyboard buffers, 61 (fig.)
Keyboard enhancers, 729
Keyboarding, 285–289
Keyboard macros, 729. See Also Macros
Keyboards, 73–79, 88
  QWERTY vs. Dvorak, 75, 76–77
  redefining keys on, 729
Keyboard templates, 225
Key fields, 555
Kettronics keyboards, 77
Keywords, in macro languages, 521–523, 525
Kilby, Jack, 50
Kildall, Gary, 36, 37
Kilobytes (KB), 45, 50, 51, 52
Knowledge-based systems. See Expert systems
Kurtz, Thomas, 36

Label entry spaces, 474
Label mode, 430
Label prefixes, 437–439
  for formatting text, 471–472
Labels, 423 (fig.)
  defined, 415
  entering, 416, 417 (fig.), 436–437, 439, 484
  merge printing, 375–376
  truncated, 437
Land, Richard, 77
Landscape mode, 243, 468
LANs. See Local area networks (LANs)
Laptop computers, 53, 54 (fig.)
Large scale integration (LSI), 28–29, 50
Laser printers, 103–104, 106
  boldfacing and, 337
  for desktop publishing, 390
  emulation, 251
  typewriter mode and, 293
Lashlee, George, 37
Leading, 349, 351
Learn mode, 521, 525
LED printers, 104
Left aligned text, 330–331
Left margins, 351
  calculating, 347
  changing, 345 (fig.)

entering text to left of, 346–347
  setting, 344
Legal characters, 171, 175
Legal file names, 232
Leibniz, Gottfried Wilhelm, 19–20
Leibniz calculator, 20
Letter quality printers. See Fully formed character printers
Lexitron, 271
Libraries. See Glossaries
Licensing, of applications programs, 260, 265
Light-emitting diodes (LEDS)
  displays, 92
  touch screens and, 88
Light pens, 85
Line adjust. See Automatic paragraph reforming
Linear data series, 438
Line blocks, 303–304
Line drawing, 380–381
Line feed, 240
Line formats, 320
Line graphs, 630, 631 (fig.)
Line printers, 103
Line spacing, 349, 351, 351 (fig.)
Lines per inch, 348, 351
Lines per page, 348, 351
Linked database tables, 537 (fig.)
Linking models, in spreadsheets, 511–512, 513
Link protocols. See Communications protocols
Liquid crystal displays (LCDs), 92
Lisa computer, 31
Lists, automatically generated, 397–398
Literal dictionaries, 316
Local area networks (LANs), 124, 667–675
  architecture, 668–670
  connections, 670–672
  defined, 130
  connections, 670–673
  signals, 670–673
  software, 675
  traffic control, 673–674
Local echoing, 694, 695
Locked titles. See Fixed titles
Logic, symbolic, 23
Logical fields, 558
Logical operators, 581
  in searches, 577–578, 579 (fig.)
  in spreadsheets, 461–462
Logical storage, 537, 538
Logic chip, 69 (fig.)
Longfellow, Henry Wadsworth, 42
Look command, 234
Lookup tables, 500–503
  horizontal, 500, 502
  offsets in, 500–503
  vertical, 500, 501
Loops, 23
Lotus 1-2-3, 38, 39, 432, 435, 545
  creating graphs with, 643–645
  date and time functions, 507
  graph menu commands, 515 (fig.)
  macros in, 524

Lotus 1-2-3 (Release 2), 467–468
   student edition, 426–427
Lotus Agenda, 720 (fig.)
Lotus Development Corp., 37, 38
Lovelace, Ada Augusta, 23
Lowercase letters, 74, 75
Lower memory. *See* Conventional
   memory
LSI. *See* Large scale integration (LSI)
Lucid 3D, 434, 435

Machine languages, 524
Macintosh. *See* Apple Macintosh
Macro languages, 521–523, 525
Macros
   branching commands, 523–524, 525
   entering, 522–523
   keyboard, 729
   learn mode for, 521, 525
   operator input and, 523
   record mode for, 521, 524
   Scroll Lock key and, 523
   in spreadsheets, 432, 521–525
   step mode for, 523
   for user-defined menus, 526–527
   in word processing, 409–410
Magnetic core storage, 27, 28 (fig.)
Magnetic disks, 29, 108, 115
Magnetic tape, 26, 108, 116, 122
Mailing labels, 543 (fig.)
Mainframe computers, 125–127
   downloading from, 413
   security problems and, 126–127
Main menus, 227, 229
Management information systems
   (MIS), 10, 124
Manual recalculation, 498, 499
Margin release, 347, 351
Margins. *See also* Left margins; Right
   margins
   calculating, 350
   changing, 345 (fig.)
   gutter, 346, 351
   line length and, 345 (fig.)
   page layout and, 344–351
   in spreadsheets, 467
   top and bottom, 348, 350, 351
Master document, 378, 379
Master models. *See* Dependent models
Mathematical functions, 459–460
   in word processing programs,
     394–396
Mauchly, John, 24, 26
MCI electronic mailing services, 678
Mechanical computers, 17–24
Megabytes (MB), 45, 50, 51, 52
Megahertz, 66
Memo fields, 558, 560
Memory, 54 (fig.), 57–62. *See also*
   RAM; ROM
   conventional, 207, 208
   data files and, 254–255
   expanded, 207, 208
   extended, 207–208
   internal, 57–58, 71
   virtual, 60, 71
Memory-based data files, 254, 258

Memory-based programs, 252, 253
   (fig.), 258
Memory caches, 62
Memory management, in spreadsheets,
   426–428, 430
Memory mapping. *See* Bit mapping
Memory resident programs, 150, 434
Menu-driven programs, 226, 551–552
Menu pointers, 226
Menus
   vs. commands, 228
   executing commands from, 157
   Main, 227, 229
   multilevel, 226, 227 (fig.)
   pull-down, 226 (fig.)
   in spreadsheets, 423 (fig.), 428, 430
   sticky, 226–227, 229
   user-defined, 526–527
   using, 226–227
   in word processing programs, 281
     (fig.)
Menu trees, 226
Merge printing, 370–376
   defined, 376
   envelopes and labels, 375–376
   process of, 374–375
Message areas, in word processing
   programs, 281 (fig.)
Metal-oxide-semiconductor (MOS). *See*
   MOS
Mice, 31, 87, 391
Micro channel architecture (MCA), 65,
   67
Microcom Networking Protocol (MNP),
   700
Microcomputers. *See also* Computers
   applications of, 11–15
   in business, 5–6, 10–15
   care of, 68
   compatibility of, 135–136
   components of, 54 (fig.)
   defined, 2
   for desktop publishing, 390
   early acceptance of, 11
   hardware, 30–35
   issues, 131–137
   mainframe computers and, 125–127
   software, 36–38
   standalone, 124
   training on, 133
   turning on and off, 68, 221
   types of, 53
   vision and, 132–133
Microcomputer systems, 2
Micro Instrumentation and Telemetry
   Systems (MITS), 30
MICRONIX, 148
MicroPro, 37
Microprocessors, 29
   8-bit, 64, 65
   16-bit, 64, 65
   32-bit, 65
   4004, 55
   8000 series, 30
   8008, 30
   8086, 56
   8088, 55, 56, 66

   80286, 55, 56, 65, 136, 146, 207
   80386, 55, 56, 65, 66, 70 (fig.), 136,
     146, 207
   80486, 55
   bits processed by, 55–56
   CISC, 57
   co-processors and, 57
   defined, 39, 71
   development of, 68–70
   differences among, 55–57
   first, 55
   functions of, 53–54
   history of, 30, 55, 68–70
   household uses of, 48
   instruction set, 56–57
   Intel, 55
   introduction of, 30
   Motorola, 55
   RISC, 57
MicroPro International, 271
Microsoft, 36, 38, 144, 146
   BASIC, 36
   Chart, 636 (fig.)
   Excel, 433, 435, 444
   Windows, 150, 151 (fig.)
   Word, 10, 280, 282 (fig.)
   Works, 280, 284 (fig.), 434, 435, 547,
     687
Microspace justification, 332, 335
Minicomputers, 29
Minimal recalculation, 497, 499
Misspellings. *See* Spelling checkers
Mistakes. *See also* Errors
   correcting, 157 (fig.), 289, 451
   undoing, 200 (fig.), 298
MITS Altair, 30, 36, 37, 39
Mixed references, 480, 493
MKDIR (MD) command, 197–199
Mode indicators,, 430
Models, database. *See* Database models
Models, spreadsheet. *See* Spreadsheet
   models
Modems, 62, 127-128, 672, 682–684
   acoustic coupler, 130
   auto-answer, 677, 683
   auto-dial, 677, 683
   baud rates, 690–691, 695
   calling other computers with,
     676–677
   command sets, 685
   communications settings for,
     689–695
   DIP switches on, 683–684
   direct connect, 130
   dumb, 683
   Hayes-compatible, 685, 688
   high-speed, protocols, 700
   serial ports and, 62, 63
   setting up, 683–684
   setup strings, 690
   smart, 683
   status lights, 682
   types of, 128
MODIFY COMMAND command, 611
Modulation, 706–707, 708 (fig.)
Monochrome displays, 92
Moore, Gordon, 50

Morrison, Philip, 50
Morrison, Phylis, 50
Morse, Samuel, 43–44
MOS, 59–60
Motorola microprocessors, 55
Mouse. *See* Mice
Moving
  blocks, 306, 308–310
  data, in spreadsheets, 476–478, 479
MS-DOS, 38, 140, 143, 143–146,
  144–146
  versions, 149 (fig.)
  See also DOS
MS-OS/2, 143, 146–147
Multifinder OS, 150
Multifunction boards, 66–67
Multilevel menus, 226, 227 (fig.)
MultiMate, 283 (fig.)
MultiMate Advantage II, 280
Multiplan, 433, 434 (fig.), 435
Multiple on-screen forms, 566 (fig.),
  567
Multisync monitors, 653
Multitasking, 136, 149, 150
Multiuser systems, 125, 126 (fig.)
  databases, security and, 618
  vs. LANs, 667
  operating systems, 149, 150

Nader, Ralph, 77
@NA function, 528, 530
Naming
  documents, 273–274
  files, 232–233
National Institute of Occupational
  Safety and Health (NIOSH), 133
Natural language queries, 574
Natural recalculation, 498, 499
Near-letter-quality (NLQ) printing, 102
Nelson, Ted, 619
Nesting, 379
Network architecture, 668–670
Network database models, 537
Network management programs, 124,
  675
Networks, 124–125
  baseband, 672, 675
  broadband, 672, 673 (fig.), 675
  local area (LAN), 124
  sneaker, 125
Network servers, 669–670
Network traffic control, 673–674
Newman, Robert, 43
Newspaper-style columns, 384–385
Nodes, 668–669, 673–674
Noncontiguous sectors, 194, 196
Nonimpact printers, 101–104, 106
Noninterlaced displays, 654
Nonvolatile memory, 58. *See also* ROM
Note command, for annotating
  formulas, 453
Noyce, Robert, 50
Null-modem cables, 677, 680
Number lists. *See* Enumerations
Numbers, 423 (fig.). *See also* Values

entering, 416, 417 (fig.), 437–438,
  439, 484
  formatting locally, 485
Numeric fields, 558
Numeric functions, 459–460
Numeric keypad, 75
Numeric keys, 75
Num Lock key, 74, 78

OCR characters, 81 (fig.)
OCR devices, 80–81, 88
OCR scanner, 82 (fig.)
OEMs, 146
Office of Charles and Ray Eames, 50
Office of Technology Assessment, 5
Offsets
  in lookup tables, 500–503
  in spreadsheet databases, 519, 520
Olivetti, 271
On-line computers, downloading from,
  413
On-line help, 229, 549
On-screen forms, 407–408, 561–567
Open architecture, 66
Open codes, 247
Operating-environment-aware
  programs, 152
Operating-environment-specific
  programs, 152
Operating System/2. *See* OS/2
Operating system environments,
  150–152
Operating systems
  applications programs and, 140,
    257–258
  commands, 156–158
  compatibility, 207
  defined, 140, 142
  development of, 36
  external commands, 156
  functions of, 141–142
  IBM computers, 143–147
  internal commands, 156
  issues, 207–208
  legal file names and, 232
  loading (booting), 153–155
  multitasking, 149, 150
  multiuser, 149, 150
  portable, 143
  prompts, 156
  proprietary, 143
  single-tasking, 149–150
  typical, 143–152
  versions, 149
Operators
  logical, 461–462
  relational, 461, 462
  in spreadsheets, 447–448, 453
  in word processing programs, 395,
    396
Optical character recognition devices.
  See OCR devices
Optical disk drives, 108
Optical disks, 108, 116–118, 122
  CD-ROM, 116–118

erasable, 116, 118
  WORM, 118
Optional hyphens. *See* Soft hyphens
Order of operations
  in spreadsheets, 448, 453
  in word processing programs, 395,
    396
Order of recalculation, 498, 499
Order processing programs, 727
Orphans, 326, 327, 329
OS/2, 140, 150
  commands, 158–160, 161
  Extended Edition, 146, 147
  loading, with Presentation Manager,
    155
  Standard Edition, 146–147
  versions, 149 (fig.)
Outline programs, 717, 718
Outliners, 404–406
Outlines, 356, 357 (fig.), 404–406
Outline view, 404–406
Output cells, 504–506
Output devices, 2, 90–106. *See also*
  Display screens; Printers
  display screens, 90–97
  printers, 97–105
Output range, 518 (fig.)
Output stage, of data processing, 9
Overhead transparencies, 662
Overlay files, 254, 258
Overtype mode. *See* Typeover mode
Overtyping, for special characters, 382
Owl International, Guide, 620

Packet-switching networks, 679–680
Packing, 584, 587
Page breaks, 325–327, 329
  conditional, 327
  controlling, 325–326
  in document-oriented programs, 291
  hard, 326–327, 327
  incorrect, 326 (fig.)
  soft, 326–327
Page composition programs. *See*
  Desktop publishing programs
Page description languages, 389, 391
Page display, dynamic, 326
Page formats, 320
Page layout, 344–351
  horizontal, 344–347
  vertical, 347–350
Page length, 349, 351
  in spreadsheets, 467–468
PageMaker, 38
Page makeup programs, 388–391. *See*
  also Desktop publishing programs
  graphics-handling capabilities, 389
  text-handling capabilities, 388–389
Page numbers, 327–328, 329
  in headers and footers, 360
  printing, 328, 329
Page offsets, 345, 346 (fig.), 351
Page-oriented programs, 291, 292 (fig.),
  294
  hard page breaks and, 327

page numbering and, 328
Page printers, 103
Page processing programs. *See* Desktop publishing programs
Paging, 208
Paired codes, 247
Palo Alto Research Center (PARC), 31
Pantographs, 84
Paper, 104
  continuous form, 104, 240
Paragraph indents. *See* Indents
Paragraphs
  aligning, 300, 330–333
  formats, 320
  hard carriage returns and, 287
  indents, 354, 355 (fig.)
  joining, 299–300
  reforming, 299–300
Parallel cables, 64
Parallel ports, 63–64, 71
Parallel-style columns, 384–385
Parity, 691–692, 695
Parity errors, 692
Park program, 114, 122
Pascal, Blaise, 18–19
Pascal, Etienne, 18
Pascaline, 18, 19 (fig.)
Passwords
  in database management programs, 616
  for remote computing, 677
  for spreadsheets, 510
Pasting, 306. *See also* Copying
PATH command, 202-203
Paths, specifying, 167, 169 (fig.), 170, 235
Paul Revere's Ride, 42–43
Payroll programs, 726–727
PC-DOS, 37–38, 38, 140, 143, 144–146, 149. *See also* DOS
PC-Talk, 686–687
PDP-1, 29
Pennsylvania, University of, 24–25
Peripherals, 2
Perseus Project, 620
Personal computers. *See* Microcomputers
Personal information managers, 719–720
Perspective views, in CAD, 649
PERT charts, 714, 715 (fig.)
PgDn key, 78, 295, 424
PgUp key, 78, 295, 424
Phase modulation, 708 (fig.)
Phase shift keying (PSK), 708
Philco Transac S-2000, 28
Phone numbers, communications settings for, 689–690
Photographs, scanning, 83
Phrase storage area. *See* Glossaries
Physical storage, in database management programs, 536–537, 538
Picture elements. *See* Pixels
Pie charts, 633–634, 639

distortions in, 640 (fig.)
Pin feeds, 105
Piracy, 260, 265
Pitch, 92, 340, 343
  fixed, 341, 343
Pixels, 106
  display screens and, 93 (fig.), 94
  graphics scanners and, 83–84, 656
  raster graphics displays and, 654
Planar transistor element, 69 (fig.)
Plan views, in CAD, 649
Plotters, 656–657
Plug compatibility, 62
Plug-in ROM chips, 59 (fig.)
Pointers, 592, 594
Point Foundation, 620
Point mode, 430, 450–451
Points, 340–341, 343
Polaroid Palette, 663
Popular Electronics, 30
Portable computers, 53, 54 (fig.)
Portable operating systems, 143
Portrait mode, 243, 468
Ports, 54 (fig.), 62–64, 71
  parallel, 63–64, 71
  serial, 62–64, 71
PostScript, 389
Powers, raising to, 50–51, 52
Powers of Ten, The, 50
Precedence, 448, 453
Precedent cells, 529, 530
Prefixes
  functions, 455, 462
  labels, 437, 439, 471–472
Presentation Manager, 38, 140
  commands in, 157–158
  default drive in, 164
  file display in, 174
  File System, 155
  loading a program from, 220
  menus, 157
  OS/2 and, 147, 155
  printing files listings, 174
  quitting a program in, 221
  selecting files in, 177–178
  Start Programs, 155
  Task Manager, 155
Presentations, interactive graphics and, 661–663
Pressure-sensitive screens, 88
Preview command, 234
Primary documents, 370, 371–373, 376
  secondary file and, 374
Primary keys, 516, 588, 589 (fig.), 590
  in word processing programs, 401–403
Print buffers, 61. *See also* Print spoolers
PRINT command, 200–201
Print direct mode. *See* Typewriter mode
Printer commands
  for filling out forms, 407–408
  in spreadsheets, 466
Printer drivers, 250
Printer emulation, 251

Printers, 62, 63, 97–105
  character formation, 98
  column widths, 97
  dot-matrix, 98–100, 102, 106, 342, 658
  electrostatic, 104
  fonts for, 105
  fully formed character, 98, 100, 101, 102, 106
  impact, 100–101, 106
  ink-jet, 102
  install program for, 244
  laser, 103–104, 106, 251, 337, 390
  LED, 104
  nonimpact, 101–104, 106
  page vs. line, 103
  paper for, 104
  plotters, 656–657
  ports and, 97
  ribbons for, 104
  settings, 239–240, 244
  sheet feeders for, 105
  soundproof enclosures for, 105
  specifying, 244
  speed of, 102
  stopping, 469
  switches for, 105
  testing, 244
  thermal, 102–103
  toner for, 104
  tractor feeds for, 105
Print files, 241, 244, 256
Printhead, 99, 100–101
Printing. *See also* Merge printing
  ASCII text files, 200–201
  assembling documents while, 378–379
  cell contents, 529, 530
  in columns, 384–385
  database reports, 597–604
  directory listings, 174
  to disk, 241
  documents, 239–245, 276–277
  models, 463–469
  options, 242–243, 467–468, 469
  queued, 241–242
  screen display, 160–161
  spreadsheets, 418, 467–468
Printing modes
  landscape, 243, 468
  portrait, 243, 468
Print quality, 99, 240
Print queues, 241–242, 244
Print servers, 670
Print spoolers, 728. *See also* Print buffers
PRINT/T command, 201
Print wheels, 98
PROCOMM PLUS, 687, 700–702
ProDOS, 148
Program disks, 249
Programming
  errors (bugs), 263
  first, 23
  hypermedia, 620

Programming languages
    assembly, 524
    fourth-generation, 524
    generations of, 524
    high-level, 524
    machine, 524
Programs, 3. *See also* Applications
        programs
    stored, 25–26, 39
Program updates, 262
Project management, 713, 714
Project management programs,
        713–716
Prompt areas, in word processing
        programs, 281 (fig.)
PROMPT command, 161
Prompt line, in spreadsheets, 423 (fig.)
PROMPT PG command, 169 (fig.),
        170
Prompts
    changing to indicate directory, 169
        (fig.)
    operating systems, 156
    responding to, 228, 229
PROMs, 59
Proportional spacing, 335, 341, 343
Proprietary operating systems, 143
Protected mode, 136, 137, 147
Protection, of cells in spreadsheets,
        509–511
PrtSc key, for printing graphics, 387
Pseudo full-duplex modem protocols,
        700
/P switch, 173
Public access message systems. *See*
        Bulletin board systems (BBSs)
Public Switched Telephone Network
        (PSTN), 676. *See also* Wide area
        networks
Pull-down menus, 226 (fig.)
Punched cards, 20–23

QDOS, 38
Quad-density disks, 112
Quantitizers, 656
Quarterdeck DESQview, 150
Quattro, 434, 435
Queries
    criteria in, 576–581
    databases, 517–519, 520, 542, 543,
        573–575
    example, 585–587
Query by example (QBE), 574, 578
        (fig.), 580 (fig.),
Query languages, 573–575, 577 (fig.),
        578 (fig.), 580 (fig.)
    natural, 574
    program-specific, 574
    structured, 574
Question mark (?) wildcard, 176, 177
        (fig.), 178
Queues, printing, 241
Quick reference cards, 223
Quit command, 220–221, 222, 277
Quitting

database management programs, 552
    spreadsheets, 418, 419
    word processing programs, 277
QWERTY keyboard, 75, 76–77
    redefining keys on, 729

Ragged left alignment, 331
Ragged right alignment, 331
RAM, 59–60, 71, 252
RAM chips
    dynamic, 59–60
    static, 59–60
RAM disks, 728–729
Random-access memory. *See* RAM
Range checking, 617
Range commands, 440–442
Ranges, 440–442
    copying, 476, 477 (fig.), 479
    defined, 440, 441 (fig.)
    formatting, 470, 485
    moving, 476–478, 479
    naming, 442
Raster graphics, 654–655, 658
Ratliff, Wayne, 37
Read-only memory. *See* ROM
Read/write heads, 110
Read/write slot, 109
Ready mode, 430
Real mode, 136, 137, 147
Recalculation, 497–499
    automatic, 497, 499
    background, 497, 499
    iteration and, 498, 499
    manual, 498, 499
    minimal, 497, 499
    order of, 498, 499
    problems with, 528
Record locking. *See* File locking
Record management programs,
        534–536, 538
Record mode, 524
Record pointers, 568–569, 592, 594
Records
    adding, 583–584, 586, 587
    current, 569
    in database management programs,
        540, 553, 554
    deleting, 584, 586, 587
    displaying, 568–572, 585–586
    editing, 586
    entering, 561–567
    flagging for deletion, 584, 587
    indexing, 591–596
    inserting, 584, 587
    in merge printing, 374
    sequentially filed, 591–592
    sorting, 588–590
    in spreadsheet databases, 516, 520
    updating, 584, 587
Recovering files, 192, 193
Rectangular blocks, 304–305
Redirection character, 174, 175
Redlining, 318, 319
Reduced instruction set chips (RISC),
        57, 71

Reform paragraph command, 300, 302
Relational database models, 537–538
Relational operators, 581
    in spreadsheets, 461, 462
    using in searches, 577, 579 (fig.)
Relations, 537–538
Relationships, 537
Relative references, 480, 481 (fig.), 489,
        493
    copying, 481 (fig.), 487 (fig.), 488,
        489
    specifying, 482
Remington Rand, 26
    Univac Division, 26
Remote computing, 677, 680
Remote echoing, 694, 695
RENAME (REN) command, 191
Repagination, 300, 301, 302
Repeat command, 289, 294
Replace command. *See* Search and
        replace command
Replace mode. *See* Typeover mode
Replacing text, 297
Reports (accounting), 722
Reports (database)
    creating, 542, 543, 597–601, 604
    formatting, 599–601, 602, 604
    printing, 597–604
Required hyphens. *See* Hard hyphens
Required page ends. *See* Hard page
        breaks
Required returns. *See* Hard carriage
        returns
Resolution, 92–93, 94, 106
Restructuring databases, 605
Retrieve command, 233–234
Return key, 78
Reverse video, 306
Revising, 295. *See also* Editing
RGB displays, 93, 106
Ribbons, 104
Right aligned text, 330–331
Right margins, 351
    calculating, 347
    changing, 345 (fig.)
    setting, 344
Ring architecture, 669, 670 (fig.)
RISC chips, 57, 71
RMDIR (RD) command, 197–199
Roberts, Ed, 30
ROM, 58–59
    defined, 71
    EPROMs, 59
    plug-in chips, 58, 59 (fig.)
    PROMs, 59
Root directories, 165, 168 (fig.), 170
Root word dictionaries, 316
Routing servers, 670
Rows, 422 (fig.)
    deleting, 445–446, 457
    inserting, 444–445, 446, 457
Rowwise recalculation, 498, 499
RS-232-C ports. *See* Serial ports
Rubenstein, Seymour, 37
Ruler lines, 281 (fig.)

Running feet, 358, 360
Running heads, 358, 360
Run-time programs, 612, 615
Russell, Virginia, 77

Sachs, Jonathan, 38
Saving
    documents, 276
    files, 231–232, 237
    spreadsheets, 418
Scanners, 79–81, 88
    for desktop publishing, 391
    graphics, 82–84, 88, 656
    text, 79–81, 88
Scanning rate, 653
Scatter graphs, 630–631
Schools, microcomputers in, 13 (fig.)
Schrayer, Michael, 37
Screen display
    printing, 160–161
    spreadsheets, 421–423
Screen dump, 160
Screen fonts, 343
Screen intensity, 68
Script languages, 621
    in communications programs, 686, 688
    in hypermedia programming, 620
Scrolling, 289–291, 294, 295–297
    with cursor, 296
    horizontal, 289–291, 294
    in spreadsheets, 424–426
    vertical, 289, 290, 294
Scroll Lock key
    macros and, 523
    in spreadsheets, 424–426
Search command, 234, 311–312
    indexed files and, 591–592
Search and replace command, 311, 312–313, 314
Search criteria. See Criteria
Seaton, Donald, 77
Seattle Computer Products, 38
Secondary files, 370, 373–374, 376
Secondary keys
    in sorting database records, 588–589, 590
    in spreadsheet databases, 516
    in word processing programs, 401–403
Secondary storage. See External storage
Second generation computers, 28
Sector holes, 110
Sectors, 112, 183, 184
    noncontiguous, 194, 195
Security, 134–135
    of database management programs, 616–618
    of files, 118–119
    mainframe computers and, 126–127
SELECT command, 606–607, 607
Selecting blocks, 305–306, 310
Self-booting disks, 182, 184
Self-booting programs, 218, 222

Semiconductors, 50
Sensitivity analysis. See What-ifs
Sequential access, 59
Sequential files, 591–592
Serial cables, 64
Serial numbers, for date and time functions, 507–508
Serial ports, 62–64, 71
Setup strings, 467–468
Set variables, 372–373
Shareware, 687
Sheet feeders, 105
Shells. See DOS, shells
Shift key, 74, 75, 79, 225
Shift-PrtSc command, 160
Shockley, William, 49
Sholes, Christopher Latham, 76
Shorthand, 45
Side-by-side columns. See Parallel columns
Sidekick, 720 (fig.)
Silicon chips, 27, 54. See also Microprocessors
    history of, 50, 68–70
    production of, 68
Silicon wafers, 70 (fig.)
Simplex transmission, 693
Single-density disks, 112
Single-tasking operating systems, 149–150
Site licensing, 260, 265
Slide shows, interactive graphics and, 661–662
Smart modems, 683
Snaking columns. See Newspaper-style columns
Sneaker nets, 125
Sockets. See Ports
Soft carriage returns, 286
Soft fonts, 343. See also Downloadable fonts
Soft hyphens, 288, 298, 294, 333
Soft page breaks, 326–327
Soft spaces, 288, 294
Software, 3–4. See also Applications programs
    microcomputers, 36–38
    names for, 39
Software Arts, 37
Solid-state transistors, 39
Soloman, Les, 30
SORT command, 174, 175
Sorting
    databases, 516–517, 588–590
    vs. indexing, 591, 594–595
    order of, 589–590, 402–403
    in word processing programs, 401–403
Sort keys
    primary, 588, 589 (fig.), 590
    secondary, 588–589, 590
    in word processing programs, 401–403
Soundproof enclosures, for printers, 105

Source disk/drive, 158, 161
Source range, 476, 479
Spacebar, 78, 287–288
    typeover mode and, 297
Spaces
    entering, 287–288
    hard, 288, 294
    soft, 288, 294
SPARC chip, 57
Sparse memory management, 428, 430
Special characters, 382–383
Special education, microcomputers in, 15 (fig.)
Spelling
    checking with search command, 312
    spelling checkers for, 315–317, 319
Split screens, 280
    vs. windows, 494–495, 496
    in word processing programs, 284
Spreadsheet control area, 421, 422, 423
Spreadsheet models, 412, 415
    changing appearance of, 470–475
    changing column width in, 470–471
    combining, 512–513
    creating, 482–492, 492
    dependent, 511, 513
    documenting, 492
    editing, 443–446
    extracting, 513
    linking, 511–512, 513
    multipage, printing, 468
    printing, 463–469
    recalculation of, 497–499
    supporting, 511, 513
    troubleshooting, 528–530
Spreadsheet operators, 447–448
Spreadsheet programs, 7
    applications of, 412–414, 415–416
    database management capabilities of, 516–520, 545–546
    defined, 214, 217
    financial analysis with, 412–413
    first, 36–37
    overview of, 415–420
    typical programs, 432–435
Spreadsheets, 412, 415
    active area, 428
    cell protection in, 509–510
    clearing the screen, 418–420
    display screen, 416 (fig.)
    downloading data for, 413
    entering labels and numbers in, 436–439
    executing commands in, 428–430
    formulas in, 447–454
    functions in, 455–462
    graphs in, 414, 491, 514–515
    hiding cells in, 510
    layout hints, 428 (fig.)–429 (fig.)
    macros, 521–525
    memory management in, 426–428, 429 (fig.), 430
    menus in, 428, 430
    moving around in, 424–426

Spreadsheets (*cont.*)
order of operations in, 448
passwords for, 510
printer commands, 466
printing, 418
quitting, 418, 420
ranges in, 440–442
recalculation of, 497–499
saving, 418
screen display, 421–423
scrolling, 424–426
security of, 509–510
sizes of, 426–428
strings in, 451–452, 453
usable capacity of, 426–427, 428
user-defined menus in, 526–527
working area, 421–422
Stacked-bar graphs, 632, 640 (fig.)
Stacked-line graphs. *See* Area graphs
Stacks, 621
Stackware, 620, 621
Standalone microcomputers, 124
Standalone programs, 216
Stanford Research Center, 31
Star architecture, 669, 671 (fig.)
Start bits, 691, 695
Static RAM, 59–60, 71
Statistical functions, 458–459
in database management programs,
581 (fig.)
in spreadsheet databases, 519–520
Statistical graphs, 636
Status lines
in spreadsheets, 423 (fig.)
in word processing programs, 281
(fig.), 284
Step mode, 523
Sticky menus, 226–227, 229
Stonehenge, 17
Stop bits, 691, 695
Stop codes, for fonts, 342, 343
Stop merge code, 371–372
Storage devices, 107–122. *See also*
Magnetic core storage; Magnetic
tape
Storage envelope, 109
Stored programs, 25–26, 39
Strikeout, 318–319, 337
Strikeover mode. *See* Typeover mode
Strike-through text. *See* Strikeout
Strings, 311, 451–452, 453
Structured query language (SQL), 574
Style and grammar checkers, 317, 318
(fig.), 319
Style sheets, 361–369
Subdirectories, 165–170
Submenus, 226
Subroutines, 23
Subscripts, 337–338
Summary models. *See* Dependent
models
Sun Microsytems, 57
SuperCalc, 433, 435, 507
Superkey, 729–730
Superscripts, 337–338
Supplemental models. *See* Supporting
models

Support, 261, 265
Supporting models, 511, 513
Surface graphs. *See* Area graphs
Surge protectors, 68
Sutherland, Ivan, 646
Switches, 173, 175
in formatting, 180
LANs and, 668 (fig.)
for printers, 105
Syllable hyphens. *See* Soft hyphens
Symbolic logic, 23
Symbolic referencing, 328, 329
Synched windows, 495, 496
Synchronous data transmission,
708–709
Syntax
in database management programs,
550
of functions, 455, 462
SYS command, 182, 184
System default settings, 247–248,
322–323, 324
System disks, formatting, 182–184
System operator (SYSOP), 679

Tab key, 79, 352
Tables (word processing), 356
Tables (database)
joining, 606–607, 609–610
projecting, 608
selecting, 607–608
Tables of contents, automatically
generated, 397–398
Tab ruler lines, 281 (fig.), 284
Tabs, 352–357, 357
decimal, 353–354
setting, 354–356
text, 352
Tabulating machines, 23–24, 24 (fig.)
Tabulating Machine Company, 23
Tagged-Image-File Format (TIFF), 659,
660
Tandy Corporation, 118
Target disk/drive, 158, 161
Target range, 476, 479
Tate, George, 37
*Technology and the American
Economic Transition*, 5
Telecommunications, 127, 676–680
equipment for, 682–684
principles of, 705–709
programs, 216
standards of, 683
trouble shooting, 703
Teleconferencing, 678
Telegraph, 43–44, 705
TeleNet, 679, 680
Telephone communications
facsimile machines, 128–129
modems and, 127–128
voice mail, 129–130
Templates, 415, 474
Terabytes, 45, 52
Terminal emulation, 693
Terminate and stay resident (TSR)
programs. *See* Memory resident
programs

Text. *See also* Blocks; Documents
combining with graphics, 386–387
deleting, 298
entering, 274
formatting, in spreadsheets,
471–472. *See also* Labels
inserting, 297
joining lines of, 299–300
printing from screen, 160
replacing, 297
Text alignment, 330–333, 335
centered, 331
flush left, 330–331
flush right, 330–331
justified, 331–332, 335
Text area, 281 (fig.)
Text displays. *See* Character displays
Text editors, 270
Text emphasis, 336–338
Text fields. *See* Character fields
Text files, 697, 703. *See also* ASCII files
Text formatters, 270
Text input devices, 73–81. *See also*
Input devices
Text recapture, 698
Text scanner, 79–81, 88
Text tabs, 352
Thermal printers, 102–103
Thesauruses, 317, 319
Thimbles, 98
ThinkTank, 717
Third generation computers, 28–29
Threads, 621
Time, automatic entry of, 293, 294,
360
TIME command, 161
Time fields, 558
Time functions, in spreadsheets,
507–508
Time-series graphs, 629
Tiny Troll, 39
Titles, fixed, 495–496
Toggle commands, 74, 297
Token passing, 674, 675
Toner, 104
Touch screens, 87–88
Trace command, 529, 530
Trackballs, 87
Tracks, 112, 183, 184
Tracks per inch (TPI) ratings, 112
Tractor feeds, 105
Training, 133, 261
Transferring files, 697–703
Transistors, 28, 39
as digital devices, 44
history of, 49
mounted on boards, 49
silicon chip development and, 69
(fig.)–70 (fig.)
Transpose command, 301, 302 (fig.),
479
TREE command, 173, 175
TREE/F command, 173–174, 175
Trojan horse programs, 263
Troubleshooting, for spreadsheet
528–530
Troubleshooting charts, 731–732

Truncated labels, 437
TWIN, The, 432
Twisted pair cables, 670–672
Tymnet, 679–680
Typeball fonts, 330 (fig.)
TYPE command, 200–201
Typefaces, 339, 343
Typeover mode, 297, 302
    spacebar in, 287–288
Type scale, 347 (fig.)
Typesetting, 105, 270
Type sizes, 340–341, 343
Typestyles, 339–340, 343
Type-through mode. See Typewriter
    mode
Typewriter mode, 291–293, 294
Typewriters, QWERTY vs. Dvorak,
    76–77

Uncompressed files, 698
Underlining, 337
Undo (undelete) command, 200 (fig.),
    298
Unique command, 518–519
UNIVAC, 26, 27 (fig.)
Univak Division, Remington Rand, 26
Universal product codes (UPCs),
    scanning, 80
UNIX, 148, 150
Unsynched windows, 495, 496
Updates (upgrades), 262, 265
Uploading, 127, 697, 698–699, 703
Uppercase letters, 74, 75
Upper memory. See Expanded memory
User-defined menus, 526–527
Utility programs, 142
    DOS, 158–160
    operating systems and, 151–152
    types of, 728–730

Vacuum tubes, 27, 39, 49
Validity checks, 559, 560
Value mode, 430
Values. See also Numbers
    defined, 415
    formatting, 473
Vaporware, 38
Variables
    in formulas, 449–450, 453
    in merge printing, 370, 371, 376
Vector graphics displays, 653–654, 658
VENIX, 148
VER command, 161
Vertical alignment, 332
Vertical applications programs, 712
Vertical centering, 335
Vertical page layout, 347–350

Vertical spacing, 348 (fig.)
Very large scale integration (VLSI), 50
Video graphics array (VGA), 96
Views. See On-screen forms
Virtual 8086 mode, 136
Virtual memory, 60, 71
    disk-based data files and, 255
    disk-based programs and, 253, 258
Viruses, 263–264, 265
Visible soft hyphens, 288
VisiCalc, 36–37, 38, 39
VisiCorp, 38
VisiOn, 38, 132–133
Voice input devices, 85–87, 88
Voice mail, 129–130
Voice templates, 86
Volatile memory, 59. See also RAM
VOL command, 161
von Neumann, John, 25
VP Planner, 432, 545
Vulcan, 37, 39
Vydec, 271

Wait mode, 430
Wait states, 66, 71
Wang, 271
Warm boot, 153, 161
Watson, Thomas J., 34 (fig.)
What-ifs, 417–418, 419 (fig.), 420
    data tables and, 504, 506
    example, 490–490
    lookup tables and, 501–503
    split screens and, 495
    spreadsheets and, 412
    using, 492
Whirlwind computer, 27
Whole Earth Catalog, 620
Wico, keyboards, 77
Wide area networks, 676–680
Widows, 326, 327, 329
Wildcards, 176–178
    checking spelling with, 312
    copying files with, 186
    ERASE command, 192, 193
    previewing effects of, 178
    in search strings, 312
Winchester disk drives. See Hard disk
    drives
Windows (program). See Microsoft
    Windows
Windows (split screens), 38, 150, 280,
    282 (fig.)
    defined, 494–495
    vs. split screens, 494–495, 496
    in spreadsheets, 494–496
    synched, 495, 496
    unsynched, 495, 496

in word processing programs, 284
Wire-frame views, 649
Word count, 319
WordMaster, 37, 39
WordPerfect, 280, 282 (fig.), 546, 547
    (fig.)
WordPerfect Corp., 700
Word processing programs, 7–8, 268,
    273–278
    applications of, 269–270
    defined, 7–8, 211, 217
    desktop publishing and, 211–212,
        271–272
    document-oriented, 291, 292 (fig.),
        294, 328
    first, 37
    loading, 273
    macros in, 409–410
    math in, 394–396
    page-oriented, 291, 292 (fig.), 294,
        327, 328
    quitting, 277
    terminology, 269
    typical, 279–284
    writing with, 369
Word processors, dedicated, 268
Words, 45
WordStar, 37, 39, 271, 280, 282 (fig.),
    283(fig.)
Word wrap, 285–286, 293
Working area, in spreadsheets,
    421–422, 430
Worksheets. See Spreadsheets; Working
    area, in spreadsheets
Workstations, 123, 130, 150
WORM disks, 116, 118, 122
Wozniak, Steve, 30–31, 32 (fig.)
Write-once, read-many disks. See
    WORM disks
Write-protect notch, 109, 110, 186
Write-protect slot, 109
Writing, with a word processing
    program, 369
Writing blocks, 308
/W switch, 173
WYSIWYG, 323, 389

X.25 (X.PC), 700
XENIX, 148
Xerox Corp., 31, 271, 389
XMODEM, 699, 700, 703
Xon/Xoff, 693, 695
XY graphs, 632–633

YMODEM, 699, 703

Zuse, Konrad, 24

COMPANY TRADEMARKS

Apple, Apple II, Apple III, AppleWorks, AppleWriter II, ImageWriter, LaserWriter, Lisa, MacDraw, Macintosh, MacPaint, MacWrite, and Pro DOS are registered trademarks of Apple Computer, Inc. Atari is a registered trademark of Atari Corporation. AVS+ is a registered trademark of Information Design. Autocad is a registered trademark of Autodesk. Bernoulli Box is a trademark of Iomega Corporation. Compaq and Compaq Plus are trademarks of Compaq Computer Corporation. CompuServe is a registered trademark of CompuServe, Inc. CP/M and GEM are registered trademarks of Digital Research, Inc. Crosstalk is a registered trademark of Microstuf, Inc. Data General One is a trademark of Data General Corporation. dBASE II, dBASE III, dBASE IV, Multimate, and Framework are registered trademarks of Ashton-Tate, Inc. PC Scan, PC Scan Plus, TEXTPac, and PUBLISHPac are registered trademarks of Dest Corporation. DEC and PDP-1 are registered trademarks of Digital Equipment Corporation. DIGI-PAD and Macintizer are registered trademarks of GTCO. Dow-Jones News Retrieval is a registered trademark of Dow Jones & Company. EasyLink is a service mark of Western Union. EasyWriter II and SuperCalc 3 are registered trademarks of Sorcim/IUS Micro Software—a Division of Computer Associates International, Inc. and Basic Software, Inc. RX-80 and LQ-1000 are registered trademarks of Epson America, Inc. Excel, Microsoft Chart, Microsoft, Microsoft Windows, Microsoft WORD, MS DOS, and Multiplan are registered trademarks of Microsoft Corporation. Fujitsu is a registered trademark. The Genius is a registered trademark of MicroDisplay. Grasshopper is a registered trademark of Tallgrass Technologies. GRiD-OS is a registered trademark of GRiD Systems Corporation. Harvard Total Project Manager, PFS:Access, PFS:File, PFS:Plan, PFS:Report, PFS:Write, and PFC are trademarks of Software Publishing Corporation. Hipad is a trademark of Oberon International. HP-150 is a registered trademark of Hewlett-Packard Co. IBM, DisplayWrite 4, IBM PC/XT, IBM PC/AT, IBM Proprinter, IBM PC, PC DOS, and TopView are registered trademarks of International Business Machines Corporation. Information Update is a registered trademark. Intel 4004, 80386, and Intel Above Board are registered trademarks of Intel Corporation. IntroVoice III is a registered trademark of the Voice Connection. Kodak Diskette and Kodak Datashow are copyrights of Eastman Kodak Co. Kurta is a registered trademark. Lotus, 1-2-3, Symphony, Jazz, and Spotlight are registered trademarks of Lotus Development Corporation. Lucid 3-D is a trademark. MC68000 is a trademark of Motorola Inc. MCI-Mail is a registered trademark of MCI Telecommunications Corporation. MicroPro and WordStar are registered trademarks of MicroPro International Corp. MNP is a trademark of Microcom. NCR is a registered trademark. National Semiconductor is a trademark. PageMaker and Adobe Illustrator are trademarks of Aldus Corporation. PC-Calc, PC-File III, and PC-Type are registered trademarks of ButtonWare, Inc. PC-Talk copyright 1983 by Headlands Press. PC-Write is a trademark of Quicksoft. Qume is a registered trademark. Phillips Subsystems and Peripherals is a trademark. RightWriter is a trademark of RightSoft Inc. Sidekick is a registered trademark of Borland International. Smartmodem is a trademark of Hayes Microcomputer Products, Inc. Spinwriter is produced by NEC Information Systems, Inc. ST225 is a registered trademark of Seagate Technology. The Source is a trademark of The Source Telecomputing Corporation. ThinkTank is a trademark of Living Videotext Inc. TRS-80 and Tandy Acoustic Coupler Modem are registered trademarks of the Radio Shack division of Tandy Corporation. Toshiba America, Inc. is a trademark. UNIX and Writers Workbench are registered trademarks of AT&T Bell Laboratories. U.S. Robotics is a registered trademark. Ventura Publisher is a registered trademark of Xerox Corporation. WordPerfect is a registered trademark of WordPerfect, Inc. Z-Soft is a registered trademark.